sociology
introductory readings

sociology

introductory readings

edited by
anthony
giddens

polity press

This collection and introductory material © Polity Press 1997

First published in 1997 by Polity Press
in association with Blackwell Publishers Ltd

Editorial office:
Polity Press
65 Bridge Street
Cambridge CB2 1UR, UK

Marketing and production:
Blackwell Publishers Ltd
108 Cowley Road
Oxford OX4 1JF, UK

ISBN 0-7456-1873-1
ISBN 0-7456-1874-X (pbk)

A CIP catalogue record for this book is available from the British Library.

Typeset in 10 on 12 pt Palatino
by Wearset, Boldon, Tyne and Wear
Printed in Great Britain by TJ International Ltd, Padstow, Cornwall

This book is printed on acid-free paper.

Contents

Part XVI   Theoretical Perspectives in Sociology   423

Preface to the Second Edition

In this new edition I have tried to sustain the strengths which made the book a success the first time around. I believe the volume offers a comprehensive overview of the principal fields, and also dilemmas, of sociological thinking and research. Sociology deals with issues central to all our lives. The selections included here give a good understanding of how sociology helps us analyse personal, and even intimate, aspects of what we do. Sociology is not just about the large institutions, but about the individual and emotional textures of our activities too. At the same time, sociology does insist upon the importance of seeing our more personal make-up in the context of more inclusive social processes and forms of change. The collection gives students ample opportunities to explore the complex connections between the individual and the social, and also the local and the global. An emphasis upon the new global order in which we now find ourselves is a continuing theme of the book.

I have kept a certain number of sources intact from the first edition, particularly where they proved popular among users of the volume. Most of the material in this edition, however, is new. In contrast to the first edition, in this new version I have included a few contributions from non-professional sources in sociology, such as newspapers and weekly periodicals. Sociological discussion is not confined to those who practise sociology in an academic context. Journalists mostly write better than academics do and quite often provide interesting commentaries on social research. Of course, the vast bulk of the selections included here come from 'respectable' sociological research carried out in an academic environment.

The book includes a number of sections which either were absent in the earlier edition, or were absorbed into other chapters. The most important new sections are those on the sociology of the body, media and popular culture, and the sociology of education.

Introduction

This book has been designed to accompany my introductory text, *Sociology*,[1] but it can be read as a completely separate work. It is aimed at those who are approaching sociology for the first time and I have devoted considerable care to ensuring that all the sources included are clear and accessible for beginning students.

Although the selections are weighted towards the study of Britain, as in *Sociology* the emphasis throughout is upon the global nature of sociological thought today. Consequently the selections are not insular, but offer a broad coverage of developments affecting the industrialized societies in general. In the current era global processes impinge upon the most local and personal aspects of social life; conversely, individual actions and localized social interaction contribute to globally ordered systems. In choosing the selections represented here, therefore, I have ranged from small-scale studies of interaction right through to the analysis of the most extensive forms of social system now influencing our lives.

Many of the selections contain empirical material of a generalizing kind. I have also incorporated a substantial range of sources based upon more qualitative materials, including many in which the individuals concerned speak for themselves rather than being spoken for by the sociological researcher. 'Case studies' often reveal more of a general nature about social processes than do apparently more extensive empirical observations.

The format and sequence of the different parts of the book more or less follow those set out in *Sociology*, save that discussions of types of society, cultural diversity and socialization, which figure as the first two chapters of that book, are not included here. An extensive number of selections is provided concerning research methods and theoretical perspectives in sociology. As in the textbook, these are placed at the end of the volume. The reason for this is my belief that abstract notions in sociology cannot readily be mastered until students have had the opportunity to become acquainted with more substantive studies and debates. However, students are encouraged to consult the two concluding sections of the book at any point for amplification of methodological or theoretical issues raised in earlier selections.

Each part of the book is preceded by a description of the selections included, but I have kept these short in order to give primacy to the source materials themselves. Although every effort has been made to concentrate upon sources that are immediately accessible, inevitably there are differences in style and complexity among the selections. Some involve rather more demanding arguments than others, and the fluency with which the authors express their findings or views varies. I hope, however, that these contrasts will help to give the reader a sense of the range and diversity of sociological writings at the present time.

Many of the selections come from books or articles which might be difficult for most readers to obtain, either because of the limited circulation of the source materials concerned or, conversely, because more popular works are in such demand that access to them, even in the best-supplied of libraries, is limited. Nevertheless, I hope that readers will be sufficiently intrigued or stimulated by the readings included here to locate the original books or articles to pursue them further.

In order to maximize the readability of the selections, references and notes have been kept to a minimum. Those that are retained should provide ample opportunity for the reader to follow up lines of thought or investigation not directly analysed in the articles themselves.

Part I

What is Sociology?

Sociology is an engrossing subject because it concerns our own lives as human beings. All humans are social – we could not develop as children, or exist as adults, without having social ties to others. Society is thus the very condition of human existence. At the same time, as the opening reading in the book emphasizes, we all actively shape the society in which we live. As sociologists, we seek to understand both how, as individuals, all of us are influenced by the wider society, and at the same time how we actively structure that society in our own actions. More than most other intellectual endeavours, sociology presumes the use of disciplined imagination. Imagination, because the sociologist must distance her- or himself from the here and now in order to grasp how societies have changed in the past and what potential transformations lie in store; discipline, because the creative ability of the imagination has to be restrained by conceptual and empirical rigour.

C. Wright Mills's discussion of the sociological imagination (Reading 2) has long been the classic discussion of these issues. We cannot understand ourselves as individuals, Mills emphasizes, unless we grasp the involvement of our own biography with the historical development of social institutions. On the other hand, we cannot comprehend the nature of those institutions unless we understand how they are organized in and through individual action. It is the business of sociology to analyse the social orders which constrain our behaviour, but at the same time to acknowledge that we actively make our own history.

These ideas are echoed by Zygmunt Bauman (Reading 3). The focus of his discussion, however, is the similarities and differences between sociology and common-sense understandings of social life. Sociology, he agrees with Mills, teaches us to see our own individual experiences in relation to wider social systems, as well as to broad patterns of social change. As such, it is a distinctive way of thinking about the social world. Studying human social activity, Bauman says, is different from analysing objects or events in the natural world. We are all in some sense knowledgeable and skilful in respect of our participation in day-to-day social activity. Sociological knowledge builds upon the practical forms of knowing by means of which we organize our everyday lives. Sociological concepts, however, need to be more clearly formulated and precise than those of ordinary language.

Sociological investigation ranges over much broader arenas, in time as well as in space, than the immediate settings of interaction with which we are most familiar in the daily round. Moreover, sociologists focus attention upon unintended and unanticipated consequences of human activity, whereas in ordinary activities we concern ourselves mainly with the intentions and emotions of other people. As Mills also stresses, sociological thought must take an imaginative leap beyond the familiar, and the sociologist must be prepared to look behind the routine activities in which much of our mundane life is enmeshed.

READING 1

Anthony Giddens

The Scope of Sociology

Sociology is a subject with a curiously mixed reputation. On the one hand, it is associated by many people with the fomenting of rebellion, a stimulus to revolt. Even though they may have only a vague notion of what topics are studied in sociology, they somehow associate sociology with subversion, with the shrill demands of unkempt student militants. On the other hand, quite a different view of the subject is often entertained – perhaps more commonly than the first – by individuals who have had some direct acquaintance with it in schools and universities. This is that in fact it is rather a dull and uninstructive enterprise, which far from propelling its students towards the barricades is more likely to bore them to death with platitudes. Sociology, in this guise, assumes the dry mantle of a science, but not one that proves as enlightening as the natural sciences upon which its practitioners wish to model it.

I think that those who have taken the second reaction to sociology have a good deal of right on their side. Sociology has been conceived of by many of its proponents – even the bulk of them – in such a way that common-place assertions are disguised in a pseudo-scientific language. The conception that sociology belongs to the natural sciences, and hence should slavishly try to copy their procedures and objectives, is a mistaken one. Its lay critics, in some considerable degree at least, are quite correct to be sceptical of the attainments of sociology thus presented.

My intention in this [discussion] will be to associate sociology with the first type of view rather than the second. By this I do not mean to connect sociology with a sort of irrational lashing-out at all that most of the population hold to be good and proper ways of behaviour. But I do want to defend the view that sociology, understood in the manner in which I shall describe it, necessarily has a subversive quality. Its subversive or critical character, however . . ., does not carry with it (or should not do so) the implication that it is an intellectually disreputable enterprise. On the contrary, it is exactly because sociology deals with problems of such pressing interest to us all (or should do so), problems which are the objects of major controversies and conflicts in society itself, that it has this character. However kempt or otherwise student radicals, or any other radicals, may be, there do exist broad connections between the impulses that stir them to action and a sociological awareness. This is not . . . because sociologists directly preach revolt; it is because the study of sociology, appropriately understood, . . . demonstrates how fundamental are the social questions that have to be faced in today's world. Everyone is to some extent aware of these questions, but the study of sociology helps bring them into much sharper focus. Sociology cannot remain a purely academic subject, if 'academic' means a disinterested and remote scholarly pursuit, followed solely within the enclosed walls of the university.

Sociology is not a subject that comes neatly gift-wrapped, making no demands except that its contents be unpacked. Like all the social sciences – under which label one can also include, among other disciplines, anthropology, economics and history – sociology is an inherently controversial endeavour. That is to say, it is characterized by continuing disputes about its very nature. But this is not a weakness, although it has seemed such to many of those who call themselves professional 'sociologists', and also to many others on the outside, who are distressed that there are numerous vying conceptions of how the subject-matter of sociology should be approached or analysed. Those who are upset by the persistent character of sociological debates, and a frequent lack of consensus about how to resolve them, usually feel that this is a sign of the immaturity of the subject. They want sociology to be like a natural science, and to generate a similar apparatus of universal laws to those which they see natural science as having discovered and validated. But . . . it is a mistake to suppose that sociology should be modelled too closely on the natural sciences, or to imagine that a natural science of society is either feasible or desirable. To say this, I should emphasize, does not mean that the methods and objectives of the natural sciences are wholly irrelevant to the study of human social behaviour. Sociology deals with a factually observable subject-matter, depends upon empirical research, and involves attempts to formulate theories and generalizations that will make sense of facts. But human beings are not the same as material objects in nature; studying our own behaviour is necessarily entirely different in some very important ways from studying natural phenomena.

The development of sociology, and its current concerns, have to be grasped in the context of changes that have created the modern world. We live in an age of massive social transformation. In the space of only something like two centuries a sweeping set of social changes, which have hastened rather than lessened their pace today, have occurred. These changes, emanating originally from Western Europe, are now global in their impact. They have all but totally dissolved the forms of social organization in which humankind had lived for thousands of years of its previous history. Their core is to be found in what some have described as the 'two great revolutions' of eighteenth- and nineteenth-century Europe. The first is the French revolution of 1789, both a specific set of events and a symbol of political transformations in our era. For the 1789 revolution was quite different from rebellions of previous times. Peasants had sometimes rebelled against their feudal masters, for example, but generally in an attempt to remove specific individuals from power, or to secure reductions in prices or taxes. In the

French revolution (to which we can bracket, with some reservations, the anti-colonial revolution in North America in 1776) for the first time in history there took place the overall dissolution of a social order by a movement guided by purely secular ideals – universal liberty and equality. If the ideals of the revolutionaries have scarcely been fully realized even now, they created a climate of political change that has proved one of the dynamic forces of contemporary history. There are few states in the world today that are not proclaimed by their rulers to be 'democracies', whatever their actual political complexion may be. This is something altogether novel in human history. It is true that there have been other republics, most especially those of Classical Greece and Rome. But these were themselves rare instances; and in each case those who formed the 'citizens' were a minority of the population, the majority of whom were slaves or others without the prerogatives of the select groups of citizenry.

The second 'great revolution' was the so-called 'industrial revolution', usually traced to Britain in the late eighteenth century, and spreading in the nineteenth century throughout Western Europe and the United States. The industrial revolution is sometimes presented merely as a set of technical innovations: especially the harnessing of steam power to manufacturing production and the introduction of novel forms of machinery activated by such sources of power. But these technical inventions were only part of a very much broader set of social and economic changes. The most important of these was the migration of the mass of the labour force from the land into the constantly expanding sectors of industrial work, a process which also eventually led to the widespread mechanization of agrarian production. This same process promoted an expansion of cities upon a scale again previously unwitnessed in history. . . .

Sociology came into being as those caught up in the initial series of changes brought about by the 'two great revolutions' in Europe sought to understand the conditions of their emergence, and their likely consequences. Of course, no field of study can be exactly pinpointed in terms of its origins. We can quite readily trace direct continuities from writers in the middle of the eighteenth century through to later periods of social thought. The climate of ideas involved in the formation of sociology in some part, in fact, helped *give rise* to the twin processes of revolution.

How should 'sociology' be defined? Let me begin with a banality. Sociology is concerned with the study of human societies. Now the notion of society can be formulated in only a very general way. For under the general category of 'societies' we want to include not only the industrialized countries, but large agrarian imperial states (such as the Roman Empire, or traditional China), and, at the other end of the scale, small tribal communities that may comprise only a tiny number of individuals.

A society is a cluster, or system, of *institutionalized* modes of conduct. To speak of 'institutionalized' forms of social conduct is to refer to modes of belief and behaviour that occur and recur – or, as the terminology of modern social theory would have it, are socially *reproduced* – across long spans of time and space. Language is an excellent example of such a form of institutionalized activity, or institution, since it is so fundamental to social life. All of us speak languages which none of us, as individuals, created, although we all use language creatively. But many other aspects of social life may be institutionalized: that is, become commonly adopted practices which persist in recognizably similar form across the generations. Hence we can speak of economic institutions, political institutions and so on. Such a use of the concept 'institution', it should be pointed out, differs from the way in which the term is often employed in ordinary language, as a loose synonym for 'group' or 'collectivity' – as when, say, a prison or hospital is referred to as an 'institution'.

These considerations help to indicate how 'society' should be understood, but we cannot leave matters there. As an object of study, 'society' is shared by sociology and the other social sciences. The distinctive feature of sociology lies in its overriding concern with those forms of society that have emerged in the wake of the 'two great revolutions'. Such forms of society include those that are industrially advanced – the economically developed countries of the West, Japan and Eastern Europe – but also in the twentieth century a range of other societies stretched across the world. . . .

In the light of these remarks, a definition can be offered of the subject as follows. *Sociology is a social science, having as its main focus the study of the social institutions brought into being by the industrial transformations of the past two or three centuries.* It is important to stress that there are no precisely defined divisions between sociology and other fields of intellectual endeavour in the social sciences. Neither is it desirable that there should be. Some questions of social theory, to do with how human behaviour and institutions should be conceptualized, are the shared concern of the social sciences as a whole. The different 'areas' of human behaviour that are covered by the various social sciences form an intellectual division of labour which can be justified in only a very general way. Anthropology, for example, is concerned . . . with the 'simpler' societies: tribal societies, chiefdoms and agrarian states. But either these have been dissolved altogether by the profound social changes that have swept through the world, or they are in the process of becoming incorporated within modern industrial states. The subject-matter of economics, to take another instance, is the production and distribution of material goods. However, economic institutions are plainly always connected with other institutions in social systems, which both influence and are influenced by them. Finally, history, as the study of the continual distancing of past and present, is the source material of the whole of the social sciences.

. . . Although this type of standpoint has been very pervasive in sociology, it is one I reject. To speak of sociology, and of other subjects like anthropology or economics, as 'social sciences' is to stress that they involve the systematic study of an empirical subject-matter. The terminology is not confusing so long as we see that sociology and other social sciences differ from the natural sciences in two essential respects.

1 We *cannot* approach society, or 'social facts', as we do objects or events in the natural world, because societies only exist in so far as they are created and re-created in our own actions as human beings. In social theory, we cannot treat human activities as though they were determined by causes in the same way as natural events are. We have to grasp what I would call the *double involvement* of individuals and institutions: we create society at the same time as we are created by it . . . .

2 It follows from this that the practical implications of sociology are not directly parallel to the technological uses of science, and cannot be.

Atoms cannot get to know what scientists say about them, or change their behaviour in the light of that knowledge. Human beings can do so. Thus the relation between sociology and its 'subject-matter' is necessarily different from that involved in the natural sciences. If we regard social activity as a mechanical set of events, determined by natural laws, we both misunderstand the past and fail to grasp how sociological analysis can help influence our possible future. As human beings, we do not just live in history; our understanding of history is an integral part of what that history is, and what it may become.

READING 2

C. Wright Mills

The Sociological Imagination and the Promise of Sociology

The sociological imagination enables its possessor to understand the larger historical scene in terms of its meaning for the inner life and the external career of a variety of individuals. It enables [the sociologist] to take into account how individuals, in the welter of their daily experience, often become falsely conscious of their social positions. Within that welter, the framework of modern society is sought, and within that framework the psychologies of a variety of men and women are formulated. By such means the personal uneasiness of individuals is focused upon explicit troubles and the indifference of publics is transformed into involvement with public issues.

The first fruit of this imagination – and the first lesson of the social science that embodies it – is the idea that the individual can understand his[1] own experience and gauge his own fate only by locating himself within his period, that he can know his own chances in life only by becoming aware of those of all individuals in his circumstances. In many ways it is a terrible lesson; in many ways a magnificent one. We do not know the limits of man's capacities for supreme effort or willing degradation, for agony or glee, for pleasurable brutality or the sweetness of reason. But in our time we have come to know that the limits of 'human nature' are frighteningly broad. We have come to know that every individual lives, from one generation to the next, in some society; that he lives out a biography, and that he lives it out within some historical sequence. By the fact of his living he contributes, however minutely, to the shaping of this society and to the course of its history, even as he is made by society and by its historical push and shove.

The sociological imagination enables us to grasp history and biography and the relations between the two within society. That is its task and its promise . . .

No social study that does not come back to the problems of biography, of history and of their intersections within a society has completed its intellectual journey. Whatever the specific problems of the classic social analysts, however limited or however broad the features of social reality they have examined, those who have been imaginatively aware of the promise of their work have consistently asked three sorts of questions:

1   What is the structure of this particular society as a whole? What are its essential components and how are they related to one another? How does it differ from other varieties of social order? Within it, what is the meaning of any particular feature for its continuance and for its change?
2   Where does this society stand in human history? What are the mechanics by which it is changing? What is its place within and its meaning for the development of humanity as a whole? How does any particular feature we are examining affect, and how is it affected by, the historical period in which it moves? And this period – what are its essential features? How does it differ from other periods? What are its characteristic ways of history-making?
3   What varieties of men and women now prevail in this society and in this period? And what varieties are coming to prevail? In what ways are they selected and formed, liberated and repressed, made sensitive and blunted? What kinds of 'human nature' are revealed in the conduct and character we observe in this society in this period? And what is the meaning for 'human nature' of each and every feature of the society we are examining?

Whether the point of interest is a great power state or a minor literary mood, a family, a prison, a creed – these are the kinds of questions the best social analysts have asked. They are the intellectual pivots of classic studies of man in society – and they are the questions inevitably raised by any mind possessing the sociological imagination. For that imagination is the capacity to shift from one perspective to another – from the political to the psychological; from examination of a single family to comparative assessment of the national budgets of the world; from the theological school to the military establishment; from considerations of an oil industry to studies of contemporary poetry. It is the capacity to range from the most impersonal and remote transformations to the most intimate features of the human self – and to see the relations between the two. Back of its use there is always the urge to know the social and historical meaning of the individual in the society and in the period in which he has his quality and his being . . .

Perhaps the most fruitful distinction with which the sociological imagination works is between 'the personal troubles of milieu' and 'the public issues of social structure'. This distinction is an essential tool of the sociological imagination and a feature of all classic work in social science . . .

In these terms, consider unemployment. When, in a city of 100,000, only one man is unemployed, that is his personal trouble, and for its relief we properly look to the character of the man, his skills and his immediate opportunities. But when, in a nation of 50 million employees, 15 million men are unemployed, that is an issue, and we may not hope to find its solution within the range of opportunities open to any one individual. The very structure of opportunities has collapsed. Both the correct statement of the problem and the range of possible solutions require us to consider the economic and political institutions of the society, and not merely the personal situation and character of a scatter of individuals.

Consider war. The personal problem of war, when it occurs, may be how to survive it or how to die in it with honour; how to make money out of it; how to climb into the higher safety of the military apparatus; or how to contribute to the war's termination. In short, according to one's values, to find a set of milieux and within it to survive the war or make one's death in it meaningful. But the structural issues of war have to do with its causes; with what types of men it throws up into command; with its effects upon economic and political, family and religious institutions, with the unorganized irresponsibility of a world of nation states.

Consider marriage. Inside a marriage a man and a woman may experience personal troubles, but when the divorce rate during the first four years of marriage is 250 out of every 1,000 attempts, this is an indication of a structural issue having to do with the institutions of marriage and the family and other institutions that bear upon them.

Or consider the metropolis – the horrible, beautiful, ugly, magnificent sprawl of the great city. For many upper-class people, the personal solution to 'the problem of the city' is to have an apartment with a private garage under it in the heart of the city and, forty miles out, a house by Henry Hill, garden by Garrett Eckbo, on a hundred acres of private land. In these two controlled environments – with a small staff at each end and a private helicopter connection – most people could solve many of the problems of personal milieux caused by the facts of the city. But all this, however splendid, does not solve the public issues that the structural fact of the city poses. What should be done with this wonderful monstrosity? Break it all up into scattered units, combining residence and work? Refurbish it as it stands? Or, after evacuation, dynamite it and build new cities according to new plans in new places? What should those plans be? And who is to decide and to accomplish whatever choice is made? These are structural issues; to confront them and to solve them requires us to consider political and economic issues that affect innumerable milieux.

In so far as an economy is so arranged that slumps occur, the problem of unemployment becomes incapable of personal solution. In so far as war is inherent in the nation-state system and in the uneven industrialization of the world, the ordinary individual in his restricted milieu will be powerless – with or without psychiatric aid – to solve the troubles this system or lack of system imposes upon him. In so far as the family as an institution turns women into darling little slaves and men into their chief providers and unweaned dependants, the problem of a satisfactory marriage remains incapable of purely private solution. In so far as the overdeveloped megalopolis and the overdeveloped automobile are built-in features of the overdeveloped society, the issues of urban living will not be solved by personal ingenuity and private wealth.

What we experience in various and specific milieux, I have noted, is often caused by structural changes. Accordingly, to understand the changes of many personal milieux we are required to look beyond them. And the number and variety of such structural changes increase as the institutions within which we live become more embracing and more intricately connected with one another. To be aware of the idea of social structure and to use it with sensibility is to be capable of tracing such linkages among a great variety of milieux. To be able to do that is to possess the sociological imagination.

READING 3

Zygmunt Bauman

Thinking Sociologically

The central question of sociology, one could say, is: in what sense does it matter that in whatever they do or may do people are dependent on other people; in what sense does it matter that they live always (and cannot but live) in the company of, in communication with, in an exchange with, in competition with, in co-operation with other human beings? It is this kind of question (and not a separate collection of people or events selected for the purpose of study, nor some set of human actions neglected by other lines of investigation) that constitutes the particular area of sociological discussion and defines sociology as a relatively autonomous branch of human and social sciences. Sociology, we may conclude, is first and foremost a *way of thinking* about the human world; in principle one can also think about the same world in different ways.

Among these other ways from which the sociological way of thinking is set apart, a special place is occupied by so-called *common sense*. Perhaps more than other branches of scholarship, sociology finds its relation with common sense (that rich yet disorganized, non-systematic, often inarticulate and ineffable knowledge we use to conduct our daily business of life) fraught with problems decisive for its standing and practice.

Indeed, few sciences are concerned with spelling out their relationship to common sense; most do not even notice that common sense exists, let alone that it presents a problem. Most sciences settle for defining themselves in terms of boundaries that separate them from or bridges that connect them with other sciences – respectable, systematic lines of enquiry like themselves. They do not feel they share enough ground with common sense to bother with drawing boundaries or building bridges. Their indifference is, one must admit, well justified. Common sense has next to nothing to say of the matters of which physics, or chemistry, or astronomy, or geology speak (and whatever it has to say on such matters comes courtesy of those sciences themselves, in so far as they manage to make their recondite findings graspable and intelligible for lay people). The subjects dealt with by physics or astronomy hardly ever appear within the sight of ordinary men and women: inside, so to speak, your and my daily experience. And so we, the non-experts, the ordinary people, cannot form opinions about such matters unless aided – indeed, instructed – by the scientists. The objects explored by sciences like the ones we have mentioned appear only under very special circumstances, to which lay people have no access: on the screen of a multi-million-dollar accelerator, in the lens of a gigantic telescope, at the bottom of a thousand-feet-deep shaft. Only the scientists can see them and experiment with them; these objects and events are a monopolistic possession of the given branch of science (or even of its selected practitioners), a property not shared with anybody who is not a member of the profession. Being the sole owners of the experience which provides the raw material for their study, the scientists are in full control over the way the material is processed, analysed, interpreted. Products of such processing would have to withstand the critical scrutiny of other scientists – but their scrutiny only. They will not have to compete with public opinion, common sense or any other form in which non-specialist views may appear, for the simple reason that there is no public opinion and no commonsensical point of view in the matters they study and pronounce upon.

With sociology it is quite different. In sociological study there are no equivalents of giant accelerators or radio telescopes. All experience which provides raw material for sociological findings – the stuff of which sociological knowledge is made – is the experience of ordinary people in ordinary, daily life; an experience accessible in principle, though not always in practice, to everybody; . . . experience that, before it came under the magnifying glass of a sociologist, had already been lived by someone else – a non-sociologist, a person not trained in the use of sociological language and seeing things from a sociological point of view. All of us live in the company of other people, after all, and interact with each other. All of us have learned only too well that what we get depends on what other people do. All of us have gone more than once through the agonizing experience of a communication breakdown with friends and strangers. Anything sociology talks about was already there in our lives. And it must have been, otherwise we should be unable to conduct our business of life. To live in the company of other people we need a lot of knowledge; and common sense is the name of that knowledge.

Deeply immersed in our daily routines, though, we hardly ever pause to think about the meaning of what we have gone through; even less often have we the opportunity to compare our private experience with the fate of others, to see the *social* in the *individual*, the *general* in the *particular*; this is precisely what sociologists can do for us. We would expect them to show us how our individual *biographies* intertwine with the *history* we share with fellow human beings. And yet whether or not the sociologists get that far, they have no other point to start from than the daily experience of life they share with you and me – from that raw knowledge that saturates the daily life of each one of us. For this reason alone the sociologists, however hard they might have tried to follow the example of the physicists and the biologists and stand aside from the object of their study (that is, look at your and my life experience as an object 'out there', as a detached and impartial observer would do), cannot break off completely from their insider's knowledge of the experience they try to comprehend. However hard they might try, sociologists are bound to remain on both sides of the experience they strive to interpret, inside and outside at the same time. (Note how often the sociologists use the personal pronoun 'we' when they report their findings and formulate their general propositions. That 'we' stands for an 'object' that includes those who study and those whom they study. Can you imagine a physicist using 'we' of themselves and the molecules? Or astronomers using 'we' to generalize about themselves and the stars?)

There is more still to the special relationship between sociology and common sense. The phenomena observed and theorized upon by modern physicists or astronomers come in an innocent and pristine form, unprocessed, free from labels, ready-made definitions and prior interpretations (that is, except such interpretations as had been given them in advance by the physicists who set the experiments that made them appear). They wait for the physicist or the astronomer to name them, to set them among other phenomena and combine them into an orderly whole: in short, to give them *meaning*. But there are few, if any, sociological equivalents of such clean and unused phenomena which have never been given meaning before. Those human actions and interactions that sociologists explore had all been given names and theorized about, in however diffuse, poorly articulated form, by the actors themselves. Before sociologists started looking at them, they were objects of commonsensical knowledge. Families, organizations, kinship networks, neighbourhoods, cities and villages, nations and churches and any other groupings held together by regular human interaction have already been given meaning and significance by the actors, so that the actors consciously address them in their actions as bearers of such meanings. Lay actors and professional sociologists would have to use the same names, the same language when speaking of them. Each term sociologists may use will already have been heavily burdened with meanings it was given by the commonsensical knowledge of 'ordinary' people like you and me.

For the reason explained above, sociology is much too intimately related to common sense to afford that lofty equanimity with which sciences like chemistry or geology can treat it. You and I are allowed to speak of human interdependence and human interaction, and to speak with authority. Don't we all practise them and experience them? Sociological discourse is wide open: no standing invitation to everybody to join, but no clearly marked borders or effective border guards either. With poorly defined borders whose security is not guaranteed in advance (unlike sciences that explore objects inaccessible to lay experience), the sovereignty of sociology over social knowledge, its right to make authoritative pronouncements on the subject, may always be contested. This is why drawing a boundary between sociological knowledge proper and the common sense that is always full of sociological ideas is such an important matter for the identity of sociology as a cohesive body of knowledge; and why sociologists pay this matter more attention than other scientists.

We can think of at least four quite seminal differences between the ways in which sociology and common sense – your and my 'raw' knowledge of the business of life – treat the topic they share: human experience.

To start with, sociology (unlike common sense) makes an effort to subordinate itself to the rigorous rules of *responsible speech*, which is assumed to be an attribute of science (as distinct from other, reputedly more relaxed and less vigilantly self-controlled, forms of knowledge). This means that the sociologists are expected to take great care to distinguish – in a fashion clear and visible to anybody – between the statements corroborated by available evidence and such propositions as can only claim the status of a provisional, untested guess. Sociologists would refrain from misrepresenting ideas that are grounded solely in their beliefs (even the most ardent and emotionally intense beliefs) as tested findings carrying the widely respected authority of science. The rules of responsible speech demand that one's 'workshop' – the whole procedure that has led to the final conclusions and is claimed to guarantee their credibility – be wide open to an unlimited public scrutiny; a standing invitation ought to be extended to everyone to reproduce the test and, be this the case, prove the findings wrong. Responsible speech must also relate to other statements made on its topic; it cannot simply dismiss or pass by in silence other views that have been voiced, however sharply they are opposed to it and hence inconvenient. It is hoped that once the rules of responsible speech are honestly and meticulously observed, the trustworthiness, reliability and eventually also the practical usefulness of the ensuing propositions will be greatly enhanced, even if not fully guaranteed. Our shared faith in the credibility of beliefs countersigned by science is to a great extent grounded in the hope that the scientists will indeed follow the rules of responsible speech, and that the scientific profession as a whole will see to it that every single member of the profession does so on every occasion. As to the scientists themselves, they point to the virtues of responsible speech as an argument in favour of the superiority of the knowledge they offer.

The second difference is related to the *size of the field* from which the material for judgement is drawn. For most of us, as non-professionals, such a field is confined to our own life-world: things we do, people we meet, purposes we set for our own pursuits and guess other people set for theirs. Rarely, if at all, do we make an effort to lift ourselves above the level of our daily concerns to broaden the horizon of experience, as this would require

15

time and resources most of us can ill afford or do not feel like spending on such effort. And yet, given the tremendous variety of life-conditions, each experience based solely on an individual life-world is necessarily partial and most likely one-sided. Such shortcomings can be rectified only if one brings together and sets against each other experiences drawn from a multitude of life-worlds. Only then will the incompleteness of individual experience be revealed, as will be the complex network of dependencies and interconnections in which it is entangled – a network which reaches far beyond the realm which could be scanned from the vantage point of a singular biography. The overall result of such a broadening of horizons will be the discovery of the intimate link between individual biography and wide social processes the individual may be unaware of and surely unable to control. It is for this reason that the sociologists' pursuit of a perspective wider than the one offered by an individual life-world makes a great difference – not just a quantitative difference (more data, more facts, statistics instead of single cases), but a difference in the quality and the uses of knowledge. For people like you or me, who pursue our respective aims in life and struggle for more control over our plight, sociological knowledge has something to offer that common sense cannot.

The third difference between sociology and common sense pertains to the way in which each one goes about *making sense* of human reality; how each one goes about explaining to its own satisfaction why this rather than that happened or is the case. I imagine that you (much as myself) know from your own experience that you are the 'author' of your actions; you know that what you do (though not necessarily the results of your actions) is an effect of your intention, hope or purpose. You normally do as you do in order to achieve a state of affairs you desire, whether you wish to possess an object, to receive an accolade from your teachers or to put an end to your friends' teasing. Quite naturally, the way you think of your action serves you as a model for making sense of all other actions. You explain such actions to yourself by imputing to others intentions you know from your own experience. This is, to be sure, the only way we can make sense of the human world around us as long as we draw our tools of explanation solely from within our respective life-worlds. We tend to perceive everything that happens in the world at large as an outcome of somebody's intentional action. We look for the persons responsible for what has happened and, once we have found them, we believe our enquiry has been completed. We assume somebody's goodwill lies behind every event we like and somebody's ill intentions behind every event we dislike. We would find it difficult to accept that a situation was not an effect of intentional action of an identifiable 'somebody'; and we would not lightly give up our conviction that any unwelcome condition could be remedied if only someone, somewhere, wished to take the right action. Those who more than anyone else interpret the world for us – politicians, journalists, commercial advertisers – tune in to this tendency of ours and speak of the 'needs of the state' or 'demands of the economy', as if the state or the economy were made to the measure of individual persons like ourselves and could have needs or make demands. On the other hand, they portray the complex problems of nations, states and economic systems (deeply seated in the very structures of such figurations) as the effects of the thoughts and deeds of a few individuals one can name, put in front of a camera and interview. Sociology stands in opposition to such a personalized world-view. . . . When thinking sociologically, one attempts to make sense of the human condition through analysing the manifold webs of human interdependency – that toughest of realities which explains both our motives and the effects of their activation.

Finally, let us recall that the power of common sense over the way we understand the world and ourselves (the immunity of common sense to questioning, its capacity for self-confirmation) depends on the apparently self-evident character of its precepts. This in turn rests on the routine, monotonous nature of daily life, which informs our common sense while being simultaneously informed by it. As long as we go through the routine and habitualized motions which fill most of our daily business, we do not need much self-scrutiny and self-analysis. When repeated often enough, things tend to become familiar, and familiar things are self-explanatory; they present no problems and arouse no curiosity. In a way, they remain invisible. Questions are not asked, as people are satisfied that 'things are as they are', 'people are as they are', and there is precious little one can do about it. Familiarity is the staunchest enemy of inquisitiveness and criticism – and thus also of innovation and the courage to change. In an encounter with that familiar world ruled by habits and reciprocally reasserting beliefs, sociology acts as a meddlesome and often irritating stranger. It disturbs the comfortingly quiet way of life by asking questions no one among the 'locals' remembers being asked, let alone answered. Such questions make evident things into puzzles: they *defamiliarize* the familiar. Suddenly, the daily way of life must come under scrutiny. It now appears to be just one of the possible ways, not the one and only, not the 'natural', way of life. . . .

One could say that the main service the art of thinking sociologically may render to each and every one of us is to make us more *sensitive*; it may sharpen up our senses, open our eyes wider so that we can explore human conditions which thus far had remained all but invisible. Once we understand better how the apparently natural, inevitable, eternal aspects of our lives have been brought into being through the exercise of human power and human resources, we will find it hard to accept once more that they are immune and impenetrable to human action – our own action included. Sociological thinking is, one may say, a power in its own right, an *anti-fixating* power. It renders flexible again the world hitherto oppressive in its apparent fixity; it shows it as a world which could be different from what it is now. It can be argued that the art of sociological thinking tends to widen the scope, the daring and the practical effectiveness of your and my *freedom*. Once the art has been learned and mastered, the individual may well become just a bit less manipulable, more resilient to oppression and regulation from outside, more likely to resist being fixed by forces that claim to be irresistible.

To think sociologically means to understand a little more fully the people around us, their cravings and dreams, their worries and their misery. We may then better appreciate the human individuals in them and perhaps even have more respect for their rights to do what we ourselves are doing and to cherish doing it: their rights to choose and practise the way of life they prefer, to select their life-projects, to define themselves and – last but not least – vehemently defend their dignity. We may realize that in doing all those things other people come across the same kind of obstacles as we do and know the bitterness of frustration as well as we do. Eventually, sociological thinking may well promote solidarity between us, a solidarity grounded in mutual understanding and respect, solidarity in our joint resistance to suffering and shared condemnation of the cruelty that causes it. If this effect is achieved, the cause of freedom will be strengthened by being elevated to the rank of a *common* cause.

Thinking sociologically may also help us to understand other forms of life, inaccessible to our direct experience and all too often entering the commonsensical knowledge only as stereotypes – one-sided, tendentious caricatures of the way people different from ourselves (distant people, or people kept at a distance by our distaste or suspicion) live. An insight into the inner logic and meaning of the forms of life other than our own may well prompt us to think again about the alleged toughness of the boundary that has been drawn between ourselves and others, between 'us' and 'them'. Above all, it may prompt us to doubt that boundary's natural, preordained character. This new understanding may well make our communication with the 'other' easier than before, and more likely to lead to mutual agreement. It may replace fear and antagonism with tolerance. This would also contribute to our freedom, as there are no guarantees of my freedom stronger than the freedom of all, and that means also of such people as may have chosen to use their freedom to embark on a life different from my own. Only under such conditions may our own freedom to choose be exercised.

Part II

Social Interaction and Everyday Life

Erving Goffman was the pre-eminent analyst of day-to-day social interaction – above all of interaction in circumstances of 'co-presence': face-to-face social engagements between individuals present in a single physical setting. Investigating co-present interaction, Goffman points out, is distinct from the study of social groups or collectivities as such (Reading 4). The analysis of interaction in situations of co-presence can be understood as a series of *encounters* into which individuals enter in the course of their daily activities. An encounter is a unit of focused interaction, in which a number of individuals directly address each other in some way. Unfocused interaction, by contrast, refers to those forms of mutual communication which occur simply because people are in the same setting – a room, a hallway, a street – as one another.

Civil inattention, discussed by Goffman in Reading 5, is an important feature of unfocused interaction between strangers. When people pass one another in the street, or experience the multitude of fleeting social contacts which make up much of city life, they acknowledge each other in subtle, yet socially very important ways. Civil inattention, Goffman argues, is a fundamental part of orderly life in public social environments. The manipulation of the gaze – how individuals look at others, and for how long – he shows to be an essential, and again extraordinarily complex, feature of everyday social interaction.

In Reading 6, Christian Heath discusses the importance of embarrassment in social interaction. Embarrassment is the emotion which results when aspects of our encounters with others go wrong – especially when an impression an individual is seeking to sustain about his or her identity comes into question. Embarrassment is essentially a form of shame about the self. Heath looks at how doctors and patients collaborate to minimize embarrassment or shame during intimate medical examinations. Someone who undresses in front of a doctor might readily feel embarrassed, but the doctor and patient tend to work at minimizing this intrusive emotion.

Much social interaction consists of routines and everyday rituals. Repetition and habit form a key part of established relationships, as they do of many other contexts of social life. In Reading 7 Michael Young investigates why habitual actions figure so prominently in our day-to-day activities. As in so many areas of sociology, what appears 'obvious', the significance of the 'force of habit', turns out when subjected to scrutiny to be puzzling.

In Reading 8, Deborah Tannen considers the differing ways in which men and women communicate. Tannen's work has made her something of a celebrity. She claims that men and women tend to bring different presuppositions into conversations they have with one another – thus leading to the frequent rejoinder 'you just don't understand!'. Women tend to live in a world of emotional networks, in which co-operation and interdependence is stressed. Their style of conversation reflects this. Men on the other hand try to establish their independence and autonomy and hence have a quite different set of assumptions.

> # READING 4
>
> ## *Erving Goffman*
>
> # Focused Interaction and Unfocused Interaction

The study of every unit of social organization must eventually lead to an analysis of the interaction of its elements. The analytical distinction between units of organization and processes of interaction is, therefore, not destined to divide up our work for us. A division of labour seems more likely to come from distinguishing among types of units, among types of elements, or among types of processes.

Sociologists have traditionally studied face-to-face interaction as part of the area of 'collective behaviour'; the units of social organization involved are those that can form by virtue of a breakdown in ordinary social intercourse: crowds, mobs, panics, riots. The other aspect of the problem of face-to-face interaction – the units of organization in which orderly and uneventful face-to-face interaction occurs – has been neglected until recently, although there is some early work on classroom interaction, topics of conversation, committee meetings and public assemblies.

Instead of dividing face-to-face interaction into the eventful and the routine, I propose a different division – into *unfocused interaction* and *focused interaction*. Unfocused interaction consists of those interpersonal communications that result solely by virtue of persons being in one another's presence, as when two strangers across the room from each other check up on each other's clothing, posture and general manner, while each modifies his own demeanour because he himself is under observation. Focused interaction occurs when people effectively agree to sustain for a time a single focus of cognitive and visual attention, as in a conversation, a board game or a joint task sustained by a close face-to-face circle of contributors. Those sustaining together a single focus of attention will, of course, engage one another in unfocused interaction too. They will not do so in their capacity as participants in the focused activity, however, and persons present who are not in the focused activity will equally participate in this unfocused interaction.

. . . I call the natural unit of social organization in which focused inter-action occurs a *focused gathering*, or an *encounter*, or a *situated activity system*. I assume that instances of this natural unit have enough in common to make it worthwhile to study them as a type. . . .

Focused gatherings and groups do share some properties and even some that are requisites. If persons are to come together into a focused gathering and stay for a time, then certain 'system problems' will have to be solved: the participants will have to submit to rules of recruitment, to limits on overt hostility and to some division of labour. Such requisites are also found in social groups. Now if social groups and focused gatherings both exhibit the same set of properties, what is the use of distinguishing between these two units of social organization? And would not this distinction become especially unnecessary when all the members of the group are the only participants in the gathering?

Paradoxically, the easier it is to find similarities between these two units, the more mischief may be caused by not distinguishing between them. Let us address the problem, then: what is the difference between a group and a focused gathering?

A social group may be defined as a special type of social organization. Its elements are individuals: they perceive the organization as a distinct collect-ive unit, a social entity, apart from the particular relationships the partici-pants may have to one another; they perceive themselves as members who belong, identifying with the organization and receiving moral support from doing so; they sustain a sense of hostility to outgroups. A symbolization of the reality of the group and one's relation to it is also involved.

Small groups, according to this conception of groups, are distinguished by what their size makes possible (although not necessary), such as extens-ive personal knowledge of one another by the members, wide consensus and reliance on informal role differentiation. Small groups themselves – let me temporarily call them 'little groups' to distinguish them from all the other phenomena studied under the title of small-group research – differ in the degree to which they are formally or informally organized; long-standing or short-lived; multi-bonded or segmental; relatively independent, as in the case of some families and gangs, or pinned within a well-bounded organizational structure, as in the case of army platoons or office cliques.

Social groups, whether big or little, possess some general organizational properties. These properties include regulation of entering and leaving; capacity for collective action; division of labour, including leadership roles; socialization function, whether primary or adult; a means of satisfying per-sonal ends; and latent and manifest social function in the environing soci-ety. These same properties, however, are also found in many other forms of social organization, such as a social relationship binding two persons, a net-work of relationships interlocking a set of friends, a complex organization or a set of businessmen or gamesters who abide by ground rules while openly concerned only with defeating the designs of their co-participants. It is possible, of course, to call any social relationship between two indi-viduals a two-person group, but I think this is unwise. A group that is just beginning or dying may have only two members, but I feel that the conceptual framework with which this ill-manned group is to be studied ought to differ from the framework used in studying the many-sidedness of the social relationship between these two individuals. And to call any two individuals a 'two-person group' solely because there is a social relationship between them is to slight what is characteristic of groups and to fail to explore what is uniquely characteristic of relationships. . . .

Given these definitions, differences between groups and encounters become apparent. Some of the properties that are important to focused gatherings or encounters, taken as a class, seem much less important to little groups, taken as a class. Examples of such properties include embarrassment, maintenance of poise, capacity for non-distractive verbal communication, adherence to a code regarding giving up and taking over the speaker role and allocation of spatial position. Furthermore, a crucial attribute of focused gatherings – the participants' maintenance of continuous engrossment in the official focus of activity – is not a property of social groups in general, for most groups, unlike encounters, continue to exist apart from the occasions when members are physically together. A coming-together can be merely a phase of group life; a falling-away, on the other hand, is the end of a particular encounter, even when the same pattern of interaction and the same participants appear at a future meeting. Finally, there are many gatherings – for example, a set of strangers playing poker in a casino – where an extremely full array of interaction processes occurs with only the slightest development of a sense of group. All these qualifications can be made even though data for the study of little groups and for the study of focused gatherings are likely to be drawn from the same social occasion. In the same way, these qualifications can be made even though any social group can be partly described in terms of the character of the gatherings its members maintain together, just as any gathering can be described in terms of the overlapping group affiliations of its participants.

In the life of many little groups, occasions regularly arise when all the members and only the members come together and jointly sustain a situated activity system or encounter: they hold a meeting, play a game, discuss a movie, or take a cigarette break together. To call these gatherings 'meetings of the group' can easily entrap one into thinking that one is studying the group directly. Actually, these are meetings of persons who are members of a group and, even though the meeting may have been called because of issues faced by the group, the initial data concern participants in a meeting, not members of a group.

It is true that on such occasions there is likely to be a correspondence between the realm of group life and the realm of face-to-face interaction processes. For example, leadership of a little group may be expressed during gatherings of members by the question of who is chairman, or who talks the most, or who is most frequently addressed. It is also likely that the leadership demonstrated in the gathering will both influence, and be influenced by, the leadership in the group. But group leadership is not made up exclusively of an 'averaging' of positions assumed during various gatherings. In fact, the group may face circumstances in which its leader is careful to let others take leadership during a meeting, his capacity to lead the group resting upon the tactful way in which he plays a minor role during gatherings of group members. The group leader can do this because 'taking the chair' is intrinsically a possibility of gatherings, not groups.

Similarly, the factions that occur in a little group may coincide with the coalitions formed during gatherings of group members. We know, however, that such 'open' expression of structural cleavage can be seen as dangerous to the group and destructive of the opportunity of accomplishing business during the gathering, so that this congruence will often specifically be avoided. Coalitions during the gathering will then cross-cut factions in the group.

Further, even when all the members of a group are the only participants in a gathering, and the gathering has been called in order to transact business pertaining to the group, we will inevitably find that the persons present are also members of other social groups and that each of these groups can claim only a subset – moreover, a different subset – of those present. Some of the positions in the gathering are likely to be allocated on the basis of these divisive group affiliations. Of course, other positions in the gathering are likely to be allocated on the basis of factors other than group affiliation, for example, recognized experience, command of language, priority of appearance in the meeting-place or age.

Finally, while the morale of the group and the solidarity of its members may increase with an increasing number of meetings, there are strong groups that rarely have focused gatherings containing all their members and weak groups that have many.

There are issues apart from those that arise because of the difference between being a member of a group and being a participant in a gathering. Some of the properties that clearly belong both to groups and to gatherings turn out upon close examination to mean two different ranges of things, in part because of a difference in level of abstraction employed in the two cases. For example, one form of leadership that can be extremely important in gatherings is the maintenance of communication ground rules, i.e. 'order'; this aspect of leadership does not seem to have the same importance in group analysis, however. Similarly, tension management is a requirement in both groups and gatherings, but what is managed in each case seems different. Tension in encounters arises when the official focus of attention is threatened by distractions of various kinds; this state of uneasiness is managed by tactful acts, such as the open expression in a usable way of what is distracting attention. There will be circumstances, then, when tactfully expressed ranklings may ease interaction in a gathering while destroying the group to which the participants happen to belong.

The preceding arguments are meant to suggest that a frequent empirical congruence between the structure of a group and the structure of a gathering of its members does not imply any invariant analytical relation between the two realms. The concepts tailored to the study of groups and those tailored to the study of encounters may be analytically related, but these relations are by no means self-evident.

I want to say, finally, that distinguishing between little groups and focused gatherings allows one not only to see that a gathering may itself generate a fleeting little group but also to examine the relation between this group and long-standing groups from which the participants in the encounter may derive.

When all and only the members of a little group come together in a gathering, the effect of the gathering, depending on the outcome of its activity, will be to strengthen or weaken somewhat the little group. The potentiality of the encounter for generating its own group seems to be expended in what it does for and to the long-standing group. Often, there seems to be no chance for the fleeting circle of solidarity to develop much solidity of its own, for it fits too well in a pattern already established. However, when individuals come into a gathering who are not also members of the same little group, and especially if they are strangers possessing no prior relationships to one another, then the group formation that is fostered by the encounter will stand out as a contrast to all other groups of which the encounter's participants are members. It is under these circumstances – when the participants in a gathering have not been together in a group before and are not likely to be so again – that the locally generated group seems to cast its strongest shadow. It is under these circumstances, too, that the fates of these two units of organization seem most closely tied together, the effectiveness of the gathering rather directly affecting the solidarity of the group.

Paradoxically, then, if a gathering, on its own, is to generate a group and have group-formation mark the gathering as a memorable event, then a stranger or two may have to be invited – and this is sometimes carefully done on sociable occasions. These persons anchor the group-formation that occurs, preventing it from drifting back into the relationships and groups that existed previously among the participants.

READING 5

Erving Goffman

Civil Inattention and Face Engagements in Social Interaction

CIVIL INATTENTION

When persons are mutually present and not involved together in conversation or other focused interaction, it is possible for one person to stare openly and fixedly at others, gleaning what he can about them while frankly expressing on his face his response to what he sees – for example, the 'hate stare' that a Southern white sometimes gratuitously gives to Negroes walking past him. It is also possible for one person to treat others as if they were not there at all, as objects not worthy of a glance, let alone close scrutiny. Moreover, it is possible for the individual, by his staring or his 'not seeing', to alter his own appearance hardly at all in consequence of the presence of the others. Here we have 'non-person' treatment . . .

Currently, in our society, this kind of treatment is to be contrasted with the kind generally felt to be more proper in most situations, which will here be called 'civil inattention'. What seems to be involved is that one gives to another enough visual notice to demonstrate that one appreciates that the other is present (and that one admits openly to having seen him), while at the next moment withdrawing one's attention from him so as to express that he does not constitute a target of special curiosity or design.

In performing this courtesy the eyes of the looker may pass over the eyes of the other, but no 'recognition' is typically allowed. Where the courtesy is performed between two persons passing on the street, civil inattention may take the special form of eyeing the other up to approximately eight feet, during which time sides of the street are apportioned by gesture, and then casting the eyes down as the other passes – a kind of dimming of lights. In any case, we have here what is perhaps the slightest of interpersonal rituals, yet one that constantly regulates the social intercourse of persons in our society.

By according civil inattention, the individual implies that he has no reason to suspect the intentions of the others present and no reason to fear the others, be hostile to them or wish to avoid them. (At the same time, in extending this courtesy he automatically opens himself up to a like treatment from others present.) This demonstrates that he has nothing to fear or avoid in being seen and being seen seeing, and that he is not ashamed of himself or of the place and company in which he finds himself. It will therefore be necessary for him to have a certain 'directness' of eye expression. As one student suggests, the individual's gaze ought not to be guarded or averted or absent or defensively dramatic, as if 'something were going on'. Indeed, the exhibition of such deflected eye expressions may be taken as a symptom of some kind of mental disturbance.[1]

Civil inattention is so delicate an adjustment that we may expect constant evasion of the rules regarding it. Dark glasses, for example, allow the wearer to stare at another person without that other being sure that he is being stared at. One person can look at another out of the corner of his eyes. The fan and parasol once served as similar aids in stealing glances, and in polite Western society the decline in use of these instruments in the last fifty years has lessened the elasticity of communication arrangements. It should be added, too, that the closer the onlookers are to the individual who interests them, the more exposed his position (and theirs), and the more obligation they will feel to ensure him civil inattention. The further they are from him, the more licence they will feel to stare at him a little. . . .

In addition to these evasions of rules we also may expect frequent infractions of them. Here, of course, social class subculture and ethnic subculture introduce differences in patterns, and differences, too, in the age at which patterns are first employed.

The morale of a group in regard to this minimal courtesy of civil inattention – a courtesy that tends to treat those present merely as participants in the gathering and not in terms of other social characteristics – is tested whenever someone of very divergent social status or very divergent physical appearance is present. English middle-class society, for example, prides itself in giving famous and infamous persons the privilege of being civilly disattended in public, as when the royal children manage to walk through a park with few persons turning around to stare. And in our own American society, currently, we know that one of the great trials of the physically handicapped is that in public places they will be openly stared at, thereby having their privacy invaded, while, at the same time, the invasion exposes their undesirable attributes.

The act of staring is a thing which one does not ordinarily do to another human being; it seems to put the object stared at in a class apart. One does not talk to a monkey in a zoo, or to a freak in a sideshow – one only stares.

An injury, as a characteristic and inseparable part of the body, may be felt to be a personal matter which the man would like to keep private. However, the fact of its visibility makes it known to anyone whom the injured man meets, including the stranger. A visible injury differs from most other personal matters in that anyone can deal with it regardless of the wish of the injured person; anyone can stare at the injury or ask questions about it, and in both cases communicate to and impose upon the injured person his feelings and evaluations. His action is then felt as an intrusion into privacy. It is the visibility of the injury which makes intrusion into privacy so easy. The men are likely to feel that they have to meet again and again people who will question and stare, and to feel powerless because they cannot change the general state of affairs.[2]

Perhaps the clearest illustration both of civil inattention and of the infraction of this ruling occurs when a person takes advantage of another's not looking to look at him, and then finds that the object of his gaze has suddenly turned and caught the illicit looker looking. The individual caught out may then shift his gaze, often with embarrassment and a little shame, or he may carefully act as if he had merely been seen in the moment of observation that is permissible; in either case we see evidence of the propriety that should have been maintained.

To behave properly and to have the *right* to civil inattention are related: propriety on the individual's part tends to ensure his being accorded civil inattention; extreme impropriety on his part is likely to result in his being stared at or studiously not seen. Improper conduct, however, does not automatically release others from the obligation of extending civil inattention to the offender, although it often weakens it. In any case, civil inattention may be extended in the face of offensiveness simply as an act of tactfulness, to keep an orderly appearance in the situation in spite of what is happening.

Ordinarily, in middle-class society, failure to extend civil inattention to others is not negatively sanctioned in a direct and open fashion, except in the social training of servants and children, the latter especially in connection with according civil inattention to the physically handicapped and deformed. For examples of such direct sanctions among adults one must turn to despotic societies where glancing at the emperor or his agents may be a punishable offence, or to the rather refined rules prevailing in some of our Southern states concerning how much of a look a coloured male can give to a white female, over how much distance, before it is interpreted as a punishable sexual advance.

Given the pain of being stared at, it is understandable that staring itself is widely used as a means of negative sanction, socially controlling all kinds of improper public conduct. Indeed, it often constitutes the first warning an individual receives that he is 'out of line' and the last warning that it is necessary to give him. In fact, in the case of those whose appearance tests to the limit the capacity of a gathering to proffer civil inattention, staring itself may become a sanction against staring. The autobiography of an ex-dwarf provides an illustration:

> There were the thick-skinned ones, who stared like hill people come down to see a traveling show. There were the paper-peekers, the furtive kind who would withdraw blushing if you caught them at it. There were the pitying ones, whose tongue clickings could almost be heard after they had passed you. But even worse, there were the chatterers, whose every remark might as well have been 'How do you do, poor boy?' They said it with their eyes and their manners and their tone of voice.
>
> I had a standard defense – a cold stare. Thus anesthetized against my fellow man, I could contend with the basic problem – getting in and out of the subway alive.[3]

THE STRUCTURE OF FACE ENGAGEMENTS

When two persons are mutually present and hence engaged together in some degree of unfocused interaction, the mutual proffering of civil inattention – a significant form of unfocused interaction – is not the only way they can relate to one another. They can proceed from there to engage one another in focused interaction, the unit of which I shall refer to as a *face engagement* or an *encounter*. Face engagements comprise all those instances of two or more participants in a situation joining each other openly in maintaining a single focus of cognitive and visual attention – what is sensed as a single *mutual activity*, entailing preferential communication rights. As a simple example – and one of the most common – when persons are present together in the same situation they may engage each other in a talk. This accreditation for mutual activity is one of the broadest of all statuses. Even persons of extremely disparate social positions can find themselves in circumstances where it is fitting to impute it to one another. Ordinarily the status does not have a 'latent phase' but obliges the incumbents to be engaged at that very moment in exercising their status.

Mutual activities and the face engagements in which they are embedded comprise instances of small talk, commensalism, lovemaking, gaming, formal discussion and personal servicing (treating, selling, waitressing and so forth). In some cases, as with sociable chats, the coming together does not seem to have a ready instrumental rationale. In other cases, as when a teacher pauses at a pupil's desk to help him for a moment with a problem he is involved in, and will be involved in after she moves on, the encounter is clearly a setting for a mutual instrumental activity, and this joint work is merely a phase of what is primarily an individual task. It should be noted that while many face engagements seem to be made up largely of the exchange of verbal statements, so that conversational encounters can in fact be used as the model, there are still other kinds of encounters where no word is spoken. This becomes very apparent, of course, in the study of engagements among children who have not yet mastered talk, and where, incidentally, it is not possible to see the gradual transformation of a mere physical contacting of another into an act that establishes the social relationship of jointly accrediting a face-to-face encounter. Among adults, too, however, non-verbal encounters can be observed: the significant acts exchanged can be gestures or even, as in board and card games, moves. Also, there are certain close comings-together over work tasks which give rise to a single focus of visual and cognitive attention and to intimately co-ordinated contributions, the order and kind of contribution being determined by shared appreciation of what the task-at-the-moment requires as the next act. Here, while no word of direction or sociability may be spoken, it will be understood that lack of attention or co-ordinated response constitutes a breach in the mutual commitment of the participants.

Where there are only two participants in a situation, an encounter, if there is to be one, will *exhaust* the situation, giving us a *fully focused gathering*. With more than two participants, there may be persons officially present in the situation who are officially excluded from the encounter and not themselves so engaged. These unengaged participants change the gathering into a *partly focused* one. If more than three persons are present, there may be more than one encounter carried on in the same situation – a *multi-focused* gathering. I will use the term *participation unit* to refer both to encounters and to unengaged participants; the term *bystander* will be used to refer to any individual present who is not a ratified member of the particular encounter in question, whether or not he is currently a member of some other encounter.

In our society, face engagements seem to share a complex of properties so that this class of social unit can be defined analytically, as well as by example.

An encounter is initiated by someone making an opening move, typically by means of a special expression of the eyes but sometimes by a statement or a special tone of voice at the beginning of a statement. The engagement proper begins when this overture is acknowledged by the other, who signals back with his eyes, voice or stance that he has placed himself at the disposal of the other for purposes of a mutual eye-to-eye activity – even if only to ask the initiator to postpone his request for an audience.

There is a tendency for the initial move and the responding 'clearance' sign to be exchanged almost simultaneously, with all participants employing both signs, perhaps in order to prevent an initiator from placing himself in a position of being denied by others. Glances, in particular, make possible this effective simultaneity. In fact, when eyes are joined, the initiator's first glance can be sufficiently tentative and ambiguous to allow him to act as if no initiation has been intended, if it appears that his overture is not desired.

Eye-to-eye looks, then, play a special role in the communication life of the community, ritually establishing an avowed openness to verbal statements and a rightfully heightened mutual relevance of acts. In Simmel's words:

> Of the special sense-organs, the eye has a uniquely sociological function. The union and interaction of individuals is based upon mutual glances. This is perhaps the most direct and purest reciprocity which exists anywhere. This highest psychic reaction, however, in which the glances of eye to eye unite men, crystallizes into no objective structure; the unity which momentarily arises between two persons is present in the occasion and is dissolved in the function. So tenacious and subtle is this union that it can only be maintained by the shortest and straightest line between the eyes, and the smallest deviation from it, the slightest glance aside, completely destroys the unique character of this union. No objective trace of this relationship is left behind, as is universally found, directly or indirectly, in all other types of associations between men, as, for example, in interchange of words. The interaction of eye and eye dies in the moment in which directness of the function is lost. But the totality of social relations of human beings, their self-assertion and self-abnegation, their intimacies and estrangements, would be changed in unpredictable ways if there occurred no glance of eye to eye. This mutual glance between persons, in distinction from the simple sight or observation of the other, signifies a wholly new and unique union between them.[4]

It is understandable, then, that an individual who feels he has cause to be alienated from those around him will express this through some 'abnormality of the gaze', especially averting of the eyes. And it is understandable, too, that an individual who wants to control others' access to him and the information he receives may avoid looking toward the person who is seeking him out. A waitress, for example, may prevent a waiting customer from 'catching her eye' to prevent his initiating an order. Similarly, if a pedestrian wants to ensure a particular allocation of the street relative to a fellow pedestrian, or if a motorist wants to ensure priority of his line of proposed action over that of a fellow motorist or a pedestrian, one strategy is to avoid meeting the other's eyes and thus avoid co-operative claims. And where the initiator is in a social position requiring him to give the other the formal right to initiate all encounters, hostile and teasing possibilities may occur, of which Melville's *White-Jacket* gives us an example:

> But sometimes the captain feels out of sorts, or in ill-humour, or is pleased to be somewhat capricious, or has a fancy to show a touch of his omnipotent supremacy; or, peradventure, it has so happened that the first lieutenant has, in some way, piqued or offended him, and he is not unwilling to show a slight specimen of his dominion over him, even before the eyes of all hands; at all events, only by some one of these suppositions can the singular circumstance be accounted for, that frequently Captain Claret would pertinaciously promenade up and down the poop, purposely averting his eye from the first lieutenant, who would stand below in the most awkward suspense, waiting the first wink from his superior's eye.
>
> 'Now I have him!' he must have said to himself, as the captain would turn toward him in his walk; 'now's my time!' and up would go his hand to his cap; but, alas! the captain was off again; and the men at the guns would cast sly winks at each other as the embarrassed lieutenant would bite his lips with suppressed vexation.
>
> Upon some occasions this scene would be repeated several times, till at last Captain Claret, thinking that in the eyes of all hands his dignity must by this time be pretty well bolstered, would stalk towards his subordinate, looking him full in the eyes; whereupon up goes his hand to the cap front, and the captain, nodding his acceptance of the report, descends from his perch to the quarter-deck.[5]

As these various examples suggest, mutual glances ordinarily must be withheld if an encounter is to be avoided, for eye contact opens one up for face engagement. I would like to add, finally, that there is a relationship between the use of eye-to-eye glances as a means of communicating a request for initiation of an encounter, and other communication practices. The more clearly individuals are obliged to refrain from staring directly at others, the more effectively will they be able to attach special significance to a stare, in this case, a request for an encounter. The rule of civil inattention thus makes possible, and 'fits' with, the clearance function given to looks into others' eyes. The rule similarly makes possible the giving of a special function to 'prolonged' holding of a stranger's glance, as when unacquainted persons who had arranged to meet each other manage to discover one another in this way.

READING 6

Christian Heath

Embarrassment and Interactional Organization

Embarrassment has received relatively little attention within the behavioural sciences. Unlike other forms of emotion, it is said to be a purely human experience, a social phenomenon, and as such less subject to physiological and psychological explanation than the less ephemeral forms of feeling. Sociology on the other hand, has paid relatively little attention to the emotions, considering feelings either inaccessible to or unworthy of analytic scrutiny . . . [However] embarrassment lies at the heart of the social organization of day-to-day conduct. It provides a personal constraint on the behaviour of the individual in society and a public response to actions and activities considered problematic or untoward. Embarrassment and its potential play an important part in sustaining the individual's commitment to social organization, values and convention. It permeates everyday life and our dealings with others. It informs ordinary conduct and bounds the individual's behaviour in areas of social life that formal and institutionalized constraints do not reach. And as with so many areas of ordinary conduct, it is Erving Goffman who directs analytic attention towards the significance of embarrassment to social life and thereby throws into relief the situational and interactional nature of the emotions.

Goffman suggests that participants in interaction have a moral obligation to sustain their own and each other's claims to relevant identities and that embarrassment emerges 'if expressive facts threaten or discredit the assumptions a participant has projected about his identity'. Goffman argues that embarrassment involves an individual losing composure, and its characteristic signs such as 'blushing, fumbling and vacillating movement' undermine a person's ability to participate in the topic or business of the encounter; embarrassment threatens the line of activity in which the participants are involved. He concludes that face-to-face interaction requires 'just those capacities that embarrassment may destroy' and provides us with a framework with which to consider how persons ordinarily avoid and dispel such difficulties. . . .

I wish to draw on Goffman's pioneering work to explore the interactional organization of embarrassment. Unlike previous work on embarrassment and the expression of other forms of emotion, the observations are based upon the analysis of actual instances of the phenomenon drawn from naturally occurring interaction. . . .

The data employed in this [study] are drawn from a substantial collection of video-recordings of naturally occurring medical consultations, collected as part of a research project concerned with visual and vocal behaviour between the doctor and patient. . . . Current work on the project is concerned with the interaction between the doctor and patient during the physical examination and it was in this rather delicate area of social life that we became interested in embarrassment and emotion and its relation to ordinary conduct. . . .

The video-recordings were reviewed to unearth instances which revealed one or other of the participants exhibiting the characteristic signs of embarrassment, in particular a loss of composure and an inability to participate, if only momentarily, within the encounter. In fact such occasions prove relatively rare and one is led, like Goffman, to consider the ways in which embarrassment is avoided. More importantly, however, in locating actual instances of embarrassment embodying the characteristics described by Goffman and others, it transpires in more detailed analysis that rather than 'flooding out', the individual's behaviour is systematically organized with respect to the surrounding configuration of action and activity. Repeatedly unearthing an interactional systematics to embarrassment undermined our confidence in the way in which the phenomenon had been characterized and conceived by Goffman and others.

A MOMENT OF EMBARRASSMENT

. . . Actual outbursts of embarrassment during the medical examination are relatively rare. If they do occur, however, they tend to happen as the participants prepare for the examination rather than as the doctor actually inspects the patient's body. It is of course following the doctor's request to examine the patient that undressing takes place, not infrequently in front of the doctor; and it is here that the patient reveals his or her body to the doctor for the first time – at least during the current consultation.

The following fragment is drawn from the juncture between the request to examine the patient and the actual inspection of the body. In this case the examination has been delayed whilst the doctor answers the telephone. The patient waits, undressed to her bra, for the examination to begin. We enter the consultation as the doctor finishes the telephone conversation and turns to the patient. . . . Of particular importance here are the length of the silences captured in tenths of a second and the rows of 'h's, which represent inbreaths if preceded by an asterisk (*hhh); outbreaths if not.

Fragment 1 Transcript 1 (simplified)

Dr: Slip your gear off an let's have a look.

.

[intervening phone conversation]

.

Dr: *[completes call and turns to patient]*
P: *hhh hhhhhh kh (0.2) *hhhh keh kh hm
(0.8)
P: khh
(2.3)
Dr: Now then, let's have a listen

The actual episode of embarrassment begins towards the end of the silence following the patient's coughing and breathlessness. As the doctor turns towards her, the patient becomes momentarily flustered and appears to lose control of her behaviour. A more detailed transcript including visual as well as vocal elements will be helpful. Unlike the previous transcript, the action is laid out across the page. The gaps are represented by dashes, each dash equivalent to 0.1 of a second. The visual behaviour of the patient is transcribed above the line used to capture the silence and vocalization, the doctor's below. The gaze of the participant is captured immediately above or below this line and a series of signs, ~~~, represents one party turning towards the other, dashes, ----, represent turning away. A continuous line or dash represents one participant looking at the other.

Fragment 1 Transcript 2 (simplified)

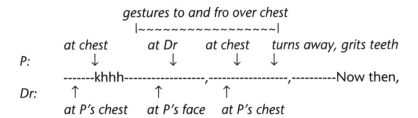

On finishing the phone conversation the doctor turns towards the patient and the patient reorientates towards the doctor. The moment her gaze arrives the patient turns from the doctor to her partially naked chest. There she begins to gesture rapidly, passing her open hand back and forth over the surface of her chest. Whilst gesturing she blinks and shakes her head. After a moment or so the doctor looks up from the chest and the patient follows, turning once more towards the doctor's face. By the time her gaze arrives, the doctor has returned his gaze to the chest. Finding the doctor looking at the chest the patient turns to the object of his gaze and once again begins to gesture, waving her open hand rapidly back and forth over the naked chest. Again the gesture is accompanied by the patient blinking and looking here and there. Less than a second passes and she turns away from her chest to one side, lowering her eyelids and gritting her teeth. The episode subsides as the doctor follows the patient and turns to one side, a second or so later the participants rearrange their seating positions as they begin the examination.

Figure 2.1
Fragment 1

(a)   (b)

Figure 2.1 – (a) showing immediately before the episode begins, and (b) during its course – may help provide a sense of the action. This brief episode embodies many of the characteristic signs of embarrassment. The patient's apparently haphazard movements, the flustered gestures, the shifting gaze and blinking eyes coupled with the head movements and, towards the end of the episode, the lowered eyelids and gritting of the teeth, capture behaviour described by both Goffman and other scholars who have addressed this form of emotional expression. For example, Goffman speaks of 'blushing, fumbling, stuttering, tremors of the hand, hesitancy and vacillating movement' as signs of embarrassment and continues by describing the associated physiological elements such as the acceleration of the heart beat and its effects on the circulation and skin colour. In the case at hand, the patient appears momentarily to lose composure and to become 'mentally confused'; she 'floods out' and undermines her ability to participate in the business at hand, the preparation for the physical examination.

In this as in other examples of embarrassment, the person's behaviour appears bizarre and idiosyncratic, unrelated to the interaction and business at hand, a moment in which the participant is overcome by a flood of emotion and unable to retain control of his or her actions. Yet however extraordinary the behaviour of the patient might appear, the moment of her emotion and its expression is systematically related to the actions of her co-participant. For example, the patient's embarrassment does not arise 'anywhere' within the developing course of the consultation but is co-ordinated with the local environment of activity. As the doctor finishes the telephone conversation and turns to the patient she too turns towards the doctor. As her gaze arrives, the patient finds the doctor looking at her chest rather than her face. She immediately turns to the object of his attention and begins to gesture. A moment or so later the doctor looks up and the patient ceases her gesture and returns her gaze to the face of the doctor, only to find him once more looking at her chest. Her embarrassment re-emerges as she once again begins to gesture and looks intermittently at the object in question.

It is the doctor's glance which gives rise to the patient's emotion, and his glance which rekindles her difficulties for a second time. The glance is 'physically' equivalent to many of the looks the doctor gives the patient during the medical examination, yet at this moment within the proceedings it fires the patient's embarrassment. The source of the difficulties arises from the state of involvement during this phase of the consultation; the juncture between the request to examine the patient and the actual inspection of the body. It is one of the few occasions during the encounter where there is no jointly co-ordinated activity in which the participants are involved; no common focus of attention. It is a sort of 'no man's land' in the interaction, a phase which frequently entails a fragmentation of involvement in which the doctor and patient attend to their distinct but related concerns in preparing for the examination. In such circumstances a glance at the body of another can gain a significance it might not otherwise have. Unlike glances exchanged between persons during the production of an activity, either talk or the examination itself, the doctor's looking does not form part of a legitimate stretch of activity to which the participants are mutually committed. Rather, the doctor's glance lies alone, divorced from the business of the consultation and, in this way, can be interpreted as 'looking at' the other, momentarily bringing the patient's chest to the forefront of mutual attention.

Thus it is not simply the temporal structure of a look which transforms glance into stare, but rather its relationship to the local configuration of activity. . . . In the case at hand the doctor's glance brings the patient's chest to the forefront of mutual attention and initiates a stretch of activity – the patient's brief episode of emotion. Whatever feelings the patient or anyone else associates with the revelation of particular parts of her or his body, it is a specific action, the looking, that renders the object embarrassable.

On finding the doctor looking at her chest, the patient produces her flustered gesture and the associated movements of the eyes and head. Though seemingly chaotic, the patient's gesture, like other movements which occur in face-to-face interaction, may be carefully designed with respect to the local circumstances and the action(s) it is performing. It will be recalled that in both its stages the patient's gesture consists of an open hand which is waved successively over the chest, the object of the doctor's attention. In both stages the gesture criss-crosses the line of regard of the doctor and in consequence intermittently conceals the chest from his view. Thus by gesturing over the chest the patient hides her chest if only partially from the doctor's view. As he withdraws his gaze she abandons the gesture. On finding the doctor once more looking at her chest, she conceals her chest from his wandering eye. The gesture therefore serves to interrupt the other's looking and perhaps encourages him to abandon his interest in her partially naked body.

If the sole concern of the gestures were to conceal the chest from the gaze of the doctor then one might expect the patient simply to place her hand on its surface or in some other way conceal the source of her embarrassment. The patient's gestures, however, may be concerned not solely with concealing the object from the doctor's view, but also with managing other demands and constraints within the local interactional environment. The moment of embarrassment occurs as the doctor finishes a telephone conversation and is about to begin the examination of the patient. Consequently, as the doctor finishes the call the patient reorientates towards the doctor and presents her chest for inspection. It is at this moment that the patient finds the doctor looking at the chest rather than moving forward to the patient to examine it. Simultaneously the patient is placed under two competing interactional demands; on the one hand, presenting the chest for examination, on the other, concealing it from the gaze of the doctor. The flustered gesture, the open hand successively passing to and fro over the surface of the chest, embody these simultaneous constraints on her behaviour; she attempts to present the chest and remain available for the examination whilst concealing the focus of her embarrassment from the unwanted attention of the doctor. In consequence, it is hardly surprising that the patient's actions appear flustered and disorganized as she attempts to settle the sequential constraints of the appropriate next activity with the implications of the doctor's gaze.

The shape of the gestures and the patient's apparent lack of commitment to concealing the chest fully may also be related to the potential consequences of such action. However strong the patient's inclination to conceal the chest from the gaze of the doctor, such an action would have significant retrospective implications and might lead to further embarrassment and difficulties. Were the patient to conceal her chest fully, it would cast aspersion on the actions of the doctor, suggesting that his glance was untoward and problematic. It would imply that the doctor's looking lay outside any warranted medical practice and suggest that less professional motives underlay the actions of the doctor. Fully concealing the chest would be tantamount to refusing to be examined for reasons which arose in the course of the doctor's behaviour, and both patient and doctor might be called to account. In such circumstances we can understand why the patient might avoid wholesale commitment to a course of action which would generate a definition of the other and his or her actions which could well undermine the very foundation of the consultation.

A characteristic of shame and embarrassment described in both literature and the sciences is of the sufferer 'not knowing where to look' and shielding the eyes from the gaze of the onlooker(s). Darwin captures a flavour of these difficulties in his classic treatise on the expressions of emotion in man and animals.

> The habit, so general with everyone who feels ashamed, of turning away, or lowering the eyes, or restlessly moving them from side to side, probably follows from each glance directed towards those present, bringing home the conviction that he is intently regarded; and he endeavours, by not looking at those present, and especially not at their eyes, momentarily to escape from this painful conviction.[1]

In fragment 1, as with many instances of embarrassment, the patient is overcome with difficulties as to where to look. She begins by turning from the doctor to her chest, quickly returning her gaze to the doctor and then once again glancing at her chest. Finally she turns to one side and lowers her eyelids as if in shame. . . . with rapid changes in the direction of her gaze, the patient successively blinks and very slightly shakes her head. As Darwin suggests, the individual who suffers embarrassment and shame becomes restless, looking hither and thither or lowering the eyes. The patient during this brief episode appears quite simply not to know where to look or rest her eyes. She appears to be simultaneously drawn and repelled by the gaze of the doctor.

The behaviour of the patient arises in part through the power of a look to affect another. The patient is . . . drawn by the gaze of the doctor to return his look, if only to check whether he is continuing to stare at the chest. Yet, were the patient to return the gaze, then the doctor might well be encouraged to look the patient in the eye; the moment of mutual gaze giving rise to a shared recognition of the doctor's preceding behaviour and an intimacy between the participants which might well generate further difficulty. Embarrassment thrives on one person seeing another see the first, and so on; the reflexive recognition kindling further the fires of discomfort.

Yet if the patient is reluctant to face the doctor she is also troubled by looking at the object of her embarrassment. No sooner does she turn from the doctor to the chest than she looks up, then, turning once again to her chest, she rapidly looks away. Looking at her chest provides little relief from her embarrassment. It is of course first noticing the object of the doctor's attention which gives rise to the initial gesture, and finding the doctor 'continuing' to look which leads to further activity across the chest. It is as if looking at the chest and sharing the focus of the doctor's curiosity generate the embarrassment and encourage it to continue; the patient's difficulty arising as she sees herself and her body in the light of another seeing her. Again, there is something in the mutual recognition of the body which fires the embarrassment. The interactional constraints which give rise to the embarrassment and feature in its organization derive from the power of the look, in particular the sequential significance of a person's gaze in environments in which persons are co-present yet not fully engaged in the mutual production of an activity.

READING 7

Michael Young

Time, Habit and Repetition in Day-to-Day Life

Why do people repeat themselves so much? Why do they do more or less the same thing every year at Christmas, or on their own birthdays, or every day as they go about their daily rounds, getting out of bed in the morning, washing, dressing, getting breakfast, reading the paper, opening the mail, walking to the garage or the station, talking to colleagues, telephoning the same people day after day, writing letters which are much like letters written on other days, stopping themselves going into the pub with a twinge of regret, as on other days? It cannot all be due to their biological clocks. People do not settle down to their Christmas dinner by measuring the day's length to the nearest few minutes: they are not birds compelled to fly to the dinner table (or into the oven) at just that precise moment.

Some additional force must be responsible for the regularity of Christmas, although it is one day in Western Europe and another in Eastern Europe, and for its absence in large parts of the world; and for keeping most people head-down at their daily tasks when it is not Christmas. I am in other words looking for a 'sociological clock' which is as powerful and omnipresent a synchronizer as the biological clock. I propose that this force is the force of habit and its extension, custom – the tendency we all have, in greater or lesser measure, to do again what we have done before. Habit is as intrinsic to the cyclic (including some of its irregularities) as conscious memory is to the linear. Habit and memory are each means of preserving the past to do service in the present, but in the main for different though complementary ends: the first to ensure continuity, and the second to open the way for change. . . .

Habits are always being created anew. As the Chinese proverb says, 'a habit begins the first time'. Habits are generated and locked into place by recurrences so that they become automatic, rather than deliberate. In his *Principles of Psychology* William James gives habit a central place as 'the enormous flywheel of society, its most precious conservative agent': 'any sequence of mental actions which has been frequently repeated tends to perpetuate itself; so that we find ourselves automatically prompted to *think*, *feel* or *do* what we have been before accustomed to think, feel or do, under like circumstances, without any consciously formed *purpose*, or anticipation of results.[1] For James habit was even more than second nature. He agreed with the Duke of Wellington:

> 'Habit a second nature! Habit is ten times nature', the Duke of Wellington is said to have exclaimed . . . 'There is a story, which is credible enough, though it may not be true, of a practical joker, who, seeing a discharged veteran carrying home his dinner, suddenly called out "Attention!", whereupon the man instantly brought his hands down, and lost his mutton and potatoes in the gutter. The drill has been thorough, and its effects had become embodied in the man's nervous structure.'[2]

This story also illustrates James's statement that 'in habit the only command is to start'. After that the actions are automatic. 'Second nature' is one term for it, despite the duke. Another popular term, in a society fancying airplanes for transport, is the phrase 'to go on automatic'.

There are degrees of automation. When it is complete, there is no need for thinking at all; there may not even be any conscious recognition of the situation that produces the habitual behaviour. No proposition is more self-evident than that people take a great deal as self-evident. I just act, without having to reason why. Without thinking about it, I scratch my head, or wink, or open my mouth when I am puzzled, and at a particular corner on my ordinary route to work I go through the routine motions with my arms and feet, all without being aware of it, unless on one occasion I put my foot hard on the accelerator instead of the brake or do something else eccentric, in which case I may remember it for life (if there is any left); and I do not do these things because I am so very notably absent-minded compared to others but because on such matters everyone is absent-minded. We are all to a considerable extent like A. J. Cook, the miners' leader in the British General Strike of 1926: 'Before he gets up he has no idea what he is going to say; when he's on his feet he has no idea what he is saying; and when he sits down he has no idea what he has just said.'[3] . . .

Habits are not usually chosen with any deliberation; they just grow, wild flowers rather than cultivated ones. They would not do this so readily and constantly without a series of overlapping advantages which assure that their growth will not be stopped. I will mention four of them. The first advantage is that habit increases the skill with which actions can be performed. The multiplication table is tiresome to learn but, once it has become habitual, reproducing it is very accurate and very quick. Reading and writing are difficult to acquire in the first place but, once acquired, both can be very efficient. To master the piano is very difficult indeed for the beginner, whose convulsive movements of the body and mangling of the keyboard make it seem impossible that any euphony will ever be achieved; but a few years later the hands may caper over the notes as though to the manner born, and all as the result of unflagging repetition. In such cases an act of will (even if abetted by the cajoling of parents or teachers) can inaugurate a habit which the will does not thereafter have to be engaged in guiding.

The second advantage is that a habit diminishes fatigue. Driving a car, or thinking about existentialism, or speaking a foreign language, or saying our prayers, is tiring the first time it is done, and if a person does not persevere because it is tiring it will always remain so. But persevere, and before too long the same person will be rattling off talk about existentialism while watching a football match or the television, or even driving a car while shouting at his children in the back to be quiet, in the hope that quietness will become as much a habit for them as shouting is for him. If fatigue could not be reduced by such means – or (to put it another way) effort invested now with an immense rate of return in reduced effort in the future – a life of any complexity could be insupportable. . . .

The third advantage is still more significant: a habit not only economizes on the effort put into the humdrum and the foreseen but also spares attention for the unforeseen. A capacity for attention is held in permanent reserve, ready to be mobilized to deal with the unexpected – the truck which appears from nowhere directly in front of one's own car, or the shout for help, or the summons to appear before the boss. Habit, by allowing predictable events or features of an event to be managed with hardly any effort, enables people to concentrate most of their attention on the unpredictable. Habit is necessary to allow this concentration. Without it, people would not be able to cope with the changes in their environments which cannot be reduced to rule; they would be without the adaptability which has enabled them to survive countless threats to their existence. Habits are one of our chief tools for survival.

The fourth advantage – the economizing of memory – in a sense encompasses all the other advantages. If Mr Murgatroyd on any morning arrived at work to find he had left his habits behind him, and had only his memory to guide him, he might as well get back into his car and go home. The same is true for the whole workforce. Without their usual collection of habits they would be looking at each other almost as if for the first time, in bewilderment, like a regiment lost in a forest, or an assembly of people with severe Alzheimer's disease for whom there was nothing in life except today, wondering what on earth to do with themselves while Mr M ransacked his memory about the organization of the factory and telephoned the head office for orders. Even if the head office were not stricken by the same disability – and if only one person was left with the capacity for habit he or she would soon rule the corporation, and perhaps the world – it would be a task indeed to translate their orders for axles into routines for everyone in the factory in time to get any made that day. Starting from scratch with only their conscious recollections to guide them, it would be miraculous if he and the other managers decided what exactly should be done, and by whom, in time for anyone else to do any work before the bell for the end of the shift. Without habit, every day would be more than fully absorbed in puzzling about what to do, with none of it available for anything else, until they all decided to give it up and stay at home for good – unless home too was similarly overtaken. It would be too much to have to rely on memory to reinvent the wheel, or the axle, even every year, let alone every day.

The head office might decide to send down for an inspection not another production manager but a psychiatrist. All of us know that some people are like the indecisive imaginary Mr M, who now does not know whether to put on sandals or boots when he arrives in his office, if he can find where it is. James was severe on such a condition:

The more of the details of our daily life we can hand over to the effortless custody of automatism, the more our higher powers of mind will be set free for their own proper work. There is no more miserable human being than one in whom nothing is habitual but indecision, and for whom the lighting of every cigar, the drinking of every cup, the time of rising and going to bed every day, and the beginning of every bit of work, are subjects of express volitional deliberation. Full half the time of such a man goes to the deciding, or regretting, of matters which ought to be so ingrained in him as practically not to exist for his consciousness at all. If there be such daily duties not yet ingrained in any one of my readers, let him begin this very hour to set the matter right.[4]

. . . Mr Murgatroyd and his men have something which is in many circumstances better than memory. They do not have to make room in their consciousness for the past. They do not have to recall what they did; instead they can be guided by the habit of what they did do. Jerome Bruner said about selectivity:

Selectivity is the rule and a nervous system, in Lord Adrian's phrase, is as much an editorial hierarchy as it is a system for carrying signals. We have learned too that the 'arts' of sensing and knowing consist in honoring our highly limited capacity for taking in and processing information. We honor that capacity by learning the methods of compacting vast ranges of experience in economical symbols – concepts, language, metaphor, myth, formulae. The price of failing at this art is either to be trapped in a confined world of experience or to be the victim of an overload of information.[5]

He might have added habits after formulae. A habit is a memory unconsciously edited for action.

READING 8

Deborah Tannen

'You Just Don't Understand'

INTIMACY AND INDEPENDENCE

Intimacy is key in a world of connection where individuals negotiate complex networks of friendship, minimize differences, try to reach consensus, and avoid the appearance of superiority, which would highlight differences. In a world of status, *independence* is key, because a primary means of establishing status is to tell others what to do, and taking orders is a marker of low status. Though all humans need both intimacy and independence, women tend to focus on the first and men on the second. It is as if their life-blood ran in different directions.

These differences can give women and men differing views of the same situation, as they did in the case of a couple I will call Linda and Josh. When Josh's old high-school chum called him at work and announced he'd be in town on business the following month, Josh invited him to stay for the weekend. That evening he informed Linda that they were going to have a house guest, and that he and his chum would go out together the first night to shoot the breeze like old times. Linda was upset. She was going to be away on business the week before, and the Friday night when Josh would be out with his chum would be her first night home. But what upset her most was that Josh had made these plans on his own and informed her of them, rather than discussing them with her before extending the invitation.

Linda would never make plans, for a weekend or an evening, without first checking with Josh. She can't understand why he doesn't show her the same courtesy and consideration that she shows him. But when she protests, Josh says, 'I can't say to my friends, "I have to ask my wife for permission"!'

To Josh, checking with his wife means seeking permission, which implies that he is not independent, not free to act on his own. It would make him feel like a child or an underling. To Linda, checking with her husband has nothing to do with permission. She assumes that spouses discuss their plans with each other because their lives are intertwined, so the actions of one have consequences for the other. Not only does Linda not mind telling someone, 'I have to check with Josh'; quite the contrary – she likes it. It makes her feel good to know and show that she is involved with someone, that her life is bound up with someone else's.

Linda and Josh both felt more upset by this incident, and others like it, than seemed warranted, because it cut to the core of their primary concerns. Linda was hurt because she sensed a failure of closeness in their relationship: he didn't care about her as much as she cared about him. And he was hurt because he felt she was trying to control him and limit his freedom.

A similar conflict exists between Louise and Howie, another couple, about spending money. Louise would never buy anything costing more than 100 dollars without discussing it with Howie, but he goes out and buys whatever he wants and feels they can afford, like a table saw or a new power mower. Louise is disturbed, not because she disapproves of the purchases, but because she feels he is acting as if she were not in the picture.

Many women feel it is natural to consult with their partners at every turn, while many men automatically make more decisions without consulting their partners. This may reflect a broad difference in conceptions of decision-making. Women expect decisions to be discussed first and made by consensus. They appreciate the discussion itself as evidence of involvement and communication. But many men feel oppressed by lengthy discussions about what they see as minor decisions, and they feel hemmed in if they can't just act without talking first. When women try to initiate a free-wheeling discussion by asking, 'What do you think?' men often think they are being asked to decide.

Communication is a continual balancing act, juggling the conflicting needs for intimacy and independence. To survive in the world, we have to act in concert with others, but to survive as ourselves, rather than simply as cogs in a wheel, we have to act alone. In some ways, all people are the same: we all eat and sleep and drink and laugh and cough, and often we eat, and laugh at, the same things. But in some ways, each person is different, and individuals' differing wants and preferences may conflict with each other. Offered the same menu, people make different choices. And if there is cake for dessert, there is a chance one person may get a larger piece than another – and an even greater chance that one will *think* the other's piece is larger, whether it is or not.

ASYMMETRIES

If intimacy says, 'We're close and the same', and independence says, 'We're separate and different', it is easy to see that intimacy and independence dovetail with connection and status. The essential element of connection is symmetry: people are the same, feeling equally close to each other. The essential element of status is asymmetry: people are not the same; they are differently placed in a hierarchy.

This duality is particularly clear in expressions of sympathy or concern, which are all potentially ambiguous. They can be interpreted either symmetrically, as evidence of fellow feeling among equals, or asymmetrically, offered by someone one-up to someone one-down. Asking if an unemployed person has found a job, if a couple have succeeded in conceiving the child they crave, or whether an untenured professor expects to get tenure can be meant – and interpreted, regardless of how it is meant – as an expression of human connection by a person who understands and cares, or as a reminder of weakness from someone who is better off and knows it, and hence as condescending. The latter view of sympathy seems self-evident to many men. For example, a handicapped mountain climber named Tom Whittaker, who leads groups of disabled people on outdoor expeditions, remarked, 'You can't feel sympathetic for someone you admire' – a statement that struck me as not true at all.

The symmetry of connection is what creates community: if two people are struggling for closeness, they are both struggling for the same thing. And the asymmetry of status is what creates contest: two people can't both have the upper hand, so negotiation for status is inherently adversarial. In my earlier work, I explored in detail the dynamics of intimacy (which I referred to as involvement) and independence, but I tended to ignore the force of status and its adversarial nature. Once I identified these dynamics, however, I saw them all around me. The puzzling behaviour of friends and co-workers finally became comprehensible.

Differences in how my husband and I approached the same situation, which previously would have been mystifying, suddenly made sense. For example, in a jazz club the waitress recommended the crab cakes to me, and they turned out to be terrible. I was uncertain about whether or not to send them back. When the waitress came by and asked how the food was, I said that I didn't really like the crab cakes. She asked, 'What's wrong with them?' While staring at the table, my husband answered, 'They don't taste fresh.' The waitress snapped, 'They're frozen! What do you expect?' I looked directly up at her and said, 'We just don't like them.' She said, 'Well, if you don't like them, I could take them back and bring you something else.'

After she left with the crab cakes, my husband and I laughed because we realized we had just automatically played out the scripts I had been writing about. He had heard her question 'What's wrong with them?' as a challenge that he had to match. He doesn't like to fight, so he looked away, to soften what he felt was an obligatory counter-challenge: he felt instinctively that he had to come up with something wrong with the crab cakes to justify my complaint. (He was fighting for me.) I had taken the question 'What's wrong with them?' as a request for information. I instinctively sought a way to be right without making her wrong. Perhaps it was because she was a woman that she responded more favourably to my approach.

When I have spoken to friends and to groups about these differences, they too say that now they can make sense of previously perplexing behaviour. For example, a woman said she finally understood why her husband refused to talk to his boss about whether or not he stood a chance of getting promoted. He wanted to know because if the answer was no, he would start looking for another job. But instead of just asking, he stewed and fretted, lost sleep and worried. Having no others at her disposal, this wife had fallen back on psychological explanations: her husband must be insecure, afraid of rejection. But then, everyone is insecure, to an extent. Her husband was actually quite a confident person. And she, who believed herself to be at least as insecure as he, had not hesitated to go to her boss to ask whether he intended to make her temporary job permanent.

Understanding the key role played by status in men's relations made it all come clear. Asking a boss about chances for promotion highlights the hierarchy in the relationship, reminding them both that the employee's future is in the boss's hands. Taking the low-status position made this man intensely uncomfortable. Although his wife didn't especially relish taking the role of supplicant with respect to her boss, it didn't set off alarms in her head, as it did in his.

In a similar flash of insight, a woman who works in sales exclaimed that now she understood the puzzling transformation that the leader of her sales team had undergone when he was promoted to district manager. She had been sure he would make a perfect boss because he had a healthy disregard for authority. As team leader, he had rarely bothered to go to meetings called by management and had encouraged team members to exercise their own judgement, eagerly using his power to waive regulations on their behalf. But after he became district manager, this man was unrecognizable. He instituted more regulations than anyone had dreamed of, and insisted that exceptions could be made only on the basis of written requests to him.

This man behaved differently because he was now differently placed in the hierarchy. When he had been subject to the authority of management, he'd done all he could to limit it. But when the authority of management was vested in him, he did all he could to enlarge it. By avoiding meetings and flouting regulations, he had evidenced not disregard for hierarchy but rather discomfort at being in the subordinate position within it.

Yet another woman said she finally understood why her fiancé, who very much believes in equality, once whispered to her that she should keep her voice down. 'My friends are downstairs,' he said, 'I don't want them to get the impression that you order me around.'

That women have been labelled 'nags' may result from the interplay of men's and women's styles, whereby many women are inclined to do what is asked of them and many men are inclined to resist even the slightest hint that anyone, especially a woman, is telling them what to do. A woman will be inclined to repeat a request that doesn't get a response because she is convinced that her husband would do what she asks, if he only understood that she *really* wants him to do it. But a man who wants to avoid feeling that he is following orders may instinctively wait before doing what she asked, in order to imagine that he is doing it of his own free will. Nagging is the result, because each time she repeats the request, he again puts off fulfilling it.

Part III

Sociology of the Body

It would seem as though the body were completely outside the scope of sociology. Our bodies are physiological systems and would therefore appear to be remote from the interests of the sociologist. In fact, however, our bodies are strongly conditioned by social influences. Consider, for example, images of the desirable body. Until quite recently in European history, and in many non-Western cultures, to be thin was regarded as a sign of poverty and undernourishment. In Western countries today, by contrast, particularly for women, thinness is held out as an ideal. The so called 'slimmer's disease', anorexia, together with a variety of other eating disorders, have become commonplace.

Keeping slim for many of us has become an obsession, as David Cohen recounts in Reading 9. For Sally, whose story Cohen tells, repeated exercise, and the cultivation of a trim body, became a means of coping with problems in her life. Men are not immune. The ideal body type for many men in the past was one of strong muscular development. Increasingly, however, the ideal of the muscle man is being replaced by one emphasizing slimness, just as in the case of women. In Reading 10 Lisa O'Kelly investigates men's attitudes towards their bodies. Male body awareness has increased dramatically in recent years. 'Looking good', surveys indicate, is still regarded as less important by men than it is by women. Yet these attitudes are starting to converge more and more between the sexes.

Exercise, slimming and controlled eating are linked not only to the desire to 'look good', but to attempts to follow a healthy lifestyle. A look back to two centuries ago provides graphic evidence of the level to which illness and the prospect of an early death haunted the lives of individuals in eighteenth-century society (Reading 11). Infectious diseases were rampant and the ordinary person suffered from a range of chronic complaints which many of us in modern social conditions would find intolerable.

Some of the great breakthroughs in the improvement of health care were made in the area of preventive medicine, particularly as a result of improvements in methods of hygiene. Other changes, however, have depended more upon the emergence of organized systems of health care. In Reading 12 Ross Hume Hall compares two contrasting systems of health care, those of the United Kingdom and the United States.

In Britain health care is provided through the National Health Service, funded through public resources. In the US, there is no government-sponsored system of health care directly comparable to the NHS. Medical care is provided by means of private insurance, or through government-supported programmes designed to help those who cannot afford to take out adequate health cover for themselves. How far either system is more effective than the other in generating adequate health care is a matter of some contention. Hall points out that the American system provides greater freedom of choice for the more affluent segments of the population, but appears considerably more expensive to run than the NHS. On the other hand, it is generally believed that the NHS provides greater medical support for poorer groups than the American system is able to deliver.

Improvements in health care partly account for the fact that there are far more older people in the population than used to be the case in the past. The body ages and dies; but what we regard as 'old age', as George Minois shows (Reading 13), is socially determined. In many traditional cultures and civilizations, older people enjoyed special privileges and a high status. In modern societies, by contrast, for many becoming old means being put on the social scrap-heap. Yet as the proportions of older people increase they become a political force to be reckoned with. Older people are likely to use their political power to re-establish a secure status for themselves in society.

READING 9

David Cohen

Could You Be a Fitness Junkie?

'Keep-it-up-keep-it-up. Up! Up! Up!' The manic, repetitive beat booms out of the fitness centre in Crouch End, north London, where evening aerobics is in full swing. Up front on a raised dais, Sally Plant ('Super Sal') drives her third class of the day to ever higher peaks of . . . work rate and leads by example. She is superbly tuned, toned, sleek, focused and driven and, to her acolytes – the twenty-five leotards and tracksuits puffing away on plastic mats – a figure to admire, perhaps desire. 'Stretch-two-three-four' . . . her torso unfurls with obscene grace, her

Plate 3.1 Keeping it up, up, up, can get you down, down, down – if you get dependent on it
Source: Kalpesh Latrigon

metronome-like chant reinforcing what we already know: that regular repeated exercise is 'boring, boring, boring', but that if we persist it will make us feel 'good, good, good'. In tight, black midriff-top and Lycra thigh-squeezing shorts, Sally, like so many aerobics and gym instructors, appears the seductive image of total health and fitness.

Nothing could be further from the truth. Sally, a 28-year-old single mother who hails from 'a middle-class cul-de-sac in the Midlands' is by her own admission a 'compulsive exerciser' who last felt good after working out more than two years ago. Her body is so run down, so exhausted, that she struggles to get up in the morning. Sex? Forget it. Last year she had flu most of the time. [At one point], a vertebra rotated out of joint and her neck got stuck. Her muscle and joint alignment was so bad that the chiropractor was convinced she had been in a car accident and was suffering from whiplash. Doctors plead with her to give her body a break, but to no avail. 'It would be sensible to stop for a while, but I can't because the physical pain I feel from training is not nearly as bad as the anxiety, self-loathing and flabbiness I feel when I don't work out', she says, munching an apple after class.

Sally started exercising as a teenager because she had a complex about her 'chubby legs', but it was only when she split up with the father of her son a few years ago that she started becoming obsessive. 'I felt demoralized and worthless when the relationship broke down, but I wanted to prove that I still had a life and that I was strong', she says. 'Initially the exercise made me feel good about myself; I got attention from men and my self-esteem was boosted. I started teaching once a week, then once a day, then two to three times a day, doing more and more to get the same high. Then the high seemed to disappear and now I need constant calorie burn just to feel normal.

'My whole life has been affected. Men don't like coming second to sit-ups, so my relationships tend to be transitory. Holidays are a disaster – I can't go anywhere unless there's a gym to work out. I push myself to the max every day and anything less is unfulfilling. I'm a case, an addict in every sense of the word.'

It is not known how many people are 'addicted to fitness' in the UK, though a few classic case-studies abound. One woman was so committed to her exercise that after having a baby, she plonked her infant in a pram in the middle of a park and ran round it. According to the Fitness Industry Association, only 10 per cent of the adult British population exercise regularly, twice as many as a decade ago, but for most of us the problem is still too little exercise rather than too much. The widespread discovery in 1975 of the existence of endorphins (endogenous morphines, the opiate-like substances produced by the body during sustained physical exercise) and the prevalence of the fitness craze since its crash-landing from the US in the 1980s has brought a growing clinical interest in exercise addiction. (Today, more than £500 m is spent annually on entrance fees for fitness facilities in the UK.)

Does addiction to exercise really exist? If so, is the addiction – defined as an inability to spend any length of time without exercise – physiological or psychological? In an attempt to raise the profile of this controversial subject, the British Psychological Society published a research book entitled *Exercise Addiction*.

Hannah Steinberg, former professor of psycho-pharmacology at University College London, now visiting professor at Middlesex University and a contributor to the book, says that much of the research is in its infancy and is still incomplete, but exercise addiction seems to resemble drug addiction in five ways: the activity is initially pleasurable and leads to repetition; the activity becomes excessive and compulsive and begins to take over [the exerciser's] life; pain thresholds are raised, withdrawal symptoms (anxiety and irritability) occur if addicts are suddenly deprived, but the feelings disappear as soon as the activity resumes; and finally, the body becomes 'tolerant' to the activity so that more and more is required to produce the same effect. (Sally Plant, interestingly, appears to satisfy all of these criteria.)

But what exactly are exercise addicts 'hooked' on? Does their addiction have a natural physiological or biochemical explanation? 'We know that exercise causes endorphins to be released into the blood and that endorphins have a similar addictive potential to opiate drugs', says Steinberg. 'Like opiates, endorphins are responsible for increased pain tolerance, favourable moods, feelings of calmness and euphoria (sometimes known as the "runner's high"). If administered externally – by intravenous injection – endorphins can induce withdrawal and craving in much the same way as morphine.

'But in order to prove that this addictive potential can cause the long-term addiction associated with drugs, we need to prove that endorphins have the same effect in the living human brain as morphine and, as yet, that has not been measured. The endorphin hypothesis is attractive but it may be that other substances, like adrenalin, are as much part of the story. It seems probable, though, that exercise addiction is a more benign addiction than drugs.'

Dr Ian Cockerill, sports psychologist at the University of Birmingham, distinguishes between two forms of addiction – positive and negative. 'Positive addiction is when individuals make exercise an essential part of their lives and their well-being is enhanced; negative addiction is when individuals organize their lives around exercise and so are ruled and ruined by it.'

People who exercise daily, the Dianas and Madonnas of this world, are not necessarily in danger. Lorenzo Blasi, interviewed below, is an example of positive addiction. But at what point, and why, does a person who is in control of their fitness suddenly cross the threshold? No one knows, though it is well documented that women with eating disorders, for example, are four times more susceptible to exercise addiction than the general populace.

Sally Plant's friend and colleague, Bonny Saunders ('Bonny Biceps'), aged 25, is a case in point. 'Aerobics became a way of controlling my weight and taking the stress off my eating disorder. I have since sorted out my eating disorder, but I'm still addicted to exercise and I am constantly worn out with it', she says.

. . . Exercise addiction is not confined to females. The conventional view was that women exercised for looks, men for athletic performance. Men jogged, ran or worked out, while women did aerobics. These distinctions are more blurred in the 1990s but, more importantly, the motives for men pursuing fitness have changed. The male body, traditionally a symbol of strength, has become a symbol of desire, with the result that the pressures on men are remarkably similar to those on women. Commercials for Levi jeans and Pepsi Cola (in which a group of women gaze lasciviously at a bare-chested man) reflect the new fetishization of the male body.

'Nowhere is this more evident than in the gay community', says Mark Simpson, author of *Male Impersonators*. 'Gay men are more likely to work out than straight men, perhaps because other men tend to be more appreciative of big muscles than women. The gay scene is a market place and the bigger your pecs [pectorals] . . . the greater your pulling power. But the pressures on men are by no means confined to the gay community. Action heroes, like Arnold Schwarzenegger and Sylvester Stallone, developed the male body to the point where muscle became body armour, something to hide behind. Men who feel inadequate and inferior in their manliness are more at risk of becoming addicted to pumping muscles because their identities start to depend on it.'

There is also new evidence that men who develop eating disorders do so after first becoming addicted to exercise. But how different is fitness addiction to, say, work addiction? Endorphins are released by stress, as much as by exercise. 'Keep-it-up! Up! Up!' is also the silent bidding of the workaholic. Do we all need to be dependent on something? If so, is there a gradation of addictions, where perhaps exercise is not as bad as, say, drug, alcohol or gambling addictions? The question is significant. Steinberg wonders whether morphine addicts can be weaned by getting them addicted to exercise (internal opiates) instead.

Dr Barry Cripps, a Devon-based occupational psychologist who has seen half a dozen cases of exercise addiction, insists it is treatable. 'I use hypnotherapy to deal with the depth issues behind the addiction and to break the link. At the same time, I treat it behaviourally, encouraging the individual to introduce other interests – hobbies, culture – into a life that's become boringly uni-focused. It's not quick or easy but patients can make a complete recovery.'

For Sally, who has been seeing a counsellor for eleven months, there is greater insight into her problem but no improvement. 'I don't hate exercise, I just hate that I have to do it. My biggest grudge is against people who eat what they like, don't exercise and have brilliant figures. They should be drowned in a sea of cellulite.'

READING 10

Lisa O'Kelly

Body Talk

The sticky toffee pudding arrived; one helping, two spoons. My companion, as they say in restaurant reviews, salivated guiltily and said: 'Bang goes the diet. I've been trying to lose weight for months, not mixing proteins and carbohydrates and so on, but I just can't seem to get any thinner. It's making me feel really bad about myself.'

It sounded like a thousand other late-night conversations between women friends. But there was a crucial difference. The person with me was a man.

You never used to hear men talking this way, at least not without a good deal of prompting. However, nowadays, such confidences come more easily. At my local sports centre in west London, George, 44, puffing after a game of squash with Richard, who is half his age, admitted: 'If I was starting from scratch, I would design everything about myself differently. I might keep my head the same, but if I could pick the rest from the catalogue, I don't think I would choose anything identical.' His opponent confessed that he, too, is unhappy with the way he looks. 'I'm too skinny. I'm always comparing myself unfavourably with the kind of men you see in those naked ice-cream ads.'

What is going on? Isn't this supposed to be female territory? Fashion historian Colin McDowell says not. 'The male peacock was the dominant figure in fashion history until mid-Victorian times, and men's self-worth was always very much tied up with their bodies and the way they looked.' However, for the past century or so, McDowell acknowledges, this has not been the case.

'The reasons why are hugely complex, to do with the lead in fashion moving away from the aristocratic classes to the middle classes, who have always been characterized by their timidity, which made men's clothes safe, sober and unremarkable. With that came a covering up of men's bodies, a denial of their importance as means of expressing the self.'

Underneath that denial, most men never stopped harbouring a secret fascination with the male body beautiful . . . As Joan Mellon observed in her book *Big Bad Wolves: Masculinity in the American Film*, Valentino was as alluring to men as women because he not only played 'the man who succeeded in the world and attracted women through the aphrodisiac of power; he embodied a sex object pursued, wooed and won by women . . . his arms muscular and well-developed, Valentino was treated by the camera itself as a desirable object.'

In many ways, then, the new male body consciousness is a historical accident that has been waiting to happen.

Male nudity is now commonplace on television and in films. Ten or twelve years ago, the bare male bottoms in *Brideshead Revisited* and Dennis Potter's *The Singing Detective* were unusual enough to attract comment. But more recently we barely blanched when Sean Bean stripped off in the BBC's adaptations of *Clarissa* and *Lady Chatterley's Lover*.

Indeed, male movie stars attract more attention these days when they remain fully clothed. Witness a recent article in Zest magazine, headlined 'Muscles Maketh the Movie', which observed: 'Action movie fans in search of steel-hard muscles . . . have to be disappointed by *True Lies* in which the bicep-brained Austrian [Arnold Schwarzenegger] . . . never takes off his shirt.'

Advertising has played a significant part in heightening male body awareness. Once advertisers would have been fearful of linking their products with images that might have been thought homoerotic. Now, even Marks & Spencer advertises its socks with pictures of hunky men.

Naturally, this shift in perception has spilled into the editorial content of glossy magazines. Mainstream women's publications such as *Marie Claire* regularly feature articles on men and their bodies, and have no qualms about including revealing pictures.

The interest starts young. Teenage mags such as *Just 17* have long featured in-depth interviews with pop icons and, increasingly, male models photographed semi-clothed. *More!* has just launched its own Mr More! competition, hard on the heels of the first Mr UK contest, which was held at the Grosvenor Park Hotel. . . .

Men's magazines are also stuffed full of features on the minutiae of their readers' bodies. [The editor of *Gentleman's Quarterly*] maintains that increasing body consciousness is a direct result of the gym culture of the 1980s which, although less pervasive now, has a strong residual influence. 'What's happening is that men are realizing the importance not so much of being muscle-bound but being fit and healthy, and turning their bodies into better living machines. They see the benefits that brings: increased longevity, a greater sense of well-being and better sex.'

He sees no evidence of any attendant insecurities or lessening of self-esteem among his readers. 'Men don't feel bad because there are increasing numbers of well-honed male torsos on show in the way that women feel bad that Cindy Crawford is so pretty. Men's minds don't work like that.' [The] editor of rival title *Esquire*, agrees. 'Men derive their sense of macho and masculinity from a much bigger range of things than women do: their job, their sporting prowess, their business acumen, their car. Looking good is just one factor for them.'

None the less, it is evidently a factor that is gaining in importance. Men are spending more on making themselves look beautiful. As well as shelling out for gym membership fees (500,000 British men belong to a gym), they are buying more cosmetics. The male beauty industry has grown by 26 per cent in value terms since 1985 to £469 million. Anti-ageing supplements and eye contour gel are no longer considered cissy, and nearly 30 per cent of men under 25 have used a moisturizer in the past month, according to recent statistics from market researcher Mintel.

There is evidence that men are beginning to exhibit patterns of behaviour traditionally associated with women. One in three diet, according to a recent Mori survey. Last year's annual conference of the British Psychological Society heard a paper which suggested that magazine pictures showing perfectly honed male models may drive men to develop eating disorders such as anorexia and bulimia. Greg Buckle, head of the male division at Storm, Kate Moss's agency, confirmed that the new look for men is 'slimmed down – the male waif is what everyone's after, no more overpumped, overdefined bodies'.

READING 11

Roy Porter and Dorothy Porter

Sickness and Health in Pre-Modern England

In the eighteenth century in particular, deadly fevers – contemporaries called them 'spotted', 'miliary', 'hectic', 'malignant', etc. – struck down hundreds of thousands, young and old alike, while the so-called 'new' diseases gained ground – some crippling, such as rickets; some fatal, such as tuberculosis. Today's minor nuisance, like flu, was yesterday's killer. 'The Hooping Cough is yet with us', wrote George Crabbe in 1829, '& many children die of it.' And all this against a background of endemic maladies, such as malaria and infantile diarrhoea, and a Pandora's box of other infections (dysentery, scarlatina, measles, etc.) that commonly proved fatal, above all to infants, to say nothing of 101 other pains, eruptions, swellings, ulcers, scrofula and wasting conditions, not least the agonizing stone and the proverbial gout, which threatened livings and livelihoods, and all too often life itself.

Resistance to infection was evidently weak. This is hardly surprising. Precipitate demographic rise under the Tudors, followed by climatic reverses and economic crises under the Stuarts, had swollen the ranks of the malnourished poor. New and virulent strains of disease possibly emerged. England's good communications network and high job and geographical mobility – it was a land of 'movers' rather than 'stayers' – proved favourable to disease spread: the market society meant free trade in maladies. Few settlements were far enough off the beaten track to escape epidemic visitations travelling along the trade routes (out-of-the-way places could, however, have impressively high life expectancies). And yet the regionality of what was still largely a rural society also meant that disease spread erratically and patchily, with the consequence that there was always a large reservoir of susceptibles, not yet immune, especially among the young, ready sacrificial victims to smallpox or scarlet fever.

Above all, pre-modern medicine had few effective weapons against the infections from which people died like flies. Once smallpox, enteric fever or pneumonia struck, doctors fought a losing battle. In the generation after 1720, the population of England and Wales actually *declined*, primarily because of the ravages of epidemic disease.

Our understanding of the biology of man in history has vastly improved. As yet, however, little attention has been paid to what this ceaseless Darwinian war between disease and populations meant to the individual, considering disease neither as a black block on a histogram nor just as a trope about the human condition betwixt womb and tomb, but as experienced torment and terror. Every soul lived in the shadow of death; indeed, being in the land of the living was itself the survivor's privilege, for so many of one's peers – one's brothers and sisters – had already fallen by the wayside, having died at birth, in infancy or childhood. Life's fine thread was ever precarious, and every statistic hides a personal tragedy. The historical record abounds with sad tales of those who ate a hearty breakfast in the pink of health, only to be dead of apoplexy or convulsions, plague or, later, cholera, before the week was out. Elizabeth Iremonger told her friend Miss Heber the sad tale of her nephew's wife, Eleanor Iremonger, whose delivery of a boy was followed a week later by a 'fever that baffled all art and, on the ninth morning, she sunk finally to this World!'

'Many dyed sudden deaths lately', lamented the late Stuart Nonconformist minister, Oliver Heywood, ever alert to the workings of Providence:

> 1, Nathan Crosly buryed Octob 25 1674, 2, Timothy Wadsworth, dyed Octob 23 suddenly in his chair without sickness, 3, Edw Brooks wife dyed under the cow as she was milking, 4, a woman at great Horton wel, had a tooth drawn, cryed oh my head laid her hand on, dyed immediately, 5, one Richard Hodgsons wife at Bradford on munday Nov. 2, dyed on tuesday the day after, &c.[1]

Over a century later, the Somerset parson, William Holland, marked the bitter fate of a father buried on the day his child was christened. Amid the bumper harvest of the Great Reaper recorded in the *Gentleman's Magazine* obituary columns, many expired when apparently in the prime of health –

cut off by mad-dog bites, by sudden strokes or through travelling accidents ('I shall begin to think from my frequent overturns', quipped Elizabeth Montagu, 'a bone-setter a necessary part of my equipage for country visiting'). Accidents are not unique to modern technology and urbanism. A Norwich newspaper noted in 1790 how:

> On Thursday last (March) a fine boy, about five years of age, fell thro' the seat of the necessary belonging to Mr. Mapes, in the Hay-market, the reservoir to which is not less than 40 feet deep; in this shocking situation he remained from a quarter past ten till three o'clock in the afternoon, before he was discovered by his cries. A person immediately went down to his relief, and when he had raised him halfway up, the bucket in which the child was, striking against a timber that had not been perceived, he was again precipitated to the bottom head forward.[2]

This child survived; so did others, for instance James Clegg, the Derbyshire minister-cum-doctor, who reported 'a very merciful deliverance when mounting [his] mare'. Many, however, fared worse, such as Thomas Day, leading light of the Lunar Society, who died after being thrown from a half-broken-in horse. Visitations came out of the blue, and some deaths were particularly cruel. A Mrs Fitzgerald went to the theatre, and laughed so much she laughed herself to death. Or take the exemplary exit of the Revd Mr M'Kill, pastor of Bankend in Scotland, so 'remarkable' that it 'made an impression upon the minds of his parishioners':

> He mounted the pulpit in good health, lectured as usual, and it being the last sabbath of the year, chose for his text these words. 'we spend our years as a tale that is told'. He was representing, in a very pathetic manner, the fleeting nature of human life, and of all earthly things, when, on a sudden, he dropped down in the pulpit and expired instantly.

'He looks much better than you would imagine', Lady Jane Coke assured a friend about her husband's convalescence on 26 February 1750: 'sleeps well, and I think I may assure you that he is better to-day than he has been for some time, so that I hope the worst is over.' She tempted fate: before sunset, he was dead.

Disease was matched by other dangers, even oncoming thunderstorms. 'William Church', writes the pious Isabella Tindal, 'was speaking to my son John at the time, and saying "The Lord cometh in his chariot, in the clouds to gather his people to himself" . . . he was struck by the lightning . . . and fell down dead.' Falls, drownings, fires, firearm explosions, mishaps with tools, knives and poisons, and traffic accidents were perpetual hazards, not least because without ambulance and casualty services, trauma or blood loss readily proved fatal before effectual medical aid was forthcoming. William III, of course, died after his horse stumbled on a mole-hill (Jacobites toasted the little gentleman in velvet), and the third Cambridge Professor of History met his end tumbling off his horse while drunk. The Revd Ralph Josselin recorded scores of such mishaps or, as he saw them, 'Providences':

> I heard that Major Cletheroe, September 21, coming homewards at Redgewell his Horse, stumbled and fell downe upon him and brake his bowells, he was taken up and spake but he dyed about 4 or 5 hours later,

Lord in how many dangerous falls and stumbles hast thou preserved mee....[3]

Most ironically of all, William Stout, the Lancaster Quaker who distrusted doctors and championed self-care, received his first blow in years – a broken leg – when he was run down by the local surgeon's horse.

Some mortifications of the flesh had their black comedy: 'Up, and to the office', wrote Pepys, '(having a mighty pain in my forefinger of my left hand, from a strain that it received last night in struggling avec la femme que je mentioned yesterday).'[4] Yet serious injuries and often death followed from apparent trifles. Erasmus Darwin's son, Charles, a promising medical student, died of septicaemia following a trivial dissecting-room cut. Unable to take life's pains, multitudes of English people took their lives instead. More philosophical minds reflected on their chances. 'The present is a fleeting moment', mused Gibbon, just turned fifty,

> the past is no more; and our prospect of futurity is dark and doubtful. This day may *possibly* be my last: but the laws of probability, so true in general, so fallacious in particular, still allow me about fifteen years; and I shall soon enter into the period, which, as the most agreeable of his long life, was selected by the judgement and experience of the sage Fontenelle.

He never did: probability, or, perhaps, Providence, was unkind, and the historian of the Roman Empire declined and fell shortly afterwards through post-operative sepsis following surgery on a hydrocele as big as a football.

Yet Gibbon was lucky: all six of his siblings died in infancy. Samuel Pepys was one of eleven children born to his parents. Only one brother and sister survived into adulthood. A single measles epidemic massacred nine members of Cotton Mather's fifteen-strong household in early eighteenth-century colonial Boston. Half a century later, Dr Johnson's friend, Hester Thrale, produced twelve children: seven of them did not reach their teens. Out of William Godwin's twelve brothers and sisters, only half survived to adult life. His contemporary, William Holland, had four children die within a fortnight of scarlet fever. Francis Place's résumé of the brief lives of his own children conveys the appalling arbitrariness of existence:

1. Ann – born 1792. Died aged 2 years of the small pox
2. Elizabeth – April 1794. Died in Chile – Mrs Adams
3. Annie – 27 Jan 1796 – ... Mrs Miers
4. Francis – 22 June 1798
5. Jane – died an infant
6. Henry – d........d [dates of birth and death unknown]
7. Mary – 6 Jany. 1804
8. Frederick Wm. – 14 Oct 1805
9. Jane – 29 Oct 1807
10. Alfred – died an infant
11. John – 1 Jany 1811
12. Thomas – 4 Augst. 1812. Died at Calcutta 16 Sept 1847. Widow and 5 children
13. Caroline – 29 July 1814. Died 1830
14. William } Twins 6 Feb. 1817 { died – 1829
    Henry }   { died an infant

The radical tailor himself outlived almost all his offspring.

Thus English people during the 'long eighteenth century' were over-shadowed by the facts and fears of sickness and by death itself. He had only three complaints, Byron bantered to his friend, Henry Drury, in 1811:

> viz. a Gonorrhea, a Tertian fever, & the Hemorrhoides, all of which I liter-ally had at once, though [the surgeon] assured me the morbid action of only one of these distempers could act at a time, which was a great com-fort, though they relieved one another as regularly as Sentinels.[5]

When John Locke's father wrote to him in 1659, assuring him of his 'health and quiet', the son – then training to be a doctor – responded that this was 'a blessing this tumbling world is very spareing of'. For sickness was all too often the unwelcome, omnipresent guest, and households doubled as hos-pitals. A letter from Lady Caroline Fox to her sister, the Countess of Kildare, sending for medicines, reads like a dispatch from the front:

> . . . as yet there is no amendment in my dearest child [Stephen]; he will be better for some hours almost a whole day sometimes then be as bad as ever again. I wonder I keep my spirits so well as I do, but my trust in Providence is great. My poor Charles was restored to me when there were no hopes left, and I will hope for the same blessing again with regard to my dear Ste. Louisa is perhaps set out by this time; seeing her will be a pleasure to me, but I fear she will find a melancholy house . . . Poor William has had a little fever, but was well again when I heard of him. . . .

'Every body is ill', exclaimed Keats to his brother in 1820. This was neither a metaphysical paradox nor a piece of poetic licence, but merely an update on his friends and family.

Not surprisingly, therefore, health was on everybody's mind and filled their conversations. Sickness challenges the stomach (the two are not unconnected) for pride of place in Parson Woodforde's diaries. 'I was very nervous today. My Cow a great deal better this morning', he chronicled on 17 January 1796. The next day:

> Poor Mr Bodham much altered for the worse. It is thought that he cannot long survive, fallen away amazingly, takes but very, very little notice of anything. Laudanum and Bark his chief Medicine. Dr. Lubbock & Dr. Donne from Norwich have both been there lately, and they say that he is out of the reach of any Medicine, he might live some little time, but is beyond recovery.

Some things improved. The day after, his cow-doctor visited her and pro-nounced 'her to be . . . out of all danger'.

Thus, in the world we have lost, sickness was a constant menace. 'One's very body', suggested Tobias Smollett – himself, of course, a doctor as well as a novelist – should be seen as a 'hospital'. Just as prudence dictated that every man should be his own lawyer, so every man should be his own physician, for he, if anyone, was expert in his own 'case' (contemporary idiom for both 'body' and 'corpse'). So it is hardly surprising that the every-day lives of ordinary people in earlier centuries reverberate with their own ailments, and those of their kith and kin.

READING 12

Ross Hume Hall

Health-Care Systems and the Medical–Industrial Complex

What drives the health-care system of industrialized countries? Is it the medical doctors, the government health bureaucracies, people's desire for good health? They all do in a sense, but the main engine that propels the health-care system is high medical technology and the industries that develop and sell the technology. The drug industry, of course, is very much part of this high-technology sector and, as we noted previously, it has become a force in the lives of consumers, the majority of whom consume its products daily. But medical technology also includes medical equipment, diagnostic services, hospitals; and medical care revolves around this technology. Medical care, in fact, could be said to be application of this technology to consumers, who in their ready acceptance of it have come to equate their health with machines, drugs and laboratory tests. This almost total reliance for health care on high medical technology is paradoxical, because in spite of its power to manipulate human biology, this technology fails to deliver on much of its promise of health. It is indeed a tribute to the almost universal acceptance of the technology that its failures are all but ignored. . . .

High medical technology by itself is neutral. It is not the technology *per se* that makes health policy good or bad: it is the institutions that use it. So this [discussion] is not to be taken as a critique of high medical technology, but a critique of its use and misuse.

The one institution that gives high medical technology its life and direction lacks a formal name but is often referred to as the *medical–industrial complex*, a group of industries that develops and markets drugs, medical equipment and supplies and provides a variety of health services. It is closely bound up with the medical profession – absolutely essential for the industry – because only physicians can legally apply medical technology and services to patients. In other words, the industry can only market its products and services through medical doctors. The companies make their money selling their goods and services, the physicians make their money applying the technology; hence the tightness of the complex.

The medical–industrial complex is no small industry. It employs some 10 million people in the United States and comparable numbers in other countries. It operates just as effectively in countries like Britain and Sweden with government-run health-care systems, because these systems are equally dependent on the technologies and services of the medical–industrial complex. It is in the United States, however, that the complex perhaps receives most attention and that public argument over its role in health care is most abrasive. But it is hard to detect in that argument any interest in a place for a preventive health strategy. Rather, public argument revolves around the efficiency of the complex – does it cost too much for the health care it delivers? . . .

Health policy in the industrialized nations for the past several decades has concentrated almost exclusively on making high medical technology accessible to everyone.

To explore this point further, we will look at two government health programmes: Medicare in the United States and the National Health Service in Britain.

First Medicare. The United States lacks a single, universal health programme comparable to the government health services of Sweden and Britain. There is a mosaic of programmes in the American health sector, but the thrust of all of them is the same – access to high-tech medical care. The method of paying for that access, however, varies, with a mixture of private and government payment. And surprisingly, although the United States is thought of as the ultimate in free-market medicine, the federal government finances 40 per cent of the country's medical bills. Medicare is the centrepiece of these programmes, providing medical cover to 33 million Americans who are disabled or 65 years of age and older. As the following anecdote suggests, this cover is not without its glitches.

In October 1987, Helen Bennett, 72, of Massapequa, New York, was diagnosed as having a tumour in her chest. Her long-time doctor, Arthur Berken, wanted to put her in hospital for chemotherapy but Mrs Bennett, living alone, did not want to leave her dog, so she asked if she could have the course of treatments in Berken's office. He agreed, and over the next three weeks, Mrs Bennett spent two hours a day, four times a week, receiving the anti-cancer drugs Adriamycin and Dacarbazine.

But the system of Medicare disbursement has become highly bureaucratic and expensive to administer, and moreover, it tries to direct treatment without regard to cost or benefit to patient. Thus, although Mrs Bennett's treatment proceeded to the satisfaction of both patient and doctor, the trouble began when Dr Berken tried to bill the Medicare plan. According to the *New York Times*, which reported the situation, Berken received an anonymous computer printout saying that his treatment 'was not reasonable and necessary'. How could Medicare make a value judgement without any knowledge of what's going on? Berken asked. He explained that chemotherapy is generally given in hospital, but Mrs Bennett being an outpatient could go home every day, a cheaper arrangement than spending three weeks in hospital. He tried phoning the Medicare office but received more unsigned printouts rejecting the claim. Exasperated, Berken contacted his Congressman, Robert Mrazek, and solicited his help in finding 'one human being to explain to me their logic'.

Mrazek, who presumably would rather be dealing with national affairs, was so overloaded with similar Medicare complaints from his constituents – 240 in the past year – that he hired a full-time assistant to help sort out the problems. In the case of Helen Bennett, it was several months before Berken, Mrazek's assistant and a *New York Times* reporter managed to track down the 'one human being' they were after: Gloria McCarthy, of a private insurance company contracted by the government to handle Medicare claims, Empire Bluecross–Blue Shield. McCarthy, head of the company's Medicare outpatient programme, said that Empire Bluecross was reconsidering its outpatient chemotherapy policy and that most such claims would now be paid. But until Berken, and apparently other doctors, complained, the Medicare insurance company tried to force patients into the more expensive hospitals by withholding payment for out-patient care.

To understand why Dr Berken had difficulty in recovering his outpatient fee is to understand one reason for the ballooning cost of Medicare. When the Medicare bill was signed into law by President Johnson in 1965, it was thought the cost to the government would be modest. In 1967 the pro-gramme cost only $3.4 billion but, by 1987, that cost had risen to $158 bil-lion and was still rising. [It has been predicted] that this one government programme alone will cost American taxpayers $600 billion by the year 2000.

As long ago as 1936, the federal government wanted to attach a health-care plan to social security legislation, but opposition from organized medi-cine, namely the American Medical Association (AMA), so cowed Congressmen that the idea of health benefits for the elderly was dropped. The AMA's lobbying against such legislation continued, and when the idea of a Medicare programme was resurrected in the 1960s, Congressmen realized that the programme would not work without the doctors' co-operation. Congress made substantial concessions to both doctors and hospitals in order to get the legislation passed, concessions that are at the root of Medicare's problems today.

AMA's main opposition to Medicare, which it called socialized medicine, was that it did not want any party coming between doctor and patient. The doctors wanted no interference in how they practised medicine or billed patients. But by the mid-1960s doctors were accustomed to private insur-ance plans that paid a fee to the doctor or hospital for each patient and for each service rendered. The major insurance carriers in this area were Blue Cross for doctors' bills and Blue Shield for hospital bills, and both carriers were structured to serve the interests of doctors and hospitals. The govern-ment, in passing the Medicare legislation, agreed that it would simply foot the bill and that administration of Medicare would be handled through the private insurance carriers. Doctors like Berken simply bill the regional insurance company administering Medicare.

Paul Starr, a Harvard sociologist who has studied the evolution of the American health-care system, noted that in this act, 'the federal government surrendered direct control of the programme and its costs'. In fact, it not only surrendered control over costs, it surrendered control over the intro-duction and use of high-tech medicine, one reason why in the United States evaluation of new medical technology is virtually non-existent. The medical–industrial complex can develop a piece of equipment or a new procedure and introduce it into wide use – paid for by Medicare or other insurance programmes – unhampered by awkward questions about whether or not it benefits people's health. . . .

Is the dominance of health care by the medical–industrial complex a phenomenon only of the freewheeling open market of the United States or is it more widespread? Let us look at the British National Health Service, a system of universal health care tightly run by the government. . . .

The National Health Service is also structured in [terms of] a two-tier system of doctors. Thirty-five per cent of British doctors practise as independent contractors, called general practitioners (GPs), that is, they are prepared to look after all members of the family. They are the equivalent of family doctors in the United States. General practitioners work in a private office or a community clinic, and each signs up a panel of patients which he or she contracts to look after. Patients select a doctor within their area, establishing a doctor–patient bond – a bond that, ironically, many United States physicians practising in corporate-run clinics have lost. Doctors are paid a capitation fee, a sum for each patient on the panel, regardless of the number of times the patient sees the doctor. A GP has on average 2,200 individuals on his panel, and in the course of a year sees 600 of them with coughs and colds, 325 with skin disorders including dandruff, 100 with chronic rheumatism, 50 with high blood pressure, 8 with heart attacks, 5 with appendicitis and 5 with strokes.

The tier of GPs acts as a primary screen for the National Health Service. GPs treat patients with minor complaints or, if they judge the complaints to be more serious, they refer patients to specialists, called consultants. Consultants occupy the second tier, the top position of privilege and power in the service. Consultants are attached to a hospital and are relatively few in number. Only about 20 per cent of registered doctors in Britain are consultants, compared with 85 per cent of doctors in the United States who practise a speciality. The National Health Service pays each consultant a salary, and in addition, consultants are allowed a percentage of time to engage in private practice on a fee-for-service basis. Consultants control their own professional standards and have a major voice in the organization and the standard of medical care delivered in their hospitals. Because of their prestige and status, they influence strongly the way the British public and government think about human health.

The work of the consultants revolves around the expensive high-tech medical care delivered by hospitals. In fact, the whole National Health Service revolves around the hospitals and about 65 per cent of the country's doctors (including the consultants) work in hospitals. This is the style of medicine determined by the machines and drugs of the medical–industrial complex. There are differences in degree between British hospitals and American ones, but the high-tech styles are identical. British hospitals tend to have fewer pieces of expensive equipment and because the number of consultant positions in each hospital is controlled, they have, for example, only half as many surgeons per capita as the United States, British doctors are less inclined to subject their patients to major operations and other high-tech procedures. A heart bypass operation, for instance, is performed about one-quarter as often as in the United States, and there seems to be no difference in outcome of patients with heart conditions. In fact, according to

Roger Hollingsworth, a sociology professor at the University of Wisconsin, who has compared the medical systems of Britain and the United States, there is no real difference in the level of care.

British doctors may use high technology to a lesser degree, but this does not suggest less faith in the technology. They are just as strong proponents of new and improved technology as their American counterparts. They use expensive high technology less because the equipment is not so readily available. But less expensive technology, such as drugs, they prescribe as freely or even more freely than doctors in the United States.

Although both US and British doctors tend to be paternalistic towards their patients – 'doctor knows best' – British doctors carry paternalism to a far greater extent. The plus side, at least from the point of view of cost containment, is that the British doctor is better able to persuade a patient not to undergo treatments for which there is no benefit. They are able to say, 'look, this is all we can do for your cancer or for your chronic arthritis' – and the patient accepts the decision. Contrast this attitude with that in the United States where treatment ends only with the patient's last breath. A British doctor who worked in an American hospital was astounded at the amount of treatment given patients: 'Rarely does an American doctor state that there is no surgery that would help, no drug that is advantageous, and no further investigation is required. There seems to be an irresistible urge always to do something, even though in many cases the doctor concerned must realize that there is no possibility of benefit.'

The more authoritarian relationship between British doctor and patient has its disadvantages. Arrogance and a faith in the infallibility of their own judgement mean that there is little likelihood of doctors questioning their own belief system of health and disease and even less of admitting that there are alternative ways of preserving health. You can see this arrogance expressed in the fate of one experiment in alternative medical care.

This experiment, set up in the London suburb of Peckham in the 1930s by two medical doctors, Scott Williamson and Innes Pearse, created a total health plan for some 2,000 families. The plan, with its own large social centre, encouraged fitness, social conviviality and good health practices. Williamson, Pearse and their medical staff got to know their families very well, giving them the kind of health maintenance that avoided illness. The plan enjoyed great success for about ten years before it was scrapped in 1948 by the newly introduced National Health Service. There were to be no funds for this type of programme.

A dogged group of British doctors and associates, some of whom once worked in the Peckham programme, have tried to rekindle a similar programme since 1948, but the idea of a wellness programme has been consistently rebuffed both by the British medical societies and by the government health bureaucracy. The belief that prevailed in 1948, that such programmes are unnecessary for health maintenance, prevails still.

The National Health Service was founded on the egalitarian principle that although most people do not mind seeing someone else drive a Rolls-Royce, everyone is entitled to a heart bypass operation. Aneurin Bevan, the minister in the British Labour government responsible for introducing the National Health Service in 1948, firmly believed that when the less advantaged citizens – those then unable to afford health care – had access to doctors and drugs, their diseases would vanish. He predicted that the need for medical facilities would decline. What he did not anticipate was the capacity of the modern health-care system to generate new demand based, in large part, on the patient's desire for access to heart transplants and CT scans. Bevan also made the mistake of equating access to doctors and their technology with access to health.

Bevan did not then, nor does the British government now, see human health in its whole relation to society and the natural environment in the way that Williamson and Pearse did. The government is satisfied to limit its focus on health to gritty debates over hospital budgets and the way the National Health Service is run. A comprehensive legislative approach to human health is just as absent as it is in the United States.

But now, forty years after the introduction of the National Health Service, slogan and fiscal reality clash: costs and demands for expensive medical technology keep pushing on the government's limits. Its response was to restrict hospital services, forcing . . . hospital managers to ration the services they offer. But now the government has gone further. It announced plans in 1989 to revolutionize the National Health Service, bringing it closer to the American free-market health-care system. 'For the first time since the NHS was founded in 1948, doctors will be encouraged to see patients as revenue sources and expense centres', said Gordon Best, director of the King's Fund College, an organization that trains health managers.

So it seems the revolution in health care has more to do with management and costs than with health; the obvious intent is to continue universal access to high-tech medical care, but to make it more revenue-effective.

READING 13

Georges Minois

History of Old Age: From Antiquity to the Renaissance

Old age: a term which generally arouses a shudder, two words loaded with anxiety, frailty and sometimes anguish. Yet an imprecise term, whose meaning is still vague, its reality difficult to perceive. When does one become old? At 55, 60, 65 or at 70 years? Nothing fluctuates more than the contours of old age, that physiological, psychological and social complex. Is one as old as one's arteries, as one's heart, as one's brain, as one's morale or as one's civil status? Or is it the way other people come to regard us – one day – which classifies us as old? The only rite of passage is a contemporary and artificial one; the passage into retirement, a moment determined more by socio-economic constraints than by actual age. Biologically speaking, people start to age from their birth onwards, but at very different speeds. Their social situation, manner of life and cultural environment accelerate or slow down bio-physiological evolution and cause us to enter old age at very different ages.

In spite of everything, growing old is still an essentially biological phenomenon to which modern medicine is paying ever greater attention, without having yet managed to understand its mechanics. While gerontologists all affirm that human longevity has not varied since the emergence of our species and is situated at around 110 years, the ageing process is still much debated. How is it that cells, which are potentially immortal, end by weakening and dying through non-regeneration? Leslie Orgel and his partisans attribute this phenomenon to the accumulation of errors in the translation of the genetic message, leading to a final catastrophe (the error catastrophe theory). Strehler proposes a related theory: with the passage of time, the cell's mechanism for decoding genetic messages weakens, and ends by modifying its bio-synthetic activity. Others, such as Burnet, promote the idea of old age being genetically programmed. For the moment, however, none of these explanations has achieved unanimous support. . . .

Whatever its causes, old age is a reality feared by those who have not yet reached it, and is often unappreciated by the old. Devalued, despised and relegated by some to the ranks of an incurable disease which serves as the harbinger of death, old age is denied by others who refuse to accept their physical transformation. They want to show that they are 'still young' and there are many examples in the performing arts, and in the worlds of sport and politics, some even bordering on the ridiculous, of elderly individuals of either sex behaving like young people, spurred on by the partisans of the theoretical equality of all mankind. But whether they exaggerate their ills or deny them against all the evidence, these old people witness to the generalized depreciation of old age in the modern world.

Our age, however, has witnessed a renewal of interest in the old. Never before have they been talked about so much or have they had so much attention paid them. Every discipline is studying this phenomenon which apparently concerns people all over the place. This is partly due to the natural growth of the range of modern scientific research, but especially to the pressure of socio-demographic conditions. Never have our Western societies included such a high proportion of old people . . . It is worth noting that the old are about to become the commonest sort of citizen.

This new market force has already aroused considerable interest. Old men and women, experienced, wise, the possessors of worldly knowledge, have penetrated advertising, recommending such and such a brand of washing machine or dog food. 'The marketers of leisure activities have taken these models of how to age well and have subtly re-injected the old into an economic circuit from which they had been definitively removed.'[1] Clubs and universities aiming at 'a new sales target', the world of the third age (our senior citizens), have also multiplied; sociologists, psychologists and doctors are attentively studying its specific problems, while economists worry about the growing volume of retirement money to be paid to this mass of non-productive persons, and demographers bemoan the grotesque upside-down age pyramid . . . in store for the beginning of the twenty-first century.

Present-day interest in old age . . . touches all spheres of life. Every discipline gradually modifies its point of view by refining it, as if surprised to find in this hitherto neglected subject an essential component of individual and social life. The case of medicine is most characteristic. For thousands of years, medicine has tried to understand the causes of ageing and to delay its effects but, given their impotence before this natural fatality, doctors had ended by limiting themselves to enumerating the pathologies typical of old people, classifying them among the incurably sick. The old were uninteresting patients because incurable, and so were relegated to hospices.

The first signs of an evolution can be distinguished in the 1950s, with the emergence of retirement schemes, and the growing intervention of the state in this domain. The traditional form of assistance was denounced as degrading; a new terminology was adopted, the 'third age', with its strong suggestion of dynamism and autonomy, replacing 'old age', which had long ago become synonymous with avarice and incapacity. Doctors who specialized in the treatment of old people began to contest the devaluation of their work and services and denounced the harmful effects of the semi-totalitarian system then reigning in the hospices. Encouraged by the state and by the new retirement funds, they gradually succeeded in promoting a new approach to the problems of old age under the name of 'geriatrics'. Based on a fundamental distinction between normal ageing and pathological ageing, the new discipline advocates a global approach to old age, taking account of the physiological, psychological, social and cultural aspects of old people. Parallel with this, psychoanalysis has undertaken a specific approach to old people, remedying Freud's silence on the subject.

As we have already said, the state was growing more aware of the extent of the problem. Old age, which had previously been an essentially private and family concern, became a social phenomenon so widespread that it could not but attract the attention of an administration anxious to endow this hitherto ignored category with status and regulations.

There have certainly always been old people, and more of them than one might think, in Egypt, Palestine, Mesopotamia, Greece and Rome; in the Middle Ages too. How difficult it is, though, to spot them in the documents of those remote ages! 'It is not easy to study the condition of old people throughout the ages. The written evidence that we have rarely mentions them: they are included in the general category of adults.' Simone de Beauvoir's remark that 'it is impossible to write a history of old age' underlines the real problem: ancient societies did not divide life up into slices as we do. Life began with a person's entry into the labour market and ended at death. Even the theories of the 'ages of life' which flourished in the Middle Ages were only abstract dissertations, intellectuals' games, which did not correspond with any practical distinctions. As long as there was no legal age for retirement, old age was not recognized as such in the texts. Given this, how is the category of the old to be distinguished? Old people were only elderly adults. The old never emerged as a social category; they dissolved into a multitude of elusive individual cases.

Let us recall further the aversion to numbers felt by traditional societies, which frequently deprives us of an individual's precise age, both through ignorance of a date of birth and through a tendency towards exaggeration. To all these imprecise quantities must be added the silence and disparity of the sources. The chronicles tell us about great acts, exploits, outstanding warriors; the archives of an economic nature count and enumerate useful and profitable things. Old people are generally absent from all these records.

The ancient civilizations . . . have been the object of only very little research into old age. They offer, however, a very interesting field of research: that of the social role of old people in traditional societies before the massive invasion of printing and state bureaucracy. A role which appears to have existed from the most distant ages onwards. Konrad Lorenz thinks it can even be distinguished among the higher primates and social animals; it is the old stag who leads the herd of deer, and no other male, however strong, dares rebel; it is the oldest crow who watches over the group; in a troop of baboons studied by researchers, two old males were in command.[2]

Anthropologists remark just as frequently on the importance of the privileges enjoyed by old people in present-day traditional societies. Georges Condominas noted concerning South-East Asia:

This privilege of old age can be found at every level. The old man, surrounded by affection, is entitled to a huge number of privileges. It is regarded as normal for him to make use of what strength is left to him to obtain all sorts of satisfactions . . . If the old man is thus surrounded by considerations, it is not on account of the duty to protect a weaker crea-ture but because happiness imbues and favours the entourage of a man thus privileged. Attaining a great age is considered a happiness and a cause of rejoicing, especially if the old man has many descendants; he has then reached the height of felicity. He cannot be put aside, as happens with us, and be sent off to an old people's home, he stays among his own people, because he is the living proof of the group's success.[3]

For his part, Louis-Vincent Thomas observed in black Africa how the old enjoyed considerable prestige among the twenty-two ethnic peoples he was able to study.

Experience, availability, eloquence, wisdom, knowledge, these all justify the idyllic picture black Africans have of old people, in spite of the reality of old people who can be senile, egoistical, tyrannical or cantankerous, just as they are everywhere in the world. This is because a purely oral society needs its old people, the symbols of its continuity, both in their role as the group's memory and as the prerequisite of its reproduction. So, in order to make their power more bearable and also to enhance one's own value by esteeming them, the group does not hesitate to idealize them. Since nothing can be done without old people, they might as well be attributed every quality – and their somnolence taken for meditative contemplation.[4]

This social role, initially so important, was to be unceasingly challenged in the historical societies of the West. The experience and wisdom of the old were contested in more complex types of society. And again, a parallel evo-lution can be observed among the African peoples we have just mentioned. Louis-Vincent Thomas has noted how the recent penetration of books, of writing, within these oral civilizations has sapped the prestige of old people: 'Nowadays however, the spoken word does not measure up to books. The power of the gerontocracy is henceforth demystified, and even attacked. The young inveigh against the old society. The old, cruelly trivial-ized, fall back into line'.[5] In the same way, the emergence of a type of demo-cratic government and the progressive elimination of religion in politics are factors contributing to the demise of gerontocracy.

Western history from antiquity to the Renaissance is marked by fluctua-tions in the social and political role of the old. What we are seeing is not so much a continuous decline as a switchback evolution; the general tendency, however, is towards degradation. The concept of a curved scale of ages was imposed on our society very early on, with its peak situated at around 40 or 50 years, preceding the irremediable and definitive decline towards a de-valued old age. This scheme includes many variants and exceptions, as will be seen, but the psychology of old people is profoundly and enduringly affected by it, making them internalize the degradation of their social status.

Every society has the old people it deserves, as is amply demonstrated by ancient and medieval history. Every type of socio-economic and cultural organization is responsible for the role and image of its old people. Every society treasures a model of the ideal man, and the image of old age depends on this model, whether it is depreciated or esteemed. Thus Classical Greece, which was orientated towards beauty, strength and youth, relegated old people to a subaltern position, whereas the Hellenistic period, which was freed from a good many conventions, allowed some old men to break with norms and taboos and return to the forefront. This fact encapsulates one of the essential opportunities of old age; it often allows one to rise above all sorts of conventions which must be submitted to in order to make one's career in adult life; freed from these constraints, an old man could give free rein to his creativity, allowing some people to reveal their genius at the age of 70 or 80.

Part IV

Gender and Sexuality

To be 'male' or 'female' seems to be something fixed for life. And for most of us it is. Some individuals, however, are so unhappy with their sexual identities that they actively change them. Precisely because it is so unusual, the experience of such people tells us a great deal about the nature of gender differences. Paul Hewitt was born as a woman, Martine (Reading 14). Describing his decision to live as a man, Hewitt shows just how wide the gulf between men's and women's lives is.

For most of history men have dominated public positions, in politics, economic life and other areas. Mostly, they still do. Yet in Western countries far more women are in paid work than ever before and have to some degree eroded pre-existing forms of male dominance. How far will such a process proceed? Some suggest that men at some point will become the 'weaker sex'. As Reading 15 indicates, in some respects they already are. For instance, men have a lower life expectancy than women and a higher proportion suffer from major diseases. Girls are starting to do better at school than boys and rates of employment of women are overtaking those of men.

Reading 16 turns to the topic of sexuality. All sexual liaisons involving certain forms of physical contact now, in principle, constitute a risk to life. No one knows how far the HIV virus, which is at the origin of AIDS, has spread through the British population or that of other countries throughout the world. Nor is there much reliable evidence about how far various categories of people have altered their sexual practices in the light of their knowledge of the risks of contracting the disease. Stuart Weir and Claire Sanders suggest that while heterosexual people are conscious of the risks that AIDS presents, this awareness does not necessarily lead them to alter their pre-existing sexual behaviour.

Reading 17 looks at the changing nature of homosexuality. Attitudes towards homosexuality have varied widely. In some cultures homosexuality, particularly male homosexuality, has been tolerated or openly approved of. In others, such as most Western countries since the Middle Ages, it has been condemned. Hence homosexuals in modern societies have had to fight long battles to achieve rights which heterosexual individuals take for granted. These rights include that of marriage. This reading discusses 'ordinary homosexuality'. Homosexuals everywhere are 'coming out of the closet': rather than wanting to be different, many simply wish to become absorbed into the wider society, without distinctions being made between them and people of a heterosexual orientation.

In the final reading, Jeffrey Weeks summarizes some important aspects of the development of attitudes towards sexuality and sexual behaviour. These attitudes, he suggests, have been affected by the ways in which sexual behaviour is discussed and debated. 'Sexology' – the supposedly scientific study of sexual activity – has had a practical impact upon what sexual behaviour means for us. 'Sexuality' as such hasn't always existed: it is in part a 'social construction', an invention of those who set out to study sex in a scientific way.

READING 14

Paul Hewitt with Jane Warren

A Self-Made Man

There were three of them. They were sitting behind me on the top deck of the bus, each of them playing the fool.

The double-decker lurched round a corner. Rain splattered down on the windows and Reading town centre became obscured behind the rivulets of grime and steamed-up glass.

The gang stood up *en masse*. I could hear the tinny wailing of their Walkmans and the squeaking of their leather coats. I tensed up, sensing trouble brewing. Then one of them slunk past my seat, half-way down on the right-hand side, and deliberately dragged his duffel bag over my head. I felt riled, but hid it.

Troublemaker two turned round to face me as he sauntered past with number three. In taunting mock apology he drawled in black man's language: 'Don't worry about it, man! They're animals.'

Something unfamiliar snapped inside me. 'Well, you're with them, so what does that make you?' I goaded, my eyes alive with menace. Then I baulked at my own defiance and began to tremble, the implications of my comment causing my heart to pump fight-or-flight messages around my tiny frame.

Then he got angry.

A huge fist in my face completely obscured my vision. For a moment I thought Mike Tyson had been let out early. Although my challenger was only 16 or 17 years old, he towered over me, and his knuckles were making intimate contact with my nose. His friends had paused on the stairs and all eyes were on me. I kept absolutely still, well aware that I had bitten off much, much more than I could chew. My palms were sweating.

'Just 'cos you got a nice suit, you think you're it', my aggressor hissed. His voice was hard now. I wisely resisted the urge to say, 'At least I haven't got a stupid haircut.'

The bus slowed to a halt. The fist quivered, then dropped away impassively. The boy spat on the floor before stepping on to the pavement with his mates. As the bus pulled away we made eye contact through the dirty window.

It took several minutes for my pulse to return to its normal rate. One day my big mouth is going to get me into serious trouble.

It was only three years ago that the 'look' through the window would have signalled something quite different: possible sexual interest. Three years ago I was a woman, Martine, and the bully could have been eyeing me up as a possible female conquest. For twenty-six years I had been used to having an advantage over these boys – but my power then was sensual, not physical. I would have slunk past their seats and attracted *their* attention. I would have heard a wolf-whistle, not a threat. I would have been the object of flirtation, not aggression.

Now, robbed of my power, I suddenly felt weak.

I certainly never expected that one day I would pose a threat as a rival male to young men on buses. Sometimes I feel a stranger here, thrust without social training into the tribal world of the male. For while I continue to see things through the same old eyes, society is reacting to me from a fresh perspective. I dress as a man now. I have facial hair. I no longer have a waist. And, yes, I can be bullied by gangs on buses.

I stand poised at the gates of manhood and the boys are beckoning me in. Beyond lies a whole world of macho ideals. He who dares wins.

Although I felt intimidated, the gang couldn't dampen my spirits – my artificial penis is in the post as I write.

I was born perfectly female, the ideal biological specimen in fact. I could appreciate my body, although I knew it not to be mine. Others loved my body far more than I ever did. When I wore a skirt I looked slinky and attractive and male attention was aplenty. And yet I have traded my feminine self for a substandard male body which will never function properly. Because of this, people find it hard to understand my motivation. But to remain as a woman would have been to deny myself my dreams and my peace of mind.

I was a man looking out through female eyes, but I played my role well. Most people, except the very perceptive ones, only ever saw me as a woman. Blending in was part of survival, or so I thought.

I will never be Arnold Schwarzenegger, yet now I feel as fully male as he. I have to accept that I will always be five feet two inches, yet inside I feel six feet tall. I have wanted to step out of my female skin all my life; there is nothing left for me there.

I am a victim of a medical condition invisible to the human eye. Women prefer to be held. I don't. I prefer to hold, and I feel a huge sense of protectiveness towards my twin sister. For a year I patiently played a waiting game for hormones to take effect. I used to liken myself to the man in the iron mask, looking out on the world through two narrow slits. He was a prisoner in a lonely tower, I was a prisoner in my own body. How could I communicate trapped in a body which certainly wasn't mine?

The truth about my real self has caught up with me with such pace that it has taken my breath away. Gasping for air in all the confusion, I have found a quiet spot in which to rest to gather my strength for the succession of operations that are to follow.

My decision to embark on a programme of gender reassignment was an act of pure survival. There have been times when I have felt suicidal, but I am too proud to quit. . . . I was born half an hour in advance of my twin sister Karen at Battle Hospital, Reading. The midwife cooed, 'Two beautiful baby girls.' Although that's what she clearly saw during her brief examination of infant genitalia, her instant assessment could not have been less accurate.

As I begin writing this diary, my outward appearance has markedly changed. Not in an overnight transformation, but in a steady sequence of social signals. Now I wear my hair cut short and manly with a slight quiff for a fringe. I am dressed in an open-necked shirt from Top Man which buttons left to right. I wear a signet ring and a single slim gold earring. There are cotton ties in my wardrobe today, three of them. They are my prized possessions, collectively symbolizing everything I have missed out on during these past twenty-six years. All three came from Top Man, a bargain at under £10 each. These slender but significant social markers are worn with a strong mix of pride and injustice. And, yes, I use the men's toilets.

Four weeks from now I will change my name by Statutory Declaration, marking for me the beginning of a new life as a man.

My new name will be Paul Hewitt, yet I was born a woman. My sister will have a twin brother. My parents a son.

I have a dream. I want to be a real man. Am I to be confined inside this foreign body with breasts forever? A female android, I mechanically sashay about, while, inside, the man stomps around this soft white body like a headless chicken shouting: 'Let me out, you bastards!'

I am 26 years old. I have an honours degree in biochemistry. I am also a female-to-male transsexual. A man born imprisoned in a female body. I suffer from a recognized medical condition called gender identity disorder. My decision to embark on a programme of gender reassignment comes down to a choice between life and death; it's an act of pure survival because my female body has always felt alien. It is not that I *want* to be male. I *am* male and, like all transsexuals, I experience an overwhelming urge to bring the gender of my body into line with the gender of my mind.

This has little to do with sex. It is not a sexual preference but an ineradicable conviction about my emotional and psychological identity. I have reached a crossing-point in my life where I have been stripped of everything. Everything except the courage to face the truth, and the courage to act upon the information I have now learned about myself.

I am not a freak. One in 15,000 people is transsexual, and sufferers are united by their total conviction that they have been born into the wrong body. Only 25 per cent of all gender reassignment patients are biological women who believe they are truly female. One hundred female-to-males like me undergo treatment every year.

The emotional pain of what I am facing is intense. It has forced me to draw on reserves of courage I never knew I had, but can it really be called courage, when I have no option? I may currently have breasts, but I ignore them. I feel as much a man as Sly Stallone – though rather more articulate. I burned my bras ten months ago and have not looked back since. Each stage I have progressed through has been symbolized by a door that has locked behind me, and since I no longer hold the keys for these doors my only way is forwards. I still can't believe this has all happened to me. The strength of my own convictions frightens me.

Now I bind up my ample 34D breasts in an elaborate chest-binding device every day and hide them beneath a suit or casual male clothes. It has taken months of experimentation and practice to create a binding device sufficient to allow me to face the world with confidence and without fear of discovery. Eight elasticated metres of the widest crêpe bandage I could find, wound from my underarms down to my stomach, flattening the breasts which I view with contempt. When they appeared late on in puberty, how could I possibly have foreseen that I would grow to hate them so much?

For so long my real self, Paul, has lain dormant and oppressed, forced into the indignity of dressing as a woman, obliged to stick to the rules, and manipulated as one of society's obedient wooden puppets. But now I am discovering reserves of power. I will be that obedient puppet no more and the world had better watch out. Fathers, lock up your daughters.

Initially, my male self wasn't as confident or expressive as it is now. When I first started cross-dressing a year and a half ago, the part of me which was Paul was happy to make a part-time appearance. Social conditioning was so deeply entrenched that, like a dog, he used to be happy with the titbits he was passed under the table. But now Paul insists on eating at the table with the rest of you. I feel as if I am being reborn, witnessing my own evolution. In two months' time, when I have lived as a man for one year, I will begin a lifetime course of fortnightly high-dosage testosterone injections. After a year of drug therapy, I plan to have a double mastectomy.

Most women get suicidal at the thought of losing a breast. To me, my enthusiasm and conviction that this is right are profound evidence of my transsexualism. It will be the final staging-post of my bid for maleness. This will be the day I will finally be liberated from my biological chains.

READING 15

The Male Dodo: Are Men Necessary?

Imagine a white, middle-class, Western couple about to pick the sex of their next child (this choice will soon no longer be a fantasy). If they are rational and thorough people, never in 1,000 years would they choose a boy. Not only is ours more and more a woman's world; by the second quarter of the twenty-first century, when a child born now will be mature, it will be time to wonder if men have a future. In many areas of life they will be marginal, in others an expensive nuisance.

If that sounds wild or overdone, consider the more glaring weaknesses in the so-called stronger sex. Start with medical ones. Boys are more often born with inherited diseases. Because they do not have a spare x-chromosome, whereas girls do, boys with a faulty gene have no back-up. The effects of this deficiency can range from colour-blindness to haemophilia.

Boys tend to have more troubled childhoods, too. More than twice as many boys as girls are autistic – meaning they so totally fail to develop normal social abilities that they cannot function independently. They are eight times as likely as girls to be hyperactive – uncontrollably jumpy and energetic. Dyslexia and stuttering are nearly five times as common among men. As most parents of both will tell you, bringing up a boy can be considerably more fraught and risky than bringing up a girl.

It is not much better at the other end of life. Until early this century, American men tended to live as long as or longer than women. Since then a gap has opened up, and it is getting steadily wider each year. Men now die on average fully seven years before women born in the same year. More strikingly, male mortality is rising in relation to female mortality in every age group.

One of the main reasons for this is that men get more of most diseases than women. Before the age of 65 men are more than twice as likely to die from heart disease as women; they are also more likely to suffer strokes, ulcers and liver failure. Half of all men get cancer, compared with only one-third of women. Smoking, which until recently was largely a male pastime, accounts for some of this difference, but not all. According to Andrew Kimbrell (*The Masculine Mystique*; Ballantine), the death rate from cancer has risen by 21 per cent in men in 30 years, while it has stayed the same for women.

For these depressing medical facts, there is a one-word explanation: testosterone. The male steroid hormone weakens the body's resistance to infectious diseases and cancer; it also seems to cause the body to age more rapidly. Eunuchs usually live much longer than other men. To the conspiracy-minded, testosterone might even look like part of an evolutionary plot on behalf of females.

Next, consider boys' educational weaknesses. Evidence is growing that on many counts girls are cleverer than boys. In 1995 the top five places – and fourteen of the top twenty – in a league table of British schools ranked by exam results were all-girl schools. In 1979 roughly equal numbers of girls and boys got five or more passes at O-level, the girls doing very marginally better. Since then the performance gap has widened. Girls now are clearly likelier than boys to get five passes.

Similar findings come from America. Boys there are half as likely again to be held back a grade in school at age 13; twice as likely to be in special education and twice as likely to drop out of high school altogether. Girls are more likely than boys to go to university, still more likely to graduate, and even more likely to do a master's degree.

TESTOSTERONE'S PEAK

After school, our putative couple's hypothetical son would then embark on another risk-fraught period of life as the output of testosterone reached a peak. Talk of violence and, more often than not, you are talking about young men. About 80 per cent of murder victims are men, as are 90 per cent of murderers. Most of these are in their twenties and the cause of most murders is hot-blooded, testosterone-induced arguments over status and love. Well aware of the connection between gender and crime, some American feminists have even proposed a male poll tax to help pay for police and prisons.

Licking wounds and drowning sorrows, young men get hooked on drugs or alcohol about twice as often as women. But that leads to more violence. More than 80 per cent of drunken drivers and those arrested for drug offences are men. The sex ratio of prisoners in United States jails is more than ten men to each woman, and men get longer sentences for similar offences. The great majority of AIDS victims in America (though not in Africa) are men. Men attempting suicide are four times as likely as women to succeed.

Should a man survive his burst of testosterone – most do – and reach the age of 30, the chances are increasing that he will find himself without steady work. The number of American men in full-time employment is falling by about 1 m a year. The number of employed women is rising at almost the same rate. If employment trends continue as now, by the end of the century, if not before, the United States will be employing more women than men.

Britain is not far behind. On Tyneside, once a byword for heavy industries employing skilled men in secure jobs while their wives stayed at home, the reversal is now so acute that a locally born playwright, Alan Plater, has written a play about it. *Shooting the Legend* is set in a colliery's social-welfare club run by unemployed men whose wives work. It is no joke. Roughly, for every new (commonly female) job in banking or airline reservation that has been created in the region since 1980, another in ship-building or heavy engineering has been lost.

One reason for this is a change in the nature of work. As each year goes by, job openings in agriculture, manual labour, metal-banging and machine-handling decline, while work in retailing, word-processing, services and health care – all traditionally female jobs – opens up. At its simplest, as computers replace tractors, brain is replacing brawn. Now that they are more and more educated, women will be almost certain to start claiming their rewards. (Conspiratorialists will recall the original idea for the modern computer was due to a woman, Ada Lovelace.)

Should some lucky male, having run this gauntlet, survive long enough to turn to sex with a woman, he will find he has entered a war zone where the enemy has many things, including law, on her side. Among many animal species males are the seducing sex; females the sex that decides whether to be seduced. Interestingly, this is less true for species where males nourish females or foster offspring – virtues females will seduce for. But a widespread pattern is that females flirt, men pounce. Among humans, this preserve is laced with rules, written or unwritten, and full of risks.

Think, to take a tricky but salient example, of date rape. According to

Andrea Dworkin, an American feminist, the big difference between seduction and rape is that 'in seduction, the rapist bothers to buy a bottle of wine'. Many evolutionary biologists would agree. To them any animal seduction is an asymmetric act of more or less forcible persuasion by a very keen seller of sperm, which comes cheap, to a discriminating buyer of impregnation, which involves huge investments of time and energy. The more asymmetric the investment, the harder the male tries. In human beings a few minutes' work by a man can be leveraged into nine months of female gestation. Whether the eager male is a rapist, an over-persistent seducer or just a husband is to the thorough-going feminist and to the evolutionary biologist of secondary interest.

Despite the nursery rhyme about Jack Sprat and his wife, another disreputable thing men do is to eat both more meat and more fat than women. The habit goes back to the Pleistocene era, when modern human beings emerged in Africa and began to spread to the rest of the world, replacing earlier forms of the species. Among modern hunter-gatherer peoples men catch most of the meat and women gather most of the plant food. Although men share meat with women, they tend to be more carnivorous.

Red meat comes these days with all the wrong cultural labels. Eating it is increasingly treated as cruel, environmentally damaging and unhealthy. Vegetarianism is on the rise, but particularly among women. Encouraged by this trend, many governments are spending large sums of money in health campaigns devoted to the demonization of red meat.

MUMMY, WHAT ARE MEN FOR?

Men are not, for all that, utter weaklings. Suppose that, under-educated, diseased, sclerotic and unemployed, the hypothetical son of our putative couple has made it to middle-age some time in the 2030s. Just as he is thinking about putting his feet on the chair and cracking a can to watch football, the beer stales and the game pales. Unaccountably he finds himself asking, 'What is it all about? What has it all been for?' But this familiar midlife twinge has a new, nasty twist. He is struck with existential doubt not just about himself, but about his gender as a whole. And the bond of male solidarity makes the question no easier to face: what are men for?

Biologically, the purpose of sex is still poorly understood. There are animals and plants that get by without one. Dandelions, for example, produce baby dandelions by themselves. Whiptail lizards in the Arizona desert practise virgin birth, though they perform a pseudo-copulation to get themselves in the mood. There is a whole class of animals, the bdelloid rotifers, that, as far as scientists estimate, have not produced a male individual for around 30 m years, and they do not just survive, they thrive.

The puzzle is less why sex (and so males) arose, but why it (and they) survive. Suppose, for a moment, sex is already present. You would think it ought to die out, and here is why. Note that, by convention, biologists call even asexual creatures that reproduce themselves female. Imagine now a population of asexual females, which pass on all their genes to the next generation; and a population of sexual ones, which mix their genes with males through copulation or some other form of sexual transmission. (This pairing of sexed and unsexed populations is not as bizarre as it sounds: snails of either sort exist side by side in New Zealand.) Suppose each female has two offspring. The asexual ones will pass their genes on to two offspring, each of which will bear two more, and so on. If the sexual females have on average a male and female offspring, only one will reproduce. In other words, the asexual gene pool should grow while the sexual one should soon die out.

But, luckily for men, it survives. There seems to be a point to sexual reproduction that counterbalances this evolutionary pressure towards femininity. That point may be summed up by saying that, once a generation, sex remixes the genes of two individuals. This spins the numbers on the genetic combination lock that seals each cell, which foils parasitic burglars such as worms, bacteria and viruses. As the main exponent of this theory, William Hamilton of Oxford University, puts it: 'Sexual species are committed to a free and fair exchange of biotechnology for the exclusion of parasites.' The reason why a defence is needed is that parasites are always trying to unlock cells using the previous generation's commonest combination.

It may sound like small comfort to a doubt-struck man to learn that he is, in effect, the female sex's health-insurance policy. But having, so to speak, invented males, our female ur-ancestors then used them for other purposes. Most strikingly, many animal species use males as genetic sieves, to sift out the good genes and discard the bad. They do this by equipping males with all sorts of encumbrances and then setting them to work in competition, either beating each other up or risking their lives against predators and parasites.

The end result, as in a deadly jousting tournament, is a lot of dead males and one or two survivors in clear possession of superior genes: thus has the species been 'sieved' for the better. Peacocks' tails and nightingales' songs are two examples of the accoutrements to these virility tests designed to get most males killed through exhaustion, disease and violence purely so that females can tell which males have the best genes.

A bull elephant seal may look to some like a male chauvinist pig – all force and no child care – but it is actually the victim of evolutionary manipulation by the female sex: to the extent that the bull seal is designed at all; it is meant to die of disease or violence trying, and usually failing, to win one chance of fathering lots of children.

The hormone testosterone, in sum, is the supreme female 'invention'. Not only does testosterone make males do dangerous things, such as fight each other or take absurd risks. It also weakens the immune system. Males, we know, are more likely to get diseases. But now we can see the biological reason why. The higher they push their testosterone levels to win fights and seduce females, the greater the risk of disease they run. The biochemical connection is direct.

MEN'S SECRET

Despite everything said so far, there is hope for men. For one thing stands in the way of a world without beer, hamburgers, pot bellies and patriarchy. Men's fate hangs by a slender thread, perhaps, but thread it is, and one of a scientifically compelling kind: for the moment, sperm is needed. If women did decide to switch to virgin birth by the simple procedure of fusing the genetic nuclei of two eggs instead of sperm and an egg, it would not actually work. At least it would not work in our species, or for any other higher mammal, though it might work, for example, in a platypus, a kangaroo or a bird.

The experiment has been done in mice. Scientists produced an embryo with a nucleus made from two sperm nuclei; and another embryo with a nucleus made from two egg nuclei. There was a remarkable difference. The all-sperm embryo developed a large and healthy placenta but a slightly deformed and rather small foetus. The all-egg embryo developed a good, healthy foetus but a small and ill-formed placenta: without a good placenta, the foetus soon died.

In other words, the placenta is largely the product of genes inherited from the father – indeed it is full of paternal genes that almost viciously set about exploiting the mother's body, not trusting the maternal genes to do so selfish a job – and without a placenta the foetus could not develop. So given the present horizons of bio-engineering, sperm remains necessary for successful fertilization and embryo growth.

But men should not sigh with relief. For a different worry looms: sperm is, or may be, disappearing. Out of the wondrous modern chemical industry flow products that appear to mimic the effects of female hormones and to reduce the sperm counts of men. (Immediately, that is a problem for both sexes; on a longer, more evolutionary scale, it is a deathknell for men.) If you believe the figures, which some scientists hotly contest, the average number of sperm in the average man's semen is falling so steadily that it 'portends the collapse of traditional means of procreation by the middle of the next century', according to one expert in the field. If that is true, it is serious. Most men spend a lot of time thinking, if that is the word, about 'traditional means of procreation'. The speed of decline is disputed. But studies done in Denmark, France and Britain all point in the same direction: fewer sperm per ejaculation each year.

What to blame for falling sperm-counts is hard to pin down. The problem is not that most chemicals are innocent but that so many are guilty. Now scientists have started looking, they are finding scores of chemicals, natural and synthetic, that mimic the effect of female hormones. When given to male rainbow trout, they cause them to start making female proteins called vitellogenins. Put a shoal of male trout downstream from a sewage farm using those chemicals and the fish are likely to start to feminize.

Just about any of the common chemicals used in making plastics seems to encourage the production of oestrogen, the female hormone. Pregnant rats fed on low doses of them give birth to male offspring with small testicles and low sperm counts. Nonylphenol, the most potent of the chemicals, first came to light in a (woman's) laboratory in Boston when some plastic tubes were traced as the source of a mysterious substance that made breast-cancer cells grow in a glass jar.

THE CASE AGAINST MEN

So is Jack Lang, France's former culture minister and a fine nose for fashion, right when he claimed – in the title of his recent book – 'Tomorrow belongs to women'? Recall, a moment, how men let the species down. They are more prone to disease, more dumb at school and more troubled at home than girls. They are more violent, die earlier, and in many walks of life are becoming less and less needed at work. Biologically, males are useful chiefly as a 'genetic sieve' for the safer transmission of the genes of the reproducing female. Male sperm, in addition, seems important to the production of the embryo-protecting placenta. But, in the longer run, there are evolutionary question-marks over the need for men to perform the first of those functions and over their capacity to perform the second.

A world of tamed, feminized or vanished men would be a world with less meat, which would reduce pressure on rain forests. It would be a world with less crime, where even the slums of Rio de Janeiro would be safe at night. Pornography would largely disappear. So would rape, classically understood. Children, true, would be brought up in fatherless homes, but the evidence suggests that it is mainly boys who turn bad in such circumstances, not girls.

Nor, as a vision of things to come, need a world without men hold out such terrible fears. Civilization owes much to men. But creating cultures and technologies is one thing, preserving them another. A sex adapted to the one is not obviously adapted to the other. In the grand sweep of things, the human race may before long have completed its evolution from a warring collection of romantic, male-dominated tribes to a peaceable, cool-headed sisterhood devoted to shopping and household management – those most feminine of arts known nowadays as economics.

Stuart Weir and Claire Sanders

Dangerous Liaisons: AIDS and Unsafe Sex

Luke is 29. He is a commodity broker in the City and earns over £200,000 a year. He is a calm and reflective man and talks very precisely about his life and feelings. Two years ago a long-standing relationship broke down.

I have been a bachelor ever since, travelling quite a bit. I work very long hours, normally until 8.30 p.m. and in my work there is a lot of tension and stress and emotion. Because of the stresses of work, I like my relationships to be as easy as possible. Emotionally, it is very difficult to carry on a strong relationship with a fixed partner because I don't have the time to deal with the consequences of that. So I have many relationships.

In the first place I was very concerned about contracting HIV. I went out with some girls I knew, who were kind of friends, and eventually I was having sexual relationships without any protection. One day I met a girl who said, 'Do you know if you have AIDS or not?' I said I don't think so. She said, 'How do you know?' and she sent me to a doctor. He tested me and I was all right. He was a specialist in this kind of disease and he explained that the main risk is with homosexuals or prostitutes. I think purely from a statistical point of view this is possibly true, but you just need one unlucky occasion and you can contract AIDS.

But in saying that, I must say that I take some risks. Although it doesn't follow any logic, I am still having sex with girls without protection. It's always with girls I have known for several months, it's very unusual for me to have sex with a person at the first meeting. And I always discuss AIDS and other relationships before I have intercourse, I ask specific questions about those kind of things. You know, 'Do you think you have AIDS, if you don't, how do you know that precisely?' The funny thing is that though I am always very honest and say that I go out with several other girls and have sex with them, and we talk very seriously about safe sex and using condoms, no bullshit – you know, we are going to do this thing seriously – the relationship kind of evolves and when it comes down to it, I have never had a girl ask me to wear a condom. Over the past year I have probably met

85

about twenty different girls, and the girls I go out with are perhaps university graduates, you know, they have very responsible jobs, but none have insisted I wear a condom.

So in effect you have a very serious discussion and then you both act entirely differently?

Well, we have a serious discussion about it and we say that it could be dangerous, you have to be careful. We don't normally talk too specifically about what we have to do. We both realize that the decision is serious, but we don't say, 'OK, we're going to do this, buy a condom.' It's more, 'OK, we have to be careful.' But eventually, having met and talked as a couple, there is no more discussion.

Why do we take such risks? I don't know, it is very difficult for me to explain. Maybe it is in our minds, or at least in mine, and it must be somewhere very remote, that using condoms is not really natural. And also if you really think about it, it is really ridiculous. So you don't want to be bothered with that, it is not pretty, it is not practical, it is not poetic. Of course, it can also save your life – but you are sure the person is OK, after all.

So in a sense you are judging each other on some notion of responsibility and respectability?

Well, for example I met a French girl and she said she hadn't had sex for quite a while. Maybe it was true, maybe it was not, for some reason I thought it was. Then I said, 'What about me? I could have AIDS, you know.' And she said, 'No, I know you haven't got AIDS.' I asked why, and she said, 'Well, because you look fairly straight.' I think that people for some reason seem to trust me. But they don't realize that by trusting me they have to trust all the partners I have been with, which is a different thing.

Do any of them ask you if you are bisexual?

No, nobody asks me that.

Or if you take drugs?

No, but I think anyone who knows me would know that I am neither of the two.

But they have only known you for weeks in some cases.

Yes, that is true. There is no doubt that there is some discrepancy in people's lives, perhaps they don't want to see some things. They may be very mature and very adult in their business life, and in taking these big risks there, but they change in their social life, they become immature, and I include myself.

Have you yourself ever decided that you don't quite trust a woman you've met?

Yes, definitely. There are a couple of girls that I didn't trust, I couldn't tell you exactly why. I just decided to stop the relationship. And perhaps in 25 per cent of the cases where I go to bed with a girl, I stop before penetration.

What about anal intercourse, does that come into it at all?

Yes, whenever it gets to anal intercourse I tend to pick the girls that somehow I trust more than the others.

And what about your partners, are they more careful with that?

That's the odd thing. When it gets down to being in bed with somebody, the whole thing is somehow not there for them any more. That kind of thought is outside the bedroom somehow.

Obviously, the women take a greater risk than you, as penetrative sex is much more dangerous for them than for you. Would you behave the same way if you felt you were running an equal risk?

I always thought I was running an equal risk. And when it comes to oral sex, when it is the man using his mouth, that is one of the great risks for the man. It is not that I have oral sex with any girl I go with, but on some occasions I have and in that particular instance I take an equal risk. I have a hard time to really pinpoint why I am taking this risk. If you think about it, it is ridiculous and I have a hard time to find out why you take risks. And I have been telling myself a hundred times never again, you know, this is crazy . . .

Do you think the risk in any sense actually makes things more exciting?

That is an interesting question, I guess I would say no, because if I thought about it during intercourse it would make me less excited. The idea that I could be contracting HIV is not the kind of thought I like to have when I am in bed with someone.

Is it your impression generally that the risk of infection has not really affected most people's behaviour very much?

In my experience, exactly. I've met girls who talk very straight about it, so you know where you are, and then you go to bed with them and they haven't got a condom. Once you get into a very physical relationship it is all over. That happens so many times. I even had a girlfriend who was a model in New York and her best friend died of AIDS and she is still suffering from that emotionally because he was a very close friend. You would think that she would be more cautious than anybody else and that is the way she talked. I said I don't like condoms, and she said, 'Don't worry, with me there is no way you won't use them, it's crazy not to.' But we met several times, and then began a physical relationship without penetration and eventually a week later we had penetration with no protection and I thought about it only later on.

But didn't you think that she might be dangerous for you?

Oh yes. I only trusted her because she was so assertive and so strict about it that I thought it was impossible she would ever take the risk. Afterwards, I thought I don't know about her any more, I got very nervous and I went and had a check. That was pushing my luck a bit too far. I did realize that somehow I would have to calm down, because if you push your luck too far one day you might get HIV, there is no question about it.

Joan is 35. She is a solicitor who concentrates on legal aid work, mostly in family law. She has been living with a regular partner for seven years and they have bought a flat in south London together.

I have a full sex life with my partner, I mean, we have probably done most things people do together. I am on the pill so he never has to use a condom. We have never discussed the question of safe sex together and I don't think that we ever would. I don't think that we have to.

87

Do you know that some people say that even people in stable relationships should discuss and practise safe sex, simply because surveys of sexual behaviour suggest that no one can actually trust their partner not to sleep with someone else?

Some people say that, do they? I can't agree with that. You have to trust somebody and surely you've got to trust the person you live with. I trust my partner completely. I am sure that he has never been out with any other woman. I know him very well and I know he thinks the world of me and I know he wouldn't – it sounds awful, but I do know him, I am 100 per cent sure of him.

Is he 100 per cent sure of you?

No. He knows that I had an affair very early on in our relationship. In fact, I knew the man – a colleague – before I moved in with Michael and we have been close friends for years. One night when I'd been with him Michael asked me if I was having an affair and I said, yes, and he was so upset that I broke the thing with Peter off. But we have remained friends since and there have been periods of time, maybe a year has gone past, when we haven't been out and haven't slept together, but then we get back together again. Over the last year or so we were seeing each other, say every two months. Peter has got his own house and he is single. He has had a long-term relationship with a woman which was supposed to be over, but then she found out she was pregnant so she has actually moved in with him now, about a month ago. Since then I haven't seen him.

So Peter was having sex with at least one other person while you were having an affair with him. Did you practise safe sex?

No.

Did you think that you might be running a risk?

No, because the way I think about it – and probably will continue to think about it – is that the people I choose to have a sexual relationship with, who now are very few and far between anyway, are people I have known for years. I know a lot about them, and they are responsible people, they don't sleep around, they have probably only had one partner for the last three or four years and I suppose that that is what makes me feel safe.

How much do you know about Peter's other lover? Do you think she may have had other lovers too?

From what he has told me, yes, I do know about her. I don't think she would have had other partners while she was seeing him – not from the way he talked about her, and what he said. I mean, it is conceivable, but she was so keen on Peter, and wanted to get married, I don't think she's the sort.

You talked about the people you have had affairs with. Has Peter been your only lover over the last few years?

There's only been one other, and that was just a one-off with my partner's best friend a few months ago. It was nothing spectacular and it was a great mistake. It took place in the afternoon and didn't last very long, and that was it. It wasn't 'safe sex', he didn't use a condom. But again, and I'm sorry if this sounds boring, I have known him for about eight years and he's been married for five of those years, and I am sure that he doesn't have other partners, except possibly a one-night stand when he's away, but I doubt that too. I mean, we have been friends for a long time and he is the sort of person who talks about it and I am very easy to talk to about it. I think I would know. So I simply didn't worry about AIDS because I know he is a responsible person.

But he has just done so with you.

Well, he knows that I have only got one partner and that I have been very good for the last so many years. And I know all about his habits with his wife. I can tell you, if I fancied somebody and was going to have perhaps a one-night stand, there is no way I would sleep with that person if I didn't know them. If I had only met them that very day at a conference or something, there is no way I would sleep with them without protection, without using a condom.

Jon is a hospital doctor in Birmingham. He is 45 and has been married for twenty-three years. He and his wife have two teenage children. He has a strong outgoing character and has always had affairs with other women.

I am in a rather complicated situation at the moment. I am going out with three women, but one of them who is married has got very, very keen and now she wants to ditch her marriage. I have been trying to drift away slightly and I haven't seen her for three weeks. I was seeing her once every week and we were speaking on the telephone four or five times a day and she was writing letters and poems.

Then there are one or two other little forays. I met a very attractive doctor, quite small, about 35, at a conference in London recently. We went back to her flat and drank some champagne and she said, 'Would you carry me into the bedroom?' I do still see her when I am in London, but she's rather neurotic. There is another one which is not so complicated in one of the provincial towns which I have to visit quite often. So when I go there that is quite a nice interlude. I would say that none of them are risky from the point of view of HIV infection.

How many women have you slept with in the past five years?

Maybe thirty, yes around thirty. I don't like using condoms, but I do if they ask me to. The doctor insists that I wear a condom, she always does. And the one in the provinces normally says I have to wear one, she thinks of some trumped-up reason, you know, she has got her period or something, but really it is because she is frightened of AIDS. Anyway, I do. But I never use a condom with the married woman that I have been seeing quite a lot. And not many people ask for it and I don't like it, I think condoms really do affect it.

But you don't think your own safety depends on it?

I still am very arrogant, I still think the risks are at the moment extremely small, you would have to be extremely unfortunate. Most of the heterosexual AIDS sufferers have contracted it through drug users or homosexuals. There are very few cases of AIDS being passed on by straight sex. Of course, in three or four years' time the risks will increase. But here at the moment the risk is very, very slight. I'm far more likely to get gonorrhoea or syphilis, or be run over or be killed in a car crash.

But if you get AIDS it doesn't just affect you, it affects all of your partners, your wife, their families and in a way your own children. Do you worry about affecting them?

Well that would be terrible, it would be an awful thing. If you start thinking about it, it would be an absolutely awful thing to have to inflict on a family. But talk to any doctor. Most doctors are basically saying there was a justifiable kind of hysteria a few years ago, but I don't think any of us now believe – apart from a small number – that AIDS is going to be anything like the scourge that people thought before.

Basically, you've got to realize there are two factors here. One, it was in the interests of the government to create a slight panic about it to try and get people to change their sexual habits. Two, some of it was generated by the gay community who didn't want to be scapegoated and wanted the whole thing to be generalized. What developed in the medical world was a small group of doctors who very cynically – this is probably not a very nice thing to say, because a lot of them I know and some of them are very decent and honourable people – but it is in their interest to maintain a kind of AIDS culture for their careers.

But at a personal level, if you consider your partner in the provincial town, she has presumably some inkling of your behaviour and she's right to be worried ...

I don't know that I have been quite so, she knows my track record very well. I think among working people, perhaps among those who don't feel they have so much to lose, that their behaviour hasn't changed as much as middle-class behaviour which hasn't probably changed an awful lot either.

Your married partner, is she too a doctor, and does she know that you have other partners?

Yes, and she knows more than the others about me.

Doesn't it alarm her?

Do you know any straight person with AIDS?

Yes, because we interviewed someone who became infected with HIV without knowing it from one random sexual encounter and she had at least one lover before she found out. Possibly you could meet someone like her who didn't know and then you could have problems.

Was she working-class?

Actually she is a middle-class person. Do you think that you're safe with middle-class people, then?

At the moment, I just think there are an awful lot of things to be frightened of which are far worse.

It's Normal to Be Queer

After the former Yugoslav army moved out of its barracks in Ljubljana, the homosexuals moved in. The gutted compound in Metelkova Road is hulking, derelict, folded in icy blackness on a winter's night because the public electricity has been cut off. But make your way through a fresh-painted door and you enter Klub Magnus, another world.

The curtains are a smart yellow, the walls cheery red; generators and portable heaters banish the winter night. Twenty or thirty young homosexuals gather at café tables smoking, drinking, chatting. One of them, Robert, sits not far from a sign saying 'All Different, All Equal'. Slovenia (population 2 m) is a shard of the former Yugoslavia; unsurprisingly, older homosexuals in this corner of Europe mostly stay out of sight. Robert, who is 25, does not.

He knew he was homosexual at 15 and began telling others at 20. 'I didn't want to have a double life', he says. 'It's more important to take the consequences and live like you want to live.' Nearby is Matej, 21, who will soon declare himself to his family. 'I don't like to hide', he says. And Zoran, behind the bar, 26 years old and living with his lover; '2QT2BSTR8', says his T-shirt ('too cute to be straight'). And Janez, who is 17. 'I have secrets,' he says impishly, 'like my bank account.'

Homosexuality was legalized in Slovenia in 1974. The first gay men's organization arrived in 1984, and a lesbian group in 1988. [In] August [1995] these hosted Slovenia's first international conference on homosexuality, which was attended by several prominent politicians and was well received in the local press. Later [in 1996], at another gay conference, there may be enough openly gay Slovenes for a small parade or demonstration.

Most striking, however, are these Slovene youths. In their casual attitude toward their homosexuality, and in their indifference to radical gay politics on the one hand and to heterosexual disapproval on the other, they might as easily be in Los Angeles or London as in Ljubljana. Or in a few years, perhaps, Lahore: a gay group opened its doors in Pakistan [in 1995] – and so too did such groups in Bolivia, Curaçao, Kenya, Moldova, Portugal, South Korea and Sri Lanka.

In Argentina last year, homosexual groups numbering more than a dozen set about forming a national organization; in Taiwan, the Asian Lesbian

Plate 4.1
Straightforwardly gay

Network met to draft its new constitution. In Tomsk, twenty-five people turned up [in] May [1995] for Siberia's first gay conference. Since the Iron Curtain fell, Eastern Europe has sprouted dozens of gay groups; [in 1995] China sprouted two. The International Lesbian and Gay Association began with seventeen member organizations in 1978; [by 1996 it had] about 300, representing seventy countries.

WE'RE HERE, WE'RE QUEER, WE'RE BORING

Sometimes, for reasons that remain but dimly understood, cultural tides wash round the world. Janez and Zoran and Matej and Robert are part of such a global cultural shift. Something new has arrived in the world: the ordinary homosexual.

Homosexuality, one may assume, is a thing. But what kind of thing? For an individual, it is a passionate longing for the erotic love of another of the same sex. For society, however, its nature is as changeable as the norms of the day.

For the ancients (among whom what would today be called bisexuality was common), and for many people since, homosexuality was a behaviour and perhaps a proclivity, but not a defining trait. To this day, many people maintain that homosexual behaviour exists but that homosexuals, as such, do not. Ironically, this 'behavioural' view is now mainly espoused by two groups of bitter enemies: right-wing anti-gay activists, who believe that everyone is naturally heterosexual, and left-wing pro-gay activists, who believe that sexual categories themselves are cramping and repressive.

Since ancient times, homosexuality has been loaded down with every kind of significance. For Christians and Jews, it was (or is) a deadly sin: one of the most vicious of vices. Later, in the nineteenth century and particularly with the work of Freud and his successors, came the scientization of sexuality, which made homosexuality a matter of diagnosis, turning it into a pathology, the sign of a disturbed personality. In the twentieth century, those two streams proceeded to mix, incoherently but potently. Homosexuality came to seem a vice and a disease simultaneously, rather as though leprosy were the fault of the people afflicted with it.

As incoherent models often do, this one broke down. Change has come over the past thirty years or so in three overlapping phases. Homosexuality, first, was in many places struck from lists of crimes and illnesses. Homosexuality, second, ceased to be shameful and became 'gay', offering for many the cultural identity of a self-aware minority. More recently, and this is perhaps the most startling change of all, homosexuality came to be accepted as an orientation like any other.

A bland word, 'orientation'. But it flags the radical redrawing of an idea. To call homosexuality an orientation presupposes that it is a neutral trait or disposition, like left-handedness: not changeable, or at least not changeable without deforming the bearer's personality; not innately harmful, though perhaps inconvenient; and not itself chosen, even if the sort of behaviour the orientation prompts is a matter of choice. In a quiet way, this latest view is more radical than any of its predecessors, because it treats homosexuals as both fundamentally distinct from the heterosexual majority and, at the same time, quite ordinary. As a minority, on this view, homosexuals may be statistically odd, but they are behaviourally normal. And that is a new synthesis.

What is new, it should be noted, is not the homosexual flowering as such, but how it is thought and talked about. One thinks of the rarefied subcultures of Wilde and Tchaikovsky a century ago, or of New York in the 1920s, where homosexual life blossomed until a backlash of police repression drove it underground. Yet in those cases homosexuality was closely linked with strangeness and cultural rebellion. It flouted, indeed inverted, bourgeois norms by defying them in secret and, for those clever enough to read the codes, tweaking them in public (as Noel Coward in his plays and songs liked to do). When (rarely) homosexuality was noticed publicly, it was associated with artists, writers, Bohemians and provocateurs.

Today the drag queen, whose flamboyant cross-dressing both sends up and pays homage to social convention, still flourishes in gay culture. Radical politics, usually of a trendy left-wing variety, still holds sway among gay activists in America and Europe, who like to see themselves as striving to liberate not just homosexuals but the whole world. What is new, rather, is the advent of banal homosexuality. If homosexuality is at root an orientation, then it may just as easily be grey tweed as purple chiffon, bourgeois as revolutionary. It can be countercultural, but it does not have to be.

So emerges that rare but proliferating species: the young woman of 20 who realizes she is a lesbian but, after a period of adjustment, shrugs her shoulders, informs her family, and plans to get on with an otherwise mundane life. Or the gay New Yorker who is more interested in bringing his lover to the company's Christmas party than in overturning corporate capitalism. He neither menaces the social order, as generations of priests and headmasters maintained, nor tartly flouts it, as generations of gay rebels have done. He is, you could say, sexually left-handed: that is all.

WITH EXCEPTIONS

And yet even this deradicalized notion of homosexuality implies a radicalism of its own. If homosexuality is just an orientation and not a cardinal sin or an unspeakable disease, there is no reason for homosexuals to hide. If it is ordinary, then it is not shameful and homosexuals can and should expect to live openly. Increasingly, they do.

The Islamic world, it has to be said, is a large exception. Militant Islam is not kind to homosexuals; in Iran, the punishment for homosexuality ranges from seventy-four lashes to death. (One Swedish report, in 1991, said that seventy Iranian homosexuals had been executed.) In most of Africa, too, homosexuality remains hidden and nameless. One might fairly add that in most other places, including America and Europe, most homosexuals keep hidden most of the time.

That said, the direction of change is unmistakable. In Japan, for example, where homosexuality is traditionally viewed as weird and distasteful but not immoral, more young homosexuals are living openly instead of marrying members of the opposite sex and then dallying with those of their own. [The year 1995] saw Japan's second gay-pride parade, whose 2,200 marchers considerably outnumbered the 1994 crowd and enjoyed corporate sponsorship (apparently a first for a Japanese gay event).

This is not anomalous. [In 1995] the first gay page appeared in a main-

Plate 4.2 In bed with Mum and Mum

stream newspaper in Turkey; an openly homosexual Pakistani poet published what may be the first book of gay verse in Urdu; and Latin America's first gay resort opened in Brazil. [In the same year] activists demanded marriage rights in Austria, Brazil, the Czech Republic and New Zealand. Estonia's all-lesbian group started in 1990, Hong Kong's in 1994 (followed by another last year), and Brazil has at least seven. Mexico's homosexual groups number more than a dozen; South Africa's, more than fifty.

Even in repressive climates, homosexuals have become bolder. In 1992, when Nicaragua criminalized same-sex relations, homosexuals responded with their first gay-pride celebration which became an annual event. More striking still is the example of Zimbabwe. [In] August [1995], Robert Mugabe, Zimbabwe's president, said he did not believe homosexuals 'have any rights at all', called them 'sub-animal' and threatened them all with arrest. The country's principal homosexual group, Gays and Lesbians of Zimbabwe (founded in 1989), rallied in self-defence instead of diving under the furniture. 'It has caused us to become stronger, more determined, more visible', says Stephen Van Breda, a 25-year-old Zimbabwean gay activist.

In short, homosexuals are emerging from the closet. And, more interesting still, they are doing it in more or less the whole world at once.

Plate 4.3 Choose your partners

DIGITALLY QUEER

To understand what is going on, begin with a catalytic, and calamitous, event. AIDS is now a problem in countries around the world; and dealing with it often prods national governments – even ones that find homosexuality distasteful – to open relations with predominantly gay groups. In Malaysia, the AIDS epidemic led to the rise of a visible gay organization (Pink Triangle), which the government grudgingly co-operates with. And it is no coincidence that, in Slovenia, the government officials who turned up for last year's conference on homosexuality came from the health ministry.

Economics is at least as important. The world as a whole, rather than just the richest bits of it, is now developing its first mass middle class; people who can afford to travel, to telephone around the world, to pick and choose from a global culture and to get a Westernized education. These are the people who are most likely to learn, and accept, the 'different-but-equal' model of homosexuality that has come to the fore in the West; and they have money to explore life choices that few subsistence cultures can allow. Before long a society that develops a largish and reasonably well-off middle class can easily 'afford' homosexuals.

A democracy, of course, is more likely to permit them: that is the story of the gay awakening in Eastern Europe, and in South Africa, where homosexual groups opposed apartheid and are now thriving. South Africa's current constitution specifically prohibits discrimination on the basis of sexual orientation, and is the only national constitution, according to the International Gay and Lesbian Human Rights Commission, which does so. In Spain, the Franco regime made homosexuality a crime; democratic Spain decriminalized it and Spain now has about three dozen openly homosexual groups.

To all of which, add the Internet.[1] Homosexuals are a small minority of any population. For all time until now, the overriding fact of life for them has been isolation: the inability to communicate with any but a few others like themselves. That has now changed, which means, in turn, that the very nature of the homosexual experience has itself changed. As the gay-friendly digital community grows, the impulse to hide recedes.

A homosexual youth in Birmingham, Alabama, may now 'chat' with peers in Birmingham, England; a fledgling group in Portugal or Pakistan may consult almost instantly with activists in London or Los Angeles. Australia's gay bulletin board took to the Net last year, and those young Slovenes, like many other gay groups, built themselves a site (electronic address) on the World Wide Web. Rex Wockner, a journalist in San Diego, runs a global gay news agency (which was used for this article); his dispatches, which may be perused on the Web, reach over 175 gay publications in more than twenty countries. A glance in the Queer Resources Directory turns up dozens of gay events from 'A Capella against AIDS' to 'Yahimba conference in Chicago' and dozens more groups. An American group founded in 1992, Digital Queers, brings other gay groups on-line.

This makes a difference. In Zimbabwe, homosexuals responded to Mr Mugabe's attack by jumping on the Internet and dispatching alarms in all directions; in London, *Out This Week*, a two-year-old BBC radio magazine for homosexuals, downloads this news (and much else) and flings it on to the air. When Mr Mugabe visited Johannesburg in August, New Zealand in November and Holland in December, he was met by crowds of Net-alerted protesters ('Two, four, six, eight, is Mugabe really straight?'). 'Without the Internet,' says a Zimbabwean lesbian, 'we would probably have just quickly faded back into oblivion.'

Looking at all this, one would be right to say that gay men and women are emerging from secrecy. The word 'emerge', however, wrongly suggests that Western-style gayness is waiting there to be unveiled. On the contrary: it is being created.

In many places, gender behaviour, not sexual practice as such, has defined sexual categories. George Chauncey, an American historian, notes that this was true in America before the Second World War: 'fairies', defined by their effeminacy rather than their sexual longings, were often seen as a kind of third gender, and a man could profligately enjoy sex with other men without being regarded as 'queer', so long as he preserved a masculine demeanour.

Today in much of Asia – Thailand and Indonesia, for instance – polite society allows a place, albeit a marginal one, for men who dress, act and socialize like women: they, too, are a kind of third gender. But such a man would not think to call himself 'gay', any more than a Westernized gay man would imagine himself to be anything but male. In the Philippines, a woman may act the part of a man, even setting up housekeeping as the 'male' side of a two-woman couple. 'They act like men, and the men who are with them don't feel threatened', says Anna Leah Sarabia, a Filippino activist. But such a woman would likely be bemused to be called 'lesbian'.

The 'orientation' view of homosexuality smashes such gender-crossing notions. It sees gay men as unambiguously male and lesbians as unambiguously female. More, it insists that homosexuality is a neutral fact, implying neither effeminacy in men nor 'butchness' in women, nor, indeed, any other particular kind of prescribed social role. This different-but-equal view of homosexuality is radiating from North America and Europe, homogenizing sexual culture as it goes. The result is not just that homosexuals are coming out. It is that they are learning to understand themselves as 'gay'.

In many places, the old and new models co-exist. In the Philippines, the word 'lesbian' is a recent transplant, and one with which many homosexual women remain uneasy. In Japan, young homosexual men see themselves in the Western 'gay' way, but many older ones do not. Still, what is remarkable is the pace of change. When Ms Sarabia, who is now 41, was growing up in the Philippines, an open discussion of lesbianism was unthinkable. Now it is far from well accepted, to be sure, but it is also not astounding. Filipino youths see homosexuality on Western media, hear about it from gay-rights groups, and may indeed write reports about it in schools.

McGAY

In effect, what McDonald's has done for food and Disney has done for entertainment, the global emergence of ordinary gayness is doing for sexual culture. One might fairly wonder whether such homogenization is entirely to the good. Anthropologists studying traditional models of sex and gender had better work quickly.

Here, however, it is well to bear in mind a distinction. The current Western concept of a gay man or a lesbian – a person who is fundamentally different in whom he or she loves, but in no other way – is a social construction. But homosexuality itself is not. Research and experience increasingly show that, for a small minority, same-sex love is not a diversion, let alone a perversion, but a basic emotional need: so basic that it persists in the face of repression even of the most violent kind. As the notion of ordinary homosexuality spreads, the ancient veil of secrecy and shame that was drawn over this love is dissolving into air.

READING 18

Jeffrey Weeks

What Do We Mean When We Talk About the Body and Sexuality?

What is the relationship between the body as a collection of organs, feelings, needs, impulses, biological possibilities and limits, on the one hand, and our sexual desires, behaviours and identities, on the other? What is it about these topics that make them so culturally significant and morally and politically fraught? These, and others like them, have become key questions in recent sociological and historical debates. In attempting to respond to them I will argue that though the biological body is the site for, and sets the limits on, what is sexually possible, sexuality is more than simply about the body. . . . I am going to suggest that the most important organ in humans is that between the ears. Sexuality is as much about our beliefs, ideologies and imaginations as it is about the physical body.

THE SUBJECT OF SEX

Although there is a strong case for arguing that issues relating to bodies and sexual behaviour have been at the heart of Western preoccupations for a very long time, until the nineteenth century they were largely the concern of religion and moral philosophy. Since then they have largely been the concern of specialists, whether in medicine, the professions, or amongst moral reformers. Since the late nineteenth century the subject has even produced its own discipline, sexology, drawing on psychology, biology and anthropology as well as history and sociology. This has been enormously influential in establishing the terms of the debate about sexual behaviour. Yet sexuality is clearly a critical social and political issue as well as an individual concern, and it therefore deserves a sustained historical and sociological investigation and analysis.

Sexology has been an important factor in codifying the way we think of the body and sexuality. In his famous study *Psychopathia Sexualis* (first translated into English in 1892), Richard von Krafft-Ebing, the pioneering sexologist of the late nineteenth century, described sex as a 'natural instinct' which 'with all conquering force and might demands fulfilment'. What can we deduce from this? First, there is the emphasis on sex as an 'instinct', expressing the fundamental needs of the body. This reflects a post-Darwinian preoccupation in the late nineteenth century to explain all human phenomena in terms of identifiable, inbuilt, biological forces. Today we are more likely to talk about the importance of hormones and genes in shaping our behaviour, but the assumption that biology is at the root of all things persists, and nowhere more strongly than in relation to sexuality. We talk all the time about the 'sex instinct' or 'impulse', and see it as the most natural thing about us. But is it? There is now a great deal of writing which suggests, on the contrary, that sexuality is in fact a 'social construction', a historical invention, which of course draws on the possibilities of the body, but whose meanings and the weight we attribute to them are shaped in concrete social situations. . . .

Take the second part of the Krafft-Ebing quote: sex is an 'all-conquering force', demanding fulfilment. Here we can see at work the central metaphor which guides our thoughts about sexuality. Sex is seen as a volcanic energy, engulfing the body, as urgent and incessant in pressing on our conscious selves. 'Few people', Krafft-Ebing wrote, 'are conscious of the deep influence exerted by sexual life upon the sentiment, thought and action of man in his social relations to others'. I don't think we could make such a confident statement of ignorance today. We now take for granted, in part because of the sexologists, that sexuality is indeed at the centre of our existence.

The following quotation from the English sexologist, Havelock Ellis, who was very influential in the first third of this century, illustrates the ways in which sexuality has been seen as offering a special insight into the nature of the self: 'Sex penetrates the whole person; a man's sexual constitution is a part of his general constitution. There is considerable truth in the dictum: "a man is what his sex is".'[1]

Not only is sex seen here as an all-conquering force, but it is also apparently an essential element in a person's bodily make-up ('constitution'), the determinant of our personalities and identities – at least, if we take the

Plate 4.4   Havelock
Ellis: Pioneer sexologist

language at its surface value, if we are men. This poses the question of *why* we see sexuality in this way. What is it about sexuality that makes us so convinced that it is at the heart of our being? Is it equally true for men and women?

This leads us to the third point that we can draw from the original Krafft-Ebing quotation. The language of sexuality appears to be overwhelmingly male. The metaphors used to describe sexuality as a relentless force seem to be derived from assumptions about male sexual experience. Havelock Ellis appears to be going beyond the conventional use of the male pronoun to denote universal experience. Even his use of metaphors ('penetrates') suggest a sublimely unconscious devotion to male models of sexuality. On one level this may seem an unfair criticism, given that the sexologists did attempt to recognize the legitimacy of female sexual experience. In fact, sexologists often followed a long tradition which saw women as '*the* sex', as if their bodies were so suffused with sexuality that there was no need even to conceptualize it. But it is difficult to avoid the sense that the dominant model of sexuality in their writings, and perhaps also in our social consciousness, is the male one. Men were the active sexual agents; women, despite or because of their highly sexualized bodies, were seen as merely responsive, 'kissed into life', in Havelock Ellis's significant phrase, by the man.

I am not attempting to suggest that definitions such as Krafft-Ebing's are the only ones, or even the dominant ones today. I have chosen this starting point to illustrate the major theme of this [discussion] – that our concept of sexuality has a history. The development of the language we use is one valuable index of that: it is in constant evolution. The term 'sex', for example, originally meant 'the results of the division of humanity into male or female *sections'*. It referred, of course, to the differences between men and women, but also to how they were related. . . . This relationship was significantly different from the one our culture now understands as given – that men and women are fundamentally different. In the past two centuries or so, 'sex' has taken on a more precise meaning: it refers to the anatomical differences between men and women, to sharply differentiated bodies, and to what divides us rather than unites us.

Such changes are not accidental. They indicate a complicated history in which sexual difference (whether we are male or female, heterosexual or homosexual) and sexual activity have come to be seen as of prime social importance. Can we therefore, with justice, describe sexual behaviour as either 'natural' or 'un-natural' in any unproblematical sense? I believe not.

. . . Our sexual definitions, conventions, beliefs, identities and behaviours have not simply evolved, as if propelled by an incoming tide. They have been shaped within defined power relationships. The most obvious one has already been signalled in the quotation from Krafft-Ebing: the relations between men and women, in which female sexuality has been historically defined in relationship to the male. But sexuality has been a peculiarly sensitive marker of other power relations. Church and state have shown a continuous interest in how we behave or think. We can see the intervention over the past two centuries or so of medicine, psychology, social work, schools and the like, all seeking to spell out the appropriate ways for us to regulate our bodily activities. Racial and class differences have further complicated the picture. But alongside these have appeared other forces, above all feminism and the sex reform movements of various types, which have resisted the prescriptions and definitions. The sexual codes and identities we take for granted as inevitable, and indeed 'natural', have often been forged in this complex process of definition and self-definition that have made modern sexuality central to the way power operates in modern society.

Part V

Crime and Deviance

What counts as a 'crime' in a given society varies widely. 'Crime' is most easily defined as any activity which breaks an existing law. Yet laws themselves change over time, fall into disrepute and are sometimes ignored; and what is defined as 'illegal' does not necessarily always reflect wider social norms. For instance, most motorists regularly break the law in the sense that they often drive over the speed limit. Mostly they do not feel themselves to be 'criminals'.

Heroin, discussed in Reading 19, is an illegal drug. Cigarettes and alcohol, which are medically at least as addictive as heroin, are not defined as illegal substances. Why? The reasons seem to be largely historical: some drugs were 'criminalized' at a certain point. Public debate continues about whether or not illegal drugs could be 'decriminalized'. In the meantime, the consumption of and trafficking in illegal drugs makes up a substantial segment of criminal activity. Illegal drug-taking, particularly among teenagers and young adults, has increased substantially in recent years, and both the supply and the consumption of such drugs tend to be heavily clustered in the poorer city areas. The idea that rising drug use is directly related to crime, however, is placed in question. According to the authors, we should understand the nature of drug-taking in terms of its place in a wider 'irregular economy', centred in households, local neighbourhoods and informal groups.

In Reading 20, Josie O'Dwyer and Pat Carlen consider the experience of women in prison. Women currently make up only a very small proportion of the total prison population in Britain, and apart from some illegal activities which are predominantly female (for instance, prostitution), the majority of offenders in all types of crime are men. Women's prisons, however, by no means form a benign environment: as O'Dwyer and Carlen describe them, such prisons are characterized by a good deal of violence and intimidation.

Reading 21 pursues the connections between gender and violence. The large proportion of crimes of violence are carried out by men. Yet one of the offshoots of increasing gender equality is the rise of female violence. This reading discusses America's new all-female gangs. Violence, the author points out, is an intrinsic part of gang activities, whether male or female.

Rape is a particular form of violent crime. And it is one almost exclusively perpetrated by men, mostly against women but in a minority of cases against other men. In Reading 22 Jane Dowdeswell emphasizes that rapists are not necessarily pathological individuals, but men who are in most respects apparently quite ordinary and 'normal'. The majority of rapes happen in familiar circumstances, rather than in dark streets or unfrequented neighbourhoods.

In the final reading, Michael Clarke discusses the phenomenon of business crime. It is easy to suppose that criminal activity is primarily a phenomenon of the underprivileged and, in fact, most of the prison population is drawn from such a group. However, 'white-collar' or business crime in various guises is an exceedingly common phenomenon. As Clarke demonstrates, business crimes – particularly those involving violations of trust – are relatively easy both to commit and to conceal. In contrast to other types of criminal activity, business crime is not immediately evident. A manager in an insurance company, for example, may be embezzling money for many years without the offence being detected, if indeed it ever is.

READING 19

John Auld, Nicholas Dorn and Nigel South

Irregular Work, Irregular Pleasures: Heroin in the 1980s

The recent period has witnessed a real and substantial increase in the use of heroin, particularly among young adults and those in their late teens. Rather than being injected, the drug has also become more typically smoked or snorted (although a relatively small proportion of recent new users are injecting). A wide variety of social groups is involved; several street agencies report seeing many more women users than in previous years. . . .

Evidence of the increased use of heroin and other drugs in the UK comes from four principal sources:

1 evidence relating to international trafficking and seizures;
2 criminal and health services statistics of persons apprehended or reported as being involved with heroin;
3 local prevalence studies, ranging in quality from the systematic to the frankly inane;
4 experience of practitioners and self-help groups in the fields of welfare, advice work, unemployment projects, etc.

A consistent picture emerges from these various forms of evidence. While there may be a 'moral panic' over heroin (following an earlier one over solvent sniffing) and while that panic may distort our view of heroin use today, there is no doubt that more people in Britain today have used heroin than ever before. Perhaps the only rough parallel in quantitative terms would be the nineteenth century, when large proportions of the population used the plant extract, opium. Admittedly, they would have been eating it, drinking it as tea or taking it as part of patent medicines rather than smoking or snorting the stronger manufactured derivative of opium, heroin. Nevertheless, what this comparison brings out is the common feature of consumption via mouth or nose, with injected use being the practice of a minority. The changes that have occurred in the dominant mode of administration in more recent times will be considered in some detail presently. Suffice it to say in the present context, however, that many more persons in Britain are familiar with opiate drugs today than has been the case for about a century.

The total international trade in opium (from which heroin is made) has been estimated as amounting to thousands of tons, with profit levels running into hundreds of billions of dollars. . . . [P]art of the explanation for third world cultivation of plant drugs, including opium, should be sought in the pressures of maintaining both personal income and the payment of interest on national debt in circumstances where there is a lack of alternative profitable crops or sources of income. However, we agree with the staff of the Drug Indicators Project when they state that while supply has increased, 'it is not being suggested that supply in itself created demand. There were a number of domestic factors which meant that increased supply would find a ready market.' We [now] examine some of these 'domestic factors' that have provided a market for heroin in Britain and other Western countries. . . .

Throughout the 1970s there developed a growing body of literature which discovered or, more accurately, rediscovered a variety of activities that seemed hidden from the official purview of the formal economy. Such activities are highly diverse. Some take place within the sphere of waged work, others in and around households, local communities and informal exchange networks. Some of the minor perks, fiddles and benefits associated with them are basically legal, others clearly not, while there are a number of other activities which occupy a great area of the law. In the absence of agreement over the matter of precise conceptual definition, we can employ the term 'informal economies' as a means of referring to these activities. Our present concerns focus upon more unambiguously illegal patterns of thieving, dealing and exchange involving a variety of commodities and centred primarily on streets and housing estates and best described, we believe, as the *irregular economy*. We suggest that it is within the context of a degree of involvement in this irregular economy that the bulk of heroin use among young people is currently taking place. The irregular economy provides multiple conduits for the distribution and exchange of drugs, and for a variety of other goods and services: prostitution, the disposal of stolen goods, and so on.

Activity within the irregular economy has as a defining characteristic a temporal sense of irregularity. It takes the form of a bunching together of intensive periods of work (buying, selling, contacting, getting money together, etc.). In between these intensive bursts of activity the business of survival requires one to be always searching for further opportunities, and to be on the look-out for potential dangers. Patterns of irregular and even sometimes 'chaotic' styles of drug use mesh with the irregularity of this economy and the subcultures that it underpins.

This perspective carries implications for the way in which one approaches two issues with which the use of heroin (and, indeed, illegal drugs in general) has traditionally been associated – namely, ill health and crime. . . .

The involvement of drug users in the irregular economy, where stolen goods also circulate, necessarily makes an important contribution to current stereotypes of drug users as being not only sick but also criminal, being pushed into crime in order to support their expensive habits. As Helmer observed of the typical response in the United States, the 'approach to the narcotics problem is the same one today as it has always been; narcotics cause crime'.[1] In London, a senior police officer discussing the rising use of heroin in a BBC news interview (19 June 1984) ventured the opinion that while there were no official figures which proved a link between rising heroin use and crime, none the less a substantial source of income is required to sustain the use of heroin, and he felt quite sure that this income was not coming from the welfare state: the clear implication being that drug users must be stealing in order to get money to supply themselves with drugs.

We would agree that there are links between widespread heroin use today and criminality. However, the nature of these links is mystified in the statement that heroin causes crime. Our argument is very simple. Social security benefits and youth training allowances are at too low a level for satisfaction of basic needs – for housing, clothing, heating and food – let alone buying much in the way of intoxicants. It is partly in order to secure a standard of living better than mere survival that people get involved in aspects of the irregular economy, and it is through their involvement in this partially petty-criminal economy that they may come to buy, exchange, sell and consume heroin. There is a sense, then, in which crime can lead to heroin use: the very opposite of the conventional view. One implication of this might be that a shift in economic policies that reduced the extent to which the irregular economy permeates increasing numbers of inner-city and other areas would reduce petty crime, and with it much heroin use in its presently expanding forms. A direct assault by law enforcement agencies against episodic heroin users, by contrast, would do relatively little to dent the criminal aspects of the irregular economy in which they play only a part.

How one responds to the activities of importers and large-scale suppliers of drugs such as heroin is another question. Organized crime of this kind is by no means new, and has been the subject of lengthy discussion elsewhere, especially with regard to the context of the USA. Here in Britain, at the same time as the street-level irregular economy has significantly expanded, there have been changes in the organization of drug supply at national and regional levels:

> The illicit market has become more organized and has attracted the attention of criminal groups who, a few years ago, would not have been willing to become involved in drugs. This is particularly true of cannabis and in the past two years of heroin.[2]

The large-scale importation and supply of drugs have always been a lucrative source of income – in this respect the illegal market simply reflects that in alcohol, tobacco and pharmaceuticals – and the combination of a ready international supply of heroin and a ready irregular market in Britain makes large-scale pushing even more attractive to established criminal organizations. What is of note is that even here – as on the lower level of the street and local community – *existing* patterns of large-scale criminal and petty criminal activity are expanding to incorporate drugs. . . .

MODES AND MEANINGS OF ADMINISTRATION

Although sample survey evidence is as lacking on this matter as it is on the issue of the total numbers of young people involved, it has come to be widely accepted that the bulk of heroin use among those whose use began during the last few years takes the form of either smoking or (less commonly) snorting the substance. Rather than being injected, in other words, the drug is heated and the smoke fumes thereby given off are inhaled.

There are a number of reasons for thinking that this particular mode of administration makes an important contribution not only to the intrinsic compatibility of heroin use with the structural features of the irregular economy, but also to an understanding of why the now widely used description of the rate of increase in the activity among young people as an epidemic might be a particular misnomer. The first and arguably most important one connects with the distinction between the categories of 'sickness' and 'irregularity' referred to earlier. Throughout the 1960s and early 1970s there was a labour market quite favourable to white males in many parts of Britain, offering opportunities for considerable freedom of movement between jobs and, significantly, ease of movement out of the labour market and back again. The adoption of the sick role in the manner made possible by being officially labelled and treated as an addict provided an important vehicle for such movements in and out of the labour market, and offered other rewards besides. The role of 'addict' was one which – provided one played one's cards right by both acknowledging the undesirability of one's predicament and at least appearing to accept the kind of technically competent medical treatment then being offered by drug treatment clinics – one might have a good chance of occupying indefinitely. There was, of course, a certain price to pay: specifically, an acceptance of the moral stigma which conventional society tends to bestow upon those whom it views as being unavoidably or irresponsibly dependent upon its beneficence, and a corresponding obligation to conform with the stereotypically defined role.

For many young people today, however, the distinction between being either 'inside' or 'outside' respectable society and the formal economy has become very blurred. They cannot easily *choose* whether to be 'in' or 'out', the choice already having been made for them. For those effectively excluded from wage employment there is little advantage to be derived in adopting the sick role, since the primary benefit of the sick role is that it allows one to evade temporarily the obligations of waged work. There is a sense, then, in which the market itself has diminished the appeal of sick/addict styles of involvement with heroin, and in doing so has undermined one possible rationalization for injecting drugs. Injection is an unappealing prospect for most people, but one that can be 'made sense of' within the context of an acceptance of oneself as a 'junkie' or addict. Injection is made less acceptable when circumstances weaken the rationale for adopting the sick/addict role.

The practice of smoking heroin, by contrast, has a number of relatively positive aspects. In the most straightforward sense, of course, it is simply easier at a psychological level to relate it to and view it as an unproblematic extension of more conventional pursuits such as the smoking of tobacco or, in the case of some young people, cannabis.

However, it is also necessary to consider certain consequences arising from the contemporary supply situation. The fact that the bulk of heroin currently entering this country is of high quality, low in cost and easily obtainable (at least in many urban areas) has been a recurrent theme in the expressions of alarm being made by the various agencies concerned with trying to deal with the problem. But it ought to be recognized that the widespread availability of cheap, good-quality heroin makes the practice of smoking it a considerably more rational activity than it would have been in former times when the supply situation was not such a favourable one from the consumer's point of view. Only when the drug is relatively plentiful and cheap can the user contemplate letting some of it quite literally go up in smoke.

It should also be pointed out that smoking has certain health advantages in comparison with injection. First, infections, sores and vascular problems sometimes associated with injection of heroin and other substances are not risks run by the smoker. Secondly, smokers may be less likely to overdose. With injection, it is sometimes difficult for the user to calculate precisely how much of the drug to inject in order to achieve the desired effect – a matter of practical inconvenience on many occasions and death by overdose on some. Smoking, by contrast, is a more easily controlled and safer mode of administration.

Summarizing our discussion, we suggest that the easing of heroin supply on an international level, the shift to the new modes of administration (most commonly smoking) that this facilitates, and the relatively casual (non-needle/non-addict) and episodic styles of involvement that emerge in the context of a more general involvement in the irregular economy may reasonably be described as contributing to a quantitative increase in the numbers of heroin users, and to a qualitative shift towards less dangerous patterns of use. Putting it in fewer and plainer words – Britain has acquired rather more of a slightly less bad thing.

Josie O'Dwyer and Pat Carlen

Surviving in a Women's Prison

Britain has six closed prisons for women: Holloway in London, Styal in Cheshire, Cookham Wood in Kent, a wing of Durham prison, Cornton Vale just outside Stirling in Scotland and Armagh Prison in Northern Ireland.

For England and Wales there is one closed Youth Custody Centre, Bullwood Hall in Essex, and an open Youth Custody Centre, at East Sutton Park. There are three open prisons for women: Drake Hall in Staffordshire, Askham Grange in Yorkshire and East Sutton Park in Kent. The three remand centres which take women and girls are: Low Newton in Durham, Pucklechurch in Bristol and Risley in Cheshire. Scotland has no open prison for women as all penal facilities – remand wing, young prisoners' wing, Youth Custody Centre and prison – are concentrated on one site at Her Majesty's Institution, Cornton Vale. In Northern Ireland a separate part of Armagh Prison is used as the female young offenders' centre. Additionally, women on remand are often held for one night (or more) in police cells and, at various times, certain convicted women prisoners have been temporarily housed in one of the male institutions. Jose O'Dwyer has served sentences (or been remanded) at Pucklechurch, Bullwood Hall, Cookham Wood, Styal, Holloway and Mountjoy Gaol in Ireland. Although she is only 28 she has, since the age of 14, spent eight of those twenty-eight years in a variety of penal institutions, including approved school, Borstal, remand centre, and four closed prisons. And Josie has survived. The purpose of this [discussion], therefore, is to describe exactly how Josie did survive those years and, in telling the story of one prisoner's survival, to describe also the violence, the injustices, the pain, the degradations and the other, different modes of survival (or not) which characterize British women's imprisonment.

On any day of the year around 1,500 women are held captive in British prisons. Many of them will be remand prisoners, only 27 per cent of whom will eventually receive a custodial sentence; over a quarter of the convicted women will be in prison for failing to pay a fine, and over half of them will be there for some minor crime of stealing. Of the remainder, less than 10 per cent of the convicted women will have been found guilty of violent crime and a sizeable number of prisoners in all categories will be those whose biographies embody accounts of all kinds of social, emotional and mental problems often either unrelated or related only tangentially to their criminal activities. A sizeable number of this latter group, too, will have either been brought up in institutions from an early age or will have been taken into either 'care' or the old Approved School system in their early teens. Either way these 'state-raised' children will have learned early on in their careers that the main name of the game in institutions is SURVIVAL.

Josie O'Dwyer is just one of the many women whose penal careers began at the age of 14 in circumstances which make a mockery of the terms 'care', 'training' and 'in the child's best interest'. Josie's account of her first taste of the penal system is one which is studded with references to feelings of fear and memories of violence. As a consequence of being apprehended by the police for 'breaking and entering' the full force of the penal and judicial machinery engulfed the adolescent Josie in a quick processing through police cell, prison remand wing and Approved School.

> They took me in a police-car, up the motorway to Bristol. I was only little: aged 14, four-feet-ten inches in height and just six stone. It seemed a long journey from Exeter to Bristol and I was terrified, absolutely terrified. But I was stroppy with it. I had already spent the night in the police-cell at Exeter and I had been in a cell with a junkie who was really sick. I got myself in the top bunk and sat in the corner clutching a pillow; I actually chewed off the corner of that pillow watching this woman thrashing about. Then in the morning they took me to Pucklechurch. They had told me that it was a remand centre but it looked like a prison. I had thought that it was going to be a kids' home, maybe with bars on the windows so that I couldn't get out, but it wasn't, it was a real prison. They took me to the women's section and the police handed me over to the prison officers. All that I wanted to do was to curl up in a corner with something over my head and stay there, but I had to get undressed. I took my clothes off and put on this dressing-gown and I felt terrified. I've never felt such fear and yet the prison officers were being really nice to me compared with how I've seen them since with other people! They eventually coaxed me out with cigarettes and took me down this long corridor with cell doors on either side. They took me to a cell, locked me up for the night and came along in the morning and said that I was to go and see the Chief. I wouldn't get dressed though. I was still terrified, still had the dressing-gown over my head. Then I looked out of the window and I saw the prisoners exercising in the yard. I couldn't believe my eyes; I really thought that some of them were men! The prison officers kept coming in and encouraging me to go out and exercise – 'Come on, love' etc., but I would not go.

Josie was terrified and, as is often the case when people are afraid, she soon realized that one effective way to counter one's own fear is to inspire fear in others. Women's prisons, no less than men's, are places of violence; places where explicit violence is the necessary currency for efficient and healthy survival. In prison, moreover, the newcomer does not have to be predisposed to violence in order to engage in violent modes of behaviour – lessons in violence come at her from all sides.

In the cell next to me there was a Pakistani woman; I think that she was waiting to be deported. They had taken her baby away from her because she had kept trying to kill herself and the baby. She actually wrecked her cell, there was a lot of blood and I was terrified. Then I wrecked my own cell. I put all the windows out and smashed all the furniture. The officers came in and told me to take all my clothes off. Then they put me in this special dress and did something up at the neck so that it could not be taken off. It took me four hours to chew through it. I wouldn't come out of that cell for ten days and then I came out to go to church. After that the prison officers managed to coax me out for the last hour of Association and I was amazed at everyone wanting to mother me because I was so tiny. They gave me chocolates and they wanted me to sit on their lap. I didn't mind at all, I liked it. Then came the bombshell. I was told that I was being moved to the Approved School.

Within the penal system those who want to survive counter their own fear by inspiring fear in others and meet violence with violence or, better still, the threat of violence. Boredom and loss of freedom, however, call for different survival tactics and, in the case of children and young people held in less secure conditions, the most obvious way to regain their freedom and self-respect is to go straight back out, either over the wall or through the gate. Josie was eventually to find that, in fact, the senior Approved School provided a good academic education but when she first arrived there was no way that she intended to stay. She became a 'runner'.

Seventeen times I ran away from that school and seventeen times they took me back. Each time they took me back I spent twenty-four hours in the detention room. I eventually dislocated my knee jumping out of a window but I still tried to run away, on crutches! Next morning they gave me a skirt to put on, but I kept my jeans on and went for the nearest window, with tennis-rackets and anything else that came to hand. The school was in Bath and I used to run back to Truro. I don't know what I was running to really; it was just an instinct. If I could get out, I got out.

But Josie, recognizing that she, like many other runners, had in reality no one and nowhere to run to, eventually settled down to O-levels, horse-riding, forced religion (it was a convent school) and more lessons in the seamier side of life.

There were girls who had been through more than me, they had been prostitutes. It was mostly sex they talked about and sex was seen as a crime anyway, because we were in a convent school. Some of those girls went on to remand centres and then to Borstal.

When Josie left the school at 16 the process of her social isolation and stigmatization as a delinquent had already begun.

I was 16 when I left. I had never had a letter or a visit all the time that I had been there. I went back to Cornwall and tried for various jobs but they soon found out about my past, what I'd done and where I'd been, and they weren't prepared to forgive and forget. I used to sit for hours and stare into space. None of my friends understood; they all thought that I was mad. After about five months I took myself back to Bath and it was there that I overdosed – I just didn't know what to do next. Then I actually went breaking and entering with the full intention of getting myself nicked.

I went to Borstal after I had been convicted on a burglary charge. They sent me off to Bullwood Hall along with two others and, again, I was terrified. This time there was real reason to be afraid. An air of viciousness pervaded the whole place. The tougher you were the better. If you weren't tough people insulted you and took your cigarettes off you. You had a dog's life. It's the way the prison officers ran it which made it like that. Inmates couldn't really retaliate, but having a go at an officer gave them some kind of credit. They tore up each other's photos and ripped up each other's clothes. I'd been on the Assessment Unit for about five days and it was my first night on the wing when I happened to be going for a bath that I saw one inmate being kicked by about five others. It was not done quickly to get it over with; they were actually thoroughly enjoying it. The message was 'Don't mix-it with us.' Everyone was frightened of everybody else. Anything could start off a fight. Everything or nothing. The officers could have stopped it if they'd wanted to. They could have run the place differently. They stood down on the ground floor and everything that went on that was bad went on either on the landings or in somebody's cell – and in the recess anyhow. Unless you were one of the toughest you were absolutely terrorized. Borstal was amazing. Whereas the grown women in Pucklechurch could take things in their stride, in Borstal the slightest little thing could make someone hit the ceiling and the officers would just go in. There would be no 'Come on, dear, calm down.' None of that. They just went in and grabbed you and took you off down to the punishment block. You got the same treatment whatever you did so you knew that you might as well hit the roof, make a big show out of it and get some credit out of it.

At that stage Josie did not have time to think about the whys and wherefores of the viciousness which permeated Bullwood. She did not realize then that the viciousness was a product of the system itself rather than of the system's victims. She only had time to suss out how best to ensure her own survival.

You weren't allowed to do your sentence quietly. You survived by being the most vicious. But you couldn't just be vicious – you also had to have no fear, to be able to take the punishment and the lock-up. At first I was probably the most frightened. I was terrified. The whole place terrified me. The air was electric, always someone doing something, alarm bells going, a fight going on, screaming, shouting, banging. They used to sing 'A . . . G . . . G . . . R . . . O . . .' It was terrible – just bang, bang, bang, bang, bang. You *had* to scream, you had to let go. You just couldn't contain it within yourself. Every single day there was some sort of trouble and people were screaming out of the windows all the time in Bullwood. If one person started banging on the door the whole wing would take it up. I discovered that if I got all wound up, ready to blow, the whole wing would be all simmering, waiting for the action and it gave me credit. But it didn't just come from me, it was there all the time, just waiting for someone to set light to it. You had to have fights with the screws as they dragged you off to punishment because you were considered a sissy if you just walked there. Everyone struggled. They bent your arms so you tried to bite and you spat and kicked. They weren't exactly gentle either. Some of the officers were a little more vicious than the others so you worked out which ones to go for. You worked out who was soft, who was hard and who would hurt you most. So when you saw them coming at you – about eight or nine prison officers and a couple of men in the background – you tried to let the gentler ones get hold of you. To me it was just a game and you had to play the game well or you got hurt. Most of my stuff looked good, but it was all bravado, all for show, to give me more credit, so that I could survive. I never really hurt anyone.

. . . By the time Josie had finished her Borstal sentence she had completed her apprenticeship in violence and she was ready for bigger things. She knew that her Borstal days were over and, like many of the other Borstal girls, she knew also that the next stop would be prison.

Most of the girls had an idea that they were going on to prison anyway so you thought that whatever crimes you did when you were out, next time you went in you'd have more 'cred'. It was happening to me like that, though I didn't realize it at the time. But now when I go back and think, I think, 'Huh! What a wally!' Because when I came out of Borstal my ambition in life was to be the top dog, the most hardened criminal, the worst, the most vicious. There was no other reason to be alive as far as I was concerned. Anything outside wasn't going to give me a chance anyway, so if I was going to make it anywhere, it had to be in there.

READING 21

Ruaridh Nicoll

Gang Babes Love to Kill

The scar on the woman's face was a neat, livid line running from her ear to her mouth and she wore it with pride. It was cut to show that she is part of a new women's gang emerging on the streets of Brooklyn.

There had been rumours about this new female club, in which members – instead of giving each other the customary beating that is usually enough to grant entry to an inner-city gang – cut their inductees' faces with a razor. The ultimate in self-loathing.

'It's pretty heavy when they start doing that to themselves', said Tony, who runs an organization of former gang members dedicated to taking kids off the streets. He has seen many things but this has taken him by surprise. His network of contacts threads New York's underworld, giving him running reports on the health of the city's ganglands.

Five years ago, girls in their early teens began joining America's inner-city gangs, attracted by the comfort of a group and the gangster image. For many, with their family lives destroyed by drugs, poverty and jail, gangs offered a sense of security, companionship and protection. They formed auxiliaries to the men's gangs and found that their status in the community suddenly shot up. 'They treated me like a little sister', said one inductee of her new gang pals. 'And if I ever had any problems, they'd help me out. I'd never had that before.'

America was shocked. The white population is used to the concept of the traditional gang made up of young, black males who expect to die violently before they are 20. But the idea of gangs of young girls, prepared to shoot, rob and sell drugs, does not fit easily into the American idea of femininity.

Yet violence is central to the girl gang phenomenon. The new Brooklyn scar-face gang shows that the violence is getting worse, and that much of it is aimed at themselves. When the gangs started forming, the girls mimicked the men by using watered-down versions of their initiation ceremonies. New members would be taken to some deserted spot where they would receive a beating for between ten seconds and three minutes. The damage would later be fixed with compacts and hairspray. If at some date in the future the inductee let the gang down, another beating would occur, but on this occasion there would be no set time limit.

Initially, their crimes were gang muggings, stealing jewellery and clothes that they could not afford themselves. 'I'd just see something I wanted so bad I'd just take it, I'd pull a knife, I'd just want things', said one 15-year-old. But as the new members have grown older, many have progressed to the killings carried out by the male gangs. A group of girls killed a 15-year-old on the New York subway for her earrings. 'The women can be as violent as the men, sometimes even more so', said a Brooklyn cop. 'When they are arrested for violent crime, they show no remorse.'

The number of girls arrested in New York for a serious felony has increased 10 per cent annually since the mid-1980s. In 1990 women made up 10 per cent of total gang membership; [in 1996] the figure is estimated to have risen beyond 15 per cent. Women are also heavily involved in drug dealing and violent crimes.

Across the Hudson River in New Jersey, where violent crime committed by women has seen a similarly dramatic rise in the past decade, a commission revealed forty-seven individual female gangs in the state. The gangs' names tell their own stories, displaying by turns self-loathing and humour – names like the 6th Street Whores, the Crochet Girls and the Wise Intelligent Sisters.

At the International Youth Organization in Newark three young mothers, one who had her first child when she was 15, talked about trying to get out of the poverty cycle. 'There is nothing out there to do but get into trouble', said Jenean Shiggs. 'When you try to do it the right way you see it's so much harder, you know there is an easier way.'

The United States Congress is currently cutting back welfare payments, increasing the squeeze on these teenage girls who are caught between the lack of job prospects, broken homes, and early pregnancy. 'It's going to get worse', said Dr Janice Joseph of Stockton State College in New Jersey. 'Ten years ago you never heard of girls in gangs, but now there are girls who if they want something from you they will kill for it.'

While many of the girls drop out of the gangs when they reach their twenties, often after they are arrested or have watched friends die, others go on to join more sophisticated gangs based in the big cities and involved in drug deals.

Nearly all the leading or 'corporate' gangs, as they are known, now have women members. For example, the Latin Kings, a huge organization born in a Chicago jail in the 1940s, has a women's corps, the Latin Queens.

Male gang members have begun to fear the women, who are starting to take key roles in many of the activities. One man, a contact of Tony's, who recently quit as a gang member, gave his own chilling conclusion on dealing with women in gangs: 'She'll set you up – men are like that with women – she'll draw you in, and then she'll kill you.'

READING 22

Jane Dowdeswell
The Act of Rape

Contrary to the stereotype image of the stranger who strikes in a dark alleyway or churchyard, you are more likely to be raped by someone you know or have seen before the assault. Strangers are involved in less than half the number of attacks, and it is more likely to be a casual acquaintance, ex-boyfriends, friends, family or neighbours. Rapists can be husbands, lovers, fathers, employers, the boy next door, the delivery man, the man you work with:

> I thought I'd be able to spot a rapist a mile off. But somehow when a man is attractive, well dressed and so pleasant, it doesn't occur to you that he could rape you. It was our office party and I got talking to this bloke who'd been working with us for just a week. He seemed really nice: very friendly. I didn't fancy him or anything, and he was telling me about his wife; they'd been married for two years. Anyhow, it turned out he lived a couple of roads away from me, so he offered me a lift home. I wouldn't just accept a lift from anyone: I'm not stupid, but he seemed so nice. Instead of driving straight home, he took another route as he said he had to call in at a friend's house. He drove to the ring road round the airport, stopped the car, and raped me. I don't remember much of what happened, I was so shocked. It was as though I'd been knocked out with chloroform. I thought of getting out of the car and running, but where to? I've not been to work since, and hardly go out in case I see him. Sometimes I remind myself that it wasn't me that did wrong. But when it's someone who's so pleasant you can't help thinking it was your own fault. (*Sandra, 28, from Slough*)

Rapists can be 'nice' men too: women are not prepared for this and find it difficult to talk about it to anyone when the man concerned is well known and well liked.

> I'd been babysitting for Dave and Ann since I was 14. They both played for the local darts team and had a regular night out each week. He had always been my childhood dream: he used to tease me and joke around with me. They only lived next door and Ann was my mum's best friend. A year ago, Dave came home early one Tuesday without Ann: he said they'd had a row and she'd gone home with a friend. I said I'd go as I was feeling tired, I went to get up and he grabbed me by the hair. I didn't know what he was doing at first, it was as if he was mucking about with

me. He pulled me up the stairs: I was so frightened I was making these little sobbing noises, trying to scream. I was on my hands and knees, trying to get away, but he was very strong. He tried to have sex with me, but couldn't do it, he got angry and started swearing at me saying I'd always led him on, teased him. He said if I ever said anything he'd tell Ann that I'd wanted him to do it, and that everyone would know that I was easy. I see him almost every day: sometimes if I'm in the garden I see him looking out of the window at me. I hate him more than I can say, but everyone else thinks he's wonderful. (*Joanne, 19, from Lewisham*)

It is generally held that being raped by a man you know is less damaging and distressing to the victim, but through talking to women it is clear this is just another myth.

Jenny, a student from Brighton, was raped when she was 18 by the person she most trusted:

My rapist wasn't the violent stranger most people imagine rapists are. This was my boyfriend. I was doing A-levels, intending to study for a degree and aiming for a good career. The last thing I wanted was a baby. I had a physical relationship with him in which I enjoyed him entering my vagina with his hand. He knew this was as intimate as I was prepared to be.

Unfortunately, this made rape very easy for him. He simply swopped his hand for his penis. I did not consent. I did not even realize what was happening. I did sense a change in his movements and was afraid of what this meant, but I was numb. In my confusion I was absolutely silent. He confirmed my fear immediately afterwards by apologizing. I can remember thinking 'This is Rape'; he looked like a stranger all of a sudden, but he was looking at me with concern and feeling in his eyes. No, he couldn't be a rapist, but then why did I feel so cold? Subtle seduction or subtle rape? I believe the latter.

Questioning ourselves about whether it is rape reveals our own confusion. Julie from Northampton would agree:

I always used to think that girls and women were raped or attacked by strangers, but I knew the boy who raped me. I was walking home with a friend at night, and on the opposite side of the road we saw a lad we knew: he had been out with one of my friends from school. We called over hello, and he came over. I thought he was drunk because he had a glass in his hand – it was Whit weekend and people were taking their glasses around with them from pub to pub. He held the glass and smashed it against the wall, holding it close to my face, and said, 'Shut up, or you'll get this.' I laughed, as I thought he was joking, but he pushed me into a garden. My friend ran off as she said she was scared, and I was screaming and had cut my hand. He was lying on top of me and I remember trying to get up and seeing my legs under his body so I couldn't move. He held me down half-way between my chest and neck, and pulled my knickers down. I just kept screaming and eventually he ran off. I had marks on my thighs for weeks after, and when I got home my face and legs were streaked with blood – I think he'd cut himself on the glass. I've not told my mum or anyone else about it, as I think a lot of people wouldn't believe me and would think I encouraged him.

Often the rape or assault seems unreal even to you. At first you may find it difficult to see it as 'rape', particularly if the man involved is known to you. In an attempt to survive, mentally, some women tell how they tried to convince themselves it wasn't really happening to them.

Sandra was raped by a man who was given her address by a friend:

> She was chatted up by this South African guy we met at a nightclub and because of some instinct or something, she tried to get rid of him, so she gave him a false name and address (mine!). The next day, Sunday, at about 9 a.m. the doorbell rang and this guy was standing there. I recognized him, and he became very angry and said my friend had been playing games with him and he didn't like it. He just pushed his way into the house and threw me down on to the hall floor, then dragged me into the living room. I had slept with a man before the rape, my second boyfriend, and I tried to think that this was what I had done with my boyfriend and tried to blank out the fact that this man was not someone I cared for. I just new instinctively there was nothing I could do to dissuade him, and in a way I just went off into a sort of a trance. It was like going out of your body, trying to disassociate myself from what was happening to me. I felt like I was in a time warp – while I could keep myself in this cocoon where it was all unreal, I'd be able to survive whatever he did to me!

This 'blocking out' of everything around them is not uncommon, says Dr Gillian Mezey from the Institute of Psychiatry, who has spoken to many rape victims in the course of her research. She says:

> There is often a narrowing of perception that occurs during attacks when women are not really aware of what is going on around them. One said, 'All I could think about was the blue button, that blue button on the rapist's shirt.' So while he was doing all these dreadful things, all the senses became narrowed down to this one single perception. I found this helps a lot of women get through it. Another woman remembers the area in the small of the back that was being rubbed up and down on concrete and the skin being grazed. She was just concentrating on that so much she couldn't remember anything else.

We are led to believe that rape occurs often in streets and dark alleys but the circumstances can be wide and varied. As examples, here are four very different settings. Read them through and decide which you think was the place and who the victim of a crime:

- 7 a.m.   a 14-year-old girl sets out on her paper-round in Sevenoaks. It's her regular route and she sees the same few joggers and workers on their way to the station . . .
- Noon   a pensioner leaves the busy shopping centre, already crowded with shoppers, calls into Woolworth's and the Post Office to collect her pension . . .
- 3 p.m.   a nurse on nightshift sleeps in the flat she shares with her friend, also a nurse, who is getting ready to leave for work . . .
- Midnight   two girls walking home after a night at the local club. They

119

stop at the bus shelter to check on the last buses. A car pulls up – it's the father of one of their friends – and offers them a lift. They are relieved: it was going to be a long walk home.

The frightening answer is that each setting we've described was witness to rape. No better proof, if it is needed, that rape can happen *anywhere*, to *any one* of us at *any time*.

READING 23

Michael Clarke
The Nature of Business Crime

The most consequential feature of business crime is the private context in which business crimes are committed. This is true almost as much of organizations in the public sector, such as schools and hospitals, as it is of private-sector business. The differences lie in the service ethic which predominates in the public sector, as against the profit orientation of the private, and in the greater penetration of public-sector organizations by oversight and funding agencies in the state hierarchy – area health authorities, local education authorities, and beyond them the relevant government ministries. Private businesses are subject to the shareholders and non-executive directors in the case of companies with shares held by the public, neither of which group has easy access to the detail of the companies' activities, and [both of which] are easily deceived, not so much by the refusal of relevant information as by not knowing the pertinent questions to ask. Both companies with public shareholders and those where shares are held privately are subject to audit by external accountants, but, as a number of decisive court cases have shown, auditors are not required, as part of their enquiries into whether the company's accounts constitute a true and fair view of the company's affairs, to ensure that they check for possible malpractices; and accountants who ask awkward questions and provoke embarrassing cover-ups may not be engaged for the following year's audit.

The principal points about privacy for present purposes – others will emerge later – are first, that members of business organizations are protected from detection by the veil of privacy. This is formally and legally the case in respect of the limited company form, which is designed to protect commercial confidentiality and not to give information away to competitors. But privacy is also inherent in the relatively complex and specialized work and context of the organization. The minutely organized, bureaucratized division of labour which characterizes modern business renders its activities opaque to outsiders, even outsiders to the section, unit, office or division within a large organization, who measure its success and probity by its inputs and outputs, not by a detailed scrutiny of its working routines. It is thus only too easy for individuals or groups within an organization to shield misconduct from prying eyes and to manipulate outputs so that all appears to be normal.

Secondly, therefore, privacy means that business offenders are legitimately present at the scene. Offences consist of violations of the trust implicit in them as officers of the organization and exploitation of the resources of the organization for personal gain. The scope for such exploitation and the ease with which it can be covered up vary partly because of chance aspects of organizational structure – individuals or groups may happen to find themselves in a position in the organization where it is particularly easy to steal organizational property or funds, where others, located elsewhere, would find this very difficult. More systematically, however, opportunities vary with discretion, autonomy and access to a range of organizational resources, and these of course increase as one ascends the organizational hierarchy. Delivery drivers, for example, may be able physically to divert goods from their vehicles, but will probably need the co-operation of the warehousing and dispatch departments to reconcile the necessary paperwork. Similarly, clerks in accounts departments may have no difficulty making use of company telephones, postage and photocopying, but, although dealing with company cheques, receipts and invoices, may find it very hard to embezzle without a collective effort. The accounts manager, by contrast, has less need to communicate such misdeeds to others, and much greater discretion, and probably also has the knowledge of the company and the expertise in accounting necessary to enable him to embezzle company funds and to manage the paperwork to disguise the fact.

This disguise of even serious offences can continue successfully for long periods, and no doubt in some cases, especially where the misconduct ceases undetected, offences are never discovered. The chief executive of the Grays Building Society was discovered in 1978 to have embezzled £2 million over a period of forty years, successfully deceiving the auditors, with whom he enjoyed a good relationship, and his staff, by always making up the books himself, sometimes working late to do so. He was discovered only because the auditors were changed on the retirement of the accountant after twenty-seven years. Similarly, the chief accountant at Pitman's Secretarial College admitted in 1987 to stealing £1.4 million over twenty years, at a rate in later years of £50,000 per annum, mostly in cash fees paid by students. He was discovered only as a result of a company reorganization and special audit, in the course of which he was made redundant.

Unlike conventional crimes, such as burglary and robbery, therefore, in the case of business crime there is not necessarily an immediate complainant. Those whose interests have been damaged may not be aware of it, or, as in the case of shops which write off stock losses through shoplifting, staff theft and accidental damage under the one heading 'stock shrinkage', not fully aware of it. Business crime is certainly not victimless, but the principal objective of the offender is to prevent the victim recognizing the loss. For, in the case of business crime, it is the offence which is difficult to discover because it is hidden by the normality of the organization's functioning and by the legitimacy of the offender's presence in the organization. Of course, some major offences emerge because their extent is so great as to cause the financial breakdown of the organization. Once the offence is uncovered, however, it is usually relatively simple to establish who committed it or at least colluded in it, as a result of checks back on individuals' actions and responsibilities. This is the reverse of the case of conventional crime, where the householder who is burgled is immediately aware of the fact of the loss but finds it extremely difficult to detect the offender precisely because he had no legitimate access to the premises.

A consequence of this is that public order is not violated in business offences as it is in conventional crime. There is normally no violence to persons or property, and the conduct in question takes place in private not public places, between people with a pre-existing and usually continuing relationship, not between strangers. This in part accounts for the much less threatening character of business offences: not only do they not involve violence, but they become possible at all only if citizens enter into a situation where they can be deceived and defrauded. While there is a substantial contemporary debate on the citizen's reasonable expectations, there is also some expectation of caution and self-protective measures against deceit. Trust is necessary between employer and employee, businessman and customer, creditor and debtor, but trust has to be established, not merely taken for granted.

This explains the relatively limited interest of the police in business crime. Its privacy and complexity make it difficult to investigate; the pre-existing relationships between victim and offender make for the likelihood of claim and counterclaim as to who occupies which role; and in many cases the police may take the view that their victims have only themselves to blame for their lack of caution, or have the necessary resources to remedy the situation by civil action. Indeed, in legal terms, the whole field of business crime is beset by ambiguity as to whether offences are to be dealt with by the criminal or the civil route. Disputes between private parties are normally dealt with through civil litigation, and the public authorities are often reluctant to act, even where a criminal offence has clearly been committed, if matters can be settled privately. There is a strong tendency for matters to be dealt with privately, and thus for the question whether the misconduct was criminal never to be raised formally. This is reflected in the disposition of manpower in the police forces: about 5 per cent of detective manpower and 0.5 per cent of overall police personnel nationally, totalling 588 police in the UK, were allocated to the fraud squads in 1987. The police see their primary responsibility as the maintenance of order in the public realm, and the pursuit of conventional crimes which violate it as well as damaging the interests of private citizens. In addition, the police and other public agencies can normally gain access to premises to pursue enquiries only where they have reasonable grounds to suspect that a criminal offence has taken place. Restraints upon the power of public authorities in a liberal democracy act to protect the accessibility of private domains.

As will become clear below, however, this tendency for business crime to be dealt with privately and often non-legally is not a matter for alarm but rather an inevitable outcome of its character. Certainly it is much more effective and flexible in coping with what are in most cases quite ambiguous patterns of conduct. Research, even on embezzlers, the most obviously criminal of business offenders, suggests a pattern not of calculated villainy but of opportunism, financial stress and, at times, an intention to repay embezzled money well before being stimulated to do so by detection. In many other areas the issue is precisely: has an offence been committed, or is it at worst error or misunderstanding, or more often a loss that the victim must accept as legitimate, as 'just business'?

It is evident from the foregoing that the detection and control of business crime are primarily, and at least in the first instance, internal to the organization, and hence private. It is up to those with a direct interest in the business to decide how much effort they devote to ensuring that probity is maintained and wrongdoing is detected and sanctioned, and as to how they define wrongdoing: does it include arriving five minutes late for work, using company phones to call home or giving lifts to friends in company vehicles, for example? When misconduct is detected or suspected, however, the mobilization of resources to deal with it internally is potentially very great. Here the privacy, enclosure and the official allocation of tasks of the business environment act to the advantage of control. The existence of rules and routines, of task responsibilities and specialized competencies, of authority clearly delimited and of extensive record-keeping and accounting makes the tracing of misconduct and its pinning down to individuals possible in a way that is immensely difficult in the case of conventional crimes. Membership of the organization requires the constant generation of evidence of activities in discharging job responsibilities, evidence that has as its counterpart the meagre traces left to scene-of-crime officers in conventional offences, which only in the fictional cases of such as Sherlock Holmes routinely provide anything like a substantial lead to the offender.

This advantage to internal control once suspicion is aroused is further enhanced by the range of sanctions available. Ideally proof and confession, and hence the introduction of effective remedies against repetition, are desirable, but even suspicion that is not cleared can be followed by, for example, the transfer of individuals to other duties, or a simple failure to promote them. Suspicions which are confirmed can be sanctioned not only by dismissal, but by demotion, involving of course recurrent loss of pay, and at worst perhaps by public exposure outside the organization, involving loss of occupational standing. In the case of professionals this may include loss of professional accreditation, but for all employees dismissal for specified misconduct will make re-employment in any position of trust very difficult. All of this is at the discretion of the organization, and its procedures for implementing investigation and imposing sanctions, while subject to the powers of the trade unions and to legislation such as the

Employment Protection Acts, usually combine the formal and the informal. The scope for the control of the employee if the organization wishes to exercise that control is hence very great, and the great majority of misconduct in organizations is dealt with in this way, by procedures ranging from a reprimand from an immediate superior to formal inquiry and arraignment before a special disciplinary panel.

The position of the employee is hence very much weaker than that of the employer. Where the employer engages in abuses, his staff have to organize strongly if their interests are affected, and may still find it difficult both to gain access to information essential to proof of misconduct, and to resist selective or even collective dismissal. Outside interests such as customers, creditors and the Inland Revenue may find all the privileges of private enterprise deployed to frustrate them: information is refused, lies are told, meetings postponed, correspondence unanswered, worthless promises made and managing directors become inaccessible. . . .

The obvious recourse of those suffering from recalcitrant and fraudulent businessmen is to the public domain of the law, usually by suing for damages or bankruptcy, or by calling on the Department of Trade to investigate the affairs of the company. As has already been remarked, the police are by no means always ready or able to act, and usually do so only if clear evidence of a criminal offence is presented to them, or where the number of complaints becomes substantial. The victims, however, are caught in a dilemma. The law is slow, uncertain and expensive; worse still, at the end of the day its use may well have the effect of closing down the business, leaving little behind but debts. This may be in the public interest in not ensnaring any more people as victims, but it does nothing to secure the interests of existing victims in recovering their money, whether this consists in repayment of the debt, the provision of goods not supplied, or supplied but defective, or in continuity of employment. There is therefore a powerful incentive for the victim to keep matters in the private realm, and to attempt to negotiate a solution. In practice recourse to the law and the public agencies is usually indicative of despair and a thirst for vengeance on the part of the victims. It is hence in the interests of the offender to continue negotiations for as long as possible by making offers, promises and part-payments. . . .

A point which has already been alluded to but needs stating more fully is the ambiguity of business crime, which ranges from calculated and single-minded fraud to hotly debated misconduct. It includes, as has been remarked, losses consequent upon incompetence, naïvety and negligence, as well as deliberate misappropriation; and misappropriation itself may be opportunist or pressured, as well as sheer, cold theft. The most comprehensive study to date of the most classically criminal of frauds, the long-term credit fraud, in which the perpetrator builds up his creditworthiness with prompt payments for a time, and then takes as much credit as he can obtain before disappearing, shows that a substantial proportion were not the unaided efforts of habitual criminals. Some cases, it is true, involve criminals financing 'front men' to set up businesses with the sole objective of building up credit and then maximizing the fraud on suppliers. Many, however, involve businessmen who have fallen on hard times and who, despairing at last of ever recovering – a corner shop squeezed out of the market by the arrival of a supermarket, for example – decide that years of honest trading deserve some substantial reward, and decide to go bankrupt for a large amount rather than a small one. Sometimes too, professional criminals prey upon such businesses by offering loans to get them through a difficult period, and then take over the business and use the proprietor as a 'front man'.

The ambiguities of business crime extend also to the corner-cutting and sharp practice from which almost no great modern business organization and business tycoon has been free at some point in their careers. Doubts and complexities here are legion. If your competitor does not realize the weakness of his position, is it your job to inform him? Is it illegitimate to obtain contracts by offering lavish entertainment to clients and key personnel? In some circumstances this may fall foul of the Corrupt Practices Acts, in others not. Goods ordered are not available and others are supplied in their stead. How does this affect the contract in respect of quality, performance and price? Are professional services to be charged at their cost plus a reasonable rate per hour, or at whatever the client can be persuaded to pay, and at what stage does this constitute fraudulent misrepresentation?

One has also to recognize the readiness of a very large sector of the public to collude in or connive at some illegal and underhand practices. Who voluntarily insists on paying VAT when they have their car serviced, their plumbing fixed or their windows repaired? Who will refuse the offer of a friend to run off some photocopies on the office machine, or do some calculations on the office computer? Who will resist the offer of the company van to move furniture or other heavy goods, or the offer of a load of 'cheap' tarmac to improve their drive? . . .

The ambiguity of business crime is hence profound and pervasive, and furthermore there is no prospect of eliminating it. . . . [D]ebate about how acceptable conduct is to be distinguished from unacceptable must be informed by the practice and practitioners of business itself.

It follows from this that business crimes have an essentially contested character. They are basically political offences, not in the parliamentary sense of the term, but in that they involve the mobilization of power to make the accusation of wrongdoing stick. Where conventional crimes are self-evidently so, business crimes, as has been outlined above, have to be shown to be crimes and not something else. The compilation of evidence and successful denunciation require the mobilization of sufficient powerful interests to overcome the offender, who will naturally secrete or destroy damning evidence, interpret his actions as legitimate (if perhaps mistaken) and counterclaim malevolence on the part of his accusers. Because he is inside the organization and may remain close to the scene of the offence, he has maximum opportunity to resist exposure, and he will of course mobilize the support of friends and colleagues if possible. Above all it is difficult to prove *mens rea* (malign intent) in business offences, even though the evidence of the records may easily show wrongful conduct. It is hard for the surprised burglar to explain forced entry, but the business offender is in the reverse position, and will use it to deny, not that he was the offender, but that the offence was an offence. Even the embezzling employee may deny theft, on the grounds that it was only a loan that he intended to repay. No burglar can credibly make such a claim; the employee's may be doubtful but not necessarily entirely so. . . .

Underlying . . . concern with the control of business crime lies a tension fundamental in all societies, but particularly characteristic of modern Western industrialized democracies: between private self-interest pursued through the institutions of business, and the service ethic of the public good, of fairness and distributive justice, developed in Britain by the civil service after the reforms of the latter part of the nineteenth century, and further developed and expanded by the welfare state. The danger of unfettered private enterprise is that it degenerates into greed, ruthlessness and deceit, to the oppression of the interests of those insufficiently cunning, skilled, wealthy or powerful to protect themselves, and so polarizes the haves from the have-nots. The danger of the service ethic and of distributive justice is that if applied to all institutions of society it imposes minimum standards but at an ever-increasing cost, while also stifling initiative with bureaucracy, restrictive practices and heavy taxation. This is not a problem that can ever be resolved. Much of political debate will continue to concern the relative balance of advantage to be given by government policy to each alternative. Whilst the demands for cost-cutting, measured efficiency and the elimination of waste constitute the assault by a business ideology upon the public sector, efforts to ensure higher standards of business conduct through regulation and public debate constitute an attempt to render business more compatible with the ideals of the service ethic.

Part VI

Media and Popular Culture

The development of the mass media – large-circulation newspapers, magazines, radio, television, videos and computer communications – has had an enormous impact upon the institutions of modern societies. Whether in the shape of news-broadcasting, soap operas, drama, documentaries, movies or music, the media have a far-reaching influence in our lives. How far people's attitudes and outlooks are shaped by the various media, however, is a controversial issue in contemporary sociology.

In Reading 24 John B. Thompson emphasizes that the reception of the 'messages' conveyed through the mass media is an actively organized one. Audiences respond to media messages selectively and in a critical fashion. The term 'mass' in mass media, Thompson points out, is somewhat misleading: media audiences may be very large, but they are also highly differentiated.

In Reading 25 Christine Geraghty analyses the nature of one of the most popular types of broadcast programme, the soap opera. Why do so many people watch the soaps? What is the source of their attraction? Geraghty questions the idea that soap operas are a substitute for 'real-life' experience or that viewers cannot distinguish between the fictional and the real. The appeal of soap opera lies partly in the very fact that it is fictional, yet it concerns 'ordinary' happenings which the audience can easily relate to circumstances in their own lives.

Sociologists have given a good deal of attention to studying the news, particularly television news. In Reading 26 Richard Ericson and his colleagues discuss how news is 'created' by the various groups of reporters, editors and producers involved. What counts as 'news' is the result of a complicated series of interchanges between these groups.

Reading 27 considers the future of public broadcasting. The BBC is such a familiar part of people's lives in the United Kingdom – and to some extent in many other countries in the world – that it is hard to believe that its position is threatened. The development of new forms of commercial television, especially those carried by cable and satellite, however, promises a future in which there may be as many as 500 television channels to choose from. How should the BBC react to such developments? Could it lose its identity altogether? The issue is partly financial – should people who do not want to watch BBC TV be forced to pay a 'tax' (the licence fee) as is the case now?

Reading 28 discusses the significance of new forms of computerized communication – in particular, the Internet. The Internet is a vast network of computers, stretched across the world. Although it began as a consciously designed project, funded originally by the US Defense Department, its growth has largely been spontaneous. Across the Internet, people communicate with one another in 'cyberspace', that is, from computer to computer. No one knows what the future of the Internet might be. Some believe its consequences will be very profound indeed, producing a situation in which people across the planet will routinely interact with one another without regard to distance. Others see a much smaller role for the Internet, which would form only one mode of communication among the other, better-established, forms.

John B. Thompson

Mass Communication, Symbolic Goods and Media Products

The advent of mass communication, and especially the rise of mass circulation newspapers in the nineteenth century and the emergence of
broadcasting in the twentieth, has had a profound impact on the
modes of experience and patterns of interaction characteristic of modern
societies. For most people today, the knowledge we have of events which
take place beyond our immediate social milieu is a knowledge largely
derived from our reception of mass-mediated symbolic forms. The knowledge we have of political leaders and their policies, for instance, is a knowledge derived largely from newspapers, radio and television, and the ways
in which we participate in the institutionalized system of political power
are deeply affected by the knowledge so derived. Similarly, our experience
of events which take place in contexts that are spatially and temporally
remote, from strikes and demonstrations to massacres and wars, is an experience largely mediated by the institutions of mass communication; indeed,
our experience of these events as 'political', as constitutive of the domain of
experience which is regarded as politics, is partly the outcome of a series of
institutionalized practices which endow them with the status of news. The
role of the media is so fundamental in this regard that it would be partial at
best to portray the nature and conduct of politics at a national and international level without reference to the processes of mass communication.

In this [discussion] I want to begin to explore some of the ways in which
the advent of mass communication has transformed the modes of experience and patterns of interaction characteristic of modern societies. . . .

Let me begin by analysing some of the general characteristics of what is
commonly called 'mass communication'. It has often been pointed out that,
while 'mass communication' is a convenient label for referring to a broad

range of media institutions and products, the term is misleading in certain respects. It is worth dwelling for a moment on some of the respects in which this term can lead astray. The expression 'mass' derives from the fact that the messages transmitted by the media industries are generally available to relatively large audiences. This is certainly the case in some sectors of the media industries and at some stages in their development, such as the mass circulation newspaper industry and the major television networks. However, during other periods in the development of the media industries (e.g. the early newspaper industry) and in some sectors of the media industries today (e.g. some book and magazine publishers), the audiences were and remain relatively small and specialized. Hence the term 'mass' should not be construed in narrowly quantitative terms; the important point about mass communication is not that a given number or proportion of individuals receive the products, but rather that the products are available in principle to a plurality of recipients. Moreover, the term 'mass' is misleading in so far as it suggests that the audiences are like inert, undifferentiated heaps. This suggestion obscures the fact that the messages transmitted by the media industries are received by specific individuals situated in particular social–historical contexts. These individuals attend to media messages with varying degrees of concentration, actively interpret and make sense of these messages and relate them to other aspects of their lives. Rather than viewing these individuals as part of an inert and undifferentiated mass, we should leave open the possibility that the reception of media messages is an active, inherently critical and socially differentiated process.

If the term 'mass' may be misleading in this context, the term 'communication' may also be, since the kinds of communication generally involved in mass communication are quite different from those involved in ordinary conversation. I shall examine some of these differences in the course of the following discussion. Here I shall call attention to one important difference: namely, that mass communication generally involves a one-way flow of messages from the transmitter to the receiver. Unlike the dialogical situation of a conversation, in which a listener is also a potential respondent, mass communication institutes a fundamental *break* between the producer and receiver, in such a way that recipients have relatively little capacity to contribute to the course and content of the communicative process. Hence it may be more appropriate to speak of the 'transmission' or 'diffusion' of messages rather than of 'communication' as such. Yet even in the circumstances of mass communication, recipients do have some capacity to contribute, in so far as recipients are also consumers who may sometimes choose between various media products and whose views are sometimes solicited or taken into account by the organizations concerned with producing and diffusing these products. Moreover, it is possible that new technological developments – such as those associated with fibre optic cables – will increase the interactive capacity of the medium of television and give viewers greater control over the transmission process, although the extent to which this will become a practical reality remains to be seen.

In the light of these preliminary qualifications, I want to offer a broad conceptualization of mass communication and to highlight some of its key characteristics. We may broadly conceive of mass communication as *the institutionalized production and generalized diffusion of symbolic goods via the transmission and storage of information communication*. By conceiving of mass communication in terms of the production and diffusion of symbolic goods, I wish to stress the importance of viewing mass communication in relation to the institutions concerned with the commodification of symbolic forms. What we now describe as mass communication is a range of phenomena and processes that emerged historically through the development of institutions seeking to exploit new opportunities for the fixation and reproduction of symbolic forms. I . . . want to analyse mass communication in a more theoretical way by focusing on the following four characteristics: the institutionalized production and diffusion of symbolic goods; the instituted break between production and reception; the extension of availability in time and space; and public circulation of symbolic forms. . . .

The first characteristic of mass communication is *the institutionalized production and diffusion of symbolic goods*. Mass communication presupposes the development of institutions – that is, relatively stable clusters of social relations and accumulated resources – concerned with the large-scale production and generalized diffusion of symbolic goods. These activities are 'large-scale' in the sense that they involve the production and diffusion of multiple copies or the provision of materials to numerous recipients. This is rendered possible by the fixation of symbolic forms in technical media and by the reproducibility of the forms. *Fixation* may involve processes of encoding whereby symbolic forms are translated into information which can be stored in a particular medium or material substratum; the symbolic forms may be transmitted as information and then decoded for the purposes of reception or consumption. The symbolic forms diffused by mass communication are inherently *reproducible* in the sense that multiple copies may be produced or made available to numerous recipients. The reproduction of forms is generally controlled as strictly as possible by the institutions of mass communication, since it is one of the principal means by which symbolic forms are subjected to economic valorization. Forms are reproduced in order to be exchanged on a market or through a regulated type of economic transaction. Hence they are *commodified* and treated as objects to be sold, as services to be paid for or as media which can facilitate the sale of other objects or services. In the first instance, therefore, mass communication should be understood as part of a range of institutions concerned, in varying ways, with the fixation, reproduction and commodification of symbolic forms.

A second characteristic of mass communication is that *it institutes a fundamental break between the production and reception of symbolic goods*. These goods are produced for recipients who are generally not physically present at the place of production and transmission or diffusion; they are, literally, *mediated* by the technical media in which they are fixed and transmitted. This characteristic is not, of course, unique to mass communication: the fixation and transmission of symbolic forms on papyrus or stone also involved a break between production and reception. But with the rise of mass communication, the range of producers and receivers affected by this process has greatly expanded. Moreover, as I noted earlier, the mediation of symbolic forms via mass communication generally involves a one-way flow of messages from the producer to the recipient, such that the capacity of the recipient to influence or intervene in the processes of production and transmission or diffusion is strictly limited. One consequence of this condition is that the processes of production and transmission or diffusion are characterized by a distinctive form of *indeterminacy*. Symbolic forms are produced for audiences and transmitted or diffused in order to reach these audiences, but these processes generally take place in the absence of a direct and continuous monitoring of the audiences' responses. In contrast to face-to-face interaction, where the interlocutors can question one another and observe one another's responses, in mass communication the personnel involved in the production and transmission or diffusion are generally deprived of immediate feedback from the recipients. Since the economic valorization of mass-mediated symbolic forms may depend crucially on the nature and extent of reception, the personnel involved typically employ a variety of strategies to cope with this indeterminacy. They draw upon past experience and use it as a guide to likely future outcomes; they use well-tried formulas which have a predictable audience appeal; or they try to obtain information about recipients through market research or through the routine monitoring of audience size and response. These and other techniques are institutionalized mechanisms which enable personnel to reduce the indeterminacy stemming from the break between production and reception, and to do so in a way which concurs with the overall aims of the institutions concerned.

A third characteristic of mass communication is that *it extends the availability of symbolic forms in time and in space*. Again, this characteristic is not unique to mass communication: all forms of cultural transmission involve some degree of space–time distanciation. But the media of mass communication generally involve a relatively high degree of distanciation in both space and time; and with the development of telecommunications, space–time distanciation is severed from the physical transportation of symbolic forms. The transmission of symbolic forms via telecommunications – for example, via a network of terrestrial and satellite relays – enables the institutions of mass communication to achieve a high degree of spatial distanciation in a minimal amount of time. Moreover, since the symbolic forms are generally fixed in a relatively durable medium, such as paper, photographic film or electromagnetic tape, they also have extended availability in time and can be preserved for subsequent use. The space–time distanciation involved in mass communication is also affected by the conditions under which symbolic forms are received and consumed. By virtue of the instituted break between production and reception, the nature and extent of distanciation may depend on the social practices and technical conditions of reception. For example, the extension of availability of a book in time and space may depend as much on the ways in which the book is received – whether it is recommended or ignored, incorporated into curricula or actively suppressed, and so on – as . . . on the channels of diffusion and the nature of the technical medium itself. Similarly, the extension of availability of a television programme or film may depend on whether potential recipients have the technical means to receive the programme, whether the scheduling concurs with the social organization of their everyday lives, and so on.

A fourth characteristic of mass communication is that *it involves the public circulation of symbolic forms*. The products of mass communication are produced in principle for a plurality of recipients. In this respect, mass communication differs from forms of communication – such as telephone conversations, teleconferencing or private video-recordings of various kinds – which employ the same technical media of fixation and transmission but which are orientated towards a single or highly restricted range of recipients. This basic difference between established forms of mass communication and other forms of electronically mediated interaction may be called into question by the increasing deployment of new communication technologies, but this is a development which has yet to be fully realized. As the institutions of mass communication have developed hitherto, their products circulate within a 'public domain', in the sense that they are available in principle to anyone who has the technical means, abilities and resources to acquire them. While the nature and scope of this public domain may be unlimited in principle, it is always limited in practice by the social–historical conditions of production, transmission and reception. The institutions of mass communication often aim to reach as large an audience as possible, since the size of the audience may directly affect the economic valorization of the products concerned. Today the audiences for some films and television programmes may amount to hundreds of millions of viewers worldwide; a single Christmas Day television broadcast can command more than 30 million viewers in Britain alone. The nature and scope of the audiences for the products of mass communication vary enormously from one medium to another, and from one product to another within the same medium. The ways in which these products are appropriated by the recipients – whether, for example, they are appropriated by a collective gathering in a cinema or by a private viewing in the home – also vary considerably, depending on the medium, the product, the channels of diffusion and the social and technical conditions of reception. One consequence of the intrinsically public character of media products is that the development of mass communication has been accompanied by attempts to exercise control, on the part of state authorities and other regulatory bodies, over the institutions of mass communication. The very capacity of these institutions to make symbolic forms available to a potentially vast audience is a source of concern for authorities which seek to maintain order and regulate social life within the territories under their jurisdiction.

READING 25

Christine Geraghty
The Appeal of Soap Opera

The close relationship between soaps and their audiences, the intimate knowledge regular viewers have of the programmes and their identification with particular characters, is . . . a source of puzzled dismay to those who do not watch soap operas. Concern is expressed that soaps are a substitute for 'real life', that viewers believe that the characters really exist and think that Albert Square and Southfork are something more than sets grown familiar through repeated viewing. Such criticisms are, as I hope to show, ill-founded, but they do at least hint at the crucial relationship which soaps have with their audiences. This [discussion] will explore the nature of that relationship through an examination of the formal narrative strategies which work to create it. Other TV programmes may deal with the traditional subject matter of soaps – personal problems, family life, relationships within a community – but only soaps invite the audience both to enter intimately into a fictional world and to stand back and view with dispassion the formal conventions through which that world is constructed. This double action of engagement and distance is the subject of this reading. By examining the way in which soaps construct their stories and in particular the manipulation of space, time and characterization in them, we shall be better placed to understand the particular pleasures of soap viewing.

SOAP NARRATIVES AND TIME

The organization of time is one of the key distinguishing features of soap story-telling and allows us to draw a distinction between soaps and the related formats of the series and the serial. The differences between a serial, a series and a soap opera have become blurred in recent years as the success of the soap format has encouraged series programmes like *Hill Street Blues* and *Cagney and Lacey* to incorporate strong elements of soap. Nevertheless, there is a distinct difference between these formats which hinges on how far the organization of time dominates the organization of the narrative itself.

A serial tells a complete story but spreads it over a number of episodes, often using the device of the cliffhanger to pick up from one episode to another. Serialization in this way has an honourable tradition in which the novels of Wilkie Collins and Charles Dickens feature. It is the format of many TV programmes, particularly the adaptations of classic novels for which British television has a reputation, and the popular mini-series (somewhat misleadingly named since they are not in fact series but serials) in which best sellers such as *Roots* and *Lace* are presented in three or four consecutive evening viewings. Thus serials, like soaps, use a set of un-resolved narrative puzzles to carry viewers across the time gap from one episode to another, but the length of the fictional time which is deemed to have passed between episodes depends on the demands of the narrative: it may be a minute, a month, a year; it may be no time at all if the following episode returns to the moment of drama on which the preceding episode ended. In addition, serials differ from soaps in having a final ending which provides a resolution to the problems which have been set up at the beginning of the story. This ending clearly subordinates the organization of time to the resolution of the narrative strands. The series format, on the other hand, is like the soap in that it offers the audience a set of characters and very often a place (the police station, the hospital) with which we become familiar. In the traditional series format, however, like *The Rockford Files* or *Minder*, the organization of time is dominated by the demand that the main story be resolved in a single episode. The classic narrative strategy of a situation which is disrupted and then restored through characters' actions is thus worked through for the viewer in one viewing and, while sub-stories may run across episodes, the audience is presented with a satisfactory resolution to a particular problem every time the programme is shown. The series, thus, lacks that sense of endless but organized time which characterizes soap operas and which shapes the way in which we respond to their narratives. In soaps, stories are never finally resolved and even soaps which cease to be made project themselves into a non-existent future. The final scene of *Crossroads*, when, after nearly twenty-four years, it came to an end in April 1988, showed Jill Chance with her new lover, John, driving away to seek another motel, another 'Crossroads'.

This lack of resolution is both an effect and a consequence of the sense of a future which is another mark of the difference between soaps and serials and the traditional series. *The Jewel in the Crown* and *Rich Man, Poor Man* may be long, complex serials but we expect that in the end the significance of what we are watching will be revealed and each strand tied into a resolution. This is not to say that the resolution will always be effectively accomplished or that the story's pressures will necessarily be contained by its ending. It is the expectation of resolution which is important here. Soap operas do not encourage such expectations and the longer they run the more impossible it seems to imagine them ending. Instead of narrative time being subordinate to the demands of the story, it dominates the narrative process and enables other formal structures to be brought into play. Time rather than action becomes the basis for organizing the narrative. At its most classic, a soap opera would appear daily and its organization of time would be based on the yesterday, today and tomorrow of the viewer. Prime-time soaps are not so strict in their adherence to 'real' time as this model suggests. Nevertheless, unlike the serial, the time which elapses between episodes of a soap is dependent not on the organization of the story (what happens next?) but on some sense of time passing in the programme which parallels the time which has passed for the viewer between episodes. Characteristically, such soaps are introduced by the announcer inviting us to 'drop in on the Square' or 'find out what's been happening in the Street' as if life has been going on there without us. In addition, the passage of time is marked by references to the 'real' world of the viewer. The time of the year and the passing of the seasons are faithfully reflected; in *EastEnders*, plastic daffodils are planted in the Square when filming takes place in early March to ensure that the flowers will be correctly in bloom in April when the episode is shown. The appropriate festivals are marked; Sheila Grant visits Rome at Easter for the pope's blessing; summer holidays are discussed and taken in July and August; the families of *EastEnders* and *Coronation Street* eat Christmas lunch and watch the Queen's speech along with the rest of the population. Important events in the 'real' world may also be referred to, although this is more of a risk since cancellation or rearrangement between the date the episode is completed and its transmission could be embarrassing. A royal wedding can usually be safely marked and there have been references to political activities such as elections; the participation of fictional characters in such national events increases the sense of a soap world which runs parallel with the world outside the programme.

The organization of soap time in a way that seeks to reflect the viewers' experience of time in their own lives may seem to be more characteristic of British soaps than of US programmes such as *Dallas* and *Dynasty*, but it is one of the purposes of this [discussion] to show that it is not necessary for each soap to display to the same degree all the characteristics which they share. In this case, as in others, it is possible to see differences between the various programmes in the soap spectrum. Not all soaps mark out the passage of time as clearly as, for instance, *EastEnders* and *Brookside*. Even among the British soaps, *Crossroads* was much less likely to measure the passage of days between episodes, and clearly the US prime-time soaps do not use the strategy at all consistently. Nevertheless, I would argue that they do the minimum to ensure that they operate as soap operas and not as series. Although the US prime-time soaps are organized in terms of a season of programmes rather than appearing regularly throughout the year like their British prime-time equivalents, the cliffhanging departures at the end of each season ensure that the audience is more concerned with continuance than resolution. There is never, for instance, a sense that a resolution is possible or imminent. Even apparent narrative closures such as a wedding or a death merely offer the opportunity for more problems to fuel the narrative, and stories are not resolved, as they are in a series, in a single episode. The US prime-time soaps do also acknowledge, in however limited a way, the passage of time as reflected in events both inside and outside the programmes. The regular Ewing barbecue and the Oil Barons' Ball help to create a calendar in the *Dallas* year, while JR's excursions into terrorism and the lobbying of Washington over the price of oil would be examples of references to the outside world, as would the gubernatorial elections in

Dynasty. Thus, within the spectrum of soaps, the organization of time follows the same pattern even if there are differences in the degree to which it
is the dominant factor.

SOAP NARRATIVES AND SPACE

The way in which soaps handle the passing of time has implications for their
organization of space and setting. Soaps can run (potentially) forever and
their lack of resolution can make them aimless and repetitious. One way of
handling the problem of repetition is to make it enjoyable, to give the audience a sense of familiarity with setting and characters so that to return to
them is pleasurable. The establishment of narrative space so that viewers
know in a detailed and intimate way the layout of the setting in which the
stories take place is thus a crucial consequence of the soap opera's use of
time. Repetition permits a familiar geography to be established through
camera-work and cutting which allows the audience to build up a sense of
the fictional space. This sense of space is almost inevitable in programmes
that run for years when for economic reasons, if for no other, the same sets
must be used again and again. . . . The close-up, which allows emphasis on
an individual's face, and the two-shot, which enables the viewer to see two
characters in the same shot, are used frequently in prime-time soaps, but a
third shot is also important – the establishing shot, often the first in a scene,
which establishes the geography of the programme's fictional world. In
Dallas and *Dynasty* the regular establishing shot of, for instance, Southfork or
the Carrington mansion is crucial, not only in fixing the location of a scene
but also for alerting the audience to what is likely to happen. In both *Dallas*
and *Dynasty*, for instance, particular decors are associated with specific characters and activities so that space and setting take on a narrative function.
The Southfork patio offers a setting for the outdoor breakfasts which often
set up future actions in *Dallas*, and the regular use of the mansion staircase
in *Dynasty* as a setting for Blake and Krystle made its appropriation by
Alexis, when she took over the house, the more scandalous. What tends to
be missing in the US programmes, however, is a sense of the geographical
relationship between these familiar domestic settings or of the space
between the interiors which represent office and home.

Such a lack of integration is not inevitable in US prime-time soaps. *Knots
Landing* showed how a sense of the geography of the programme could be
established through the aerial shots in the credits and through the use of
the public spaces between the houses for narrative events. It may be, however, that such an integration of space is more difficult when it is the public
and the private, office and home, which have to be linked. *Crossroads*, which
paralleled the public work of the motel with the personal lives of its staff,
had the least well-established space of the British soaps. Although the spatial link between the motel bar and the reception, for instance, was clearly
elaborated, the position of the motel in relation to Jill's home or Di's cottage
was much less clear. At the other extreme, the opening credits of the British
soap *Brookside* clearly invite us into a geographical space, Liverpool with its
cathedrals and municipal buildings, and then, in a series of shots, directs us

to Brookside Close, the heart of the drama, clearly established by the street nameplate. Aerial shots give us access to the layout of the Close, the positioning of the houses and the relationship between the neighbours, and throughout the programme conversations and actions take place in the communal space between the houses. Similar care for geographical space is apparent in *EastEnders* and *Coronation Street*, where again the outdoor spaces of the streets provide an arena for narrative action as well as a link between characters' homes.

SOAP NARRATIVES AND CHARACTERS

The endlessness of soap time and the familiarity of its space has its effect on the construction of its characters. One of soap's most striking qualities is the way in which the audience becomes familiar with the history of certain characters and has access to knowledge which is well beyond that given in a particular episode. The audience may be aware for instance of traumatic events in a character's past which affect how they are currently behaving and can ascribe reasons for behaviour beyond that of dramatic necessity or the demands of plotting. Such awareness is based not only on knowledge of key events – that a woman has in the past lost a child or been married to a cruel husband – but also [on] an understanding of the way in which a particular character fits in to the network of relationships which make up a soap. It is easy to underestimate the pleasure of predictability but very often the repetition of plots, so tedious to the casual viewer, is part of a pattern based on the well-established character traits of particular individuals. To see Cliff Barnes embark on yet another ill-fated attempt to foil JR, or Angie in *EastEnders* begin another emotional and fraught battle with her husband, Den, is to set off on a roller-coaster whose ups and downs are reassuringly predictable because the viewer has been gaining knowledge of them for years. Familiarity with the characters allows the viewer to bring meaning to the narrative rather than having to rely on what is shown in a particular episode. It is the viewer who brings richness and density to material which on the surface can look thin and unrewarding.

If the presence of well-established characters leads soaps to value familiarity and predictability, the audience is also invited to relish change and disruption. The familiar world which soaps work so hard to establish is disrupted by new characters and changing story lines. What happens may be predictable but the interest lies in the many variations on how it will happen. A soap's endless future means that an ultimate conclusion can never be reached and soaps are thus based on a premise of continuous disruption. The stability of a conclusion is always threatened by the next event, the marriage by divorce, the unified family by the children's departure, the community celebration by quarrels and disharmony. Various formal factors contribute to this sense of the possibility of change. New characters are introduced on a short-term basis to feature in a particular story; long-term characters leave and their tracks have to be suitably covered. In US prime-time soaps, an actor is replaced and the character is reworked to accommodate a new face. On both sides of the Atlantic, well-established characters change as the soap develops and the audience is offered a different perspective on them. Thus, in *Brookside* the treatment of Bobby Grant and his stubborn insistence on his role as head of the family became more critical and harsh, and in *Dallas* Sue Ellen changed dramatically from an out-of-control drunk to a high-powered executive. Some of the most moving moments in soaps come when a regular acts out of character – JR remorseful, at least for a moment, at Sue Ellen's bedside or Mavis, in *Coronation Street*, summoning up dignity and courage to stand up, for once, for her rights. Such moments are brief but offer the regular viewer a different facet to a familiar character which can be drawn on in future episodes.

These moments of change and disruption are made possible by the interweaving story lines in which lacunae in plotting or characterization conveniently go unnoticed. The British soaps traditionally run two or three stories together, sometimes linked by a common theme or counterpointing a serious story with a more comic one. These interleaving stories make it appear quite natural for characters to come and go, for regulars to disappear for a while and return, for new light to be shed on familiar characters. Even in US prime-time soaps, where the dynamic of the narrative is more unified, the complexity of the overall narrative means stories can run parallel with each other. Thus Pam's search for her mother clearly had links with other stories in *Dallas* but was treated largely as a series of events which were separate from other elements in the overall plot. Such flexibility allows soaps to extend their range of stories, establish new characters and provide the audience with change and variety without losing the stability provided by the setting.

This ability to handle both repetition and disruption, familiarity and change, is important in establishing the audience's relationship with a soap narrative and its characters. Soaps can survive major changes because the audience's commitment is engaged across a range of characters and stories and not dependent on one or two individuals. The importance of key characters, such as JR in *Dallas*, Den and Angie in *EastEnders* and Meg in *Crossroads*, can be overestimated. Certainly . . . the departure of a well-established character such as Meg Mortimer, the matriarch of *Crossroads*, arouses strong feelings in an audience for whom the change is just too disruptive. Nevertheless, *Crossroads* did survive the departure of a major character and Angie's disappearance from *EastEnders* offered the possibility of new stories for her husband and daughter. Pamela Ewing's departure from *Dallas* meant that Bobby's relationship with Southfork was strengthened and also allowed his character to be available for new romantic encounters. The organization of space, time and character means that the audience is engaged with the programme as a whole, with its overall narrative and its established space; it is no accident that the titles of soaps refer to a geographical area or group of people (*EastEnders, Dallas, Dynasty, Coronation Street*) rather than one or two individuals (*Kojak, Cagney and Lacey, Bergerac*). While the viewer's engagement with particular characters is clearly important it is perhaps more diffuse than is usually recognized. Identification is decentred; it is invited across a range of characters, not with a particular central figure. It is thus possible for regular viewers to be torn between two characters, to endorse the position of some characters but not others, and indeed to find some tedious as well as dislikable.

Richard Ericson, Patricia Baranek and Janet Chan

Visualizing the News

VISUALS FOR TELEVISION

Television reporters have special requirements in obtaining visuals. These constitute both constraining and enabling features of reporting peculiar to television.

Reporter–cameraman relations

The cameraman is a highly valued member of the television newsroom. This was symbolized by the fact that while he was formally under the direction of the reporter, he was paid substantially more than the reporter, sometimes double or more. Moreover, the reporter was very dependent on the cameraman to understand what the story was about so it could be visualized appropriately. 'While the presence on the screen of the television reporter gives the story journalistic credibility in the traditional sense, it is heavily reliant on the news judgement of the cameraman.'[1]

The basis of the reporter–cameraman relationship was tacit understanding of requirements. The cameraman has to become part of the newsroom culture and learn the vocabulary of precedents of reporters, editors and producers. He must learn the approach of each reporter and the subtle differences in the way each works. Over time a reporter develops a preference for working with a particular cameraman and vice versa. However, since reporter and crew assignments were done on the basis of situational availability rather than keeping a team together, it was not possible to expect a regular matching of those who felt that they worked well together.

Beyond tacit understandings and cues in the field, cameramen often offered specific advice and direct assistance. Advice was given freely on what shots to take, what clips or source quotations to use from shots taken, and what reporter voice-over phrasing might be appropriate for particular visuals. The cameraman also helped to encourage sources to co-operate generally, and to phrase particular notions when they stumbled or seemed unable to articulate in the manner expected.

As would be expected where aesthetic preferences are constantly being worked at rather than already worked out, reporter–cameraman relations were often marked with tension and conflict. Reporters carped about cameramen who took poor shots; packed up too early and therefore missed something of relevance; did not follow directions well; and failed to 'hustle' in the face of time limitations. In turn, cameramen were critical of reporters' judgements about the selection of sources; questioning of sources; overshooting, and otherwise obtaining too much information that risked missing the slot; and making stories where there were none in the opinion of the cameraman. Some of these disputes were taken to the level of supervisors. Underlying the reporter's concern was the fact that he was dependent on the cameraman for a good public face, while the cameraman could remain invisible after completing his visualization work.

On locations

One picture may not be equivalent to a thousand words, at least not in television news. However, television does have the ability to show as well as to tell. It can show the location of an event and can also picture what the people involved look like, thereby providing for the audience readings of their moral character. It provides a form of tertiary understanding not available to print except through still photographs: during our observations, efforts ranged from committing a crew for hours to obtain a visual of a suspect leaving court with a bag over his head, to hiring a helicopter so a crew could obtain an overview of a fire.

Television actuality shots are quite rare. Visuals rarely capture an actual event in the world, only talk of an event. Hence, most often the choice of a location is a matter of finding some place or someone that will stand for what is being talked about. In terms of physical locations, these were termed 'generic spots'. The release of a government report on domestic violence was represented by a reporter stand-up in front of the legislative building. A politician whose election campaign included disputing a high-rise building development was interviewed near the site of the development to represent this point of the campaign. When a place of a type could provide the sign, then the most convenient one would do: for a story about the contamination of a pharmaceutical product sold in drugstores, the handiest local drugstore was chosen for the visuals; for a story about lawyers' fees for real estate transactions, a street near the newsroom was selected for shots of houses with 'for sale' signs.

If official reports or other documents were being talked about, these were sometimes also shown to exist. These visuals focused on title pages or bold headings, as well as taking key words or phrases to print across the screen with the document shown above or in the background. As in showing events and people, this treatment did not provide documentation of the matter being addressed but only a sign that the document being talked about actually existed and appeared in a particular form.

Most television stories were built around interview clips with a few sources, 'the talking head'. While the key aspect of these clips was in the person's words rather than the context in which they were said, as shown in the visuals, the context was often deemed by the reporter to be a relevant component of his visualization of how the source was to be represented. An important consideration for the reporter was how to represent the source's authority, in the context of the matter being reported and the other sources involved. The basic choice was whether talking-head visuals should be 'on the street', or in the physical office which represented the source's official office. One executive producer encouraged 'on-the-street' accounts from ordinary folk, the vox pop. He circulated memos to reporters to this effect, including one that stressed the need generally of 'going to the street' rather than letting 'institutional mouthpieces get air time with no real people'. However, what was done in this respect depended on the particular story and the contexts in which sources were dealt with.

In stories of the basic point/counterpoint format, involving leading representatives of each of two organizations in dispute, the usual approach was to represent each in the authority of their physical office. An instance of this, in which complications arose, is illustrative. A representative of a citizens' organization trying to establish a half-way house for prisoners was also an executive of a large corporation, but did not want visuals to be taken in his corporate office because the matter did not pertain to that corporation. Similarly, the representative of a citizens' organization in opposition to the establishment of this half-way house did not wish to have his unrelated corporate office used for visuals. The reporter, wishing to represent both as men of significance, found alternative physical space to convey the authority of their offices visually. One person agreed to come to the television station for interview. He was interviewed sitting behind the desk of one of the station's senior executives, appearing as if it was his own. The other interview was done in the lobby of a quality hotel across the street from the source's corporate offices, with permission of the hotel. The lobby furniture was rearranged so that the source could be suitably visualized sitting in a solid wingback chair, indicating that he too was talking from, and within, an authoritative office.

A reporter was assigned to do a story on the reaction of various ethnic groups to the revelation that RCMP security services had an 'ethnic list' of suspicious persons connected to various ethnic types. The reporter planned to do the story by filming the representatives of different ethnic groups 'on the street' to emphasize the 'voice of the people', against what was portrayed as a possible sign of totalitarian practice of government. The first representative agreed to a street interview. The reporter then proceeded to interview a doctor who said that in his practice he had many patients who complained of abuse by immigration and RCMP policing authorities. However, upon arriving at this doctor's office it was discovered to be in a poor part of town and the doctor himself did not look the part: he was in his late twenties or early thirties, and casually dressed without tie or jacket. The reporter decided that a street interview with this person would undercut his authority as a family physician speaking sympathetically about aggrieved patients. In spite of crew grumblings about having to set up their lights inside, the reporter insisted on representing the source in the authority of his office to add credence to his story. In contrast, the third source, a representative of a Polish group, was wearing a quality business suit. He refused an interview on the street in spite of the reporter's efforts to convince him. Instead he insisted on being shot behind his desk, flanked by flags of Poland, Canada and Ontario that were placed there by him for the purpose of the interview. In this instance the source's desire to appear authoritative won out, and the reporter ended up, against her initial wish, with two of three sources 'off the street'.

It was a convention to shoot two sources with opposing views from opposite angles. On one occasion a reporter thought that the cameraman tacitly understood this procedure when he asked him to obtain a clip from each of two opposition-party leaders making statements outside the legislature. When he discovered that the cameraman had taken shots of both from the same angle he was most annoyed, stressing that it was simply 'common sense' to shoot from opposite angles.

When sources were not available to be filmed, or a crew was not available to film them, other means were devised. A common practice was to telephone a source and obtain a voice recording that could be used along with a still photograph of the source and/or a shot of the reporter in the newsroom making the call. This was done in particular when a source was some distance from Toronto and the newsroom did not want to go to the expense of obtaining something that they knew could be captured in essence through a voice clip. In these circumstances something had to be shown with the voice clip, and if a still photograph of the source was lacking, that something was usually the reporter shown to be doing his job. While this representation was useless in terms of its relation to the source's statement, it was at least useful in showing the authority of the reporter's office.

Staging

The imperative of television journalists to represent visually people doing things related to the story often poses difficulties. Crews cannot always be on time at the place where the events are occurring, and even if they are they often face technical difficulties in obtaining shots with proper lighting, sound and focus. When such difficulties arise the solution is to have sources stage their activities, or in the words of the vocabulary of precedents, do a 'fake'. Indeed, the resource limitations and technical requirements of television news are so well known to sources that they usually take elaborate measures to script the event in advance and stage everything so that television crews can obtain their clips expeditiously. In this activity Goffman's dramaturgical model of social life is acted out in considerable detail.

When the requirement is talk about events, and 'talking heads' for television visuals, the news conference is a standard format. Well-prepared and well-groomed organizational representatives represent what is organizationally in order. After the basic presentation at a news conference, sources are asked by a television journalist to repeat a part of their performance for the purposes of a television clip. This approach saves film and editing time, since shooting the entire presentation expends a lot of film and requires a lot of sorting out back in the film-editing room.

The two leaders of the Guardian Angels citizen-patrol organization, based in New York City, came to Toronto on several occasions to stage news events that might help them with their cause. They chose significant locations – such as the city-hall square, the main indoor shopping precinct, and a space in a park where a woman had been sexually assaulted – to conduct interviews and give displays of self-defence techniques. On these occasions television journalists co-operated in the staging of each event by helping with locations, props, and suggestions for the enactment of representative action such as self-defence-technique displays.

Similar staging techniques were employed by citizens' groups with other causes. Groups in opposition to nuclear weapons held several marches and demonstrations, engaging in acts guaranteed to result in arrest by police, and equally guaranteed to be visually represented as the dominant frame of television-news items. At one demonstration television reporters from two different outlets discussed the various staging techniques being employed. They were very negative about the sources' representations, but nevertheless felt 'forced' to treat them as a central aspect of how they visualized the deviance. They pointed out that the source organization selected a key location (a plant involved in weapons manufacture); a good day in summer when 'news' was likely to be 'slow' because key source bureaucracies were in recess; and sent a release, along with promises via telephone calls, that there would be 'violence' of some sort. One television station had three crews on location. The source organization arranged for five people to jump over a fence to throw red paint, signifying blood, on a wall. They were stopped and arrested for trespass or public mischief. Meanwhile two women were able to paint with stencils six green doves on a wall before they were arrested for public mischief. A spokesperson for the organization, wearing a shirt displaying an anti-nuclear statement, was asked by a reporter why these acts were necessary. The source replied that it was a way of educating the public, through the media, about the role of Toronto-based firms in the manufacture of nuclear weapons. The reporter asked what acts of civil disobedience had to do with educating the public and was told that the organization wanted to remind employees of these firms, as well as the general public, that people have strong feelings about disarmament. The source organization had also come equipped with a variety of props – including banners (e.g. 'Ban the Bomb') and a coffin – all of which were focused on by cameramen, along with shots of the paint on the wall and the persons responsible being arrested. The reporters recognized that they were simply following the script of their source, and one remarked while editing that this item was a prime example of creating the news.

Virtually all sources work to create appearances for visuals in some way. Persons are selected who photograph and speak well. Background materials are also attended to, for example, piling papers and documents on the office desk to sustain the dominant cultural impression that good people work hard. If television crews are to be allowed inside private space to visualize what goes on there, it is in the terms of public culture.

Reporters did on occasion object to a source's staging techniques or props and were sometimes able to get rid of them. Ultimately it was for the reporter to decide what was an appropriate sign, and whether it was useful or in good taste. A reporter doing a story on a citizens' group campaigning against anti-Semitism included an interview with a source who had a collection of artefacts that were anti-Jewish, such as bumper-stickers, pamphlets and a Nazi flag. The source offered to hold the Nazi flag as she was being filmed, but the reporter regarded this as out of place and rejected it.

Reporters sometimes moved into the director's seat and used equally elaborate techniques of perfecting the 'fake'. A reporter doing a story on the introduction of a major foot-patrol-beat system for police arranged through the public-relations office of the police to meet two officers on patrol. The location selected was the 'Yonge Street strip', a segment of a street widely visualized in the city as a centre of vice and disorderliness. One police officer was wired up with a tape recorder, and two were followed down the street by the reporter, cameraman and researcher. Shots were taken of the officers going into stores, talking to people on the street, interviewing people in an automobile accident, and writing a traffic ticket.

Efforts to film events occurring 'naturally' sometimes ran into difficulty so that staging was necessary. Television crews waited in the mayor's office for the arrival of two people who represented an organization wanting to meet the mayor's executive assistant about a social problem. When the two people arrived and entered the office of the secretary to the executive assistant, they and the television crews 'broke up' laughing at the effort to appear 'natural' in face of a pack of reporters and cameramen. After everyone had regained composure, one television reporter asked the two people to go out of the office and enter again. A proper representation of the event was made on this 'retake'.

Reporters sometimes set out to recreate what had occurred previously without always stating to the audience that it was a recreation. The RCMP had sent some illegal drugs to an incinerator, but part of the shipment was lost. A reporter decided to visualize the incineration process on film. At the incineration plant, she had visuals taken of the fire itself, a 'pretend' run of a crane picking up the garbage and dropping it into the incinerator, the temperature gauge, and a conveyor belt carrying indestructible materials left behind after the ashes were washed away. These visuals, visualizing the process, were then used by the reporter in juxtaposition with a description of what was believed to have taken place weeks before, when the drugs went missing. The result was a blend of illusion and accounts of reality, as is evident in the following script of the story.

Anchorperson roll-up:	The RCMP had it . . . but it slipped out of their hands. In the process of destroying the largest-ever cache of drugs seized in Canada . . . one million dollars' worth went missing. The mounties had wanted to get rid of the stuff but not in the way it disappeared. It has been recovered . . . but police are still trying to figure out how it got lost. (Names reporter) has more.
Reporter:	They tried to burn it away . . . faced with the problem of disposing six tonnes of methagaeline . . . heroin substitute . . . (fire burning in furnace). RCMP took it to the Metro Toronto incinerating plant (Sign: Metro Inc. Plant). On that day in June, an RCMP truck arrived with its precious cargo . . . (truck dumping garbage) it

came and went four times with 200 million dollars' worth of drugs, packed in Sunlight detergent boxes . . . (Sunlight detergent box).

While three RCMP officers supervised . . . a crane picked up the drugs with the other garbage and dropped it into the hopper leading to the incinerator. But inside the incinerator . . . (a Metro works official) explains, the drug made it too hot (crane and hopper travelling and dropping) (Metro works official talking head).

Reporter: When the temperature went up to a critical point they shut down the incinerator . . . One truck load was turned away and the RCMP were informed the drug clogged the incinerator. Somehow one box was neither burned away nor returned to the RCMP (temperature gauge, followed by shot of truck coming down ramp).

The RCMP didn't even know one million dollars' worth of drugs was missing . . . that is until Metro Toronto police stopped a car three weeks later and found hidden in a suitcase thirty-five pounds of meth . . . three people were subsequently charged for possession of drugs and one of them is an employee of the incinerating plant . . . (stand-up) Inspector (name) and his staff were the ones who announced the huge heist of meth . . . last October . . . (Super: stock film showing RCMP) it was a dramatic seizure of drugs at Collingwood airport . . . (still graphic: police firing guns with an airplane in the background).

Even though the missing box went unnoticed for three weeks . . . (the inspector) says he's sure there isn't any more on the streets . . . (box).

RCMP Inspector: I would be very surprised if there's another box missing . . . (etc.) (talking head).

Reporter: The RCMP has used this plant three times . . . (Sign: Metro Inc. Plant) workers don't have special security clearances . . . the RCMP assumes full responsibility (truck going down ramp).

RCMP Inspector: Our procedure . . . (etc.) completely recalculated to make sure they get into the fire box. (talking head).

Reporter: The remaining drugs will be neutralized by a chemical process (pick up drug in box . . .).

This story used visuals of the incineration process – including 'fakes' – to represent what happens in talking about what happened. The audience was offered the illusion of watching the actual dumping of the drugs, the detergent box used, etc., at the time. There was no mention that this was a reconstruction of what *may* have happened. Similarly, the artist's graphic of the original seizure of drugs ten months before was simply his visualization of what happened at the time. Apart from the talking heads, all the visuals were simply visualizations of how events might have appeared, and of how things might have looked in the improbable event a 'live-eye' television crew had been there at the time. Faced with the impossibility of being 'everywhere', television news is left to visualize things as if they are.

Stocks

Time and space considerations influenced decisions about whether to use stocks (old visuals) from previous stories to represent something. A reporter faced with a distant event, an event that had already occurred, an event occurring in a physical space he could not penetrate, and/or an encroaching deadline, often turned to the stocks for something to add vision to his story. A considerable amount of 'research' in the television newsroom consisted of searches for appropriate stocks, and special 'researchers' were employed to assist reporters in this regard.

The choice of stocks also involved 'fake' elements. A reporter doing a story on an Ontario government report concerning domestic violence, including police response to it, had difficulty finding appropriate shots of police attending a domestic call. He and an editor searched for and eventually found stock footage from a story done five months earlier, involving the domestic-response team for the city of Detroit, Michigan. This footage visualized police officers talking with a woman, and was used with a voice-over stating: 'The report says wife battering must be treated as a crime ... that the onus for laying charges in such cases should be with the police.' Of course the reporter's intention was not to lie with these shots of police – not to indicate that Detroit police should be seen to be helping Ontario women – but that the police institution should be doing more of what was represented in these pictures.

The only real concern in using this form of representation was that it not be seen through as an obvious fake. Thus, there was concern that repeated use of the same stock clip, especially to represent aspects of different stories rather than the same continuing story, would look bad. Moreover the stock clips usually had to look as if they appeared to have been taken at the time of the shots actually taken on the day. A reporter was preparing a story about an accused person, released after a preliminary hearing, who had decided to sue various officials for malicious prosecution and negligence. The reporter relied on stocks of the attorney general's office building to use with a voice-over stating this office was named in the suit. This story was in August, but the stock shot of the building showed it to be winter. The reporter had a close-up 'freeze' of the building edited to get rid of the snow in the wider shot. The reporter relied on stocks of police officers on motorbikes to use with a voice-over stating the chief of police and investigating officers were also named in the suit. This stock film had a background of trees with no leaves, indicating that it was not in August, but in this case the reporter did not ask for it to be 'frozen'. The regular memos from the executive producer included critiques about the use of stocks which laid bare the fact that they did not represent the time the story was done. One such memo complained that a particular reporter had all day to shoot new footage, but had relied on stock footage with snow on the ground when it was summer. Even though everyone could see that a particular visual clip was a representation, it was not to appear as a 'fake'.

VISUALS AND TEXTS

The research literature emphasizes that television journalism is still dominated by the written text, and most of the conventions of print journalism are therefore applied in television journalism. If anything, the visual requirement serves as a limiting factor on television texts, meaning that they have less depth and range of opinion than is available in the quality press. Nevertheless the construction of a coherent text is paramount in most instances. . . . The early news broadcasts of BBC television included sound only and, even a decade after its establishment in 1957, the BBC television news bulletin was in essence a radio bulletin read to camera, with a few illustrations. Even in the contemporary period television news has been portrayed as 'visual radio' . . . because the spoken word predominates, linking and ultimately binding the visual images. . . .

The traditional interpretive role of the print journalist is sustained through the considerable degree to which the journalist himself appears, or voices-over, other visuals, talking about things that happened elsewhere. While clips with sources are termed 'actualities', they too involve the source talking about what has gone on, or is going on, in another time at a different place. The need for talk from sources, and for the reporter to connect their talk in the maintenance of a flow, means the text forecloses on the range of visual options. Visuals only rise to the forefront 'when the material is exclusive, exceptionally dramatic and has unusual immediacy' . . . A shot of a person leaping from a building that is in flames may speak for itself. However, most visual material consists of people speaking for themselves. In this respect, television most often pictures the sources who form part of the text, a capability also available to newspapers through still photographs.

The reporter constantly visualizes what visuals can be obtained in relation to the text he imagines to be appropriate and what can fit with what his sources have said. This relation is dialectical, with amendments to both text and visuals being made at every stage of the reporting process. The extent to which one or the other predominates is related to the nature of the matter being reported on. In a story on a public demonstration several video cameramen were sent to obtain copious material; video was selected because it does not require processing and can be edited with much greater speed. The reporter then returned to the newsroom to screen the videotapes and in that process took notes for an accompanying text. Only after the screening was the text prepared, with the reporter indicating explicitly to the researcher how the script was written in accordance with the visuals obtained. In contrast we witnessed scripts being written in advance and then tinkered with as required by source-interview material obtained and stocks available. When the requirement was simply to update a continuing story, then the updated information – augmented by background information, usually from newspaper clippings – was the core of the matter and written much [as] a newspaper journalist would write it. However, because something had to be put up on the screen, the journalist scrambled to obtain generic visuals, stocks, graphics, or whatever else would fill the bill.

The importance of visuals was revealed when there were problems in obtaining them. If particular visuals could not be obtained, or if obtained were deemed to be lacking in drama, immediacy or exclusivity, then the entire story was sometimes dropped. Thus a reporter assigned to a story on Monday regarding a murder on the previous weekend initially screened some film a weekend crew had obtained. The film was of poor quality and there were only two things shown: the apartment building where the incident occurred, showing a third-floor balcony, and two detectives looking around for evidence. With no body and no police-car visuals, the reporter said he did not think he could build a story around it and the item was eventually dropped.

When there were inadequate visuals – often in the face of severe time limitations to search for stocks or to dispatch a crew, or in face of the material limitation of no crew available – one option was to do a script for the anchorperson to read. This script was sometimes accompanied by whatever visuals were available, but usually only included a head-on shot of the anchorperson reading what the reporter had written for him. This situation arose also when physical space was difficult or impossible to penetrate for visuals. For example, reporters doing court stories were prevented from filming in the courtroom or courthouse. They usually relied upon a graphic artist's representation of the key actors during the day in court, supplemented if possible by source interviews outside the courtroom and stocks of the original incident or investigation related to the court hearing. A typical court story we observed entailed the use of five graphics with the reporter's voice-over. We also observed instances in which not even an artist's conception was obtained, and the anchorperson was left to say what the reporter had written.

Visuals were used to make statements beyond the scripted text. A reporter was doing a story on fear among women, in the context of a reported series of incidents of attacks on women. She decided to take shots of a 'secluded' area in a park where a woman had been raped while sunbathing in her swimming suit. On location, there were approximately 100 men, women and children in the area. The reporter had the cameraman isolate two women in swimming suits sitting on a bench, with no other people in the background. This clip was later used in the story, suggesting that even after the rape there were women foolhardy enough to be in this 'secluded' area of the park and wearing only scanty clothing.

In the ideological use of visuals there was usually textual material to set the stage and give preferred readings of what the reporter was representing. . . . A reporter covering a well-policed demonstration by persons opposed to nuclear weapons began his item with a series of shots of police dragging demonstrators off a roadway. Instead of his own words, he used a background audio clip of demonstrators elsewhere on the site singing 'Give

Peace a Chance'. A shot of a woman being led by a policeman who had hold of her hair was selected to fit with a textual statement, 'For the most part police used as little violence as possible.' Here the reporter was suggesting visually that this was a possible instance of excessive use of force, even while the text standing by itself was less suggestive of police excesses.

In a story on local residents' opposition to the establishment of a halfway house for prisoners, the reporter wanted to visualize a view that people felt threatened and there was potential for danger. In order to do so she not only obtained a talking head of a spokesperson for the citizens in opposition, but went to the location of the house proposed for this use to obtain suggestive visuals. On location she had the cameraman picture the house alongside the one next door, which had a for-sale sign on it. This was done in the context of a newspaper story which cited the potential centre's next-door neighbour as being concerned about the safety of her two children. 'Are they sex offenders, drug offenders, or what?' The suggestion to be left was that the house was for sale because the neighbour was concerned about 'criminals' moving into the neighbourhood. Shots were also taken of young children walking through the park across the street from the house, suggestive that with the park so accessible to the house, children might be easy prey. Visualizations of deviance of this type were rendered more easily and subtly with the aid of television visuals. In print, reporters would be quite unlikely to say, 'Since this park is directly across the street from the house, criminals are likely to watch for children playing in the park and calculate whom they can victimize.' They might obtain a quotation from a local resident expressing this fear, but even that is arguably less immediate and dramatic than *showing* the physical possibility with visuals.

Time to Adjust Your Set

When Parliament first debated ending the BBC's monopoly of television by allowing a channel supported by advertising, some compared the prospect to the coming of the Black Death. Lord Reith, the corporation's first director-general, talked of 'betrayal and surrender'. Just two years after the launch of a commercial channel in 1955, the BBC's share of the audience had collapsed to 28 per cent.

The BBC survived, and recovered some of its lost viewers. Now it faces a far more serious challenge. Increasingly, it will have to compete with hundreds of new television channels. As they erode the BBC's audience, they will inevitably erode the corporation's legitimacy. Most of the BBC's considerable income comes from the licence fee – a flat tax, which will rise [in 1996] to £89.50, on every home with a television set. People who do not pay and cannot meet the consequent fine can be imprisoned, as 1,555 people (one-third of them women) have been in the . . . two years [before 1995]. How can this tax possibly be justified once viewers desert the BBC?

The BBC's share of the national television audience has already fallen to 42 per cent, from 50 per cent in 1989. In the 20 per cent of homes that receive cable or satellite television, it accounts for only 28 per cent of total viewing. In radio, where lots of new commercial services have become freely available, its share has dropped from 66 per cent in 1990, when commercial radio was deregulated, to just under 50 per cent.

But the legitimacy of the licence fee is not the only problem that the multiplication of channels creates for the BBC. The newcomers will have revenues that are more cyclical but also more buoyant than the licence fee. The corporation's revenue has long been bolstered by the switch from monochrome to colour sets, which carry a higher fee. That change is over. From now on, the BBC's licence-fee revenues – £1.7 billion out of a total income of £2.1 billion ($3.2 billion) – will be determined purely by the increase allowed by the government. Inflation-linked increases have been promised only until 2001.

While the BBC's revenues are constrained, those of its competitors, the regional independent television companies (ITV) and BSkyB, the subscription satellite service part-owned by Rupert Murdoch's News International, are not [Figure 6.1]. Even the BBC expects the net advertising revenues of its commercial rivals to grow 50 per cent in real terms over the next decade,

Figure 6.1 Retuning:
Television market share
Sources: David Graham &
Associates; Zenith Media;
London Economics

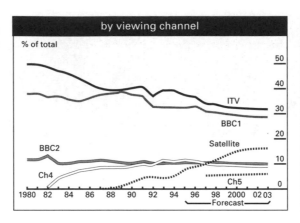

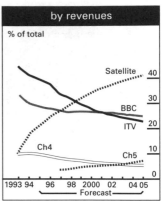

and their subscription revenues to quadruple. As a result, the BBC's competitors will be able to outbid it in any battle to buy sports rights, film rights or new programmes. They have already begun to do just that. On 13 December [1995] the ITV companies jointly bought the rights to screen Formula One motor racing for five years from 1997. They paid £60 m, ten times what the BBC currently pays for the privilege. The BBC has already lost many rights to football, cricket and rugby.

The Beeb's dilemma is acute: it has to compete for audience share, which costs money, but it receives no direct financial reward if it succeeds. Advertising-supported television can charge advertisers higher rates for big audiences; subscription television can bill viewers directly for channels they particularly want to watch, and in future for particular programmes. But whether the BBC snares an audience of 23 m, as it did for its interview with Princess Diana, or 2 m makes no difference to its main source of

Plate 6.1 When
Auntie was queen of
the airwaves

Plate 6.2 Once the eyes and ears of the nation

revenue. In spite of a licence fee that costs the equivalent of a penny on income tax, it may be unable to afford the programmes that people most want to watch.

A MAN WITH A MISSION

The BBC's problems are not unique. All over the world, public broadcasters are in retreat from the onslaught of new commercial channels. For example, Germany's two public networks, ARD and ZDF, together lost 44 per cent of their audience between 1990 and 1994. Spain's TVE lost almost 20 per cent. NHK, Japan's public broadcaster, found in a survey [in 1995] that, although 90 per cent of people in their fifties and sixties watched its programmes at least once a week, the 'contact rate' dwindled with each succeeding age group, to a mere 50 per cent among people in their twenties. Perhaps with hindsight public-service broadcasting will seem a freak of technology: for a rare half-century, it was possible for one medium to communicate the same material to most of a country's population. If so, is there any role for the BBC?

The man with the job of answering that question – John Birt, the corporation's director-general – has neither the broad-mouthed antipodean aggression of Sam Chisholm, BSkyB's chief executive, nor the arbitrary irascibility of Michael Green, chief executive of Carlton Communications, Britain's biggest commercial broadcaster. But Mr Birt probably arouses more ire among his staff than just about any boss in Britain.

In spite of a notorious enthusiasm for management theories, Mr Birt's most obvious shortcoming is his lack of previous management experience. He came to the BBC in 1987 as deputy director-general, having been a director of programmes at London Weekend Television, one of the ITV companies. From there, he went in 1993 to the top BBC job, with responsibility for an organization employing 25,000 people – more than the rest of the broadcasting industry combined. He has proved a skilful political lobbyist, but less successful as a manager. Up to now, since most of the BBC's revenues come from a single tax, lobbying politicians has probably been the more important skill.

Mr Birt's main concern has been to secure the renewal of the BBC's royal charter, the document which sets out the conditions under which it operates. When he arrived, it looked as though the government might sell or dismantle the BBC. Instead, not only did the government renew the charter, it gave the BBC another ten years of guaranteed life. In the eyes of many outsiders, the renewal of the charter has been Mr Birt's outstanding achievement. In the eyes of many of his staff, on the other hand, it was a foregone conclusion. This complacency was helped along by a book by Steven Barnett and Andrew Curry (*The Battle for the BBC*, Aurum Press), which argued that the government's enthusiasm for privatizing the BBC had waned by the time Mr Birt arrived. If such complacency prevails, it will be hard to press on with the changes which are still needed at the BBC if it is to survive the transition that lies ahead.

MIND THE GAP

Mr Birt identifies the BBC's dilemma accurately. The licence fee has not risen in real terms since 1985–6. 'But we have to buy rights, and raise pay, and invest in programmes and expand our services. We have been able to do it by reducing over-capacity. That is coming to an end.' He accepts that, over the ten-year life of the new charter, a 'yawning gap' will emerge between the revenue available to the BBC and the cash available to advertising-supported and subscription broadcasting. The question is how to bridge that gap.

Mr Birt is surely correct that cost-cutting has its limits. But has he gone about it in the right way, or gone far enough? The centrepiece of his cost-control strategy has been the development of an internal market, called 'producer choice': programme makers are told to work within a set budget but allowed to buy services from outside the BBC. As in the National Health Service, which has tried to control costs in a similar manner, the attempt has aroused plenty of criticism. Programme makers complain (as do doctors) that they waste time on paperwork that would be better spent practising their craft, and that bureaucracy has flourished while their budgets have been constrained.

The system has, however, had the great virtue of drawing the attention of programme makers to the financial implications of their actions. On one occasion at the Edinburgh television festival, a producer complained of having to pay £140 because somebody on a set had hurriedly needed a bow tie: the initial cost of the tie had been inflated by a taxi fare and a handling fee. Somebody else pointed out that the fee was a reasonable penalty for poor planning.

A more serious charge, made by Patrick King, head of entertainment and media consulting at Price Waterhouse, is that the internal market lacks safeguards to stop programme makers taking decisions which may make sense for their budgets, but cost the BBC as a whole more money. As a result, newspaper diary columns frequently carry tales of musicians rehearsing in a cheap church hall while the BBC's own rehearsal rooms go unused, or of the BBC's expensively trained designers resigning their jobs at the corporation to do the same job for the same programme maker, but as private subcontractors and at a higher charge.

Moreover, the fact that the BBC's own production staff cannot readily tout for outside work to help to support their overheads, for fear of being seen to use the licence fee to undercut rivals, inevitably tilts the balance against them. And, while private-sector competitors can price their services on the basis of marginal cost to win additional business, the corporation's own departments have to incorporate their full share of overheads in their pricing.

The real test of 'producer choice', though, is whether it has cut costs without jeopardizing quality. Certainly there is little sign that the quality of the corporation's main output has declined; and the hours broadcast have risen. Meanwhile the cost of production facilities has fallen, the BBC claims, by around one-third since 1989. Staff numbers, which had been rising at the end of the 1980s, have fallen: almost 6,000 people were made redundant between 1991 and 1995. More recently, the headcount has been static. In March 1993 the corporation (excluding the World Service) employed 21,945 people; two years later, 22,160. Yet bleats from programme makers about a shortage of cash have reached a crescendo.

Moreover, the central bureaucracy remains largely unscathed. Many signs of flabby management remain: large premises, low morale, squads of policy advisers tripping over armies of outside consultants, and a board of management too large and divided to do its difficult job effectively. The personnel department sees its job mainly in terms of pay-slips and numbers. Indeed, the clearest sign of management failure is the poverty of internal communications. 'Producer choice' might work better if more programme makers were persuaded of the case for it.

WHERE TO CUT?

Preserving morale while cutting costs is never easy. For the BBC, the difficulty has been compounded by its public role. It is hemmed in by government-imposed obligations. When, for example, it decided earlier this year to merge CWR, its local radio station in Coventry, with Radio WM in nearby Birmingham, there was uproar: protests by both the Mayor and the Bishop of Coventry, and a motion in the House of Commons signed by over 100 MPs. A long list of advisory bodies had to be informed. The BBC's extensive regional offices would be one of the first places that a commercial owner would look for savings. Yet it is BBC policy to move one-third of network production outside London. When the licence fee is paid by viewers all over the country, what makes poor financial sense may still be prudent politics.

If not in the regions, where else are savings to be found? Mr Birt hopes that a big increase in efficiency can be achieved with new digital technologies, which will allow a single programme maker to gather material and edit it. He wants to digitize the corporation's vast archive of programmes, and to install broadband links connecting the BBC's various outposts. But all this will require heavy capital investment over the next two years. On top of that, the BBC will have to invest in digital transmission if it is to take advantage of the provision in the government's new broadcasting bill for it to be awarded the most desirable frequencies for digital terrestrial television.

Where is the money to come from? Some will be drawn from the privatization of the BBC's transmission capacity. The corporation will be allowed to keep 80 per cent of the proceeds, provided they go towards making a success of digital television. (This device will steer an additional subsidy to public broadcasting past the grasping hands of the Treasury.) Some may come from the 'private finance initiative', the government's plan to encourage the private sector to invest in public-sector projects. But a third source may also be tapped. Some of the BBC's managers are starting to wonder whether the BBC's production facilities – design, costume, lighting – should be privatized. The presumption is still in favour of keeping them in-house. But the effect of 'producer choice' has been to create semi-independent business units that would be relatively easy to spin off.

. . . AND WHERE TO RAISE REVENUE?

One of the remarkable aspects of the BBC's new charter, published in draft in November [1995], is that it gives the corporation the right to provide, alone or with a partner, services which are financed by 'advertisements, subscription, sponsorship, pay-per-view system or any other means of finance'. The aim is clear: the BBC has to become more commercial, hitching itself to more buoyant sources of revenue.

In time, the BBC may have to do without the licence fee altogether. But no government will find it easy to remove, at one fell swoop, a £1.7 billion subsidy to broadcasting. More probably, the BBC will eventually offer a mixture of publicly financed and subscription-supported programming. Indeed, the BBC's eagerness to get into digital television (in marked contrast to the nervous hesitation of most ITV companies) springs from the fact that it sees in digital broadcasting a chance to build an array of lucrative new subscription services.

Developing these services entails two obvious risks. First, the government may simply subtract the revenue which the BBC raises from subscription television from the licence fee. Secondly, the BBC's rivals will watch like hawks to see whether the revenue from the licence fee is being used to subsidize its commercial activities. Parliament too will take a dim view of the use of licence-fee money to finance commercial risks. Keeping the BBC's commercial activities and public-service operations completely separate will be difficult. In any case, the stubbornly public-sector culture of the BBC may well thwart its attempts to develop commercial activities.

Undeterred, the BBC has made a start. Bob Phillis, the deputy director-general recruited from commercial television, heads BBC Worldwide, a division set up in 1994 to develop commercial revenues. One aim is to market BBC programmes more effectively. Both Mr Birt and Mr Phillis rue the fact that two successful American cable channels, Discovery and Arts & Entertainment, were launched with the help of underpriced BBC material. Another is to develop global television services. In January 1995 two new services were launched outside Britain: BBC World, a news channel and, in a joint venture with Pearson (part-owners of the *Economist*), BBC Prime, an advertising-supported channel devoted to entertainment.

This commercial division paid a contribution of £72 m to the BBC in 1994–5. Of that, about £50 m represented revenues from co-productions, channelled through it to the BBC. Mr Phillis hopes to be able to triple the £72 m total in real terms over the next decade. As income from co-production is unlikely to rise much, that will be a tall order. It will certainly require a cultural revolution in the corporation.

For, without capital, the corporation must proceed mainly through joint ventures. But those who have done business with the BBC in the past year sound apoplectic. 'Frankly, they couldn't run a bath', says one manager at Pearson. Michael Grade, a BBC alumnus who is boss of Channel 4, a broadcaster supported by advertising which also has a public-service mission, describes with despair the correspondence that followed his attempt to buy some archive material from the corporation. ('I have recently recruited a director of distribution strategy and as soon as he arrives he will be reviewing our strategy.') Another argues that joint ventures are possible 'only if the BBC is bound and gagged in the back seat; not if it gets its hands anywhere near the steering wheel'.

Such anecdotes augur badly. They suggest that radical change will be needed if the BBC is to develop commercial instincts. Yet far from entering a period of crisis, the BBC may be about to enjoy an Indian summer. The ITV companies face competition from Channel 5, a new commercial terrestrial channel which is due to start broadcasting by early 1997. BSkyB, although it is prosperous, has now signed up the most eager viewers and will have a harder time recruiting new ones. Meanwhile the BBC has ten years of guaranteed subsidy. Although a Labour government might resent the unfairness of the licence fee, it would be unlikely to be tougher on the BBC than the Tories have been.

The warmth of an Indian summer would be dangerously beguiling. Britain's biggest broadcaster has huge advantages: an astonishing array of talent, a deserved reputation for quality and a world-famous name. It operates in English, the global language of media. Its guaranteed finance gives it the security and the shelter from market pressures to experiment and to invest in unusual programmes.

But it lacks the two essential ingredients for building on these advantages: an entrepreneurial instinct and access to capital. The deals that will shape global broadcasting in the first quarter of the next century are being done now – by the likes of Rupert Murdoch, Time Warner, Disney and Bertelsmann. The BBC, in its present public-sector, tax-financed form, has no hope of participating. That is why the BBC's Indian summer may only presage a sad and wintry death.

READING 28

Steven Levy with Katie Hafner and Adam Rogers

The Internet and Global Communications

Tucked in the back of a low-slung building off a highway service road in Mountain View, California, is one of the few physical epicentres of the virtual monster that ate 1995: the Internet. Walk past a handful of windowless offices – some of them populated by exhausted programmers in sleeping bags – turn left at the mountain bikes and enter the eerie, air-conditioned serenity of a small room stuffed with racks of dull metallic monitorless computers.

'This is one of the most populated nodes on the Net – there's a million visitors a day here', says Jerry Yang, co-founder of Yahoo!, an electronic guide to the Internet that has established itself as one of cyberspace's hottest addresses. Yes, the consciousness of 1 million human beings is moving through this undistinguished square of sheet rock. Such is the magic of the Net. Less than two years ago Yang was a slacker grad student at Stanford who with his friend David Filo started listing favourite destinations on the then cutting-edge World Wide Web. Now Yahoo! is a venture capital-backed corporation with a lofty business plan, marketing executives and a recent development deal with magazine giant Ziff-Davis. Yang gives speeches to audiences of gape-jawed entrepreneurs, gets profiled in *People* and *Rolling Stone* and is on the fast track to joining the burgeoning pool of Internet multi-millionaires. It was as if Yang and Filo had opened a lemonade stand in a hayfield and a year later found themselves surrounded by skyscrapers. They were positioned in exactly the right place during the Year of the Internet.

Can you recall a day when there *wasn't* some gee-whiz Internet story in the newspapers? Was there ever a time when surfing was performed in a bathing suit, outdoors? When advertisements on buses did not emblazon a string of puzzling letters beginning with HTTP:// and getting weirder from there? When Java meant coffee, and showbiz insiders used the term

Web to refer to a saurian entity known as a television network? When you didn't know how to verbally articulate the @ sign? If you strain, perhaps you can remember such a time – 1994. There was an Internet then, but it lurked under most of our personal radar screens. When we heard of the Information Highway, we thought of 500 channels of cable television, half of which would be home-shopping networks or pay-per-view movie channels showing Hugh Grant comedies in staggered time slots.

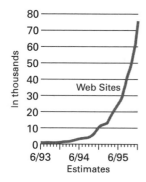

Figure 6.2 Widening Web
Sources: Mathew Gray, Net.Genesis

But in 1995, the Internet ruled. Early on it became clear that the explosive growth of the Web – the part of the Internet that enables even neophytes to embark on digital tours of the world's computers [Figure 6.2] – was the killer application that would push the already-growing Net to new levels of activity. One of the first on the bandwagon was Speaker Newt Gingrich, who fulfilled his vow to put Congress on the Web. It was part of a blitzkrieg of home pages (the opening screens of WWW sites), created by everyone from high-school students to non-profit organizations – and especially businesses. 'When we launched [late in 1994] there was no such thing as a commercial Web site', says Chip Bayers, executive editor of *HotWired*, *Wired* magazine's Web-based sibling. Now the number is in six figures. Yahoo! gets 3,000 submissions of new Web sites a day.

'I date the big transition as sometime [in 1995]', says Eric Schmidt, VP [Vice President] of technology for Sun Microsystems, of the time when the Net shifted from geekhood to coolness. 'One day before, the Internet was a specialized thing. Then there was a day when it got into the public consciousness. All of a sudden every business publication had the majority of its ads listing the company's URL [the arcane code that signifies a Web address].' Around that time, the stock market went bonkers with Internet fever. Netscape Communications had the most successful public offering in history; a year-old company with no earnings was instantly valued at more than $2 billion. That began a spiralling updraft in Internet stocks – Netscape would rise to more than $6 billion – creating millionaires by the bushel. (You can track these rich guys, if you want, on an Internet Millionaires home page, where the fortunes of Netscaper Marc Andreessen and other new moguls are recalculated several times daily.) It was also this summer that the media frenzy about so-called cyberporn exploded, and people began worrying whether little Stuart or Janie was using the Performa to download hard-core binaries from some offshore newsgroup.

By November, at the huge Comdex computer trade show, all anyone wanted to talk about was the Internet. Earlier in the year the industry talk was centred on Microsoft's power – was its domination of the computer industry so thorough that the government should break it up? Now people were wondering whether Bill Gates's company was a trapped mastodon, unable to compete in the open-standards world of the Internet. Microscoft gave its reply on 7 December [1995], announcing that it was throwing all its considerable weight towards the Internet 'tidal wave'. It endorsed Java, Sun Microsystems' competing computer language for generating lively inter-active Web pages, and announced that it would gear its applications to work with the Internet. 'The Internet is pervasive in everything we're doing', said Bill Gates.

Then came the news that Microsoft would buy half of an NBC cable channel to establish a two-pronged joint venture – an all-news cable service with an Internet counterpart. Executives from both companies breathlessly described how, on the video-channel report from Bosnia, viewers would see pointers to sites on the Microsoft/NBC on-line venture offering 'great maps' of Bosnia, and perhaps a report on the art museum in Tuzla. It was a perfect symbol of where, in the new Info Highway wisdom, television stood in relation to the Net – Microsoft was buying a cable-TV channel to provide content for its Internet effort!

During the course of the year the discussion of the Internet ranged from sex to stock prices to software standards. But the most significant aspect of the Internet has nothing to do with money or technology, really. It's us. 'The Internet mediates human interaction better than any other medium', says futurist Paul Saffo. 'Getting in touch with each other is more fun than the coolest computer game, or the hottest information.' Just look at the

Plate 6.3
Communication: The best aspect of the Internet has nothing to do with technology. It's us. Getting in touch is more fun than the coolest computer game or the hottest information.
Source: Michael Llewellyn

various things you can do on the Internet. You use e-mail to zip messages to friends and associates, most often at no charge per letter, sending them across the world in a few seconds. You play elaborate games on role-playing 'MUDs', submersing yourself into the guise of a fantasy *doppel-gänger*, and even making virtual love with other people's jerry-built personae. You go on a Usenet newsgroup to flame the scum who disagreed with you on the virtues of last night's episode of *Deep Space Nine*. You use a software browser like Netscape Navigator to cruise the Web, an awesome construct where the publishing efforts of thousands of people are inter-linked into a massive seething monument to human expression, enabling everything from shopping for a new car to keeping track of Madonna's bio-logical clock. And when you create your own Web site, you enjoy the same access to millions as do powerful entities like Sears, IBM or the US govern-ment. In fact, if you didn't start a Web site in 1995, your status may be endangered. 'The technology is successful because it's based on people's natural emotions, including fear, greed and vanity', says Sun's Schmidt. 'They want to show off. If you don't have a Web server, you're nothing in cyberspace.'

You talk about a revolution? For once, the shoe fits. 'In the long run it's hard to exaggerate the importance of the Internet', says Paul Moritz, a Microsoft VP. 'It really is about opening communications to the masses.' And 1995 was the year that the masses started coming. 'If you look at the numbers they're quoting, with the Web doubling every 53 days, that's bio-logical growth, like a red tide or population of lemmings', says Kevin Kelly, executive editor of *Wired*. 'I don't know if we've ever seen technology exhibit that sort of growth.' In fact, there's a raging controversy over exactly how many people regularly use the Net. A recent Nielsen survey pegged the number at an impressive 24 million North Americans. But Donna Hoffman, a business professor at Vanderbilt University, charged that the Nielsen numbers were skewed towards the upscale demographic that dom-inates the Net, and therefore the estimate was too high.

'But there is *no* controversy about what on-line users look like', says Hoffman, explaining why businesses are desperately trying to catch the Internet wave. 'They're demographically attractive – upscale, over-educated people. And the market is now moving into the mainstream – regular people are starting to come on-line. The Internet is clearly racing toward full-fledged status as a commercial medium.'

For all of this, many people, including some experienced Net riders, don't have a good grasp of what the Internet really is. It's sort of a virtual embodiment of Gertrude Stein's description of Oakland, California: there's no there there. Strip away the peels of the Internet onion, and all you have are layers of technology – a bunch of rules for moving data around. These rules, or protocols, were developed by the United States government for research use, but over the past few years government support has been gradually scaled back. Users hook up to the Net through Internet service providers (ISPs) like Netcom or PSI, but those are only middlemen who hook into big regional data lines called backbones. At the top of the pyra-mid, there is no CEO [Chief Executive Officer] of the Internet – the real power lies in those open protocols that ensure that all the information moves smoothly. The closest thing to a ruling body is the Internet Engineering Task Force, though its influence is being overtaken by big-time commercial players. They met earlier this month in Dallas: a group of hippie-hackerish computer scientists. Many had been participants in the forerunner to the Internet: the ARPAnet, a Defense Department network that linked various research sites in the early 1970s. Their unofficial motto is emblazoned on a T shirt: WE REJECT KINGS, PRESIDENTS, AND VOTING, WE BELIEVE IN ROUGH CONSENSUS AND RUNNING CODE.

The miracle of the Internet is that that credo permeates the virtual world. 'There's something about the environment that tends to make people leave their existing culture at the door', says John Barlow, co-founder of the Electronic Frontier Foundation. The components of the Net ethic are easy to identify: voraciously free expression, a drive for individual empowerment, a loathing for authority and a strong libertarian strain that actually welcomes commerce – as long as it follows the live-and-let-live spirit of the Net. Indeed, as a higher share of the population gets wired, business will reshape itself to take advantage of the instant communication with customers the Net will provide.

No one really know what it means to connect hundreds of millions of people together. Whole industries might go away, particularly those involved in modes of distribution that will evaporate when businesses can send the same materials direct to customers over the Net. New sorts of ventures will certainly emerge, but we can't be sure what they'll be. Some projections of where the Internet will take us are so sweeping that the only response is a dumb nod. 'The Net will include TV, radio, all the cash-register data in the world, every traffic sensor in the world', says *Wired*'s

Plate 6.4 Commerce: Businesses salivate at the prospect of reaching customers world-wide from a virtual storefront. But the Net Economy will force every company to change its ways.
Source: Michael Llewellyn

Kevin Kelly. 'It won't be just people talking to each other. It will be people talking to machines, and machines talking to each other.' If all of this is true, much of the world we know is about to fade into the rear-view mirror. Before any of this happens, however, the Internet still has serious obstacles to overcome.

OVERHYPE

Perhaps the biggest short-term danger to the Net is the prospect of millions of newbies jumping on the boat so fired up by, uh, laudatory magazine articles that they confuse the promise with the current reality. The former is a wonderland where set-up is a breeze, Web pages load instantly, junk e-mail does not exist and you can buy any item imaginable with untraceable digital cash. The present-day reality is baffling to install, requires a love of staring at hourglass-shaped cursors and maybe lets you buy Monty Python jokes with an insecure credit-card transaction. Travelling the Net in these pioneer days is like a journey to a rugged, exotic destination – the pleasures are exquisite, but you need some stamina.

Despite this, an oceanload of serious investment is being showered onto the Internet, both in the stock market and into the development of fancy, and increasingly expensive, Web operations. (A classy site will commonly set you back six figures.) A recent study by the Yankee Group claims that most of the businesses venturing into the Net do so with 'little more than a back-of-the-envelope calculation', and some don't even bother with the envelope. Zima liquor can't put interactive ads in *all* of these sites – what happens when the revenues don't pour in?

REGULATION

Go figure – the vice-president and the speaker of the House both swoon with enthusiasm about the Net, but the [US] government's behaviour towards the burgeoning Internet ethic seems more in sync with Sid, the sadistic kid next door in *Toy Story*. The cyberspace crowd is most infuriated with the efforts of Sen. James Exon and Rep. Henry Hyde to ban so-called indecent speech on the Internet. Arguments rage *ad infinitum* over the amount of digital pictures of naked people on the Net and whether high-tech filters can enable parents to zap the filth. But the language approved by the House-Senate conference committee in early December would slap six-figure fines and jail terms for digitally uttering a nasty word.

The proponents of such censorship, urged on by Christian-right activists, make no bones about it – they do not wish to grant the same speech rights in cyberspace that are permitted in newspapers, movies, magazines and books. Despite an Internet Day of Protest where more than 20,000 people flooded congressional offices with phone calls, faxes and e-mail, it's possible that by next year plain speaking on the Net will be illegal. 'People like us are going to litigate', says Marc Rotenberg, head of the Electronic

Privacy Information Center. 'The court is where First Amendment issues belong.' In the meantime, anyone using the unrestrained language that is now as common on the Internet as those smiley-face emoticons will face serious risks. 'My worst nightmare would be to have the Internet turn into something that eroded civil liberties and free speech', says Vint Cerf, an Internet pioneer who now heads MCI's efforts on the Net.

While legislative efforts to make the Net squeaky clean have received all the attention, the question of copyright promises to be, as Lotus Development founder Mitch Kapor puts it, 'the Vietnam of the Net'. The interconnectedness of cyberspace works best when there are no barriers to the free movement of words, images and sounds, but originators of these creations understandably want money for their efforts. Almost everybody agrees that new rules are required to restore some balance. But the Clinton administration's solution, outlined in a recent white paper, wants to apply the old rules, an approach that seems to side so firmly with the copyright owners that Net denizens are alarmed that its provisions will chill the exchange of ideas so essential to the Net. Despite the outcry, the Clintonites aren't budging. 'It's not a culture clash', says Bruce Lehman, the US commissioner of patents and trade-marks. 'It's that people are accustomed to a certain environment on the Internet and they can't quite envision a time when the Internet will be a market-place in which people want to sell valuable products.'

SECURITY

A recent Yankelovich survey of cybersavvy respondents brought more proof of what everybody already knows: security, not porn, is the No. 1 concern of Internet users. As we rush headlong toward electronic commerce, the basic infrastructure of the Internet – which was designed to zip data around unpoliced – still hasn't been modified to make sure that snoops and thieves can't grab private information off your computers or read your e-mail. Meanwhile, dozens of companies are making plans to introduce digitized forms of money – but can we trust them?

On 10 December [1995], there was yet another report of a potential hole in the Internet wall. Paul Kocher, a 23-year-old security consultant, discovered that under certain circumstances a predator, by carefully measuring the amount of time it takes a potential victim to scramble data, can get enough information to get the victim's cryptography key. Once a crook or a snoop has your key, it's easy to read all your messages and monitor your transactions. 'It's a significant security problem but it can be addressed', says Kocher. Then it's on to whatever bug is discovered next. 'It's a process of continual improvement', says Jim Bidzos, president of RSA Data Security Co. 'Perfect security on the Internet will never exist.'

TECHNICAL OVERLOAD

Will the waves of new users overwhelm the Internet? It doesn't take a stop-watch to notice that things are going s-l-o-w-e-r than they used to – despite more high-speed data 'backbones' added to the Internet and a general user upgrade from pokey 9600-baud modems to faster models. Owners of popular Web sites are noticing that it takes longer for their users to download information than it took only a few months ago. Milo Medin, a vice president of @Home, a company planning to exploit high-speed cable modems on the Internet, compares the phenomenon to the heat death of the universe, where entropy dissipates the available heat to unusable levels: in this case so many people are competing for bandwidth that almost no one gets enough. Blame it on the Web – with sound, images and even video, a whizzy home page requires people to shove ever more bits through the wires, just to view family pictures or hear a punk-rock melody.

Is it possible that the whole Net might totally crash, leaving millions of computer screens with the dread 'Host Contacted: Waiting for Reply' message frozen upon them? Unlikely, say the Internet wizards. 'The network is wired to route around trouble', says Einar Stefferud, a networking consultant. But the Net is also prone to glitches, as occurred last spring [1995] when apparently someone in Florida trying to access a computer at MIT flubbed the process in such a way that for 30 minutes all the voluminous Internet traffic destined for MIT wound up going into a tiny wire in Florida. (Picture all the flights destined for O'Hare landing in your driveway.) Eventually, the Net will handle all these problems, but for now 'there's no relief in sight', says Medin. 'It's like the New York City infrastructure – you can fix things but it takes time. As fast as we network people add capacity there's new applications.'

These obstacles will have their effect on the Internet, but the expanding base of true believers is certain that the Net's growth, as well as its impact on our society, will only accelerate. Maybe the Net really is evolving to some sort of self-healing organic system, made of wires, silicon and a superb collection of human brains and emotions. Though some folks are making millions – billions! – on the Net, the real fuel for the excitement is the connectedness, the thrill of putting one's own brick into the ultimate edifice of human creation. Only if this essential collaborative aspect of the Net is compromised can any company or individual dominate it. Adherents believe that the Net will never let that happen. 'I have heard people say the hype can't last', says Sun's Eric Schmidt. 'But so far if you were to bet on that point of view you would have lost all your money. There are stakeholders in the Internet. They fix the problems. The bandwidth isn't wide enough, we give more. If government tries to stop it, the Net reconnects around [borders].'

It's bad news for neo-Luddites and low-techers: you'll have to put up with a continued fusillade of hyperbole about this new medium. In the next twelve months you'll be hearing plenty about 'hot' Web pages, blazingly fast cable modems, $500 Internet terminals and cyberspace coverage of the [US] presidential election. No matter that most people in the United States have yet to log on, let alone net-surf. In 1996, maybe they will.

'If this year seemed like a big one for the Net, wait till the next one', says the EFF's John Barlow. 'You ain't seen nothing yet.'

Part VII

Marriage and the Family

Among the changes now affecting modern societies few are more profound than those acting to transform the nature of personal life. Over the past several decades, in virtually all the industrialized countries, divorce rates have risen sharply, while the proportion of people in the 'orthodox' family (biological father and mother living with their children in the same household) has declined very substantially. There is a great deal of experimentation in personal life, and no one can be sure where patterns of family development will lead in the future.

The first selection (Reading 29) considers the implication of the changes happening in the family. Is the family indeed collapsing? The author considers comparative evidence from several different societies to assess this question.

Reading 30, by Gwynn Davis and Mervyn Murch, considers the causes of marriage breakdown in current times. The authors identify several factors which might underlie high rates of divorce. Possible influences include a reduction in the stigma associated with divorce; the movement from marriage as an economic division of labour towards a personal relationship valued for the intimacy it provides; and the increasing emancipation of women. As the authors point out, the majority of divorce petitions are now lodged by women rather than men – a reversal of major proportions, when considered in historical terms.

In spite of growing gender equality, the income of men is on average much higher than that of women. What impact does this differential have upon control of finances and patterns of spending within marriage? Jan Pahl (Reading 31) studied the issue by interviewing more than a 100 married couples from varying class backgrounds. She found that the higher the income group, the more likely the husband is to control the family finances. Where finances are pooled, women tend to be more responsible for domestic expenses, while husbands are more likely to determine major financial decisions.

The family is often associated in people's minds with a cosy environment of warm domesticity. While the image may frequently be an appropriate one, the family is often the site of violence. Most such violence, although not all, is directed by men against women. As Elizabeth Stanko (Reading 32) points out, only a tiny proportion of wife-battering ever comes to the notice of the authorities. The phenomenon is extremely widespread; yet many women, for a mixture of practical and psychological reasons, find that escaping from a violent marriage or relationship is difficult.

In Reading 33 Joan Chandler examines the various circumstances in which women live alone, giving particular attention to the separated, divorced and widowed. A high proportion of women living alone, or living as a lone head of household, find themselves in poverty. Well over half of women over 65 and lone mothers live below the poverty line, compared to about 30 per cent of all other households.

READING 29

Home Sweet Home: The Debate About Family Values

To European ears, America's 'family values' debate can sound shrill, even surreal. It is taken as a sign that the citizens of the new world remain considerably less sophisticated, and more moralistic, than those of the old. But Europe would do well to listen. In many American neighbourhoods, the family has collapsed: among households with children in poor inner cities, fewer than one in ten has a father in residence. If there are lessons from this awful experience, they are worth learning.

Many argue that the plight of the inner cities reflect a wider social malaise. America and Europe alike are witnessing profound changes in the structure of the family – increases in divorce and in births outside marriage. Great economic and social forces, combined with policy itself partly shaped by those forces, have weakened the link between parenthood and partnership. Compared with thirty years ago, it is easier for women to raise children without men, and for men to escape the burdens of fatherhood.

Plate 7.1

The weakening of that link has hurt children. Multi-generational studies in Sweden, Britain and America all seem to show that, compared with their peers of the same economic class, children in lone-parent families do less well in school, get in trouble more often and have more emotional and health problems. They are also more likely to become single parents themselves.

Demands for government to arrest the decline of the family are mounting. If governments were to heed these calls, what could they do?

SOLO SWEDES AND GERMAN GROUPINGS

Governments act in ways that, intentionally or otherwise, affect the family: in this sense, every country has a 'family policy'. In Britain and America, these policies are a mess. To see how they might be changed, it is helpful to look at systems elsewhere. In Europe, the most distinctive approaches are those of Sweden and Germany. These start from very different assumptions about what such policy should be, but each acts upon a relatively coherent philosophy. Both manage to do moderately well by their children.

Sweden defines itself as a nation of individuals; its policy reflects that outlook. There is no married-couple's allowance, no tax deduction for children, no way to file jointly for income tax. Benefits are also assessed on an individual basis.

This treatment dates from reforms in the early 1970s. Sweden had a labour shortage and wanted to encourage married women into the job market. High marginal tax rates on joint filings, however, took an enormous bite out of a second income. By taxing both incomes independently, a major disincentive to work was removed; and as tax rates increased, two incomes became the norm. As a considered national policy to get women into work, it worked. Sweden has a higher proportion of working women than any other country. Everyone is expected to have a job. Mothers with young children generally work part-time.

Swedes are not particularly religious, and with such an individualized tax structure it is no surprise that many couples do not bother to marry. About half the babies in Sweden are born to unwed mothers, though very few are born to young girls. And although nineteen out of twenty babies will go home to a father, many will not grow up with one. Half of Swedish marriages end in divorce, and unmarried parents split up three times as often as married ones. The result is that the number of lone-parent families as a proportion of all families with children has increased steadily, to 18 per cent in 1991.

The children in those families will not necessarily be in material need, though they do tend to be slightly worse off. Generous benefits mean that if one parent leaves, the other parent and children do not slip into poverty. Child support enforcement is ferocious. In 1990, only 6.8 per cent of Swedish children lived in families with less than half the average income. Though there are no premiums for children in the Swedish tax code, there are numerous state-supported goodies for them – parental leave, subsidized day care, leave to care for sick children and so on. This may be why

Swedish women have more children than their European sisters. It is the only OECD country in which the birth rate has increased since 1970.

Germany, by contrast, is a nation of families. People are legally required to help elderly parents and hard-up family members. There are tax allowances for dependants and a high level of child benefit. A minimum subsistence level for children is exempt from taxation.

Marriage is rewarded in the tax code. A parent who stays at home to care for a child can keep many of the perks of her job. And it is, normally, hers not his; the old idea of a woman's world dominated by '*Kinder, Küche, Kirche*' – children, kitchen and church – still persists, albeit to a diminishing extent. A full-time parent keeps her pension rights, and cannot be dismissed from her job for three years. When fathers fail to pay up, the state covers the child-support payment and enforces collection.

It is hardly surprising, given its dramatically different policies, that compared to Sweden Germany has: fewer births to unmarried mothers [Figure 7.1]; a higher rate of marriage; a divorce rate a third lower; a smaller percentage of children being raised in one-parent families [Figure 7.2]; and a smaller percentage of women in the workforce. The gaps between the two countries are shrinking, though. Taxes and benefits have an effect on

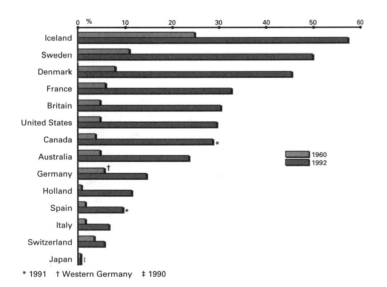

Figure 7.1 Fewer gold rings: Births to unmarried mothers, as percentage of total
Source: Senator Daniel Patrick Moynihan

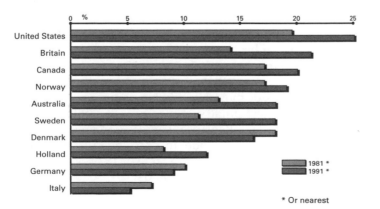

Figure 7.2 More missing fathers: One-parent households with dependent children, as percentage of total households with children
Sources: UNICEF; UN; US Bureau of Labor Statistics

behaviour, but not a decisive one. If government policy was the only factor in such decisions, Sweden would never see a wedding.

NOT BACK TO BASICS

British family policy combines aspects of the Swedish and the German approaches without the coherence of either. The Tory government has preached 'back to basics', an alliterative nostrum not that far in feeling from Germany's three Ks. At the same time, its tax policies have been anything but encouraging to families with children, particularly those in which the father works and the mother stays at home. Since the late 1960s, Britain has steadily moved towards a tax system that treats adults as individuals, not as part of a family unit.

Critics say that these changes have made policy hostile to nuclear families. They have a point. Single adult occupiers pay 25 per cent less local council tax than a married or cohabiting couple, and those with children may be given higher priority for public housing. Taxes have increased more steeply for the married. In 1964 a married couple with two children making the national average paid 9 per cent of its income in tax; now it pays 22 per cent, a faster rise than for single people or childless couples. The married-couple's tax allowance is probably doomed.

According to Patricia Morgan of London's Institute of Economic Affairs, a lone parent may end up with more income after tax than a working father with the same number of children and a dependent wife – even though in the latter case there is an additional adult in the house. Although Ms Morgan's conclusions have been hotly contested, there is little argument that, at lower levels of income, marriage becomes uneconomic. Parents with little money do better on benefit if they live apart than if they live together; boyfriends vanish when social workers come calling. As the Labour-affiliated Institute for Public Policy Research put it in a 1994 study, young mothers may be making a realistic assessment of the available options when they choose not to marry.

This realistic assessment lies behind the most dramatic change in patterns of marriage and parenting. While most British children live with their two natural, married parents, 20 per cent of households with children now contain only one parent. The majority of these single parents are divorced, but an increasing proportion never married, and many became mothers when very young (though the birth rate among teenagers has recently levelled off). One in three British births is out of wedlock. Half those children start life with no father at home; the others run an increased risk of losing him – unmarried fathers are more likely to walk out than married ones.

Almost three-quarters of those households depend on state income support, comprising the largest single group on benefit. Child benefit, itself less generous than the child tax allowance/family allowance it replaced in the mid-1970s, has been allowed to erode. In 1992 one in three British children lived in a poor household, three times the rate of 1979. More than half those poor children live in single-parent households.

AMERICA FIRST

In America families are valued tremendously – so much so that most people will have at least two of them. Americans are religious, but have one of the highest divorce rates in the world. They are ambivalent about abortions but have a lot of them. Government has worked hard to make public policy as contradictory as private choices.

There is a marriage penalty at the middle to upper end of the income-tax schedule: married couples pay more tax than two single people with the same income. Under other conditions there is a marriage bonus. Divorce is easy. Three out of ten American children will sleep in a different home from their father tonight. Among black children, the rate is six out of ten.

Child benefits are low – the government spends four times as much on the elderly as on children, although old people are much better off. Lone parents are six times more likely to be poor than married couples. Benefits designed to alleviate that poverty have put the family under further strain. Until quite recently, women could not get income support if there was a man in the house. The welfare cheque, with its attendant medical benefits and food stamps, became considerably more valuable to have than a low-wage husband and father.

With the breakdown of marriages has come a breakdown in the idea of marriage as a precursor to family life. Half a million teenagers have babies every year; very few of them go home to their father. More than half the 5 m women on welfare started as teenage mothers. Their daughters often follow in their mothers' footsteps; their sons often follow in their fathers'.

WHEN DID YOU LAST SEE YOUR FATHER?

The only common thread to America's chaotic policies is that they are intended to allow adults freedom. That goal is now being questioned. There is widespread agreement that the design of America's modest safety net has helped to destabilize the family. Republican redesigns on offer include time limits and no increase in benefits for additional children; Democrats are talking about work requirements and group homes for teenaged mothers. Few, however, are talking about family policies that affect the middle class, such as state laws on divorce or the erosion of the dependants' allowance.

The problem with the American and British approach is not that benefits are too generous; they are stingy. The fundamental mistake is that fathers have been airbrushed out of the picture. Although there cannot be lone mothers without a roughly equivalent number of fathers lurking some-where, the latter are mostly ignored.

Throughout the world, the lack of fathers is a key factor in the impoverishment of children. In Britain, almost half the single-parent families have incomes of £100 ($155) a week or less, compared with only 5 per cent of couples with children. This is not simply because the poor are more likely to become single parents. As the Rowntree Foundation, a British research organization, notes: 'Poverty is more obviously one of the consequences of breakdown than a cause.' The result of divorce or abandonment is often two poor households rather than a single struggling one. Children bear the brunt: when money is tight, studies show, parental discipline gets harsher and more arbitrary.

A father is not just a cash cow. Daniel Patrick Moynihan, a Democratic senator who has taken these problems seriously for thirty years, says that a community without fathers 'asks for and gets chaos'. As an American, he has been able to see that chaos for some time, but it is now visible elsewhere. There are neighbourhoods in Britain where more than two-thirds of homes with children lack fathers; some of Paris's wilder *banlieues* are not that different.

Humans have long childhoods in order to learn; they are very sensitive to the environment in which they grow up. In most societies, quite possibly throughout the evolution of the species, that environment has contained men – and, in particular, a man who is their mother's partner. If the environment is not like that but society tries to act as if it is, it should be no surprise that the child is affected in all sorts of ways. For boys, the absence of men can induce what sociologist Elijah Anderson calls 'hypermasculinity', characterized by casual, even predatory, sex and violence. Fatherless girls, like their brothers, tend to do less well in school and have greater difficulty in making the transition to adulthood; they are much more likely than girls who grew up with a father to be young and unmarried when they first get pregnant.

Asserting the value of fathers is not to say that lone mothers are rotten; it is to recognize that their children tend to have more of the kinds of social, economic and academic difficulties that a generous society would seek to spare them. But if that idea moves society to prefer faithful fatherhood, it will face two big problems: divorce and low pay.

At all levels of income, divorce destroys fatherhood. When men do not live under the same roof as their children, they find it more difficult to maintain a relationship. Researchers from Exeter, in Britain, found in a 1994 study that more than half the children of divorce did not see the non-custodial parent – almost always the father – on a regular basis. A quarter did not even know where he lived. Studies from other countries confirm that Britain's divorced fathers are not unique in their isolation from their children. Never-married fathers are even more remote. Stepfathers and boyfriends are, as a group, a poor substitute. They tend to offer less emotional and financial commitment than resident fathers. They are many times more likely to abuse the children with whom they live.

Low incomes may also discourage men from living with any family they have fathered. In the 1992–3 British Social Attitudes survey, men without an academic qualification were far more likely than those better educated to think that the husband's role was to earn money, and the wife's to stay at home. Unfortunately, many less-educated men cannot find work that pays enough to allow them to play this role. This is particularly true in Britain and America, less so in Sweden and Germany, where wage differentials are narrower.

In America, the earnings for black male high-school drop-outs fell by half, in real terms, in the period 1973–89. Roughly a third of all American men aged between 25 and 34 earn too little to lift a family of four out of poverty. American research has found that men's willingness to live as part of a family rises as their income does. When women get used to the idea that the state is a better breadwinner, they come to devalue fatherhood. 'How do you get a bloke to make a go of it with his girlfriend if the wage he can get is no more than welfare?' asks Frank Field, a Labour MP who chairs the House of Commons Select Committee on Social Security.

The Swedish response has been to nationalize the family. This may deal with the economic side of the problem. It is little help on the psychological front. And it is expensive. Britain and America, with their low tolerance for high taxes, are unlikely to choose the Swedish road. Nor are they likely to favour the heavy-handed approach that Germans accept. It should be possible, however, for these countries to build a consensus around three principles: first, that tax-and-benefit policies should not discriminate against the family; secondly, that fathers should be obliged to face up to their parental responsibilities; and thirdly, that the working poor should be given every opportunity to achieve financial self-reliance.

Proposed British legislation to make the welfare of children the first priority in divorce is a step in the right direction. Looking at ways to boost the take-home pay of working parents makes sense, as does getting lone mothers into work, something which Sweden does excellently, and which helps break down the belief that men must either be sole earner or nothing. Rules that are hostile to fathers staying with their families should be scrapped.

Even if all this was done, the effects might be disappointingly limited: far larger forces are at work. But incentives do matter. Sweden's marriage rate more than doubled in 1989 as couples married in order to take advantage of a one-off pension reform. Since people do respond to the tax-and-benefit structure, a systematic attempt to stop that response being socially destructive is not unreasonable. It is difficult for democratic government to create incentives so strong that they greatly change the behaviour of lots of people. But, as the effect of too many bad incentives in Britain and America has made it clear, it is not impossible.

READING 30

Gwynn Davis and Mervyn Murch

Why Do Marriages Break Down?

In this [discussion] we pose the deceptively simple question: why do marriages break down? There is a tendency *either* to provide answers in terms which are broadly sociological (such as the 'emancipation of women') *or* to offer psychological explanations based on the individual personalities of husband and wife, or on the interaction between them. Both these ways of describing the causes of marriage breakdown may have validity, but there is an inevitable distortion if they are considered separately. We shall try, wherever possible, to relate the private trouble to the public issue.

One set of explanations has to do with the gradual reduction in the social pressures to remain married. There is certainly less of a social stigma attached to divorce, and even, some would argue, a process of social imitation. Clearly the view of marriage as a religious sacrament, entered into for life, is no longer as potent or as widespread as it once was. It is also suggested that the development of urban living, leading to uprooting and greater social isolation, has both contributed to the stresses within marriage and made it easier to leave. There is, indeed, some evidence that marital breakdown and divorce are more prevalent in urban, especially metropolitan, than in rural areas.

Secondly, it can plausibly be argued that there has been a change in our explanations of what marriage ought to provide. This can be summarized as a move from 'institutional' to 'companionate' marriage. If the essence of marriage is seen as a personal relationship, and if it is no longer necessary to preserve the bond for *economic* reasons, fulfilment may legitimately be sought in a second union. It has been suggested that it was much easier to fulfil the demands of institutional marriage, these being largely economic, or entailing the provision of basic domestic services, than it is to meet the expectations of companionate marriage (intimacy, sexual gratification, shared friends and interests). As Rheinstein puts it, 'In all these more subtle aspects of marriage we need more, we expect more, and we are more easily disappointed.'[1] Brigitte and Peter Berger are likewise of the view that

> the high divorce rates indicate the opposite of what conventional wisdom holds: people divorce in such numbers *not* because they are turned off marriage, but rather because their expectations of marriage are so high that they will not settle for unsatisfactory approximations. In other words, divorce is mainly a backhanded compliment to the ideal of modern marriage, as well as a testimony to its difficulties.[2]

Thirdly, we might point (as many others have done) to 'the emancipation of women'. There are a number of key areas where it is possible for a growing proportion of women to have the same opportunities and to behave in the same way as do men – in education, in employment and in marriage. These steps towards equality have been accompanied by the granting of increased legal rights, in marriage as in other spheres. Even more important, women now enjoy greater financial independence of their husbands. Three obvious examples which bear directly on the incidence of divorce are, first, the provision of state-financed legal advice and representation, allowing women to petition for divorce in large numbers; secondly, the availability of Supplementary Benefit, allowing women to leave their husbands without fear that they (or their children) will starve; and thirdly, a pool of local authority accommodation, generally awarded on the basis that children (and their carers) should have priority.

All this only matters to the extent that women *want* to abandon their marriages. Jessie Bernard has suggested that

> we do our socialising of girls so well . . . that many wives, perhaps most, not only feel that they are fulfilled by marriage but even hotly resent anyone who raises questions about their marital happiness. They have been so completely shaped for their dependency and passivity that the very threat of changes that would force them to greater independence frightens them. They have successfully come to terms with the condition of their lives. They do not know any other. They do not know that other patterns of living might yield greater satisfactions, or want to know. Their cage can be open. They will stay put.[3]

The most fundamental aspect of 'emancipation' may be that a growing proportion of women appear to be dissatisfied with marriage as they experience it. Bernard has referred to 'his' and 'her' marriage in order to suggest the idea that there are two marriages in every marital union and that these do not always coincide. Furthermore, in Bernard's view, 'his' marriage is better than 'hers'. Our own research evidence lends support to the by now familiar idea that marriage means something rather different to men than it does to women. 'The emanication in women' has therefore had an impact on divorce rates in two ways: first, in provoking more women to question the terms of the bargain which they appear to have struck and, secondly, in giving them freedom to leave.

The relative number of men and women who initiate divorce proceedings has fluctuated dramatically throughout this century. Prior to 1914, more decrees were granted on the petition of husbands than of wives. The proportion of husband petitioners increased after the First World War, reaching over 76 per cent in 1920, the highest this century. In 1923, wives were, for the first time, enabled to petition for divorce on the same footing as their husbands. In the following year, over 50 per cent of divorces were, for the first time, granted to wives. World War II again saw a substantial increase in the proportion of decrees granted on petition of the husband (64 per cent in 1946), but since 1949 more women than men have petitioned for divorce. Indeed, the proportion of female petitioners has risen steadily since 1960, reaching 74 per cent in 1982. This has coincided with the seemingly inexorable rise in the overall number of divorce petitions.

Financial assistance to litigants of limited means who wished to divorce was first introduced in 1950 and has been uprated a number of times since then, with the most generous increase in real terms coming in 1960. It has therefore been suggested that the thirty-year trend towards an increased proportion of female petitioners is due to the way in which the Legal Aid fund operates, with both parties being separately assessed so that it pays them (quite literally) to ensure that the poorer of the two (in terms of current assets and income) does the petitioning. But while the way in which the Legal Aid fund operates is bound to have an influence, we found that the high proportion of women petitioners does indeed reflect the woman's role as the key decision-maker, determining if and when the marriage should end.

	View of wives		View of husbands	
	No.	%	No.	%
Wife's decision	104	72	77	61
Husband's decision	25	17	36	28
Joint decision	14	10	14	11
Not recorded	1	1	–	–
Total	144	–	127	–

TABLE 7.1 Who took the decision to divorce? (Conciliation in Divorce survey)

We asked all those interviewed in the course of the Conciliation in Divorce study[4] whether it was they or their former spouse who had taken the decision to divorce. The results, broken down by sex, are given in Table 7.1. . . .

Can we assume from this that men are, in general, more committed to sustaining the marital relationship? Not necessarily. It was clear from a few cases which we studied that while the husband had not wanted a divorce, he had not wanted much of a marriage either – and it was this which had prompted his wife to issue proceedings. As one husband recalled:

> Well, I was going out with somebody, but she didn't know anything about it – you know, sort of once, twice a week. I don't think that would have broken my marriage up. I was quite happy, until she started hearing rumours about it, like. She questioned me about it and I denied it all. But she got up one Monday morning and started ranting and raving again and then she just up and went.

This was not the only man whom we interviewed who confessed to having had a somewhat 'laid back' approach to his marriage. This was the husband's account in a different case: 'I didn't really want a divorce. I was happy going on as I was. I mean, I wasn't a good husband. The fact is I was always out, always drinking, but I mean she never went without. It wasn't a wonderful marriage. I'd have carried on.'

It also appeared in a few instances that the wife's filing of the divorce petition was a kind of desperate last throw, hoping against hope that it would make her husband realize the enormity of what he was doing. Perhaps because we were interviewing members of the divorced population, we gained the impression that, as a strategy for achieving reconciliation, this was not to be recommended. This was one woman's account:

> I never really took the decision. I never actually sat down and thought about it. It just happened. When I first went ahead and filed for a divorce I thought it might pull him to his senses. Everybody kept saying, like friends would say, 'Ah, this'll make him think', but it didn't make him think. It just didn't affect him at all.

But these cases were the minority. In general, we found that not only were women the initiators of divorce, they were correspondingly less likely to regret the ending of the marital relationship. We asked everyone whom we interviewed in Bristol in the course of the Conciliation in Divorce study whether they would have preferred to have remained married. The breakdown of replies is given in Table 7.2. The figures certainly suggest that it is women who, by and large, resolve to end the marriage tie. This has also been found to be the pattern in Australia, where it is reported that divorced husbands are much more likely to regret the ending of the marital relationship than are their wives. This may in turn have implications for second marriages, since we found that even among the thirty-eight men in our Conciliation in Divorce sample who had remarried, 37 per cent said that they wished they had remained married to their former partner (21 per cent of remarried women said the same thing). Apart from throwing a new light on the alleged high failure rate amongst second marriages, these findings reinforce the general impression of male regret.

TABLE 7.2 Would you have preferred to have stayed married? (by sex)

	Women		Men	
	No.	%	No.	%
Yes	41	28	65	51
No	99	69	52	41
Uncertain	1	1	6	5
Other, e.g. reconciled, spouse died	3	2	4	3
Total	144	–	127	–

These responses lead one to wonder whether there might not be another section of the married population, perhaps just as large, who soldier on rather unhappily together. Certainly our interviews suggest that in many of these cases the impulse to divorce had existed for some years prior to the eventual decision to separate. Our evidence is consistent with the arguments advanced by Brigitte and Peter Berger, who describe marriage as the creation of a world in which the individual may achieve power and intelligibility, enabling him or her to become 'a somebody'.[5] As these authors note, this is not an aspiration that one gives up easily; or, as one of the women whom we interviewed remarked, 'Who would willingly subject themselves to this indignity and heartbreak?'

Very few of the people whom we interviewed had taken a *sudden* decision to end their marriage. For example, one couple had separated three times altogether: on the first occasion they had two children; when they finally divorced they had four – one extra, it appeared, for each reconciliation. Women, especially, were inclined to suggest that the cause of the problems lay far back in the marriage, perhaps unacknowledged for years.

> As the years go by . . . I suppose if you look into every nook and cranny, it starts off with one thing, which leads into another, which goes on to something else, and then you go and do something – and that's the end. And it's only that actual end bit that anybody knows about – 'Oh, she went off with somebody else' and that's it. Nobody asks 'why?' That's what amused me – they are all too busy making up their own stories. This all sort of started a few years after [child] was born and I was pregnant and my husband made me have an abortion. That's where it all began. If it hadn't happened, if he hadn't kept on nagging and nagging until I had the blasted abortion, it would never have come to this. In the end, you felt you didn't want him to touch you. You'd had enough, sort of thing.

One of the strongest messages to emerge from these interviews is that people will put up with an extraordinary amount – years of unhappiness – in order to try to keep their marriage and family together. If divorce is 'too easy' . . . this can only be in relation to crossing the legal boundary; one could never accuse the couples in our sample of having taken the decision lightly. One woman, for example, had been married for nineteen years to a very violent man – a heavy drinker – who used to terrify her. She had tried to divorce him fifteen years previously but, in the face of cross-examination from her husband's barrister, had fled the courtroom in tears – to return to her husband for what she regarded as another fifteen wasted years.

The final decision to leave was often prompted by this sense of waste – of time wasted in the past and of being unable to bear such waste in the future.

> I really didn't want it [divorce]. My mother had been divorced and I thought when I eventually got married, I didn't want that to happen to me. I tried very, very hard for it not to happen. I had left a couple of times and gone back, just because I thought I should stay and I should try as much as I possibly could – especially having a child. I was so unhappy by then, I would drink a bottle of wine during the day just to make life more bearable, you know. I suddenly decided, well look, if I don't leave now, I will sacrifice the rest of my life just to live with someone I feel sorry for. I didn't want to hurt him, but I didn't want to stay with him and perform the duties of a wife. It wasn't a thing to take lightly – it meant a lot to me to get a divorce.

This was the view of one husband in a different case.

> The biggest thing was the waste of time, the years we were married. Getting married at 20 and divorced at 30, you've lost ten years. We were a long time in ignorance. It took us a lot of time to wake up. Once we had taken stock of ourselves and realized what we were doing to each other, then it didn't take very long at all [to be divorced]. We spent a lot of time destroying each other until we realized what we were doing: that sort of creeps up on you gently, like old age.

Many of the people we spoke to were at pains to point out that they took the responsibilities of marriage very seriously. As another husband explained, 'I'm the only person in my family that has ever been divorced. My mother and father have been married for donkey's years. My grand-parents are still alive and they are still married. I'm the only one of five children that has ever been divorced – and I've been divorced twice. I feel it's not a family tradition.' Others were keen to distance themselves from any suggestion of radicalism in personal relations; they were certainly not critical of marriage as an institution. As one woman put it to us, 'If you haven't got it right, then it's best to do something. But to me, marriage and a family is everything. I'm not a burn-your-bra type – I don't want to go it alone. I like to think there's someone around.'

There was also, even among some of those who had clearly been the instigators of their divorce, a sense of profound regret that they had felt bound to take such a step. The wife in a different case, asked why she left, replied:

> That's difficult. I loved him and the security is very important – especially when you have children. I'd have preferred none of it to happen. I'm a very loving person and I try to see the good in everyone. I loved my hus-band with all my heart, but the drink won. It's one thing you can't fight. There'll always be that little something between us. You can't love like that twice. We had the best from each other. It only comes once. I haven't found anyone else to love like him.

181

READING 31

Jan Pahl

Household Spending, Personal Spending and the Control of Money in Marriage

The aim of this article is to examine the extent to which money is shared within marriage and to consider the implications of this for patterns of spending. The article draws on my own study of the control and allocation of money within marriage. Two sets of quotations from the interviews carried out in the course of the study may serve to set the scene: in both cases it is the husband who is speaking.

> My wife is totally dependent on me. We are basically traditional: she has a set amount of housekeeping money and I pay the bills as they come in. I wouldn't want a joint account: I like to feel I'm in control of the family scene and I feel more in control this way.

> Marriage is a joint partnership: the money is there for both of us. I wouldn't want to keep our incomes separate. I earn more than my wife and it equalises incomes putting them in a joint account. My wife controls the money and decides how much she needs to spend on house-keeping.

These quotations raise complicated issues about the transfer of resources within households and about responsibility for spending. Where one partner is the main earner and the other the main spender, what social and economic processes shape the transfer of resources from earner to spender? We know that household spending patterns reflect household income levels: do they also reflect the control and allocation of money *within* the household? The working hypothesis which underpins the article is summarized in Figure 7.3.

[I examine] these issues in the light of data drawn from a study of the control and allocation of money within the household. The study focused on households containing two adults, who were married in all but one case,

Figure 7.3 Earning, sharing, spending

and at least one dependent child. The words 'household', 'family' and 'couple' may be used interchangeably in the pages which follow. However, it is important to remember that both households and families can take many different forms. The extent to which money is shared within our social groups offers a rich field for further research.

The main aim of the study was to gain a better knowledge of patterns of allocation of money within households and to investigate the significance of different allocative systems for individual members of households. Husband and wife were interviewed first together and then separately, and interviews were completed with 102 couples. The small number of respondents means that it would be rash to claim that they were representative of a wider population of families; it is likely that unhappy marriages and couples with money problems were underrepresented. However, in many respects the study couples had characteristics which one would have hoped to see in a representative sample.

There are many different criteria which might be used to create a classification of household financial arrangements. However, for the purpose of this analysis it seemed important to focus on the extent to which income was pooled and on the control of the pool, if there was one. The existence of joint and separate bank accounts offered a relatively objective way in which to assess the jointness or otherwise of a couple's financial arrangements. Having a joint bank account suggested some degree of pooling, so couples with a joint account were divided from those without.

Next the couples were sorted according to the wife's answer to the question 'Who really controls the money that comes into this house?' The possible answers to this question were 'wife', 'husband' and 'both'. However, where 'both' were said to control finances, the analysis showed that husbands were likely to be responsible for paying major bills, checking the bank statement and financial arrangements which most closely resembled those where husbands controlled finances. In the analysis which follows, 'both' and 'husband' have been combined in order to reduce the number of categories. Support for the choice of the wife's answer came from the interviewers, who at the end of the joint interview noted discreetly which partner had been the most authoritative in talking about money. A very significant correlation existed between the husband appearing authoritative in the joint interview and his being described by his wife in her separate interview as controlling the money: conversely, wives who appeared authoritative were likely to control the money.

Sorting in this way the 102 couples in the sample produced four categories. The first category contained couples where there was a joint bank account and where the wife described herself as controlling the money. There were twenty-seven of these and they were described as 'wife-controlled pooling'. Among these couples it was usually the wife who paid the bills for rates, fuel, telephone, insurance and mortgage or rent. In the majority of cases, neither partner had a separate bank account and all finances were handled from the joint account.

The second category was described as 'husband-controlled pooling'. This contained couples where there was a joint bank account, but where the wife considered either that the husband controlled the finances or that they were jointly controlled. There were thirty-nine couples in this category. Among this group husbands were typically responsible for the bills for rates, fuel, telephone and insurance and for paying the mortgage or rent.

Lack of a joint account implied one of two things. Either the couple were paid in cash and were too poor ever to need a bank, or one or both partners rejected the idea of a joint account. The third category contained couples where there was no joint account and where the wife considered that control was in the husband's hands. There were twenty-two couples in this category, which was described as 'husband-controlled'. Typically the husband had his own personal bank account and he was responsible for all the main bills.

Finally, there was a small group where there was no joint bank account and the wife considered that she controlled the finances. This category contained fourteen couples and was described as 'wife-controlled'. These couples typically had no bank accounts at all and operated in cash, with the wife controlling and managing the finances and taking responsibility for the major bills.

Wife control of finances was particularly common in low-income, working-class households where neither partner had any qualifications. Wife control was associated with the payment of wages in cash and with the absence of any bank accounts. Typically the wife also managed the money, paying for food and for rent, fuel, insurance and so on, while the husband had a set sum for his personal spending money. Thus in many respects wife control was synonymous with wife management.

Husband control was associated with relatively high income levels. . . . Most of these couples kept their money separate. When the wife was earning her wages typically went into the housekeeping purse, while the husband was responsible for larger bills. Husband control was characteristic of couples where the husband was the main or sole earner, and there was a tendency for it to be associated with marital unhappiness for both partners.

There were interesting differences between wife-controlled pooling and husband-controlled pooling. Wife-controlled pooling was associated with medium income levels, while husband-controlled pooling was more typical of higher income levels. Wife-controlled pooling was associated with the employment of both partners; when only the husband was in employment he was likely to control the pool. Table 7.3 shows that the more the wife contributed to the household income the more likely it was that she would control household finances; this effect was particularly marked among pooling couples. Where wives' earnings were 30 per cent or more of their husbands' earnings, wives were twice as likely as husbands to control the pool; where wives had no earnings, husbands were three times more likely than wives to control the pool. When neither partner was employed there was a tendency for wives to control finances; however, the term 'wife control' of finances seems a misleading way to describe what was essentially a struggle to make ends meet in very poor households.

TABLE 7.3 Control of finances by wife's earnings as a proportion of husband's earnings

	Wife's earnings		
	Over 30% of husband's earnings	Under 30% of husband's earnings	Wife had no earnings
Wife control	6	–	8
Wife-controlled pooling	12	8	7
Husband-controlled pooling	5	14	20
Husband control	5	5	12
Total	28	27	47

The effect of social class was particularly marked among pooling couples, especially where husband and wife were of different classes. Social class was defined according to the Registrar General's Classification. Where the husband was classified as middle-class and the wife as working-class, the husband always controlled the pool, or joint account. Where the wife was middle-class and the husband working-class, she controlled the pool in all but one instance. The same pattern occurred for qualifications. If one partner had more qualifications than the other he or she was likely to control finances: where both partners had gained some qualifications after leaving school there was a tendency for the husband to control finances.

To sum up this section, then, where a wife controls finances she will usually also be responsible for money management; where a husband controls finances he will usually delegate parts of money management to his wife. Thus where a wife controls finances she will usually be responsible for paying the main bills and for making sure that ends meet, as well as for buying food and day-to-day necessities. Where a husband controls finances he will typically delegate to his wife the responsibility for housekeeping expenses, sometimes giving her a housekeeping allowance for this purpose. Marriages where the wife controls the money and the husband manages it are rare. There were no examples of this pattern in the study sample, nor were there examples of the small number of marriages where the husband both controls and manages the money. Evidence from other studies suggests that in these circumstances there is likely to be extreme inequality between husband and wife and deprivation on the part of the wife and children.

What is the relationship between the control of money within the household and patterns of spending by individual household members? Patterns of spending were investigated in the joint interview, when each couple was asked who was responsible for spending on each item in a long list. They were asked 'who actually buys each item or pays each bill?' Patterns of spending were differentiated by gender. Wives were likely to pay for food, clothing for themselves and their children, presents and school expenses such as dinner money. Husbands were likely to be responsible for paying for their own clothing, the car, repairs and decorating, meals taken away from home and alcohol. Joint responsibilities, paid for by either partner or by both together, included consumer durables, donations to charity and Christmas expenses. This pattern is similar to that found by Todd and Jones: the main difference between the two studies lies in the increase in goods purchased by 'either or both', a change which reflects the spread of joint bank accounts.[1]

Responsibility for spending varied significantly according to the control of finances within the household, but only for some items of expenditure. In general the person who controlled finances, whether or not there was a joint account, was also responsible for the major bills. This applied in the case of the bills for mortgage or rent, rates, fuel, phone and insurance. However, the pattern for consumer goods was rather different: where there was a joint account, whether it was controlled by husband or wife, it was likely that they would both be responsible for buying the washing machine, refrigerator or other household item. However, where there was no joint account, husbands were likely to be responsible for spending on consumer goods. . . .

In this study the question of spending on leisure was approached in various different ways. In the joint interview each individual was asked to identify a source of money for personal things 'like cigarettes, tights, a drink out with friends, a present for your spouse'. In the separate interviews each was asked about their personal spending money, the sums involved and the items it had to cover: each was asked what leisure activities he or she pursued and how much was spent on each activity. Each was then asked to describe their partner's leisure pursuits and to estimate how much he or she spent on them.

What determined the amount of money which each person felt they could spend on leisure and personal needs? [The] part of the household budgeting system [from which] each person drew her or his personal spending money [appears to be an important factor]. Husbands were more likely than wives to take their personal spending money from their earnings, while wives were likely to use housekeeping money for their personal needs, especially if they were not earning. The source of personal spending money varied according to how the couple organized their finances. Where there was a joint account and money management was shared, both partners tended to get their own spending money from the pool. When money was managed independently both partners took their personal spending money from their earnings. Where there was an allowance system the husband's personal spending money tended to come from his earnings, while the wife's money came from the housekeeping money, a situation which was particularly likely to make a woman feel that she had no right to spend on herself.

. . . Spending on leisure varied depending on the control of money within the household. In the sample as a whole husbands were likely to spend more than their wives, but this was especially so when there was no joint account. Husbands were particularly likely to spend more on leisure than wives in those households where wives controlled finances, that is, in households with the lowest incomes. A rather unexpected result was found, however, when wife-controlled pooling couples were compared with husband-controlled pooling couples. It was among the latter category that wives who spent more on leisure than their husbands were most commonly found. Of the seventeen women who spent more on leisure than their husbands, ten were found in those households where the husband controlled finances and there was a joint account. Perhaps these were the households where a larger-than-average income was combined with an ideology of financial sharing?

READING 32

Elizabeth A. Stanko

Wife Battering: All in the Family

More than anything else, the experiences of women battered by husbands, boyfriends or lovers expose the underside of the ideal family or the happy couple. To hear battered women recount these experiences is to hear stories of abuse which are often characterized as 'normal' interaction of intimate couples. Blinded by patriarchal notions about the privacy of family matters, deafened by the rhetoric which maintains these notions, society once again focuses blame on individual women who, because of their assumed weakness, 'choose' battering relationships. Masochistic women, they are called. Battered women live within their own state of siege; they know, to the core of their being, the weight of the contradictory demands of their roles as women. . . .

Physical intrusion within intimate relationships reflects a pattern similar to sexual intimidation and violence: women are overwhelmingly the recipients of 'domestic violence'. So too, women are blamed for their powerlessness, and labelled as passive, submissive, even desirous of their own harm. Hence dominant stereotypes of women provide the common-sense information to divide women in two categories, those who are nurturers and care givers, and those who are nagging, selfish and in violation of women's expected role. And men's behaviour? Too often, it is seen as 'typical'.

While the stereotype of the blameworthy battered wife remains steadfast, researchers have found that wife beating is perhaps the most under-reported crime. One estimate suggests that only one out of 270 incidents of wife abuse is ever reported to the authorities. When incidents do come to police attention, they compose a significant proportion of assault complaints. [An] analysis of 3,020 reported cases of violence in two Scottish cities, for instance, found assault against wives to be the second largest category of assault that comes to police attention. Researchers who examine violent incidents outside police involvement find even higher incidence of wife abuse. [Another] random survey on women's experiences of sexual assault revealed that 21 per cent of women who had ever been married reported physical violence by a husband at some time in their lives. [A third] random survey of 2,143 households in the US found evidence of 'domestic violence' in 28 per cent of households. It is important to note here, however, that domestic violence and wife-battering are different concepts. In one – domestic violence – the researcher assumes that all violence is experienced by men and women alike and that the damage administered by a wife is equivalent to that administered by a husband. In fact, the [last-mentioned] survey found that the incidence of husband battering exceeded that for wife battering. As Russell points out in her critique of these findings, [the authors] 'fail to distinguish between offensive and defensive violence', ignoring strength differences, variation in fighting skills and the sustained injuries of women and men. The term 'wife abuse', then, stresses the social position of women *vis-à-vis* men. The context of women's position is what needs to be explained, not 'exchange' of physical abuse. Furthermore, wives who fight back might be more severely injured. Women who are beaten either try to defend themselves or remain physically passive: there is no set pattern. What remains a 'social fact' . . . is that violence between adults in the family is directed at women.

Common among women's experiences of physical assault are reports of sexual assault. Approximately 10 per cent of [currently or previously married] respondents [to the second survey mentioned above] reported being raped and beaten by their husbands. [Another recent study in the US] reveals widespread sexual abuse among . . . battered women . . . one of every three women . . . interviewed had been battered. Of the battered women, one-third of . . . respondents had been raped, two-thirds felt they had been pressured into having sex with their husbands and 40 per cent felt sex was unpleasant because it was forced. Clearly men's sexual intimidation and violence toward women goes hand in hand with physical intimidation and violence.

Behaviour referred to as wife-battering – the violent action on the part of husband against wife – includes forms of pushing, kicking, slapping, throwing objects, burning, dragging, stabbing or shooting. Assaults over time may have cumulative physical effects; severe bruising and all-round bodily soreness accompany emotional distress. For example, in answering 'What kind of injuries were inflicted on you?' asked by a member of the Select Committee on Violence in Marriage, UK, one woman replied:

I have had ten stitches, three stitches, five stitches, seven stitches, where he has cut me. I have had a knife stuck through my stomach; I have had a poker put through my face; I have no teeth where he knocked them all out; I have been burnt with red hot pokers; I have had red hot coals slung all over me; I have been sprayed with petrol and stood there while he has flicked lighted matches at me. But I had to stay there because I could not get out. He has told me to get out. Yet if I had stood up I know what would have happened to me. I would have gotten knocked down again.

. . . Research on Scottish women in prison, [found] many women's accounts of violent attacks at the hands of men. These attacks included severe beatings, with a range of bodily injuries from the loss of an eye and a tooth to physical mutilation: a carved swastika on one woman's forehead. Women's discussions about their lives eventually focused on the common occurrence of male violence, which some women attributed to 'Scottishness'. (Some American, English and Welsh women subjected to violence might also attribute it to that which arises from a particular cultural context. The similarities across cultures, however, reinforce the commonness of male violence in both British and American societies.) The 'cult of aggressive and assertive masculinity' is attributed to a Scottish working-class ethos; women's experiences of male violence elsewhere show how this cult crosses class boundaries. Equally important, the cult of aggressive and assertive masculinity is taken by some women to be typical male behaviour.

Ultimately, women's injuries reflect the effects of aggressive masculinity. In [a recent] study, nearly 80 per cent of the battered women reported going to a doctor at least once during their marriage for injuries resulting from attacks by their husbands; nearly 40 per cent stated they sought medical attention on five separate occasions. . . . The medical profession too participates in perpetuating wife-battering by ignoring women's complaints of physical injury as symptomatic of a pattern of battering. So do those who feel that the sanctity of marriage is, above all, more important than a woman's physical safety.

By late afternoon I still hadn't come up with a specific plan of action. All I knew was that I would have to get away from Florida. Just before dinner my mother said she wanted to talk to me.

'Chuck has been calling all day', she said. 'I've talked to him a few times now and all I know for sure is that he really loves you.'

'Mother, you don't know what you're talking about.'

'Oh, you never think that I know what I'm talking about', she said. 'I've been married a good long time, longer than you've been alive, and after all this time I guess I know a thing or two about husbands and wives. You don't want to forget that he's your husband and you're his wife. No matter what little difficulties you've been having, you should be able to work them out.'

'Little difficulties? *Little* difficulties!'

'Chuck has told me everything', my mother said. 'He told me enough so that I know this is just a lovers' quarrel.'

All day I had been thinking about how I could tell my parents what was going on in my life. I felt that I should break it to them gently. Well, all those plans just flew out the window. I laid the situation flat-out, using the bluntest words I knew.

'Mom. Chuck has beaten me bloody', I began. 'He has held a gun to my head and made me do awful things. He has forced me to have sex with women and other men. And now he is talking about making me have sex with animals. He has made me pose for dirty pictures and he is turning me into a prostitute. He is always threatening to kill me. He has even threatened to kill you and Daddy.'

'But, Linda, he's your *husband*.'

That women are to blame – the strongly entrenched male point of view often held by many doctors, police, neighbours, parents and so forth – is difficult for battered women to confront. Many women still envision a life of domestic tranquillity. Yet the economic and emotional ties wrap tightly around women's uncertainty about the domestic tranquillity when violence arises. All too often, battered women's responses, similar to incestually assaulted or raped women's responses, end up in self-blame. . . . Battering may be interpreted by the woman as an indication, not of her husband's problem but as her failure as a wife. Mortified, ashamed, humiliated, a woman may then remain silent about her abuse to others, fearing most of all that she is ultimately to blame.

> I don't know. I kept thinking he was changing, you know, change for the better. . . . He's bound to change. Then I used to think it's my blame and I used to lie awake at night wondering if it is my blame – You know, I used to blame myself all the time.

> I was concerned, I didn't do anything to deserve it. I mean, I never went out. I never went out of the house, you know. I never looked at anybody.

> The feeling of helplessness due to the fact that it was my fault that I got battered, which I think is common that a woman is blamed because she provoked him. Certainly my husband immediately blamed me. 'If you had done so and so; if you hadn't done so and so.' And the fact that he did almost kill me and threatened if I said anything to the police he *would* kill me, and the destruction of confidence or any way out. I had no money, I had kids. I couldn't for years see my way out of this situation, in myself I didn't have any sense of it. If I left, he'd follow me. He'd take my kids away. He threatened to do that. I believed all that. Getting the strength came with my finally deciding that I was dying, and that if I was going to die, I was going to die fighting, which meant I had to leave. I could not die this way any longer in this relationship and if he came after me, damn it, I was going to give him what he was trying to give me. It was a giving up of his power over me and my acknowledgement of his power over me [that] gave me power to move. It was a long time before I was able to – ten years – get over really being afraid of that man. I'm just now getting to a point to where I am not afraid of him, and move forward into my life. My life has always been attached to this kind of powerlessness. If I do this, what's he going to do? It's a reaction instead of an action. It's always a reaction instead of moving with the confidence of no matter what he does I can somehow manage, maybe get killed in the process. I don't think that any more but I did for a long time. And I talk to other women who have had other experiences like that who have the same kind of hopelessness and in many instances, without resources, without the ability to make a living, find a house, to solve all these terrible problems, these real problems, practical problems. Where they are as bad as this, it is better than that [the battering situation], better than going into an absolute abyss of nothing.

For a period of time – days, months, years – many battered women are caught within the web of violence, unable to predict when more violence will occur or to understand why violence is occurring in the first place. During this period, many report symptoms of stress, such as lack of sleep, weight loss or gain, ulcers, nervousness, irritability, and [for] some even thoughts of suicide. Moreover, depression slows down a battered woman's ability to escape the battering, an act that, by its very nature, is an assertive one. . . .

Keeping the relationship together, despite the violence, is also important for practical reasons – financial support, shelter, even access to the ability to earn a living many times rest with the husband/boyfriend. Getting out is almost as bad as staying in the relationship. Women often feel inadequate to cope with self-sufficiency; the lack of self-confidence often acts as a trap to keep women within a violent home.

Women stay within battering situations because of the real conditions of their lives within a male-dominated world. Men's power is not an individual, but a collective one. Women's lives are bounded by it. The threat of male violence outside the home . . . is an acutely intimidating reality of women who endure violence within their own homes. . . . Having women react instead of act, as the woman stated above, is a response pattern fostered by women's dependence upon men.

Many women do leave violent husbands/boyfriends. In doing so, many women leave, return, leave again, return again and leave never to return. The process could take years, or it could happen immediately after the first beating.

> I went to my parents and of course, he came – I left him because of his hitting and kicking me – and I went home to them, but he came there and I had to go. I went back really to keep the peace because my parents weren't able to cope with it.

> [I returned to my husband] because I was sure there was something in me that could make the marriage work. I was quite positive about that.

Reasons for returning are similar to those for staying: hope that the husband will change or, because he has apologized, hope that he will never strike again; concern for the children; worry over financial difficulties; resignation to the 'inevitability' of violence; fear for the safety of others; fear of being outside the home; fear of losing the status of 'wife'; just plain fear – these are but a few of the motivating forces affecting women's decisions to leave or stay.

READING 33

Joan Chandler

Women Outside Marriage

There is a widespread feeling that 'something' is happening to the marriage patterns of modern Western society, but what the 'something' is is rather ambiguous and the interpretations placed upon the trends are yet more contradictory. Traditional marriage is in decline and more individuals are living alone [Figure 7.4, Table 7.4]. But there is also a growth in cohabitation and 'the couple' remains central to personal life and domestic arrangements. It remains relevant in the lives of the non-married as well as the married and to homosexuals as much as heterosexuals.

Changing marriage patterns touch all but, it could be argued, they are more keenly felt by women. Family ideology continues to link women's identity to hearth and home and to emphasize the importance of their domestic relationships with men and children. Even when in paid employment women retain residual identities as marital and economic dependants. This ensures that women are more married than men inside marriage and it limits the social autonomy of women outside marriage. As the structure

Plate 7.2 Traditional marriage continues to be attractive to many young couples

As percentage of all households

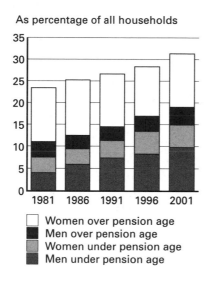

Women over pension age
Men over pension age
Women under pension age
Men under pension age

Figure 7.4 Single-person households, 1981–2000
Sources: DOE, SDD, Mintal 1992

and ideology of marriage and domestic partnership are central to the gendering of women, the changing nature of marriage and non-marriage will have a profound effect upon their lives.

THE NORMALITY OF MARRIAGE?

Despite the pluralism of living arrangements, marriage remains a normal and expected part of female biography in Britain . . . although the vast majority of women still expect to marry at some time, and at least once, in recent years there has been some decline in the popularity of marriage. . . .

TABLE 7.4 Households by size, Great Britain, 1961–91: more home alone

Household size	Percentages and numbers			
	1961	1971	1981	1990–1
1 person	12	18	22	26
2 people	30	32	32	35
3 people	23	19	17	17
4 people	19	17	18	15
5 people	9	8	7	5
6 or more people	7	6	4	2
All households:	100	100	100	100
Average household size (number of people)	3.09	2.89	2.17	2.46
Number of households (thousands)	16,189	18,317	19,492	9,623[1]

1 Sample size (number).
Source: Office of Population Censuses and Surveys. Crown copyright.

193

However, much of this debate hinges on the differences drawn between cohabitation and formal marriage. In historical and cross-cultural studies . . . the differences more obviously blur. But they are also not that clear in contemporary analyses. Here it is useful to note that the Census uses self-identification to place people in the combined category of married or living as married, while the Registrar records only formal marriages, counting only those entering and leaving marriage as a legal estate. Consequently, it is important not to assume that marital status is synonymous with living arrangements. Not only do the non-married cohabit, but the married may live apart, separated, for example, by the demands of employment or because their husbands/partners are in prison.

Whatever the complexities of these trends one thing is sure – the changing patterns of marriage and the relative longevity of women are increasing the numbers of women without husbands and blurring the boundaries between marriage and non-marriage . . . In discussion of marriage and 'the family' there is often a clear delineation: women are either married or they are not. In reality women not only have a variety of marital statuses, they also have a range of domestic and sexual relationships with men.

COHABITATION

Cohabitation is increasingly popular; during the 1980s, the proportion of single women cohabiting increased from 8 per cent to 17 per cent. Also half of first-time marriages and 70 per cent of subsequent marriages were preceded by a period of cohabitation. The growth of cohabitation in part accounts for the fall in marriage figures. The time couples spend cohabiting is lengthening and increasingly they appear to be choosing cohabitation as a long-term alternative to marriage.

The preference for consensual unions rather than formal marriage is also influential in interpretations of the growing numbers of children born outside marriage [Figure 7.5]. Illegitimacy as a legal status was abolished in 1987, thus giving the same rights to children born inside and outside mar-

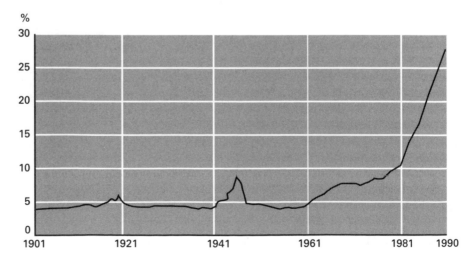

Figure 7.5 Live UK births outside marriage, as a percentage of births *Source:* Office of Population Census and Surveys. Crown copyright.

riage. This change was again indicative of the blurring of distinctions between customary and legal unions. In the past pregnancy was a prompt to marriage, but this is less so today; in 1977, 25 per cent of women were pregnant at the time of their wedding, compared with 12 per cent in 1987. Many of today's parents have detached child-bearing and rearing from traditional marriage and 28 per cent of children are now born to unmarried mothers. However, many fewer are born to residentially lone parents, as 70 per cent of these children are jointly registered by parents who usually share the same address.

Cohabitation is often seen as an emergent trend, whereas historical analyses describe its constant popularity. . . . Cohabitation [always] thrived amongst those who could not afford the expense of the big wedding, among migrant workers and those already married. Local practices of self-marriage and self-divorce flourished; the best-known of these were the 'besom marriages' of couples 'living over the brush'. [One study] estimates that consensual unions constituted a quarter to a third of all 'marriages' in the eighteenth century and a fifth of them at the turn of the nineteenth century.

In terms of people's own definitions, cohabitation is not a single phenomenon. There are those who deliberately choose cohabitation as an alternative to marriage, where couples have less sense of merging into a single domestic unit and feel more loosely committed, and there are those who regard it as equivalent to marriage. In Afro-Caribbean society, with its history of slavery, consensual unions have long been a cultural norm. But whatever the range of attitudes among the population, the law is more ambiguous on this point. When relationships end and cohabiting partners go their separate ways, legal recipes for the division of the domestic unit are less clear and rely more on proof of financial contribution and individual ownership.

SEPARATION AND DIVORCE

Divorce and separation are distinct marital statuses, although separation may be seen as a half-way house, part of the dynamics of marriage or a prelude to divorce. It is estimated that 40–50 per cent of couples who separate become reconciled, although this reconciliation is often only temporary, a

TABLE 7.5 Divorce[1]: women taking the lead

	Petitions filed[2] (thousands)									
	1961	1971	1976	1981	1984	1985	1986	1987	1988	1989
England and Wales										
By husband	14	44	43	47	49	52	50	50	49	50
By wife	18	67	101	123	131	139	131	133	134	135
Total	32	111	145	170	180	191	180	183	183	185

1 This table includes annulment throughout.
2 Estimates based on 100 per cent of petitions at the Principal Registry together with a two-month sample of county court petitions (March and September).
Sources: Office of Population Censuses and Surveys, Lord Chancellor's Department, General Register Office (Scotland). Crown copyright.

TABLE 7.6 Marriage and divorce: EC comparison, 1981 and 1989

	Rates			
	Marriages per 1,000 eligible population		Divorces per 1,000 existing marriages	
	1981	1989	1981	1989
United Kingdom	7.1	6.8	11.9	12.6[1]
Belgium	6.5	6.4	6.1	8.6
Denmark	5.0	6.0	12.1	13.6
France	5.8	5.0	6.8	8.4
Germany (Fed. Rep.)	5.8	6.4	7.2	8.7[2]
Greece	7.3	6.1	2.5	–
Irish Republic	6.0	5.0	0.0	0.0
Italy	5.6	5.4	0.9	2.1
Luxemburg	5.5	5.8	5.9	10.0
The Netherlands	6.0	6.1	8.3	8.1
Portugal	7.7	7.1	2.8	–
Spain	5.4	5.6	1.1	–

1 1987.
2 1988.
Source: Statistical Office of the European Communities. Crown copyright.

rehearsal for a later and more permanent marital dissolution. In the twentieth century divorce rates have peaked and if trends continue, approximately 40 per cent of marriages presently being formed will end in divorce. Divorced women are a growing sector of the population: one in twenty women are divorced, a proportion slightly higher than that for men. Also in recent years the gap between first marriage and divorce has been narrowing. In 1981 only 1.5 per cent of divorces occurred within two years of marriage; in 1990 the proportion had risen to 10 per cent. Today most divorces will occur within five to nine years of marriage.

In recent years women have been more likely to petition for divorce than men and in Britain over 70 per cent of petitioners are women [Table 7.5]. This may be seen as evidence of women's greater dissatisfaction with marriage. Alternatively it may be a product of the types of negotiation between ex-partners and their legal representatives and the conventional format in which to request dissolution. Not only have divorce rates risen [Table 7.6], but the nature of the divorce process has also changed. These changes have altered the operations of the courts, the bases of legal argument between men and women and the experience and the aftermath of divorce. High remarriage rates produce a rapid turnover in the populations of both the married and the divorced. Three-quarters of all women married in the 1970s were remarried within six years, and at current rates, half of these will divorce again. But the 1980s have seen a new trend, with rates of remarriage in decline, a decline which may well contribute to future reductions in overall divorce rates.

WIDOWS

Another large and growing group of non-marriage women in Britain are widows. Here Britain is representative of other Western nations: 14 per cent of women over 16 are widows, compared with 4 per cent of men. Furthermore over a third of women aged 65–74 and nearly two-thirds of those over 75 are widows. This reflects the increased life expectancy of women, the tendency of women to marry older men and the fact that widowers marry more frequently. There is little discussion of widowhood, despite the large numbers of women who will experience it. This is indicative of the wider invisibility and low social valuation of older women in our society.

Child-bearing is completed earlier in today's families and women live longer than in earlier centuries. Consequently, children will usually have left home for a number of years prior to the death of their father and their mother's bereavement will follow life in an 'empty nest' household. This colours the associations of widowhood. It is seen as a natural end to women's lives and, being associated with ageing, it relates to loss of social contact and the closure of the social world. There are a number of questions and issues that are raised by a greater awareness of the range of marital/non-marital relationships. The instability and pluralism of marriage patterns is influential in the biographies of women, their economic circumstance, their domestic relationships with partners and children, the organization of domestic routine and the home, and the exchange of social support.

MARRIAGE, NON-MARRIAGE AND BIOGRAPHY

One dimension of the present trends in marriage is the flux that it introduces into the domestic biographies of women. Given the present trends in marriage, many women will spend the bulk of their life outside conventional marriage and many more will experience a wide range of marital identities. To roll forward social time for a woman who is presently 18 may give the hypothetical biography detailed in [Box 7.1], if current trends remain unchanged.

PROPERTY

Central to marriage are rights of property transfer. Engels argued that 'marriage' resulted from the need to control private property and to ensure its ownership by legitimate heirs. Contemporary discussion of marriage which emphasize its personal and emotional side ignore its continuing role in inheritance. The changing pattern of marriage and non-marriage has a number of implications for women's control over property and the growth of home-ownership makes this an increasingly relevant issue. Amongst

Box 7.1 The complexities of modern relationships: the example of Jane

Years of age

17 Jane begins her sexual career. Before she is 19 she has a series of sexual partnerships with varying degrees of commitment. During this time she is living at home with her parents.

19 Jane briefly shares a flat with female friends and then moves into rented accommodation with her boyfriend, Kevin.

20 Jane has a son and she gives up full-time employment but works in the evenings, filling shelves in a supermarket.

21 Jane's relationship with her boyfriend breaks up and with her child she temporarily moves back to live with her parents. She finds this situation unsatisfactory, but efforts to secure alternative accommodation prove difficult. After an argument she leaves home, is judged homeless by the local housing department and given bed and breakfast accommodation. At this time Jane's only source of income is income support.

23 Jane begins another relationship with Eric. He has been divorced for two years and has two children by his first marriage who live with his ex-wife. Jane and Eric decide to live together. Jane's mother has now retired and agrees to look after Jane's son; Jane returns to working part-time as a secretary in an insurance office. Jane and Eric take out a mortgage on a house.

25 Jane and Eric get married.

29 Jane has had two more children and temporarily decides to give up employment.

31 Jane and Eric separate.

32 After a brief and unsuccessful attempt at reconciliation, Jane and Eric divorce. Their house is sold and Jane and her three children are rehoused in local authority rented accommodation.

34 Jane meets Edward who eventually moves into Jane's house.

40 Jane and Edward get married.

62 Edward dies and Jane becomes a widow.

Thinking about Jane's life

- How does Jane's changing partnership and marital status connect to other aspects of her life?
- How do past and present relationships influence biography?
- What are the implications of these changes for Jane's children and stepchildren?
- How relevant are class and ethnicity to marital biographies?

non-married women, widows are the group best placed in terms of property. Marriage gives widows inheritance rights but, in the absence of a will, this will not necessarily include all their husband's assets.

The division of marital assets is central to divorce procedure. With the introduction of no-fault divorce the court is rarely deciding if a marriage shall or shall not be dissolved, but presiding over the division of assets and the responsibilities of ex-partners in the care and control of their children. However, the courts' deliberations reflect social judgements about the role of women in and outside marriage. First, the concept of no-fault applies more to men than women, since conduct in marriage will be ignored only when there is agreement and in so far as the courts consider it fair or 'equitable' to do so. In practical terms, faithless wives do not seem to have the same right to family assets as faithful and blameless ones.

Secondly, the unpaid contribution that women make to the family and household has been increasingly recognized in the distribution of family property but is still seen as giving them a smaller entitlement. [A] study . . . of solicitors' perceptions and assumptions shows that, whatever their professional appreciations of the law, they have considerable sympathy for husbands and a conventional and traditional view of the division of domestic labour, in which women are primarily dependants and not contributors.

Living together is often regarded as a form of unofficial marriage, but it is an area where the operation of the law remains confused. The laws of inheritance and property distinguish between marriage and cohabitation, where women not married to their partners have few, if any, rights. Here cohabitation contracts may be necessary to protect the rights of women. By contrast, welfare law regards marriage and cohabitation as more equivalent and assumes that cohabitees are economically supporting one another. This limits independence in claiming income support.

HOUSING

Change in marital circumstances has important consequences for housing. Women commonly move on the dissolution of their marriages and partnerships, have problems securing or keeping new accommodation, and are housed in poorer conditions. Widows are the most likely to remain in their homes, though some still move, typically because they have difficulty with mortgage payments and/or because their accommodation is tied to their husband's job. Nearly half of the women who divorce move from the marital home . . ., a proportion which rises substantially when the women are in younger age groups. Here the presence of children has little effect, as 41 per cent of women with children move at this time.

In housing, cohabiting women have fewer rights and [a recent study] argues that only if women have children, whose needs are prioritized by the courts and local authorities, will they be seen to have *de facto* rights of the married. The type of tenure women had while married is also important. With a dissolution of domestic partnership there is a gravitation towards local authority housing. This is because, as existing local authority tenants, women tend to remain in their accommodation, but few women

Plate 7.3 A derelict housing estate in North London: the poverty trap for lone mothers is clear

who are owner-occupiers can continue to shoulder the costs of a mortgage alone. In these circumstances, women in privately rented accommodation are the most insecure and the most at risk of homelessness. Also, in their frequent moves between accommodation the support of relatives, however temporary, remains crucial.

POVERTY

Many women outside marriage live in poor households and this is especially true for lone mothers and the lone elderly. . . . Analyses of the 1983 Family Expenditure Survey [showed] that 61 per cent of elderly women and lone mothers were living below the poverty line, compared with 28 per cent of all other households. Together these two groups comprised a third of all poor households, a fact which supports wider evidence for the feminization of poverty. It also has economic implications for children, as the gap between the average income of one- and two-parent households is immense: in 1986 the average income of one-parent households was less than 40 per cent of that of two-parent households.

Furthermore, the economic and welfare policies to which women outside marriage are subject are rife with contradictions as they are variously treated as self-sufficient workers and as family dependants. Women's greater participation in paid employment has led them to be considered economically self-sufficient and to weaken their claim to continued financial support from former husbands. As a result, divorce marks a cleaner financial break from marriage. However, as workers they rarely earn the equivalent of male wages and are less likely to build up entitlement to an occupational pension in their own right.

Although in financial terms divorce may be a cleaner break, there are strong pressures to continue co-parental responsibilities and where there is continuing economic support, this is for children. However, the proportion of women receiving child maintenance payments from their former husbands fell from 50 per cent to 23 per cent between 1981 and 1986, and almost none are now reliant on maintenance from husbands as their main source of income. For women leaving cohabiting relationships the sums involved are even smaller.

The poverty trap for lone mothers is clear, as many face the chance of earning only low wages, especially in a recessionary economy, while paying high child-care costs and forgoing entitlement to meagre welfare benefits. Hence increasing numbers of lone mothers are choosing the welfare option: the proportion wholly dependent on benefit rose from 38 per cent to 60 per cent between 1981 and 1988. In 'conventional' families women are assumed to be benefiting from their access to overall household income, an assumption that has been shown to be unwarranted. [. . . A] study of families in Northern Ireland . . . found that 47 per cent of divorced women, 41 per cent of the separated and 39 per cent of the widowed claimed to be in the same financial situation or a little better off once their marriages had ceased. This was despite the fact that 70 per cent of the sample were judged to be living on or below the poverty line. So, analyses of lone women may say as much, if not more, about the visibility of female poverty as it does about its incidence.

HOUSEHOLD ROUTINES AND DOMESTIC POWER

Conventional marriage is associated with a traditional and patriarchal division of labour. However, cohabitation seems to do little to alter informal work in the domestic economy. This is especially so if the couple regard themselves as 'married' and see their relationship as long-term. Women without husbands often have more personal elbow-room and control over domestic resources. Marriage absorbs the time and energy of women and in conventional marriage the amount and nature of housework relates to the servicing of men. Here domestic routines are fitted around male schedules and career patterns. Hence the absence of men or marriage may mean less housework and offer women more domestic control. At the very least it reshapes domestic routines, such as meals and mealtimes. There are fewer 'proper meals' and more snacks, less formal mealtimes and more 'grazing in the fridge'.

However, although there may be less housework, there is also no possibility of dividing domestic chores, however uneven that division may be in conventional marriage. Here shared living is more important than whether couples are formally married or not. Living alone gives women more unchallenged domestic power, but it also means they have to shoulder the burden of domestic responsibility largely unaided. . . . Irrespective of the quality of the marriage, there are painful adjustments in learning to shop and cook for one and to adjust to the fact that there is no longer a domestic division of labour.

RELATIONSHIPS WITH FAMILY AND FRIENDS

Dissolving or loosening ties with partners is deeply influential on relationships between parents and children and with kin. Many children live in one-parent households. Presently in Britain 17 per cent of households with children under the age of 16 are headed by a lone parent, the majority of whom are women. In decisions about custody, the move in recent years has been from the rights of the father towards the 'best interests' of the child, and these 'best interests' have been interpreted as children remaining with their mothers. In 90 per cent of cases children remain with their mothers and this is especially so for younger children and girls. However, although

Plate 7.4 A child playing in a stairway in a bed and breakfast hotel

children may routinely live with their mothers, jointness in care and control is increasingly being favoured by the courts in an effort to strengthen ties with non-residential fathers.

This presents a number of issues for women and their children. The adjustment to parental absence or loss and the restructuring of the household and its routines is often accompanied by stress and conflict. Furthermore, lone parenting is often stigmatized and regarded as a poor substitute for 'proper parenting'. But it is perhaps more helpful and illuminating to ask what are the qualitative differences in styles of parenting outside conventional marriage. The power structure of the lone-parent household is unlike that with two resident parents: children are often expected to be more self-reliant and more involved in family decision-making, and such households appear more permissive. Furthermore, single parenting may enable women to be more child-centred. But there is a cost and lone-parenting also reduces the amount of adult space in the home.

Lone-parenting may be the experience of mothers with little or no contact with the non-residential parent, but it may be a poor description of relationships where contact is maintained. Here the child frequently moves between households and experiences multi-parenting and different domestic regimes. The growth of joint-custody orders demonstrates the determination of the state to encourage co-parenting, even in the absence of marriage. This may produce more pluralism in styles of parenting. However, it may also extend men's powers in controlling the lives of their ex-partners . . . As partnerships dissolve, so wide kinship relations alter. Ties and patterns of exchange with one's own kin may strengthen as they provide at least temporary support. Here younger, never-married women, may find themselves reincorporated into their parents' household. However, relations with in-laws are often severed, especially if the dissolution has been accompanied by bitterness and recrimination . . .

Women without partners may have a greater need of wider friendships and a greater opportunity to participate in friendship groups. As a partnership dissolves, so often the joint friendships associated with it also fade and new circles of acquaintanceship are built up. Relationships in these networks are less intense than those in kinship networks. They are more fleeting, reciprocal and *ad hoc*, in contrast to the more all-encompassing and obligatory understandings of kinship support. Among friends the exchanges are also less gendered, with a greater range of services being supplied by other women.

Part VIII

Race and Ethnicity

Ethnic divisions – divisions between groups based upon differences of culture and/or physical appearance – are frequently linked to profound social tensions and conflicts. There are few multi-cultural societies that have no history of antagonism between the members of their constituent ethnic communities. Lines of opposition and prejudice frequently centre upon 'racial' differences between whites and non-whites. In Reading 34, Frances Aboud discusses the development of ethnic awareness in childhood, concentrating upon 'racial' difference. She finds that ethnic awareness develops at an early age, although the differentiations that are drawn are complex and shift quite rapidly.

In Reading 35 Tariq Modood and his co-authors analyse ethnic diversity in Britain. 'Britishness' is a complicated matter. A white Briton who does not understand the accents of, say his or her Afro-Caribbean co-citizens is as incompletely 'British' as is someone of South Asian background ignorant of the ways of the white population. Modood's survey indicates something of the cultural diversity which now exists in Britain. Second-generation immigrants are likely to differ from their parents, but most tend to preserve cultural practices distinct from those of the white majority.

The prejudices which whites have entertained towards blacks have to be understood in a broad historical context. In substantial part their origins are bound up with Western expansionism and colonialism. In Reading 36, Paul Gilroy emphasizes that the cultural development of black groups in Britain similarly has to be seen against an international backdrop. Black cultural styles in the United Kingdom form part of a 'diaspora' – a network of cultural connections and oppositions spanning many countries. Blacks in Britain are linked by many ties to blacks elsewhere:

something which is also the case, however, Gilroy argues, for whites within British culture.

In Reading 37, Christian Jopke seeks to understand ethnic relations in Britain in the context of the country's imperial past. Most immigrants in Britain since 1945 have come from countries which once formed part of the British Empire. Britain's history as an immigrant society has been strongly affected by the fact that many citizens of the British Empire have been denied rights of immigration into Britain itself.

READING 34

Frances Aboud

The Development of Ethnic Awareness and Identification

Applying an ethnic label correctly or identifying which person goes with a given ethnic label is usually measured by showing pictures or dolls from different ethnic groups and asking the child to point to, for example, the white, the black and the Native Indian person. A significant proportion of children make correct identifications at 4 and 5 years of age and this proportion increases with age. By 6 and 7 years the children reach close to 100 per cent accuracy especially when identifying whites and blacks. Two studies found that 3-year-olds were very inaccurate in that less than 25 per cent of them correctly pointed to the white and black when given those labels. However, 4- and 5-year-olds reached close to 75 per cent accuracy or better in both white and black samples. Most of these studies also indicate a significant improvement with age, suggesting that 3–5 are the critical years for acquiring this form of label awareness. By improvement, I mean that a larger proportion of children made accurate identifications. Older white and black children of 6, 7 and 8 years usually reached a level of 90–100 per cent accuracy.

. . . It is also between the ages of 5 and 7 years that white and Chinese Americans acquire the ability to identify Chinese people. However, the identification of Hispanics or Mexican Americans seems to be more difficult for both white and Hispanic children. They improved in accuracy between 4 and 9 years of age and reached asymptote around 9 or 10 years. Similarly, the identification of Native Indians by both white and Indian children was fairly good by 6 years of age but continued to improve during the next three years. Presumably the children were using features such as skin colour and hair type for whites and blacks and so found Hispanics, Indians and whites less distinctive in these features than whites and blacks.

The child's awareness of ethnic groupings also takes the form of perceiving certain similarities between members of the same group and perceiving certain differences between members of different groups. Vaughan gave children sets of three pictures of people and asked them which two were similar and different from the third. By 6 years of age the children had reached a level of 68 per cent accuracy and this improved to 83 per cent by 11 years.[1] Similarly, Katz, Sohn and Zalk asked children to rate the degree of similarity between pairs of people. At 8 years of age, white and black children rated same-ethnic pairs as more similar than different-ethnic pairs.[2] That is, two whites were perceived as very similar and two blacks were perceived as very similar despite their different facial features or different shades of skin colour. Black children rated two whites as slightly more similar than two blacks. However, a white and a black were always perceived as very different. An interesting result from the Katz et al. study was that in later years, perceptions of dissimilarity were not always based on race but were sometimes based on individual features such as emotional expression. In other words, the children had acquired perceptions of racial similarity and difference by 8 years, had continued to use these perceptions for the following three years, and then abandoned them at 11 or 12 years in favour of perceptions of individual features. Thus, we must keep in mind the fact that racial awareness is often overused when it is first acquired, but that it may lose its salience later on when other types of awareness become more useful.

Another method was used by Aboud and Mitchell to examine how children perceive similarities and differences among different ethnic members.[3] The Native Indian children in this study were first asked to place photographs of men from four different ethnic groups on a similarity board to indicate how similar the men were to themselves. Then a peer from each ethnic group was placed (one at a time) at the end of the board. The children were asked to repeat the rating procedure, this time to indicate how similar the men were to each ethnic peer. The children, who ranged from 6 to 10 years of age, accurately perceived the same-ethnic man as most similar to the peer and the three different-ethnic men as equally dissimilar. On a second task, they were asked whom each ethnic peer would most want as an uncle or brother. It was expected that these kinship selections would closely parallel the similarity ratings as indeed they did.

When white children of the same age were given the same task they made a number of interesting errors. Younger children often made egocentric errors in that they assigned the uncle they wanted, a white uncle, to another ethnic peer. Both younger and older children also made mismatch errors in that they assigned an incorrect non-white uncle to the peer. These mismatches were especially frequent when the peer came from a disliked ethnic group, or when the peer, whether from their own or a disliked group, spoke his non-English native language (e.g. the Asian child spoke Chinese, the Hispanic Spanish and the white French). Perceptions of ethnic similarity or kinship received interference both from the child's own strong preferences and from his or her strong dislikes. It seemed that the older children were able to control their own strong preferences but not their dislikes. The errors for the disliked group were probably due a lack of knowledge or attention to details. [Another study] also found that children possessed least knowledge about national groups that they disliked. This lack of knowledge or attention to detail has manifested itself in several different ways. For example, in the Aboud and Mitchell study, many children chose the wrong, but not their ingroup, ethnic uncle. In [one] study, it was reported that British children from 7 to 11 years were egocentric in suggesting that a disliked outgroup peer would prefer a British person. The opposite was found by [another investigation], where more ingroup preference or ethnocentrism was attributed to disliked nationalities. The egocentric judgements of British children support Piaget's observations of Swiss children, but not the reports of North American children. Perhaps egocentrism persists longer when one is assigning preferences to national groups with whom one has little contact rather than ethnic groups living in one's community.

Vaughan found that children were able to categorize by race and to give appropriate labels to people only after they were relatively accurate at perceiving similarities.[4] He claimed that categorizing and labelling required certain cognitive skills, such as classification, that matured later than perceptual skills. For example, Vaughan asked children to sort white and Maori dolls by race. At 5 and 6 years of age, only 60 per cent of the children could do this correctly. However, by 7 years of age 85 per cent of the children were accurate, and 100 per cent were at 8 years. Similarly, when Vaughan showed them a doll and asked 'What sort of doll is this?' not until 7 years of age did a significant proportion of the children give the correct racial label: 85 per cent at 7 years of age and 100 per cent at 8 years.

Other researchers have used the sorting task but they have used it to measure the salience of race over other cues such as sex and age rather than as a measure of awareness of categories. [One group] presented children with pictures of people who varied in race, sex and age. The children sorted these pictures into two boxes of people who 'belong together'. Almost half the children sorted the people according to race; this was true for white, black and Asian children who ranged from 6 to 10 years of age. Sorting by race increased with age for the white children only. Given Vaughan's data, we cannot be sure whether the younger children sorted by sex or age because they were unable to sort by race or because sex and age were more salient to them. However, the older children were presumably capable of sorting by any one of the categories but chose race because it was the most salient. We might expect, then, that sorting by race or ethnicity increases from 4 to 7 years as children develop a cognitive awareness of racial categories. Whether it increases or decreases thereafter depends on the other categories available. Relative to sex and age, race remained salient for Davey's children. However, relative to personality or individual features, race became less salient for the white children in Katz et al.'s study.

A more mature form of ethnic awareness involves understanding that race and ethnicity are tied to something deeper than clothing and other superficial features. Adults think of a person's ethnicity as being derived from his or her family background. However, young children are not aware of this deeper meaning of ethnicity; they are fooled by superficial features. For example, not until the age of 9 or 10 do black children seem to be aware that a person remains black even though she puts on white make up or a blond wig, or even though she may want to be white. This deeper awareness manifests itself in many ways. One of these is constancy or the constant identification of a person's ethnicity despite transformations in superficial features. Aboud examined constancy by showing children a photograph of an Italian Canadian who was labelled as such. Then a sequence of four photos was shown of the Italian Canadian boy donning Native Indian clothing over the top of his ordinary clothes. In the final photo, the boy's appearance had changed except for his face. The children were asked to identify the boy in the final photo. Constancy was said to be present if the child said that he was Italian and not Indian (label), that he was more similar to photos of other Italian children than to photos of Indians (perceived similarity), and that he should be put into the pile of other Italians (categorization). Constancy increased from 5 to 9 years of age but was not really present until 8 years. Most children younger than 8 years thought the boy was Indian.

Furthermore, when asked if the boys in the first and last photos were the same person or two different persons, half the 6-year-olds said they were two different persons. Over 90 per cent of the 7-year-olds knew they were the same boy, but not until a year later did they attain ethnic constancy. Children of 8 years and older were certain that the boy was Italian and not Indian. Consistent with our previous discussion, the two cognitive identifications of labelling and categorization were more difficult than the perceived similarity identification. At 8 years they not only identified the boy as Italian but also inferred that he would prefer an Italian over an Indian playmate. However, although the 8- and 9-year-olds understood that ethnicity was deeper than clothing, they were not able to articulate the reason for this. When asked what makes a person Italian or Indian, only a few mentioned country of birth or family but most did not know.

Another manifestation of children's maturing awareness of ethnicity is that they understand the cause of skin colour. [One group] tested the notion that with age children dispense with their early view that skin colour is caused supernaturally or through arbitrary association (e.g. being American or being bad) and begin to understand that it is transmitted via a physical mechanism from parents to children. Children were asked. 'How is it that this person is white . . . this one black?' Their answers were coded in terms of seven levels of understanding the cause of skin colour. Children became aware that there were physical origins of a person's skin colour after the age of 7, though they did not make the link to parents till some time later. Understanding the physical basis of skin colour was acquired after they had mastered conservation. This awareness developed around the same time as identity constancy, measured here as the understanding that kinship remains constant despite a change in age and family size. It is clear, then, that ethnic constancy and a mature understanding of skin colour are later developments and require a fairly mature level of cognitive development. [It has been] found that this level of awareness [is] necessary for the decline in white children's prejudice towards blacks.

READING 35

Tariq Modood, Sharon Beishon and Satnam Virdee

Changing Ethnic Identities in Britain

We sought, through interviews and group discussions with seventy-four people, to build an understanding of what their ethnic background means to members of the main minority groups. For the South Asians, the two variables were national/regional origins and religion. With the Caribbeans, they were regional origins and African descent. Additionally, the study was structured so that we could compare the migrant with the British-born generation and focus on the changes that have been and are taking place in the various ethnic identities, especially in how they relate to conceptions of Britishness.

FAMILY AND SOCIAL CONTACTS

We found that family structures have undergone considerable change from the pre-migration period. The extended family networks of the Caribbeans have not been carried over to Britain and there is no longer a collective solving of child-care and financial problems within the wider family or the wider community. Half of the Caribbean respondents were in regular contact only with immediate family members. There was a strong feeling of mutual obligations, however, within the immediate family, but here too change was evident. The first generation felt that their children, growing up in Britain, did not give them the automatic respect *they* had given to their own parents. Parents had, in the main, adapted to this generational change and had come to have, with their children, more of a relationship between equals with advice and support flowing in both directions. Feelings of financial independence were present in both generations.

Between the two Caribbean generations the church has declined in favour of education and work as the place where friendships are made and sustained. Most Caribbean respondents had friends from other ethnic groups, though half of the first generation and a third of the second generation had only other Caribbeans as close friends. In both generations friends were chosen on the basis of shared experience, real or imagined, including that of ethnicity. Moreover, the experience of racism was often extremely important to the second generation in choosing friends. There was little if any difference in the type of activities shared between family members and friends regardless of ethnicity. Caribbeans were, on the whole, not committed to an ethnic preference in any absolute sense in the context of giving or receiving help, but some respondents felt that the inadequacy of existing mainstream services in meeting the needs of Caribbean people had left them with no option but an ethnic group basis for self-help and voluntary community work. Some of those who were active in organizations set up specifically for Caribbean people saw their work as contributing also to the wider goals of black cultural pride and black unity.

For the first-generation South Asians the extended family was an important institution of mutual support and transmission of values, and the main sphere of social life. Members of an extended family had high levels of contact with each other, seeing at least some other members once or twice a week, and would expect to give financial assistance to each other, including sending money 'back home'. If social life extended beyond the extended family it was within the ethno-religious community and was likely to be focused around a local temple or mosque. The absence of friends outside their own community was explained by first-generation respondents by reference to language and the importance of shared values and norms as a basis for friendship; some respondents were also discomforted that a lot of socializing in Britain involved the imbibing of alcohol.

The second-generation Asians, however, had much less contact with the extended family which was, at least up to this stage of their lives, hardly conceived of as a support system. Much of the value that the first generation placed on the extended family, the second generation placed instead on the immediate family, meaning parents, siblings and probably grandparents. While this probably means that their lives are more centred around the family than their non-Asian peers in Britain, it also means that their social life is unlikely to be centred around the extended family but rather around relationships formed through work or educational institution. Most of this generation, consequently, had friends from outside their ethnoreligious communities, particularly if they were or had been in higher education. For most respondents, however, their closest friends were from their own ethnic background or were at least Asian. The reasons given for this were to some extent similar to those of the first generation, namely the importance of similar backgrounds, interests and values; but some mentioned the need for mutual support against racism and cultural isolation, and others that it was a consequence of their ethnic identity.

COMMUNITY LANGUAGES

Both the South Asian generations thought it important to maintain the learning and use of their ethnic group languages. It was generally perceived that the use of these languages was in decline, with increasing numbers of second-generation respondents not only unable to read or write in the relevant language but also restricting the spoken language to home and family. But some counteraction was being taken. For example, some communities were organizing classes and most Asian respondents wanted Asian languages to be taught in state schools.

The Caribbean first generation on the other hand were relatively unworried by the decline in the use of Patois and Creole. There was, however, a resurgence of interest amongst the second generation in Creole and Patois as part of a new emphasis on cultural identity. The first generation took a predominantly practical approach to language, judging a language by its utility in offering career opportunities. The second generation valued their ancestral languages for putting them in touch with a history, a culture and a part of the world that for some was only ever seen on rare holidays and on television screens.

RELIGION

For the majority of the first-generation Caribbeans and nearly all first-generation Asians religion was of considerable importance as to how they lived their lives. It gave them a moral structure, with its emphasis on familial obligations and opposition to a materialist, hedonist or selfish view of life. The Caribbeans were more likely to emphasize the power of prayer in bringing them close to God, in giving strength to cope with difficulties that arose and in celebrating joyful occasions. Some also spoke of the church as a family group to give and take support from when needed. The Asians were more likely to emphasize the regularity of prayer and attendance at a place of worship and the restrictions on food and drink, though they also spoke of the celebration of holy festivals. For most first-generation Asians religion was central to their cultural identity and for some it was of more importance than any other aspect of ethnicity.

Virtually all the first-generation respondents had brought their children up within their faith and, while the Asians expected their children to live within it, the Caribbeans hoped they would but expected them to decide for themselves upon reaching adulthood. All the second-generation Caribbeans had been brought up as practising Christians but over half felt that religion no longer played an important part in their lives. They viewed religion as a set of behavioural restrictions out of touch with their daily realities. The importance of Christianity for those second-generation respondents who were still influenced by it centred on the supportive nature of the church community. They also attributed a sense of stability in their lives to adherence to their faith. It was considered central to educational and career progress because it kept them 'out of trouble' and away from negative influences. While some of the first generation spoke of Christianity as an important part of their cultural heritage and identity, in general the second generation did not. Neither the minority who were practising Christians nor the majority who were not made any special connection between Christianity and their ethnicity.

The Asian second generation too did not give religion the same kind of importance as the Asian first generation. This was particularly so with the Sikhs, only one of whom thought that religion was important. Even she, however, confessed that like the rest of her peer group she did not attend the temple or pray regularly. In fact the young Sikhs attended the temple only when required to do so for a festival or a wedding. Yet, in differing degrees, they held the view that Sikhism was part of their ethnic heritage and they would wish to hand it on to their children.

The second-generation Hindus were more likely to say that religion was important in the way they led their life, yet they, too, rarely attended a temple. For them religion was a matter of personal spiritual fulfilment and therefore each individual had to practise it in the way it suited them. Some did, however, also emphasize the religious basis of their code of behaviour concerning food and drink, dress and socializing, some of them instancing pubs and mini-skirts as things with which they were not comfortable. Even so they tended to observe the Hindu prohibition on beef more than the prohibition on alcohol. Other second-generation Hindus, particularly men, frankly admitted that religion was an irrelevance to them and regretted that to please their parents they would have to restrict their choice of marriage partner to Hindus. Yet they were not inclined to deny that Hinduism was part of their cultural heritage and they expected to want to pass it on to their children.

Among the second-generation Asians it was the Muslims who spoke most positively about the value and centrality of their religion. Most said that Islam was 'very important' to how they lived their lives. But it was obvious that beyond this emphatic affirmation there were currents of questioning, revision and even a pressured conformity. Nearly all the second-generation Muslims said they were not strict in the observance of the various requirements of their faith, and several felt a tension between the demands of their faith and the life they thought appropriate in contemporary England. One of them, encouraged by her father, had gone a long way in reinterpreting Islam as an ethical philosophy without an array of petty rules. Like their Hindu peers, they were less likely to perform formal worship and prayer and more likely to have a more personalized approach. Even more than the other Asian groups they did not doubt that a religious identity would be part of what they would wish to inculcate in their children, for Islam was central to their minority identity.

Despite the importance that the three sets of first-generation Asians claimed for religion, there was little support for the idea of religious schools. The only group that could see any value in the idea were the Muslims, and even then only two of the eight first-generation Muslims said they would send their children to such schools. Everyone else either questioned the quality of academic education that such schools would provide or thought that they would exacerbate communal divisions and racial prejudice. The second generation of each of the three faith communities was of this view and many of them were passionately opposed to such schools. Most of both generations thought that state schools should make better provision to meet the religious needs of minorities and to include their heritage within the curriculum, though some thought that the transmission of religions and languages was the responsibility of families and communities alone. Similarly, the majority of the first generation, including all of the

Muslims, were in favour of single-sex secondary schools, especially for girls. A number of second generation women too thought that girls-only schools were academically better for girls.

MARRIAGE PARTNERS

A further topic of study was mixed marriages and relationships. In both the Caribbean generations there was some ambivalence about these. Most did not express disapproval and it was generally felt that the choice of partners was down to the individual person. Respondents pointed out, however, the problems that mixed couples would face. Other peoples' attitudes towards mixed relationships and the children were highlighted. Indeed, even the attitude of the white partner was said to be potentially troublesome. Cultural differences were also mentioned as a possible problem. Two respondents argued that mixed relationships should be encouraged as they break down barriers between groups in society. The most emotive issue, however, was a feeling among the second generation of betrayal by those successful black people who had chosen white partners because they thought other black people not good enough for them or likely to be a social handicap.

The marriages of the first-generation Asian respondents had been arranged by their parents within their own ethno-religious group. They expected the same for their children, believing this was a sounder basis for a life-long marriage than 'falling in love'. Additionally, Asians voiced several objections to mixed marriages. It was envisaged that the partner in such a marriage would not be interested in or able to fully join the Asian family with its mutual responsibilities. This would weaken family ties and the children would drift away; conversely, in order to succeed in a mixed marriage and a predominantly non-Asian social environment, the Asian partner would lose or suppress his or her culture or religion. Children of such unions would have even fewer roots in Asian family, cultural and religious life. Finally, the first-generation respondents pointed to the disapproval in their communities [of] such marriages, as a result of which a family in which such a marriage took place might suffer a considerable loss of standing. The position of the Muslims was modified by the fact that it was at least theoretically recognized that marriages outside the ethnic group were endorsed by religion as long as the partner was or became a Muslim. The position of the Sikhs and Hindus had undergone some change in that very few respondents mentioned caste as a legitimate consideration.

The second-generation Asians took a less clear-cut view, though many of them held diametrically opposed views to those of the first generation. Nearly all of the second generation gave some support to the view that marriage was ultimately a matter of individual choice, and some explicitly argued that colour or ethnic origin was not relevant. On the other hand, most also recognized that the problems mentioned by the first generation were real enough; a few said that romantic love was overvalued and they could not happily marry someone not culturally compatible with their family. Some Indians thought that the problems of drifting away from one's family and culture were not insuperable if sympathetic non-Indian partners were chosen. The majority of the second-generation Indians had no objections to mixed marriages and about half of them (though few Muslims) positively approved of cohabiting with a partner as a form of 'trial marriage'. Muslims seemed to entertain least the possibility of marriage to non-Muslims who did not convert to Islam though some thought that conversion was too great a demand to make on one's partner.

The most marked difference between first-generation expectations and second-generation aspirations, especially among the Indians, was on the custom of parentally arranged marriages. If Asian families have so far avoided serious internal conflict over arranged marriage, this is probably because when it came to the crunch the children accepted their parents' authority, perhaps fearing the consequences of outright conflict, and wanting to avoid the community censure and shame their actions might bring upon the whole family. Parents may be modifying traditional arrangements by incorporating some element of consultation and compromise with the children, but endogamy continues to be the norm, and for the time being marriage remains a principal means of affirming and maintaining an ethnic identity amongst the South Asian groups.

DIFFERENCE, COMMONALITY AND EXCLUSION

The predominant term of self-identity amongst the Caribbean respondents was black, though slightly more common amongst the first generation was West Indian and, amongst the second generation, hyphenated terms like Afro-Caribbean had replaced West Indian and some made reference to British, as in black British. Black is now firmly established as a term of positive self-identification, colour having replaced specific island origins, and being allied to a pan-Caribbean identity. For colour is the conspicuous difference noted by the white British and the basis of exclusion. Some second-generation respondents thought of themselves as black British even while appreciating that the white British did not necessarily accept this sharing of an identity. Two respondents, however, felt that a colour identity was too restrictive and could not encompass the totality of their identity.

Thus, while most had transformed a negative racial description into a positive identity, some worried that even a positive racial identity restricted one's total identity and encouraged the white British to see one as a 'type'. There was little interest in an 'African' identity, unlike in the United States, where 'African-American' is largely replacing 'black' in public discourse. For some second-generation respondents 'black' referred to all who suffered racism and thus included South Asians. In any case, most thought that, despite the considerable cultural dissimilarities, the experience of racism was a basis of commonality with Asians and some thought that food and family offered other forms of commonality, while others that British youth culture was creating new fusions.

Despite a strong sense of social and cultural commonality with the white British, most Caribbeans found it difficult to lay claim to [being] British. The difficulty was almost entirely based on the knowledge that the majority of white British people did not acknowledge the commonality and really believed that only white people could be British. The Caribbeans felt that they were constantly reminded that they were not accepted in a variety of ways including discrimination in employment, harassment, invisibility and stereo-typing in the media, and glorification of an imperial past in which they were oppressed. This racism rather than any sense of distinctive ethnic heritage was seen as an obstacle to feelings of unity with the white British majority.

Most South Asians, especially amongst the first generation, identified with their specific ethnic or religious identity rather than with a pan-Asian ethnicity or British nationality. Religious identification was virtually absent amongst the Punjabi Sikhs who predominantly described themselves as Indians. Pakistanis were alone amongst the first generation in using a hyphenated Pakistani-British description. Such hyphenated descriptions were used by some second-generation individuals in each of these groups, and amongst the second-generation Punjabis and Gujaratis, 'Asian' was also used. On the whole, the South Asians were as conscious of differences as of similarities between Asians. The Sikhs and Hindus were most likely to refer to each other as the group with whom they had the most in common, and Pakistanis and Bangladeshis pointed to their commonality in Islam. Those who emphasized the differences between Asian groups referred to religion, language, dress and cuisine; those who emphasized the similarities spoke of Asians having religion-centred cultures based on similar family structures and moral codes.

While those for whom Asian was a positive identity were a minority (only half the sample expressed a view), those who rejected the idea were few, and most used the term to describe themselves and their community. A small number of second-generation persons, mainly Punjabis, emphas-ized the importance of a 'black' political identity; for them it highlighted the importance of racism rather than minority cultures in shaping the lives of the non-white minorities, and offered a basis of uniting all these groups in effective anti-racism beyond an emphasis on cultural differences. Most of them, and some other second-generation Asians, felt culturally close to young Caribbeans, especially in terms of music, friendships and social life. Most of the second-generation respondents and all of the first-generation respondents, however, felt there were major dissimilarities between them-selves and Caribbeans, instancing religion, language, family structure, marriages, dress and food, and felt that the Caribbeans were much more integrated into British life.

Most Asian respondents thought that being British depended upon more than a legal definition, for example, most first-generation Asians thought that their children, schooled and socialized in Britain, were more British than themselves. Equally, they thought that white people did not allow non-whites to be fully British. For themselves, most of the first generation did not claim to be, nor wanted to be, British in this extra-legal sense. They had a strong sense of belonging to the society in which they had been brought up and saw themselves as law-abiding, hard-working citizens at peace with British society but culturally distinct from it. Other first-generation respon-dents, more often male and more educated, saw their citizenship as imply-ing an active interest in British institutions and society, adopting British ways and mixing with all kinds of Britons socially, whilst still maintaining some of their religious and ethnic traditions in a bi-cultural way.

217

Some of the second generation too saw themselves in terms of a bi-culturalism but the majority felt they were culturally more British than anything else. Few, however, felt they could call themselves British in an unproblematic way. By thinking of Britishness in terms of 'whiteness', backed up by violence, racial discrimination, harassment, abusive jokes and cultural intolerance, some white people made it very difficult for non-whites to identify with Britain in a positive way. Those who saw themselves in terms of a bi-cultural or hyphenated identity were, however, usually positive about being British and did not think that there was an inevitable conflict between the two sides of their identity. A minority of second-generation Asians, however, felt alienated from British culture, which they perceived as hostile to their family-centred and religious values.

ETHNIC IDENTITY AND THE FUTURE

This study, then, shows how ethnic identity, far from being some primordial stamp upon an individual, is a plastic and changing badge of membership. Ethnic identity is a product of a number of forces: social exclusion and stigma and political resistance to them, distinctive cultural and religious heritages as well as new forms of culture, communal and familial loyalties, marriage practices, coalition of interests and so on. Hence, the boundaries of groups are unclear and shifting, especially when groups seek to broaden an ethnic identity or to accommodate membership in a number of overlapping groups. And this leaves out the broader social, economic and political forces.

What is clear is that, while considerable cultural adaptation has taken place and is still taking place, the predictions of an unproblematic assimilationist 'melting pot' have proven to be sociologically naïve . . . Minority ethnicity is neither simply a racist attribution nor a set of private practices but, symbolically and materially, has become a feature of British society with all that implies for public identities, political solidarities and competition for resources. It also means a rethinking of Britishness and the varieties and forms that it can encompass.

Our research shows, we believe, that the emerging and evolving plurality on the ground, especially when allied to developments in mixed ethnicity relationships which we have not explored, belies those who argue that the infusion of new cultural groups is disruptive to social cohesion and British identity. It challenges those who think in terms of the simplistic oppositions of British–alien or black–white. A significant population on the ground is living in ways that refute these dualisms. It is time for social analysts and policy-makers to catch up. We need a new vision of Britishness which allows minorities to make a claim upon it, to be accepted as British regardless of their colour and origins, and without having to conform to a narrow cultural norm.

READING 36

Paul Gilroy

'There Ain't No Black in the Union Jack'

As black styles, music, dress, dance, fashion and languages became a determining force shaping the style, music, dress, fashion and language of urban Britain as a whole, blacks have been structured into the mechanisms of this society in a number of different ways. Not all of them are reducible to the disabling effects of racial subordination. This is part of the explanation of how [black] youth cultures became repositories of anti-racist feeling. Blacks born, nurtured and schooled in this country are, in significant measure, British even as their presence redefines the meaning of the term. The language and structures of racial politics, locked as they are into a circular journey between immigration as problem and repatriation as solution, prevent this from being seen. Yet recognizing it and grasping its significance is essential to the development of anti-racism in general and in particular for understanding the social movements for racial equality that helped to create the space in which 'youth culture' could form. The contingent and partial belonging to Britain which blacks enjoy, their ambiguous assimilation, must be examined in detail for it is closely associated with specific forms of exclusion. If we are to comprehend the cultural dynamics of 'race' we must be able to identify its limits. This, in turn, necessitates consideration of how blacks define and represent themselves in a complex combination of resistances and negotiations, which does far more than provide a direct answer to the brutal forms in which racial subordination is imposed.

Black expressive cultures affirm while they protest. The assimilation of blacks is not a process of acculturation but of cultural syncretism. Accordingly, their self-definitions and cultural expressions draw on a plurality of black histories and politics. In the context of modern Britain this has produced a diaspora dimension to black life. Here, non-European traditional elements, mediated by the histories of Afro-America and the Caribbean, have contributed to the formation of new and distinct black cultures amidst the decadent peculiarities of the Welsh, Irish, Scots and English. These non-European elements must be noted and their distinctive resonance must be accounted for. Some derive from the immediate history of empire and colonization in Africa, the Caribbean and the Indian subcontinent from where postwar settlers brought both the methods and the memories of their battles for citizenship, justice and independence. Others create material for the processes of cultural syncretism from extended and still-evolving relationships between the black populations of the overdeveloped world and their siblings in racial subordination elsewhere.

The effects of these ties and the penetration of black forms into the dominant culture mean that it is impossible to theorize black culture in Britain without developing a new perspective on British culture *as a whole*. This must be able to see behind contemporary manifestations into the cultural struggles which characterized the imperial and colonial period. An intricate web of cultural and political connections binds blacks here to blacks elsewhere. At the same time, they are linked into the social relations of this country. Both dimensions have to be examined and the contradictions and continuities which exist between them must be brought out. Analysis must, for example, be able to suggest why Afrika Bambaataa and Jah Shaka, leading representatives of hip-hop and reggae culture respectively, find it appropriate to take the names of African chiefs distinguished in anti-colonial struggle, or why young black people in places as different as Hayes and Harlem choose to style themselves the Zulu nation. Similarly, we must comprehend the cultural and political relationships which have led to Joseph Charles and Rufus Radebe being sentenced to six years' imprisonment in South Africa for singing banned songs written by the Birmingham reggae band Steel Pulse – the same band which performed to London's [Rock Against Racism] carnival in 1978.

The social movements which have sprung up in different parts of the world as evidence of African dispersal, imperialism and colonialism have done more than appeal to blacks everywhere in a language which could invite their universal identification. They have communicated directly to blacks and their supporters all over the world asking for concrete help and solidarity in the creation of organizational forms adequate to the pursuit of emancipation, justice and citizenship, internationally as well as within national frameworks. The nineteenth-century English abolitionists who purchased the freedom of Frederick Douglass, the distinguished black activist and writer, were responding to an appeal of this type. The eighteenth-century settlement of Sierra Leone by blacks from England and their white associates and the formation of free black communities in Liberia remain an important testimony to the potency of such requests. The back-to-Africa movements in America, the Caribbean and now Europe, Negritude and the birth of the New Negro in the Harlem Renaissance during the 1920s all provide further illustrations of a multi-faceted desire to overcome the sclerotic confines of the nation state as a precondition of the liberation of blacks everywhere.

Technological developments in the field of communication have, in recent years, encouraged this desire and made it more powerful by fostering a global perspective from the memories of slavery and indenture which are the property of the African diaspora. The soul singers of Afro-America have been able to send 'a letter to their friends' in Africa and elsewhere. The international export of new world black cultures first to whites and then to 'third world' markets in South America and Africa itself has had effects unforeseen by those for whom selling it is nothing other than a means to greater profit. Those cultures, in the form of cultural commodities – books and records – have carried inside them oppositional ideas, ideologies, theologies and philosophies. As black artists have addressed an international audience and blues, gospel, soul and reggae have been consumed in circumstances far removed from those in which they were originally created, new definitions of 'race' have been born. A new structure of cultural exchange has been built up across the imperial networks which once played host to the triangular trade of sugar, slaves and capital. Instead of three nodal points there are now four – the Caribbean, the US, Europe and Africa. The cultural and political expressions of new-world blacks have been transferred not just to Europe and Africa but between various parts of the new world itself. By these means Rastafari culture has been carried to locations as diverse as Poland and Polynesia, and hip-hop from Stockholm to Southall.

Analysis of the political dimensions to the expressive culture of black communities in Britain must reckon with their position within international networks. It should begin where fragmented diaspora histories of racial subjectivity combine in unforeseen ways with the edifice of British society and create a complex relationship which has evolved through various stages linked in different ways to the pattern of capitalist development itself.

The modern world-system responsible for the expansion of Europe and consequent dispersal of black slave labourers throughout Europe and the new world was from its inception an international operation. Several scholars have pointed to its uneasy fit into forms of analysis premised on the separation of its economic and cultural subsystems into discrete national units coterminous with nation states. The social structures and processes erected over the productive and distributive relations of this system centred on slavery and plantation society and were reproduced in a variety of different forms across the Americas, generating political antagonisms which were both international and transnational in character. Their contemporary residues, rendered more difficult to perceive by the recent migration of slave descendants into the centres of metropolitan civilization, also exhibit the tendency to transcend a narrowly national focus. Analysis of black politics must, therefore, if it is to be adequate, move beyond the field of enquiry designated by concepts which deny the possibility of common themes, motives and practices within diaspora history. This is where categories formed in the intersection of 'race' and the nation state are themselves exhausted. To put it another way, national units are not the most appropriate basis for studying this history, for the African diaspora's consciousness of itself has been defined in and against constricting national boundaries.

As the international slave system unfolded, so did its antithesis in the form of transnational movements for self-emancipation organized by slaves, ex-slaves and their abolitionist allies. This is not the place to provide a full account of these movements or even of the special place within them occupied by ideas about Africa. However, that continent has been accepted by many, though not all, who inhabit and reproduce the black syncretisms of the overdeveloped world as a homeland even if they do not aspire to a physical return there. Ties of affect and affiliation have been strengthened by knowledge of anti-colonial struggles which have sharpened contemporary understanding of 'race'. These feelings, of being descended from or belonging to Africa and of longing for its liberation from imperialist rule, can be linked loosely by the term 'pan-Africanism'. The term is inadequate as anything other than the most preliminary description, particularly as it can suggest mystical unity outside the process of history or even a common culture or ethnicity which will assert itself regardless of determinate political and economic circumstances. The sense of interconnectedness felt by blacks to which it refers has in some recent manifestations become partially detached from any primary affiliation to Africa and from the aspiration to a homogeneous African culture. Young blacks in Britain, for example, stimulated to riotous protest by the sight of black 'South Africans' stoning apartheid police and moved by scenes of brutality transmitted from that country by satellite, may not feel that shared Africanness is at the root of the empathy they experience. It may be that a common experience of powerlessness somehow transcending history and experienced in *racial* categories; in the antagonism between white and black rather than European and African, is enough to secure affinity between these divergent patterns of subordination. As Ralph Ellison pointed out long ago: 'Since most so-called Negro-cultures outside Africa are necessarily amalgams, it would seem more profitable to stress the term "culture" and leave the term "Negro" out of the discussion. It is not culture which binds the people who are of partially African origin now scattered throughout the world but an identity of passions.'[1]

. . . [These struggles] have, since the very first day that slaves set out across the Atlantic, involved radical passions rooted in distinctly African history, philosophy and religious practice. Passions which have, at strategic moments, challenged the political and moral authority of the capitalist world-system in which the diaspora was created. The ideologies and beliefs of new world blacks exhibit characteristically African conceptions of the relationship between art and life, the sacred and the secular, the spiritual and the material. Traces of these African formulations remain, albeit in displaced and mediated forms, even in the folk philosophies, religion and vernacular arts of black Britain.

READING 37

Christian Jopke

The Legacy of Empire: The British Case

In the wake of the Brixton riots of 1981, the worst urban unrest in British history, Salman Rushdie launched a bitter attack on the 'new empire' that had arisen within Britain. Branding the government's liberal 'race relations' policy as 'the latest token gesture towards Britain's blacks', the Indian-born author announced that the 'new colony' would rise up against the 'one real problem' that aggrieved its involuntary members: '[the racism of] white people'.[1] A few years later, Rushdie's *Satanic Verses* were publicly burned by an angry Muslim crowd in the city of Bradford, under the approving eyes of the Asian-born lord mayor; at Westminster, young Muslim demonstrators demanded that 'Rushdie Must be Chopped Up'. The incriminated author had to go into hiding, protected by Thatcher's white police against the anger of his fellow inmates of Britain's 'new colony'. What became known as the 'Rushdie affair' may epitomize more dramatically than [other events] the seamier side of a multi-cultural society. But the apparent ethnic assertiveness of parts of Britain's immigrant community is also the result of uniquely British conditions.

While the immigrant and colonialism perspectives usually exclude one another, they do closely overlap in Britain. This is because former colonial subjects – Caribbean blacks and Asian Indians – formed the bulk of postwar immigration. The legacy of empire created a unique linkage between immigration and multi-culturalism. In contrast to the United States, Britain has a race problem because it had immigration – the two are not separate here. This may explain why Britain has opted for an exceptionally restrictionist immigration policy from early on. In contrast to Germany, Britain complemented its restrictionist immigration policy with an American-style liberal 'race relations' management, which stopped short of granting affirmative action privileges to ethnic minorities but saw them as a legitimate part of a 'multi-racial' society in which 'mutual tolerance' should be the norm. The conjunction of a restrictionist immigration policy, which was conditioned by Britain's devolution from multi-racial empire to ethnic nation state, and liberal race relations management has both fuelled and frustrated the aspirations of Britain's immigrant minorities. Excluded by Britain's national community as 'blacks' or 'immigrants', even in the second generation, but endowed with equal citizenship status from the beginning, Britain's immigrant minorities have become more militant and ethnicized than elsewhere, as . . . became evident from Brixton to Bradford.

The first parameter shaping Britain's treatment of immigration is the devolution from empire to ethnic nation state. This went along with the exclusion of a 'coloured' immigrant periphery from an ethnicized British national community. Originally, Britain, with its English nationalist core, had adhered to a 'civic' model of nationhood, forged in an interstate struggle against Catholicism and absolute monarchy, with 'liberty' as core value . . . The acquisition of a vast empire had never been easy to reconcile with the civic nation model, and according to the national mythology it had occurred in a 'fit of absentmindedness'. In the post-imperial period after World War II, when Britain faced the double challenge of economic and geopolitical decline and potentially huge post-colonial immigration, Britain refashioned itself from a 'civic' to an 'ethnic' nation, in which membership became defined by birth and ancestry. Analysing the anti-immigrant rhetoric of Enoch Powell, Tom Nairn even finds that 'in the obscene form of racism, English nationalism has been re-born'.[2]

The flat 'racism' charge obscures the very real problem of immigration and national membership in post-imperial Britain. At the end of World War II, 800 million persons, born outside the UK on a territory that covered 25 per cent of the land surface of the globe, could claim the equal status of 'British subjects', with the concomitant right of settlement in Britain. A shift of membership definition from the feudal-dynastic principle of 'allegiance to the crown' to the national principle of territorial citizenship was not only a requirement of political modernization, but also corresponded to the right of a national collectivity to regulate its boundaries. Such a shift of membership definition was necessarily exclusive. Tragically, in the British constellation of a 'coloured' colonial periphery and a 'white' core nation it was impossible to accomplish without, in effect, [dividing] the 'ins' and 'outs' along racial lines.

The British political élites were initially unwilling to perform the shift from dynastic 'subjectship' to national 'citizenship', and it took the British Nationality Act of 1981 to accomplish it. After World War II, the negative example of 'racist' Nazi Germany and a certain nostalgic clinging to Britain's past Great Power status prevented Tories and Labourites alike from questioning the status quo. The British Nationality Act of 1948 solemnly affirmed the existence of a single Commonwealth citizenship in Britain and (post)colonies, with the equal right to enter Britain freely, work and settle. The non-nationalism of the centre was deliberately held against the nationalistic strivings of the decolonizing periphery. In a Westminster debate over immigration policy, a Conservative minister expressed the Commonwealth ideal then prevalent among the British élite: 'In a world in which restrictions on personal movement and immigration have increased we can still take pride in the fact that a man can say *civis Britannicus sum* whatever his colour may be, and we take pride in the fact that he wants and can come to the Mother Country.'

The reality of a country in decline undermined the noble Commonwealth idealism of the political élite. The Suez Crisis, where Britain was not followed by its coloured Commonwealth allies, exposed the hollowness of the

Commonwealth rhetoric. The snubbing of Britain's hesitant application to enter the European Community reinforced its isolationist and inward-looking leanings. Long-term economic stagnation soured the mood of the public. In the 1950s, 'no blacks, no dogs' signs were no rare sight in houses and shop windows across Britain. The Notting Hill riots of 1958, instigated by whites against blacks, convinced the élites of the ugly mood of the public. The following restrictions on New Commonwealth immigration reinstated a 'fundamental congruence between public attitudes and public policy',[3] as Gary Freeman dryly comments. The Commonwealth Immigrants Act of 1962 restricted entry to people holding work permits, and to the close families of residents and permit holders. In 1968, when British Asians faced expulsion from newly independent Kenya, a new Commonwealth Immigrants Act was [pushed] through Parliament in just three days, to deny these people entry to Britain, in clear violation of earlier promised protection. The Immigration Act of 1971 introduced the infamous 'patrial' clause, which tied the right of residency to the existence of at least one British grandparent – an indirect way of saying that 'Britain preferred white immigrants', as the *Economist* wrote. Finally, the British Nationality Act of 1981 adjusted nationality law to the restrictive immigration regime already in place, establishing a three-tier system of British, dependent territory, and overseas citizenship, with the right of entry and residence for 'British citizens' only.

Since it was fused with the creation of boundaries to define and encompass the British nation, immigration policy was necessarily restrictive and discriminating *vis-à-vis* members of its former colonies. With the exception of the 1968 Immigration Act, which was passed by a Labour government, all major legislation was passed by Conservative governments. But immigration policy was carried by a remarkable consensus among the major political parties, and there was a general attempt to keep the topic out of partisan politics. The two exceptions to this – Enoch Powell's notorious 'river of blood' speech in 1968, and Mrs Thatcher's no less notorious 'swamping' statement in 1978 – only confirmed the general pattern. Tellingly, Powell was thereafter removed from the Conservative shadow cabinet and, once elected as prime minister, Mrs Thatcher largely abstained from addressing race relations and immigration matters.

Yet Mrs Thatcher coined the phrase that best characterizes the general thrust of British immigration policy: 'firm but fair'. British immigration policy, which emerged as a result more of *ad hoc* adjustments than of a grand design, has at least two distinct characteristics: the complete absence of considering economic and labour market needs, and an obsession with control and 'detect[ing] or keep[ing] out that one extra black'.[4] The absence, if not explicit denial, of economic considerations reflects the general climate of decline and uncertainty about Britain's place in the world, in which immigration policy has been crafted. The obsession with border controls has deep roots in geography and history, i.e. the concentration of entry controls at a few port cities in conjunction with the absence of an internal passport system. But the antics of preventing illegal entry, often in breach of international human rights conventions, from denying visas to visiting family members, fingerprinting and 'virginity tests' to rabid acts of detention, which mostly happen to be directed against coloured persons of New Commonwealth origins, carry a clear message: that blacks are unwanted.

While it has been a declared government principle that 'good race relations' are dependent on 'strict immigration control', critics have repeatedly pointed at the inconsistency of a policy that 'discriminates against ethnic minorities at the point of entry while seeking to remove discrimination against them internally'.[5]

Part IX

Class and Stratification

All social systems are stratified – that is, material and cultural resources are distributed in an unequal fashion. In modern societies, class is the most significant (although by no means the only) form of social stratification. In spite of, or perhaps because of, its centrality in sociology there is no general agreement over how the concept of class should best be formulated.

Reading 38 compares the two most influential conceptions of class advanced in classical social thought, those of Karl Marx and Max Weber. According to Marx, class is above all linked to control of private property and 'surplus production'. Class relations are not just incidental to modern social orders, but absolutely essential to them, as are mechanisms of class conflict. Weber accepted a good deal of Marx's viewpoint, but argued that economic factors other than ownership or control of property are important in determining class divisions. Class concerns the differential distribution of 'life-chances', and these are affected by economic influences such as the structure of labour markets as well as by who controls property in the means of production.

John Scott's contribution (Reading 39) is directed at the upper echelons of the class structure. At the core of the upper class is the 'Establishment', a network of people who wield power in a diversity of major institutions. In terms of social mobility, the Establishment is substantially self-recruiting, such social reproduction being achieved primarily through the influence of the public schools and ancient universities. Within the business sector, Scott demonstrates, similar patterns of recruitment are found to those in other élite areas, such as the church, army or judiciary.

In Reading 40 Mike Savage discusses the problem of the middle class.

Who exactly is to be included in the category 'middle-class'? Is there in fact a distinct and separable middle class in Britain today? There is, he concludes, but it is not a unity; rather, it is composed of a variety of different occupational groupings which, while they share certain class characteristics in common, are also often in conflict with each other.

The final contribution discusses the vexed issue of the underclass. The notion of the underclass – a class of people more or less permanently unemployed and living in poverty – is a controversial one. Andy Pilkington accepts that inequality has been increasing in Britain over the past two decades. However, he concludes, there is not as yet evidence of a clearly distinct underclass. The poorest groups in society have probably not – yet at least – become clearly separated out from the larger category of the working class.

READING 38

Anthony Giddens
Marx and Weber on Class

According to Marx's theory, class society is the product of a determinate sequence of historical changes. The most primitive forms of human society are not class systems. In 'tribal' societies – or, in Engels's term, 'primitive communism' – there is only a very low division of labour, and such property as exists is owned in common by the members of the community. The expansion of the division of labour, together with the increased level of wealth which this generates, is accompanied by the growth of private property; this involves the creation of a surplus product which is appropriated by a minority of non-producers who consequently stand in an exploitative relation *vis-à-vis* the majority of producers. Expressed in the terminology of Marx's early writings, alienation from nature, which characterizes the situation of tribal society, yields place to an increasing mastery of the material world, whereby [human beings] both 'humanize' [themselves] and develop [their] culture; but the increasing dissolution of . . . alienation . . . is attained only at the price of the formation of exploitative class relationships – at the price of an increase in human self-alienation'.

Marx was not always careful to emphasize the differences between capitalism and [the] forms of class system which have preceded it in history. While it is the case that all (written) history 'is the history of class struggles',[1] this most definitely does not mean that what constitutes a 'class' is identical in each type of class society (although, of course, every class shares certain formal properties which define it as such), or that the process of the development of class conflict everywhere takes the same course. Marx's rebuke to those of his followers who had assumed the latter is instructive in this respect. Several of the factors which characterized the origins of the capitalist mode of production in Western Europe in the post-medieval period existed previously in Ancient Rome, including the formation of a merchant/manufacturing class and the development of money markets. But because of other elements in the composition of Roman society, including particularly the existence of slavery, the class struggles in Rome took a form which resulted not in the generation of a 'new and higher form of society', but in the disintegration of the social fabric.[2]

The diverse forms and outcomes of class conflict in history explain the different possibilities generated by the supersession of one type of society by another. When capitalism replaces feudalism, this is because a new class system, based upon manufacture and centred in the towns, has created a sort of enclave within feudal society which eventually comes to predominate over the agrarian-based structure of feudal domination. The result, however, is a new system of class domination, because this sequence of revolutionary change is based upon the partial replacement of one type of property in the means of production (land) by another (capital) – a process which, of course, entails major changes in technique. While capitalism, like feudalism, carries 'the germ of its own destruction' within itself, and while this self-negating tendency is also expressed in the shape of overt class struggles, their underlying character is quite different from those involved in the decline of feudalism. Class conflict in capitalism does not represent the struggle of two competing forms of technique, but stems instead from the incompatibility of an existing productive technique (industrial manufacture) with other aspects of the 'mode of production' – namely, the organization of the capitalist market. The access of a new class to power does not involve the ascendancy of a new form of private property, but instead creates the conditions under which private property is abolished. The proletariat here is the equivalent of Saint-Simon's *'industriels'*: because it becomes the 'only class' in society, its hegemony signals the disappearance of all classes.

The problem of Marx's usage of the term 'class' is complicated, given the fact that he does not provide a formal definition of the concept. In approaching this matter, it is valuable to make a distinction between three sets of factors which complicate discussion of the Marxian conception of class – factors which have not been satisfactorily separated in the long-standing controversy over the issue. The first of these refers simply to the question of terminology – the variability in Marx's use of the word 'class' itself. The second concerns the fact that there are two conceptual constructions which may be discerned in Marx's writings as regards the notion of class: *an abstract or 'pure' model of class domination*, which applies to all types of class system: and *more concrete descriptions of the specific characteristics of classes in particular societies*. The third concerns Marx's analysis of classes in capitalism, the case which overwhelmingly occupied his interests: just as there are in Marx 'pure' models of class, so there are 'pure' and 'concrete' models of the structure of capitalism and the process of capitalist development.

The terminological issue, of course, is the least significant of the three sets of questions here. The fact of the matter is that Marx's terminology is careless. While he normally uses the term 'class' (*Klasse*), he also uses words such as 'stratum' and 'estate' (*Stand*) as if they were interchangeable with it. Moreover, he applies the word 'class' to various groups which, in theoretical terms, are obviously only parts or sectors of 'classes' properly speaking: thus he speaks of intellectuals as the 'ideological classes', of the

Lumpenproletariat as the 'dangerous class', of bankers and moneylenders as the 'class of parasites', and so on. What matters, however, is how far this terminological looseness conceals conceptual ambiguities or confusions.

The principal elements of Marx's 'abstract model' of class domination are actually not difficult to reconstruct from the generality of his writings. This model is a dichotomous one. In each type of class society, there are two fundamental classes. Property relations constitute the axis of this dichotomous system: a minority of 'non-producers', who control the means of production, are able to use this position of control to extract from the majority of 'producers' the surplus product which is the source of their livelihood. 'Class' is thus defined in terms of the relationship of groupings of individuals to the means of production. This is integrally connected with the division of labour, because a relatively developed division of labour is necessary for the creation of the surplus product without which classes cannot exist. But, as Marx makes clear in his unfinished discussion at the end of the third volume of *Capital*, 'class' is not to be identified with source of income in the division of labour: this would yield an almost endless plurality of classes. Moreover, classes are never, in Marx's sense, income groupings. Modes of consumption, according to Marx, are primarily determined by relations of production. Hence his critique of those varieties of socialism which are directed towards securing some kind of 'distributive justice' in society – which seek, for example, the equalization of incomes: such forms of socialism are based on false premises, because they neglect the essential fact that distribution is ultimately governed by the system of production. This is why it is possible for two individuals to have identical incomes, and even the same occupations, and yet belong to different classes; as might be the case, for example, with two bricklayers, one of whom owns his own business, while the other works as the employee of a large firm.

It is an axiom of Marx's abstract model of classes that economic domination is tied to political domination. Control of the means of production yields political control. Hence the dichotomous division of classes is a division of both property and power: to trace the lines of economic exploitation in a society is to discover the key to the understanding of the relations of super- and subordination which apply within that society. Thus classes express a relation not only between 'exploiters and exploited', but between 'oppressors and oppressed'. Class relations necessarily are inherently unstable: but a dominant class seeks to stabilize its position by advancing (not usually, of course, in a consciously directed fashion) a legitimating ideology, which 'rationalizes' its position of economic and political domination and 'explains' to the subordinate class why it should accept its subordination. This is the connotation of the much quoted assertion that:

> The ideas of the ruling class are in every epoch the ruling ideas: i.e., the class which is the ruling *material* force of society, is at the same time its ruling *intellectual* force. The class which has the means of material production at its disposal, has control at the same time over the means of mental production, so that thereby, generally speaking, the ideas of those who lack the means of mental production are subject to it.[3]

In the abstract model, classes are conceived to be founded upon relations of mutual *dependence* and *conflict*. 'Dependence' here means more than the sheer material dependence which is presupposed by the division of labour between the classes. In Marx's conception, classes in the dichotomous system are placed in a situation of reciprocity such that *neither class can escape from the relationship without thereby losing its identity as a distinct 'class'*. It is this theorem, heavily influenced by the Hegelian dialectic, which binds the theory of classes to the transformation of types of society. Classes, according to Marx, express the fundamental identity of society: when a class succeeds in, for example, elevating itself from a position of subordination to one of domination, it consequently effects an overall reorganization of the social structure. In the dichotomous system, classes are not, of course, 'dependent' upon each other in the sense of being collaborating groups on a level of equality; their reciprocity is an asymmetrical one, since it rests upon the extraction of surplus value by one class from the other. While each class 'needs' the other – given the continued existence of the society in unchanged form – their interests are at the same time mutually exclusive, and form the basis for the potential outbreak of open struggles. Class 'conflict' refers, first of all, to the opposition of interests presupposed by the exploitative relation integral to the dichotomous class relationship: classes are thus 'conflict groups'. This is, however, a point at which Marx's terminology is again variable. Whereas in his normal usage a 'class' represents any grouping which shares the same relationship to the means of production, regardless of whether the individuals involved become conscious of, and act upon, their common interests, he occasionally indicates that such a grouping can be properly called a 'class' only when shared interests do generate communal consciousness and action. But there is not really any significant conceptual ambiguity here. On the contrary, by this verbal emphasis, Marx seeks to stress the fact that class only becomes an important social agency when it assumes a directly political character, when it is a focus for communal action. Only under certain conditions does a class 'in itself' become a class 'for itself'.

Most of the problematic elements in Marx's theory of classes stem from the application of this abstract model to specific, historical forms of society – that is to say, they turn upon the nature of the connections between the 'abstract' and 'concrete' models of class. The first question to consider in this respect is the relationship between the dichotomous class system, presupposed by the abstract model, and the plurality of classes which, as Marx admits, exist in all historical forms of (class) society. Although Marx nowhere provides an explicit discussion of this matter, there is no serious source of difficulty here. Each historical type of society (ancient society, feudalism and capitalism) is structured around a dichotomous division in respect of property relations (represented most simply in each case as a division between patrician and plebeian, lord and vassal, capitalist and wage-labourer). But while this dichotomous division is the main 'axis' of the social structure, this simple class relation is complicated by the existence of three other sorts of grouping, two of which are 'classes' in a straightforward sense, while the third is a marginal case in this respect. These are: (1) 'transitional classes' which are in the process of formation within a society based upon a class system which is becoming 'obsolete': this is the case with the rise of the bourgeoisie and 'free' urban proletariat within feudalism; (2) 'transitional classes' which, on the contrary, represent elements of a superseded set of relations of production that linger on within a new form of society – as is found in the capitalist societies of nineteenth-century Europe, where the 'feudal classes' remain of definite significance within the social structure. Each of the first two examples results from the application of two dichotomous schemes to a single form of historical society. They represent, as it were, the fact that radical social change is not accomplished overnight, but constitutes an extended process of development, such that there is a massive overlap between types of dichotomous class system. (3) The third category includes two principal historical examples: the slaves of the ancient world, and the independent peasantry of the medieval and post-medieval period. These are 'quasi-class groupings', in the sense that they may be said to share certain common economic interests; but each of them, for different reasons, stands on the margin of the dominant set of class relationships within the societies of which they form part. To these three categories, we may add a fourth 'complicating factor' of the abstract dichotomous system: (4) sectors or sub-divisions of classes. Classes are not homogeneous entities as regards the social relations to which they give rise: Marx recognizes various sorts of differentiations within classes.

It should be noted that none of these categories involves sacrificing the abstract conception of the dichotomous class system: but they do make possible the recognition of the existence of 'middle classes', which in some sense intervene between the dominant and the subordinate class. 'Middle classes' are either of a transitional type, or they are segments of the major classes. Thus the bourgeoisie are a 'middle class' in feudalism, prior to their ascent to power; while the petty bourgeoisie, the small property-owners, whose interests are partly divergent from those of large-scale capital, form what Marx sometimes explicitly refers to as the 'middle class' in capitalism. If the terminology is again somewhat confusing, the underlying ideas are clear enough. . . .

For the most significant developments in the theory of classes since Marx, we have to look to those forms of social thought whose authors, while being directly influenced by Marx's ideas, have attempted at the same time to criticize or to reformulate them. This tendency has been strongest, for a combination of historical and intellectual reasons, in German sociology, where a series of attempts have been made to provide a fruitful critique of Marx – beginning with Max Weber . . . As in Marx, we find in Weber's writings treatments of 'classes' and 'capitalist development' as abstract conceptions; and these can be partly separated from his specifically historical discussions of the characteristics of particular European societies.

In the two versions of 'Class, status and party' which have been embodied in *Economy and Society*,[4] Weber provides what is missing in Marx: an explicit discussion of the concept of class. There are two principal respects in which this analysis differs from Marx's 'abstract model' of classes. One is that which is familiar from most secondary accounts – the differentiation of 'class' from 'status' and 'party'. The second, however, as will be argued below, is equally important: this is that, although Weber employs for some purposes a dichotomous model which in certain general respects resembles that of Marx, his viewpoint strongly emphasizes a *pluralistic conception of classes*. Thus Weber's distinction between 'ownership classes' (*Besitzklassen*) and 'acquisition classes' (*Erwerbsklassen*) is based upon a fusion of two criteria: 'on the one hand . . . the kind of property that is usable for returns; and, on the other hand . . . the kind of services that can be offered on the market', thus producing a complex typology. The sorts of property which may be used to obtain market returns, although dividing generally into two types – creating ownership (*rentier*) and acquisition (entrepreneurial) classes – are highly variable, and may produce many differential interests within dominant classes:

> Ownership of dwellings; workshops; warehouses; stores; agriculturally usable land in large or small-holdings – a quantitative difference with possibly qualitative consequences; ownership of mines; cattle; men (slaves); disposition over mobile instruments of production, or capital goods of all sorts, especially money or objects that can easily be exchanged for money; disposition over products of one's own labour or of others' labour differing according to their various distances from consumability; disposition over transferable monopolies of any kind – all these distinctions differentiate the class situations of the propertied ...[5]

But the class situations of the propertyless are also differentiated, in relation both to the types and the degree of 'monopolization' of 'marketable skills' which they possess. Consequently, there are various types of 'middle class' which stand between the 'positively privileged' classes (the propertied) and the 'negatively privileged' classes (those who possess neither property nor marketable skills). While these groupings are all nominally propertyless, those who possess skills which have a definite 'market value' are certainly in a different class situation from those who have nothing to offer but their (unskilled) labour. In acquisition classes – i.e. those associated particularly with the rise of modern capitalism – educational qualifications take on a particular significance in this respect; but the monopolization of trade skills by manual workers is also important.

Weber insists that a clear-cut distinction must be made between class 'in itself' and class 'for itself': 'class', in his terminology, always refers to market interests, which exist independently of whether men are aware of them. Class is thus an 'objective' characteristic influencing the life-chances of men. But only under certain conditions do those sharing a common class situation become conscious of, and act upon, their mutual economic interests. In making this emphasis, Weber undoubtedly intends to separate his position from that adopted by many Marxists, involving what he calls a 'pseudo-scientific operation' whereby the link between class and class consciousness is treated as direct and immediate. Such a consideration evidently also underlies the emphasis which Weber places upon 'status groups' (*Stände*) as contrasted to classes. The contrast between class and status group, however, is not, as often seems to be assumed, merely, or perhaps even primarily, a distinction between subjective and objective aspects of differentiation. While class is founded upon differentials of economic interest in market relationships, Weber nowhere denies that, under certain given circumstances, a class may be a subjectively aware 'community'. The importance of status groups – which are normally 'communities' in this sense – derives from the fact that they are built upon criteria of grouping other than those stemming from market situation. The contrast between classes and status groups is sometimes portrayed by Weber as one between the objective and the subjective: but it is also one between production and consumption. Whereas class expresses relationships involved in production, status groups express those involved in consumption, in the form of specific 'styles of life'.

Status affiliations may cut across the relationships generated in the market, since membership of a status group usually carries with it various sorts of monopolistic privileges. None the less, classes and status groups tend in many cases to be closely linked, through property: possession of property is both a major determinant of class situation and also provides the basis for following a definite 'style of life'. The point of Weber's analysis is not that class and status constitute two 'dimensions of stratification', but that classes and status communities represent two possible, and competing, modes of group formation in relation to the distribution of power in society. Power is *not*, for Weber, a 'third dimension' in some sense comparable to the first two. He is quite explicit about saying that classes, status groups and parties are all 'phenomena of the distribution of power'.[6] The theorem informing Weber's position here is his insistence that power is not to be assimilated to economic domination – again, of course, a standpoint taken in deliberate contrast to that of Marx. The party, orientated towards the acquisition or maintenance of political leadership, represents, like the class and the status group, a major focus of social organization relevant to the distribution of power in a society. It is, however, only characteristic of the modern rational state.

Weber's abstract discussions of the concepts of class, status group and party, while providing the sort of concise conceptual analysis which is missing in Marx, are nevertheless unfinished expositions, and hardly serve to do more than offer a minimal introduction to the complex problems explored in his historical writings. In these latter writings, Weber details various forms of complicated interconnection between different sorts of class relationships, and between class relationships and status group affiliations. In the history of the European societies, there has been an overall shift in the character of predominant types of class relationship and class conflict. Thus in ancient Rome, class conflicts derived primarily from antagonisms established in the credit market, whereby peasants and artisans came to be in debt-bondage to urban financiers. This tended to cede place, in the Middle Ages, to class struggles originating in the commodity market and involving battles over the prices of the necessities of life. With the rise of modern capitalism, however, relationships established in the labour market become of central significance. It is evident that for Weber, as for Marx, the advent of capitalism dramatically changes the character of the general connections between classes and society. The emergence of the labour contract as the predominant type of class relationship is tied to the phenomenon of the expansion of economic life, and the formation of a national economy, which is so characteristic of modern capitalism. In most forms of society prior to modern capitalism, even in those in which there is a considerable development of manufacture and commerce, status groups play a more important role in the social structure than classes. By creating various sorts of restriction upon enterprise, or by enforcing the monopolization of market privileges by traditionally established groups, status affiliations have in fact, as is shown in Weber's studies of the Eastern civilizations, directly inhibited the formation of modern capitalist production.

John Scott
The Old Boy Network

The Establishment has been defined as 'a body of people, acting, consciously or subconsciously, together, holding no official posts through which they exercise their power but nevertheless exercising a great influence on national policy'. That is to say that whatever formal power its members may or may not have, the Establishment has a considerable amount of informal power and influence. The influence is based upon its role as a means of opinion formation: it facilitates communication among those who are familiar with one another, share a common social background and meet in numerous formal and informal contexts. . . .

The Establishment is not simply a group of people: it is a group of people allied around certain social institutions. These institutions are the Conservative Party, the Church of England, the public schools and ancient universities, the legal profession and the Guards regiments; and the lifestyle of Establishment members has traditionally been expressed in the 'season' of social activities in London, the gentlemen's clubs and country-house life. The dominant status group can be termed 'an establishment' so as to bring out the 'assumption of the attributes of a state church by certain powerful institutions and people'. In its informal aspect the Establishment is the 'old boy network', the system of social contacts which stem from family and education. Such contacts 'are maintained largely in an informal manner by membership of the London clubs, by the social round of dinners and parties as well as, more formally, in business meetings and at official events'. The contacts which constitute this informal network of social relationships are important in the determination of the life-chances of those who go through the public school and Oxbridge system. Their contacts 'both facilitate their careers and enable them to have more influence in the posts where they eventually land'. . . .

The public schools and the ancient universities are crucial mechanisms for the integration and recruitment of both the Establishment and the wider business class. They maintain a high level of closure in access to positions of privilege, and they ensure the assimilation of those newcomers who have necessarily to be granted entry. Directly through their 'old boys', and indirectly through the influence which they exert on the older grammar schools, they bring about a social and cultural unity among those who possess superior life-chances. In the monopoly sector of the economy; in Parliament, government, the military and paramilitary forces, and the civil service; in the church and the legal profession; and in the various bodies and agencies which bridge the gap between the state and the economy are to be found people with a similar social and cultural background and a similar set of life-chances. Within and between these various occupational milieux, intragenerational and intergenerational mobility is frequent. It is with a description of these milieux and the connections between them that the rest of this section will be concerned.

For most of this century government has been dominated by the Conservative Party; and over that period the Conservative Party has been dominated by the products of the public schools. . . . [T]he proportion of public-school MPs on the Conservative benches dropped immediately after 1950 from 83 per cent to 70 per cent and fluctuated between 75 and 80 per cent after 1955. Within this figure the role of Eton has been particularly great, though the proportion has fallen from 26 per cent to 17 per cent. While the proportion of all boys attending public schools is extremely low, three-quarters of all Conservative MPs in the postwar period were public-school boys. Similarly, over 50 per cent of Conservative MPs attended Oxford or Cambridge colleges: and the proportion of Oxbridge MPs was actually higher in 1974 than in 1945. Almost a half of all Conservative MPs in the postwar period have followed the public school and Oxbridge route. The public-school MPs tend to have the safest seats and to form a core of long-serving Conservative MPs whose numbers are periodically enlarged by the arrival at Westminster of non-public-school, non-Oxbridge men when the party wins sufficient marginal seats to attain power. For this reason those from the public schools are likely to be the more established and influential MPs. Other things being equal, they are more likely to attain ministerial posts. At this level, and especially in the Cabinet, the products of Eton and Harrow have been particularly prominent.

In the period 1901–57 a total of 317 MPs moved on to the House of Lords. Allowing for inheritance of titles and for MPs who died in office, about one-fifth of MPs could expect to end their careers with a peerage. Of these 317 peers, 180 had been backbench MPs and 137 had been ministers. Given the small number of ministers – 89 ministers out of 635 MPs in 1980 – it is clear that the chance of attaining a peerage is greater for those who reach ministerial posts. The normal grade of peerage for a minister or backbencher is a barony, nowadays a life peerage, and backbenchers have also qualified for the lesser titles of baronet and knight. Those who have held senior posts as Leader of the House or Home Secretary, and those who have been Speaker, have traditionally been able to expect a viscountcy; and a prime minister has usually been able to claim an earldom. As well as a peerage being a reward at the end of a political career, it can be used in the time-honoured way for building up a bloc of support in the Lords – though the declining power of the Lords makes this less necessary than in the past. More usually a peerage can be a short cut to a parliamentary career, obviating the need for selection and election in a parliamentary constituency. . . .

[Outside government, t]he scions of the privileged classes have monopolized the military profession from the time that it became established as an integral part of the national state. The same is true of the church and the law, which have provided profitable sources of income for the younger sons of the great families and have acted as essential adjuncts of the state's social control functions of legitimation and discipline. While the declining salience of religion in British life and the increasing bureaucratization of the church have perhaps restricted the power and influence of the Church of England in modern Britain, it remains the established church and, as such, retains an important role in state ceremonials. There were, in 1980, 144 Church of England bishops, of whom the twenty-six most senior sit in the House of Lords. The bishops, still appointed by the Prime Minister and the Patronage Secretary, stand at the head of a formal hierarchy in which many important managerial functions have been delegated to the numerous deans, provosts and archdeacons. The legal profession does not have this hierarchical structure, though the judicial bench remains the position of highest status in the profession and the members of the judiciary are themselves formed into a hierarchy of superior and subordinate courts. The number of top judges is similar to the number of Church of England bishops: in 1980 there were 136 people holding the most senior judicial appointments (see Table 9.1). Those judges who are required to sit in the House of Lords to enable it to fill its role as a court of law have, since 1850, been accorded peerages for life. The House of Lords does, of course, include many other former lawyers and judges among its membership, just as it includes former churchmen who have received peerages in their own right.

TABLE 9.1 The senior judiciary,[1] 1980	
	Number
Law Lords	13
High Court	95
Scottish Court of Session	21
Northern Ireland Supreme Court	7
Total	136

[1] With the Law Lords are counted the Lord High Chancellor, the Master of the Rolls and the Lord Chief Justice of England. The Court of Appeal is counted with the High Court.
Source: Calculated from Whitaker's Almanack.

Both the law and the church show a high degree of self-recruitment, showing the existence of church families and lawyer families. Those who fill the senior posts within the professions tend to be recruited from the business class, and especially from its dominant status group. In the years 1900–9 there were 43 per cent of judges whose fathers had been in the legal profession and 18 per cent whose fathers or uncles had been judges. By the period 1960–9 both of these figures had increased: 52 per cent of judges had lawyer fathers and 29 per cent had fathers or uncles who were judges. In terms of their general patterns of recruitment the judiciary of the 1960s and 1970s had four-fifths of its members drawn from the public schools, with 39 per cent of judges in 1963 coming from Eton, Winchester, Harrow and Rugby alone. In the same year 18 per cent of judges were the sons or close relatives of peers. For the period 1947–70 it has been found that a consistent two-thirds of bishops were public-school products, though the proportion of Oxbridge bishops declined slightly from nine-tenths in 1920–39 to four-fifths in 1960–70. Bishops remain a university-based group, but the proportion of university men among the clergy as a whole has decreased. This has led to a greater educational separation of the episcopacy from the parochial clergy. At the same time the tendency for bishops to come from church families has increased to a current level of over one-half.

Within the business world itself the same patterns of gentlemanly recruitment are to be observed. [It is clear] that business leaders tend to be drawn from the wealthiest levels of society and that the inheritance of wealth plays a crucial role in the perpetuation of business fortunes. Among the business leaders there is a high degree of self-recruitment, and the top positions tend to be monopolized by members of the Establishment. Erickson's widely cited study of intergenerational mobility among steel executives suggests that there may have been a move towards relatively greater openness.[1] Erickson's study shows that the proportion of steel executives whose fathers were major landowners declined towards the end of the nineteenth century and has since remained at a level of between 7 and 10 per cent. The main group of steel executives consisted of those whose fathers had come from a business background, though she shows that the proportion declined from 55 per cent in the period 1905–25 to 34 per cent in 1953. Although the proportion of steel executives drawn from the professions may have increased, the main increase was in those who came from clerical and skilled manual backgrounds. Erickson argues that the decline in the proportion coming from a background of business leadership is mainly due to the failure of sons to take up positions in family firms. During the interwar years, she argues, the heirs of these family businesses found more congenial career lines available to them and so began to abdicate . . . control in their own firms. Further light is thrown on this by two other discoveries from Erickson's research: the proportion of steel executives from public schools remained constant at about one-third, and the proportion of Oxbridge executives increased from 15 per cent in 1905–25 to 21 per cent in 1935–47. These figures suggest that a gentlemanly education was important for the second- and third-generation steelmen who remained in the industry and for the financiers who dominated the boards of the steel companies in the interwar years. That is, the entrepreneurial capitalists and finance capitalists continued to follow the public-school and Oxbridge route, though Erickson gives no information on how important this route might be for those internal capitalists who enter business leadership from outside the ranks of the business class.

Erickson's findings are drawn from one particular industry and relate to those who are actively involved in management; they have less relevance to the question of the social background of other participants in business leadership. In particular, the finance capitalists whose interests spread across the monopoly sector as a whole are not covered by the research. Fortunately, a number of recent studies have concentrated their attention

TABLE 9.2 Social origins of business leaders, 1906–70

	From propertied and wealthy background (%)					
	1906	*1920*	*1946*	*1952*	*1960*	*1970*
Top 50 industrials	62	61	53	48	50	39
Top 30 financials[1]	78	73	71	68	69	55

[1] In the original source the figure for financial companies in 1952 was incorrectly given as 48. This has been corrected above.

on precisely these groups. Whitley has shown that one-half of the directors of the largest industrial companies in 1970 were former public-school boys, with one-sixth coming from Eton alone. Among financial companies it was found that about one-half of the directors of clearing banks and large insurance companies in 1957 came from six major public schools, with one-third from Eton alone. Among clearing-bank directors of 1970 three-quarters were public-school products: one in three from Eton and one in ten from Winchester. Between one-half and three-quarters of bank directors had graduated from Oxford or Cambridge. The most recent figures on the social origins of business leaders, presented in Table 9.2, seem to show that the proportion of directors of top companies coming from a background of 'substantial property or wealth' has declined over the period 1906–70 for both industrial and financial companies. An important qualification to be made about these figures, however, is that those whose fathers were in the professions were classified as being of upper-middle-class origins. In view of the monopolization of the higher levels of the older professions by members of the business class, this is an important qualification. . . . While only 6 or 7 per cent of directors were from such a background in 1906, fully a quarter were in 1970. Indeed, the total of 'upper-class' and 'upper-middle-class' origins over the period shows virtually no decline at all. Clearly, any alteration in the openness of recruitment to positions of business leadership must be far less than the figures in Table 9.2 suggest.

It has been argued that the business class has exercised a high degree of closure over recruitment to a number of privileged occupations, and that members of the establishment have been able to monopolize those positions of greatest privilege through the mechanisms of sponsored mobility. The business class, despite the diversity in occupations followed by its members, has been able to achieve a high degree of unity and cohesion because of the amount of circulation that takes place between positions of privilege. Mobility between the various class situations, both intergenerationally and intragenerationally, has been frequent enough to counteract any tendency towards the formation of distinct class fractions. Although there are to be found church families, army families, political families and business families, there is sufficient circulation to prevent the formation of separate groups. While this is true for the business class as a whole, it is particularly true for the Establishment. Members of the Establishment have been able to perpetuate its position as a group with an extremely high degree of social solidarity. Table 9.3 shows the occupations of Conservative MPs prior to their election. The fact that many of these occupations are continued concurrently with membership of the House of Commons is a further source of solidarity between the various positions of privilege. It can be seen that the largest groups of Conservative MPs in 1945 were those from the law, the armed forces, business and the land. By 1974 the number of military MPs had fallen away considerably, even after allowing for the inflation of the figures in the immediate postwar period by those who were commissioned for war service. The law, business and industry all held their positions over the thirty-year period, indicating that the social composition of the Conservative Party has altered only very slightly. It is perhaps particularly significant that two-thirds of Conservative MPs in the 1970s held a business directorship at the time they sat in the House.

The solidarity and cohesion of the business class has depended on the

TABLE 9.3 Occupational background of Conservative MPs, 1945–74

Occupation	Numbers of MPs at each election[1]									
	1945	1950	1951	1955	1959	1964	1966	1970	1974a	1974b
Barrister	37	51	55	60	66	58	48	50	50	47
Solicitor	4	10	11	11	12	13	13	13	11	9
Civil service	3	2	2	1	1	0	0	0	1	1
Diplomatic service	8	11	12	14	14	17	14	12	11	8
Military	30	30	31	36	30	20	11	12	4	4
Director	67	100	109	113	122	85	74	94	83	81
Banking and finance	1	4	2	2	3	3	4	7	13	13
Commerce and insurance	7	8	10	14	17	13	9	13	11	9
Farmer, landowner	25	28	32	30	36	36	34	35	28	22
Other	31	53	56	62	64	56	46	94	85	83
Total	213	297	320	343	365	301	253	330	297	277

[1] The two entries for 1974 relate to the two elections of that year.

extent to which it could maintain its social distinctiveness. Members of the business class have, however, increasingly tended to eschew the language of class division in formulating images of their own social positions. Instead, they have projected a view of themselves as part of an extensive 'middle class'. Such a claim is made realistic by the formal position of business executives and directors at the head of managerial hierarchies, and by the absence of any obvious distinctions between those professional employees who do and those who do not come from a background of wealth and privilege. Unequal life-chances are, in many respects, invisible; and this invisibility lends plausibility to the image of a continuous and hierarchical middle class. The business class, then, has a degree of social anonymity: it no longer sees itself and is no longer seen by others as constituting a distinct social class. Business class and service class appear to merge into a unified middle class. . . . Although it makes sense to speak of a partial normative convergence between business class and service class, there remains a crucial economic and relational difference between them – and the survival of the Establishment involves the survival of distinctive normative standards and a distinct lifestyle. Centred on the honours system and its gentlemanly values, this meaning system is a crucial aspect of social legitimation. The hierarchical character of the system of honours, leading from the peerage through the knightage to the 'officers' and 'members' of the Order of the British Empire, overlays the formal hierarchies of authority which permeate modern British society. In this way the norms of the Establishment are an important condition for the plausibility of the image of a hierarchical middle class. The social anonymity of the business class is, paradoxically, enhanced by the survival of the gentlemanly meaning system. The relational differentiation of the business class from the service class is apparent in the myriad contexts of informal interaction, in patterns of intermarriage, and in political and leisure activities. The lifestyle of the Establishment constitutes a paradigm of social behaviour for other members of the business class. Those who are outside the established social circles may follow the precepts of this paradigm because they aspire to the higher social status with which it is associated, or they may simply accept

241

the activities it enjoins as being normal features of a civilized lifestyle. The tendency for members of the business class to live in half-timbered houses in areas commonly referred to as the 'stockbroker belt' or to live in carefully modernized cottages in 'rural' areas, their preference for private education and private health care, and their regular involvement in such sporting activities as golf, racing, shooting and hunting are all reflections of the salience of the Established lifestyle. . . .

[However, despite such differences in lifestyle, it] would be wrong to depict the business class as totally closed to outsiders. The evidence shows that this is not the case. While members of the business class are able to pass on their own privileges to their children, the growth in size of the occupational groups which they have traditionally monopolized has necessitated relatively high rates of recruitment from other sectors of society. As a result, many newcomers are to be found in the fringes of the business class, and together with others who reach high managerial and professional positions they may be able to secure access to the business class for their children. It is difficult to judge the full extent of such openness at the upper levels, since studies of those reaching the peaks of their careers in the 1960s and 1970s are concerned with people who were educated before World War II and whose fathers were educated before World War I. The new entrants to the business class are still likely to have followed the public-school and Oxbridge route and so are likely to be endowed with the appropriate habits of class behaviour, but they are far less likely to owe their positions to the operation of the old boy network. Educational assets and technical expertise are increasingly prominent factors in executive recruitment and in recruitment to the professions. Any changes in rates of upward mobility into the business class may not yet be apparent in the available statistics. The relative decline of the Establishment and the possibility of increased openness mean that the traditional means of representing the interests of the business class within the political system are likely to prove increasingly inadequate.

READING 40

Mike Savage

The Middle Classes in Modern Britain

Contemporary discussions of social class still tend to be couched within the theoretical frameworks laid down by Karl Marx and Max Weber in the late nineteenth and early twentieth centuries . . . The world has, however, changed in significant ways since the days when they were writing. Perhaps most importantly, in the early twentieth century manual workers (in manufacturing and agriculture) formed the over-whelming majority of the working population, and it was therefore the character of the working class which held the attention of sociologists and social commentators. Even down to the 1980s, much sociological debate on social class has focused upon whether the working class has changed – think of the discussion of the 'Affluent Worker' studies in the 1960s . . ., arguments about the way that consumption-sector cleavages were possibly dividing the working class . . . and, more recently, interest in whether the working class is being divided into an underclass and a more prosperous group of workers . . .

However, as we approach the twenty-first century, the relevance of this focus is in serious doubt. Since 1945, and especially in the past two decades, the number of people employed in 'middle-class' jobs has increased rapidly, so that any attempt to understand the social relations of modern Britain really cannot avoid seriously examining the position and activities of the middle classes. It comes as something of a shock to realize that there are now more university lecturers than coal miners! In 1991, 29.4 per cent of those in the workforce worked in professions and management, a figure only marginally smaller than the 32.7 per cent who worked as manual workers. If one were to include the self-employed (10.7 per cent) and the routine white-collar workers (27.2 per cent) as part of the middle class, we would have to conclude that the middle classes now comprise a substantial majority of the employed population.

Thinking about the middle classes is therefore of fundamental import-ance for understanding contemporary social change, and in recent years a lively debate has taken place on the significance of current trends for the way sociologists talk about social class. Indeed, there is some suggestion

Plate 9.1
Gentrification in a
street in Hackney

that recent debates about the middle classes have given a new lease of life
to rather tired old debates about class . . . In this [discussion] I shall point to
some of the main issues and findings from recent research.

MIDDLE-CLASS BOUNDARIES

Studies of the middle classes have always been bedeviled by the 'boundary
problem' . . ., the problem of deciding which types of people can helpfully be seen as part of the middle class. In recent years a considerable
amount of agreement has been reached on this tricky issue, however.
Traditionally, the most common way of differentiating the working
classes from the middle classes was to claim that the working class
were manual workers, whilst the middle classes were non-manual
workers. This difference is occasionally referred to as the 'collar line', the
distinction between blue-collar (manual) and white-collar (non-manual)
workers. Today, this stress on the collar line has largely been discredited.
It is generally agreed that many routine white-collar workers (especially
women) now have rather similar conditions of work and remuneration

to blue-collar workers, and cannot helpfully be seen as being in a higher class.

The rise in employment in the service sector confuses the division between manual and non-manual workers anyway, and it is possible to argue that many of the most extreme forms of 'proletarianization' – in the sense of poor wages, irregular employment, and bad working conditions – are found amongst service workers. By the 1980s only 8 per cent of British unskilled workers were employed in industry! Furthermore, it can be argued that many forms of supposedly 'working-class' activity, such as trade union membership and industrial action, are now as strong, possibly stronger, amongst white-collar workers as they are amongst manual workers. In short, the idea of a 'collar line' being used to differentiate the middle from the working class has now been largely discredited.

The self-employed also pose interesting puzzles for thinking about the middle classes. Both Marx and Weber recognized the existence of the *'petit bourgeoisie'* as a distinct middle-class fraction, lying between workers on the one hand and large property-owners on the other. Marx assumed that self-employed farmers, small business owners, small shopkeepers and so forth would increasingly be 'squeezed out' by the rise of large business. And indeed, for much of the twentieth century Marx's view seemed to be borne out, as the number of people working on their own account fell gradually, but steadily. However, there has been a remarkable turn-around [since 1970]. Between 1971 and 1981 the numbers of self-employed bottomed out, at around 6.7 per cent of those in the labour market; whilst in the years between 1981 and 1991 the numbers rose by a staggering 45 per cent, to comprise over 10 per cent of the workforce. The difficulty resides, however, in knowing what to make of this rise in numbers. Does it indicate a flourishing petty economy, and the expansion of opportunities for entrepreneurs? Or is there a bleaker portrait to be painted? Perhaps as workers have lost their jobs they have had to turn to self-employment as a last resort (possibly encouraged by Conservative government support of small business in the 1980s), with the result that this shift to self-employment masks the growth of marginal, insecure employment which can hardly be seen as middle-class in any meaningful sense.

One way of considering which of these perspectives is correct is to see whether the self-employed tend to be a stable or unstable group. Do they continue in self-employment over a period of years, or do they tend to slip into more marginal forms of employment (or unemployment)? Recent research . . . examines what the self-employed in 1981 were doing ten years later in 1991 – and therefore allows us to consider whether self-employment was a temporary phase in a person's working life . . . [This] shows that – rather against expectations – the majority of the self-employed in 1981 (67.2 per cent, though a smaller proportion of women than men) who were still in the labour market in 1991 were still in self-employment. They therefore appear, on the whole, to comprise a relatively stable and secure part of the workforce. In fact this is a much higher figure than was found for the period 1971–81, where less than half the self-employed lasted the ten-year course . . . Around 12 per cent of the self-employed had become unemployed by 1991, and a further 10 per cent were working as manual workers. Putting these figures together suggests that, in general, the *petit bourgeoisie* are becoming a more secure, distinct and visible group in British society. This marks a very significant shift which reverses a long-term trend.

There is a further point to make here. In the past self-employment tended not to carry high status, and (with the exception of 'independent' professionals in legal or architectural practice and so on) most professional and managerial employees preferred to achieve rewards and standing by working for a large organization. This seems to have changed, however. Considerable numbers of managers now seem to prefer to work for small firms or for themselves; and the proportion of managers moving into self-employment rose considerably in the 1980s. Many areas of expanding self-employment were in 'glamorous' areas, such as consultancy work in financial services, or in 'high-tech' industry. Some writers argue that many firms now prefer to contract services to outside consultants and agents rather than to carry them out in-house, with the result that the self-employed gain a further boost. Furthermore, it has become easier to have a 'business on the side', whilst continuing to be an employee (one survey . . . suggests that as many as one-third of managers in one firm had a side-business). In short, a group which had been regarded as recently as the 1970s as part of the 'traditional' *petit bourgeoisie*, a legacy of the past, seems to have found a new lease of life.

What does this mean for thinking about the size of the middle class? It seems sensible to see manual workers, the unemployed, and most routine white-collar workers as occupying largely working-class positions, which means that the majority of the population can still usefully be seen as working-class (. . . around 60 per cent of the workforce). None the less the middle classes employed in the professions, administration, management – and the self-employed – do now constitute a very sizeable proportion of the workforce. Let us now consider their sociological significance.

THINKING SOCIOLOGICALLY ABOUT THE MIDDLE CLASSES

Major issues of interpretation are posed by the changing positions of the professions and management – a group which accounts for nearly one-third of the workforce. The rise of people employed in these groups is striking. In 1971, 10.2 per cent of those in the labour market were employed in the professions; by 1991 this figure had risen to 15.2 per cent. Comparable figures for managers indicate a rise from 7 per cent to 11.3 per cent over the same twenty-year period. What do these trends indicate for the shape of British society? Here a number of different theories have recently been advanced.

Perhaps the best-known account is the 'service-class' thesis, developed especially by John Goldthorpe . . . and in a rather different way by Abercrombie and Urry. . . . Goldthorpe argued that professional, managerial and administrative workers form a distinctive social class, which separates them from all other social groups. He calls this class the 'service class' (or occasionally, and perhaps more helpfully, the 'salariat'). This term 'service class' can be confusing. It makes us think of workers in the 'service sector', such as catering. However, Goldthorpe uses a different definition which refers instead to workers who provide specialist 'services' (hence the title) to their employer. These services involve providing either specialist knowledge (in the case of professionals) or delegated authority (in the case of managers). In return for these specialist services these workers are granted special privileges, such as a high salary, job security, fringe benefits, and 'prospective rewards' – the potential for career development. Professionals and managers are relatively secure and privileged; and for this reason Goldthorpe argues that the service class will become a major conservative force in society as it seeks to defend and consolidate its own advantages. In short, the expansion of the 'service class' has helped bring about a new social group who can be expected to play a conservative role as bulwarks of the status quo and the presence of this class will tend to damp down pressures for any fundamental social change.

In direct opposition to Goldthorpe's views is the work of some – mainly American – sociologists (notably Alvin Gouldner), who talk about the rise of a new class (occasionally called a 'professional-managerial class' or PMC) which stands outside traditional class divisions and is therefore able to sustain forms of social dissent and new ways of living. Gouldner . . . argues that this 'new class' is able to generate a 'culture of critical discourse'. Other writers suggest that these new groups are bearers of 'post-materialist' values. Since they have 'solved' the problem of affluence, and no longer have to worry about such basic issues as feeding, clothing and housing themselves, their attention switches to other, more 'expressive', issues – such as ecology, personal well-being, better ways of living and relating – and so on. In short, the development of these professional and managerial groups is seen by Gouldner as a 'progressive' development, which augurs well for the future. . . .

[Another group of writers] argue that it is not helpful to talk about professionals and managers as a distinct class of their own, because there are in fact major divisions within their ranks. Perhaps the best-known example of this view is [Pierre] Bourdieu's emphasis upon the differences between economic and cultural capital. Bourdieu stresses that some groups within the middle classes succeed by emphasizing their cultural distinction and taste, which, amongst other things, allows them to succeed in the education system and therefore gain qualifications to move into professional jobs. Other members of the middle classes (for instance, managers who work their way up from the shop floor), however, do not do well at school and succeed for other reasons.

Bourdieu emphasizes the conflicts between the 'cultured' and the 'moneyed' groups which this can lead to. Savage et al.[1] draw upon this framework to argue that in Britain there are major long-standing divisions between managers and professionals which, if anything, are becoming rather more distinct. Managers are becoming rather marginalized; whilst professionals have been able to defend their existing privileges and find new areas to deploy their expertise, by selling their services on the market. Savage et al. . . . suggest growing tensions and conflicts within the middle classes as they struggle to improve their position.

Before evaluating these different views, it is noteworthy that none of them draws directly on the 'classical' class theory of either Marx or Weber. The pedigrees for each of these theories is hybrid. This does suggest that as the middle classes increase in size, so the sociological debates themselves shift. Let us now consider which of these theories offers the best way of understanding the contemporary middle classes.

HOW ARE THE MIDDLE CLASSES CHANGING?

There is now a substantial body of research devoted to exploring various facets of middle-class life. Here I only have scope to deal with a few of the salient issues.

Traditionally both professionals and managers tend to have enjoyed predictable, secure careers in large bureaucracies. The idea of the organizational career refers to the way that these middle-class employees could expect to work their way up a job ladder within a large firm or within a public organization. Such employees often strongly identified with their employer, who in turn 'cocooned' their salaried workers with generous pension and fringe-benefit systems. However, the idea of predictable job movement in the course of one's career has radically changed in recent years. Professionals and managers alike are increasingly paid on the basis of their performance, and payment is also increasingly arranged on an individual basis and is subject to renegotiation.

A good example of these changes is in banking. Until the later 1980s bank managers were paid a salary which reflected their seniority in the bank and the size and importance of the branch or unit they were employed in. Salaries (for junior managers) were negotiated between unions and management, and contained an incremental component, which meant that they automatically rose each year. In the later 1980s the banks began to change this system. Managers' salaries were determined in part by whether they were able to achieve targets (for instance, a certain level of sales) which were set annually. Automatic increments, paid regardless of performance, were largely abandoned. A considerable number of managers, especially those over the age of 50, also lost their jobs during the recession of the early 1990s. Cases such as this are not unusual. Throughout much of the public sector, similar innovations – which question the security and privileges of senior staff – were introduced. Some local authorities, for instance, employed their chief executives on five-year renewable contracts.

These developments suggest that Goldthorpe's view of the 'service class' as characterized by 'prospective rewards', which stands above the rough-and-tumble of the labour market, is today misplaced. One might also suggest that an emphasis upon the way these groups have 'solved' their economic problems is also misleading. In fact, increasing levels of labour-market insecurity may well have accentuated the struggle of middle-class employees to look after their own position!

This increasing instability means that professionals and managers now have more mobile and uncertain careers than hitherto. The significance of increasing levels of job mobility have been much debated in recent work . . . Considerable evidence has now accumulated which suggests that the careers of managers have changed markedly. During the 1980s and 1990s many firms have cut management jobs . . . Organizations have increasingly recruited managers from outside, rather than promote their own staff. Surveys of managers in private industry suggest that until the 1970s around 40 per cent of managers had only ever worked for one firm. By the 1980s only between 10 and 20 per cent of managers had worked for one firm. [One recent study] has shown that no less than 24 per cent of managers in 1981 actually moved down the social ladder by 1991, indicating increasing proportions of instability. The comparable figures for professionals were much lower, at 14 per cent. It has also shown that a significant number of managers have been able to move into professional employment and that substantial numbers of managers were downwardly mobile between 1981 and 1991. Over 20 per cent of male managers in 1981 had moved to routine white-collar work, manual employment or unemployment by 1991. For women managers, the figure is an astonishing 38.2 per cent. In short, it would appear that, although the managerial wing of the middle classes may have grown in size, it has become a rather insecure group. The professional middle class, by contrast, is rather more stable, with markedly lower rates of downward mobility for both men and (especially) women.

There is also evidence that professional and managerial groups have rather different cultural outlooks and political viewpoints, though much further research remains to be done here. One interesting example of fragmentation concerns the residential preferences of the middle classes. For much of the twentieth century the middle classes were an archetypically suburban class, and many aspects of middle-class identity were forged out of common residential patterns. From the 1960s social scientists began to detect that growing numbers of the middle classes were attracted to what has been called the 'rural idyll', as many professionals and managers have moved into the countryside. Indeed, one recent research project suggests that as many as two-thirds of migrants to selected rural areas are from the middle class. However, by contrast, there is also a contrary movement, whereby some parts of the middle classes have moved back to the cities – a process known as 'gentrification'. During the 1980s it became fashionable for members of the affluent middle classes to move to central urban locations in London (such as Islington) and other large cities. Middle-class lifestyles appear therefore to have fragmented.

Finally, let us consider the case of politics. Goldthorpe[2] argues that the service class is increasingly conservative, whilst the 'new class' theorists point to its radical potential. Research on political alignments suggest that the political alignments of the 'salariat' have actually changed little, despite the major political upheavals of recent years. Around 50–55 per cent appear to identify with the Conservative Party and around 22 per cent with the Labour Party. There are also significant differences within the 'service class' . . . Public-sector workers tend to be more left-wing than private-sector workers. Welfare and creative workers, such as journalists, teachers, artists and so on, are distinctive in being relatively left-wing. The highly educated appear to be more left-wing than the less highly educated, a fact which appears to endorse the 'new class' idea, at least for some fractions of the middle classes.

CONCLUSIONS

Let us return to the theoretical accounts of the middle classes. Goldthorpe's arguments about the 'service class' do appear to ignore the multiple axes of division within the middle classes, which I have briefly highlighted here. On the other hand, 'new class' ideas do not take account of the fact that only a small proportion of the middle class – the highly educated, people working in the arts and higher education etc. – appear to exhibit much 'culture of critical discourse'. So it would appear that an emphasis upon fragmentation is the most useful, though we need to know more about the sources of such division.

Further, it is important to recognize the way that different types of class position are linked by mobility chains. The fact that around 60 per cent of the workforce are in working-class positions and 40 per cent in middle-class ones should not blind us to the fact that many people move between such positions. Of all the routine male white-collar workers in 1981, over a third had moved into management or the professions by 1991 – though the figures for women are much lower. There is also evidence that people from the middle classes are downwardly mobile. The processes facilitating and constraining mobility are therefore of fundamental importance for thinking about the meaning of class today. And, it might be added, given that gender, race and ethnicity appear to be important forces affecting mobility, it may be suggested that class cannot be seen as standing totally apart from these other social forces.

One final point is this. It should not be thought that the rising number of people in 'middle-class' jobs means that class itself is less important. What we have seen is the erosion of the 'collar line' as a meaningful axis of social division. However, it would appear that the expansion of professional and managerial employees has led to new types of conflict and division. As traditional 'middle-class' privileges are called into question, and middle-class employees need to compete more intensively in the labour market, they are forced to engage in 'positional' conflicts to market themselves and their skills. The important conclusion is to suggest that even if it is true that the middle classes are forming a larger proportion of the workforce, this does not mean that we live in a more stable or harmonious society.

READING 41

Andy Pilkington

Is There a British Underclass?

A major preoccupation of British sociology is social class. What is becoming noticeable is that, in addition to the conventional triumvirate of upper, middle and working classes, a further class is increasingly identified – an underclass. There are two main reasons for this focus. First, economic changes since the mid-1970s have entailed class polarization. This development has been particularly evident since 1979 with the dominance in government of the Conservative Party, whose economic restructuring involved significant unemployment and whose New Right ideology justified welfare cuts. While, for most of the population, economic restructuring and growing inequality have been accompanied by an increase in standards of living, a growing stratum has become relatively deprived . . . It is this stratum which some wish to call an underclass. Secondly, evidence continues to accumulate that ethnic minorities and women face significant disadvantage. The persistence of racial and sexual discrimination is severe enough to suggest to some that ethnic minorities and/or women constitute or are at least overrepresented in an underclass . . .

'DISCOVERING' THE UNDERCLASS

Much of the current concern with the underclass was anticipated in a major text on class theory in the 1970s.[1] In the course of arguing that capitalism was characterized by a three-class structure, Giddens suggested that in advanced capitalist societies a new division was opening up between the working class and a growing underclass. The latter, comprising those whose low-status position entailed restriction to a secondary labour market (itself characterized by low pay, poor promotion prospects and little job security) was, for Giddens, in a different economic situation from the working class, whose members were located in a relatively privileged primary labour market. This division meant that while the working class sought to protect its relative advantage, the underclass – deprived of support and denied equal rights – resorted to 'hostile outbursts'.

Giddens was not alone in the 1970s in detecting the arrival of a new subordinate class. The notion that those dependent on welfare benefits constituted a new 'claiming class' . . . was put forward and the contention that ethnic minorities constituted a new 'underclass' became increasingly widespread. In this context, mention must be made of one study which purported to show that ethnic minorities comprised an underclass . . . On the basis of their study of Handsworth in Birmingham, Rex and Tomlinson argued that there were clear differences of life-chances between ethnic minorities and the white British, which meant that the former had 'a different kind of position in the labour market, a different housing situation, and a different form of schooling'. Subject to racism and distinctly disadvantaged in these three sectors, the minorities constituted an underclass in British society, increasingly conscious of their subordinate position and the need to pursue their interests in a distinct and militant fashion. Given the increasing racism among white people, who saw the newcomers as responsible for the deterioration of the inner city, and the absence of any community-wide organizations, the authors pessimistically concluded that 'the greatest likelihood is that conflict in the community will grow'.[2]

Some writers in the 1970s referred to the emergence of an 'underclass', and the term has been much more widely adopted since. Thus, in two recent accounts of the class structure . . ., the authors identify an underclass as one of their key social classes. In two popular articles, highly esteemed social scientists detect the development of such a class, which is seen as a severe threat to social order . . . In a . . . (4 November 1991) *Panorama* programme about the disturbances in the Meadow Well Estate in Newcastle the term was used freely to describe those involved in the disorders. Even in [academic] journal[s] the concept has been used quite routinely to clarify what are seen as significant changes in the inner city . . . But, if the term itself has been utilized only relatively recently by many writers, the notion of a subordinate and dangerous stratum at the bottom of the economic order has a long ancestry.

THE CULTURE OF POVERTY

The distinction between the deserving and undeserving poor has underpinned much of the development of British social policy, and the division between the respectable and rough working class is part of British folklore. This image of an undeserving and rough stratum was given academic credibility in the 1960s by [O.] Lewis, when he sought to explain the persistence of poverty by positing the existence of a 'culture of poverty' . . . He argued that individuals socialized within this distinct culture were psychologically incapable of taking up opportunities open to them and thus free themselves from poverty. Lewis's contention – which was taken up in Britain by Sir Keith Joseph and popularized as 'the cycle of deprivation' – has been severely criticized. It seemed to blame the poor for their deprivation; it failed to account for the fact that people move in and out of deprivation and was unable to show that is was to any significant extent transmitted intergenerationally; it ignored the structural roots of deprivation; and it did not demonstrate that the cultural values which may develop in response to deprivation cannot be altered through structural changes.

Despite the criticisms which have been levelled at Lewis's contention and have resulted in fewer references being made to a supposed 'culture of poverty', his ideas still live on, albeit transposed into (some variants of) the notion of an underclass. This is evident in a book by an American journalist who first promulgated the concept to a wide audience in the 1980s.[3] A picture was drawn of a group – many of them black – whose members lived in poor inner-city ghettos and within a culture where dependency, criminality and family breakdown were the norm. While Auletta expressed some sympathy for the plight of the underclass, the American New Right theorist who recently helped to popularize the notion in Britain was less charitable.[4] The underclass were defined not by their poverty but by their 'deplorable behaviour in response to that condition'.

The transposition of the notion of the culture of poverty into that of an underclass is clear from the following: 'If illegitimate births are the leading indicator of an underclass and violent crime a proxy measure of its development, the definitive proof that an underclass has arrived is that large numbers of young, healthy, low-income males choose not to take jobs.'

STRUCTURAL VIEWS OF AN 'UNDERCLASS'

Despite the fact that the notion of an underclass has been propagated by writers who favour a cultural view and question the need for structural changes or, indeed, the value of a welfare state, it should not be assumed that the concept is used only in this way. One American sociologist, for example, has argued that structural changes have created an underclass of poor black families who live in inner-city ghettos and are effectively isolated from the rest of society.[5] The 'deplorable behaviour' of such people 'should be analysed not as a cultural aberration but as a symptom of class inequality', for 'if underclass blacks have low aspirations or do not plan for the future, it is not ultimately the result of different cultural norms but the product of restricted opportunities'.

Of the two major approaches which seek to account for the growth of an underclass – the cultural and the structural – it is the latter which has been more prominent in Britain. [F.] Field's book[6] is typical in this respect. An underclass, comprising the long-term unemployed, single-parent families and elderly pensioners, has resulted from the government's economic and social policies. This stratum is effectively excluded from citizenship rights enjoyed by the bulk of the population. What is needed is a return to full employment, a redistribution of income and wealth and a revamped welfare state. If Field's approach is distinctive, it is in that he tends to play down – relative to other structural theorists – a racial dimension in his account of the emergence of an underclass.

While the cultural approach to the underclass has been severely criticized, this is not the case with the structural approach. The reasons for this are twofold: first, structural explanations of poverty and racial disadvantage are better evidenced and, secondly, structural explanations are ideologically more acceptable to British sociologists. None the less, such an approach to the underclass can also be questioned.

First, the concept is nebulous: Ruth Lister warns that it is imprecise and disturbing. She describes its use as an example of the language of disease and contamination, which encourages a pathological view of people in poverty rather than one which links the poor to a denial of the full rights of citizenship.[7] To the extent to which it is defined at all (and definitions differ significantly, from Giddens's wide category, which comprises those in the secondary labour market, to Runcimann's more restricted one, which relates to those more or less permanently dependent on welfare benefits), it is a very heterogeneous stratum. Even taking a restricted definition of the concept gives us Fields's three distinct groups, one of which, the long-term unemployed, is itself diverse, comprising young and old constituents.

Secondly, the concept is frequently used to link together a number of phenomena, such as the growth of relative poverty, the persistence of racial disadvantage, the increase in criminality, the rise of one-parent families and changes in housing patterns in the inner city. There is a tendency to see patterns developing in British inner cities comparable to those in the United States. Such an approach not only fails to do justice to the differences between the two societies but also assumes links which need to be established empirically. There may, for example, be an association between the growth of an underclass and a rise in criminality, but surely not all the groups which characterize the underclass are equally involved? Are we talking about the young unemployed? Or elderly pensioners?

Thirdly, there is a danger – if links are made too readily – of taking on board inadvertently a picture of the underclass which flows from a cultural approach. Thus, even Field, who is at pains to distance himself from Dahrendorf's (partially) cultural approach, takes on trust that a 'culture of dependency' exists and that the underclass are particularly involved in the black [sic] economy – this despite the fact that he sees their aspirations as 'centred on gaining work and admittance to the mainstream of ordinary life' and the fact that other evidence indicates that opportunities for participation in the informal economy are greater for 'work-rich' households ...

Finally, for the underclass to constitute a group with a distinctive set of attitudes there must be a degree of stability in its social composition ... The only group this seems to apply to is the long-term unemployed, which is indeed an expanding category. Although some attitudes, such as fatalism, may become accentuated by long-term unemployment, it should be remembered that these are by no means unique to this group (being found among the unemployed generally and sections of the working class who are most at risk of unemployment) and that these people share most of the same aspirations as the rest of society ...

The structural version of the underclass thesis cannot easily be discounted, despite the arguments which can be levelled at it. Note needs to be taken, in particular, of the way it takes seriously the persistence of racial disadvantage and seeks to clarify the class position of ethnic minorities. The view that 'racism is probably the most basic cause of the underclass condition' . . . is one which receives the assent of many sociologists on both sides of the Atlantic. And the association of race and underclass is now so prevalent that even a *Sunday Times* editorial (1985) has pointed to 'alarming signs that Britain is well on the road to creating a new black underclass'.

RACE AND THE UNDERCLASS

Of the two major European theoretical traditions on class – the Marxist and the Weberian – it is the latter which has been more willing to depict ethnic minorities as an underclass. Drawing upon Weber's distinction between three dimensions of stratification, racial inequality is seen as an example of status inequality and, as such, may be as significant as class inequality.

A status division between whites and blacks, with its concomitant belief in the superiority of whites, developed alongside imperialism. This division still persists and is reinforced when social groups (including the white working class) attempt to maximize their rewards by restricting the access of other groups, defined as racially different, to resources and opportunities . . . If racial discrimination results in black people being restricted to those occupations which are characterized by low pay, poor job security and few promotion prospects, status disadvantages are being translated into class disadvantages and we can talk of a black underclass.

Marxists are more reluctant to talk of an underclass. In line with their stress on the primacy of class and the division between capital and labour, they locate ethnic minorities in the working class. Some, indeed, go so far as to argue that the minorities are integral members of the working class. [Some studies] see racial discrimination as merely increasing the impact of otherwise common disadvantages. However, most Marxists who have addressed the issue of racial disadvantage believe that this position underestimates the significance of racism and, instead, highlight divisions within the working class which migration accentuates.

Two studies, in particular, have been influential in propagating such a view. The first involved a study of migrant workers in Western Europe and reached the conclusion that the new ethnic minorities comprise 'a lower stratum of the working class' . . . The primary emphasis is on their economic distinctiveness. They constitute a 'reserve army of labour', concentrated either in non-skilled manual work or unemployment. Such a disadvantaged economic situation is matched by a correspondingly low political and ideological position: politically, they do not have full citizenship rights and, ideologically, are subject (even when white) to racism. The authors' suggestion that their findings are at least partially applicable to Britain is taken up in a study by Miles . . . [H]is conclusion is remarkably similar. 'Migrants occupy a structurally distinct position in the economic, political and ideological relations of British capitalism, but within the boundary of the working class. They therefore constitute a fraction of the working class.'[8]

UNDERCLASS OR CLASS FRACTION?

While the Weberian thesis that ethnic minorities in Britain constitute an underclass may seem very different from the Marxist theses that they comprise either a lower stratum of the working class or a fraction of the working class, what is more noteworthy is the similarity of their analyses. On four key issues, they are in accord. First, they agree that 'economic and social requirements of British society create disadvantaged positions in the class structure and it is the racism of British society that ensures that black people continue to fill them.'[9] Secondly, they concur in recognizing that racism is extremely pervasive, affecting the position of the minorities not only in the labour market but also in other areas, such as housing and education. To comprehend fully the class situation of minorities entails, therefore, an acknowledgement of the wider impact of racism. Thirdly, there is agreement that in locating ethnic minorities in the class structure, particular attention needs to be placed on the field of employment. What is apparent here, it is argued, is that they still constitute a 'replacement population', employed (if at all) in non-skilled manual work which white people are not willing to undertake. Fourthly, there is a shared recognition that the distinctive position of ethnic minorities means that their interests are not always congruent with [those of] the white working class. The result is that the minorities develop distinct forms of consciousness and action.

To discover similarities between the underclass and Marxist theses does not mean that their conclusions are well founded. The most reliable recent data we have come from the Policy Studies Institute (PSI) survey of black and white Britain in 1982 . . . A comparison of the job levels of white men and men of West Indian and Asian origin . . . indicates that the job levels of the latter do indeed tend to be skewed towards lower levels, so that they tend to be underrepresented in non-manual jobs, especially the higher ones, and overrepresented in manual jobs, especially the lower ones. A similar pattern is apparent when the job levels of women are compared, although the differences here are less striking, probably because 'for those who already suffer the disadvantage . . . of being women, there is little scope for racial disadvantage to have a further, additive, effect'.[10] While the data clearly point to racial disadvantage in employment, they do not, however, indicate that the ethnic minorities are overwhelmingly concentrated in non-skilled manual work. Indeed, if we disaggregate men of Asian origin and calculate the proportion in semi- and unskilled work for each group, we find 35 per cent of West Indian men, 41 per cent of Indian men, 43 per cent of Pakistani men, 69 per cent of Bangladeshi men and 25 per cent of African Asian men in this kind of work. Compared to the 15 per cent of white men in this kind of work, each of the minorities is overrepresented at this level, but in only one case – that of Bangladeshis – is a majority of men in such jobs. Although this finding glosses over the disadvantage faced by minorities within each job level, a phenomenon which becomes manifest when average earnings or the risks of unemployment are compared, it 'certainly prohibits the notion that they are all in an underclass in occupational terms.'[11]

DIVISIONS WITHIN THE ETHNIC MINORITIES

Once it is accepted that the underclass thesis has heavily overstated the concentration of ethnic minorities in non-skilled work, the question arises as to whether the situation has deteriorated over time so that they are now more likely to find themselves in such work. [S.] Field . . . summarizes the situation well.

> If attention is confined to the top end of the job spectrum – say, one third of men with jobs – racial inequality appears to have diminished markedly. Within this top third, the socio-economic profiles of Afro-Caribbean and Asian men improved and became more similar to whites between 1974 and 1982, and within each category of job, the earnings gap narrowed. Looking at the bottom third, the opposite result emerges. The socio-economic profiles remain distinct, and an earnings gap has opened up in manual work. Moreover, ethnic minority workers in these lower status jobs have borne the brunt of the rise of unemployment.[12]

While the data – which focus on the fact that the proportion of both Afro-Caribbean and Asian men in non-skilled manual work has actually increased, when the unemployed are included on the basis of their last job – point to increasing racial disadvantage in employment, they do not indicate that ethnic minorities are becoming overwhelmingly concentrated in non-skilled manual work. Although the inadequacy of the existing information on such issues is clear, two conclusions, nevertheless, seem justified. First, just as economic changes since the mid-1970s have entailed class polariza-tion among whites, so a similar process has occurred within the ethnic minorities. Secondly, it is apparent, when the minorities are disaggregated, that some have been relatively successful. The third survey of black and white Britain indicates that African Asians have a similar socio-economic profile to [that of] whites, while labour force survey data for Spring 1986–8 suggest that the same is true of Indians . . . In view of such economic divers-ity, it is scarcely surprising that cultural differences between the minorities have not been overriden by a shared colour consciousness and need for united black action, as anticipated by some versions of the underclass thesis.

CONCLUSIONS

What conclusions can we come to? There is no doubt that Britain has become a more polarized society, but whether this has resulted in the growth of a distinct underclass, cut off economically from the working class and characterized by distinct attitudes and behaviour, is debatable. An analysis of the way the term has been used raises doubts about its utility, and an examination of that section of the community most associated with the notion points to too much economic diversity to enable us to speak, unproblematically, of a black underclass.

Part X

Work and Economic Life

Work is central to most people's lives. Almost everybody works, although by no means everyone at any point in time has a paid job. 'Work' is a very wide category, including not only those in paid employment, but children who work in school, housewives who work in the home and people in unpaid voluntary work. People work in many different settings also: factories, offices, shops and a diversity of other contexts.

People work for many different reasons. Some put up with dull, repetitive, poorly paid jobs because they have no other way of earning a livelihood. Others have more privileged work circumstances and may focus most of their lives upon their job. In Reading 42, Nicholas Abercrombie and Alan Warde concentrate upon the experience of industrial work. While a good deal of such work may appear uninteresting and uninvolving, the majority get some satisfaction from it – for example, from mixing with others, if not from the actual work task itself. Industrial jobs vary a great deal, however, in terms of how monotonous the tasks involved are, how much control each worker has over what he or she does, and the forms of managerial discipline to which they are subject.

Women are increasingly doing jobs once the sole preserve of men. In Reading 43, Anna Coote describes one such work situation. Lesley Smith set out to undertake a job normally regarded as exclusively within the male domain. Smith trained to drive large long-distance lorries. She found that mastering the technical skills needed to control the vehicle was a relatively minor problem compared to coping with the antagonism and puzzlement with her adoption of the career of lorry driver aroused in the male fraternity.

The 'formal economy' of the labour market, as J. I. Gershuny and R. E. Pahl (Reading 44) show, exists alongside a complex series of informal economic arrangements. The informal economy, they argue, should be thought of as involving three main components: the household economy, the 'underground' or 'hidden' economy and the 'communal' economy. In each of these three segments, goods and services are created, modified and exchanged without passing through orthodox economic institutions. For instance, a neighbour might help repair a part of another person's house in exchange for produce which the first individual has grown in his or her garden. As the authors indicate, the informal economy is not only fundamental to modern industrial production, but tends to grow in a way parallel with the formal economic system.

Reading 45 discusses the changing shape of work careers. Some observers are suggesting that full-time, long-term jobs will become less and less common. In fact in the UK already less than 50 per cent of the working population are in such jobs. The same trends are observable in other industrialized countries. What seems on the face of it a problem – insecure careers – can also be an opportunity. If there is less and less lifetime work on offer, people might be able to develop more flexible and autonomous working careers.

Modern industrial production was pioneered in the West, but today, of course, has spread widely throughout the world. Among non-Western countries, Japan in particular has emerged as an extremely strong producer and exporter, able to compete in a more than effective way with Western firms. Japanese styles of management differ in certain important ways from those characteristic of most Western countries. In recent years, some Japanese corporations have begun to initiate joint ventures with Western companies, others to set up their own production facilities in Europe and the United States. Reading 46, by Jeremy Seabrook, looks at a joint endeavour established by the Japanese firm Mitsubishi and the American carmaker Chrysler in Illinois. The study indicates that the US employees adapt fairly quickly to the Japanese type of administrative system. A feature of that system, in this particular plant at least, is a very high level of technological sophistication and automation.

David Lyon (Reading 47) analyses the possible implications of a further set of technological changes now affecting industrial production: the widespread use of information technology. Many have claimed that modern economies no longer depend centrally, as they once did, upon the production of manufactured goods; in place of manufacture, the production of information becomes a core resource. Lyon submits to critical scrutiny the idea that we are moving from an industrial order towards an 'information society'. As he says, it is impossible to resist the conclusion that information technology has already changed our lives significantly and is likely to alter them further in the future. Yet, as Lyon shows, upon examination the idea of the information society turns out to be a complicated one, and there is good reason to be cautious about some of the wilder claims which have been made about its potential consequences, good and bad.

Nicholas Abercrombie and Alan Warde

The Labour Process

THE EXPERIENCE OF WORK

Consider this description, given by a man who works on the assembly line at Ford, fixing the trim on to motor cars:

> It's the most boring job in the world. It's the same thing over and over again. There is no change in it, it wears you out. It makes you awful tired. It slows your thinking right down. There's no need to think. It's just a formality. You just carry on. You just endure it for the money. That's what we're paid for – to endure the boredom of it.
>
> If I had the chance to move I'd leave right away. It's the conditions here. Ford class you more as a machine than men. They're on top of you all the time. They expect you to work every minute of the day. The atmosphere you get in here is so completely false. Everyone is downcast and fed up . . .

For many people, the factory symbolizes a debased work environment. A woman employee cooking meals on a large community-centre site with several canteen and snack-bar outlets observed of the kitchens she worked in:

> It's just like a factory making radios. It *is* a factory. When we prepare the food, we don't think that someone is going to sit down and enjoy it. As long as it looks right we are not making any effort to improve the quality. There is no variety . . . Everything by the book, always the same way . . .

Boredom, lack of variety and the absence of opportunity to make decisions about how to set about work tasks are typical complaints.

Plate 10.1 An industrial kitchen
Source: Camera Press

But not everyone finds work as unpleasant as this. Another woman working in a small snack-bar on the same site said:

> I like working in this small bar better than anywhere else; you get to know the students who come here, we have a laugh and a chat. The bosses leave us alone; it's a first-rate job . . .

Many people derive intrinsic satisfaction from their work. A study . . . of agricultural labouring found that 93 per cent of those interviewed in East Anglia considered their job either 'mostly interesting' or 'interesting all the time'. Most workers like some part of their work and dislike others. This was true of the sample of agricultural workers who appreciated the variety of their jobs, enjoyed using farm machinery, and liked seeing crops and animals grow, but disliked aspects of the hours and conditions under which they had to labour.

Workers' reactions to their jobs are understandably mixed. The deprivations resulting from not having a job – poverty, social isolation and low social status . . . – are sufficiently severe to persuade people that any work is better than none. In this sense people want to work. Similarly, most people will say that they are satisfied with their job, partly because the realistic alternatives are not much better. Previous experience, qualifications and the local availability of other employment all severely limit any individual's choice of work. On the other hand, employees usually feel that their talents and skills are poorly utilized in work which they perceive as dull and monotonous. As one study of unskilled work in Peterborough observed, 95 per cent of the workers used more skill driving a car to work than they exercised on their job . . . Variation in the experience of work is considerable. Most people accept, instrumentally, the financial necessity of having a paid job. But they also expect to derive other benefits – self-satisfaction, self-actualization, performance of a duty and companionship among them – from their employment.

Adults typically spend a lot of time working, so that the actual quality of the experience of work deeply affects both personal and social relationships. Sociologists have, therefore, examined closely the precise content of jobs and the kind of relationships established between employers, supervisors and employees. These are elements of the so-called *labour process*.

In order to chart the consequences of work experience, it is necessary to compare the qualities of jobs. Since there are thousands of jobs, each distinctive, we need to reduce differences to a few, important dimensions. For sociological purposes, jobs may be grouped in terms of:

1 the range of tasks involved;
2 the degree of discretion given to the worker to decide how to accomplish those tasks; and
3 the mode of control used by managers and supervisors to try to ensure that those tasks are completed satisfactorily.

In these respects, the workers in the Ford assembly plant of Halewood and a schoolteacher are involved in very different types of labour process. Assembly work in car production entails that a single task be repeated, in a tightly prescribed manner, under the close surveillance of a foreman. The schoolteacher, by contrast, undertakes a wider range of tasks; the way of working is left to the teacher's initiative, i.e. *how* teachers teach varies from one person to the next; and supervision is distant, headteachers interfering infrequently in what happens in the classroom . . .

ORGANIZATIONS, TECHNOLOGY AND THE QUALITY OF WORK

The nature of work is partly dependent upon the organization of the enterprise providing employment. Generally, large firms are more complex, rules and procedures are formally specified, and the element of administrative authority is more prominent. Thus there is a tendency for work to be more specialized and authority relations more impersonal than in small firms. Work may then be more fragmented, with less discretion left to the worker. However, the effect of size should not be exaggerated, for . . . there are differences between large firms, some being more bureaucratic, others more flexible, depending upon the economic environment in which they operate.

The type of technology (equipment and machinery) used by an enterprise is obviously one important cause of the quality of work experience. A teacher's work might be much altered by the introduction of new electronic technology. In higher education, the Open University offers an instructive example. The use of television means that proportionately little of teachers' time is spent personally teaching students. The same lesson can be broadcast to thousands of students simultaneously. Teachers thus become relatively specialized: as writers of the course materials, as presenters of programmes, or as tutors corresponding with students about their work. Indeed, it is conceivable, with developments in communication technology, that in the near future people will be educated mostly at home, using televisions, microcomputers and direct-link telephones. Under such circumstances, the work of teachers would be transformed. Similarly, the tedium of assembly work in automobile manufacturing is a direct result of a decision to use production-line techniques to make cars. There are, however, other ways of manufacturing cars: some are still effectively hand-built by craft workers. But, among mass manufacturers, Volvo, for example, launched a well-publicized and successful experiment in the 1970s to abandon assembly-line production. Instead, flexible work-groups were created, each collectively responsible for a wide range of tasks, which were rotated frequently among members of the group. The results, according to the firm, were lower levels of turnover and absenteeism, reflecting greater work satisfaction, without any loss of efficiency.

It is important to realize that enterprises have a degree of choice about what technology to use. Such choices are not purely technical matters. Of course, there are economic constraints over the choice: goods have to be sold at competitive prices, privately owned firms insist on making profits, and workers demand adequate wages. Nevertheless, as the Volvo example illustrated, there is often a choice. What determines the decision? Some sociologists have argued that employers and managers, when selecting technology, are especially concerned with establishing and maintaining *control* over the workforce. Decisions about technology are an aspect of so-called managerial *strategies*.

The effects of technology should not be exaggerated. It used to be thought that work satisfaction was directly determined by the technology used: manual workers on assembly lines were likely to be bored and discontented, while those involved in craft work or in automated-process production would derive more satisfaction from their work. In turn, it was argued, greater work satisfaction would lead directly to a reduction in industrial and political conflict. Reality, however, is more complicated. Not merely the machinery but also the social organization of the workplace and the general political culture beyond the factory strongly affect workers' attitudes.

One analysis which demonstrates that technology itself does not determine people's experience of work or their political attitudes is that of Gallie.[1] Gallie compared the attitudes of workers in four oil refineries, two in France and two in Britain. All the refineries used advanced, automated, continuous-process technology; to all intents and purposes the technological situation was identical in each. But the industrial and political responses of the British and French workers differed sharply. The French workers identified strongly with the working class, expressed greater resentment of class inequality, were more hostile towards the management and believed that redress of their industrial grievances required political action. The British workers, by contrast, whilst recognizing the existence of class inequality, showed significantly less resentment about it, and were more likely to seek remedies for their dissatisfaction at the local level, within the plant, through trade union representation. This shows that the same technology can have quite different effects on workers in different contexts. The greater radicalism of the French workers, Gallie thought, derived from the interaction of a high level of work grievance and the exposure over time to the radical messages of the parties of the French left.

It was particularly important that trade unions were unable effectively to redress grievances in France, collective bargaining procedures being very weakly developed. As Gallie . . . says:

> The most striking difference in the work situation of French and British workers lay in the structure of managerial power. French employers had retained virtually intact their traditional rights to determine unilaterally both the terms of payment and the organization of work with the firm. It was an institutionalized system in which the representatives of the work-force were given minimal influence over decision-making. In other terms, it was a system in which there was a very low level of institutionalization of industrial conflict. In Britain, on the other hand, the employers had made much more substantial concessions to the trade unions. Traditional conceptions of managerial prerogative had been considerably eroded and issues relating to both salaries and work organization had become subject to procedures for joint regulation . . . The British cases had seen a deliberate attempt on the part of employers to develop procedures for institutionalizing industrial conflict.

Gallie, then, demonstrated that technology alone determines neither the nature of the experience of work nor the character of the workers' responses. Rather, national political culture is important, as are, especially, the strategies which managers use to control their workforce.

MANAGERIAL STRATEGIES AND CONTROL AT WORK

Managerial strategies are ways of getting workers to spend their hours at work in a fashion which advances the economic goals of management. Given that much work is unpleasant, management has a problem of motivating workers to complete their allotted tasks quickly and effectively. Care and effort on the part of workers are not guaranteed merely by their presence at work. A major source of industrial conflict is the so-called 'effort bargain', the negotiable definition of what constitutes a 'fair day's work'. Management has two, intertwined, resources at its command – payment and authority.

Management's control is based ultimately on the threat to stop paying wages to ineffective workers, i.e. if the worker's effort falls beneath a certain acceptable minimum, he or she can be sacked. There are, however, more subtle ways in which payment can be used to generate effort. Payment by piece-rates, for example, whereby a worker gets a certain amount for each article completed, means that wages are directly related to work effort. The productivity deal is the equivalent system in large-scale manufacturing industry where, since no individual completes any particular product, collective financial incentives are provided to encourage high output. The other main way of regulating effort by financial incentive is by constructing promotion ladders within companies. If promotion can be made to depend upon performance then workers have an incentive to work hard and obediently.

The other major managerial resource is authority, which is exercised in association with payment. By and large, workers accept that management has some right to instruct them what to do. The presence of managers and supervisors watching over workers is, thus, legitimate. At the same time, though, in practice that authority is frequently resented and challenged by workers. The concept of managerial strategy refers to the various ways of exercising authority at work, of making managerial control effective in the face of resistance . . .

There is currently extensive debate about the ways in which increased competition between firms during the protracted and repeated economic recessions since the mid-1970s has affected industrial organization and work practices. A difficult economic climate has encouraged enterprises to adopt new arrangements to suit trying circumstances. The adaptation most discussed has been the pursuit of greater *flexibility* . . .

TOWARDS POST-FORDISM?

Some authors consider the growth of flexible organization and working practices so significant as to constitute the basis for a major new phase in the development of capitalist societies. Various terms are used to describe the new phase: 'flexible accumulation', 'neo-Fordism' and 'post-Fordism' all imply slightly different scenarios . . ., but each identifies a transition away from Fordism, as described by Braverman,[2] to a more flexible *system* of production, the ideal-typical characteristics of which are listed in Table 10.1. As can be seen, the characteristics of Fordism are precisely those that Braverman argued were becoming more general in the late twentieth century. Fordist production describes a system of mass production in mechanized workplaces (including offices) where work is routinized and closely supervised and where deskilled workers come to share a common proletarian condition.

TABLE 10.1 Ideal types of production system

	Fordist	Post-Fordist
Technology	Fixed, dedicated machines	Micro-electronically controlled multi-purpose machines
Product	For a mass consumer market Relatively cheap	Diverse specialized products High quality
Labour process	Fragmented Few tasks Little discretion Hierarchical authority and technical control	Many tasks for versatile workers Some autonomy Group control
Contracts	Collectively negotiated rate for the job Relatively secure	Payment by individual performance Dual market: secure core, highly insecure periphery

Source: A. Warde, 'The future of work', in J. Anderson and M. Ricci (eds), *Society and Social Science: A Reader* (Milton Keynes: Open University Press, 1990), p. 88.

Post-Fordism offers a different prospect. If the new scenario is accurately identified, then it certainly sweeps away many of the industrial conditions identified by Braverman. In some cases it entails the return of the craft worker: the pattern of work in the 'Third Italy' is one in which craft workers use their experience and very advanced technology to work in small, quasi-domestic workshops. In all instances, flexible organization and working practices entail the abandonment of the technical control that contributed to the degradation of labour on the dedicated assembly line. It means the contraction of mass production and, some authors suggest, a significant change in patterns of consumption as new products, designed to suit special tastes or needs, are made available. Also it signifies the end of secure full-time employment for a substantial portion of the labour force.

These accounts of new flexible practices identify *tendencies*. Flexible production describes the leading edge of industrial innovation on a world scale. Scarcely anyone thinks that mass production has yet been superseded; it is, rather, that this is the way things are developing. Employment figures show a decline in unskilled manual work and an increase in white-collar occupations. Subcontracting has increased somewhat. There has also been a considerable increase in the number of small businesses: self-employment comprised about 12 per cent of total employment in 1992 . . . A growing proportion of jobs are part-time and there are more temporary jobs than there used to be.

However, there are two kinds of objection that may be raised about this view of the future of industry. First, there is an empirical problem of how many people are being affected by these changes. Secondly, there is an explanatory problem: do these things have anything in common? Are they a unified set of changes with a common cause, or is the apparent power of this trend more a function of sociologists' concepts?

The extent to which these tendencies have developed in Britain remains doubtful. Relatively few firms have introduced a complete flexible package on the model of the Japanese, for example. B. Jones . . ., studying the engineering industry, argued 'that British industry has not yet made a systematic shift to flexible automation. The systems that have been implemented have not yet been accompanied by a corresponding revolution in work roles, or the functional and authority aspects'.[3] This may be an indication of Britain being somewhat backward, since comparative studies show far more examples of integrated flexible production systems in Germany and Japan. In all countries there can be no doubt that mass production survives in many industries, for instance in food processing. In addition, the new international division of labour has seen some of the most routinized of mass production processes developed in factories owned by the Western multinational corporations but located in the less-developed countries.

Nor is it entirely clear that these changes are part of a coherent or unified system of manufacturing production, still less that they are the harbinger of a new age. In Britain, conditions of employment have altered in the last ten years, with some functional flexibility and many more insecure jobs. However, these features may have other causes than attempts by firms to move towards flexible accumulation. Part-time work has been increasing since the early 1960s, before flexible production had been thought of, and has more to do with the movement of more low-paid women workers into the labour force. Moreover, most part-time work is not in manufacturing industry, where it has been declining recently, but in the service industries. Agency work, a form of flexible contract, is largely restricted to a couple of occupations – nursing and secretarial work. Temporary contracts are more prevalent in the public sector than in the capitalist sector, contrary to the logic of competitiveness that lies behind flexible accumulation. This suggests that changes in employment conditions may have more to do with state policy than capitalist reorganization. Indeed, it might be proposed that, in Britain at least, what we have seen [since the late 1970s] is a consequence less of advanced technology and new products than of a change in the balance of power between employers and unions. Declining membership, the loss of legal immunities, unemployment, and fewer jobs in traditional manufacturing industries with high union density have swung the balance of industrial power significantly in favour of employers.

READING 43

Anna Coote

Lesley Smith: Lorry Driver

'Have you got a single room for the night?'
'Yes, indeed, Madam.'
'Is it all right if I leave my vehicle in your car park?'
'Certainly, Madam.'
'It's the one with the forty-foot trailer behind it . . .'

It was Lesley's first long-distance trip. She had to deliver 18 tons of frozen food from a Doncaster cold store to two depots in Scotland. And it was getting late. She had made her first drop in Edinburgh and phoned through to the Glasgow depot to make sure it didn't close down for the night leaving her with a lorry full of carrots and peas. When she arrived in

Glasgow it was dark. The depot was on the edge of the Gorbals and she'd heard alarming stories about the area. A small boy asked her for 10p to guard her wagon for the night and she remembered another driver telling her how he'd turned down a similar offer – and found all his wheels gone the next morning.

Most of the transport lodging-houses in that part of town were full, except the ones with three beds to a room. In desperation, she headed out towards Renfrew where she was due to reload the following day, stopped at the big hotel near the airport and asked for a room for the night.

When they'd recovered their composure, the hotel staff were most helpful. Could Madam park her lorry round the back? It would be safer there. The night porter would keep an eye on it. Lesley was grateful – the vehicle was worth around £30,000.

That hotel room cost Lesley's firm £5 more than a regular stop-over, but they didn't complain as it was the first time and it never happened again. Soon she was making regular long-distance trips down to Cornwall via Avonmouth and up to Fort William in the Highlands where the roads got narrower and narrower, calling on all her skills at manœuvring. Like the other drivers, she got to know the best lodging-houses along her routes, and established her favourite transport cafés where the faces were familiar and she didn't have to keep explaining herself.

It was always the same when she went into a café for the first time. The drivers all fell silent. Then they looked out into the park for a car. when they saw no car, they assumed she was a hitchhiker and asked her where she wanted to go. She would then explain and wait for the usual handful of jokes about women drivers. On the whole, however, the men were a lot friendlier and more courteous once they learnt that she too was a driver. They were careful with their language, and always curious. After a while Lesley wished she could carry a tape-recorded message, so she wouldn't have to answer the same questions again and again: Why did she want to be a lorry driver? How did she start? Where did she learn?

Her dad is a lorry driver, but it was never her intention to follow in his footsteps. She was brought up in a small mining village outside Doncaster, an only child and thoroughly spoilt. Her mother has worked, since well before Lesley's birth, as a nurse in the local hospital.

> My parents gave me everything I wanted. I was crazy about horses, so they saved up and bought me horses of my own. I left school at 15 without taking any exams because I was determined to start working with horses as soon as possible. I was sent to the local riding school to train as an instructor. My dad built me some stables on the land behind our house – we had a four-acre smallholding left to us by a relative. When I was 17, I started working from home, training other people's horses and giving a few free lessons to kids who helped me out in the stables.

It was her friend Hilda who introduced her to lorry driving. An unconventional woman herself, being managing director of a local sand and gravel company, Hilda gave Lesley a rather unusual twenty-first birthday present: a ten-day training course for the heavy goods vehicle driving test. So Lesley went to the training centre in Rotherham and took the course to please her friend. She learnt to drive Class 1 vehicles, the biggest on the road.

The main practical skill she learnt was how to manœuvre a large vehicle, reversing and turning a 10-ton lorry which was 12 feet wide, 40 feet long and 14 feet high – in spaces more suited to Minis and Escorts. 'When you turn a corner you don't stay close to the kerb as you do in a car. You're taught to use more of the road you're leaving than the one you're entering, and to stick to your own side of the road once you've made the turning. And you're told never to use the weight and size of your vehicle to get you around – in other words, don't play Big Brother with the little cars, they pay for use of the road too.' She had to learn the relevant sections of the Highway Code, what the law said about juggernauts, and the restrictions on hours of driving. She didn't need any detailed knowledge of motor mechanics, although she was expected to know what was wrong if, for instance, black smoke was pouring from the exhaust. In fact, she knew a lot more than that, as she had often watched her father strip down engines when she was a child.

'It's a hard test. Quite a lot of people fail. I managed to pass first go and then started to look for a job. I can't explain why – I just wanted to go on driving.'

She telephoned or visited one local company after another. 'I'll be truthful with you, love', said one old Doncaster trucker. 'There's no way I'm going to trust 20,000 quids' worth of my vehicle in a woman's hands.' At least he was honest. There were others who tried to fob her off by saying they might have some work in a week or two. They never did.

In the end, Lesley's father had to step in. He'd telephone a company, as if there was a job going and find out all the details. When they said 'come and see us', he'd casually mention the job was not for him but for his daughter. Six weeks later, she was hired by a general haulage company. When the boss first saw her, he felt sure she wouldn't last for more than a fortnight. She certainly didn't look the part – a slim, delicately built young woman with pale blonde hair, dressed in neat pretty clothes. (If she turned up at your door you might think she was the Avon lady, never the driver of a 32-ton truck.) But looks can deceive, of course, and Lesley stayed in her first job for more than a year. . . .

The driving itself wasn't physically taxing. With power steering and smooth gears, the lorry was no heavier to handle than the average family car. But power steering is a fairly recent innovation. Not long ago drivers really did need a lot of muscle, as Lesley discovered on the one occasion when she had to drive a very old vehicle. 'It was an ancient 32-ton truck. It had no power steering, there seemed to be nothing powered about it at all! I had to drive 17 miles to the Hull docks. When I came to the first roundabout I found I couldn't steer and change gear at the same time. I had to stop in the middle of the road, put it into gear, then lean on the steering wheel with all my weight to ram it round. Nowadays a child could get into a truck and steer with one hand.'

After thirteen months she moved over to Hull to work for a container firm. It was easier than her last job. She picked up the loaded containers at the docks and drove them to various destinations, up to 100 miles away, where they were unloaded so she could return them empty to the docks. The only drawback was that she had to live in digs during the week. Hull was fifty miles away and she couldn't do a day's work and get back to Doncaster each night without breaking the legal limits on driving hours.

(The maximum time was ten and a half hours with a half-hour break after five hours; now it's eight hours, under EU laws.) She was very attached to her home and she missed her boyfriend Robert, a young farmer with whom she'd been going steady since she was 17. So after six months she moved back to her old firm in Doncaster.

It wasn't long before another local company offered her a better job. This was the one which took her to Scotland, delivering frozen food from the Doncaster cold store. It was the main depot for all the farmers in the area, who sent in their produce to be frozen and stored. When the produce was purchased, the farmers employed Lesley's firm to make the deliveries which usually went in 18-ton loads to one or two customers at a time. Lesley was in charge of a larger and newer vehicle with a 40-foot refrigerated trailer which didn't need roping or sheeting. . . .

Though she travels all over the country, she is still based in Doncaster with her parents and manages to get back there most nights of the week. When I last saw her she told me she and Robert were about to get engaged. 'He's been looking at houses, and we want to wait until he's found one before we get married; it may take a while because he wants to buy a small farm. Robert's been on about buying me my own lorry when we're married – just the front without the trailer – so that I could contract to pull grain vehicles and potato carts for the local farmers. There'd be plenty of work. I like the idea – as long as it would leave me time to look after Robert. I'm quite looking forward to being a housewife. Mind you, I'm like my mother. She never gave up her job, she couldn't bear to stay in the house all day.'

READING 44

J. I. Gershuny and R. E. Pahl

Implications and the Future of the Informal Economy

People have always fiddled, had perks, worked on the side, and helped a neighbour with 'cheap goods'. This is the way the workers have always survived and, at another level and in a different style, the rich have got richer. (Those in the middle may have missed out.) Attempts by the state to organize, tax and control have shifted various activities from the formal economy or the domestic economy into the informal economy. Yesterday's 'enterprise' becomes part of today's hidden economy. But the political parties huff and puff about the importance of getting people into employment rather than helping people to do their own work.

Obsession with what can be easily counted leads to false ideas about the British disease and our national performance. The political agenda ignores, or misunderstands, the main economic tendencies in our society. This would not matter much if the 'formal' and 'informal' modes of production maintained a constant interrelationship over time. If the informal economy grew at the same rate as the formal economy, then the significance of GNP as an indicator of change would be unaffected by the fact that it only measures formal activity. And if the amount of work done in the two economies rose or fell in parallel, then statistics of formal employment levels would indicate the overall availability of work.

But our thesis is that, on the contrary, the two economies develop at different rates. A consequence of social and technological development is the transfer of particular spheres of production between them.

We must first deal with some definitional problems. We are using the term *informal economy* to cover the following three areas, of which the first two are the most important for our argument:

1 *Household economy:* production, not for money, by members of a household and predominantly for members of that household, of goods or services for which approximate substitutes might otherwise be purchased for money.

2 *Underground, hidden or black economy:* production, wholly or partly for

money or barter, which should be declared to some official taxation or regulatory authority, but which is wholly or partly concealed.

3 *Communal economy:* production, not for money or barter, by an individual or group, of a commodity that might otherwise be purchasable, and of which the producers are not principal consumers.

Like any economic definitions, these have fuzzy edges. Where, for example, do we place those small businesses which rely heavily on family workers, and are less than absolutely scrupulous in their VAT returns? But the definitions will stand up for our present purpose – which is to demonstrate that there are good reasons for expecting the informal economy to grow at the expense of the formal.

In most of the developed world, the massive increase in material production over the last 150 or 200 years has been associated with technological developments and with an increasing scale in organization. Now this process is showing clear signs of breaking down. With new technology, production can be cheaper, more efficient and often more convenient when it is carried out on a small scale. Work can be done in the household or in the hidden economy which once was done only in the formal economy.

The man who finds that it pays him to take a week off to paint the house, or rebuild the engine in his car, will probably do a better job than if he went to a firm in the formal sector. With sewing machines, power drills and food mixers, we can (if we have the skills) get smart clothes, fine carpentry and gourmet food by working in our own time with our own tools. Technology has created this new freedom.

Technology is not the only driving force. Legal changes also push production from the formal into the informal economy. VAT means that money payments in cash become illegal and unrecorded. Steep rates of personal taxation, obligations to pay high national insurance contributions, and employment protection legislation: all these encourage both casual work 'for cash' and do-it-yourself. Changes in relative prices increase DIY, too. Technical innovation has pushed down the price of goods. But rising wages rates have pushed up the price of services. And the satisfactions of informal work – relative autonomy, self-direction and self-pacing – also encourage its growth.

Seen in this perspective, development is not a one-way progress – from reliance on primary production, through manufacturing production, to a society whose major efforts are devoted to the production of services. Nor is there a simple transition from a society in which economic relationships are based on custom to a modern society in which an increasing proportion of social relationships are cash-based – i.e. converted from generalized to specific exchange. The pattern is less tidy. [Figure 10.1] shows that, instead of a steady one-way flow of economic activity – whereby things move, over time, from the household to the industrial production system – there is a whole series of little transformations of production (perhaps taking place simultaneously) between the formal economy, the household economy and the underground economy. The direction of flow is determined by the social and technical conditions for the production of particular commodities at particular times. As [Figure 10.1] shows, this involves six possible flows among three types of economy.

Here are some examples. The washing of clothes and linen, which moved

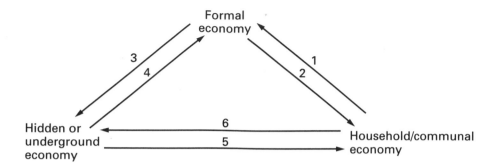

Figure 10.1 The three economies

from the wash-house at home into the laundry, and then back into the home with the technological help of a washing machine, illustrates the two-way flow between households and the formal economy (1 and 2 in the [figure]). The current prevalence of household construction work paid for in cash may indicate a shift from formal to underground or 'black' production (3 in the [figure]). And if unemployment levels rise, the cost of black work will drop and some jobs, now DIY, will move across (6).

There is much discussion about the 'deskilling' of the workforce in the formal economy. But there may be a reskilling in the informal one. Some people who in the past might have called in a plumber or a carpenter are now more ready to try to do the job themselves. 'How-to' books democratize skills in the informal economy. Hiring a cook or a chauffeur has always been a minority pastime. The same is now coming to apply to carpenters and glaziers.

Though we argue for a wide range of different sorts of flow between three types of economy, we wouldn't deny that over the last couple of centuries, the aggregate effect has been an overall shift from household/communal production to formal industrial production. But it may be that the most significant transformation in the future will be from the formal economy to the underground and household economies.

We are both engaged in research work, attempting to explore the implications of this hypothesis. One of us (Gershuny) is analysing published and unpublished data to assess more precisely the growth of informal economic activity. For example, the official Family Expenditure Survey shows that, rather than buying formal transport, household and entertainment services, the British have increasingly bought *goods* like cars and TV sets – which are used in the informal household production of services.

Another source is the national sample of people's activity patterns, carried out by the BBC Audience Research Department. Re-analysis of the diaries which respondents kept over a number of weeks in 1961 and 1974–5 shows that time spent working for money declined; time devoted to the informal production of services increased.

The other author (Pahl) is exploring the detailed social and economic transactions within and between families in one community. He is trying to document a new kind of rationality, which allocates time and energy between the three economic spheres according to a very subtle calculus. There is employment for which one gets money, and perhaps social satisfaction; and there is work with one's own tools in one's own time, for which one gets much satisfaction and perhaps some money as well.

Work and sociability can get more intertwined in the informal economy than in the formal one. A woman calls on her sister and looks after her [sister's] child while she has her hair done; [the woman] returns with some commodity got through her sister's employment. A man who goes to the pub for a drink and a chat gets suggestions from people who will help him build his house extension.

The whole of everyday life is suffused with contacts, exchanges and reciprocities. Yet the standard economic model is of a market-place in which you sell your labour for money, and this in turn pays for the goods and services you need. Certainly, that is one option. But, for many people, it is not very satisfactory or rewarding. Any government which assumes that everyone is longing to sell their labour to an employer ought to get closer to the people.

But what will it be like to live in a world dominated more by the household and hidden economies, and less by the formal economy? Let us construct some alternatives. Two grim ones, and a pleasant one.

The first kind of future goes like this. If current trends continue, the 'self-service' sector of the economy will continue to grow at the expense of the formal sector. The demand for commodities from the formal sector will be concentrated in the manufacturing sector, which is also the sector with high growth in manpower productivity. This productivity is dependent on shedding labour, which in turn may produce faster growth in the underground economy.

The non-manufacturing and less productive part of the formal economy will be forced to pay minimal wages and to use part-time labour – probably women, and children still at school or the retired. They will expect to augment their wages through tips and fiddles.

This will produce a dual labour market: (a) a high-technology sector, aiming at an international market and obliged to be as efficient and productive as possible, and probably paying relatively high wages; paired with (b) a low-wage sector, largely relying on female and part-time workers.

Below this dual labour market, the informal economy will flourish uncontrolled, and perhaps uncontrollable. This would be a world of *mafiosi*, of big bosses and little crooks. The working class will become divided within itself. The new labour aristocracy of the high-technology growth industries in the manufacturing sector will get high wages and be able to afford an expensive, even ostentatious lifestyle. Those less fortunate, in the low-wage sector, may sink yet further.

Women obliged to work part-time, a shifting workforce of young people or immigrants, and a fluctuating and unstable pattern of employment – all these help to provide the ingredients of a nasty, increasingly inegalitarian world.

The second glimpse into the gloomier side of the crystal ball is perhaps not so much an alternative to the first – rather, a consequence of it. On this view, the state, fearful of the unstable situation in the first scenario, increases its power of surveillance and control. It attempts to enforce taxation and employment legislation by increasing the penalties for non-compliance, and by bolstering the police force and other law-enforcing agencies. It keeps up employment in the formal sector by spending the increased tax yield on more public services, and developing a larger bureaucracy. This creates more resentment among the mass of the population. The social satisfactions of the informal economy could not be re-created in the formal economy. People would feel much like those caught in the 'socialism' of Poland or Czechoslovakia.

Both these forecasts are extremely disagreeable and unpleasant prospects. What is the third and better route? This would be based on the state's recognizing certain realities in our new economic life, encouraging the most desirable features, and mitigating the less desirable. Governments are now uncomfortably caught. On the one hand, they feel they should try to maintain, or increase, the present number of jobs. On the other hand, the efficient industrial production which is necessary to compete in international markets means reducing employment. The dilemma can only be resolved by a deeper understanding of the socially good aspects of the informal economy, and then by encouraging them.

The formal economy can provide efficient material production, but the informal economy can provide services which, since they are not widely traded, need *not* be efficient in their use of labour. So the state could adopt a 'facilitative' role. It would support community-based services in such fields as care for old people, children and the chronically sick. It would modify the laws relating to very small companies in order to relieve them of administrative and tax burdens. It would change social security benefits, in order to reduce the high tax rates on low-wage earners, and to protect anyone working exclusively in the small-scale informal sector. Above all, the state would *encourage* people to participate simultaneously in both the formal and the informal sectors. There would be job-sharing schemes in the formal economy; and education and training schemes to develop the skills needed for the informal economy.

Clearly, some aspects of the way the informal economy is developing are unpalatable. Some people are expelled or excluded from the formal economy. Their participation in the informal economy is not voluntary. They do not gain any intangible, personal benefits from informal production. They are vulnerable to exploitation by those with access to jobs (and therefore cash) from the formal economy. The growth of the informal economy is no grounds for complacency about formal unemployment.

But positive government action could extend the range of genuine options open to people. Action should be taken to reduce the discriminatory impact of unemployment, and to promote shorter working hours. This would improve things. It is the only kind of strategy that will cope with rising levels of unemployment in the formal economy.

The problem that still faces us is lack of knowledge. We do not thoroughly understand the social processes that underlie the flows between the formal and informal economies. We need new concepts as well as more detailed ethnography. The scale of adjustment in intellectual frameworks is enormous. The only reason we have for thinking that this adjustment will take place is that it is necessary. If we are to cope with a world in which jobs are lost inside the formal economy, we must come to understand the nature of work outside it.

READING 45

Chris Brewster

You've Got to Go With the Flow: The Changing Nature of Jobs

Only a minority of jobs in Britain now fits our idea of a 'normal' or 'real' job. We are only just beginning to understand the implications of this. [Since the late 1970s] the labour market in the UK has undergone more radical changes than occurred in the previous half a century. The nature of these has been so substantial – but comparatively so sudden – that many people still have only a vague idea what has happened.

Many employers, too, are only now beginning to understand the variety of ways, other than 'standard' employment, in which they can get work done; and many employees and potential employees are still struggling to realize that 'normal' jobs are frequently not on offer.

Less than 50 per cent of the working population in Britain has a full-time, long-term job with a traditional employment contract. Nor is the UK alone in this; although patterns of employment vary widely across Europe, the same trends are visible everywhere.

There has been a sharp rise in the variety of ways in which work is organized. We cannot describe it as 'the way people are employed' because many of these expanding forms of working arrangements (subcontracting, franchising, self-employment) break the link between work and employment.

The story is one of increases in almost every form of work – except the traditional full-time, long-term job. One million people have more than one job. Part-time work has more than doubled in the last fifteen years, and so has self-employment. Temporary employment and fixed-term contracts have significantly increased. And new working arrangements, such as job-sharing and annual hours contracts, have been established [Figure 10.2].

The increase in these forms of working is not just a matter of changes in the industrial structure: it is evidence of their spread into new areas.

Figure 10.2 Flexible friends: Percentage of organizations using flexible working practices, UK, 1995
Source: Chris Brewster, Cranfield

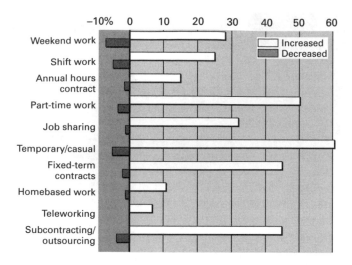

Shift working, for example, always existed in the emergency services and where manufacturers wanted to use expensive equipment over more than eight hours per day. It has now spread into shops which stay open in the evenings to meet customer requirements, and to offices concerned with global operations and which need to be in touch with people in different time zones. Similarly, subcontracting was always common in the construction industry, but it is now common in the computing, scientific and local authority sectors.

According to government statistics, around 27 million people now make up the UK's working population, of whom around 2.5 million are unemployed. The Trades Union Congress and others might argue that another several hundred thousand, who don't appear in the official statistics, should also be counted as out of work.

We know that unemployment is a significant problem for all European countries. In the UK, there are 1 million fewer men in jobs now than in 1990. Since 1990, the manufacturing sector alone has lost almost a million jobs, although even in manufacturing there have been pockets of growth. British Aerospace, for example, has made well-publicized job reductions recently, while its former subsidiary, Rover, . . . increased jobs by 2,000 [in 1995]. And there is certainly growth in other sectors.

The world of work is changing and the range of options increasing. For employers, the need to think strategically becomes more important; to end the discussions about headcounts and to begin thinking about how to get the work done in the most cost-effective manner; and there is evidence that this is beginning to happen.

For employees and potential employees, the changes mean they have to be prepared to work in different ways and to be more flexible about their work arrangements. Already, a majority is in other than 'standard' or 'typical' employment. Also employees have realized that the days of a job for life have, in most cases, disappeared. Much more rapid movement in and out of work takes place now than it used to (around 10 per cent of the working population leave a job, and a roughly similar proportion start a job, every year). It is no surprise, therefore, to find that the job market is becoming more varied and more volatile. How we deal with this situation will be one of the touchstones of social and economic success over the next few years.

PART-TIME WORKING

In the past two years, well over two-thirds of all the jobs that have been created have been part-time jobs. Of those that are employed, about 6 million (one-quarter) have part-time jobs. Women fill more than eight out of ten of these, and research shows that most people are in part-time employment because they prefer to work that way.

Part-time working enables them to fit work in with other responsibilities, such as caring for young children or elderly relatives, which many see as a major part of their lives. Employers prefer it because it allows them to match the jobs on offer to the work that needs to be done. Not all work comes in neat, seven-and-a-half hour blocks; if the work a particular employer has only lasts for part of the day, why pay for a full day? Employers also know that if the tasks are not varied and interesting, employees find it easier to work with commitment and enthusiasm for a few hours rather than for a whole day. Nor do part-timers have to take time off for visits to the dentist or the doctor; so part-timers are more productive.

TEMPORARY JOBS

These account for well over 1.5 million employees, around 7.5 per cent of all jobs, including an additional 0.5 per cent increase last year. Few employers can predict whether a job will continue into the next decade; none can be sure that a particular recruit will succeed in a job – so it makes little sense to make a promise of permanent employment they may be unable to keep. A further 3 million people (more than 12 per cent) are self-employed, while more than 400,000 people are involved with some form of government-subsidized training.

OTHER OPTIONS

A wide range of other forms of work exist, which sometimes overlap with part-time or temporary employment. Some involve quite small variations to the standard employment contract. But others are organized with no employment contract at all.

Shift working is not just becoming more widespread, it is also becoming less standardized. The days when nearly all shifts consisted of ten or twelve hours are gone. 'Twilight shifts', usually for women working in shops, are now widespread. Shifts can be of different and varying lengths, brought about by increasing pressures on managers, changing employee expectations, and the advent of computer programs which enable managers to organize and check that everyone works a specified number of hours, no matter how complicated the shift patterns.

Annual hours working has taken a firm foothold in recent years. If work in places such as travel agencies, food-processing firms and accounts departments is on a cyclical pattern, it makes little economic sense to employ staff for the same number of hours each day. Varying the hours to suit the work demand avoids paying for overtime in some periods – and also avoids the workers suffering boredom in others. Phillips, British Gypsum and some in the paper industry now pay their employees for the total number of hours they do during a year, while continuing to pay the same salary every month.

Job sharing is a form of part-time working where two people share the same full-time employment pattern. Job sharers working for Hewlett Packard, for example, guarantee that if one of them is away the other will fill in for them. The employer gets full cover for only a little extra cost.

Homeworking and teleworking have grown, but only a little. Some of the wilder predictions that large numbers of us would be working this way by the end of the decade will be wrong. Although the technology would allow this to happen, the predictions failed to take account of the necessary social side of work. More and more people will work at home, but the main growth will be among those who do so only occasionally, to complete a specific report or prepare for a meeting.

Term-time working has been successful at the NatWest bank. Female employees retain their contracts, without pay, during the school holidays, resuming their usual full- or part-time jobs during school terms.

Franchising, subcontracting and the use of consultants are all ways of getting work done without actually taking on the responsibility of employing people. The organization gets its work done (at a cost, of course), but without having to employ anyone extra. Those doing the work are either employed by other organizations or work for themselves.

Then, finally, there is the unlawful economy, or informal economy, which on any measure is a substantial part of the UK economy. Someone – although not you or me, of course – must be involved in making their living there.

Jeremy Seabrook

House of the Rising Sun: The Nature and Impact of Japanese Corporations

The joint venture between Mitsubishi and Chrysler looks incongruous set in the rich black earth of McLean County in central Illinois. The plant is one of the most highly automated and robotized in the world. Ninety per cent of welding is done robotically, releasing the associates (there are no workers) from dangerous and tedious operations. Almost half a billion dollars' worth of investment has gone into the 636-acre site. This has produced just under 3,000 jobs.

There is a stamping shop, body shop, plastic moulding shop, paint shop and final assembly area; the conveyor lines are eight miles in length. A 1.5-mile track allows for the test-driving of every vehicle. The low white building is surrounded by a wire mesh fence and rows of barbed wire. It looks like something between a military installation and a hospital.

Although this is an equal venture, few people in the plant can be unaware that Mitsubishi accounts for almost 10 per cent of the gross national product of Japan. One in ten of the Diamond Star Mitsubishi (DSM) workforce will be trained in Japan for a period up to thirty-seven weeks. There are about fifty Japanese employees at present, and 100–150 technical assistants on short-term visits to help production under way. The plant opened in the autumn of 1988.

The Japanese say they have been surprised by the dedication of the Bloomington workforce. It is no accident that the site chosen is the middle west, where the work ethic remains strong. The office hours of DSM are 7.30 a.m. until 4.12 p.m. When the first 300 jobs were advertised, there were more than 30,000 applicants. You don't have to travel far in Bloomington before you meet disappointed aspirants. Those accepted are the object of envy and admiration, forming, as they do, a new aristocracy of workers in a community whose egalitarianism is only apparent.

All applicants are screened by the Illinois Department of Social Security for information about their work record and basic skills. The next step is a battery of State-administered general aptitude tests before further screening at the DSM Assessment Center. A physical examination and routine drug test are also mandatory.

It goes against the grain for many people in the middle west to acknowledge the industrial superiority of the Japanese. There is some overt xenophobia, and an understandable reserve on the part of those who were on the death marches of World War II. Others insist that it is now time for Japan to share the burden of defending the free world.

There is also much criticism of the Japanese for having unfairly protected their industries. But perhaps the most common response would be familiar to us in Britain. It clearly echoes the proprietorial tolerance with which Britain once regarded the US, seeing in it an extension of an energy and vigour which originated in Britain. In the US, the reasoning goes like this: 'We are the true initiators and innovators, the Japanese take over our inventions, improve upon them, perfect them.' In this way, the Americans feel that they remain the original source of all that is most vital in the world, even though they get less of the credit for it, and little of the profit.

It turns out that Japanese management can be seen as simply a matter of common sense. 'Kaizen', or continuous improvement, is at the heart of the Mitsubishi philosophy, and who could quarrel with that? As an employee of DSM, your advice and suggestions are sought for the enhancement of safety and efficiency. All suggestions are considered; if they are not implemented, you are given an explanation. It is easy to buy into such a system, so different from traditional manufacturing plants, where suggestions boxes grew dusty with disuse.

The training manual applies to all 3,000 associates. There is a common programme of work discipline. All wear the grey and maroon DSM uniform, which removes the last traces of any 'them and us' attitude. All are part of the Diamond Star family. The United Auto-Workers' Union of America was recognized by the Company in 1988; although it is hoped that the need for it will wither away.

The team concept pervades the plant. There are teams of ten to fifteen people, who all work together under a team-leader. Each team has twenty to thirty job responsibilities. People are trained in all of these, and work rotated on a two-hourly basis, so that the working day remains varied. It also means that there is flexibility: if an employee is absent, someone else can cover. It is the antithesis of the monotony of the assembly line, where people have always been given one simple, repetitive function. Naturally, the strong sense of belonging means there are many collective social activities. On the Friday I was there, I was told 'tomorrow some people are going to the ball-game in Peoria, there is a golf outing to Chicago, some women are shopping in Chicago, and there is a trip to the home of Abraham Lincoln in Springfield'.

Among the associates are former bank-tellers, farmers, housewives, day-care workers, students. The level of educational attainment is relatively high. There is sophisticated equipment to operate and no quality inspection is carried out until the vehicle is completed. The teams themselves are responsible for quality, which is superb.

Donald Schoene is Executive Vice-President of Finance, and Treasurer. Before joining Diamond Star, he spent more than twenty-five years with

Chrysler, and was Controller for Chrysler UK. He says: 'Our eastern friends are very good at learning our western trades. They know how to modify and enhance our technology. This places us in the role of teachers, and the knowledge we impart is then transferred back, improved, to the USA.'

While the robots take care of the work that is monotonous and dangerous, the associates become responsible only for what is most creative. There are three key words in Japanese: 'Muri' means unreasonable; 'Mura' means uneven; 'Muda' means unnecessary. The approach is to remove all these from the workplace experience. This gains their loyalty.

> In the past, the typical US plant would try to control waste by making the worker responsible for it; the workers became estranged from the company's ideals by having to do tasks that were not enhancing. The Japanese believe in consensual decision-making. This is also more efficient: our plant is two-thirds the size of the average US car plant. We have two million square feet, producing 240,000 cars a year, one thousand a day. The flow of work is so well planned that it can be carried out in a smaller space. It is a process-driven product and plant.

... When Diamond Star settled on Bloomington, they were anxious not to arrive in the middle west like a whirlwind. They wanted to stay on a par with the community, not offer sky-high wage rates that would disrupt the local economy. Everything has been discreet and without ostentation. The wage rates are comparable to those in the area, lower than in traditional assembly plants. The associates are paid $9.95 an hour, and skilled maintenance people $11.74. DSM didn't want to strip other industries of their employees. Even so, there have been complaints in Peoria and Springfield that some heavy industrial works have lost people to DSM. The Japanese believe in 'wa', harmony among people at all levels, and have sought to insert themselves as unobtrusively as possible in Bloomington-Normal.

In spite of its compactness, the workplace is so big that it is difficult to see from one end of the building to the other. A subdued white light pervades the space, from where the great rolls of metal arrive in the press shop to the finished product. In the press shop, the panels are delivered to a computer-controlled storage area; they are stored robotically, and distributed to the body shop by automatic guided vehicles. Front and rear bumper fascias are moulded in the plastic shop. In the body shop, panels and undercarriage are welded together. There are more than 250 robots, and 90 per cent of the operations are automated. The conditions in the paint shop are said to be 'hospital clean'.

More than seventy robots seal the welded seams of the car body. The doors are then removed and the 'operating hardware' is installed; instrument panel, heater, air conditioner are also set in place automatically. There is a 'just in time' inventory management practice, which means that local suppliers can be alerted automatically when a new consignment of seats or tyres or some other component is due. This saves storage space.

The whole process moves forward at considerable speed: one vehicle is produced for every twenty-three work hours. There is something disturbing about the robots: they are installed like some vast giant human body. They emerge from their place of rest in the form of skeletal arms, fingers, claws, eyes, an exposed musculature deftly lifting and placing with the greatest precision. Each movement goes forward at a precisely calculated pace, and is preceded by an electronic warning tune that sounds like 'Mary Had a Little Lamb', so that the employees can be clear of the arena of operation. When this is completed, the people move in to add their touch – so much lighter than the machines. The vehicles emerge in such a way that those who must work beneath them can work at eye level.

The guided vehicles taking the parts to the body shop emit a euphonic robotized warning as they go, following predetermined, computerized tracks along the floor. Although it all seems smooth and effortless, enormous force is used. The robotic welding process with its cascade of blue sparks is noisy and dazzling, the thud of the metal each time the whole ensemble moves forward demands ear-plugs, hard hats and goggles. There is little space for the employees to communicate beyond co-ordinating their specific function. Some of the operations are spectacularly graceful – the double- or triple-jointed flexibility of metal arms that lift the windshield with suction-pads and dexterously place it in the aperture of the car.

Yet the subordination of the people to the process remains: the dwarfing, indeed, the inferiorizing of human beings who must wait until the warning music comes, and then, with precision, accomplish their task, and then withdraw, so that the whole lot can proceed to the next work station.

There are two eight-hour shifts at present, with a 42-minute meal break (this because time is measured in tenths of one hour). The shifts begin at 7 a.m. and 3 p.m. and are preceded by ninety seconds of stretching exercises. Thirty-five per cent of the employees are women. Most are young. There has been only one serious accident so far – one associate thought a robot was in a training mode, i.e. was still being taught the operation it had to perform, when it was already in the production mode.

That production can take place with such scant human intervention is both exalting and appalling: exalting because it makes the possibilities seem endless; appalling because so little of the labour saved is of any benefit to all the under-occupied and unemployed in the world. The finished products, the Eclipse and the Laser, stand on plinths in the reception area, a place of bare functional metal and marble, with only photographs of the Illinois countryside on the walls as ornament.

The embodiment of such power and strength in these robots is disturbing, because it represents the successful neutralization of the working class, and celebrates the triumph of international capital which has, contrary to some predictions, proved itself to be the gravedigger of labour. This is perhaps the meaning of that dispersal of disembodied energies and powers in these tame machines. The flesh and blood has been liberated into the benign functions required by the service economy of Bloomington-Normal.

No wonder the associates of DSM must have intelligence, communicative ability and psychosocial skills. As well as doing their job, they are custodians of the funerary monument of a defunct working class.

READING 47

David Lyon

Information Technology and the 'Information Society'

The 'information society' expresses the idea of a novel phase in the historical development of the advanced societies. Not just a 'postindustrial' society, but the advent of new social patterns is predicted, consequent upon a 'second industrial revolution' based above all on microelectronic technologies. A growing proportion of people, it is claimed, is involved in an unprecedented variety of information-related jobs. Scientific and technical workers gather and produce information, managers and supervisors process it, teachers and communications workers distribute it. From domestic life to international relations, and from leisure activities to industrial relations, no sphere of social activity is left untouched by this 'informatizing' process.

Notions such as Alvin Toffler's 'third wave' – virtually synonymous with 'information society' – have entered popular imagination. A television film has been made of the *Third Wave*, and in the UK, the 'Third Wave' is the slogan for a British Telecom advertising campaign. The 'information society' is increasingly used as a handy catch-all for focusing discussions of 'the future' as we approach the third millennium. Government policy also draws upon this concept, particularly with regard to education. The British are assured, for instance, that 'Our educational system will be a major, perhaps the dominant factor in ensuring the economic prosperity of the UK in a world-wide information society.'[1]

However, certain questions are too frequently left unanswered or treated only to oblique or opaque responses. What are the connections between new technology and society? To what extent and under what circumstances does technological potential become social destiny? Is it warranted to see an epochal social transformation in the kinds of economic and social restructuring currently taking place? And whether or not we are witnessing the emergence of a 'new kind of society', are its advocates correct to assume, as they often tend to, that the social effects of information technology are generally benign? . . .

All manner of vested interests are involved in [information technology]

(IT), but the concept of the information society is all too often used in ways that obscure their role. Sometimes those interests are intertwined in ways that have yet to be carefully explored. The coincidence that defence funding supports so much research in IT *and* that the world of IT frequently excludes women deserves just such exploration. Technology in general is undoubtedly associated with maleness, socially and culturally; IT no less so.

Secondly, the information society concept papers over not only the cracks but also opposing movements in society. Underlying contradictions are even less likely to be exposed than inequalities and conflicts on the surface. Opposing movements may be seen, for instance, in the IT context, along the fault-line of information as public good versus saleable commodity. The real threats of current IT development to public service broadcasting and to public libraries are manifestations of deeper dynamics of opposition.

Thirdly, the coming of the information society is viewed (by its popular proponents at least) as an entirely natural occurrence. It is the obvious way forward. The future lies with IT. The new technologies must be 'whole-heartedly embraced', declare the captains of industry. This is why educational systems have to be reorientated, the market unshackled and high-technology research and trading deals engineered. It is also why Luddism has to be stamped out.

This particular ideological aspect – information society as a natural and logical social advance – is further buttressed by the typically Western belief in progress via unlimited economic accumulation. What Shallis calls 'silicon idolatry' resonates with this still-strong belief. As Bob Goudzwaard observes, if indeed this faith is a driving force within economic and techno-logical expansion then two things follow. One, the 'overdevelopment' of both spheres comes as no surprise, and two, it is 'accompanied by an expectation of happiness that relativises anything that might raise objections against them'.[2]...

Anyone worried about the encroaching tyranny of technocratic power embodied in IT should not ignore countervailing movements also present in contemporary societies. True, the information society idea is strong and popular, but there are many for whom it is remote and unreal, and yet others who regard it with suspicion and hostility. For them, the critique of ideology may itself appear as a less than central task; more urgent is actual resistance to the adoption of new technology. Examining forms of resistance – particularly the 'Luddism' scathingly referred to above – is one thing, however; joining the quest for alternatives is another. I shall argue that both strategies are required if the information society as depicted here is not to become a self-fulfilling prophecy.

The intrusion of IT into numerous areas of life – only this week I discovered that my plastic card could buy a train ticket at the local station and that my office is soon due to be connected with a central IBM computer – has revived interest in Luddism as a mode of opposing technology. While some use it as an epithet to be directed at all 'anti-progressives' who quite irrationally wish to 'put the clock back' by refusing to adapt to new technology, others – both conservative and radical – willingly accept the label as correctly portraying their stance. 'If Luddite means the preservation of all that is good from the past and the rejection of things that destroy good', says Michael Shallis, 'then I would welcome the term.' ...

What form should be taken by 'alternative visions' to the 'information society' idea? At least two criteria should be satisfied. One, the normative basis of the alternative(s) must be made clear. Two, the different levels on which intervention might take place, and modes whereby policies may be implemented, must be indicated. This involves offering practical examples of altered practice and of the potential for choice in technological innovation.

Technocratic thought, especially that embodied in today's computer logic, tends to minimize or exclude debate about ethics. Discussion of 'alternatives' brings this into the foreground. Unfortunately, . . . an ethic suited to the global and long-term aspects of today's technology is largely lacking. The ethics of the personal is far better developed. That said, once it is recognized that the 'information society' gives the false impression that we are entering an *entirely* novel social situation, then certain long-trodden ethical paths become pertinent.

A further problem here is the relative lack of contexts within which such moral debate may take place. Professions, for instance, have always provided such opportunities (even though they have sometimes been self-interestedly abused). Medicine, involving 'technologies of the body', has traditionally been hedged by moral qualification, dating back to the Hippocratic oath. Today's computer professionals evidence a very low level of membership or interest in any comparable organizations.

It may be that IT raises new moral problems. The ease with which data can be permanently and untraceably erased may be one, the way in which privacy is invaded by computers, another. But among the most pressing issues is that of the status of information itself. This raises old questions about the proper relation between data, information, knowledge and a fourth category, which has a low profile today, wisdom. But IT gives their ethical consideration a new urgency, and also connects them with another cluster of problems to do with property: information as a commodity. 'Information' is produced for sale in the market-place. But what should rightly be defended as 'public information', as a 'resource'? What should be the limits to commodification?

The second criterion is that of realism about strategies. It is all very well for 'processed' (read 'alienated') San Francisco office-workers to parade the streets wearing cardboard visual display terminals over their heads, but such demonstrations do not exhaust the possibilities of strategic action relating to IT. The kind of realism required is that which connects possibilities for alternative action with actual conditions in a given social context. Despite the apparent cohesiveness of the 'information society' vision, it is unlikely that alternatives to it will be similarly homogeneous.

Although it may be possible theoretically to show how modern societies are increasingly divided between classes of people with and without control over and access to information, in real life their struggles are on numerous and often unconnected fronts. The labour process and industrial relations offer some obvious examples of appropriate strategies. New Technology Agreements, for whatever reason they are introduced, may be used to monitor and control the process of adapting to new technologies. Demonstrations of automation and robotics whose introduction does not de-skill or displace labour are vital here.

Other strategies run through a spectrum including formal political activity within existing parties, involvement in the political process by social movements, attempts to influence communications or educational policy and local grass-roots action. Legislative change, such as data protection, clearly requires activity of the former sort. But concern for IT alternatives may also be expressed in conjunction with other movements. In Britain, the 'Microsyster' organization attempts to redress the gender imbalance within IT, while 'Microelectronics for Peace' encourages the fostering of alternatives to military developments, mainly within the big IT transnationals. Similar organizations, such as the American 'Computer Professionals for Social Responsibility', exist elsewhere.

Part XI

Government and Politics

Most modern industrial societies regard themselves as democracies. But what exactly is democracy? This issue is taken up by David Beetham and Kevin Boyle in Reading 48. Democracy, the authors argue, does not just belong to the sphere of government as such. Democratic principles can be involved in decision-making in any kind of organization. We can, and should, relate democracy in government to the level of democratic development of other institutions in society.

Jean Blondel (Reading 49) investigates the nature of political parties. Parties did not exist in traditional states, which were ruled by monarchs, emperors and the members of aristocratic groups. In virtually all modern states, however, political parties of some kind exist, although some states are 'one-party' states. Parties, Blondel suggests, represent conflict groups, including class groups, and their specific character is influenced by how far they need to seek mass electoral support.

In Reading 50, John Kingdom considers the nature of the British political constitution. Westminster is marked by much ceremony and ritual. The House of Commons is the inheritor of long-standing traditions of political debate, as well as political confrontation. Britain remains a monarchy and in formal terms the monarch retains a considerable number of traditional powers, such as appointing the government or approving legislation. In practice, of course, the monarchy has lost most of the power it once had. Is the monarchy a positive help to democracy, providing as it does for a certain stability within a society at large? Or is a monarchical society inherently anti-democratic? Debate continues about this issue.

In his contribution to this part, Ernest Gellner (Reading 51) addresses the issue of the nature of nationalism and its relation to the modern state. Nationalism, he proposes, is essentially a theory of political legitimacy, by means of which ethnic boundaries are made subordinate to the overall political integration of the state. Sentiments of nationalism, and the boundaries of nation states, he stresses, do not necessarily coincide; hence the impact of nationalist beliefs can foster the disintegration as well as the cohesion of states.

Reading 52 moves on to discuss the political transformations happening in Eastern Europe. Eastern European countries, like Poland, Hungary or Romania, used to be Communist states. How well are they managing the transition to becoming market economies and to developing democratic forms of government? Birna Helgadottir sees many difficulties standing in the way of the transition to democracy in Eastern Europe.

The final two selections discuss issues of military power and war in society. Martin Shaw (Reading 53) points out that some notions central to democracy, particularly citizenship, were defined in relation to war. Democratic rights were to some extent granted by states which wished to enlist their citizens to fight in the armed forces. Soldiers have always predominantly been male. The question of the relationship between masculinity and warfare has been extensively debated. According to Jean Bethke Elshtain (Reading 54), the relation between gender and war is complex. Women have not often fought in combat situations, but when they have, they do not seem to behave any differently on the battlefield from men.

READING 48

David Beetham and Kevin Boyle

What is Democracy?

hroughout our lives we are members of different groups or associations, from families, neighbourhoods, clubs and work-units to nations and states. In all such associations, from the smallest to the largest, decisions have to be taken for the association as a whole: about the goals to be pursued, about the rules to be followed, about the distribution of responsibilities and benefits between members. These can be called *collective* decisions, in contrast to *individual* decisions taken by people on behalf of themselves alone. Democracy belongs to this sphere of collective decision-making. It embodies the ideal that such decisions, affecting an association as a whole, should be taken by all its members, and that they should each have equal rights to take part in such decisions, Democracy, in other words, entails the twin principles of *popular control* over collective decision-making and *equality of rights* in the exercise of that control. To the extent that these principles are realized in the decision-making of any association, we can call it democratic.

Defining democracy in this way makes two things clear at the outset. The first is that democracy does not just belong to the sphere of the state or of government, as we usually tend to think of it. Democratic principles are relevant to collective decision-making in any kind of association. Indeed, there is an important relation between democracy at the level of the state and democracy in the other institutions of society. However, because the state is the most inclusive association, with the right to regulate the affairs of society as a whole, the ability to raise compulsory taxation and the power of life and death over its members, democracy at the level of the state is of crucial importance. It is with democratic government, therefore, that we shall be mostly concerned.

The second point about our definition is that democracy is not an all-or-nothing affair, which an association possesses either in full or not at all. It is rather a matter of degree; of the extent to which the principles of popular control and political equality are realized; of greater or lesser approximations towards the ideal of equal participation in collective decision-making. Conventionally we have come to call a state 'democratic' if its government is accountable to the people through competitive election to public office, where all adults have an equal right to vote and to stand for election, and where civil and political rights are legally guaranteed. However, no such state in practice realizes the two principles of popular control and political equality as fully as it might. To that extent the work of democratization is never ended; and democrats everywhere are involved in struggles to consolidate and extend the realization of democratic principles, whatever regime or political system they happen to live under.

There are many reasons why democracy should be valued. Democracy aims to treat all people equally. 'Everyone to count for one and none for more than one', wrote the English legal theorist Jeremy Bentham in his attack on the aristocratic view that some people's lives were intrinsically more valuable than others. The principle of equality requires not only that people's interests should be attended to equally by government policy, but also that their views should count equally. 'We give no special power to wealth,' spoke an Athenian in one of Euripides' plays; 'the poor man's voice commands equal authority.' Critics of democracy have always objected that the mass of people are too ignorant, too uneducated and too short-sighted to take any part in determining public policy. To this democrats answer that the people certainly need information and the time to make sense of it, but are perfectly capable of acting responsibly when required to do so. Just as we expect all adults to take responsibility for directing their own personal lives, so they are also capable of taking a share in decisions affecting the life of their society.

Democratic government is more likely than other types of government to meet the needs of ordinary people. The more say people have in the direction of policy, the more likely it is to reflect their concerns and aspirations. 'The cobbler makes the shoe', went the ancient Athenian saying, 'but only the wearer can tell where it pinches.' It is ordinary people who experience the effects of government policy in practice, and only if there are effective and consistent channels of influence and pressure from below does government policy reflect this experience. However well-intentioned the holders of public office may be, if they are immune from popular influence or control, their policies will be at best inappropriate to people's needs and at worst self-serving and corrupt.

Democracy relies upon open debate, persuasion and compromise. The democratic emphasis on debate assumes not only that there are differences of opinion and interest on most questions of policy, but that such differences have a right to be expressed and listened to. Democracy thus presupposes diversity and plurality within society as well as equality between citizens. And when such diversity finds expression, the democratic method of resolving differences is through discussion, through persuasion and compromise, rather than by forceful imposition or the simple assertion of power. Democracies have often been caricatured as mere 'talking shops'. However, their capacity for public debate should be seen as a virtue rather than a vice, since it is the best means for securing consent to policy, and is not necessarily inconsistent with decisive action.

Democracy guarantees basic freedoms. Open discussion, as the method for expressing and resolving societal differences, cannot take place without those freedoms that are enshrined in conventions of civil and political rights: the rights of free speech and expression, of association with others, of movement, of security for the person. Democracies can be relied on to protect these rights, since they are essential to their own mode of existence. At best such rights allow for the personal development of individuals and produce collective decisions that are better for being tested against a variety of argument and evidence.

Democracy allows for societal renewal. By providing for the routine and peaceful removal of policies and politicians that have failed or outlived their usefulness, democratic systems are able to ensure societal and generational renewal without the massive upheaval or governmental disruption that attends the removal of key personnel in non-democratic regimes.

The idea that ordinary people should be entitled to a say in the decisions that affect their lives is one that has emerged as an aspiration in many different historical societies. It achieved a classical institutional form in Athens in the fifth and fourth centuries BC. From the early fifth century onwards, when property qualifications for public office were removed, each Athenian citizen had an equal right to take part in person in discussions and votes in the assembly on the laws and policies of the community, and also to share in their administration through jury service and membership of the administrative council, which were recruited in rotation by lot. The example of this first working democracy has been a reference point and source of inspiration to democrats ever since. The fact that it coincided with a period of Athenian economic and naval supremacy, and with an enormous flourishing of creative arts and philosophical enquiry, put paid to the idea that giving ordinary people a say in their affairs would produce either a society of drab uniformity or irresponsible government, as the critics of democracy have often asserted.

Athenian democracy was both more and less democratic than the democracies we know today. It was more democratic in that citizens took part in person in the main decisions of the society ('direct democracy'), whereas today's representative democracies are indirect, and citizens stand at least at one remove from the decision-making processes of government and parliament. For direct democracy to be possible requires a relatively small citizen body capable of being accommodated in a single place of assembly, and one with enough time free from other responsibilities to be able to grasp the evidence and arguments necessary to make an informed political decision. Neither requirement for direct democracy is met by the citizen bodies of today, through there is scope for their involvement in direction decision-making at national level in elections and referenda, and for more continuous participation in decision-making at very local levels.

Athenian democracy was less democratic than democracies of today, however, in that citizenship was restricted to free-born males; it excluded women, slaves and resident foreigners, these groups ensuring the continuity of the domestic and productive work necessary to enable the male citizens to engage in political activity. So the active participation of a direct democracy was only possible at all because the citizenship was restricted. 'The people' certainly ruled, but they did so from a position of privilege.

It is worth recalling that similar restrictions on citizenship existed in most

Western parliamentary systems until well into the twentieth century. The principle made famous by the French Revolution that 'all political authority stems from the people' was not intended to include all the people. Thus it is only in this century that women and propertyless males have been granted the suffrage in most Western countries; and even today not all adult residents of a country are entitled to vote in its elections, however much they may contribute to its economy.

Can a representative system be really democratic? The eighteenth-century political theorist Rousseau thought not. In a representative system, he argued, people are only free once every few years at election time; thereafter they revert to a position of subordination to their rulers which is no better than slavery. This is an extreme version of the characteristic left-wing or radical criticism that representative systems are not properly democratic, in contrast to the right-wing objection that they give people too much say.

The simple response is that a representative system is the best system yet devised for securing popular control over government in circumstances where the citizen body is numbered in millions and has not the time to devote itself continuously to political affairs. The theory is that the people control the government by electing its head (president or prime minister) and by choosing the members of a legislature or parliament that can exercise continuous supervision over the government on the people's behalf, through its power to approve or reject legislation and taxation. This popular control is only effective, however, to the extent that elections are 'free and fair', that government is open, and that parliament has sufficient powers in practice to scrutinize and control its actions.

Although elections are the principal means by which people have a say in government policy in a representative system, they are not the only means. People can join associations to campaign for and against changes in legislation; they can become members of political parties; they can lobby their representatives in person. Governments in turn can be required to consult those affected by their policies or a selected cross-section of the electorate. In practice, few representative governments are immune to expressions of public opinion such as are regularly provided by opinion polls or through the press, radio and television. Yet all these channels of popular influence are ultimately dependent upon the effectiveness of the electoral process. Governments will only listen seriously to the people when there is a realistic possibility that they will be turned out of office if they do not.

So popular control in a representative system is secured by the direct influence people exercise over the direction of government policy and personnel at elections, through the continuous supervision exercised over government by a representative assembly or parliament and by the organized expression of public opinion through a variety of channels, which governments have to take into account.

What about the second democratic principle . . . that of political equality? A representative system involves inequality at least in this respect, that it gives a small number of the population the right to take political decisions on behalf of the rest. Within these limits, however, political equality can be achieved to the extent that there is an effective equal right for all citizens to stand for public office, to campaign on public issues and to obtain redress in the event of maladministration; and that the electoral system gives equal value to each person's vote. In practice most representative democracies do

not fully satisfy these criteria, since political equality is substantially qualified by systematic differences in the wealth, time, access and other
resources possessed by different groups of the population. It is one of the
tasks of democrats in a representative system to find ways to reduce the
political impact of these differences, as well as to make more effective
the various mechanisms of popular control over government.

In a large society people can exercise little public influence as individuals,
but can in association with others. Political parties bring together those who
share similar views and interests to campaign for political office and influence. They perform a number of different functions. For the *electorate* they
help simplify the electoral choice by offering broad policy positions and
programmes between which to choose. For *governments* they provide a
reasonably stable following of political supporters to enable them to
achieve their programmes once elected. For the *more politically committed*
they provide an opportunity for involvement in public affairs, a means of
political education and a channel for influencing public policy.

READING 49

Jean Blondel

What are Political Parties For?

Parties are groups – but how does one distinguish them from other
groups which seem close to parties? A national liberation movement
in a colonial territory may not be called a party, but is it very different
from a political party? What about organizations like the Campaign for
Nuclear Disarmament in Britain in the 1950s or anti-war movements in the
United States in the 1960s? There is a distinction between pressure groups,
such as trade unions or employers' organizations, and political parties.
There are other intermediate groups whose aims are openly political, and
the boundary between parties and such groups is not very precise.

To approach these questions realistically, it is better to eschew a theoretical definition or description of goals and concentrate more practically on the existence of parties. Political parties emerge under different conditions and with different viewpoints. Behind the façade lie conflicting desires, which may explain some of the difficulties faced by political parties.

Parties exist in some countries and not in others. Given certain conditions parties are more likely to exist; these conditions are of three types.

... [First, p]arties are more likely to exist where many members of the society *perceive* the existence of social conflict and perceive these conflicts to be large and long-standing. There is no need for parties if everyone agrees about everything. This is why, typically, parties do not emerge in traditional societies. The elders of tribes are expected to take the decisions which need to be taken. Social conduct and order are their province by right. There are few new problems; past experience is the best guide. Within tribes, at least, social conflicts are either few or non-existent.

For parties to develop there must be broad social conflict. Parties organize large sections of society for major battles; if conflicts involve only a few individuals, parties will not be formed. For parties to emerge conflicts must run deeply into the fabric of society and sharply divide its members. Parties might emerge, for example, if there are conflicts *between* tribes or *between* ethnic groups within the same country, as in Nigeria, Ghana and many other African countries. Deep conflicts between religious groups or between social classes may produce the same effect. When this occurs, members of the society are not simply confronted with isolated clashes over one issue; on the contrary, individual conflicts can become absorbed into one major social conflict. In Northern Ireland, for instance, conflicts over housing and job discrimination are sucked into a broad religious conflict. Similarly, in many Western democracies, numerous conflicts become branded as part of a class conflict between workers and the 'bourgeoisie'.

Perception of the conflict is more important than actual conditions; antagonisms become acute only when they are perceived as such by members of the society. This is true of all major types of social conflict. In two countries where income and status as between rich and poor are objectively similar, perception of class conflict may be very different. It may be very weak in one of them, very strong in the other. Broadly speaking, despite large income differences on both sides of the Atlantic, perception of class conflict is much greater in Europe than it is in North America. Thus it is hardly surprising that parties in Europe are based on class conflict while this is not so marked in the United States and Canada. Indeed, there are gradations in the perception of social conflict as there are gradations in objective differences. Only in traditional societies is conflict hardly perceived at all; in modern societies, variations in the intensity of social conflict can be very wide. There is some perception of class conflict in the United States, where to some extent parties are based on class. Conversely, in Europe class conflict is dominant, but not overwhelming; parties are not exclusively based on class, they may also be based on religion. But religious conflicts also vary in intensity: the religious composition of Glasgow and Belfast is almost the same, for example, yet religious conflict is strikingly higher in Belfast than it is in Glasgow.

Since social conflict is based on the perception of this conflict, it can be engineered. The development of class consciousness is an endeavour to engineer social conflict where it has not been perceived. Marxists often say that class consciousness must be increased. They mean that efforts have to be made to increase the perception of objective conflicts, because the basis for a class party will be more assured when class conflict is perceived to be high. But Marxists are not the only ones wishing to increase the perception of conflict. The Nazis encouraged conflict with the Jews. In many countries, especially third world countries, conflict with 'foreign elements' is deliberately fostered. More generally, single-party systems are often set up with a view to increasing some conflict: social conflict may thus be perceived intensely even when there is one party only . . .

Parties are unlikely to emerge if there is little or no perceived conflict. But, even if conflict is relatively high, parties will only arise if politicians need popular support and if traditional social hierarchies are weak. In a traditional society, the absence of social conflict accounts in part for the absence of parties; but, even if there are conflicts, for instance *between* tribes, the existence of a well-defined tribal structure which is accepted by members of the various tribes makes a party organization superfluous. Those in government can rely on these hierarchies to implement their decisions. Feuds only occur between the leaders of tribes, or between aristocrats. In an absolute monarchy, politics is therefore limited to the factions of courtiers, and so long as no political leader wishes to appeal to the people, parties will not be created.

A party is thus more than a faction or a conspiracy, although it may originate from one. It results from the desire or the need to obtain or strengthen support among the population. It entails trying to attract, if not the 'common man', at least many helpers and followers. A party is to a faction or conspiracy what the army is to a band.

All parties face problems of organization and leadership which differ from, and are more complex than, those of a faction. Members of a faction know each other, face-to-face. Decisions are taken among friends although some members of the group may be more influential than others. In a party, there are followers as well as leaders; following may merely execute leaders' decisions. Only some members are directly involved in party activities; others, the majority, are less active. Leaders do not know more than a small fraction of these followers and communication between leaders and followers becomes difficult and complex. Questions of organization therefore cannot be avoided in a political party. Indeed, they tend often to be one of the major aspects of the life of political parties.

The extent to which a party needs popular support varies: the complexity of party organization varies accordingly. Some parties have little popular support; in some, the leader commands – or wants to command – the allegiance of millions. What begins as a faction – for instance, near or around the palace – may slowly become a party with outside support. A party is created when supporters of a faction acquire followers. Parties emerged in this way in Britain in the seventeenth and eighteenth centuries; they developed, in a similar way, in Western Europe in the eighteenth and nineteenth centuries.

Traditional societies do not need parties, as we saw, because existing tribal or feudal links are sufficient for day-to-day government. A party is only formed when some individuals want to change the social structure, achieve more power for themselves or the group to which they belong, or develop the country economically or socially. The response to these efforts may be slow, however; people may not understand or agree with party goals. The party may not take roots in the community. This happened in Europe in the past and currently happens in the third world. Parties may be set up to achieve popular involvement, but traditional bonds – tribal, for instance – may scarcely be touched. The new parties are artificial, and easily disbanded or abolished by a *coup d'état*.

We need to account for the link between the formation of a party and expectation of political victory. Why do many believe that, by setting up a party, they are more likely to achieve their political goals? The reason lies in the fact that it is usually *assumed* or *believed*, not just by political leaders but by most of us, that 'unity is strength'. We feel that good results will be achieved if we unite with like-minded people.

This belief is general. Many organizations exist because men believe it is worthwhile to unite with others. Yet it is worthwhile remembering that this is only an assumption for which little real 'proof' can be given. Indeed, there is evidence for and against the assumption. For example, members of trade unions believe that workers should be 'organized' because they will obtain better living conditions as a result. The causal link is not proved. It is true that workers have obtained better living conditions in the last 100 years *at the same time* as trade unions developed; but there is no appreciable difference between the workers' standards of living in those industrial countries where they are well organized and those where they are not. From the examination of policies and achievements it is even more difficult to prove that the conditions of the poor are better in those countries where they are politically united than in those where they are not.

Most of us believe that 'size is strength'. Most men and women who are concerned with social and political action feel that, in order to win, they must enlist the support of large numbers. This belief is rarely questioned. We are told that support attracts more support and brings victory nearer. Parties often use their current support as bait for prospective followers. We are thus told, for instance, that we will find hundreds or thousands of friends and comrades if we join a party.

Although the belief in the necessity of large numbers is very common, it is not universal. Indeed, all of us are probably inconsistent in this respect. For instance, some men profess to believe in the value of 'active minorities' rather than in large groups. Many small groups – factions, conspiracies – have attempted to take power and some have succeeded. The supporters of this view place greater stress on the dynamism and dedication of a few than on the role of large numbers. They point to the limited achievements of trade unions and established political parties and state that 'real' revolutions are only made by a few men.

Moreover, even if we believe that 'size is strength', we are also often prepared to be somewhat inconsistent and not to consider ourselves defeated when we fail to muster large numbers of supporters. In the West the principle of majority rule is applauded and institutionalized. But, even in the West, this principle is often thwarted, one way or another, by the action of minorities. Outside the West, the principle of majority rule plays a less significant part; it is often not legally entrenched. Everywhere in the world minorities are very powerful, in political parties and in other associations, and use dubious tactics to undermine majority groups. It seems as if, the more one feels unable to muster a majority, the more one uses conspiratorial tactics to achieve one's aims. Thus, we are coming close to recognizing that only those who can rally support of large segments of the population really adhere to the principle that 'size is strength'; the minority live by different principles.

Indeed, political parties exist precisely because of this inconsistency. The need for both large support and smaller groups is at the origin of political parties. Parties exist only where there is conflict; but conflict means disunity. Parties thrive both on the disunity of the society and on a popular desire to rally to a common cause....

At first sight, the function of parties seems straightforward: they exist to propose and implement policies. But what policies? The British Labour Party may exist to improve the conditions of the common man in Britain, but what are the conditions which need improvement? And who exactly is the common man or the 'working man'? And what does 'improvement' mean?

These are questions which we usually brush aside because no one really knows the answers. If we talk about improvement, we must have some goal, some ideal, some general principles. This may be equality for all, or a hierarchy of classes and groups, or a combination of various goals. But one thing is certain: an understanding of human nature must precede any improvements. It is no good saying that some situations are scandalous and obviously need redress. First, if they are so obvious, why were they not redressed before? Is it only because our forefathers were wicked or stupid? And secondly, do we know really what our goals are? Can we say that any party really knows what its goals are?

But this is not all. Policies are based on a principle – be it conservative, socialist or liberal. It is difficult to see the link between these principles and specific policies. If a party states that pensions should be increased because older citizens should not be allowed to live in poverty, we see a relationship between principles and policies. But the link is imprecise because we do not know *by what amount* pensions should be increased. It is also imprecise because we do not know whether pensions, rather than sickness benefits for instance, should be increased. A party may propose social improvement as a general principle, but this proposal does not help in deciding on pension increases or choosing between pensions and sickness benefits.

There is another question: should party supporters decide on policies or should policies be 'sold' to supporters? Which do we think should come first, the policies or the supporters? In practice, most parties follow both strategies at one and the same time; they are influenced by supporters and adopt some policies as a result, while they also adopt policies and 'sell' them afterwards. This messy practical approach does not answer the question: who should decide policy?

These three problems – general principles, links between principles and policies, the relationship between policies and support – are not easily solved. They are rarely solved except in a pragmatic, muddled way. As parties need support, they 'bend' their principles, they 'bend' even more their policies and postpone their goals. Popular support is seen as indispensable and the first priority; policies based on principle recede into the background.

Parties are often tempted to go further and see organization as an end in itself. Lukewarm or passive followers must be encouraged to be more active. Party organization becomes separated from principles and policies: 'If only our branches and sections would increase, if only our members could be more active at branch meetings, we would be closer to victory.' In almost all parties, party organization is as important as the search for policies and the analysis of ideology.

In a subtle fashion, all parties are thus infected by the curse of oversimplification. For the most dedicated party activists, the 'goodness' of the party cause seems obvious. If the party's goals are obviously good, popular support should automatically be forthcoming. If it is not forthcoming, this can only be because people cannot see what the party wants to do. Why should anyone not see the bright sunshine? Because the curtains are drawn. Thus lack of support is not seen as a lack of policies or goals, but as a lack of good public relations. Party activists rarely ask themselves why people do not automatically support the party. They have to avoid the issue; they can answer only in terms of 'enemies' or a lack of understanding, lack of awareness, lack of 'consciousness'.

Oversimplification creeps in, and it does so in two ways. It creeps in because party activists always have a ready-made answer to the problem of lack of support: people are not aware, opponents beguile the masses; if only people could see, if only we could lift the curtain, there would be no problem. And oversimplification also affects the party programme. The message must be simple; by saying that 'if only such and such were done, a solution would be found', party workers hope to find more support. Parties tend to oversimplify every problem, idea or difficulty. They oversimplify ideologies because they believe that people will understand matters better this way, and they oversimplify solutions by not showing problems of priorities, or constraints. To win the contest, parties always underestimate the case of their opponents and overestimate their own programme.

This, in turn, has two consequences. First, it reinforces the importance of organization. Ideas, principles, programmes and policies are less important than the need to put the idea across. Principles become subservient to the need to communicate them; they are gradually simplified into simpler messages. And, secondly, party activists and leaders become infected by the message which they try to put across. They, too, come to believe that matters are simple, that principles are clearly defined, that priorities are self-evident and that time is unimportant.

READING 50

John Kingdom

Pomp and Circumstance: The Living Dead of the Constitution

THE PHYSICAL SETTING

Parliament formally comprises the monarchy, the House of Lords and the House of Commons, with a very tangible presence as the picturesque Palace of Westminster situated grandly on the bank of the Thames at the end of Whitehall. It is one of the major landmarks of London, and during the holiday season a permanent queue of visitors (about a million each year) wait to be conducted on guided tours and purchase trinkets marked with the prestigious portcullis logo (which is also found on MPs' official notepaper). Within the palace the two great chambers, the Commons and the Lords, exude a cathedral-like aura calculated to intimidate all but the initiated, and around them a labyrinth of corridors, quadrangles and staircases lead to offices, committee rooms, smoking rooms, tea-rooms and, of course, bars. MPs can be seen variously talking in intimate clusters, meeting groups of eager constituents, playing host to interest group representatives, or in secretive places of refreshment trying to avoid such encounters.

The chambers are surprisingly small and could not seat all members if they were to descend simultaneously. This is quite deliberate; the opportunity to rebuild was presented by the German *Luftwaffe* in 1941, but the decision was taken to retain the sense of intimacy conducive to debate. Figure 11.1 shows how the benches are arrayed in a hostile, confrontational manner and, in the Commons, commemorating a more colourful age, the front ranks are set a sword's length apart with the Mace, the symbol of authority, resting on the intervening table.

Figure 11.1 The chamber of the House of Commons
Source: Constructed from Halsey et al., *Origins and Destinations*

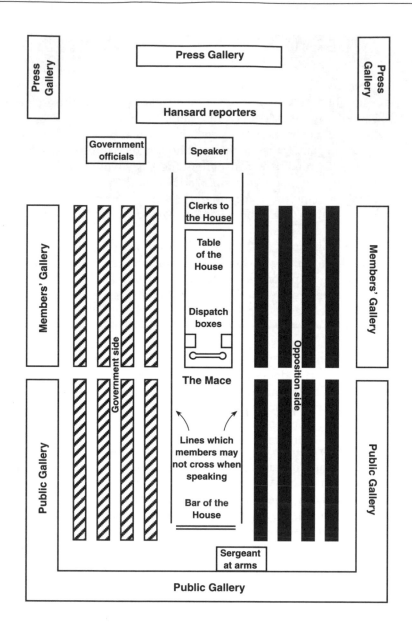

PARLIAMENTARY MUMBO-JUMBO

Westminster is a great home of ceremony and ritual. It is formally opened every year with a procession led by Black Rod, the officer responsible for maintaining order in the House of Lords, who carries an ebony cane for the purpose. He summons the Commoners to the Lords to hear the Queen's Speech, and all is conducted in Norman French. When he approaches the lower house the doors are slammed in his face (because in 1642, the last time the Commons allowed the monarch into their chamber, he arrested five members). Undeterred, he gives three solemn knocks, the doors are opened, and the MPs emerge in pairs, advancing like a *corps de ballet* towards the Lords, led by the Prime Minister and Leader of the Opposition.

THE EVOLUTION OF PARLIAMENT

The three elements of Parliament represent the great estates of the realm which have fought over the centuries for control of the state: the crown, the aristocracy and the common people. Its origins lie in the assembly of Anglo-Saxon kings which met as the *Witangemot*. In Norman times kings governed with only their officials to assist them, although the country was divided into territorial units ruled by barons whom the kings would call together as the *Magnum Concilium* for discussion, advice and to raise money. The barons began to demand more control over the royal authority and secured this through the Magna Carta signed at Runnymede in 1215. Herein lies the origin of the House of Lords.

The House of Commons was conceived in the kingly practice, from the thirteenth century, of calling additional meetings of the less-important local representatives, the commoners – knights from the shires and burgesses from the incorporated towns – as a further source of revenue. They would assemble humbly before the king, surrounded by his lords and nobles, who would tell them how much money he required and dispatch them to find it, leaving the aristocracy to discuss important matters of state.

However, the Commons, recognizing a source of power, demanded that the king listen to certain demands before payment. Expensive wars forced Edward III (1327–77) to summon frequent Parliaments, and the commoners took the opportunity to attach a list of desired reforms when approving the tax demands. As they held meetings of their own, away from the king and lords, the House of Commons began to materialize as a distinct entity. At the beginning of the fifteenth century Henry IV agreed that grants of money would only be initiated in the Commons, recognizing the lower house as part of Parliament.

The crucial power which the Commons held over the purse-strings saw the gradual erosion of the monarch's position. Coming soon after the profligate Henry VIII (1509–47), Elizabeth I (1558–1603) fully recognized this, and was careful to court Parliament with flattery and charm. However, the Stuarts lacked the Tudors' realism and Charles I sought to reassert royal authority and govern without parliamentary consent, by raising 'ship money' from all towns. John Hampden, a squire and member of Parliament, refused to pay this highly unpopular tax in a legendary and eloquent stand in the parliamentary cause. However, by this time the Commons had become powerful enough openly to oppose the king, and events led to the Civil War between the supporters of royal authority (Royalists or Cavaliers) and the parliamentarians (Roundheads), lasting from 1642 until 1652. It resulted in Charles losing not the crown, but a head upon which to rest it. Britain entered upon a brief period as a republic with the Puritan Oliver Cromwell (1599–1658), though declining to be king, supreme as 'Lord Protector'.

The decision to restore the monarchy in 1660 saw Charles II return in glory from exile to be a *constitutional monarch* constrained by Parliament. In a grizzly ceremony that did not augur well for the future, Cromwell's corpse was disinterred and hung on the infamous gallows at Tyburn in January 1661, to mark the anniversary of Charles I's execution. The remaining Stuarts were too stupid and arrogant to accept the principle of constitutional monarchy, further skirmishes culminating in the Glorious Revolution of 1688, which placed William (of Orange) and Mary on the English throne with clearly restricted powers. Yet it was not until the 1701 Act of Settlement that the subordinate position of the monarchy *vis-à-vis* Parliament was satisfactorily established, made easier by the fact that the Hanoverian line (established in 1714 when the succession failed owing to Anne dying without an heir) produced kings with little interest in British affairs. . . .

The struggles also saw an increase in the power of the Commons over the Lords as a result of its control over the supply of funds. By convention going back beyond 1688 the upper house has acquiesced to the claim that money supply is in the sole gift of the Commons and could not be interfered with. Many lords had sided with the king and the upper house was abolished after the victory of the parliamentarians, only to be reinstated with Charles II's restoration. However, the Commons remained under the control of aristocratic and royal factions, both exercising a corrupt influence on elections and nomination. It was not until the great nineteenth-century Reform Acts that the lower house delivered the ultimate *coup de grâce*, through the supremacy derived from the moral authority of the popular vote.

Yet the message was not immediately clear to their lordships. In 1883 they rejected the second Irish Home Rule Bill and, when the reforming Liberal government replaced the Conservatives in 1905, eighteen of its bills were rejected. Lloyd George's 1909 budget, in which he showed the temerity to tax the landed aristocracy, roused the lords to purple-faced indignation and a furious constitutional (or unconstitutional) battle ensued, in which a reluctant monarch was told he would have to rat on his aristocratic kinsfolk by threatening to create sufficient new government-supporting peers to quell their opposition. The result was the Parliament Act of 1911, which not only legalized the existing convention regarding financial legislation, but reduced the Lords' veto over other legislation to a power to delay for two years. In 1949 the Labour government, nearing the end of its life and fearful of the fate of its steel nationalization bill, shortened this to a year. . . .

Britain has a *constitutional monarchy*, meaning that, although the Queen may be said to *reign*, she does not *rule*. Perhaps its last dying gasps as an agency of real government were heard under Victoria. First under the influence of her consort Albert (who took his authority very seriously), and later encouraged by the flattery of Disraeli, she made several efforts to exert the royal prerogative. It was the lot of the austere Gladstone, preaching the gospel of capitalism, to school the Queen in the art of constitutional rule and he can claim 'the main share of the credit for cutting the modern pattern of British democratic kingship'. . . .

A number of textbooks and commentaries on British politics and sociology omit the monarchy altogether. This may be intended to betoken a jettisoning of meaningless symbolism in order to concentrate on the hard world of reality, but it is a mistake, betraying a dangerously short-sighted and superficial vision focusing no further than Downing Street. The monarchy affects the nature of politics and policy by being a significant element in British political culture. The capitalist class needed it as a symbol to unite society while pursuing economic inequality. . . .

Today the monarch continues formally to hold the powers of old (the royal prerogatives), but they are generally exercised on the advice of the Prime Minister. They include appointing the government; patronage; legislation; emergency powers; and summoning, proroguing (dismissing), and dissolving Parliament. . . .

Though the succession has faltered from time to time, it is based on the hereditary principle, Queen Elizabeth II being the fortieth monarch since the Norman Conquest.

Today Buckingham Palace, the main royal residence, stands at the end of the Mall in some forty acres of gardens. Together with Horse Guards' Parade, Westminster Abbey and the Palace of Westminster, all of which are within a cannon's shot of each other, it is part of a baroque Disneyland of the past, sleeping while it is gradually overgrown by a towering office-block jungle. Inside the palace, courtiers and flunkeys, with titles and sometimes costumes of a bygone age, perform the tasks of running the monarchy industry. Many of these, from the Queen's private secretary down, are themselves nobly born and treasure their families' links with the sovereign, passing the positions down through the generations. This modern monarchy is distinguished by the following characteristics.

- *Ceremony:* While Britain is not alone in having a constitutional monarchy (The Netherlands, Belgium, Spain, Sweden, Denmark and Norway all do the same), it is unique in the degree to which the pomp and ceremony of old has been unctuously preserved. (The Scandinavian monarchies have been slightly dubbed 'bicycling monarchies' by the British, because of their deliberate paring away of ostentation and display.) The British monarchy, although never able to match the French in its extravagant prime, can on great occasions in the royal life-cycle (births, weddings and funerals) reach a scale only matched in Hollywood epics.
- *Political impartiality:* Although informed on a weekly basis by the Prime Minister, the Queen remains insulated from the rough and tumble of politics. She (like all members of the aristocracy) does not vote, neither is she expected to express partisan opinions on the issues of the day. This is not to say that the mask does not sometimes slip. In May 1977 the Queen inserted some criticisms of the government's devolution proposals into a public speech. It was also widely reported in 1987 that she was disturbed by Mrs Thatcher's refusal to go along with other Commonwealth leaders on economic sanctions against South Africa. In 1988 Prince Charles criticized some of the implications of the government's social policy, earning a rebuke from Norman Tebbit, who alleged that the prince's sympathy for the unemployed stemmed from his own absence of gainful activity (presumably a plea for a bicycling monarchy).
- *Popularity:* Before World War II, shaken by the abdication crisis, the monarchy was in an uncertain condition. However, in the postwar era, with the coronation, weddings and many royal offspring, the public appetite for its dignified constitution grew to gargantuan dimensions. In addition to the sychophantic tabloid reporting, quality newspapers regularly carry the 'Court Circular', confident that readers will pore over the royal engagements with earnest concern. . . .

It must be recognized that by any reckoning the monarchy does not come cheap. In 1761 George III agreed to surrender the income from the Crown Estate in exchange for a regular grant from Parliament, to be known as the Civil List. Although remaining constant for a considerable time, it was revised during the reign of Elizabeth II to keep pace with inflation (see Table 11.1). In addition there are other expenses, including the upkeep of five palaces and the maintenance of the aircraft of the Queen's Flight. . . . Yet royal wealth goes well beyond income received from the Civil List. The Queen possesses a considerable personal fortune . . . and enjoys an independent annual income of several hundred thousand pounds. Over the years this has been exempt from tax and death duties, giving the Queen a touch similar to that of King Midas, and enabling her to outdistance all aristocratic rivals, some of whom, even after World War II, were actually richer than the king. Today, while they collect the tickets for the roller-coaster and zoos in their estates, the wealth in the royal coffers continues to swell. The Queen also owns an internationally renowned art collection, a stamp collection worth well over £1 million, the fabled royal jewellery, and two of the royal residences, Sandringham and Balmoral.

TABLE 11.1 The Civil List, 1988 and 1989

Name	Amount (£)	
	1988	1989
The Queen	4,500,000	4,658,000
Queen Mother	390,300	404,000
Duke of Edinburgh	217,000	225,300
Duke of York	86,500	155,400
Prince Edward	20,000	20,000
Princess Royal	135,600	140,000
Princess Margaret	132,100	136,700
Princess Alice	53,500	55,400
Duke of Gloucester	106,300	110,000
Duke of Kent	143,500	148,500
Princess Alexandra	136,800	141,600
Refund by Queen	386,600	400,100
Total	5,635,000	5,794,800

READING 51

Ernest Gellner

Nations and Nationalism

Nationalism is primarily a political principle, which holds that the political and the national unit should be congruent.

Nationalism as a sentiment, or as a movement, can best be defined in terms of this principle. Nationalist *sentiment* is the feeling of anger aroused by the violation of the principle, or the feeling of satisfaction aroused by its fulfilment. A nationalist *movement* is one actuated by a sentiment of this kind.

There is a variety of ways in which the nationalist principle can be violated. The political boundary of a given state can fail to include all the members of the appropriate nation; or it can include them all but also include some foreigners; or it can fail in both these ways at once, not incorporating all the nationals and yet also including some non-nationals. Or again, a nation may live, unmixed with foreigners, in a multiplicity of states, so that no single state can claim to be *the* national one.

But there is one particular form of the violation of the nationalist principle to which nationalist sentiment is quite particularly sensitive: if the rulers of the political unit belong to a nation other than that of the majority of the ruled, this for nationalists, constitutes a quite outstandingly intolerable breach of political propriety. This can occur either through the incorporation of the national territory in a larger empire, or by the local domination of an alien group.

In brief, nationalism is a theory of political legitimacy, which requires that ethnic boundaries should not cut across political ones, and, in particular, that ethnic boundaries within a given state – a contingency already formally excluded by the principle in its general formulation – should not separate the power-holders from the rest.

The nationalist principle can be asserted in an ethical, 'universalistic' spirit. There could be, and on occasion there have been, nationalists-in-the-abstract, unbiased in favour of any special nationality of their own, and generously preaching the doctrine for all nations alike: let all nations have their own political roofs, and let all of them also refrain from including non-nationals under it. There is no formal contradiction in asserting such non-egoistic nationalism. As a doctrine it can be supported by some good arguments, such as the desirability of preserving cultural diversity, of a pluralistic international political system and of the diminution of internal strains within states.

In fact, however, nationalism has often not been so sweetly reasonable, nor so rationally symmetrical. It may be that, as Immanuel Kant believed, partiality, the tendency to make exceptions on one's own behalf or one's own case, is *the* central human weakness from which all others flow; and that it infects national sentiment as it does all else, engendering what the Italians under Mussolini called the *sacro egoismo* of nationalism. It may also be that the political effectiveness of national sentiment would be much impaired if nationalists had as fine a sensibility to the wrongs committed by their nation as they have to those committed against it.

But over and above these considerations there are others, tied to the specific nature of the world we happen to live in, which militate against any impartial, general, sweetly reasonable nationalism. To put it in the simplest possible terms: there is a very large number of potential nations on earth. Our planet also contains room for a certain number of independent or autonomous political units. On any reasonable calculation, the former number (of potential nations) is probably much, *much* larger than that of possible viable states. If this argument or calculation is correct, not all nationalisms can be satisfied, at any rate at the same time. The satisfaction of some spells the frustration of others. This argument is further and immeasurably strengthened by the fact that very many of the potential nations of this world live, or until recently have lived, not in compact territorial units but intermixed with each other in complex patterns. It follows that a territorial political unit can only become ethnically homogeneous, in such cases, if it either kills, or expels, or assimilates all non-nationals. Their unwillingness to suffer such fates may make the peaceful implementation of the nationalist principle difficult.

These definitions must, of course, like most definitions, be applied with common sense. The nationalist principle, as defined, is not violated by the presence of *small* numbers of resident foreigners, or even by the presence of the occasional foreigner in, say, a national ruling family. Just how many resident foreigners or foreign members of the ruling class there must be before the principle is effectively violated cannot be stated with precision. There is no sacred percentage figure, below which the foreigner can be benignly tolerated, and above which he becomes offensive and his safety and life are at peril. No doubt the figure will vary with circumstances. The impossibility of providing a generally applicable and precise figure, however, does not undermine the usefulness of the definition.

Our definition of nationalism was parasitic on two as yet undefined terms: state and nation.

Discussion of the state may begin with Max Weber's celebrated definition of it as that agency within society which possesses the monopoly of legitimate violence. The idea behind this is simple and seductive: in well-ordered societies, such as most of us live in or aspire to live in, private or sectional violence is illegitimate. Conflict as such is not illegitimate, but it cannot rightfully be resolved by private or sectional violence. Violence may be applied only by the central political authority, and those to whom it delegates this right. Among the various sanctions of the maintenance of order, the ultimate one – force – may be applied only by one special, clearly identi-fied and well centralized disciplined agency within society. That agency or group of agencies *is* the state.

The idea enshrined in this definition corresponds fairly well with the moral intuitions of many, probably most, members of modern societies. Nevertheless, it is not entirely satisfactory. There are 'states' – or, at any rate, institutions which we would normally be inclined to call by that name – which do not monopolize legitimate violence within the territory which they more or less effectively control. A feudal state does not necessarily object to private wars between its fief-holders, provided they also fulfil their obligations to their overlord; or again, a state counting tribal popula-tions among its subjects does not necessarily object to the institution of the feud, as long as those who indulge in it refrain from endangering neutrals on the public highway or in the market. The Iraqi state, under British tutelage after World War I, tolerated tribal raids, provided the raiders dutifully reported at the nearest police station before and after the expedi-tion, leaving an orderly bureaucratic record of slain and booty. In brief, there are states which lack either the will or the means to enforce their monopoly of legitimate violence, and which none the less remain, in many respects, recognizable 'states'.

Weber's underlying principle does, however, seem valid *now*, however strangely ethnocentric it may be as a general definition, with its tacit assumption of the well-centralized Western state. The state constitutes one highly distinctive and important elaboration of the social division of labour. Where there is no division of labour, one cannot even begin to speak of the state. But not any or every specialism makes a state: the state is the special-ization and concentration of order maintenance. The 'state' is that institu-tion or set of institutions specifically concerned with the enforcement of order (whatever else they may also be concerned with). The state exists where specialized order-enforcing agencies, such as police forces and courts, have separated out from the rest of social life. They *are* the state.

Not all societies are state-endowed. It immediately follows that the prob-lem of nationalism does not arise for stateless societies. If there is no state, one obviously cannot ask whether or not its boundaries are congruent with the limits of nations. If there are no rulers, there being no state, one cannot ask whether they are of the same nation as the ruled. When neither state nor rulers exist, one cannot resent their failure to conform to the require-ments of the principle of nationalism. One may perhaps deplore stateless-ness, but that is another matter. Nationalists have generally fulminated against the distribution of political power and the nature of political bound-aries, but they have seldom if ever had occasion to deplore the absence of power and of boundaries altogether. The circumstances in which national-ism has generally arisen have not normally been those in which the state itself, as such, was lacking, or when its reality was in any serious doubt. The state was only too conspicuously present. It was its boundaries and/or the distribution of power, and possibly of other advantages, within it which were resented.

This in itself is highly significant. Not only is our definition of national-ism parasitic on a prior and assumed definition of the state: it also seems to be the case that nationalism emerges only in milieux in which the existence of the state is already very much taken for granted. The existence of politically centralized units, and of a moral–political climate in which such centralized units are taken for granted and are treated as normative, is a necessary though by no means a sufficient condition of nationalism.

By way of anticipation, some general historical observations should be made about the state. Mankind has passed through three fundamental stages in its history: the pre-agrarian, the agrarian and the industrial. Hunting and gathering bands were and are too small to allow the kind of political division of labour which constitutes the state; and so, for them, the question of the state, of a stable specialized order-enforcing institution, does not really arise. By contrast, most, but by no means all, agrarian societies have been state-endowed. Some of these states have been strong and some weak, some have been despotic and others law-abiding. They differ a very great deal in their form. The agrarian phase of human history is the period during which, so to speak, the very existence of the state is an option. Moreover, the form of the state is highly variable. During the hunting–gathering stage, the option was not available.

By contrast, in the post-agrarian, industrial age there is, once again, no option; but now the *presence*, not the absence of the state is inescapable. Paraphrasing Hegel, once none had the state, then some had it, and finally all have it. The form it takes, of course, still remains variable. There are some traditions of social thought – anarchism, Marxism – which hold that even, or especially, in an industrial order the state is dispensable, at least under favourable conditions or under conditions due to be realized in the fullness of time. There are obvious and powerful reasons for doubting this: industrial societies are enormously large, and depend for the standard of living to which they have become accustomed (or to which they ardently wish to become accustomed) on an unbelievably intricate general division of labour and co-operation. Some of this co-operation might under favourable conditions be spontaneous and need no central sanctions. The idea that all of it could perpetually work in this way, that it could exist without any enforcement and control, puts an intolerable strain on one's credulity.

So the problem of nationalism does not arise when there is no state. It does not follow that the problem of nationalism arises for each and every state. On the contrary, it arises only for *some* states. It remains to be seen which ones do face this problem.

The definition of the nation presents difficulties graver than those attendant on the definition of the state. Although modern man tends to take the centralized state (and, more specifically, the centralized national state) for granted, nevertheless he is capable, with relatively little effort, of seeing its contingency, and of imagining a social situation in which the state is absent. He is quite adept at visualizing the 'state of nature'. An anthropologist can explain to him that the tribe is not necessarily a state writ small, and that forms of tribal organization exist which can be described as stateless. By contrast, the idea of a man without a nation seems to impose a far greater strain on the modern imagination. . . .

A man must have a nationality as he must have a nose and two ears; a deficiency in any of these particulars is not inconceivable and does from time to time occur, but only as a result of some disaster, and it is itself a disaster of a kind. All this seems obvious, though, alas, it is not true. But that it should have come to *seem* so very obviously true is indeed an aspect, or perhaps the very core, of the problem of nationalism. Having a nation is not an inherent attribute of humanity, but it has now come to appear as such.

In fact, nations, like states, are a contingency, and not a universal necessity. Neither nations nor states exist at all times and in all circumstances. Moreover, nations and states are not the *same* contingency. Nationalism holds that they were destined for each other; that either without the other is incomplete, and constitutes a tragedy. But before they could become intended for each other, each of them had to emerge, and their emergence was independent and contingent. The state has certainly emerged without the help of the nation. Some nations have certainly emerged without the blessings of their own state. It is more debatable whether the normative idea of the nation, in its modern sense, did not presuppose the prior existence of the state.

What then is this contingent, but in our age seemingly universal and normative, idea of the nation? Discussion of two very makeshift, temporary definitions will help to pinpoint this elusive concept.

1 Two men are of the same nation if and only if they share the same culture, where culture in turn means a system of ideas and signs and associations and ways of behaving and communicating.
2 Two men are of the same nation if and only if they *recognize* each other as belonging to the same nation. In other words, *nations maketh man*; nations are the artefacts of men's convictions and loyalties and solidarities. A mere category of persons (say, occupants of a given territory, or speakers of a given language, for example) becomes a nation if and when the members of the category firmly recognize certain mutual rights and duties to each other in virtue of their shared membership of it. It is their recognition of each other as fellows of this kind which turns them into a nation, and not the other shared attributes, whatever they might be, which separate that category from non-members.

READING 52

Birna Helgadottir

Eastern Europe Tires of Capitalist Promises

In the years since the fall of the Iron Curtain [in 1989] many countries in the region – particularly in the former Soviet Union, Baltics and Balkans – have sunk into almost complete civil disorder.

In most of Eastern Europe, economies have made great advances, according to the recent Transition Report from the European Bank for Reconstruction and Development (EBRD). The report praised the speed of reforms and, although despairing glances were cast at those former Soviet republics still suffering four-figure inflation rates, the general forecast was of buoyant rates of growth for the years ahead.

But despite these glowing commendations, the 'feel-good' factor is definitely missing. The dream of democratic capitalism has turned into a nightmare for many East Europeans.

According to a recent Unicef report, these economic reforms have created not only growth but also 75 million 'newly poor'; that is, people who have slipped below the poverty line since 1989. (This figure does not include the populations of former Yugoslavia.) The EBRD report conceded, amid the economic optimism, that mortality rates in Russia and the Baltics had risen by up to 70 per cent in the last five years [Table 11.2].

Such statistics, which experts on the region call 'crisis indicators', abound. Birth rates are at an all-time low in most countries. Life expectancy for men in Russia is now 58.2 – the same as Pakistan.

In some countries the crime and homicide rates have increased tenfold in the past five years [1990–5].

Unexpectedly, it is not the most traditionally vulnerable, old people and children, who have suffered the highest rises in mortality, but young and middle-aged men. Many of these deaths are due to cardiovascular, heart, digestive and infectious diseases which are now epidemics, says Unicef, of 'frightening dimensions, almost unique for sheer magnitude in peacetime'. Poverty, the breakdown of health services, deteriorating nutrition and increased stress levels are all to blame.

The extent of the welfare crisis took the economic reformers who came to power after 1989 by surprise and, in the past couple of years, many have found themselves ejected in favour of members of the pre-revolutionary

TABLE 11.2 Crisis after Communism

	Albania	Armenia	Azerbaijan	Belarus	Bulgaria	Czech Republic	Estonia	Georgia	Hungary	Latvia	Lithuania	Moldova	Poland	Romania	Russia	Slovakia	Slovenia	Ukraine
Real wage levels (% fall since 1989)	70.2	38.3	81.8	34.6	37.6	14.2	–	56.0	11.7	47.5	67.2	71.0	27.5	47.5	36.2	28.4	26.4	71.5
Birth rate (% fall)	22.3	37.3	18.9	28.7	26.1	16.4	38.7	35.9	3.6	34.9	23.7	19.3	15.5	32.3	35.6	18.7	16.2	25.9
Mortality rate 20–39-year-olds (% change)	–	33.9	126.2	34.7	13.6	6.1	76.6	9.3	37.2	69.4	41.8	18.5	–6.9	–1.4	72.8	–13.2	–1.4	27.8
Crime rate (% change)	–	10.4	17.5	78.6	297.4	209.3	95.4	0.5	78.1	44.7	86.2	–9.0	63.0	401.3	61.9	193.7	–3.4	65.8

Source: Unicef report 'Central and Eastern Europe in Transition', 1995.

élite. Former Communist Aleksander Kwasniewski was . . . elected president of Poland. Communists are now in power, or make up part of a coalition, in Bulgaria, Latvia, Lithuania, Hungary and Georgia, although they are not necessarily pursuing policies that are identifiably Communist.

The Czech Republic has long been regarded as the most stable of the former Warsaw Pact states, a fact reinforced when it became the first Eastern European country to join the Organization of Economic Co-operation and Development. It is also one of the few countries of the region which still excludes former Communists from power. But in [the 1996] elections this could change. Crisis indicators can be found even in this relatively prosperous economy.

Some would have it that the Western world betrayed the nascent democracies to the East. During the initial post-1989 euphoria, many East Europeans believed that largesse from their friendly neighbours would pour in to help them on the road to capitalist prosperity.

The actual aid forthcoming was on a much meaner scale than had been hoped.

There was, however, advice and not all of it helpful. The Unicef report, for example, talks about 'untimely, naïve, partial, poorly sequenced and, at times, completely erroneous policies, some of them introduced on the advice of western experts'.

'There is more to industrial restructuring than just opening up the market', says Dr Kirsty Hughes, head of the European programme at the Royal Institute of International Affairs in London. 'The advice was often given not by industrial experts but by theorists, applying an undergraduate-level model of the free market.' Although there was an element of 'the quick consultancy buck', she says, lack of experience was also to blame: the transition phenomenon was unique in economic history. 'This was a huge upheaval in society, in peoples' lives', she says. 'There was perhaps not enough respect for people.'

The question of funding is another controversial point. Some critics feel that a Marshall Plan-type aid programme should have been implemented. When the EBRD was founded four years ago, many European governments wanted it to be a restructuring agency, but American wishes that it should act primarily as a bank – giving loans only to commercial initiatives – prevailed.

However, Hughes believes that any large-scale aid programme would have faced absorption problems. Even the relatively modest EU Phare programme for Eastern and Central Europe, which has a budget of Ecu4.2 billion ($5bn), has had difficulties finding worthy investment projects. But, she says, more needs to be done. Western Europe should, for example, remove some of the trade barriers it has constructed.

'The West is probably not concerned enough about the fragility of transition to democracy in Eastern Europe', she concludes. 'The EU enlargement process is going very slowly.'

READING 53

Martin Shaw

Military Conscription and Citizenship

The idea of citizenship, as the way in which the individual's relationship to the state is defined, has developed over the two centuries since the French Revolution. It has been very much in evidence in recent discourse: many have seen the revolutions of 1989 as successful reclamation by the peoples of Eastern Europe of the rights and duties of genuine citizenship. No longer mere subjects of an authoritarian state, they now have the chance to act as responsible citizens, participating individually and collectively in a democratic polity. The duties of citizens to the state will be defined no longer in terms of blind obedience, but as conditional on the accountability of the state to a democracy.

Recent debate has not been exclusive to Eastern Europe. a new concern with citizenship has been apparent in some Western societies. In the German Federal Republic the consolidation of a democratic polity has involved, from the 1950s, the creation of new relationships between civil rights and military duties. The provisions for non-military alternatives to conscription have been fuller than in any other country; in recent years they have been further liberalized, and in the 1980s, . . . about a third of young men of military age were opting for the non-military form of national service, the *Zivildienst*.

In the USA a debate on national service has developed, in which a persuasive case for a voluntary scheme of non-military national service has been made by military sociologist Charles Moscos. The lobby for national service, which claims the ear of possible Democratic presidential contenders, argues for a scheme that will develop civic values and participation, especially among young people, in a society which has moved beyond 'the draft'. Whether such a scheme can really gather widespread political support is debatable, however.

In Britain, where the call for a form of national service is not on the mainstream political agenda, a rather different debate on citizenship developed on the centre-left under the Thatcher government. The British debate about citizenship has traditionally focused on the extension of rights from the narrowly political to the social and economic. Recent concern has reflected alarm, first, that the postwar extension of citizens' rights in the 'welfare state' is being threatened; and, second, that the political freedoms of the British are inadequately protected by their 'unwritten constitution' and unreformed electoral system.

The British debate has been limited in that it has rarely grappled with the military dimension of citizenship. This is largely because Britain has known only relatively short periods of conscription, and the right of the state to demand military service – although conceded in practice – has not been fully incorporated into the understanding of citizenship. Recent debate has parochially assumed that this issue, because it no longer pertains directly to Britain, no longer needs to be addressed. And yet the echoes of conscription linger on in British society, raised periodically in the demand for some form of national (even if non-military) service and in the recently advanced concept of 'active citizenship'. These represent the continuing importance of the idea that the state must demand duties of citizens in return for the rights they enjoy.

In other European societies this side of citizenship is a much more concrete question, for, as we have seen, states everywhere continue to demand military service of their young men. In the politically united European Community of the future, the issue of military service as an element of citizenship will have to be faced. In many countries this will involve a challenge to long-established traditions.

For a century or more conscription has been viewed, in most European states, as an essential part of citizenship. The origins of modern conscription lie in the French Revolution, when the revolutionary state introduced the *levée en masse* of 1793, followed by the general Law of Conscription of 1798, under which all unmarried Frenchmen between the ages of 18 and 25 were made liable to service, although in practice only a minority served. Universal conscription in the modern form, in which all young men (with whatever exceptions) underwent a period of military training and then remained liable to recall until they reached middle age, was first introduced by Prussia in the nineteenth century. By the last quarter of the century, this system was universal among the great states of continental Europe: Italy, Russia and Austro-Hungary as well as France and Germany. Conscription came to be seen . . . as one of the 'pillars of the democratic state': a foundation of social order, a school of political socialization, an essential bond between citizen and state.

The inadequacies of conscription, as an ingredient of citizenship, are quite evident with the benefit of twentieth-century experience. Conscription has proved as effective a tool of the authoritarian and totalitarian as it has of the democratic state. And even in the 'democracies', as Kiernan points out of the late nineteenth century, 'within armies anything democratic was firmly ruled out'.[1] The picture has not changed so dramatically even in the late twentieth century: few conscript armies allow their recruits many rights, although some Western European armies, such as the Dutch (with their soldiers' organizations) and the German (with largely token trade union organization), are more democratic than most. Even these militaries, however, are hardly 'democratic' institutions: hierarchy remains their essential principle. Whatever 'democratic' political education is given within a military context is in a fundamental sense negated by the way in which military organizations actually operate.

Various solutions were offered to this problem by classical socialist and anarchist thought, centring on the concept of the 'democratic army' (or, more commonly, workers' or peoples' militia) with officers elected by the soldiers themselves, and other measures to break down the hierarchical model. 'Militias were to be set up', says Deutscher, summarizing Jean Jaurès, 'on the basis of productive units, factories and village communities; the militia-men were to receive their training locally and were to continue to live and work as normal citizens, devoting themselves part-time and intermittently to the art and craft of war.'[2] (This type of organization was an early casualty of Bolshevik centralization, when Trotsky, as founder of the Red Army, seemed 'to be burning all that he had worshipped and worshipping all that he had burned'.[3] Centralization returned with a vengeance in the successful prosecution of the civil war.)

Although the purists would argue that democratic militias have never been fully tested (for example, they were supplanted by a centralized Republican army in the Spanish Civil War, again at Stalinist insistence), their military potential is at the very best unproven. They have continued to have their devotees – in Britain the ex-Communist Tom Wintringham advocated turning the Home Guard into a democratic militia during 1939–45, and this was seen by Peter Tatchell as a possible model for 'democratic defence' in the 1980s. The Swiss army (also untested in modern war) is in fact probably closest to realizing these ideas. It is doubtful, however, that they really have a relevance today. The whole problematic of 'democratizing warfare' is the wrong one for a period in which warfare itself is ceasing to be a viable option in relations between European states (if not so fully in other regions of the world).

A good instance of this problem is the issue of women's participation in the military. A central defect of conscription as a facet of citizenship is that it has applied almost always only to men. To be fully democratized, it would have first to be extended to the majority of women who are now excluded from a military role, and these women would have to be allowed to participate in the military on an equal basis with men. There are few armed forces of any kind in which anything approaching such equal participation occurs, and one side of the feminist debate about the military is precisely the demand for equality in this as in all other spheres. One does not have to go to the other extreme in the feminist debate, to claim a uniquely caring, maternal-pacifist role for women, to see the problem of this perspective. A democratization of conscript armed forces to include women would amount to a massive militarization of one-half of society. It is much more relevant to think of the exclusion of the majority of women from the military as positive sign of the limits of militarization, and to look at how these limits can be pushed further into the world of men. A genuinely sex-equal citizenship will be post-military, not military.

READING 54

Jean Bethke Elshtain
Women and War

We know women can be brave but doubt they can be ruthless. We know those made of sterner stuff will defend themselves and their children in the final redoubt, the home/land itself, but doubt women will march out to a nation's defence. We know women have been in uniform, but think of auxiliary services, support, non-combat duties. We can accept female spies, for that is a sexualized and manipulative activity given our Mata Hari-dominated image of it. We think rarely of women who have actually fought, who have signed up by disguising themselves as men or volunteering their services to resistance and guerrilla movements; and these, too, get slotted as exceptions that prove *the* rule.

The woman fighter is, for us, an identity *in extremis*, not an expectation. Joan of Arc proves this truism through her challenge to it, as her uniqueness as myth and legend in Western history shows. Joan gripped my childhood imagination, but as much for her brave martyrdom as for her warrioring. I suspect it was and has been so for many who have cherished her story in the nearly six centuries since her death. She didn't enter sainthood until this century. Her martyrdom figured centrally. So did her virginity. She may have donned male garb, but she was a *pure* woman whose violence, or leadership of violence, was sanctified officially once others granted her voices the epistemological privilege she gave them . . .

Should the few [female fighters] become not merely many but more – and yet more? Join the ranks of male combatants? In France in World War II, '*in the tradition of Joan of Arc*, women led partisan units into battle . . . During the liberation of Paris women fought in the streets with men'.[1] Some 'regulars', members of the armed services, recalling events forty years later, remain vexed by restrictions on what they could and could not do – for example, women pilots for Britain's Air Transport Auxiliary – as others detail wartime camaraderie and equality with men. 'I was considered a comrade, just the same as them', reports one French Resistance fighter. But she adds that this was true only in the Resistance: the professional army never accepted a woman as equal.

Women have described their wartime activities as personally *liberating* despite pervasive fears and almost paralysing anxieties. None regrets her choice to fight or to be in the thick of the fighting. They would, to the woman, do it all over again. But they hope no one else will have to in the future. All report gaining respect, in the words of a Soviet woman fighter, for 'men – soldiers – born not out of idolatry from afar, but out of sharing this with them, exposed to their weaknesses, seeing how they coped, and showed more human sides . . . They cried, they were frightened, they were upset about killing.' So were the women. But they did what they had made their duty.[2]

Today the United States Marines are training women for combat despite the no-combat rule because women 'can be assigned to support units that might unexpectedly come under attack and since there is always a danger of terrorist activities'. Because women Marines are not assigned to units that are likely to be direct combat units, they are not instructed in 'bayonets, offensive combat formations, offensive techniques of fire', and a few other skills. Women comprise about 5 per cent of the active-duty strength of the Marine Corps.

More interesting than almost-Marines or future conflict is the little-known or remembered story of Soviet women in combat in World War II. Soviet women formed the only regular female combat forces during the war, serving as snipers, machine-gunners, artillery women, and tank women. Their peak strength 'was reached at the end of 1943, at which time it was estimated at 800,000–1,000,000 or 8 per cent of the total number of military personnel'.[3]

Soviet women formed three women's air regiments and participated in mine-sweeping actions. Nadya Popova, a Soviet bomber pilot, has recounted her wartime experience in the language of pure war, the classic language of force Clausewitz would recognize and endorse: 'They were destroying us and we were destroying them . . . That is the logic of war . . . I killed many men, but I stayed alive. I was bombing the enemy . . . War requires the ability to kill, among other skills. But I don't think you should equate killing with cruelty. I think the risks we took and the sacrifices we made for each other made us kinder rather than cruel.' Despite this unusual – given the numbers of women involved and the tasks to which they were assigned – experience with women as wartime combatants in regular forces, the Soviets have returned to the standard model, with women designated as non-combatants and vastly outnumbered by the men, fewer than

10,000 by estimate. Just as the Greek term for *courage* is elided to the word for *man*, in Russian *bravery* is by definition masculine. Pointing this out, Shelley Saywell has noted that all the woman fighters she interviewed said that women 'do not belong in combat', and that they took up arms only because Russia faced certain destruction.

Part XII

Education

Mass education is a phenomenon of the relatively recent past, dating in most industrial countries only from the late nineteenth century. In pre-modern societies, the majority of the population was non-literate. Mastery of formal educational skills was confined to a very small stratum. Education became generalized partly through the efforts of liberal reformers, who wished to extend the benefits of education to the working class, and partly because it became generally recognized that the functioning of a complex society depends upon a populace having at least minimal educational qualifications.

In Reading 55, Nicholas Abercrombie and Alan Warde provide a discussion of the relationship between inequality and academic achievement. Education has often been regarded as a means of escaping from the limitations of a lowly class background. For some people this is true; on the other hand, education often reinforces class divisions rather than overcomes them.

The private schools, discussed by Geoffrey Walford in Reading 56, play a part in this process. About 7 per cent of the population are educated at fee-paying schools. Since the cost of such education is high, not many parents can afford to send their children to such schools. The evidence strongly suggests that the private schools play an important part in transmitting wealth and privilege from generation to generation.

The intrinsic value and social importance of education are not always evident to those obligated to attend schools – more specifically, children from underprivileged backgrounds, who often see the authority system of the school as oppressive rather than liberating. Paul Willis's study (Reading 57) describes the outlook of a group of working-class boys ('the lads') in a school in Birmingham. The lads feel alienated from the dominant culture of the school and seek every opportunity to challenge or contest it. They have developed an informal culture of their own, the main tenets of which diverge radically from the orthodoxy of the school. The lads seek every opportunity, Willis points out, to frustrate the formal objective of the school, which is to make pupils 'work'.

Children from minority group backgrounds commonly face a clash of values when attending school. Parents and children may wish to keep alive cultural values and practices which the school system, in combination with the wider social environment, tends to dissolve. Reading 58, by Saeeda Cahanum, discusses an instance in which the members of an Asian community in the north of England took an active approach to the question of education and cultural development. The Bradford Muslim Girls' School was established as a means of providing Asian girls with an educational setting which would stress the religious and cultural values of Islamic life. Although the context of the school is a 'protected' one, both the teachers and pupils experience problems in following a set of subcultural practices in a society whose overall values are very different.

READING 55

Nicholas Abercrombie and Alan Warde

Inequality and Selection in Education

Educational qualifications are a principal determinant of job opportunities. Employers use examination results as a way of screening
applicants, usually prescribing a minimum level of qualification for
any position. Schools are thus a vital link in the allocation of individuals to
places in the workforce. Achievement is a continuous process, but is
symbolized by decisions made at key stages in a child's educational career.
The type of school attended, the stream within the school to which a
pupil is allocated, and the age of leaving full-time education all affect the
acquisition of the certificates important in determining long-term life
chances.

Levels of achievement are systematically related to the social characteristics of pupils. Thus Table 12.1 shows differences in qualifications by ethnic
origin and gender at the end of the 1980s. White men and Indian men are
better qualified than female counterparts, though the gender difference is
reversed among people of West Indian and Guyanese origin. Inter-ethnic
differences indicate that men of West Indian and women of Pakistani and
Bangladeshi origin are much more disadvantaged. Indians are, on average,
better qualified than whites, though this is partly a consequence of their
being younger: younger generations have higher levels of qualification
because educational provision has expanded rapidly in the recent past.

Class origins are also important, as Table 12.2 indicates. The children of
white-collar workers are very much better qualified than their peers from
manual backgrounds. Ethnicity and gender interact with class in the determination of educational attainment. To understand the causes of unequal
attainment requires attention to all three factors.

TABLE 12.1 Highest qualification level of the population,[1] by ethnic origin and sex, Great Britain, 1988–90

Highest qualification held[2]	White (%)	West Indian/ Guyanese (%)	Indian (%)	Pakistani/ Bangla- deshi (%)	Other[3] (%)	All[4] (%)
Males:						
Higher	15	–	19	8	22	15
Other	57	58	51	40	56	57
None	29	36	30	52	21	29
Females:						
Higher	13	16	13	–	20	13
Other	51	52	46	28	52	51
None	36	32	41	68	28	36
All persons:						
Higher	14	11	16	6	21	14
Other	54	55	49	34	54	54
None	32	34	36	60	25	32

[1] Aged 16 to retirement age (64 for males and 59 for females).
[2] Excludes those who did not know or did not state their qualifications.
[3] Includes African, Arab, Chinese, other stated and mixed origin.
[4] Includes those who did not know or did not state their ethnic origin.
Source: Social Trends, 1992, p. 65; from *Labour Force Survey* data. Crown copyright.

CLASS INEQUALITIES IN EDUCATION

Origins and destinations: a case study

One major landmark in the development of education during the twentieth century in England and Wales was the 1944 Education Act, which required that all children be provided, free of charge, with a place at secondary school. Previously most children had remained in elementary education (until age 14) throughout their schooldays, as selective secondary schools, which charged fees, were available only to a minority. The 1944 Act reorganized schooling on a tripartite system: with the exception of those in private education, children were to be transferred at age 11 to either a grammar, a technical or a (secondary) modern school, on the basis of their individual abilities and aptitudes. The expressed wish was that all three types of school should be accorded 'parity of esteem'; each should cater for different kinds of children by offering different training. It was imagined that this system would provide better, and more equal, educational opportunities, eradicating the waste of talent among working-class children. Halsey et al.[1] studied the workings of the tripartite system, inquiring into the extent to which inequalities in education had been reduced for boys born between 1913 and 1952. This study remains the most authoritative regarding the nature and change in the relationship between social class and educational attainment in England and Wales.

Halsey et al. examined the educational biographies of 8,526 men aged between 20 and 60 in 1972, a part of the national sample taken in the Nuffield Mobility Project. These men were assigned to groups by their *social class of origin* and by *age cohort*. The class categories used were the same as

TABLE 12.2 Highest qualification level attained,[1] by socio-economic group of father, Great Britain, 1989

Highest qualification level attained	Professional (%)	Employers and managers (%)	Intermediate and junior non-manual (%)	Skilled manual and own account non-professional (%)	Semi-skilled manual and personal service (%)	Unskilled manual (%)	All persons (%)
Degree	38	17	18	5	4	3	11
Higher education	18	16	16	12	7	6	13
A-level	10	14	13	9	8	6	10
O-level	20	24	27	22	20	14	22
CSE	4	8	9	13	13	13	11
Foreign	5	5	3	3	2	3	3
No qualifications	6	17	14	37	47	54	31
Sample size (=100%) (no.)	440	1,656	835	3,383	1,059	438	7,811

[1] Persons aged 25–49 not in full time education.
Source: Social Trends, 1992, p. 66; from *General Household Survey* data. Crown copyright.

in Goldthorpe et al.,[2] based upon the father's occupation when the respondent was 14 years old. An age cohort is a group of people born between two given dates. Halsey et al. considered four separate cohorts, of those born in the years 1913–22, 1923–32, 1933–42 and 1943–52. Thereafter, the educational experiences of each cohort were compared, to test whether equality of access and attainment had *changed over time*. This comparison was made in order to assess the argument . . . that the organization of schooling made little difference to the chances of success of working-class pupils. The cohorts were chosen so that all men in the last two cohorts (born between 1933 and 1952) would have experienced the tripartite system, since the men born earliest, in 1933, would have passed into the secondary system, at age 11, in the year of the introduction of the new Education Act. If the organization of the education system did affect social inequalities, Halsey et al. reasoned, then comparison between the first two and the last two cohorts should show this to be the case.

The findings of Halsey et al. suggested that the 1944 Act made very little difference to inequality between classes. Of course, the total number of places in educational establishments increased, which allowed more children of all classes to attend selective schools and universities, with corresponding increases in the qualifications achieved. But the differentials between classes hardly changed. In general the proportions of children from each class remained more or less the same. Among the 1913–22 cohort, 7.2 per cent of sons of the service class (classes I and II [Registrar General's Classification]) attended university but only 0.9 per cent of the working class (classes VI and VII). Of the 1943–52 cohort, who would have gone to university between 1961 and 1970, 26.4 per cent of the sons of the service class reached university but only 3.1 per cent of working-class boys. The *rate* of increase is thus more or less the same for each class: the proportion of sons going to university grew 3.5 times for both classes. As with some of the other reforms associated with the growth of the welfare state after World War II, the dominant rather than the subordinate classes benefited most. Not *all* trends confirm the hypothesis of constant class differentials: the chances of working-class boys, relative to their service-class peers, staying at school a year beyond the minimum leaving age did improve substantially over time, for example. None the less, in most respects the service class maintained its educational advantages, relative to both intermediate and working classes, over the forty-year period examined.

Halsey et al. sought to show how, and to a lesser extent why, such unequal educational selection takes place. Dealing successively with the key 'decisions' which define an educational career (private or state primary school; selective or modern, private or state secondary school; when to leave school; whether to enter higher or further education), they evaluated explanations of educational inequality.

Despite much debate, it has never been established conclusively whether the cause of working-class under-achievement is material poverty or the cultural attributes of typical working-class families. Halsey et al. approached this question by attempting to separate out the effects of material circumstances and cultural background. They measured the former by family income, the latter by the cultural characteristics of parents (particularly their educational experiences). They found that cultural background, and specifically parental values, were of principal importance in determining the child's progress up to age 11. Whether a child went to a private primary school, and whether he subsequently entered a selective secondary school, were most clearly related to cultural background. After age 11, however, material circumstances became much more important in determining at what age, and with what qualifications, a boy was likely to leave school. This reflects the financial expense of keeping a child at school, a cost more difficult for working-class parents to bear. This discovery undermines arguments that working-class children have inadequate cultural preparation for engaging in the intellectual pursuits required of academically successful children.

Success in secondary schooling was, according to Halsey et al., most importantly determined by the school which a pupil attended. [Earlier studies] had argued that the type of school attended made no difference to achievement because all schools were merely 'class confirming' institutions. Halsey et al. disagreed. They found that it did not matter whether a child went to a private or a state *primary* school. However, the kind of *secondary* school a boy attended was considerably more important than any other factor, including the material circumstances of the family. The chance of a boy in a secondary modern school surviving past the minimum school-leaving age, or of obtaining any certificates, of course, was much lower than for a boy at grammar school. What Halsey's analysis showed, however, was that this fact is accounted for directly by neither social class composition nor IQ. Rather, it is an effect of the type of school. Under the tripartite system, survival past the minimum school-leaving age was usual if a child attended a selective secondary school. It was thus the case that the 'decision' made at age 11, by the 11-plus examination, was the critical point in determining whether children 'succeeded' or not.

Incidentally, this does not imply that social class and IQ are irrelevant. What Halsey et al. did was to *standardize* for these variables, showing that if class and IQ were held constant for any two children there would still be a very significant difference in educational outcome depending upon which schools were attended. Thus, for example, *holding social class constant*, the success of boys in gaining O-levels was the same in state-maintained grammar schools as in the leading public schools; but the *actual* proportion of boys gaining O-levels at these two types of school was quite different, since the public schools took in boys from higher class backgrounds. Hence, Halsey affirms that type of school *does* matter. Box 12.1 illustrates the main determinants of educational success according to Halsey et al.

Box 12.1 Main determinants of the educational careers of men born 1933–52

This model shows the *main* causal determinants only. It indicates that a child's cultural background is mainly relevant to explaining the nature of primary schooling and entry into secondary school. When considering qualifications, the material circumstances of the child's home become important, along with the type of secondary school attended. The qualifications obtained are the primary determinant of entry into the various forms of further and higher education.

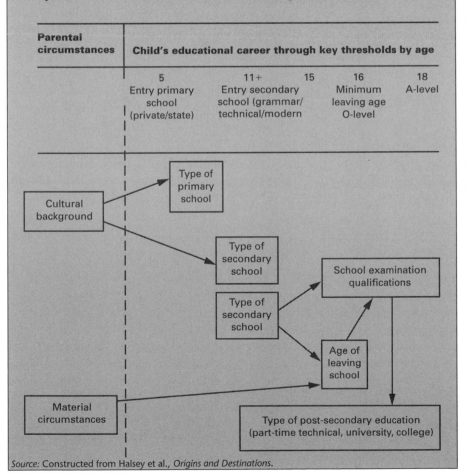

Parental circumstances	Child's educational career through key thresholds by age			
	5	11+ 15	16	18
	Entry primary school (private/state)	Entry secondary school (grammar/ technical/modern)	Minimum leaving age O-level	A-level

Source: Constructed from Halsey et al., *Origins and Destinations*.

327

Critics of Halsey et al. have tended to concentrate on whether the limited biographical information collected in the study was sufficient to test the theoretical positions which they evaluated. In particular, it is argued that their measures of cultural background were too crude for the purpose. Two other limitations are apparent: Halsey et al. have almost nothing to say about either comprehensive schools or girls. The first limitation was unavoidable: of their sample only 121 boys attended comprehensives because such schools, having developed only recently, were unavailable to most men born between 1931 and 1952. To have neglected girls was very disappointing.

Social class and comprehensive schooling

Since the later 1960s significant numbers of pupils have been educated at comprehensive secondary schools. The reasons for their introduction were partly that, as Halsey et al. conclusively demonstrated fifteen years later, the tripartite system did not seem to ensure equal educational opportunity: the segregation of 11-year-olds into the three different types of school did not produce a meritocracy. But also, the movement for comprehensive education had social objectives, particularly that class divisions and prejudices might be dissolved if there was greater mixing between those social classes at school.

Whether a fully comprehensive system of secondary education was ever likely to achieve its meritocratic and social goals will remain a matter of speculation, for recent policies have changed direction. Incentives for schools to opt out of local authority control, city technology colleges and encouragement of independent fee-paying schools have entailed greater selectivity. The percentage of pupils in private schools increased from 5 per cent in 1976 to 7 per cent in 1990 (although there are signs of a fall in the recession of the early 1990s).

Informed opinion was fairly pessimistic about the likely success of the comprehensive system. The survival of selective schools, and private schools, itself was detrimental to the comprehensive project. It was also frequently observed that streaming and banding within comprehensive schools segregated pupils within those schools, thereby replicating the old tripartite divisions. Most comprehensive schools were internally organized in a way that facilitated differentiated treatment of pupils, permitting teachers to transmit different hidden curricula. Beachside Comprehensive, [for example], had a policy of putting children into 'bands' on the basis of their performance at primary school. This resulted in the top band initially containing a disproportionate number of middle-class children. Because the bands were taught different subjects (i.e. the formal curriculum was different) there was very little movement between bands. Thus, the bands tended to coincide with social class differences and to generate different patterns of interaction between pupils and teachers as an oppositional culture emerged within the lower band. During the time that Beachside [was being studied], the school's policy changed to mixed-ability grouping. For the first three years in the school, pupils were put into classes without reference to their academic abilities. This system seemed to prevent the emergence of an oppositional, anti-school culture and to increase social interaction between pupils with different class backgrounds. However, at the time of entry into their fourth year, the pupils' friendship networks were sharply delimited by social class and academic attainment.

The transitions from compulsory schooling of young people aged 16–19, in the years between 1985 and 1988, [have been] investigated . . . Most respondents had attended comprehensive schools. Results in exams at 15 or 16 indicated that class differences in performance persist. Besides the fact that girls were more successful than boys, household social class and the educational levels of both mother and father were the principal social determinants of attainment. However, household class characteristics explained only a small proportion of the variance in pupil performance.

READING 56

Geoffrey Walford

Education and Private Schools

In 1990, John Major campaigned for the leadership of the Conservative Party on the platform of a classless society. He spoke of his hope of building a society of opportunity where individual success would depend on talent and hard work, rather than on the luck or good fortune of birth. John Major's own rise to power might be seen as a reflection of his desire for this classless society, for he left school at 16 with few qualifications; yet the choice of members for his first cabinet showed that the classless society has not yet arrived.

Of the twenty-two members of Major's first cabinet, nineteen had attended private schools, mostly of the status that usually confers on the school the somewhat confusing title of 'public' school. Included within the cabinet group were former pupils of Marlborough College, Shrewsbury School, Loretto, Dulwich, Sedbergh, George Heriot's, Charterhouse and

Plate 12.1 John and Norma Major with their daughter Elizabeth

St Paul's. Two schools – Rugby and Eton – had two members each. Most of these men, selected by John Major for the highest political positions in the country, thus spent their early years as boarders at one of a select group of highly prestigious and élite schools. Moreover, only one of the members of the cabinet had entrusted the education of his own children entirely to the state-maintained sector. Sixteen of them used the private sector alone for their children, while the rest used a judicious mixture of state-maintained and private schools. Clearly the government as a whole was not uniformly supportive of the idea of a classless society, for these members of cabinet were prepared to pay high fees in the belief that private schooling would ensure success for their own children.

TRENDS IN PRIVATE SCHOOLING

Traditionally, the élite private schools have been known as 'public' schools, and most sociological study has concentrated on these schools. While there are good sociological reasons for such a concentration, the élite schools are only part of a diverse range of schools which are not directly maintained by the state. The term 'private' schools is the most appropriate one for this whole range. In Britain, these schools are officially designated as 'independent' schools, which encourages the idea that they are not dependent upon local or central government for financial or other support. In practice, the term 'independent' is not particularly appropriate, for many of these schools now derive a large proportion of their funding from the state through such means as the Assisted Places Scheme and the Aided Pupils Scheme, and are also highly dependent on the government's ideological support, which sustains the idea that they are almost automatically superior to maintained schools. In many cases, their degree of independence is less than they might wish their customers to recognize. In practically every other country, schools not directly maintained by the state are designated as private schools, and this designation is gradually becoming more acceptable here as well.

In 1991 there were 2,287 registered private schools in England. They educated just over 565,800 children, about 7.4 per cent of the school-age population. Although there was a slight decrease in pupil numbers in 1992, there has been a significant overall increase of 13 per cent since 1984. Figure 12.1 shows the number of pupils, by age and type of school, for England in 1990. It can be seen that for school-age children the percentage in private schools gradually increases from 5.6 per cent of 5–10-year-olds, to 8.5 per cent of 11–15-year-olds, and to 19.6 per cent of those aged 16 and over.

The figures at secondary level are particularly interesting, where over the last decade or so there has been a small increase in private secondary pupil numbers even though there has been a large decline in the overall secondary school age population. Nationally, the number of 13-year-olds reached its peak in 1978 and declined by over 30 per cent from that year until 1990. That the secondary schools have been able to maintain their pupil numbers and actually increase their market share might at first seem to indicate a major growth in popularity. However, the decline in secondary school age population has been predominantly to parents of

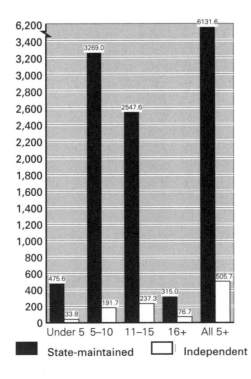

Figure 12.1 Full-time pupils in English schools, 1990 (thousands)
Source: DES, *Independent Schools in England – January 1990 and Statistics of Schools in England – January 1990*

331

social classes III to V (Registrar General's Classification), while the number of 13-year-old children of social classes I and II has remained far more constant. Since children from these top two social classes dominate the private sector, the private schools have not experienced the same decline in potential customers as has the state sector. Indeed, the proportion of the population in social classes I and II has also actually risen over the years with changes to the social structure, so there are more parents able and likely to consider private education. Both of these factors have protected the schools from the decline in enrolments experienced in maintained schools, such that the proportion of children aged 11–15 within the private sector has risen from 6.7 per cent in 1976 to 8.5 per cent in 1990.

The previous discussion of the whole of the private sector is only partially illuminating. It inevitably gives the impression of homogeneity within the sector, when this is far from correct. In practice, the private sector in Britain is highly diverse and the study of this variety is unexpectedly fascinating. There are some obvious ways in which schools differ, in terms of clearly observable variables such as age range, gender of pupils, size, religious denomination and geographical location. Some, for example, are small, isolated boarding schools attached to Roman Catholic religious houses, while others are large day schools set in the centre of busy cities. But the schools also differ greatly in their culture, history and traditions and in the experience of private schooling that the pupils receive. While some are heavily academic and highly selective by academic ability, others are more comprehensive in their intakes or may cater for children with learning difficulties such as dyslexia.

DIVERSITY IN TEACHING

Private schools also offer diversity in what is taught. Following the 1988 Education Reform Act, all state-maintained schools are now forced to follow a standardized National Curriculum and take part in its associated testing of pupils at ages 7, 11, 14 and 16. The nature of this imposed curriculum and testing has led to fierce opposition from many teachers and culminated in the teachers' strike action against the tests in summer 1993. Yet, in spite of representatives from the private sector being involved in the construction of the National Curriculum and in the development of testing, private schools do not have to follow either aspect. Private schools are free to teach whatever they like and are under no obligation to test pupils. In practice most of the schools have decided to follow the broad outline of the National Curriculum and some have been involved in testing. Others have ignored both and continue to prepare pupils for GCSE and A-level, largely unaffected by the changes.

While the most highly prestigious private schools are generally boarding schools, the percentage of children who board is not uniformly high throughout the private sector. In 1990, only 19 per cent of pupils in the private sector boarded, and 38 per cent of boarders were girls. Moreover, there has been a steady decline in the total number of children who board over the last two decades. There are some differences between girls and boys, with a gradual increase in the proportion of girls who board, but this has been overwhelmed by the decrease in boy boarders of a regular 2–3 per cent each year. The result is that many schools, even some of the well-known names, now find it difficult to attract enough pupils of sufficiently high academic ability to fill their boarding places. There have also been changes in boarding arrangements such that, even within those classified as boarding pupils, some 10 per cent are actually weekly boarders and return to their homes for each weekend.

HEADMASTERS' CONFERENCE SCHOOLS

Sociological research on the full range of schools is still very limited, and most research has been concerned with the major schools and, in particular, the boys' boarding schools. . . . The usual definition of an élite (or public) school is through the headmaster's membership of the Headmasters' Conference (HMC), an organization formed in 1871 in a successful attempt to ward off a political attack on the schools. The total number of members was limited, initially to fifty, but the total is now 233. As the number of schools grew, so did the diversity of schools involved. The range is now from the well-known names such as Eton and Winchester, which are of ancient foundation and provide a full boarding life for highly academic boys at very high cost (both had fees of nearly £11,000 per year in 1992), to several day schools which cater for children of more moderate abilities at about a quarter of the cost of the historic schools. The HMC group includes both day and boarding schools, but only about 28 per cent of the total number of pupils are either full or weekly boarders. Day pupils predominate. Day schools usually take the age range 11–18, while boarding schools often start at the later age of 13, although they increasingly have their own linked preparatory schools to take younger children.

Even though the HMC schools only educate about a quarter of all privately educated children, the concentration of sociological research on them is justified through their historic position in educating the nation's élite. Research . . . has shown that a large proportion of high-ranking judges, civil servants, diplomats, directors of major banks, and other similar highly prestigious and powerful people were educated at HMC schools. In 1984, for example, 84 per cent of the top judiciary, 70 per cent of bank directors and 49 per cent of high-ranking civil servants were from HMC schools. A similar analysis of the twenty-seven appointments of Judges to the House of Lords, Court of Appeal, and High Court between 1989 and 1991 showed that 84 per cent had been to HMC schools. Additionally, together with some prestigious girls' private schools, HMC schools still provide about 25 per cent of university undergraduates and about 50 per cent of the home undergraduates at Oxford and Cambridge universities. It is worth noting, though, that while a disproportionate number of members of present-day élites attended private schools some forty or fifty years ago, this does not mean that present-day pupils will necessarily have advantaged entry to élite positions in the future. Moreover, as the major schools were at that time highly socially selective, privileged entry to élite positions may have nothing to do with the schools themselves. At the time when these people went to school, privileged children probably had a good chance of entering élite occupations irrespective of the effect of the school.

Until the 1960s, all HMC schools were for boys only, and occupational élites were even more dominated by men than they are now. The decision of Marlborough College to admit girls into its sixth form meant that the HMC was forced to change its policy of excluding schools which accepted girls. By 1992 about two-thirds of the HMC schools taught girls as well as boys, with more than half of these schools admitting girls of all ages, rather than just into the sixth form. Nineteen per cent of pupils in HMC schools are now girls. This has been a fundamental change, and has been the result of varying reasons and circumstances in different schools. For some schools, the 1970s brought a need to expand numbers to remain economically viable, yet there was a shortage of boy applicants. This was often a particular problem in boarding schools, which are frequently sited in isolated rural areas. Other schools introduced girls to act as a 'civilizing' influence on the boys, while yet others wished to enhance or maintain their academic standards by taking in girls who were often academically more able than many of the boys. More recently, schools have become co-educational as a result of parental pressure within a changing social environment where mixed schooling is seen as more 'natural' and acceptable than single-sex schooling. Lastly, some schools have admitted girls for genuine equal opportunities reasons at a time when parental demands for the education of their daughters has grown to more nearly match those for their sons . . .

GIRLS' PRIVATE SCHOOLS

There has been less sociological research work on private schools for girls, where the organization taken to be roughly analogous with the HMC is the Girls' Schools Association (GSA) and the related Governing Bodies of Girls' Schools Association (GBGSA) . . . In 1992 there were 257 schools in membership of GSA/GBGSA, with an even wider range of size, academic emphasis, geographical location, religious affiliation, and so on than in the HMC. There is less variation in the date of foundation as the great growth in the number of girls' schools was linked to the greater emancipation of women in the nineteenth century. Of greatest importance was the work of Frances Mary Buss, who started the North London Collegiate School in 1850, and Dorothea Beale, who developed Cheltenham Ladies College after she became Head in 1858. These schools served as models for many others.

Fewer girls attend private schools than do boys and there are fewer girls in GSA/GBGSA schools than boys in HMC schools, even though there are more schools in membership. In England, in January 1990, 47 per cent of private school pupils were girls. The proportion of girls being privately educated has increased faster than that for boys, which has enabled some girls' schools to expand, even though they have suffered a considerable loss of girls to the HMC schools as the latter have become co-educational. The few former girls' schools which have attempted to become co-educational have been markedly unsuccessful. About 18 per cent of girls in GSA/GBGSA are boarders, but both day and boarding schools tend to start at age 11 rather than 13.

PREPARATORY SCHOOLS

Separate private schools for children below the age of 11 or 13 are often called preparatory schools. Traditionally, these schools have also been single-sex. However, the moves towards greater co-education at this age were great and led, in 1981, to the amalgamation of the two separate preparatory schools associations into the Incorporated Association of Preparatory Schools, which was formerly the name of the boys' association. The new body now has 526 schools in membership. All pupils must leave these schools by age 14, but most boys leave by 13, usually to the various HMC schools, while girls may leave at any time between 11 and 13. Most of these schools are far smaller than the secondary schools, and about 18 per cent of the pupils are either full or weekly boarders. Although there is now a good history of the preparatory schools, there have been no sociological studies. It is in this preparatory school age range that the main recent increase in private school pupil numbers can be found, particularly at the pre-school and pre-prep school levels. In 1992, about 12 per cent of IAPS pupils were under age 5. Schools within other groupings have also moved to exploit this market – for example, some 8 per cent of HMC pupils were under 11 in 1992.

A GROWING DIVERSITY

About two-thirds of all private school pupils are in schools within these three major groups, but there are several other small groups of schools worthy of consideration. For example, the heads of fifty of the boys' and co-educational senior schools together form the Society of Headmasters of Independent Schools (SHMIS). These schools are smaller than those in the major associations, and generally have a higher percentage of boarders. The list includes some unusual schools such as the Jewish Carmel College and Chetham's School of Music. The heads of a further 282 private schools catering for all ages come under the umbrella of the Independent Schools' Association Incorporated. The majority of these schools are for day pupils only, and fees are usually considerably lower than those of the other groups. Only a few pupils leave from these schools to go to university or other forms of higher education. Finally, some seventeen schools hold membership of the Governing Bodies Association (GBA) and not of any other organization, and hence are often categorized together.

All of the schools in the groups described above are members of the Independent Schools Information Service (ISIS) and the Independent Schools Joint Council (ISJC), which represent about 80 per cent of the private school population. Far more is known about these pupils and schools than the rest of the private sector. Indeed, it is ISIS Annual Census figures from which I have drawn much of the above information and which are yearly paraded in the press and media. Many commentators wrongly take them to be indicative of the entire private sector. There is a great diversity of experience for the remaining 20 per cent of private sector pupils who are accommodated in about 40 per cent of the total number of private schools. These schools are sometimes very different from the larger and longer-established schools, and offer anything but privilege for those children unlucky enough to be consigned to them.

The number of small private schools is increasing rapidly; in particular, there are now more than eighty Evangelical Christian schools and about twenty Muslim schools. Most of the religiously based schools are run by parents who argue that the state-maintained sector does not offer an educational experience to their children which is congruent with their group's religious beliefs. They believe that the state-maintained system has become secularized, while education should centre around religious and moral teaching. A further group of new lower-fee private schools has developed in response to parents who do not want their children to go to comprehensive schools. In some cases these schools act to replace the grammar schools not available in the comprehensive system, but others trade more upon snobbery and a modicum of social exclusivity.

PRIVATIZATION

Since election in 1979, the Conservative governments have gradually encouraged what may be seen as a 'privatization' process for schooling, by supporting existing private schools, both ideologically and financially, and by reducing the psychological barrier between the state and private sectors. The 1980 Education Act, for example, introduced the Assisted Places Scheme to enable some children to attend academically selective private schools, their parents paying no fees or only a part of the fees on a means-tested scale. Some £65 million was spent on this scheme in 1991/2. The scheme has acted as a firm financial and ideological support for the private sector. A further £5 million was spent on private music and ballet schools.

The 1988 Education Reform Act further softened the dividing line between the maintained and private sectors by legislating for the introduction of City Technology Colleges and Grant Maintained Schools. The CTCs are designated as independent schools, but are funded jointly by the state and industry and commerce, while the Grant Maintained Schools are still officially within the state system, but are funded directly by the Department for Education rather than through the local education authority system. At the same time, there has been an increasing need for parents of children in the state-maintained sector to make donations to the schools to ensure that adequate facilities are available. All of this blurs the boundary between the state and private sectors . . . such that, increasingly, the state-maintained sector cannot be understood without reference to the nature and diversity of the private sector. The private sector is not an isolated oddity of voyeuristic interest, but directly interacts with the nature and quality of education available in the maintained sector.

READING 57

Paul E. Willis

Dossing, Blagging and Wagging: Countercultural Groups in the School Environment

On a night we go out on
the street
Troubling other people.
I suppose we're anti-social,
But we enjoy it.

The older generation
They don't like our hair,
Or the clothes we wear
They seem to love running
us down,
I don't know what I would
do if I didn't have the gang.

(Extract from a poem by Derek written in an English class)

. . . Counterschool culture is the zone of the informal. It is where the incursive demands of the formal are denied – even if the price is the expression of opposition in style, micro-interactions and non-public discourses. In working-class culture generally opposition is frequently marked by a withdrawal into the informal and expressed in its characteristic modes just beyond the reach of 'the rule'.

Even though there are no public rules, physical structures, recognized hierarchies or institutionalized sanctions in the counterschool culture, it cannot run on air. It must have its own material base, its own infrastructure. This is, of course, the social group. The informal group is the basic unit of this culture, the fundamental and elemental source of its resistance. It locates and makes possible all other elements of the

337

culture, and its presence decisively distinguishes 'the lads' from the 'ear'oles'.

The importance of the group is very clear to members of the counter-school culture.

[In a group discussion]

Will: [. . .] we see each other every day, don't we, at school [. . .]

Joey: That's it, we've developed certain ways of talking, certain ways of acting, and we developed disregards for Pakis, Jamaicans and all different . . . for all the scrubs and the fucking ear'oles and all that [. . .] We're getting to know it now, like we're getting to know all the cracks, like, how to get out of lessons and things, and we know where to have a crafty smoke. You can come over here to the youth wing and do summat, and er'm . . . all your friends are here, you know, it's sort of what's there, what's always going to be there for the next year, like, and you know you have to come to school today, if you're feeling bad, your mate'll soon cheer yer up like, 'cos you couldn't go without ten minutes in this school, without having a laff at something or other.

PW: Are your mates a really big important thing at school now?

– Yeah.

– Yeah.

– Yeah.

Joey: They're about the best thing actually.

The essence of being 'one of the lads' lies within the group. It is impossible to form a distinctive culture by yourself. You cannot generate fun, atmosphere and a social identity by yourself. Joining the counterschool culture means joining a group, and enjoying it means being with the group:

[In a group discussion on being 'one of the lads']

Joey: [. . .] when you'm dossing on your own, it's no good, but when you'm dossing with your mates, then you're all together, you're having a laff and it's a doss.

Bill: If you don't do what the others do, you feel out.

Fred: You feel out, yeah, yeah. They sort of, you feel, like, thinking the others are . . .

Will: In the second years . . .

Spanksy: I can imagine . . . you know, when I have a day off school, when you come back the next day, and something happened like in the day you've been off, you feel, 'Why did I have that day off', you know, 'I could have been enjoying myself'. You know what I mean? You come back and they're saying, 'Oorh, you should have been here yesterday', you know.

Will: [. . .] like in the first and second years, you can say er'm . . . you're a bit of an ear'ole right. Then you want to try what it's like to be er'm . . . say, one of the boys like, you want to have a taste of that, not an ear'ole, and so you like the taste of that.

Though informal, such groups nevertheless have rules of a kind which can be described – though they are characteristically framed in contrast to what 'rules' are normally taken to mean.

PW: [...] Are there any rules between you lot?

Pete: We just break the other rules.

Fuzz: We ain't got no rules between us though, have we?
      [...]

Pete: Changed 'em round.

Will: We ain't got rules but we do things between us, but we do things that y'know, like er . . . say, I wouldn't knock off anybody's missus or Joey's missus, and they wouldn't do it to me, y'know what I mean? Things like that or, er . . . yer give 'im a fag, you expect one back, like, or summat like that.

Fred: T'ain't rules, it's just an understanding really.

Will: That's it, yes.

PW: [...] What would these understandings be?

Will: Er . . . I think, not to . . . meself, I think there ain't many of us that play up the first or second years, it really is that, but y'know, say if Fred had cum to me and sez, 'er . . . I just got two bob off that second year over there', I'd think, 'What a cunt', you know.
      [...]

Fred: We're as thick as thieves, that's what they say, stick together.

There is a universal taboo among informal groups on the yielding of incriminating information about others to those with formal power. Informing contravenes the essence of the informal group's nature: the maintenance of oppositional meanings against the penetration of 'the rule'. The Hammertown lads call it 'grassing'. Staff call it telling the truth. 'Truth' is the formal complement of 'grassing'. It is only by getting someone to 'grass' – forcing them to break the solemnest taboo – that the primacy of the formal organization can be maintained. No wonder, then, that a whole school can be shaken with paroxysms over a major incident and the purge which follows it. It is an atavistic struggle about authority and the legitimacy of authority. The school has to win, and someone, finally, has to 'grass': this is one of the ways in which the school itself is reproduced and the faith of the 'ear'oles' restored. But whoever has done the 'grassing' becomes special, weak and marked. There is a massive retrospective and ongoing reappraisal among 'the lads' of the fatal flaw in his personality which had always been immanent but not fully disclosed until now:

[In a group discussion of the infamous 'fire extinguisher incident' in which 'the lads' took a hydrant out of school and let it off in the local park]

PW: It's been the biggest incident of the year as it's turned out, hasn't it?

Joey: It's been blown up into something fucking terrific. It was just like that [snapping his fingers], a gob in the ocean as far as I'm concerned when we did it, just like smoking round the corner, or going down the shop for some crisps.

PW: What happened [. . .]?

– Webby [on the fringes of the counterschool culture] grassed.

Joey: Simmondsy had me on me own and he said, 'One of the group owned up and tried to put all the blame on Fuzz'. But he'd only had Webby in there.

Spanksy: We was smoking out here.

Spike: He's like that, you'd got a fag, hadn't you [to Fuzz].

Spanksy: And Webby asks for a drag, so he give Webby the fag. Rogers [a teacher] walked through the door, and he went like that [demonstrating] and he says, 'It ain't mine sir, I'm just holding it for Fuzz'.

Will: Down the park before, [. . .] this loose thing, me and Eddie pulled it off, didn't we, me and Eddie, and the parky was coming round like, he was running round, wor'he, so me and Eddie we went round the other side, and just sat there, like you know, two monkeys. And Webby was standing there, and the parky come up to him and says, 'Come on, get out. Get out of this park. You'm banned'. And he says, he walks past us, me and Eddie, and he says, 'I know you warn't there, you was sitting here'. And Webby went, 'It warn't me, it was . . .', and he was just about to say summat, warn't he?

Eddie: That's it, and I said, 'Shhh', and he just about remembered not to grass us.

Membership of the informal group sensitizes the individual to the unseen informal dimension of life in general. Whole hinterlands open up of what lies behind the official definition of things. A kind of double capacity develops to register public descriptions and objectives on the one hand, and to look behind them, consider their implications, and work out what will actually happen, on the other. This interpretative ability is felt very often as a kind of maturation, a feeling of becoming 'worldlywise', of knowing 'how things really work when it comes to it'. It supplies the real 'insider' knowledge which actually helps you get through the day.

PW: Do you think you've learnt anything at school, has it changed or moulded your values?

Joey: I don't think school does fucking anything to you [. . .] It never has had much effect on anybody I don't think [after] you've learnt the basics. I mean school, it's fucking four hours a day. But it ain't the teachers who mould you, it's the fucking kids you meet. You'm only with the teachers 30 per cent of the time in school, the other fucking two-thirds are just talking, fucking pickin' an argument, messing about.

The group also supplies those contacts which allow the individual to build up alternative maps of social reality, it gives the bits and pieces of information for the individual to work out himself what makes things tick. It is basically only through the group that other groups are met, and through them successions of other groups. School groups coalesce and further link up with neighbourhood groups, forming a network for the passing-on of distinctive kinds of knowledge and perspectives that progressively place school at a tangent to the overall experience of being a working-class teenager in an industrial city. It is the infrastructure of the informal group which makes at all possible a distinctive kind of *class* contact, or class culture, as distinct from the dominant one.

Counterschool culture already has a developed form of unofficial bartering and exchange based on 'nicking', 'fiddles', and 'the foreigner' – a pattern which, of course, emerges much more fully in the adult working-class world:

> *Fuzz:* If, say, somebody was to say something like, 'I'm looking, I want a cassette on the cheap like'. Right, talk about it, one of us hears about a cassette on the cheap, y'know, kind of do the deal for 'em and then say, 'Ah, I'll get you the cassette'.

Cultural values and interpretations circulate 'illicitly' and informally just as do commodities.

Opposition to the school is principally manifested in the struggle to win symbolic and physical space from the institution and its rules and to defeat its main perceived purpose: to make you 'work'. Both the winning and the prize – a form of self-direction – profoundly develop informal cultural meanings and practices. By the time a counterschool culture is fully developed its members have become adept at managing the formal system, and limiting its demands to the absolute minimum. Exploiting the complexity of modern regimes of mixed ability groupings, blocked timetabling and multiple RSLA options, in many cases this minimum is simply the act of registration.

> [In a group discussion on the school curriculum]
>
> *Joey:* [. . .] of a Monday afternoon, we'd have nothing right? Nothing hardly relating to school work, Tuesday afternoon we have swimming and they stick you in a classroom for the rest of the afternoon, Wednesday afternoon you have games and there's only Thursday and Friday afternoon that you work, if you call that work. The last lesson Friday afternoon we used to go and doss, half of us wagged out o' lessons and the other half go into the classroom, sit down and just go to sleep [. . .]
>
> *Spanksy:* [. . .] Skive this lesson, go up on the bank, have a smoke, and the next lesson go to a teacher who, you know, 'll call the register [. . .]
>
> *Bill:* It's easy to go home as well, like him [Eddie] . . . last Wednesday afternoon, he got his mark and went home [. . .]
>
> *Eddie:* I ain't supposed to be in school this afternoon, I'm supposed to be at college [on a link course where students spend one day a week at college for vocational instruction].
>
> *PW:* What's the last time you've done some writing?
>
> *Will:* When we done some writing?
>
> *Fuzz:* Oh are, last time was in careers, 'cos I writ 'yes' on a piece of paper, that broke me heart.

341

PW: Why did it break your heart?
Fuzz: I mean to write, 'cos I was going to try and go through the term without writing anything. 'Cos since we've cum back, I ain't dun nothing [it was half way through term].

Truancy is only a very imprecise – even meaningless – measure of rejection of school. This is not only because of the practice of stopping in school for registration before 'wagging off' (developed to a fine art among 'the lads'), but also because it only measures one aspect of what we might more accurately describe as informal student mobility. Some of 'the lads' develop the ability of moving about the school at their own will to a remarkable degree. They construct virtually their own day from what is offered by the school. Truancy is only one relatively unimportant and crude variant of this principle of self-direction which ranges across vast chunks of the syllabus and covers many diverse activities: being free out of class, being in class and doing no work, being in the wrong class, roaming the corridors looking for excitement, being asleep in private. The core skill which articulates these possibilities is being able to get out of any given class: the preservation of personal mobility.

[In a group discussion]
PW: But doesn't anybody worry about your not being in their class?
Fuzz: I get a note off the cooks saying I'm helping them [. . .]
John: You just go up to him [a teacher] and say, 'Can I go and do a job'. He'll say, 'Certainly, by all means', 'cos they want to get rid of you like.
Fuzz: Specially when I ask 'em.
Pete: You know the holes in the corridor, I didn't want to go to games, he told me to fetch his keys, so I dropped them down the hole in the corridor, and had to go and get a torch and find them.

For the successful, there can be an embarrassment of riches. It can become difficult to choose between self-organized routes through the day.

Will: [. . .] what we been doing, playing cards in this room 'cos we can lock the door.
PW: Which room's this now?
Will: Resources centre, where we're making the frames [a new stage for the deputy head], s'posed to be.
PW: Oh! You're still making the frames!
Will: We should have had it finished, we just lie there on top of the frame, playing cards, or trying to get to sleep [. . .] Well, it gets a bit boring, I'd rather go and sit in the classroom, you know.
PW: What sort of lessons would you think of going into?
Will: Uh, science, I think, 'cos you can have a laff in there sometimes.

This self-direction and thwarting of formal organizational aims is also an assault on official notions of time. The most arduous task of the deputy head is the construction of the timetables. In large schools, with several options open to the fifth year, everything has to be fitted in with the greatest of care. The first weeks of term are spent in continuous revision, as junior members of staff complain, and particular combinations are shown to be unworkable. Time, like money, is valuable and not to be squandered. Everything has to be ordered into a kind of massive critical path of the school's purpose. Subjects become measured blocks of time in careful relation to each other. Quite as much as the school buildings the institution over time *is* the syllabus. The complex charts on the deputy's wall show how it works. In theory it is possible to check where every individual is at every moment of the day. But for 'the lads' this never seems to work. If one wishes to contact them, it is much more important to know and understand their own rhythms and patterns of movement. These rhythms reject the obvious purposes of the timetable and their implicit notions of time. The common complaint about 'the lads' from staff and the 'ear'oles' is that they 'waste valuable time'. Time for 'the lads' is not something you carefully husband and thoughtfully spend on the achievement of desired objectives in the future. For 'the lads' time is something they want to claim for themselves now as an aspect of their immediate identity and self-direction. Time is used for the preservation of a state – being with 'the lads' – not for the achievement of a goal – qualifications.

Of course there is a sense of urgency sometimes, and individuals can see the end of term approaching and the need to get a job. But as far as their culture is concerned time is importantly simply the state of being free from institutional time. Its own time all passes as essentially the same thing, in the same units. It is not planned, and is not counted in loss, or expected exchange.

READING 58

Saeeda Cahanum

Finishing School: Asian Girls in the British Educational System

I hail a taxi to go to spend the day at Bradford Muslim Girls' School. The Asian taxi driver smiles and turns his gaze away from my face. This is a mark of respect on his part and a change from the normal flirtatious attitude of Asian drivers to a Westernized Asian woman with uncovered hair. He commends me on my choice of school and hopes that I will make a good student.

More than thirty girls attend this private school which is in an old stone building in the city centre. Parents pay for their daughters to receive a strong grounding in Islam in a place that sustains the religious and cultural values of Muslim home life. The school also acts as daytime custodian to ensure that the girls do not have the opportunity to stray from orthodoxy.

The school's existence owes much to the row in 1983 when an article by Bradford headmaster Ray Honeyford entitled 'Multiracial influences' appeared in the right-wing *Salisbury Review*. Asian parents complained that Bradford Education Authority's multi-racial policy had failed to accommodate the religious beliefs of Muslim students. Some suggested separate schooling for girls and the Bradford Muslim Girls' School was born.

After assembly, the girls disperse to rooms named after the Prophet's wives and daughters to begin their studies. The classrooms are spartan, small and decorated with posters showing details of prayer, pilgrimage and the life of the Prophet. The school costs £100,000 a year to run – but only £28,000 is raised in fees. Private donations and school merchandizing help cover some of the costs but the school is run on a deficit. It employs seven part-time teachers and a headmistress, Nighat Mirza. Last year pupils were able to take GCSEs in Urdu, child care and religious studies. This year, French and English have been added. Next year maths and science are promised.

'Sacrifices have to be made,' says Mrs Mirza. 'I'm not sad that the girls in previous years left with no qualifications, but proud that they have the satisfaction of knowing that they did something for someone else.'

Mrs Mirza began her career after marriage and motherhood. She denies that by teaching the girls to be good wives and mothers she is placating Muslim men. 'By teaching the girls about Islam we are giving them tools with which to challenge and fight for their rights. Empowering women doesn't frighten men but creates a more stable society', she says. 'Islam teaches us that men and women are equal but different.' Girls are also taught to understand the restrictions on their lives and that Islam is a preparation for the life hereafter.

Molly Somerville, a charismatic white women, dressed in a *shalwaar-kameez* and wearing earrings shaped like the continent of Africa, teaches French and the Christian element of religious studies. The only presence of Islam in the French lesson is the press cuttings of the three French Muslim Alchaboun sisters involved in the campaign to allow them to wear the *hijab* (veil) to school. In the afternoon the same classroom doubles as a room for religious studies. Today the girls are learning about leprosy. They are told to look it up in the Bible and the Koran and compare the two. The girls then discuss modern-day equivalents of outcasts. Suggestions made include people with AIDS, the homeless and people with disabilities.

During the lunch hour I am surrounded by girls in their maroon uniform. What do they like about the school? 'We get to learn all about our religion and can pray when we like. There is no racism here. No one laughs at the way we dress, because we are all the same', they say.

Fcw dispute the fact that they could get the same religious education by going to an ordinary state school during the day and attending a supplementary school run by the mosque in the evenings. They agree that they would not be getting an education unless it was compulsory. They say they are educating themselves because 'they might need it one day'. 'If I am lucky I might get married to a man who will let me use my education and get a good job', says one 15-year-old. A 16-year-old can't decide whether she wants to be a doctor or a lawyer, but says it will depend on what her parents allow her to do. This strikes a familiar chord with all of them. 'I want to be a hairdresser', says another. Does she think she'll realize her ambition? 'No, because my parents won't let me.'

One tiny 14-year-old with freckles has hopes of being a journalist. I take to her immediately. She doesn't think her dream will come true because 'Asian parents don't allow their daughters to go into such professions'. A moment of silent confusion follows when I point out that they're talking to such a woman.

Mrs Mirza says she wants her 10-year-old daughter to get the best education possible. So will she send her to the school? 'Yes, but only if things improve.' Her daughter, she claims, doesn't need to come to the school to get the good grounding in Islam, because, says Mrs Mirza, 'I can provide that at home for her.'

The dilemma for the Muslim community is that having an educated daughter has a particular value, if only for the prestige in the marriage market. The conflict arises when education leads to independent thought among women and so a desire for independence. In response, parents opt for separate schooling as a means of social control. The girls, too, believe in education but end up aborting their own aspirations when faced with massive pressures.

At Belle Vue Girls' School, a Bradford comprehensive where most of the girls are Muslim, there are similar conflicts. Yet none of the girls wishes to go to a segregated school.

They see themselves as the 'lucky ones' for they have been brought up to see education as a privilege, not a right. They are unsure of the future. 'We all have our own plans, but we don't actually know what will happen', says one lively 17-year-old about to sit her A-levels. Girls who lack qualifications discover that the only alternative is marriage. These girls see marriage as the end of their individual identity and describe it as a form of death. One 18-year-old is getting involved in as many activities as possible before she gets married this summer. 'My in-laws are sexist and won't let me do anything once I'm married.' Yet she doesn't see herself as being oppressed. 'My parents' choice is my choice. My freedom is in my mind.'

Community pressure plays an overwhelming role in their lives, and 'mistakes' by other women in the community cause more restrictions. 'Asian parents don't understand the concept of individuality, we're always judged by someone else's standards, never our own', says Farrah, a 17-year-old Muslim and former heavy metal fan who found her identity at 13 when she became a practising Muslim. Dressed in a *hijab*, she says Islam has taught her her rights, that she no longer lets people take advantage of her and that religion is the dominant force in her life. 'It answers all my questions, makes sense and is perfectly logical.' Muslim women, she adds, are oppressed not because of religion but through a lack of religious education. 'Women have to be educated to use religion as a tool and not leave the interpretation up to men.'

For Asian women teachers, social pressures impose particular restrictions and difficulties. The younger generation of women teachers in particular work hard to challenge their students' cultural and religious upbringing and to use their own experience as a model and guide.

Saira had been teaching in a Bradford state school for one year when a colleague reprimanded her for challenging an Asian girl who said arranged marriages work because there are hardly any divorces. The white teacher accused Saira of 'arrogance' and told her to stop confusing the girl and learn to be more 'objective' about cultural concerns. 'As a black teacher in this school . . .' began Saira. 'You're not a black teacher, you're *a* teacher', came the response.

This incident, says Saira, highlights the complexities and contradictions of her position. 'As a professional I'm expected to detach myself from the concerns of Asian pupils. However, as an informed insider who has experienced the intolerable pressures the community brings to bear on girls, I feel I have a duty to encourage pupils to hope for more from life.'

Some girls assume that because Saira is young, drives a car, wears Western clothes and teaches a subject other than Urdu her experiences are completely different to theirs. To them she's distant and totally 'free'. 'This is just one step away from seeing me as an Uncle Tom, a mere token', says Saira.

Asian parents also have different expectations of an Asian teacher. On the one hand, they welcome the fact that Saira is Asian, but they also expect her to police their daughters on behalf of the community. 'Tell me straight away if you see her hanging around with boys after school won't you?', they say.

Saira's ambivalent relationship with her pupils is paralleled by a story told by Asha, a 24-year-old teacher in a Leeds state school. A stone was recently thrown at her in the classroom in what she describes as a display of 'tabloid fundamentalism'.

'I have an extremely good relationship with my 14-year-olds. They love a teacher who relates to them in both language and experience. On this particular day, a new Asian girl had joined the class and I suppose the others were trying to impress her by seeing what they could do to rile me', says Asha. 'I turned to the blackboard and felt this stone whiz past my head and hit the board.' Asha's calm response resulted in the culprit coming forward to confess the full story. The girls had had a meeting during break and collected nine stones each, the size of pebbles, and decided that if 'Miss' gave a negative response to the question 'Are you fasting?' then they would discharge their missiles at her. All but one lost their nerve.

Asha and another teacher tried to make sense of the episode and there is talk of bringing parents in to discuss it and reiterate the school's philosophy of tolerance. She now thinks that all the girls have an ambivalent attitude towards her. 'Part of them finds me and all I stand for enticing, yet another part of them finds me threatening. It was this conflict and in-bred conditioning that made them respond to me in what I regard as a fundamentalist way.'

The Rushdie episode has put Muslim girls' schools back on the agenda and the gains made in state schools since 1984 are under threat. Although the Bradford Muslim Girls' School was set up in 1984 it did not represent the feelings of the majority of Asians. Polls taken by the Commission for Racial Equality in 1984 found little support for separate schooling in Bradford. This put paid to plans by the Muslim Parents' Association to buy four state girls' schools and transform them into separate Muslim girls' schools. At that time, the Bradford Council for Mosques also opposed the demand for separate schooling, opting instead for a compromise with Bradford council in which they accepted concessions in dress and food. In public, the Bradford Council for Mosques said the proposal had not been thought out properly.

Other Asian organizations said the idea smacked of 'educational apartheid'. Privately, it was rumoured that the Council for Mosques decided tactically that the time was not right to pursue the campaign because of the atmosphere created by the Honeyford affair.

The Rushdie affair has reinforced the Bradford Muslims' siege mentality and with this has come talk of separate schools. A culture besieged in this way throws up its own notions of what a 'good Muslim woman' should be. Religion then becomes a substitute for a kind of cultural conformity. In practice, Islam comes to represent what is allowed rather than what is possible. For women the idea of *Izzat*, or chastity and honour, has become the means of social control, and separate schools the perfect institutions for exercising that control. And as Saira and Asha have learnt through their own experiences as Asian teachers, intellectual freedom is meaningless unless it goes hand in hand with social freedom. The girls of the Bradford Muslim Girls' School have yet to learn the lesson but if – and when – they do, they too will go on the offensive in their fight for self-determination.

Part XIII

Religion

The classical social thinkers, such as Marx, Weber and Durkheim, believed that with the progressive development of modern societies, religion (at least in its traditional sense as the belief in supernatural beings) would disappear. This has not happened: religious beliefs and ideals seem not only to have remained strong, but in certain contexts to have undergone a significant revival and further elaboration.

Yet everyone agrees that the role of religion in modern societies is substantially different from its role in pre-modern times, and that in some respects the hold of religion over people's day-to-day lives has weakened. It remains widely debated how far such a process of weakening, or secularization, has occurred, and what its implications are for other social institutions.

In the first selection in this part (Reading 59) Jeffrey Hadden considers different aspects of the question of secularization. Hadden provides a balanced assessment of the various arguments involved in the secularization debate. He points out that the major difficulty with the thesis of progressive socialization is that there is little accurate historical evidence about patterns of belief and religious practice in the past. If we cannot be sure how strong religious beliefs used to be, and whether or not individuals regularly took part in religious practices, we cannot easily assess how far profound changes have taken place.

Hadden concludes that secularization has almost certainly occurred in certain spheres, and in respect of particular aspects of religious organization and practice; but he argues that other aspects of religion remain of basic importance. Religion and political movements, he points out, have become closely intertwined. An example is provided by Emmanuel Sivan (Reading 60) in his discussion of Islamic fundamentalism. This religious orientation, Sivan makes clear, has to be understood in some part as a reaction against the impact of Western culture upon other parts of the world.

Andrew Brown (Reading 61) discusses the question of gender and religion. While the Anglican church has now admitted women priests, the Roman Catholic church still bans women from ordination to the priesthood. At least for the moment, the Pope and other major church leaders seem determined to resist the growing demand for equal female rights within the religious sphere. Brown suggests, however, that the promotion of equal rights for women within the religious domain should be seen as part of the more general process of social democratization, and in that sense in the end is likely to prove irresistible.

In the final reading Serge Moscovici returns to classical social thought to inquire into the origins of religion. Durkheim saw the centrality of religion as lying in the fact that religions express basic social values. In his studies, he analysed the most 'primitive' form of religion, totemism – the worship of animal species or plants. The idea of the 'sacred' does not spring from the totemic object, plant or animal, itself, but from the feelings inspired by collective processes of ceremonial. The notion of the sacred, Durkheim says, is present in all religions.

READING 59

Jeffrey K. Hadden
Challenging Secularization Theory

CRITIQUE OF THE THEORY

Here's a translation of secularization theory in three short sentences:

Once the world was filled with the sacred – in thought, practice and institutional form. After the Reformation and Renaissance, the forces of modernization swept across the globe and secularization, a corollary historical process, loosened the dominance of the sacred. In due course, the sacred shall disappear altogether except, possibly, in the private realm.

Secularization, thus understood, is properly described as a general orientating concept that causally links the decline of religion with the process of modernization. That is, it is more appropriately described as a proposition than as a theory.

Beyond its use as a general orientating proposition, secularization has been used in many ways ranging from the 'decline' or 'loss' of religion, to the 'differentiation' of the religious from the secular, to an Enlightenment myth 'which views science as the bringer of light relative to which religion and other dark things will vanish away'.[1]

Two decades ago David Martin argued for the abandonment of the concept. Later, Larry Schiner reviewed the uses of the term secularization and found six discrete meanings. Noting that several of these meanings were infused with polemical and ideological overtones, Schiner, too, thought abandonment was a reasonable way of dealing with the problem.

Encased within this general orientating proposition are the elements of a theory. Many scholars have highlighted one or more of these elements, but for all that has been written about secularization, probably only Martin, who decided not to abandon the concept, has written a treatise that would qualify as a theory.[2]

More recently, Karel Dobbelaere has achieved a remarkably thorough and systematic review of secularization literature which reveals the absence of a general theory.[3] Dobbelaere's review differentiates three distinct levels of use: (1) societal, (2) organizational and (3) individual. A Belgian, Dobbelaere sees the evidence of secularization all around him and is reluctant to challenge the utility of the theory. Rather, he concludes that we need to be more conscious of the fact that different theorists, working with different paradigms, mean different things . . .

Dobbelaere's analysis is extremely useful. More clearly than anyone else, he has illuminated the sad fact that in the lexicon of sociological enquiry, 'secularization means whatever I say it means'. But Dobbelaere's solution to the problem seems ill-advised. He seems prepared to give the idea of secularization a life of its own, free to yoke or splinter in as many directions as there are crafters with moulds and chisels. I think the sounder conclusion to be reached from his work is the same that Martin and Schiner reached two decades ago.

To summarize, the idea of secularization is presumed to be a theory, but literature reviews support this assumption only in a very loose sense. This, however, does not diminish its importance. It is believed to be a theory and is treated as such. The fact that the theory has not been systematically stated or empirically tested is of little consequence. It has dominated our assumptions about religion and guided the types of research questions scholars have asked. Its imagery is powerful, and it is unlikely that it will disappear from our vocabulary or thought processes. But developments in the social scientific study of religion have begun to erode its credibility.

I turn next to the empirical evidence we have about secularization in support of this prediction.

EXAMINING THE DATA

Charles Glock not only warned us about the limited utility of data on religion, he further counselled that 'It is extremely doubtful that accurate statistics can be produced through manipulating the unreliable ones.'[4] A decade later, N. J. Demerath III thoroughly documented the point that Glock had only asserted. In a 95-page contribution to Eleanor Sheldon and Wilbert Moore's *Indicators of Social Change*, Demerath meticulously examined indicators of church membership, religious belief, organization and ecumenical activity.

Some types of data are more reliable than others, Demerath concluded, but for every argument that can be made in defence of a data set, there exists a rebuttal. The result of Demerath's extensive evaluation and critique of many data sources leaves us with a single plea: 'If there is a single recommendation that emerges from this review,' Demerath pleads, 'it is that *the Census should include questions concerning religion in its regular enumerations*.' 'Indeed,' Demerath continues, 'this recommendation is so urgent . . . that it deserves a postscript of its own.'[5]

In the face of such a passionate admonition, one must be cautious in trying to build a case either for or against secularization with existing data. But if we must not throw caution to the winds, neither are we compelled to silence, or forbidden from examining and interpreting the data.

To me, the data, with all their recognized faults, speak clearly. And their most important message is that *the data cannot confirm the historical process predicted by secularization theory*. One must also add the caution that neither can the data disconfirm the process. But when one examines the large corpus of literature that provides some longitudinal perspective, I don't see how one can fail to conclude that religion stubbornly resists the prophecies of its early demise. If that simple proposition is entertained, then we open the door for alternative ways of thinking about religion in the modern world.

Marking 1935 as the beginning of scientific polling, the Gallup Organization's annual *Religion in America* report for 1985 highlights a half-century assessment of religion. In the introductory essay, George Gallup, Jr, concludes: '. . . perhaps the most appropriate word to use to describe the religious character of the nation as a whole over the last half century is *"stability"*. Basic religious beliefs, and even religious practice, today differ relatively little from the levels recorded 50 years ago.'

Unfortunately, early polling included only sporadic questions about religion, and when they were included, the wording was frequently changed just enough to leave one wary about comparability. Most of the items for which Gallup now provides trend data were not available in the early years of polling. But when one picks one's way through the poll data, plus other types of data that permit some inferences, Gallup's conclusion of stability seems to me a prudent assessment.

Still, within the general context of stability, there are some important changes. I shall briefly identify *six significant deviations from the theme of stability*.

1 The most reliable indicators we have confirm the existence of a *religious revival in the post-World War II era*. We can't precisely pinpoint the beginning, but it seems to have lost steam by the end of the 1950s.

2 During most of the second half of this century, the 'mainline' or *liberal church traditions* have struggled and mostly *lost membership and influence*.

3 During this same time period, *conservative religious traditions*, evangelicals and fundamentalists, have *experienced sustained growth*. Growth continues within these groups, although there is some evidence of a slowing of the process.

4 *The Second Vatican Council dramatically affected the beliefs and behaviour of Roman Catholics in America*. Attendance at mass and confession fell dramatically. Catholics became much less likely to report that religion was 'very important' in their lives. But these indicators of decline now seem to have levelled off and stabilized.

5 While Catholics now seem positioned to fight among themselves over the essentials of belief, meaning and purpose of the church, and the authority of their leaders, the *authority of the Roman Catholic leadership is now greater than at any point in American history*.

6 Primarily as a result of immigration from Central America and the Caribbean, *Catholics have increased their proportion of the American popula-*

tion from roughly 20 per cent in 1947 to almost 30 per cent in 1985, *and their proportion* of the total population *can be expected to continue to grow.*

Each of these patterns of change either has had or will have important implications for the future of religion in America. Nested within these trends and countertrends are social forces that portend changes which could alter the face of religion during the next fifty years. But the indicators of stability also provide clues to the future. I shall identify five among many possible indicators of stability.

1 The overwhelming proportion of Americans report that they *believe in God*, and that proportion has fluctuated very little over the forty years for which we have data. The proportion professing belief in God has never dipped below 94 per cent and has moved as high as 99 per cent during the revival period of the 1950s [according to the Gallup poll].

2 Church *membership* statistics have fluctuated only a little over the past forty years. Self-reported membership surveys consistently run a little higher than statistics reported by religious organizations. By Gallup survey estimates, church membership was 73 per cent in 1937 and 68 per cent in 1984. A high of 76 per cent was reached in 1947 and the low was 67 per cent in 1982.

3 *Church attendance* has fluctuated in some religious sectors, but the overall picture of church attendance is amazingly stable. Essentially the same proportion reported attending church in 1984 as was the case in 1939. After the revival of the 1950s, reported church attendance dropped back to the range of 40 per cent and has remained at that level since 1972.

4 Some differences in *personal devotion* can be noted, but the bigger picture is again one of stability. In 1985 almost as many people reported that they prayed (87 per cent) as in 1948 (90 per cent). Whereas fewer people reported frequent prayer (twice a day or more), the proportion who read the Bible at least daily was half again as great in 1984 as in 1942. And religious knowledge grew significantly between 1954 and 1982: this during a period when most types of cognitive skills seemed to be declining.

5 Contributions to charitable or voluntary organizations are higher in the United States than any other country in the world. And there is but scant evidence that either proportional or per capita giving to religion has declined. In 1955, 50 per cent of all charitable contributions were given to religious organizations. That proportion slipped to 44 per cent in 1975, but has since climbed back to 46.5 per cent. On a per capita basis, *in constant dollars, Americans gave almost 20 per cent more to religious organizations in 1982 than they did in 1962.*

During the period for which we have data, some dramatic shifts in people's perceptions about religion have occurred. For example, the proportion believing that the influence of religion was increasing in society peaked at 69 per cent in 1957 and then plunged to only 14 per cent in 1970. Since that date, the figure has risen steadily to 48 per cent in 1985. Also, people are less likely to report today that religion is 'very important' than in the revival period of the 1950s. But after a significant plunge following the revival period, these figures now have stabilized, even risen slightly.

Other short-term trends may be interpreted as supportive of the secularization hypothesis. Space permitting, I could comment on each. In the absence of that opportunity, I would offer two general conclusions. First, there is abundant evidence to support the conclusion that *what* people believe and *how* they practise religion is a dynamic, ever-changing process. For example, over the past twenty years we have experienced a significant decline in the proportion of Americans who believe that the Bible is the actual word of God and is to be taken literally, word for word. But, as we have seen, rejecting biblical literalism does not mean that people cease to believe. Similarly, weekly attendance at mass has fallen dramatically for Roman Catholics in the quarter of a century since the Second Vatican Council. But this is not *prima facie* evidence that people are ceasing to be Catholic or that they are 'less religious' because they don't go to mass every week.

Second, it is clear that some indicators are affected by the broader cultural milieu. Demerath noted this possibility in his essay on religious statistics: 'There may be a self-fulfilling prophecy crescendoing as the phrase "religious revival" is trumpeted from steeple to steeple. The tendency to conform artificially to this newly religious image in a poll response may be a factor in documenting the image itself.'[6] It should be equally obvious that downside trends may be triggered by media-pronounced prophecies of religious demise. The Gallup question on the perception of the importance of religion seems to support the self-fulfilling prophecy generalization.

Claims about trends in religions are not likely to be sustained and reinforced for long in the face of contrary evidence, but we can hypothesize that any trend is likely to get some self-fulfilling action from mass public perceptions. But the general conclusion this suggests is that we can expect indicators of religious behaviour to continue to fluctuate.

To summarize this all too brief assessment of trends in religious behaviour, I would say that the balance of data supports the proposition that religion is changing within a context of broad stability. There is a general absence of indicators which would support the long-term secularization hypothesis. Religion is dead in the minds, hearts and feet of large sectors of American society. But just as certainly, religion is alive for other broad sectors. There is no evidence to support a decisive shift either towards or away from religion.

NEW RELIGIOUS MOVEMENTS

A third factor which has served to challenge the secularization thesis has been the emergence of new religious movements. The countercultural movement of the late 1960s involved a wholesale rejection of our materialistic world and its concomitant secularized ethos. The search for a 'new consciousness' took many bizarre turns, but there was a profound religious quality to the search for new meaning.

This happened on the heels of a radically different perception of what was happening in America. In the early 1960s, a small group of theologians proclaimed the 'death of God', and their proclamation captured substantial national media attention. Arguing that man is by anthropological nature a religious animal, Harvey Wheeler concluded that 'a death-of-God era is also a god-building era'.[7] And certainly the late 1960s and early 1970s were an era of frantic 'god-building.'

The growth of new religions was stimulated in part by Lyndon Johnson's repeal of the Oriental Exclusion Acts in 1965. The disorientated but searching counterculture became a missions field for gurus of Eastern religions. Their seeds multiplied, as did the seeds of many new sectarian visions of the Christian faith and the indigenously manufactured religions and quasi-religions.

[By the mid-1980s] many of the more prominent new religions [had] collapsed. Most of the others [were] struggling. At the moment it does not seem likely that any of the new religions of the 1960s and 1970s will experience the kind of sustained growth that has characterized the Mormons, the most successful of several surviving new religious movements of the nineteenth century.

In the final analysis, the significance of the new religious movements of the 1960s may be not so much their contributions to religious pluralism in America as the fact that their presence stimulated a tremendous volume of scholarly inquiry. And the result of those enquiries has been an enrichment of our understanding of the process of sect and cult formation and dissolution.

Many scholars have contributed to this literature. The single most important development to emerge out of these studies has been the comparative study of new religions over time and across cultures....

I offer here four important generalizations that are emerging from the research on new religious movements:

1 Historical investigations have led us to understand much more clearly that sectarian fissures (splintering from established traditions) and cults (newly created or imported) have been forming for the whole of human history.
2 Furthermore, the parallelisms in the patterns and process of sect and cult formation appear to be highly similar over a very long period of time.
3 'Religious schisms are inevitable.' In a free market-place, new religious organizations will spring abundantly from established traditions. Even under conditions of an established state church and the suppression of unsanctioned religions, new groups spring forth.
4 Cults (new inventions or exports from another culture) flourish where traditional established religions are weakest.

The last proposition is less well documented with cross-cultural evidence. Nevertheless, the comparative ecological research of Stark and Bainbridge for the US during the nineteenth and twentieth centuries, with more limited data for Canada and several European nations, provides some provocative conclusions. 'Secularization, even in the scientific age,' they argue, 'is a self-limiting process.'[8]

Referring to the West Coast region as the 'unchurched belt' in America, Stark and Bainbridge demonstrate that this pattern has persisted for a century. Cults, thus, do not automatically 'fill the void' in areas that have experienced a high degree of secularization. But cult activity is greatest in those areas with the lowest levels of 'established' religious activity. With but a slight twist on Egyptian mythology, the phoenix may be consumed by the fires of secularization, but it is sure to rise again from its own ashes.

The study of new religious movements introduces a certain irony to the view that our heritage from the founding generations provides ample evidence that religion will eventually fade from our collective consciousness. Durkheim, perhaps more than any other founding scholar, took us into the abyss which follows discovery that society itself is the object of collective worship. How can we believe once we have discovered we are the creators of the gods?

In the context of scepticism, if not open antagonism toward religion, perhaps we sociologists have parted from our guide before the journey was finished, presuming we had learned all there was to learn. 'There is something eternal in religion,' concluded Durkheim, 'which is destined to survive all the particular symbols in which religious thought has successively enveloped itself.'[9]

RELIGION AND POLITICAL AUTHORITY IN GLOBAL PERSPECTIVE

One way that secularization theorists have accounted for the persistence of religion in the midst of the secular is with the notion of *privatization*. Within [Thomas] Kuhn's conception of 'normal science', this concept may be viewed as a 'mopping-up' operation; the filling in of details and accounting for anomalies.

According to this reformulation, religion becomes a personal matter in the modern world, anchored in individual consciousness, rather than a cosmic force. Religion may be capable of maintaining its traditional function as a mechanism of social control, at least in some sectors of human societies. But certainly religion is not to be taken seriously as an earth-moving force.

This assignment of religion to the private sphere is rather like having your cake and eating it too. One can hold steadfastly to the Enlightenment image of the demise of religion and still account for its embarrassing persistence. It is not necessary to establish a timetable for the disappearance of religion. In due course it will happen. And in the meantime, its only significant effects are in the private sphere.

The anomalies have been ignored for a long time. Notwithstanding the omnipresence of religious leadership during the civil rights movement of the 1960s, we tended not to think of this as a religious movement. The periodic outbursts of violence in Northern Ireland have something to do with historical conflict between Protestants and Catholics. The present conflict involves only a small minority of fanatics. We got over our differences earlier this century, and surely they will too.

Jews have been fighting Arabs since the establishment of the state of Israel, but that's a struggle over turf. After all, the Zionist leaders of Israel were highly secularized. What do their quarrels with their neighbours have to do with religion? Mohandas Gandhi was a religious leader, of sorts, but the nation he led in revolt against colonialism was hardly a modern secular state. And besides, with Hindus and Muslims and Sikhs all fighting one another, it didn't make much sense. And if one thought about it at all, it was much easier to see India's ongoing unrest grounded in the great ethnic diversity of the Asian subcontinent. One thing is for certain, the Europeans know how to have a good brouhaha without bringing religion in. Remember World War II?

Examples of such myopic analysis could go on and on. Because of our assumptions about secularization, we have systematically engaged in a massive wholesale dismissal of the religious factor when considering socio-political events in the modern world.

In 1979 and 1980, the United Stated encountered two nearly simultaneous developments which radically altered our consciousness about religion. In 1979, fanatical Muslims overthrew the Shah of Iran, a man and government believed to symbolize the modernization of the Middle East. That same year, Jerry Falwell heeded the call of secular right-wing leaders and formed the Moral Majority. In 1980 a small band of Ayatollah Khomeini's followers held hostage more than 400 Americans from the diplomatic and military corps. And Falwell held captive the attention of the mass media with claims that his organization registered millions of conservative voters.

Since these developments at the turn of the decade, our consciousness has been bombarded almost continuously with evidence of religious entanglement in the political. The Roman Catholic Church [played a central role] in the overthrow of the corrupt regimes of Ferdinand Marcos in the Philippines and Jean-Claude Duvalier in Haiti. Pope John Paul II is a tormented man trying to curb ecclesiastical involvement in the praxis of liberation theology in Nicaragua and Brazil while tacitly encouraging political engagement in Poland and the Philippines.

The remarkable Kairos Document signed by more than 150 South African clergymen confesses prior timidity even as it charts a bold course of engagement in the political crisis of that nation. Like Martin Luther King, Jr, Nobel Peace Prize winner Bishop Desmond Tutu is but a symbol of courageous religious leadership.

Not all of the religion and politics stories of the 1980s involve courageous voices speaking out for peace and justice. And in many tension spots, distinguishing the heroes from the villains is very much an ideological issue. In Lebanon, Egypt, Iran and Iraq, we mostly agree that the Muslim extremists are villains. But when the same Islamic zealotry is unleashed against Soviet invaders in Afghanistan, we see them as heroes and seek to minimize the similarities with their Middle East brothers. Turning to Central America, if you are a 'liberal', you're likely to admire the courage of the priest brothers Ernesto and Fernando Cardenal. If you are a 'conservative', they are traitors to their church and dupes of the Sandanista regime.

In many tension-ridden areas there is the tendency to reduce religious conflict to 'just ethnic hostilities', and there are no heroes at all. Sikhs assassinating Hindu leaders, Hindus doing battle with Muslims, Buddhists oppressing Tamils and Tamils striking back with guerrilla warfare tactics are all part of a complex mosaic of ethnic conflict.

Such simplistic explaining by labelling reduces our need to come to grips with one of the most important developments of the second half of the twentieth century. But the extensiveness of political entanglement around the globe is simply too great to be ignored. Each episode cries out for explanation, not as an isolated event, but as part of a global phenomenon. The present data base for comparative analysis consists mostly of case-studies. We do not yet have a very good conceptual model, much less a theory, to account for the tumultuous entanglement of religion in politics all around the globe. The one thing that is clear is that the classical imagery of secular-ization theory is not very helpful.

READING 60

Emmanuel Sivan

Radical Islam

Islamic revival – while activist and militant – is essentially defensive; a sort of holding operation against modernity. And though it has no doubt a sharp political edge, it is primarily a cultural phenomenon. Its very strength proceeds from this alliance of political and cultural protest.

The refrain of all fundamentalist litanies is 'Islam is isolated from life.' This is nowhere more evident, in their eyes, than in the mass media. Television comes in for most of the blame because it brings the modernist message in the most effective, audio-visual form into the very bastion of Islam – family and home. But the same holds true for radio and for tape cassettes, be they specially produced or recordings of radio programmes. The electronic media carry out a 'destructive campaign' that overwhelms the efforts of religious militants by 'broadcasting indecent and vulgar songs, belly-dancing, melodramas on women kidnapped in order to serve in the palaces of rulers, and similar trash'.[1] Pop music, Arab style, comes in for more criticism than explicitly sexual plays (or films), perhaps because of its popularity. According to a field study quoted by _al-Da'wa_, preference for variety programmes was expressed by 60 per cent of Egyptian viewers and listeners (as against 54 per cent for Koran reading). They are all the more dangerous for being indigenous and at the same time impregnated with 'the Western poison'. A content analysis of the lyrics propagated by popu-lar singers like Umm Kulthum. Muhammad 'Abd al-Wahhab and 'Abd al-Halim Hafiz comes up with 'terms and ideas diametrically opposed to Arab and Islamic concepts, encouraging loose morality and immediate satisfaction, placing love and life and its pleasures over everything else, totally oblivious of religious belief, and of punishment and reward in the Hereafter'.

Sociological surveys revealed indeed that love songs take up to 37.8 per cent of Egyptian broadcasting time compared with 9 per cent for religious programmes. Worship of TV, film and singing stars – generated by the media itself – only tends to make things worse, as it creates idols that subsume the superficial character of this popular culture, lionized for achievements based on image and not on substance. Popular mourning over the death of 'Abd al-Halim Hafiz, given an aura of respectability by the participation of prominent intellectuals and pundits, made one commentator scoff: 'All the martyrs of Sinai and Golan . . . did not get the same amount of solicitude from the media. . . . To hear their eulogies, one could think that insipidity is heroism, vulgarity is an uplifting experience, and singing is tantamount to glorious struggle. The populace learned that their problems, grief, and suffering are of no significance, compared with the death of that entertainer.' TV 'personalities' build up a trivialized hero-worship around themselves, enabling them to spread consumerism all the more efficiently by incorporating commercial publicity into their talk shows. Even worse is professional sport, which brings the idolatry of pagan-inspired body worship to a peak.

Not that the sexually explicit products of popular culture are made light of; it is only that as Islamic criticism of modernity became more sophisticated, it learned that the indirect approach is sometimes more dangerous, precisely for being implicit. But articles on the permissive morality of TV dramas and films (let alone underground pornographic films, whether imported or produced locally) are legion. Here Egypt is no doubt the most prolific centre of production in the Arab world, although Lebanese writers find much to complain of about Beirut. This is less true of pulp novels and popular magazines – whether of the implicitly or explicitly sexual variety – but their availability to the public, even in the proximity of mosques, is often lamented. Buttressed by other forms of popular culture such as beauty contests, the result is inevitable: 'the weakening of family bonds battered by the unleashing of carnal appetites'. 'Rare are the films and plays in which one cannot watch at least one of the following: seminude dancing, wine cups filled, easy-to-learn tricks to woo young females, criticism of the conservative older generation for blocking marriage between lovers, description of the beloved merely in terms of sex appeal, justification of the adultery of a young woman given in marriage to an old man or that of an older woman married to one she does not love.'

Other forms of 'recreation' – that hated term which signifies, for the fundamentalists, an attempt to divert the mind from the moral values – have their share in this [discussion]. Foremost is the nightclub industry, which prospered as a result of the growing tourism from puritanical oil states (encouraged by the demise of Beirut). This is a case where moral protest is linked with an economic one: criticism of an unbridled 'open-door policy' bent on maximization of foreign-currency income by every means. The 'commerce in the human body', bordering on, or even incorporating, high-class prostitution, is rendered all the more obnoxious to the True Believers, as alcoholic beverages can be sold in the same tourist precincts. This 'cancerous growth' is bound to spread to the indigenous society as well as through those natives who are associated with the tourist trade or with foreigners.

Religion does figure in the Syrian and Egyptian mass media, but significantly enough, it is a religion made of externals, of gestures shorn of values: prayer, fast, pilgrimage. This is particularly evident in the context and manner of their presentation. The call for the daily prayer comes over television and radio in the middle of entertainment programmes (whether belly-dancing or a love scene) with no introductory and concluding presentation designed to separate the holy from the profane. Koran readings are not only much shorter than they used to be, but are also not reverently separated from the preceding (and following) pop songs; they are often recorded 'live' in mosques, making them part of show business, complete with the non-aesthetic cries and wailings of ignorant men in attendance. During the month of Ramadan, while more attention is given to religious programmes, their impact is neutralized by quiz and prize shows that foster 'material obsessions', and by belly-dancing and erotic films. Small wonder that the few, supposedly serious, religious talk shows deal with technicalities of devotional acts and seldom with the application of Islam in daily life. . . .

A much more systematic introduction of modern culture is detected in Syrian and Egyptian education. Concerning school curricula, the radicals voice the all-too-expected complaint that the teaching of science, though not openly critical of religion, is subverting Islam quite efficiently, precisely by being oblivious to it. Science offers an alternative explanatory model, supposedly value-free and objective; it does not even deign to try to reconcile this model (as, they claim, could be done) with Islam. The implication is, of course, that by transfer through training, the same approach will be applied to other spheres. In like vein, the radicals attack the teaching of philosophy for giving too much place to Western thinkers and above all for having Islamic philosophy represented by rationalistic, Greek-style medieval philosophers such as the Mu'tazila school, Avicenna and Averroes, branded as deviationists in their own times. This is deemed a victory for Orientalism and its disciples, who had tried to trace back a sort of proto-modernist strand in Islam. Traditional philosophy of the Ash'ari and Ghazzali variety is barely taught.

Somewhat less expected is the critique of Arab language and literature studies. Arabic is, after all, the sacred language of Islam, heavily permeated with its terminology, history and culture. Yet the language in question is the classical literary one. Schools and universities do not do enough to promote it, with the result that most university graduates cannot speak it properly and prefer the colloquial or the 'middle language' (*wusta*), an amalgam of colloquial dialects, modern vocabulary and syntax, and a debased classical (*fusha*) backdrop. Quite often, it is reported, dissertation defence – even in departments of Arabic – is held in the colloquial ('*amiyya*) medium for lack of ability to converse formally in *fusha*. The schools, of course, did not unleash this danger, for the mass media tend toward a growing use of the '*amiyya* and *wusta*, as do political leaders in assemblies. It is not unusual for an imam in his Friday sermon to resort to the colloquial whenever at a loss for *fusha* terms and structures. Modern literature – increasingly taught in the schools – is moving in the same direction, towards a language not far from that of journalism. This so-called contemporary (*mu'asira*) language is rapidly losing historical – that is, Islamic – connotations.

As for the content of literary studies, it is quite in tune with ambient popular culture. Not only are junior high school students taught an ode to Umm Kulthum, 'making singing appear a sublime value', but modern poetry anthologies include works in praise of physical culture 'where struggle is equated with playing football and happiness with healthy bodies'. Other poems praise the beauty of nature in the pagan manner of pop songs, with no mention of any values other than self-gratification. Prose is skewed by a heavy dose of political speeches of the president-of-the-day, part of the ritual of state worship. No attempt is made to produce separate texts for boys and girls to foster the values that suit each sex (courage and endurance, family orientation and chastity, and so on); schools thus enhance the growing promiscuity typical of mass culture. (The education system, it is lamented, is almost completely integrated at the elementary and university levels, and is becoming increasingly so at junior and senior high school levels.) Religious texts tend to be relegated to 'religious culture' classes, and at the university level there are even cases where Syrian and Egyptian students of Arabic are no longer required to take courses in [the] Koran and Sunna.

Teaching 'religious culture' cannot help matters. Treating it as a separate topic legitimizes the separation between religion and daily life, which is much more bothersome for the Muslim radicals than the more formal separation between religion and state, a danger they do not consider imminent. Moreover, religious culture is a 'parasitic teaching matter': its time allocation is small; its prestige low because it is not judged by schools to be a criterion of scholarly aptitude; the calibre of teachers is low (mostly Arab-language teachers who treat it in an offhand manner); the curriculum is dull, designed to have students memorize a few sacred texts and learn some acts of devotion rather than inculcate values. The 'religious vacuum' so many youth suffer from – and which was the most popular topic in a youth essay contest organized recently by the Egyptian Muslim Brethren – is certainly not being filled by what is judged a perfunctory endeavour. Not that it would have been an easy task, for as one teacher remarked to an investigative reporter:

> What if I teach that taking interest is forbidden by the Shari'a when our whole economic structure, consecrated by law, is based on it? What if I teach Koranic verses on the virtues of modest dress when my students see décolleté and miniskirts in public places? And what about teaching Islamic doctrine that the rich are morally and legally bound to help the poor when inequity in income distribution is steadily growing?[2]

Andrew Brown

And the Word was All Male

Pope John Paul II has once more addressed his 'Venerable Brothers in the episcopate' on the infinitely troublesome subject of women. In a letter to bishops published [in 1966], he reiterated the Roman Catholic Church's ban on the ordination of women to the priesthood. 'Wherefore, in order that all doubt may be removed regarding a matter of great importance . . . in virtue of my ministry of confirming the brethren, I declare that the Church has no authority to confer priestly ordination on women and that this judgement is to be definitively held by all the Church's faithful.'

This is about as authoritative as a pope can get without claiming infallibility. The curious phrase 'confirming the brethren' is a reference to Luke 22: 32, where Jesus tells Peter that he has prayed that his faith may not fail; and that he in turn is to strengthen the faith of his brothers. Since the root of the papacy's power is the claim that the pope today is the linear successor of Peter, the use of this phrase entails a claim that John Paul II is faithfully transmitting the will of Jesus in this matter.

'The question is one of discerning the mind of the Lord. In his treatment of women, Our Lord emphasised their dignity without conforming to the prevailing customs of the time, yet he still did not choose them as apostles', explained Monsignor Philip Carroll, the General Secretary to the Bishops' Conference of England and Wales.

This is the letter that some Catholic feminists have been dreading, since they think it makes it a great deal more difficult for any subsequent pope to change his mind on the issue. Others are more upbeat. One, who did not want to be named, said: 'The more feminist people are, the less distressed they are, because it's so ridiculous; there's nothing new.'

In fact, the latest papal letter ties in with the signals that have been coming from the Catholic church in recent years. The English translation of the new catechism, which has just been published, was delayed for nearly two years by the successful attempts of American anti-feminists and their allies in the Vatican to remove 'inclusive' language from it. The inclusive language in the original draft was never about God, but about men and women, or 'men' as the Vatican calls them. Even this was too much of a concession for the Vatican, which found an elderly archbishop in Tasmania to rewrite the whole thing without reference to modern usage. The rewriting reaches an exquisite climax on page 500, where the devout reader learns that 'everyone, man and woman, should acknowledge and accept his sexual identity'.

The pattern is one of almost pathological hostility to feminism. It was especially clear in reactions to the one concession the Vatican has made in recent years to any sort of feminist sentiment: the decision . . . that women could serve as altar girls. This only regularized what had been the practice in many dioceses, yet it was greeted with hysterical outrage by the anti-feminist political right in America.

Any weakening of the laws that exclude women from the priestly domain of the altar threaten, it seems, all order in the church.

Otherwise, the line has been clear ever since *Humanae Vitae*, the encyclical banning artificial birth control that was produced in 1968. *Humanae Vitae*, too, was only reaffirming the teaching of the church throughout previous ages. It marked a watershed, though, for two reasons: first, it followed a really intense period of consultation and research by a specially appointed commission, whose members had decided, rather to their own surprise, in favour of contraception within marriage, before the pope overruled them; second, after he had overruled them, most Catholics in the developed world carried on using contraception exactly as if nothing had happened.

Humanae Vitae has had almost no effect on the birth-rate in countries where Catholics have access to some form of contraception. But it has had a shattering effect on papal authority.

It has vastly weakened the church's ability to resist abortion by tangling two very different issues together. For many intelligent self-reliant women who grew up as Catholics, it was simply too much to be told the meaning of sex by celibate old men. They have left the church, concluding that since it is obviously wrong about this, it must be wrong about everything else. Similarly, the choice of bishops has been drastically diminished, since any suspicion that a man doubts the teaching is a bar to promotion in the church.

However strange this attitude of passionate resistance to plain justice and common sense may seem, it is not new. There is almost an exact parallel in the attitude that the Catholic Church adopted in the last century. Then, the object of its scorn and hatred was democracy rather than feminism.

For most of the latter half of the past century and the first half of this, successive popes did all they could to stamp out the idea that discussion had any place in the discovery of truth. Free Thought, in the sense of atheism, was confused with free thought in the sense of unsupervised, or grown-up thought (a conclusion that suited the atheists as much as anyone else).

In 1861 Pope Pius IX solemnly denounced the theory that a pope 'ought to reconcile and adjust himself with progress, liberalism and modern civilisation'. Papal infallibility was defined (infallibly) in 1870. The papacy gloried in being chief among the forces of reaction. In 1961, however, at the Second Vatican Council, all this came tumbling down, or seemed to. The church had been full of progressives all along, we discovered; and only a tiny minority under Archbishop Lefebvre left in protest against the great renewal.

Humanae Vitae represents the hinge at which the Vatican, without perhaps even realizing it, stopped struggling against democracy, and started to struggle against feminism instead. There are, of course, anti-democratic elements involved in the struggle against artificial contraception. But it is primarily a struggle against feminism; against the dignity and moral sense of women. The same attitude lies behind the pope's repeated defence of a celibate priesthood.

If this parallel is correct, then it should be most heartening for women who want their granddaughters to have the option of becoming priests. After all, the resistance to democracy did crumble when it was safe for the church to drop its guard: no one, it could be argued, has done more to spread democracy than the present pope, who played such a large part in the fall of Communism. In 2094, perhaps, onlookers may be arguing that no one has done more for women's rights than the pope. But not before.

READING 62

Serge Moscovici

Durkheim on the Origins of Religion

What better way to proceed [in analysing religion] than by turning our attention to the most simple religion, the most archaic and, in this sense, the most original one that we believe we know of? In it we hope to find the fundamental, common components that are at the basis of the great religions of more recent creation. Is this not what physicists do when they search for the elementary particles of matter, or naturalists when they are exploring the most primitive forms of life, and even cosmologists when they scrutinize the surface of the planets in order to decipher the evolution of the earth? In the same way we hope to perceive, greatly refined, the relationship between sacred beliefs and rituals on the one hand, and societies on the other. Thus Durkheim arrived at the idea that totemism embodies the seeds of every religion. The other religions, Christianity and

Buddhism for example, have then developed them, bringing them to fruition. By examining these seeds very minutely under the microscope of the mind we can arrive at general conclusions. He formulated this idea in the following terms:

> Then we are not going to study a very archaic religion simply for the pleasure of telling its peculiarities and its singularities. If we have taken it as the subject of our research, it is because it has seemed to us better adapted than any other to lead to an understanding of the religious nature of man, that is to say, to show us an essential and permanent aspect of humanity.[1]

A page or two later he continued: 'Thus, in the end, there are no religions that are untrue. All are true in their own way; all respond, although in different ways, to the actual conditions of human existence . . . All are equally religions, just as all living creatures are equally alive, from the humblest amoeba to man himself.'[2]

No one will readily concede that such an intellectual leap can be made. Hence the interest lies in attempting to do so. What is there apparently more simple than an Australian tribe? It is a kinship group not formed on the basis of consanguinity. The group occupies more or less permanently an area of land, gives itself over to hunting and gathering, acknowledges one chief and employs its own dialect. It might be conceived of as an atom or a socially isolated entity, if it did not maintain a multiplicity of neighbourhood relationships and exchanges with other similar clans. Each of these identifies itself by the name of its totem, to which it pays respect. The individuals that make up the clan consider they are united through this totem. It serves them as an emblem or coat of arms in the same way as do for us the tricolour or the Gallic cockerel. The connection is immediately discernible. Values and emotions always tend to be awakened by an object. If this object is not easily accessible another is substituted for it, the sign or symbol of that object. Thus we are moved by the sight of the flag, and we rally round this symbol of our native land, even forgetting that this flag is no more than a substitute and a sign. When we meet together it is the colours of the flag and not the representation of our native land that rise to our highest level of consciousness. For the clan this role is taken by the totem. At one and the same time it is the external and visible form of the god and the symbol of that kind of society. There is an upsurge of fervour and affection towards it that is felt for the clan itself. If it is thus perceived as the representative of the divine and the social, must one not say that the divinity and society are one?

How are totems chosen? The Australian aborigines take as emblems for their clans the most lowly of the creations that surround them, whether animals or plants. Let us make it plain that the totem does not represent a single entity but indeed an animal or vegetable *species*. It is considered to epitomize the distinctive characteristics of the clan and is consequently hedged round with certain rituals and prohibitions. Among other things, care is taken not to harm it or the eat it. Thus the clan expresses its identity by linking itself to a species, such as the kangaroo or the frog, the bamboo or the spinach plant. In reality, representations of these species are venerated more than the creatures or the plants themselves. They are represented as long poles made of wood or stone, often in the shape of shuttles, the *churinga*, some of which are carved with symbolic signs or pierced with holes and utilized as a kind of horn. Ritual practices that recall those observed for the totemic creatures themselves are devoted to them. One may even assert that the clan exercises great vigilance in insisting on this respect for these material images or artefacts. It is as if it were less serious to touch or consume the totem, if the need should arise, than to destroy a duplicate or a substitute for it. No one can equal its power, or can disobey it, whether the material it is made of is real or symbolic.

Considering it more closely, we see that the totem takes on a religious character. Durkheim observed:

> These totemic decorations enable us to see that the totem is not merely a name and an emblem. It is in the course of the religious ceremonies that they are employed; they are a part of the liturgy; so while the totem is a collective label, it also has a religious character. In fact, it is in connection with it that things are classified as sacred or profane. It is the very type of sacred thing.[3]

It is as sacrilegious for the Australian aborigine to attack the totem, to infringe the prohibitions regarding it (to eat it if it is an animal, to pick it if it is a plant) as it is for us to destroy or burn the flag, to smash the emblems of the Republic – Marianne is our totem, just as the kangaroo can be the emblem of the Australian aborigine. The prohibition does not apply to books, which may be torn up or burnt, for they are not sacred things.

Finally, besides the totem itself and the objects that it represents, sacred qualities are attributed to a third category of creatures: the members of the clan. In this way they form a community of the faithful united by a real bond of kinship, as Durkheim made clear:

> Every member of the clan is invested with a sacred character which is not materially inferior to that which we just observed in the animal. This personal sacredness is due to the fact that the man believes that while he is a man in the usual sense of the word, he is also an animal or plant of the totemic species. In fact, he bears its name; this identity of name is therefore supposed to imply an identity of nature.[4]

A human being is therefore sacred not in his own right but through the totem to which he is attached. Hence to infringe prescriptions and religious practices is not only to expose oneself to physical reprisals. It is unerringly to draw censure, to unleash against oneself the vengeance of the gods, which is both harsh and implacable. Whoever would be tempted to do so is held back by the fear of certain punishment.

What is it therefore that is revered and consecrated through the totem? The totem is a principle that orders the whole universe. By analysing the materials at his disposal concerning the Australian tribes and other tribes originating in America, Durkheim established that they did not make the same distinction as we do between the human and the non-human world. For these tribes, the natural elements form a part of society, and the members of the tribe part of nature. On each occasion a terrestrial phenomenon or a heavenly body are assigned to a particular clan. They belong to its domain and have the same totem as the members of the clan. A different terrestrial phenomenon or another heavenly body are allocated to another clan and bear its totem. Thus, for example, the sun and the moon have not the same totem. Accustomed to this procedure, Australian aborigines classify everything surrounding them – things, plants, animals – according to the model in which human beings are grouped in society. Thus they arrive at an overall view of the universe, in which everything fits together and everything is explicable. Do they not even go as far as to derive this universe from some distant ancestor and an event recounted in their myths? Such insights reveal to us that the totemic principle reduces cosmology to a concept, elevates language to an instrument for classification, and attributes an intelligible meaning to reality. We can go still further. By constructing a system on the basis of diverse human and material phenomena totemism has made possible philosophy and science. At least we find in it the beginnings of our logic of relationships and categories, as well as our idea of force. For a long time we were unwilling to see in it any more than a welter of aberrations and exotic superstitions. However, through the descriptions and analyses he made Durkheim transformed what was considered either as 'a collection of curiosities or observations, or as relics of the past'[5] into a coherent picture of beliefs, notions and modes of behaviour. It suffices for the field he studied to be revealed for the first time as a way of life that was fully social and wholly religious. As such, these primitive classifications and archaic notions constituted in his view the first philosophy of nature.

We have stated that the Australian aborigines saw the domain in which religious forces were exercised as the whole of nature. Thus what is sacred does not spring from the totemic object, whether plant or animal. Furthermore, the feelings the sacred inspires are shared both by the members of the clan and the representations that they make of it. Their religious character has its source in an element common to everybody. It confers upon them a spiritual power without the latter losing its peculiar nature. Aboriginal beliefs do not separate this power from the objects (men, animals, plants) in which it is embodied. More advanced societies, in Melanesia, call it *mana*. *Mana* is a diffused energy, anonymous and impersonal, which permeates humans associating together and whose psychological influence is set free and intensified during ritual ceremonies. On it depend also the success or failure of an action. The man who possesses it vanquishes his foes in war, and his herds and cultivated fields thrive. The arrow that hits its target and the canoe that moves along the water are charged with *mana*.

What is present here is the totemic principle within each individual, in some way his soul, which through contact is suffused into the objects he possesses. We should understand that this principle is the clan, is society itself. Imagination personifies it, giving it the visible characteristic of the animal or plant totem. Society is a representation everywhere, in every name, every image, every species that individuals hold in veneration. It has indeed all the attributes needed to awaken in human beings the sense of the divine, 'for to its members it is what a god is to his worshippers'.[6] It enjoys absolute power over those who have learnt to depend on it, and imposes upon them ends that are its own. It can exact sacrifices and at every moment a compliance that life in common makes possible:

Whether it be a conscious personality, such as Zeus or Jahveh, or merely abstract forces such as those in play in totemism, the worshipper, in the one case as in the other, believes himself held to certain manners of acting which are imposed upon him by the nature of the sacred principle with which he feels that he is in communion. Now society also gives us the sensation of a perpetual dependence. Since it has a nature peculiar to itself and different from our individual nature, it pursues ends which are likewise special to it; but, as it cannot attain them except through our intermediacy, it imperiously demands our aid.[7]

Society therefore enjoys the same privileges and exercises the same tyrannical hold over us as do the gods of religions. In other words, the Old Covenant that the Jews had entered into and the New Covenant of the Christians are in reality alliances not with a conscious transcendental personality, but with their immanent, flesh-and-blood community. If the community lacked that moral authority that the sacred confers upon it, it would not arouse in individuals that unanimous obedience. Individuals would not turn to it on every occasion when they felt threatened and abandoned. To conceive of that authority as outside themselves, all-powerful and absolute, requires a vast series of transformations. Since neither material constraint nor external power can succeed in subjugating them to rules of behaviour and thought, a moral attachment and an internal influence are needed, as Durkheim asserted once again:

> Even if society were unable to obtain these concessions and sacrifices from us except by a material constraint, it might awaken in us only the idea of a physical force to which we must give way of necessity, instead of that of a moral power such as religions adore. But as a matter of fact, the empire which it holds over consciences is due much less to the physical supremacy of which it has the privilege than to the moral authority with which it is invested. If we yield to its orders, it is not merely because it is strong enough to triumph over our resistance; it is primarily because it is the object of a venerable respect.[8]

It is in this way that religion justifies itself, and justifies and elevates society in all our eyes. Yet, and I stress this, if it welds together the lives of human beings, it is not because it is a set of beliefs; on the contrary, it is because of our inner sense of belonging and participation in the collectivity. It ensures for its members an upsurge of life. It exalts the ardour and enthusiasm which all of us need in order to carry on our tasks. The believer not only knows things of which the unbeliever is ignorant, but can also accomplish more. We feel ourselves surrounded by superior forces that hold sway over us and sustain us, and we share in their superiority. We think ourselves capable of overcoming the difficulties of existence, of imposing our will upon the world, forcing it to satisfy our desires: 'The trials of existence find within [a man] more strength to resist: he is capable of greater things and demonstrates this by his behaviour. It is this dynamic influence generated by religion that explains his ability to endure.[9] And it is through it that society transmits to the individuals of which it is made up a share of its all-powerfulness and personality. A part of its aura shines through each one of them.

I do not know whether it is easy to experience such an exceptional feeling and whether it has the effects that are ascribed to it. Nevertheless let us follow the logic of the hypothesis. You will note that totemism as conceived by

Durkheim is, recalling one of Bergson's ideas, a religion placed at the service of the group for its own preservation. Through its mediation the group ensures its unity and remains present in the consciousness of its members. At the same time it marks out the boundaries within which they must live. Now, we should note carefully that the totem that establishes a kinship between the members of a clan sets them apart from the rest of humanity. It is the sign of the collective personality, which identifies all those who share in it in any way whatsoever – individuals, animals, plants – and through this all others are excluded. These can be abhorred and despised, since they do not possess the same inheritance of beliefs and gods. Thus the sacred puts people in touch with one another, bringing them together, on condition of prohibiting all contact, of separating and opposing. Thus Raymond Aron rightly concludes: 'Hence, if a religious cult is aimed at societies, there exist only national tribal religions. In that case the essence of religion might be to inspire in human beings a fanatical attachment to partial groupings and to dedicate the attachment of each individual to a collectivity and, at the same time, to manifest his hostility to other groupings.[10]

Thus no religion is one of love if it is not one of hatred, unless it is one of a kind completely different from those occurring throughout history. These are religions whose vocation is the preservation of society, conferring upon it extraordinary power over individuals. Totemism might no longer be the simple form, appearing at the dawn of humanity, of all the sacred beliefs and practices that have emerged since then. It is certain that nothing justifies our deciding in favour of continuity or discontinuity in this matter. Bergson tended to favour a discontinuity. He refused to grant totemism the privilege of enshrining, so to speak, the genetic code of revealed religions, whether Islam or Christianity. This choice has no longer for us the importance it once possessed.

Durkheim's hypothesis shocks in some respects. It assumes that all religions are sacred as soon as social conditions correspond to them. It abolishes the distinction between true religions and those in which some see only peculiar beliefs and superstitions. Moreover, it supposes a unity in religious facts and a determining role throughout history. In order to believe in the reality of a group and its goals, one must first believe in the power of its illusion, and of the emblem or symbol that it represents. A society that disdains it or gets rid of it grows weaker, crumbling away and losing its authority over its members. No phenomenon has appeared during the course of history that has not created sacred things and sought at all costs to impose them on societies. In spite of its caveats and its hostility towards religious sects the French revolution was obliged to set up the cult of the Supreme Being and of the goddess of Reason. Men imbued with the philosophy of the Enlightenment constructed altars, invented symbols and proclaimed festivities in honour of these new deities. The difficulty is that natural selection is at work for the gods as it is for mortals – and these gods scarcely survived the events that gave them birth.

The hypothesis shocks yet again because it asserts that we render divine what most religions hold to be sacrilege. If, by adoring sacred creatures, human beings have done no more than worship their own society transfigured and personified, this means that they have been either idolaters or impious. Moreover, it is not enough to possess the faith: you must possess it in common with others, within the community. According to Durkheim, the individual on his own could not believe in or respect a god. He could certainly pray to it, kneel to it, and humble himself before it. But such a situation removes the constraint imposed by the sacred. To illustrate this, if we say that today we have become less religious and attend churches and chapels less frequently, it is not because we have become unbelievers, and have been enlightened by modern science and civilization. On the contrary, it is because modern science and civilization have isolated us, making us solitary and individualistic, that we have become unbelievers. The terms Durkheim employed could not be more categorical:

> We can say of it what we just said of the divinity: it is real only insofar as it has a place in human consciousness, and this place is whatever one may give it. We now see the real reason why the gods cannot do without their worshippers any more than these can do without their gods; it is because society, of which the gods are only a symbolic expression cannot do without individuals any more than these can do without society.[11]

Part XIV

Social Change and Global Crises

Social change occurs as a result of many factors. Some sorts of social change are actively and consciously brought about – for example, through the activities of social movements. Many changes, however, are unintended and unanticipated. Such is the case, for instance, with most political revolutions. Revolutions involve the active engagement of political groups or movements, but usually the sweep of events outdistances anything they originally proposed or sought.

Modern industrial society is a revolutionary society in several aspects (see Reading 1). It is associated, first of all, with political revolution, beginning with the American revolution of 1776 and the French revolution of 1789. It is also associated with industrial and technological revolution. The industrial revolution – the widespread transfer from agricultural to industrial production – was essential to the early development of modern society. Thereafter, revolution in technology has been more or less continuous, from the early days of the invention of steam and electricity through to the current 'information revolution'.

The selection by Michael Kimmel focuses specifically upon political revolution (reading 63). It is not easy to define what should count as a revolution. Revolutions are usually considered to involve the activities of a mass movement which succeeds in overthrowing an established government by force. However, it is not easy to separate revolution, defined in this way, from a *coup d'état*, which also involves a forcible seizure of power. The 1989 revolutions in Eastern Europe mostly did not involve the use of force, nor was there in any of these instances an organized revolutionary movement.

None the less, in terms of the definition which Kimmel arrives at – that revolutions are 'attempts by subordinate groups to transform the social foundations of political power' – the 1989 transformations in Eastern Europe would be instances of genuinely revolutionary activity.

The second item in this part provides a direct discussion of the recent changes in Eastern Europe (Reading 64). Deirdre Boden acknowledges that these events in some ways resembled other patterns of revolutionary change, but she insists that they also had new and unusual characteristics. The course of their development, she proposes, has to be understood in terms of the influence of the mass media. (The reader might at this point like to refer back to part VI, in which general aspects of modern mass communications are discussed.)

Boden points out that the changes of 1989 were more intensively analysed and reported in the media than any comparable set of events hitherto. In the age of satellite communications, images from one context are rapidly transmitted to another, setting up broad waves of mutual influence. We meet yet again here the theme of globalization: according to Boden, the changes of 1989 were triggered and shaped by mediated interactions. The global reporting of events provided models for challenges to pre-existing political orders that would otherwise have seemed unrealizable.

The third selection in this part, Reading 65 by Johan Galtung, examines a social movement which is not revolutionary in terms of the above definition, but which certainly has radical objectives. The ideals of the Green movement, Galtung points out, cross-cut orthodox political mechanisms. Most Western countries now have 'Green parties' but their aims and objectives can hardly be confined to the normal limits of the political arena. In general terms, the 'Green movement' actually consists of a diverse, and to some extent internally heterogeneous, collection of parties, groups and associations. None the less, there are clear similarities in the aims and ambitions of different sectors of the Green movement. In this reading Galtung offers an overall portrayal of some of these common characteristics, noting how far-reaching are the social changes they imply.

The final selections in this part all concentrate upon global risks and insecurities. Many of the unintended consequences brought about by industrial and technological development are potentially disturbing or disastrous for the future of life on the earth. In Reading 66, Tom Horlick-Jones discusses new aspects of risk created by the interdependent nature of a highly advanced technological society. The new 'megacities' – cities with populations above 8 million – present many new hazards. For instance, the release of nerve gas by terrorists in the Tokyo underground in 1994 put many thousands of people at risk. Natural hazards, like earthquakes, can be much more dangerous than before if they happen in areas containing millions of people.

Global warming presents an even more threatening risk scenario (Reading 67). Scientists are not completely agreed over whether or not global warming is occurring and, if it is, how advanced it is likely to become. The majority of scientists studying the issue, however, believe that global warming is a reality and that its consequences in many parts of the world will be disastrous. Among those consequences are a marked increase in the numbers of tropical storms, droughts, floods and hurricanes. The phrase 'global warming' sounds innocuous, even welcoming to those who live in cooler climates; but its environmental implications are extremely serious and little has so far been done to combat the phenomenon.

Reading 68, by John Skow, discusses a further environmental worry – the destruction of millions of acres of fertile farming land. In many areas of the world, farmers are destroying forest land and clearing it for agriculture. A good deal of forest soil, however, is not really suitable for farming and after a few seasons the land is exhausted. The peasants then move on, repeating the process. Some such land could be reclaimed, but a much wider global effort to achieve this needs to be instituted than has been contemplated so far. As the German sociologist Ulrich Beck has observed, we now live in a global 'risk society' in which threats abound that humanity has not had to face before. For hundreds of years, human beings worried about risks coming from nature – risks of natural disasters, plagues or bad harvests. Today, as a result of the impact of human industry and technology upon a natural environment, we have to worry much more about what we have done to nature.

READING 63

Michael S. Kimmel

What is a Revolution?

There's a well-known story about King Louis XVI of France. As the king observed the protests in the streets of Paris in 1789, he turned to his friend, the duc de La Rochefoucauld-Liancourt, and exclaimed, 'My God! It's a revolt!' 'No, Sire', La Rochefoucauld is said to have replied. 'That is a revolution.'

La Rochefoucauld's reply is justly celebrated because it revealed how the king was unable to perceive what was occurring beneath his window, but it also suggests several questions – questions that lie at the heart of social science thinking about revolution. How could La Rochefoucauld know the difference between a revolt and a revolution? What are the distinguishing features of each? If we were standing at the window with the king and his duc, would we have known enough to agree with the duc?

The central questions in the study of revolution have plagued social scientists, philosophers and even kings, for centuries. What are revolutions? Why do they occur? Why do some succeed and others fail? Are revolutions necessarily violent upheavals, or can there be non-violent revolutions? Why do people rebel? What motivates them to risk their lives for such a cause?

Revolutions are of central importance for social scientists not only because they are extreme cases of collective action, but also because revolutions provide a lens through which to view the everyday organization of any society. '[T]he understanding of revolution is an indispensable condition for the fuller knowledge and understanding of society'. Revolutions are also important for us to understand not as social scientists but as citizens: we live in a world in which over half of the inhabitants of the planet live in a country that has undergone a revolution in this century. Our age is a revolutionary age, and in order to be responsible citizens, it is imperative that we begin to understand this phenomenon. Revolutions are events which deeply affect our lives. In fact, 'excepting war, religion, and romantic love, nothing in ordinary human experience has so inflamed the imagination of men, encouraged so many romantic illusions, or broken so completely with the ordinary routine of existence, as has been true of revolution'.[1]

What is more, revolutions make a moral claim on our sensibilities. Revolutions demand that we take sides, that we commit ourselves to a political position. It is difficult to remain neutral during a revolution. At the more international level, revolutionaries often make large claims about what they will accomplish if they are successful in an effort to enlist support from those of us in advanced industrial countries. The support of the major industrial powers, or at least the withdrawal of support for the established regime, has historically been central to the success of revolutions in the twentieth century. So revolutionaries will make moral and political demands of us, even if we do not live in a revolutionary society ourselves. . . .

Revolutions are a central phenomenon to all theories of society, and have proven a popular subject to study. As the editorial foreword to an issue of *Comparative Studies in Society and History* put it in 1980, '[o]utbursts of violence attract social scientists the way volcanic eruptions draw geologists, as specific events inviting measurement that promise to reveal subterranean forces which may in turn reflect still more basic structures'. As a result of this popularity, and the different theoretical postures which social scientists assume, there seem to be as many theories of revolution as there are theorists. . . .

The first question [we must ask] about revolution concerns what we mean by the term. Definitions abound, and there is little consensus about what a revolution is, let alone why it may occur. Let's start with a definition drawn from a non-social-scientific source: the *Oxford English Dictionary* defines revolution as 'A complete overthrow of the established government in any country or state by those who were previously subject to it; a forcible substitution of a new ruler or form of government.' This definition implies that revolutions take place on the political level, involving governments and rulers, and that they must be 'complete' and successful in order to count as revolutions. It also equates the imposition of a new ruler with a revolutionary transformation of society.

Aristotle understood revolutions to be qualitatively different from these simple changes in political leadership, although he agreed that success was a criterion of the term. In *Politics*, Aristotle wrote that there were 'two sorts of changes in government; the one affecting the constitution, where men seek to change from an existing form into something other, the other not affecting the constitution when, without disturbing the form of government, whether oligarchy or monarchy, they try to get the administration into their own hands'.

These two definitions resonate with many of those offered by social scientists. Most definitions, for example, imply that in order to be labelled a revolution, the uprising must be successful. Baecheler defines revolution as a 'protest movement that manages to seize power',[2] and Neumann expands the definition to include a 'sweeping, fundamental change in political organization, social structure, economic property control and the predominant myth of a social order [thereby] indicating a major break in the continuity of development'.[3] Trimberger calls revolution 'an extralegal takeover of the central state apparatus which destroys the economic and political power of the dominant social group of the old regime', which again implies success in the definition.[4]

The last definition also implies the use of violence in a revolution, and many social scientists have placed violence in the centre of their analysis. Thus Friedrich defines revolution as 'the sudden and violent overthrow of an established political order',[5] and Huntington calls it 'a rapid funda-mental and violent domestic change in the dominant values and myths of a society, in its political institutions, social structure, leadership, government activity, and policies'.[6] Skocpol offers perhaps the most comprehensive and succinct structural definition: 'Social revolutions are rapid, basic trans-formations of a society's state and class structure; they are accompanied and in part carried through by class-based revolts from below.'[7] One writer attempts to modify this requirement of violence by arguing that revolution refers to events 'in which physical force (or the convincing threat of it) has actually been used successfully to overthrow a government or regime'.[8]

But is success a *requirement* for a revolution to be called by that name? Such a definition would mean that revolutions that fail be called something else, thus restricting the number of empirical cases to about twenty. This would be unfortunate, because revolutions that fail can provide as many clues to the causes and the process of revolutions as those that succeed.

To posit success of the revolution as a definitional criterion also leads to a serious teleological problem, in which the theorist interprets the origins by their outcomes. During a potential revolution, an 'urban mob' or a mass of 'traditional peasants' may attempt to seize power, and they may think they are making a revolution. Why would social scientists only permit a success-ful attempt to be labelled a revolution? Are not all such efforts revolutions – some that succeed and some that fail? Does the content of the revolutionary effort change after the fact if the rebels are unsuccessful?...

One useful suggestion might be to hold a distinction between revolution-ary situations and revolutionary outcomes. We can of course imagine situ-ations in which a revolution takes place, but the outcome does not yield the type of society envisioned by the revolution, or in which the forces of the old regime are victorious, either by their own strength or by soliciting aid from abroad. But these are revolutions also, and they are far more numer-ous than the successful transformations. To include them in the definition, and to draw contrasts between them and the successful revolutions, will, I believe, prove instructive to students of the phenomenon.

. . . I offer a fairly fluid and simple definition . . . *Revolutions are attempts by subordinate groups to transform the social foundations of political power.* Such efforts require confrontation with power-holders, and must stand a reason-able chance of success to differentiate a revolution from other acts of rebel-lion, such as a social movement or terrorist act. Such a definition is sufficiently broad to include successful and unsuccessful revolutions, to embrace a large number of sequences over various amounts of time, and yet it is specific enough to allow us to distinguish between revolutions and other forms of social change, such as *coups d'état* and rebellions. Although a revolutionary event must stand a reasonable chance of successfully carry-ing out a programme of social transformation, success is not inevitable. Social movements and seemingly isolated acts of rebellion may trigger wider movements and become revolutions themselves.

READING 64

Deirdre Boden

Reinventing the Global Village: Communication and the Revolutions of 1989

The revolutions of 1989 in Eastern Europe have been among the most intensively recorded and extensively observed collective moments in human history. At the heart of the discussion that follows is a concern with the role of communication, in the broadest sense, in the making of revolution. Clearly, there are vast differences between the social events I am characterizing as 'the revolutions of 1989', in terms simultaneously of their concrete historical origins, their immediate conditions and their local political ideologies, as well as the vast differences of language, tradition and culture, to say nothing of the actual outcomes of which we have only a glimmer of insight at this point. For all their important differences, the revolutions of 1989 have shared a common variable: they have been significantly affected by the globalization of information technology and have, in their turn, interactively shaped those media.

I am thus interested, quite specifically, in the role of the mass media and telecommunications in the tumultuous social change to which we [were] all . . . witness . . ., indeed, primarily through those same media. The revolutions of 1989 are like no others in human history in certain highly suggestive ways. The [1980s] have seen a radical break with past history; it is one which, I believe, has gone largely unnoticed not only by academics but by the very social actors engaged in these activities. Not only did no academic or government specialist predict any of the revolutions of 1989, none of the revolutionaries themselves would have predicted their relative achievements at any specific point during those same world-changing activities. Indeed, an interesting motif of 1989 has been the recurrent astonishment of expert and subject alike. One reason, I believe, for this remarkable underestimation of the direction, rate and ultimate totality of social transformation in that year was a lack of appreciation of the now global, instantaneous, simultaneous and total effect of the telecommunications media as a primary agent of social change.

In the classic sociological literature on the subject, revolutions are generally described as involving fundamental changes in ideology and values, as well as in social structures and relations of power. More recently, from a structural perspective, social revolutions have been defined by Skocpol as 'rapid, basic transformations of a society's state and class structure . . . accompanied and in part carried through by class-based revolts from below'.[1] These massive transformations necessarily, according to Skocpol, involve mutually reinforcing changes in both the political and social realms, that is at the level of both the state and its citizens. In the revolutionary rhetoric of Marxism and a variety of related conflict theories, rapid social change depends, on the one hand, on contradictions in the objective structural conditions of a given society and, on the other, on the ability of a particular class or coalitions of classes to mobilize their common interests. Many theories are thus structural in the causes and explanations of revolution, while some are 'actor-oriented' and an emerging few are both. In these and other writings in revolution, sociologists and their founding fathers have had a distinct tendency to characterize such upheavals as occurring from within, from economic conditions, internal class conflict, relative and perceived deprivation within a social system and so forth. They are, by and large, endogenous models of social change.

The revolutions of 1989 are nothing of the kind, in at least one irreversible and unavoidable way. They are global in their inspiration and in their consequences, as well as in their immediacy and intensity. That is to say that they are, to some considerable degree, exogenously triggered as well as being endogenously driven. . . .

In a most cursory way, I shall now trace the essential sequencing of events in Central and Eastern Europe in the autumn of 1989. It is the sequence and sequential timing of these tumultuous moments that I want to examine, in relation to what I take to be a multi-media environment of these chained events. The world is not only wired in some diffuse and general sense. The unfolding properties of human action, in their finest detail, are temporally, serially and, especially, sequentially interconnected in such a way as to significantly change the consequences. In today's wired world, people do indeed make history, and in new ways. This single, seamless world in which we all live is interactive – continuously, simultaneously and reflexively. While speculative, my assumption is that there was, in effect, a chain reaction triggered by the media images of China in April, May and even June, and of the triumph of Solidarity in the June elections. That 'reaction' was the altogether human one of hope, at first faint, finally filling hearts from Berlin to Baku; in the short span of six months, from June to December 1989, the face of Europe was to light up with it. And, every night, Europeans and others tuned in to that ever-brightening world, as images of human action bounced across satellites and fed along telephone lines into once-dim living-rooms and lives. At the same time, shortwave radio services of the BBC World Service, Radio France, Radio Free Europe, and Voice of America also stepped up transmission and, in some cases, wattage and the number of broadcast hours in Eastern European languages. The medium had not so much become the message as the many messages, across many media, had merged to become a seemingly unstoppable single signal of hope.

The hearts and minds of the peoples of Central and Eastern Europe are just that: European. Their cultures belong to the West, to Roman Christianity, to the traditions and values of Old Europe. Indeed, many of the peoples and languages of the region we conveniently call 'Western' Europe have their roots in the depths of what we now call 'Eastern' Europe. For a Hungarian, a Czech or a Pole, 'the word "Europe" does not represent a phenomenon of geography but a spiritual notion synonymous with the West';[2] if not part of the West, Kundera argues, they are driven from their destiny. Thus, the lure of the West in recent revolutions cannot be seen as a simplistic craving for consumer culture or for essentially 'foreign' ideals. If we are to treat the notion of 'hearts and minds' seriously, we need to engage ideology with emotion, trust with risk, hope with despair. Here we are on tricky ground to be sure, both theoretically and empirically, but it is my suggestion that the dynamism and intensity of the revolutions of 1989 find little explanation in conventional notions of structural conditions or constraints. If, too, we are to be genuine in our theoretical interest in the 'return of the actor', in 'action and its environments', and, most generally, in the nature of human agency, we must examine what people actually do at the intersections of history. Here, this pervasive problematic is presented as the meeting of people and information. The hearts and minds of the people of Eastern Europe have been lit up by the kinetic effects of global communications and local conditions.

In important ways, of course, the immediate events in Eastern Europe in late 1989 were shaped initially by Solidarity's revolution in the shipyards of Gdansk in 1980–1, which led to the military government of General Jaruzelski and culminated in the suppression of Solidarity in late 1981. Although crushed, Solidarity caught the attention of the world during those dark months, and Lech Walesa was to become a major figure in the years that followed. While some have argued for primarily structural explanations for the Polish revolution at that time, it is equally clear that the reflexive articulation by individual Poles of their emerging independence critically shaped Polish discourse in the years to follow, as well as Polish–Soviet relations, especially with Gorbachev's arrival on the Soviet scene in 1985. Scholars have also argued that these early events in Poland were greeted with considerable hostility in East Germany and Czechoslovakia. By 1988 and 1989, it was nevertheless against the backdrop of Solidarity's successful struggle and extended international image that the unfolding of events across Eastern Europe took place.

It may be useful to consider some of the everyday underpinnings of this largely unpredicted shift in national identifications. Note, as an almost simplistic geographic starting-point, that the key countries of Central Europe all share borders with West European countries that now have a considerable mix of radio and television facilities, with enhanced transmission capacities, cable linkages and other penetrating technology. East Germans, for example, have long and longingly viewed the lives of their compatriots, not merely in Berlin but all along their borders with West Germany. In recent years, cable TV services have linked all of East Germany to the images from West German television, and thus with Eurovision and full-scale international satellite connections. Hungary shares television borders with Austria, Yugoslavia with Austria and Italy, Bulgaria with Turkey and Greece, Estonia with Finland, and so on. In addition, Radio Free Europe is located in Munich and staffed by expatriates of each of the East European countries who, in recent years, have mostly travelled freely in their former homelands. Their sophisticated knowledge, combined with the considerable cosmopolitan skills of the BBC, Radio France, Voice of America and other similar services, also contributed to the high-tech saturation of information in the critical weeks of 1989. Indeed, these routine windows on the West were to take on special significance in the tense moments of October and, especially, November. In addition, video-recorders have become an important aspect of Soviet-bloc life. In Poland and elsewhere in Eastern Europe, a major vehicle for the dissemination of ideas and images has been videotapes and VCRs, and Poland soon earned the name of the 'VCR proletariat'. Videos provided a means for developing a kind of 'magnitizdat' of information and alternative ideology. Rock music and jazz have also played an important role, from Budapest to the depths of the Russian continent.

Throughout the summer of 1989, first in Poland with Solidarity's election success, then in Hungary with demonstrations to commemorate the 1956 uprising and in East Germany with early waves of emigration to the West, a series of relatively sporadic changes began to occur. . . . The key telecommunication connections were television, radio, telephone, print media and – profoundly, I suspect – the complex and highly collaborative exchange of information, news, rumour and deep-seated fear in face-to-face settings. It was, in fact, a time when the long privately held fears, opinions and hopes of the peoples of Eastern Europe moved from personal and intimate settings into the public domain – from backstage to centre stage – in city squares and on world television. . . .

Were we to rerun the events of 1989 in slow motion and with the retrospective clarity of hindsight, the connections between the execution scenes in Bucharest, the crowds on the top of the Berlin Wall and the vision of the Goddess of Democracy in Tiananmen Square might seem obvious. But are they? We know, for example, that the leaders of East Germany and Romania, to name but two, certainly considered the 'Chinese solution' when confronted with the growing physical presence and psychic pressures of their peoples; yet they did not use it. Why not? Certainly part of the reason is that, in Eastern Europe, that sort of solution would depend on the support of the Soviet Union; indeed, in the past, it had been Russian tanks that had imposed just such 'solutions' on the peoples of Hungary, Czechoslovakia and Poland, to name but three prominent examples. But the Soviet relationship with its Eastern-bloc satellites has changed in recent years and, even in the early days of Hungary's border relaxation and the demonstrations in Prague, the role of the Russian Bear was more removed and less menacing than it had been for forty years.

Similarly, if we look for a 'cause' of the revolutions of 1989, it can hardly be located simply in political ideology and economic structure, since the countries involved – despite their journalistic label of 'Communist-bloc' – are far from monolithic. Nor are their relationships with the Soviet Union identical, though it may be fair to say that the most notable common connection may be the person of Mikhail Gorbachev. The latter has certainly loomed large if rather benignly above the heads of the masses of demonstrators – as a central symbol in Eastern Europe, and as a physical presence in Beijing and East Berlin at the height of the demonstrations. But, apart from subscribing to a 'great man' theory of social change, neither Gorbachev's programmes nor his presence can have 'caused' the sort of contagion of ideas and actions that we have seen. Although the causes of these revolutions may elude us for many years to come, the conditions of these extraordinary events clearly involve one element which has been the central focus of attention in this essay: world-wide communication. As noted earlier, any assessment of the conditions of these multiple revolutionary events, or occurrence of a 'revolutionary situation', must surely include careful attention to the interlaced role of information and communication in 1989. In this world of intense and intensive mass communication and social change, 'everyone must change'.[3]...

It is not my purpose to suggest that the media *caused* the revolutions. The political and economic crises in both China and Eastern Europe have been years in the making. The countries of Central and Eastern Europe especially, although treated *en bloc*, are far from identical in their relative economic crises, political sophistication, degree of dependence on the Soviet Union and even level of religious solidarity. [All] of these factors, and more, play crucial roles in both the emergence and the eventual resolution of these historically located events. And these are 'events', in the fullest sense suggested by Foucault, in that they appear to be not only singular occurrences but instead represent 'the reversal of a relationship of forces, the usurpation of power, the appropriation of a vocabulary . . ., the entry of the masked "other" '.[4] Today, there are union leaders and playwrights as presidents and premiers in Eastern Europe, and a population larger than Western Europe or North America attempting to appropriate the vocabulary of democracy and of capitalism. There are also, in Romania and Bulgaria for instance, considerable signs of resistance to the proposed shift of power. The outcomes of these watershed events will be complex and far from automatic. Indeed, there is a very real danger of anarchy and a return to highly autocratic structures and political solutions, as well as a well-grounded concern for losing the benefits of socialism in the harsh reality of capitalism.

I have been concerned simply to highlight what I take to be a largely invisible yet new and significant aspect of these spontaneous events: the globalization of communication. A central feature of recent global social change has been the instantaneous, simultaneous and essentially non-linear explosion of images, information and, ultimately, ideology. Historically, revolutions have a number of identifying features including the mobilization of new resources in loyalty, political power, terror and, in modern times, education. We can now add a new and, I believe, prospectively powerful dimension to the revolutionary situation: communication. No society, as noted above, can now operate in the sort of secrecy that was possible barely ten years ago. At the time of writing, the unfolding events in the Baltic republics are but a small sample of the shape of things to come. The role of mass media is, as we have seen, largely unanticipated and unintended, so much so that the functional notion of 'role' is largely misplaced. It would also be a mistake to think of mass media as either monolithic or hegemonic. The media's considerable influence is, moreover, so intertwined with other telecommunication innovations as to be compounded by them. The making of the news has been accelerated to such a degree that careful empirical studies will be needed to disentangle the technological from the social.

READING 65

Johan Galtung

The Green Movement: A Sociohistorical Exploration

The Green movement is puzzling people today, particularly when it takes the form of a Green party, and most particularly in connection with the German party, by far the most important one, *Die Grünen*. They are said to be unpredictable and unable/unwilling to make any compromises with any other actors on the party political scene; consequently they are not really in politics, they are only political. For a party launched in 1981, to break through the 5 per cent barrier (they made 5.6 per cent) already in the elections of March 1983, and then move on to 7, 8 and 9 per cent in subsequent elections is already an achievement and leads to three obvious hypotheses about the future: the Greens will continue their comet-like career; they will find their natural level as a party below 10 per cent but possibly still above 5 per cent; they will dwindle down to zero again which is where they belong.

The following is an effort to explore the phenomenon, particularly directed at . . . readers very used to conceiving of politics in terms of blue and red; market forces, protected by conservative parties, and *étatiste* forces with planning and redistribution protected by socialist parties; both of them found in democratic and dictatorial versions. The Greens are obviously different, neither blue nor red, neither dictatorial nor democratic in the parliamentarian sense of [those words]. In spite of participating in parliamentary elections, mass action, direct democracy, local autonomy, self-reliance and so on are obviously closer to their heart.

Hence, what do they stand for, where do they come from, and who are they? This paper does not claim to have conclusive or any novel answers to these questions, but they are certainly worth exploring: the Greens have probably come here to stay, and to expand. Hence, three analytical approaches: *idcological, historical* and *sociological*; not necessarily compatible, not necessarily contradictory, but well suited to shed some light on the phenomenon.

[Table 14.1 sets out] 'a survey of Green policies', divided into twenty points, organized in packages with four points each. The mainstream

Table 14.1 A survey of Green policies

Mainstream characteristics	Green policies, movements
Economic basis:	
1 Exploitation of *external proletariat*	Co-operative enterprises, movements; labour buyer/seller difference abolished, customers directly involved
2 Exploitation of *external sector* relations: liberation movements	Co-existence with the third world; only equitable exchange
3 Exploitation of *nature*	Ecological balance person–nature; building diversity, symbiosis; complete or partial vegetarianism
4 Exploitation of *self*	More labour- and creativity-intensity; decreasing productivity in some fields; alternative technologies
Military basis:	
1 Dependency on *foreign trade*	Self-reliance; self-sufficiency in food, health, energy and defence
2 Dependency on *formal sector*, BCI-complex	Local self-reliance, decreasing urbanization, intermediate technology
3 *Offensive* defence policies, very destructive defence technology	Defensive defence policies with less destructive technology, also non-military non-violent defence
4 *Alignment with superpowers*	Non-alignment, even neutralism: decoupling from superpowers
Structural basis:	
1 *Bureaucracy*, state (plan) strong and centralized	Recentralization of local level; building federations of local units
2 *Corporation*, capital (market) strong and centralized	Building informal, green economy: • production for self-consumption • production for non-monetary exchange • production for local cycles
3 *Intelligentsia*, research strong and centralized	High level non-formal education, building own forms of understanding
4 MAMU factor; BCI peopled by middle-aged males with university education (and dominant race/ethnic group)	Feminist movements, justice/equality and for new culture and structure; movements of the young and the old; movements for racial/ethnic equality
Bourgeois way of life:	
1 *Non-manual work*, eliminating heavy, dirty, dangerous work	Keeping the gains when healthy, mixing manual and non-manual
2 *Material comfort*, dampening fluctuations of nature	Keeping the gains when healthy, living closer to nature
3 *Privatism*, withdrawal into family and peer groups	Communal life in bigger units, collective production/consumption
4 *Security*, the probability that this will last	Keeping security when healthy, making lifestyle less predictable
Chemical/circus way of life:	
1 Alcohol, tranquillizers, drugs	*Moderation*, experiments with non-addictive, life-enhancing things
2 Tobacco, sugar, salt, tea/coffee	*Moderation*, enhancing the body's capacity for joy, e.g. through sex
3 Chemically treated food, *panem*, natural fibres removed	Bio-organic cultivation, health food, balanced food, *moderation*
4 *Circenses*, TV, sport, spectatorism	Generating own entertainment, *moderate* exercise, particularly as manual work, walking, bicycling

characteristics in first-world societies are then confronted with their counterpoints, Green policies and movements. The list is self-explanatory; suffice it here only to add some remarks about how the list came into being.

The point of departure is a simple model of mainstream society with an economic basis, a military basis and a structural basis. The [last] is particularly important, for this is where the pillars of the Western social formation are found: the state with its bureaucracy and its plans, capital with its corporations and its markets, and the intelligentsia with its research, serving both of them. In addition to that there is a peculiar selection of people for these institutions: middle-aged males with university education from the dominant racial/ethnic group being preponderant almost everywhere. It is this structure, then, and composed in that particular manner, that organizes the economic and military basis of society. And all of this is done, manifestly, in order to achieve what is here called the 'bourgeois way of life', with its four characteristics, and the somewhat empty 'chemical way of life', with booze, with *panem et circenses*, in ways known to everybody in the first world.

Let me now formulate two assumptions about the Green movement: (1) the Green movement is an umbrella movement for a number of partial movements, each one of them attacking one or more elements on this list; and (2) the Green movement differs from many other social movements in denying that basic social problems can be solved attacking one single factor; a much more holistic approach is needed.

Thus, the Green movement is a federation of constituent movements and aims at an alternative society roughly characterized by the right-hand column in the survey of the policies. Many such lists can be made. This is one of them, not necessarily better or worse than most others; probably somewhat more comprehensive. To be a 'Green', one does not have to subscribe to all of these ideas; one probably has to agree with more than just one of them, however. There is a correlation in the ideological universe and not only because ideas happen to be held by the same people. There is some kind of internal consistency. For one's inner eye is conjured up the vision of a decentralized society, probably some kind of federation, with strongly autonomous units using the local bases in a self-reliant manner, trying not to become dependent on the outside, including for military purposes. Inside this social formation an alternative way of life is supposed to come into being, more or less as described here.

READING 66

Tom Horlick-Jones

Urban Disasters and Megacities in a Risk Society

INTRODUCTION

Much concern has been expressed about the disaster vulnerability of the new 'megacities' in developing countries. . . . These rapidly growing urban developments, with populations (according to the UN definition) exceeding 8 million, combine structural poverty and fragile infrastructures to create a worrying susceptibility to the impact of natural hazards. Events like the gas explosions in Mexico City (1984) and Guadalajara (1992) warn of the potential for technological disasters in such cities.

In contrast, megacities in the technologically advanced countries, cities like London and New York, are commonly regarded as relatively free of such concerns. But is this the case? What trends, if any, are creating greater vulnerability or resilience to hazards in these urban environments? Cities like Los Angeles and Tokyo continue to be exposed to potential earthquake hazards, and the recent Kobe earthquake revealed extensive vulnerability, despite use of advanced building codes. The recent Tokyo underground railway nerve gas release, together with events such as the New York City World Trade Center bombing, demonstrated the vulnerability of complex urban infrastructures not only to terrorist attack, but also, perhaps, to technological failure.

The modern city may present relative freedom from risk for some, yet for others it conjures up a host of 'man-made' and social risks. David Harvey has nicely characterized this contradictory environment:

> The city is the high point of human achievement, objectifying the most sophisticated knowledge in a physical landscape of extraordinary complexity, power, and splendour at the same time as it brings together social forces capable of the most amazing sociotechnical and political innovation. But it is also the site of squalid human failure, the lightning rod of the profoundest human discontents, and the arena of social and political conflict.[1]

Paradoxically, these cities present both a rich array of potential hazards and relative safety. They also provide an arena in which certain visions of doom are selected for special attention and concern, leading Douglas and Wildavsky to ask 'are the dangers increasing or are we more afraid?'[2]

The perception of risks is now recognized as being framed in social and cultural formations . . ., and the consequent mismatch between 'objective' measures of potential harm and degree of risk aversion has been the subject of much discussion . . . The degree to which modern urban environments can be said to be more or less safe is, then, a matter deeply fashioned by the politics of risk tolerability.

This recognition certainly does not deny the potential physical harms associated with a given risk. Rather, it reflects the extent to which risk perception and resulting decision-making [are] deeply embedded in cultural consciousness and practices. Indeed a direct correspondence has been observed between patterns of risk adjustment identified in the classical geographical literature and the distinct risk-handling behaviour of specific lifestyles . . .

It has been argued that the 'late modern' postindustrial societies, in which the megacities to be considered in this paper are embedded, are experiencing profound structural changes which will have an increasingly significant impact on the way risk is regarded and handled. Writers such as Beck . . . and Giddens . . . have begun to map out the contours of societal forms in which risk plays a central role. However, as Beck puts it: 'It is not clear whether it is the risks that have intensified, or our view of them. Both sides converge, condition each other, strengthen each other, and because risks are risks in knowledge, perceptions of risks and risks are not different things, but one and the same.'[3]

This conception of the 'Risk Society' poses an important challenge to our understanding of risk tolerability and the practice of risk management. It has important implications for hazard adjustment in megacity environments.

URBAN SYSTEMS AND RISKS

To what extent do physical hazards pose serious difficulties for megacities in the developed world? Adopting a relatively flexible definition of 'megacity' leads to consideration of about half a dozen cities – New York City, Tokyo, Los Angeles, London, Paris and possibly Osaka and Moscow . . . This paper will focus on the first four. Together they offer an interesting series of similarities and contrasts with regard to a number of relevant factors, including age of infrastructure, spatial distribution, built environment and exposure to natural hazards.

A city may be regarded as a complex nexus of socio-technical systems, all interacting with shared physical and socio-economic environments. Risks may be posed by technological failures, such as train crashes, natural agents – perhaps the result of winds or floods – or by social activity, such as crime. All may be regarded as resulting from the undesirable outputs of such systems . . .

The scale and complexity of these cities together with their population densities can generate physical vulnerability to unusual perturbations . . ., for example the disruption that can be produced by freak weather conditions. This effect is, however, rather unpredictable. The 1992 'urban nightmare' of a 'Jumbo' jet crash in Amsterdam produced relatively little damage beyond the immediate vicinity of the crash site; however, it generated disruption necessitating a complex process of crisis management . . .

The literature on technological systems failure is of relevance here, there being a multitude of opportunities for the 'incubation' of latent failures . . ., and many examples of tightly coupled subsystems with the potential for complex interactions . . . Indeed, Sylves and Pavlak . . . have suggested that the failure of elaborate security and safety systems following the World Trade Center bombing may have been characteristic of one of Perrow's 'normal accidents'.[4]

Studies of New York City . . . and London . . . reveal the range of possible risks posed by extensive transport infrastructures, places that attract large crowds, such as shopping and entertainment centres, and industrial hazards, whether at fixed sites or in transit. The built environment complicates matters considerably, with the substantial resource implications of infrastructure maintenance, the possibility of major fires, evacuation difficulty from high-rise structures and the problem of road congestion sometimes leading to gridlock.

Exposure to extremely violent perturbations presented by natural hazards is relatively limited for New York City and London. However, the 1992 and 1993 East Coast storms presented major difficulties for New York City, and development on the London floodplain has heightened the risk of severe flash flooding . . . The catastrophic risk to London presented by Thames tidal flooding is significantly reduced by the Thames Barrier, although the effectiveness of this measure may be challenged by the impact of global warming early in the next century.

Both Los Angeles and Tokyo have suffered massive destruction from earthquakes in the past; however, the degree of protection to earthquake hazard that can be afforded by advanced building codes was graphically demonstrated in Los Angeles early in 1994, where, despite the collapse of a section of interstate highway, a 6.6-Richter-scale earthquake resulted in relatively few casualties. It has been suggested that the same level of protection does not apply to Tokyo, which possesses significantly more vulnerable infrastructure . . ., although studies of the impact of the recent Kobe earthquake may provide useful lessons for future preparations, and prompt appropriate action. Direct comparisons between North America and Japan may, however, be misleading in view of possible differences in the utilization of building techniques.

Paradoxically, the ageing infrastructures of New York City and London, spared by most violent disruptions (with the exception of the World War II 'Blitz'), present a range of risks from leaks, structural weaknesses and other failures . . . These potential hazards arise from the interaction between socio-technical systems and their socio-economic environments, which, it has been suggested, can erode the systems in such ways as to create a metastability to sometimes apparently innocuous perturbations . . . Such 'real-world' features of urban hazard management can prove particularly intractable and the resource implications of maintaining complex socio-technical systems may be significant. In times of financial stringency or economic turbulence ensuring the safe functioning of such systems may be more difficult than expected . . .

CHANGES IN RISK PROFILES

Whilst some city structures tend to receive inadequate levels of investment and maintenance, powerful economic forces can drive rapid developments in the built environment and associated new infrastructures. This is particularly true in the dramatic changes in urban form associated with global economic restructuring that have occurred in the four cities in question over recent years. All have been transformed into so-called 'postmodern urban landscapes' . . . by these processes, the term reflecting radical social, cultural and spatial changes. All these changes may have important implications for disaster vulnerability, manifesting themselves in the gentrification of the older megacities like London and New York, and the creation of a 'Disney World' like form of a 'stage set for consumption' in Los Angeles.

Whereas London and New York City possess concentrated, high-rise centres, the evolution of Los Angeles has followed a more decentralized pattern over a wide geographical area. A relentless process of suburbanization has increased the proportion of city dwellers exposed to wildfire, landslide and flood hazards, whilst an associated extensive road transport infrastructure has led to severe air pollution . . .

New York City, London and Tokyo now form the apex of the organization and management of the world economy. This development is based especially upon the rapid growth of the international financial market and the trade in services. A host of support industries has developed to facilitate these activities, bringing significant changes to the local economies of these cities . . . In terms of urban form, the need for management and servicing of a huge and complex volume of financial transactions leads to high building densities, rapid building of high-rise offices and extremely high land prices. Massive telecommunication infrastructures have also been introduced. These dramatic changes bring new potential for complex system failures in parts of the urban infrastructure.

The Cold War may have ended; however, the former possibilities of aerial bombardment or nuclear attack have been replaced by 'para-warfare', or terrorism, as the major threat of hostile attack. The February 1993 World Trade Center bombing in New York City and, two months later, the huge amount of damage created by the City of London bombing, together with the recent nerve gas attack in Japan and bombing of the Federal building in Oklahoma City, have demonstrated the possible scale of such events. Bombings of industrial plant or transport systems, for example, invalidate conventional risk assessments, yielding results that can be radically different in nature, likelihood and severity from accidents.

THE SOCIAL DIMENSION

Processes of gentrification of once-poor parts of London, New York City and Tokyo have taken place, together with the development of associated shopping and entertainment facilities, like South Street Seaport in Manhattan and Covent Garden in London. Yet the glittering glass palaces of the financial institutions and the conspicuous consumption of fashionable stores are but one side of these cities. Recent changes have sharpened the contrasts behind the new well-off and an increasingly marginalized poor. Homelessness is now present in London, New York City and Tokyo and, as Sassen puts it, 'How many times do high-income executives have to step over the bodies of homeless people till this becomes an unacceptable fact or discomfort?'[5]

In Los Angeles, staggering contrasts of wealth exist in a city that combines high-tech industry with extensive areas of virtual shanty town characterized by drugs, crime and violence. The recent riots were indicative of the level of inter-ethnic and class tensions in some parts of the city and its suburbs . . .

The influence of the socio-economic environment on these urban systems is profound. Consider fire risk. Research in both the United States and Britain has demonstrated the correlation between the high frequency of fires and resulting casualties with those parameters of poverty associated with the urban inner city: the unemployed, those on low wages, single parents, the old, those living in overcrowded, shared accommodation or in rented or local authority accommodation. These are the people most likely to fall victim to domestic fire . . . Direct comparisons with cities in Japan, for example Tokyo, might, however, be misleading in view of the use of wood-based construction and high prevalence of fires.

These categories of urban dwellers, together with the homeless, are also most exposed to risks resulting from various criminal activities, whether drug-driven, interethnic violence and so on (*New Statesman & Society*, 1988). They are extremely vulnerable to the hostile environments created by a range of natural and technological hazard agents.

Vulnerability for urban dwellers is not, however, simply a matter for the poor. The relatively wealthy are exposed to certain risks by virtue of their work or leisure activities. Flying, commuting by train, enjoying a party on a river boat, going to the theatre by underground railway or working in a high-rise office block can all be risky activities.

Clearly a wide variety of risks and vulnerability to hazard exists in these cities. The new concentration of built environment, financial investment and associated infrastructure has brought the possibility of massive losses. A sharpened division between rich and poor has generated 'risk ghettos' that expose classically vulnerable groups to relatively high levels of risk. Turbulent socio-economic environments erode the resilience of complex socio-technical systems leading to the unexpected effects of 'system vulnerability'.

URBAN LIVING IN A RISK SOCIETY

The economic changes responsible for the restructuring in urban form discussed above also provide some of the sources of turbulence that may be responsible for eroding the resilience to failure of a multitude of urban systems. In social terms, they also contribute towards shifting risk *perception* into a position of central importance by encouraging the development of 'reflexivity'.[6] Such changes create significant uncertainties and doubts, and, as Giddens put it: 'To live in the "world" produced by high modernity has the feeling of riding a juggernaut.'[7] So he describes the experience of contemporary life, referring primarily to the technologically advanced societies, with their bewildering doubts and multiple risks. It is a theme developed at length by Beck . . . in his celebrated work on the so-called 'Risk Society'; a recognition of transitions taking place from postindustrial societies to new societal forms in which the perception and management of hazards and risks become a central organizing dynamic.

Beck's 'risks' are not, however, the traditional blights on humanity such as disease, famines, natural hazards or other 'Acts of God'. Rather, they are the (actual or perceived?) uncontrollable and dysfunctional side-effects of technology, 'the dark side of progress'.[8] According to these theories, the emergence of 'Green' politics is one significant outcome of social processes that erode trust in institutions and produce uncertainties about identities and ways of life. Of course, such processes are rather more complex, with 'Green' politics also being associated, for example, with the rise of a 'knowledge class' with distinct cultural characteristics . . .

It has been argued . . . that the concept of disaster in the technologically advanced societies has been socially constructed from traditional notions relating to catastrophic events. Building upon themes explored by Giddens and Beck, this work concludes that the social and political impact of contemporary 'disasters' corresponds with a release of repressed existential anxiety resulting from a perceived betrayal by trusted individuals or institutions. Blaming mechanisms are used to restore trust . . .; however, the events fuel the imagery of the 'nightmare' and the generalized sense of threat. In practical terms, the social impact of such events may be out of all proportion with the physical harms generated by them.

The media seem to have an important role to play in amplifying certain risks and 'disasters' for special attention . . . Indeed, urban disasters form powerful motifs in works of fiction, and the imagery of the *Towering Inferno* and other such stories are used by the media to retell topical stories, complete with associated myths. Reality begins to mirror fiction, as in the *London Evening Standard*'s coverage following the October 1992 'Jumbo' crash in Amsterdam. 'Like a plane disaster movie' read the headlines. 'Here they lived in fear of a disaster from the jets that roared overhead. Here they died, when the nightmare became true.'

Since the work of Weber it has been recognized that cities play a key role in social change. Harvey reminds us that 'Big cities have long been important arenas of cultural production, forcing-grounds of cultural innovation, centres of fashion and the creation of "taste".'[9] One might conclude that the advanced megacities, bringing together a variety of risks and potential 'modern disasters' with the most pronounced worries and uncertainties of the Risk Society, play a central role in creating new patterns of behaviour with regard to risk in the technologically advanced countries. How might such changes manifest themselves? Can they be observed today?

THE IMPLICATIONS FOR ADJUSTMENT TO HAZARD

. . . Burton et al. in their classical examination of adjustment to environmental hazards, argued that urbanization leads to vulnerability to natural hazards.[10] They observed that urban dwellers appear to be less sensitive to the possibility of extreme natural events than rural people. This, they note, might reflect a preoccupation with other, apparently more pressing, problems associated with urban life.

Kirby . . . suggests that such vulnerability arises from a combination of an economic imperative and a belief that 'civilization' leads to the safety of almost any location. Indeed, urbanization is based on the use of technology, which in turn is legitimated by ideas of control. The city is, then, a zone where technological risks are under control. The key question now seems to be what happens to individual and collective hazard adjustment strategies when trust in such controlling influences is eroded.[11]

In the advanced societies adjustment to hazard has largely been determined by institutions that are related to individuals by power and trust relationships. If such trust is eroded, then it follows that individual and small-group adjustment strategies may begin to be adopted. If so, what form will they take? Horlick-Jones and Jones drawing on the work of Mary Douglas and her collaborators, have discussed the cultural roots of risk aversion strategies embedded as they are in chosen ways of life, leading to a number of distinct approaches – denial, passive acceptance, action to reduce future losses and radical action to remove the risk.[12]

In practice, individual actions will be constrained by personal circumstances and a range of contextual factors. Such factors also contribute to the social framing of risk perception. Individuals are exposed to a portfolio of risks, from the mundane to the catastrophic, and corresponding sources of information are integrated into a pragmatic assessment of contingencies and possibilities . . .

The emergence of 'Green' politics would correspond to some individuals adopting the 'radical action to remove the risk' strategy. Changes in insurance-purchasing behaviour, for example, could be an indicator of the influence of an 'action to reduce further losses' strategy. There is clearly a need for more empirical investigations in order to investigate possible evidence for these hypotheses, in particular ethnographic-type investigations of community risk perception, the design of which recognizes the social and cultural framing effects in risk perception and handling.

Turning now to the role of hazard and emergency management agencies, it is important to consider how their behaviour might be affected by social changes in risk perception behaviour. The planning agendas of such organizations are determined by a combination of resource constraints, the experience of day-to-day crises and the political dynamics of risk tolerability. The impact of past disasters may be very significant in shaping institutional agendas . . ., and arguably such processes may shift hazard adjustment in unhelpful ways if they provide a 'distorting lens' that skews priorities away from hazards that generate less 'dread' in the imagination of the public, politicians and administrators.

Perhaps this point needs to be developed a little. Many spectacular 'modern disasters' arise from technological failures of one sort or another, and they tend to produce an intense 'zone of harm' of rather limited geographical extent. There are important counter-examples, of course, such as the Chernobyl nuclear power station accident. Nevertheless, a host of train and aircraft crashes, sports ground tragedies and sundry fires and explosions do generate rather different patterns of harm from, for example, the impact of a range of natural hazard agents, although, of course, such impacts can themselves precipitate technological failures.

The point here is that geographically large-scale hazards, producing both acute and chronic effects, may require rather different forms of emergency response from local, acute catastrophes. It has been suggested that discontinuous shifts occur in the resource burden of responding to progressively greater-scale contingencies . . .

Equally, various sorts of unusual contingencies may present challenges that exceed capabilities corresponding to the usual and the routine. In megacities such as London and New York, the dynamism, speed of change and concentration of activities lead to the routine occurrence of emergencies of one sort or another. Whilst regular response to such 'routine' emergencies assists the development of effective operational procedures, it does tend to reinforce a view that major crises require simply an extended application of day-to-day emergency procedures. Such unusual contingencies may require extensive and co-ordinated response, [with] scale problems described above, unanticipated effects and considerable situation uncertainties . . .

Finally, the insurance industry may [prove] both an interesting indicator and [a] significant player as the impact of the Risk Society makes its presence felt more keenly in megacity environments. Concern about losses resulting from fires in large urban supermarkets has recently been expressed by the industry (*Financial Times* 1994a) together with a warning that cover against flooding in London may be increasingly difficult to obtain (*Financial Times* 1994b). Changing perceptions of risk clearly play a central role in the operation of the industry, and concerns about the potential losses in the developed megacities may lead to the disappearance of some cover and the need to develop new, preventive, risk management strategies.

CONCLUSIONS

Global economic restructuring has impacted on the physical form, socio-economic environment and socio-cultural structures of developed megacities in complex and interacting ways, as gentrified wealth and relative safety from physical harm exist in close proximity to 'risk ghettos'. An increased propensity for the spectacular failure of socio-technical systems combines with a social fluidity and insecurity to create 'modern disasters'; events with significant social and political impact such as catastrophes become media spectacle.

Such events erode trust in institutional risk management and generate a convoluted risk politics as individuals and small groups tend to adopt a fragmented range of risk management strategies, whilst hitherto hegemonic institutions come under pressure to address those contingencies associated with popularly perceived 'dread', resulting in possibly distorted risk management priorities.

Clearly these conclusions have potentially very important implications for hazard adjustment in the megacities of the developed world. There is an urgent need for more empirical investigation of the hypotheses discussed in this paper.

Finally, it is important to note that the risk politics in developed countries discussed in this paper is associated with powerful global processes. These will impact in significant ways on the vulnerability to both natural and technological hazards of the megacities of the developing world, leading to an even sharper contrast between developed and developing countries. Beck argues in graphic terms that this impact will rebound upon the wealthy countries, as the poor ones 'become the breeding grounds of an international contamination, which, like the infectious diseases of the poor in the cramped medieval cities, does not spare even the wealthy neighbourhoods of the world community'.[13]

READING 67

George Monbiot and Tim Radford

Last Warning on Earth

As memories of the scorching summer are soothed away by snow and rain, the 600 water tankers trundling around Yorkshire have been all but forgotten. Yorkshire Water regards the situation as exceptional – the Met Office has told them the drought was a 'once in 500-year event'. The possibility that it might reflect a long-term trend, the company confesses, hasn't even been raised.

The findings of the world's foremost climate scientists, officially unveiled in Rome recently, expose a strange disjunction. We've all heard about global warming. Most of us are aware that the world has basked in nine of its ten warmest recorded years since the early 1980s, and everyone knows that our own summers have been exceptional. But these considerations don't seem to connect in our heads. When two Englishmen meet, they talk about the weather, but somehow they seem to have missed the point.

The Intergovernmental Panel on Climate Change (IPCC) has now managed to agree that 'the balance of evidence suggests a discernible human influence on global climate'. While they are properly hedged with cautions and uncertainties, its members' data should be enough – poor thermal insulation notwithstanding – to throw us all into a muck sweat.

Some of the events the IPCC's climatologists have observed in the last five years have, with uncomfortable accuracy, fulfilled their predictions of what would happen if global warming were to begin. In the 1970s, scientists proposed that an early sign of warming would be the disintegration of the Wordie and James Ross ice shelves in the Antarctic. Both have dutifully broken up. Thirty per cent more tropical storm activity was forecast for the Atlantic in 1995 – it came. Glaciers in New Guinea are retreating at the rate of 45 metres per year; snow cover in the northern hemisphere has declined by 10 per cent in the last twenty years; less ice formation in the Greenland Sea means that its convection currents have virtually stopped. [In 1995] the Hadley Centre in Bracknell found that the temperature record of the last 130 years doggedly tracked the predicted effects of the carbon dioxide and sulphur emissions in that period.

The IPCC climatologists predict that a doubling of carbon dioxide in the atmosphere – which would take about 100 years – would mean a world-wide temperature rise of between 1 and 3.5°. This sounds trifling, until you hear that the difference between the average temperatures of the last Ice Age and those of today is 4°. No one can be certain quite what this warming would do, but the scientists' predictions include droughts, floods and hurricanes, a severe decline of harvests in some poor countries, the retreat of forests and invasions of tropical diseases.

No one can say whether change will progress steadily towards 2100 or flip into sudden convulsions, such as the postulated disruption of the Gulf Stream, which could leave Britain with a climate like Labrador's. But the message, repeated again and again, is that global warming is likely to mean not just the odd inconvenience here and there, but the end of the life we know.

So why aren't we panicking? Why aren't we mobilizing? Part of the reason is that while we are waiting for government, government is waiting for us. Cowed by oil, transport and power lobbyists, governments won't act until they hear people baying for change. Worried about the loss of our comforts, we won't bay for change until it is cheaper and easier to conserve fossil fuels than to waste them. This means more public transport, more incentives for energy saving and alternative energy generation, and more expensive fossil fuel. All these depend on government.

Both the scale of what might be happening and its complete disproportion to the apparently innocuous causes – switching on the lights, Christmas shopping, trucking water round Yorkshire – take effort and imagination to grasp. Never before have such trivial pursuits had such vast implications. Never before have we been so well insulated from the consequences of our actions.

Our inability to respond to what seems to be happening has been compared by the environmentalist George Marshall to our refusal to understand that Germany was preparing for war. The comparison is a good one. Stanley Baldwin's complaint that the people would not rally to the cry of rearmament will doubtless find echoes in Rome. The American fixation with sea walls is horribly reminiscent of the French reliance on static defences, while the governments and missions of most of the big industrialized nations seem to be stuffed with Chamberlains, Hendersons and Halifaxes.

The crisis of 1939 arose from a failure to apply what environmentalists call 'the precautionary principle'. We can't afford to wait for certainty. The time to start sweating is now.

HOW TO BRING PEACE AND GOODWILL TO ALL MEN

First, all governments must now encourage ways of burning less fossil fuels, because that is where the carbon dioxide comes from. This does not necessarily mean a nuclear future, because fossil fuels are burned to mine and process uranium and build nuclear power stations. Cement making also releases carbon dioxide from limestone. The hunt should be on for neat new tricks for harnessing solar, wind, water, tidal and geothermal energy. What else?

- Since people cannot get by without burning coal, oil, gas and wood and other fuels, governments will need to think up ways of getting more bang from each buck spent on energy. This means new kinds of building, insulation and cooling systems. This means that public transport, energy distribution and resource management really will have to be efficient. This means understanding that oil – already the basis of sophisticated manufacture – really is too precious to burn. This means that peace and stability will seem to be economically desirable things, so that wasteful military spending will seem just that – wasteful.
- All these things are economic opportunities for rich, resourceful nations. Since 93 million new mouths need to be fed each year, and since 90 per cent of these are in the developing world, and since low population growth is probably linked with high economic security, the rich world will have not just an incentive but an imperative to share the new technologies with the poor.
- There is more to the carbon dioxide problem than simply lowering population growth rates and economizing on petrol. Planetary warming could release stupefying quantities of carbon and methane locked in the tundra, or the ocean floor. So warming has to be slowed. But it is accelerated by the burning and clearing of forests. Trees are a great way to abstract atmospheric carbon and store it, so vast undisturbed forests and eruptions of woodland wherever possible will again be desirable. Since these shelter the other millions of threatened species on earth, provide medicines, building materials and food, and limit soil erosion, this will be a good thing. Cattle produce vast quantities of planet-warming methane, and grazing is an inefficient food provider. It looks good for vegetarianism.
- All these solutions involve (a) a new world order, (b) a diversity of local ingenuity, (c) peace, (d) economic fairness, (e) new jobs, (f) sustainable development and (g) plenty of forests. Even if the global warming threat turned out to be a huge mistake, would these things be a waste of time and money?

READING 68

John Skow

The Land: Less Milk and Honey?

Every year hordes of Brazil's land-starved peasants press deeper and deeper into the Amazon rainforest, clearing patches of earth by putting torches to the trees. It's a largely self-defeating exercise, since the forest soil is unsuitable for farming. After a few seasons, when the land plays out, the peasants move on, clearing more ground and cutting a swath of devastation across one of the world's most precious ecosystems. Although international opinion has condemned the torching of the Amazon for years, and the Brazilian government has pledged to protect the forest, [1995]'s burning season was one of the most destructive ever.

The land is under even greater pressure in Bangladesh, where a population of 120 million crowds into a river-delta region at the mouth of the Bay of Bengal. Rain running off deforested northern hills has badly eroded the soil, and low-lying areas are flooded much of the time. Even though Bangladeshis shed so much blood to win their independence from Pakistan in 1971, thousands of them are now leaving the homeland they prize and migrating west to India.

In Burundi, Hutu farmers have long prided themselves on passing their land to the next generation; holdings are typically divided equally among the three eldest sons. Today that patrimony is often almost worthless. As the country's population has exploded, the land has been subdivided so many times that the tiny plots that sons inherit may not be sufficient to feed even one family. Intense competition for land in Burundi and neighbouring Rwanda is one of several forces fanning the ethnic conflicts that have led to the slaughter of hundreds of thousands of people in this turbulent region of central Africa.

Is the human race running out of land? At first the thought seems absurd, given the vast open spaces that are still found on the planet. Indeed, the earth's entire population of 5.7 billion people could stand upright within the 576,500 hectares of Brunei with a bit of elbow room to spare, but people need extra room to roam – and especially to grow food. Much of the world's land is too rocky or arid or salty for agriculture. And forests that haven't already been cut deserve protection: they harbour the habitats of earth's endangered wildlife. With the supply of prime turf for farming so tight, according to Washington's Worldwatch Institute, the average amount of grainland per person has dropped in thirty years from more than 0.2 hectares to little more than 0.1 hectare. Only a boom in agricultural productivity has kept the burgeoning population fed.

Much of the arable land becomes less arable by the minute, assaulted by urbanization, chemical pollution, desertification and the overuse of limited water supplies. The exhaustion of land in many areas has created a new class of displaced person: what experts call the environmental migrant. And while wars have always been fought over territory, the future may see 'green wars' triggered by shortages of such basic resources as topsoil or water.

Driving the competition for land, of course, is the historically unprecedented explosion of human population. It took the species about 150,000 years of fits and starts to reach the 1 billion mark around 1800. Since then, an additional 4.7 billion have been added to the head count, and if trends continue, the population could pass 10 billion before the middle of the next century.

One consequence is certain to be continued pressure on woodlands, especially the tropical forests that are the reservoirs of the majority of earth's animal and plant species. Between 1980 and 1990, an estimated 8 per cent of the world's tropical-forest cover was cut, burned or otherwise destroyed. The loss of such irreplaceable biological treasure is disturbing in its own right, but the impact of deforestation goes far beyond the felled trees. As a region loses its forests, it loses its ability to trap and absorb water, and so runoff from denuded woodland worsens the natural process of soil erosion. If, at the same time, farmers harvest crops year after year, the soil is constantly exposed to wind and water. Result: the world wears away 24 billion tons of topsoil a year – roughly equal to the topsoil on the Australian wheatlands.

When dry areas are worn down by the wind, by intensive farming or by the hooves of too many grazing animals, the region may eventually become a sterile desert, a fate that has befallen 30 per cent of the world's dry lands. Three-quarters of dry lands in Africa and North America are in some stage of desertification.

Farmers the world over have boosted their yields and fought against desertification by using heavy doses of fertilizer, pesticides and irrigation water, but that strategy has side-effects. Agricultural chemicals may gradually poison the soil, and irrigation also deposits a harmful residue: when the water evaporates, it leaves behind various salts. They contribute to the natural build-up of salty compounds in the soil, and the salinization process can render the land useless for farming. The World Bank reported in 1993 that some degree of salinization affects 28 per cent of the US's irrigated land, 23 per cent of China's and 11 per cent of India's.

Where are all these worrisome trends leading? Many environmental scientists, including Stanford biologist Paul Ehrlich and Worldwatch president Lester Brown, have long maintained that the earth's farmers are struggling against the limits of their ability to feed the population. Brown notes that global grain production has been stagnant for five years because of water scarcity and diminishing returns from the use of fertilizer. To meet food needs, agricultural exporters have drawn down their ample grain reserves, but in the years ahead, Brown expects to see rising prices, less grain devoted to meat production and ultimately more hunger in the world. 'We're in the early stages', he says, 'of a food transition from surplus to scarcity.'

While most agricultural experts are concerned, few are as gloomy as Brown. The most optimistic of his critics dismiss him as the latest in a long line of Cassandras that began two centuries ago with Thomas Malthus and his predictions of mass starvation. Optimists point out that even though the human population has more than doubled since 1950, the world's farmers have kept pace. Staying abreast of another doubling of the population would not be nearly so simple, if indeed it is possible. But the weapons of the Green Revolution are impressive: they include not only fertilizer and irrigation but also new, hybrid strains of crops that yield more bushels per hectare. Brown's critics argue that modern agricultural methods have yet to be applied on much of the land in poorer countries. Last year the Philippines' International Rice Research Institute came up with a new strain of 'super-rice', which is expected to increase the annual global rice harvest by 100 million tons, or 30 per cent.

The optimists maintain that world hunger has more to do with war, poverty and poor food distribution than with the failure of farmers to get enough grain to sprout. The difficulty, however, is that war and maldistribution are likely to remain facts of life, and poverty can often be self-perpetuating rather than self-correcting. Observes Robert Brinkman, chief of the land-and-water-development division of the UN-affiliated Food and Agriculture Organization in Rome: 'When people get poor, they put pressure on the land, and then they get poorer.'

Is the degradation of the land irreversible? Not necessarily. FAO projects over the past decade show that on a small scale, at least, even the most devastated terrain can be revived. In the early 1980s, The Netherlands, acting under the auspices of the FAO, agreed to provide $18.4 million for a fifteen-year project to promote forestry programmes in Peru, where once forested highlands had been barren since before the coming of the conquistadores. Now much of the highland region is green, and villagers have become forest activists. The FAO began with awareness programmes in schools, and it provided material for community nurseries. But all decisions about what to plant and where were made by the villagers of some 700 communities that participated. Initiative at the grass-roots level, the FAO concluded, was crucial to success.

Another model project, in the Keita Valley of Niger, began in 1983 with the ambitious goal of reclaiming some 5,000 sq km of once fertile pasture thought to be irrevocably damaged by flooding and overgrazing. The Italian and Niger governments committed $53 million, the FAO supplied technical knowledge and the people of 205 villages learned and applied modern concepts of water 'harvesting'. Keitan men, who had been migrating for six months a year to find work, received food rations from the World Food Programme for participating in the project. Small dams and anti-erosion ponds were built to reduce runoff. Trees were planted as windbreaks and riverside water sponges.

By 1990, 2,000 sq km had been reclaimed, and wildlife had returned. As villagers started growing more produce than their families needed, markets and food co-operatives flourished. Schools, community centres, shops, roads, electrical generators and a meteorological station were built. Once blighted and seemingly hopeless, the region has become a going concern.

The question is whether such successes can be replicated on a global scale. More than 100 nations have signed a UN-drafted Convention to Combat Desertification. It calls for wide creation of FAO-style 'bottom-up' programmes that help villagers with terracing, using drought-resistant crops and organizing modest irrigation and reforestation efforts. What remains to be seen is whether nations will put up the $10 billion to $20 billion that experts say is needed each year for land reclamation.

Providing sufficient food in poorer nations will be hard enough, but what about countries enjoying prosperity? Consider the 1.2 billion Chinese, many of whom are getting a first taste of affluence. Brown noted recently that China's bustling, newly capitalistic economy was starting to gobble up its food supply. Some 1.1 million hectares of grainland were lost annually from 1990 to 1994 as the grainland was converted to industrial sites and other uses. And Chinese who used to eat little but rice and wheat now have more money, which they are using to buy pork and chicken, and much more beer than before. Pigs, chickens and breweries, in turn, use a great deal of grain. By March 1994, agricultural prices in Beijing were on a steep rise. As Brown had earlier predicted, China, the world's largest grain producer, emerged overnight as the second-ranking grain importer, trailing only Japan.

The net grain imports were just 16 million tons, but, says Brown, that's only the beginning. He estimates that by 2030, China will need to import between 210 million and 370 million tons of grain annually, out of a total world production of 2.15 billion tons. Presumably China will have the money if its economy continues to thrive. But who will be the seller? The entire world produces only 200 million tons of grain for export each year. And there will be other hungry mouths: Africa, by some estimates, will need to import 215 million tons of grain annually by 2030.

Hu Angang, an economist at Beijing's Research Centre for Eco-Environmental Sciences, says, 'The problem is fairly serious but not as serious as Mr Brown depicts it.' Still, Hu does not dispute that China will become a major grain importer, since his country has only half as much arable land as the US.

If China's draconian birth-control programme is any indication, Beijing long ago started worrying about having too many mouths to feed. The mandatory one-child-per-family policy has helped China reduce its population-growth rate from 2.8 per cent in 1970 to just below 1 per cent [in 1994]. In fact, demographic experts expect that sometime in the first half of the next century, China will gladly relinquish its title as the world's most populous nation to India, whose population of 929 million is growing 1.7 per cent a year.

The rest of the world would like to emulate China's birth-control success but not its coercive methods. Charting a global strategy was the goal of last year's surprisingly successful UN population conference in Cairo. In a rare show of unity on a contentious issue, representatives of 184 nations agreed to a document that calls for freer access to birth-control methods and asks governments to spend $17 billion by the year 2000 on population-related programmes. Most important, the document identifies the education and empowerment of women as the best means of reducing family size. Says

Nafis Sadik, executive director of the UN Population Fund: 'If we respond to women and take care of their needs, demographic issues will take care of themselves.'

The best anyone hopes for is a stabilization of the population at somewhere between 8 billion and 9 billion by 2050. Even the pessimistic Ehrlich thinks that if this goal is met, the world's farmers and agricultural scientists will have a fighting chance to produce enough food. But notwithstanding that imagined achievement, threats to the land – and to the world's standard of living – are sure to grow ever more intense.

Part XV

Sociological Research Methods

Sociology is a very varied subject and a diversity of research methods is commonly used in the course of social investigation. There is no single method of research which commends itself for all types of study: some methods are more appropriate to the analysis of specific problems than are others. Sociologists do not always agree when one approach rather than another should be employed. For instance, some researchers tend to favour methods which generate rich case materials, while others have a preference for gathering data which can be easily quantified.

One of the most widely used methods for collecting information of a richly detailed kind is fieldwork, also commonly known as participant observation. Two contributions (Readings 69 and 70) discuss this approach. Robert A. Georges and Michael O. Jones provide a general interpretation of the nature of fieldwork. Fieldwork research, they stress, cannot be carried on in the way in which a natural scientist might conduct an experiment in a laboratory. The researcher must interact with, and gain the confidence of, those whose activities form the concern of the investigation. Fieldworkers face many problems, including the possibility that their research endeavours might have a strong impact upon their own personal attitudes and identity (a phenomenon which, however, some authors argue is actively desirable: the situation should be one of mutual communication). Anna Pollert's study (Reading 70) furnishes a concrete example of a fieldwork project. Her description of her experiences as a participant observer in a tobacco factory yields a graphic yet humorous account of the attitudes and outlook of those working within it.

The survey method is used as widely as fieldwork in social research. Surveys are usually carried out by means of questionnaires, either administered directly by the researcher, or sent by post to the individuals concerned. Other variations include telephone or tape-recorded interviews orientated towards a fixed range of questions. In Reading 71, Catherine Marsh gives a general description of the survey method and also points out that it is widely used in other disciplines besides sociology.

Joanna Mack and Stewart Lansley (Reading 72) employed the survey method in their investigation of poverty in the United Kingdom. Surveys of the poor formed the basis of the celebrated work by Charles Booth, who in the late nineteenth century first brought to public consciousness the level and extent of poverty in London. Mack and Lansley say that their own study reveals an important point about conceptions of poverty today: that most people now interpret poverty not in terms of the minimal material requirements for subsistence, but in terms of a minimal standard of living which everyone living in the country should rightfully expect to achieve.

The final selection in this part (Reading 73) discusses conversation analysis, a type of research investigation which recently has become important in sociology. Conversation analysis concentrates on the study of everyday talk. It not only forms a distinctive research orientation but is also linked to a specific general research programme, that of 'ethnomethodology'. Ethnomethodology is essentially the study of the lay or 'folk' methods which ordinary people use in employing language to make themselves understood and to be understood by others. 'Methodology' here, therefore, has a double sense: it refers to the practices of the research observer, but that observer is in turn studying the methodologies of ordinary day-to-day life.

READING 69

Robert A. Georges and Michael O. Jones

The Human Element in Fieldwork

Two facts about the nature of fieldwork are seldom recognized, acknowledged or discussed. First, as individuals move from the planning to the implementation stages of their field research, they discover that they must engage continuously in a process of clarifying for others and for themselves just who they are, what it is they want to find out and why they wish to obtain the information they seek from the individuals they choose as subjects. Second, as fieldworkers interact with their selected subjects, they are confronted with the necessity of being willing and able to compromise. Unlike laboratory scientists, who can control the phenomena that are the focal points of their investigations by controlling the environments and conditions under which these phenomena are examined, individuals whose research plans call for them to study other human beings while interacting with them in non-laboratory settings must surrender a certain amount of the independence and control they enjoy while they are generating their fieldwork projects. For to gain the co-operation of those from whom they need to learn if they are to succeed in their endeavours, fieldworkers must explain, again and again, their identities and intentions in meaningful and acceptable ways. In seeking assistance, fieldworkers implicitly request permission to assume, and indicate their willingness to accept, a subordinate, dependent status *vis-à-vis* those they have chosen to study.

That fieldworkers must become largely dependent upon their research subjects is one of the ironies of fieldwork, creating a source of tension as fieldwork projects are implemented. The irony stems from the fact that while it is fieldworkers who elect to study others rather than others who choose to be studied by fieldworkers, it is the subjects who are knowledgeable, and the fieldworkers who are ignorant, about the phenomena or behaviours that fieldworkers decide to study. For their project plans to succeed, therefore, fieldworkers must be willing to learn and subjects to teach; and the pupil is necessarily subordinate to the teacher. Tensions arise because fieldworkers' conceptions of themselves as subordinate to their subjects conflict with their images of themselves as investigators to whom research subjects are subordinate. Dealing with this conflict creates an ambivalence with which both fieldworkers and subjects must cope. This coping requires clarifying identities and intentions for, and compromising with, both others and self.

Feelings of ambivalence that require fieldworkers to clarify identities and intentions and to compromise arise not only from the conflict between images of self as both independent and dependent, or dominant and subordinate, in their relations with their chosen subjects, but also from differences between themselves and their subjects that fieldworkers conceive to be significant. The differentiation may be based on any one of some combination of such factors as sex, age, race, nationality, native language, religious background, occupation, social or economic status, living environment, relative degree of technological know-how or overall lifestyle. The greater the significance of differences that fieldworkers conceive to exist between themselves and their chosen subjects, the greater the amount of conflict and ambivalence that is apt to arise, and the greater the number of clarifications and compromises that is likely to occur. . . .

Because they plan fieldwork projects and commit themselves to carrying them out, fieldworkers understandably feel that they have the right to become privy to the kinds of information they set out to obtain; yet they are also aware that their selected subjects are under no obligation to provide that information. Similarly, individuals may determine in advance that the successful implementation of their fieldwork projects is dependent upon their filming, photographing, tape-recording, sketching or making written records of the phenomena or behaviours they have singled out for study; yet they know that those they have chosen to study are not obliged to permit such activities. Individuals may also decide that to accomplish the objectives set forth in their research plans, they must interact on a day-to-day basis and for an extended period of time with their chosen subjects; yet they are also cognizant of the fact that subjects are not required to welcome, accept, accommodate or co-operate with them. Fieldworkers tend to assume as well that subjects have a responsibility to keep interview appointments, provide honest and full answers to questions and submit willingly to any tests or experiments that are part of research designs; yet they also know that their subjects' principal time commitments are not to the fieldworker, but rather to those whose relationships with them are permanent instead of temporary, and that subjects need not tell or do anything unless they choose to tell or do it, regardless of its importance to the fieldworker's aims. In fieldwork involving people studying people at first hand, in sum, rights and responsibilities cannot be legislated by the fieldworker, but must instead be negotiated by fieldworkers and subjects. The negotiating is continuous and requires repeated clarification and compromise.

READING 70

Anna Pollert

Girls, Wives, Factory Lives: An Example of Fieldwork Research

When I began my study of Churchmans, a tobacco factory in Bristol, I was met with astonishment from management; what could I possibly want to know about 'factory girls'? Was I, then, a 'troublemaker'?

On the shop floor I was met with a mixture of suspicion and curiosity. I was not an employee and had to explain that I felt many people had no idea what factory life was like and I wanted to listen, learn and write about it. Slowly, I became a familiar figure, with notebook and cassette-recorder in hand, and suspicion turned to amusement, even sympathy: 'Go on, my love'; 'I think it's a good thing: people ought to know how people live – not just think about themselves.'

Churchmans was a declining part of Imperial Tobacco, producing pipe and loose tobaccos. Rationalization and insecurity were accepted parts of life, like the din of machinery, the sweet sickly smell of *rag* (the loose, shredded tobacco) and the unyielding pace of work. And indeed the factory is now shut.

It was a small factory. Most of the 140 women worked in the weighing and packing departments, the labour-intensive areas. The largest of these, the machine weighing room, was filled with long weighing machines with conveyor belts to the labellers and baggers.

Each machine contained six scales, each with a little light which went on to register the correct weight of tobacco. Machine weighing needs finger-tip precision and flying speed. Each weigher picks up tiny lumps of rag which she drops into a hole – sometimes taking back a few shreds – until the exact weight is reached. A counter records her performance. The machines clatter all day from 7.30 a.m. to 4.30 p.m., except for a fifteen-minute breakfast break and an hour for lunch, recording all the time.

Failure in performance standard or speed leads to a warning, and downgrading to a lower 'proficiency pay rate'. Each minute, ten empty foil packs pass below the scale inside the machine's belly; one weighing per woman every six seconds.

It is rowdy and pacey here. But it is also good for a laugh, and that counts in factory life. Most of the younger women are in the machine weighing room. There are other young women in the smaller, quieter hand-packing rooms, and the distinction between the 'crowds' in each came up again and again:

> Patti (from the machine weighing room): They take their work seriously, whereas we don't. If you go in there, you can't talk. *They* all keeps themselves to themselves, whereas *we* all mucks in together.

Upstairs in the stripping department, and downstairs in the spinning room, are concentrated the older women – the long-term workers, women with children, women with grandchildren.

Stripping can be done either by hand or by machine. Hand-stemming means stripping the tobacco leaf from the stem between forefinger and thumb. Fingers get cut, calloused and bent. The dust catches the back of the throat; but it isn't a noisy job. There is an intimacy of years of shared experience, with quiet talk or, sometimes, group discussion about children and families, news and personal experiences.

Machine-stripping makes a regular clacking noise. It looks like feeding washing through a mangle, as tobacco leaf is fed between two rollers operated by a foot pedal. A blade cuts out the stem, and the stripper carefully stacks the left and right halves of the leaf, avoiding tearing it, but always fighting time, and fighting to keep up to [the] proficiency standard.

In the spinning room, concentration was so intense that I was frankly told not to interfere by interviewing. There was no time to talk and keep up at the same time.

The air here is thick with oppressive fumes from the ovens which cook speciality tobacco. One woman describes it wrily as a 'slave camp'. In fact, work here is the most skilled task in the factory. You have to carry out the seemingly impossible feat of joining 'wrapper' leaves together, while twisting them round a 'filler' to produce a long roll of tobacco. But spinning wasn't paid at craftsman's rates.

Keeping up with the machines or the performance rates and coping with monotony – that was what factory work was about. Geoff, the training supervisor, thought he really 'knew' the 'girls' at Churchmans:

'They're quite happy. They're in a fool's paradise. They've got the money coming in. They've never had it so good.' And indeed it was the money that kept them there. It was very good – *for a woman*:

> Patti: We get good wages. I think I'm lucky to be working here. We ought to be grateful for having jobs.

But 'good for a woman' did not mean it was a living wage:

> Sandra: You know, I thought it was good wages in here. Well it is, I suppose, except for the price of flats and food and bus fares.

And the money didn't mean that they were not bored:

> *Patti:* I'd like to see them here. I'd like to see the manager on a weighing machine for a week.
>
> *Mary:* Not a week! An hour would be enough!

Finding escapes made factory life tolerable. You had to pretend it wasn't happening, or steal a break:

> *Val:* You gets used to it, though. I think it's imagination a lot of the time.
>
> *Sue:* Some girls'll sit up all day and weigh. But with me, well, I gets me hair off. I mucks about. I gets so fed up, I goes out the back.

Twice a day there is music. In the hand-packing room, there is an encyclopaedia under the supervisor's desk for quizzes. Some machine weighers read books while their hands continue 'on automatic'.

Most important of all, however, is companionship and collective life. As the women talked to me, it became clear that a 'good' factory was one where you found mates. The *work* could never be 'good';

> *Jenny:* You've just got to be friends with everyone. Like it's terrible if someone's not talking to you. But if you're talking to them, and friends with them, it's all right.

Mucking in together, and having a laugh, are what make a 'good' day. There are jokes, sing-songs, teasing. In the hand-stripping room sits Vi, almost 60, single, bent and quite deaf:

> *Pearl:* Vi's got the nice voice, haven't you, Vi? Come on, Vi!
>
> *Vi* (in a croaking voice, the others listening solemnly): We was waltzing together, and the stars began to fall . . . In this wonderful moment, something's happened to my heart, We was once changing partners till I'm in your arms and then . . . So we'll keep on changing partners till I hold you once more.
>
> *Pearl:* (shouting): Look, Vi, over there, your boyfriend's coming.
>
> *Vera:* (pointing to a chargehand in his glass cubicle): Ooh. Here's your boyfriend coming. Here's Jo coming. You'll have a kiss now, Ivy.
>
> *Pearl and Vera* (calling): Jo! Jo! (then like doves) Joey! Joey!
>
> *Vera:* Ah, he didn't hear, Vi. Never mind, eh.

Some of the best laughs are from turning the tables on supervisors, especially getting the upper hand with men:

> *Pearl:* Vi, sing *Robinson Crusoe*! Come over here, Stan (calling over to the chargehand).

Vi	(singing): He's a dirty old man, called Crusoe, He sat on the rock and played with his sock,
	(roars of laughter among the women, Stan looking hot under the collar)
	Oh dear old Robinson Crusoe.

Higher management, who quite often visited the shop floor, were not exempt from older women's mockery. While a visiting party of salesmen comb their hair before a photograph taken next to a hogshead of tobacco, the hand-stemmers taunt them through a glass partition:

| *Stella:* | He's combing his hair! If we combed our hair in the factory, he'd go out of his mind. |
| *Vera:* | Well, go and tell him, Stan, manager or no. |

At this point the salesmen pose with their arms round each other:

All the women:	Ah! Ah!
Vera:	Wish they could hear us! AH! Everybody together. AH!
All the women	(even louder): AH! AH!
Vera:	I'm glad he had a sauna. He's slimming; Nicholson, he's on a diet.
Me:	Which one is he?
Stella:	The manager. With his hand here. He's always got his hand down his trousers.

Chargehands have to 'deal with' the build-up of boredom and frustration:

| *Val:* | I goes to sleep. I daydream. But when we don't talk for two hours, I start tormentin the others, pulling the rag about, muck about sort of thing. With the Irish, you know, I picks on them. About Ireland – take the soldiers back, the bombings, all that – only mucking about like I don't mean it. But then we has a little row, but we don't mean what we says. But I get so bored, I got to do something, or I start going out the back and have a fag. (Music comes on.) It's the best part of the day when the records come on. |

Older women find the younger generation 'more defiant' than they used to be. 'Good thing, too, though sometimes it can go too far.' Shop-floor humour is aggressive, often sexual. 'Who were you in bed with last night?' – '*Me*? In bed with someone? Don't be disgusting.' There are quick-witted insults, jibes, competition. Sometimes there are uproarious sessions of jokes.

Once I was called over to a group helpless with splutters of laughter, red faces and watery eyes:

Cherry:	What do you think of polo?
Me:	Polo?
Cherry	(shrieks up a pitch): Yes! The mint with the hole!
(Uproar.)	

Ann: Want a banana? (shrieks)
Cherry: Oh yeh – a banana!
Ann: Can I have it peeled, please?

Then they turn on Cherry, who has a face burnt red by a sun lamp:

Rene: You've got radiation.
All: Radiation! Radiation! Radiation!
Rene: Only three weeks to live! Never mind, eh. What are you going to do?
Cherry: I don't want to be a virgin all my life. (A good minute's solid ribaldry.)
Rene: Ssh. Not so loud.
Me: What else are you going to do?
Cherry: Two weeks left? Must see the changing of the guards. Ooh aah.

READING 71

Catherine Marsh

The Value of the Survey Method

The word ['survey'] has a long tradition in the English language, and developed from being the fact of viewing or inspecting something in detail (as in a land survey) to the act of doing so rigorously and comprehensively, and finally to the written results. The idea of the social survey started with this connotation of the collection of social facts, but has undergone an evolution such that nowadays the survey method is a way not just of collecting data but also of analysing the results.

A survey refers to an investigation where:

(a) systematic measurements are made over a series of cases yielding a rectangle of data;
(b) the variables in the matrix are analysed to see if they show any patterns;
(c) the subject matter is social.

In other words, surveys have a particular method of data collection, a particular method of data analysis and a particular substance.

The only restriction made on the survey as a method of collecting data is to insist that it be systematic, looking at more than one *case*, be it individuals, hospitals, countries or whatever, and measuring the same variables on each case, so that you end up with each case having one and only one code for each variable. The data could come from observation, from fixed-choice responses to a postal questionnaire, from content analysis of newspapers, or from postcoding tape-recorded depth interviews. The important thing is that there is more than one case and that variation between cases is considered systematically. 'Survey analysis' involves making causal inferences from some kind of passive observation programme. The word 'survey' *is* sometimes used to refer to such investigations as a split-ballot question-wording trial, where there has been an experimental manipulation, but I think it is clearer if we use the word 'experiment' to describe such investigations.

Surveys and experiments are the only two methods known to me to test a hypothesis about how the world works. The experimenter intervenes in the social world, does something to a set of subjects (and usually also refrains from doing that thing to a set of controls) and looks to see what effect *manipulating* variance in the independent variable has on the dependent variable. If the subjects have been assigned in some fashion to control and experimental groups, the experimenter can be sure that it is what she did to the independent variable that has produced any differences between the groups.

The survey researcher has only made a series of observations; to be sure, as we shall come on to argue, these cannot be seen as passive reflections of unproblematic reality, but they must be logically distinguished from the manipulation that the experimenter engages in. The only element of randomness in the survey design comes in random selection of cases; *random sampling does not achieve the same result as random allocation into control and experimental groups.* The survey researcher may have a theory which leads her to suspect that X is having a causal effect on Y. If she wants to test this, she has to measure X and Y on a variety of different subjects, and infer from the fact that X and Y covary that the original hypothesis was true. But unlike the experimenter, she cannot rule out the possibility *in principle* of there being a third variable prior to X and Y and causing the variance in both; the experimenter knows that the relationship is not spurious because she knows exactly what produced the variance in X – *she* did.

In other words, in survey research the process of testing causal hypotheses, central to any theory-building endeavour, is a very indirect process of drawing inferences from already existing variance in populations by a rigorous process of comparison. In practice, one of the major strategies of the survey researcher is to control for other variables that she thinks might realistically be held also to produce an effect, but she never gets round the purist's objection that she has not definitively established a causal relationship. Furthermore, although having panel data across time certainly helps with the practical resolution of the problem of how to decide which of one's variables are prior to which others, it does not solve the logical difficulty that, in principle, any relationship which one finds may be explained by the operation of another unmeasured factor.

Finally, the subject matter of the surveys that sociologists are interested in is always social. Many different disciplines collect systematic observational data and make inferences from it. Biologists looking at correlations between plant growth and different types of environment, psychologists coding films of mother–child interactions, or astronomers drawing inferences about the origins of the universe from measurements of light intensity taken now are all performing activities whose logic is similar to that of the social survey analyst, but they would not describe their studies as 'surveys'....

Surveys have a lot to offer the sociologist. Since experimentation cannot be used to investigate a wide range of macrosocial processes, there is often no alternative to considering variation across cases in a systematic fashion. Since the processes of determination in the social world are subjective in important ways, involving actors' meanings and intentions, the survey researcher has to face the task of measuring these subjective aspects. It is not easy. Perhaps the most misguided and damaging of all the criticisms that have been made of survey research was C. W. Mills's contention that their design and implementation involved no sociological imagination, but only the mechanical skills of techniques following time-honoured formulae. Nor are surveys cheap. Because of the ever-present danger of faulty inference from correlational data, measurements of all the possible confounding variables must be made, and the sample size must be large enough to ensure adequate representation of cases in the subcells created in analysis.

The survey method is a tool. Like any tool, it is open to misuse. It can be used in providing evidence for sociological arguments or, as in any aspect of sociology, it can be used for ideological constructions. Surveys are expensive, so it tends to be people with power and resources who have used them most heavily.

READING 72

Joanna Mack and Stewart Lansley

Absolute and Relative Poverty in Britain: An Illustration of Survey Work

There has been a long tradition that has tried to define poverty narrowly in terms of health, aiming either for a universal standard or for a standard relative to a particular moment in time. There has been an equally long tradition that has seen a person's needs as being culturally and socially, as well as physically, determined. It is a view that recognizes that there is more to life than just existing. Two hundred years ago the economist Adam Smith wrote:

> By necessaries, I understand not only commodities which are indispensably necessary for the support of life but whatever the custom of the country renders it indecent for creditable people, even of the lowest order, to be without. A linen shirt, for example, is strictly speaking not a necessity of life. The Greeks and Romans lived, I suppose, very comfortably though they had no linen. But in the present time . . . a creditable day-labourer would be ashamed to appear in public without a linen shirt, the want of which would be supposed to denote that disgraceful state of poverty.

This theme was adopted and first used for a more practical purpose by Charles Booth in his pioneering surveys of poverty in London from the late 1880s to the turn of the century. He defined the very poor as those whose means were insufficient 'according to the normal standards of life in this country'. . . .

The essentially relative nature of poverty is immediately obvious when viewing people's standards of living in these broader terms. Purchases of consumer durables are specific to each generation, or even each decade, and activities involving social participation have no meaning outside the society in which people live. This has long been recognized; Karl Marx wrote in 1849: 'Our needs and enjoyments spring from society; we measure them, therefore, by society and not by the objects of their satisfaction. Because they are of a social nature, they are of a relative nature.' . . .

[Yet] a body of opinion has persisted that places emphasis only on 'absolute' poverty. The fact that the poor in Britain today are better off than the poor of the past, and than the poor of other countries today, is seen to devalue their problems. Dr Rhodes Boyson, as Minister for Social Security, gave his view of 'relative' poverty to the House of Commons in a debate on the rich and the poor called by the opposition:

> Those on the poverty line in the United States earn more than 50 times the average income of someone in India. That is what relative poverty is all about. . . . Apparently, the more people earn, the more they believe poverty exists, presumably so that they can be pleased about the fact that it is not themselves who are poor.

Others, in contrast, have argued that the facts of starvation in the poorest countries of the world and the intense deprivations suffered by the poor of the past are not relevant to the problems of the poor of the industrialized world today. Tony Crosland, for example, argued not just for the importance of a concept of 'primary' poverty but also that

> poverty is not, after all, an absolute, but a social or cultural concept. . . . This demands a relative, subjective view of poverty, since the unhappiness and injustice it creates, even when ill-health and malnutrition are avoided, lies in the enforced deprivation not of luxuries indeed, but of small comforts which others have and are seen to have, and which in the light of prevailing cultural standards are really 'conventional necessities'.

During the 1960s this view became widely accepted, as a result – at least in part – of the work of Professor Peter Townsend. For the last thirty years, Townsend has argued that poverty can only be viewed in terms of the concept of 'relative deprivation'. In his studies of poverty he has refined this concept, culminating in his 1969 survey of living standards. In his report of this comprehensive and influential study, Townsend defined poverty as follows:

> Individuals, families and groups in the population can be said to be in poverty when they lack the resources to obtain the types of diet, participate in the activities and have the living conditions and amenities which are customary, or are at least widely encouraged or approved, in the societies to which they belong.

Although something like this definition of poverty would now be widely accepted, there remains immense room for debate about what exactly it means.

The central brief given to MORI, the survey specialists commissioned by London Weekend Television to design and conduct the *Breadline Britain* survey, was as follows:

> The survey's first, and most important, aim is to try to discover whether there is a public consensus on what is an acceptable standard of living for

Table 15.1 The public's perception of necessities

Standard-of-living items in rank order	% classing item as necessity	Standard-of-living items in rank order	% classing item as necessity
1 Heating to warm living areas of the home if it's cold	97	18 New, not second-hand, clothes	64
2 Indoor toilet (not shared with another household)	96	19 A hobby or leisure activity	64
3 Damp-free home	96	20 Two hot meals a day (for adults)	64
4 Bath (not shared with another household)	94	21 Meat or fish every other day	63
5 Beds for everyone in the household	94	22 Presents for friends or family once a year	63
6 Public transport for one's needs	88	23 A holiday away from home for one week a year, not with relatives	63
7 A warm waterproof coat	87		
8 Three meals a day for children	82	24 Leisure equipment for children e.g. sports equipment or a bicycle	57
9 Self-contained accommodation	79	25 A garden	55
10 Two pairs of all-weather shoes	78	26 A television	51
11 Enough bedrooms for every child over 10 of different sex to have his/her own	77	27 A 'best outfit' for special occasions	48
12 Refrigerator	77	28 A telephone	43
13 Toys for children	71	29 An outing for children once a week	43
14 Carpets in living rooms and bedrooms	70	30 A dressing gown	40
15 Celebrations on special occasions such as Christmas	70	31 Children's friends round for tea/a snack once a fortnight	37
16 A roast meat joint or its equivalent once a week	67	32 A night out once a fortnight (adults)	36
		33 Friends/family round for a meal once a month	32
17 A washing machine	67	34 A car	22
		35 A packet of cigarettes every other day	14

Average of all 35 items = 64.1

Britain in 1983 and, if there is a consensus, who, if anyone, falls below that standard.

The idea underlying this is that a person is in 'poverty' when their standard of living falls below the minimum deemed necessary by current public opinion. This minimum may cover not only the basic essentials for survival (such as food) but also access, or otherwise, to participating in society and being able to play a social role.

The survey established, for the first time ever, that a majority of people see the necessities of life in Britain in the 1980s as covering a wide range of goods and activities, and that people judge a minimum standard of living on socially established criteria and not just the criteria of survival or subsistence.

Table 15.1 lists the thirty-five items that were tested, ranked by the proportion of respondents identifying each item as a 'necessity'. This ranking shows that there is a considerable degree of social consensus. Over nine in ten people are agreed about the importance of the following basic living conditions in the home:

* heating;
* an indoor toilet (not shared);
* a damp-free home;
* a bath (not shared); and
* beds for everyone.

The right of everyone, regardless of income, to exactly these sorts of basic minima was a key objective of postwar housing policy until the recent sharp cutbacks in public-sector housing investment.

The survey also found a considerable degree of consensus about the importance of a wide range of other goods and activities. More than two-thirds of the respondents classed the following items as necessities:

* enough money for public transport;
* a warm waterproof coat;
* three meals a day for children;
* self-contained accommodation;
* two pairs of all-weather shoes;
* a bedroom for every child over 10 of different sex;
* a refrigerator;
* toys for children;
* carpets;
* celebrations on special occasions such as Christmas;
* a roast joint or its equivalent once a week; and
* a washing machine.

This widespread consensus on what are necessities clearly reflects the standards of today and not those of the past. In Rowntree's study of poverty in York in 1899, for a family to be classed as poor 'they must never spend a penny on railway fare or omnibus'. In Britain in the 1980s, nearly nine in ten people think that such spending is not only justified but a necessity for living today.

John Heritage
Conversation Analysis

The inception and development of conversation analysis as a distinctive field of research is closely linked with problems surrounding the tendency for ordinary language descriptions to gloss or idealize the specifics of what they depict. This tendency is inherent in the use of type concepts in the social sciences irrespective of whether the types are produced by 'averaging' as recommended by Durkheim[1] or by explicit idealization as proposed by Weber in his various methodological writings. In an early paper, Sacks criticized the use of both of these categories of type concepts in sociology on the grounds that they necessarily blur the specific features of the events under investigation.[2] The result, he argued, is that sociological concepts and generalizations can have only a vague and indeterminate relationship with any specific set of events. This, in turn, inhibits the development of sociology as a cumulative body of knowledge because, given this indeterminacy, it can be difficult to decide whether a specific case in fact supports or undermines a given sociological generalization.

Sacks's response to this problem was a deliberate decision to develop a method of analysis which would keep a grip on the primary data of the social world – the raw material of specific, singular events of human conduct:

> When I started to do research in sociology I figured that sociology could not be an actual science unless it was able to handle the details of actual events, handle them formally, and in the first instance be informative about them in the direct ways in which primitive sciences tend to be informative, that is, that anyone else can go and see whether what was said is so. And that is a tremendous control on seeing whether one is learning anything. So the question was, could there be some way that sociology could hope to deal with the details of actual events, formally and informatively? . . . I wanted to locate some set of materials that would permit a test.[3]

Sacks's work on tape-recorded conversation was initiated in deliberate pursuit of this methodological aim:

> It was not from any large interest in language or from some theoretical formulation of what should be studied that I started with tape-recorded conversation, but simply because I could get my hands on it and I could

study it again and again, and also, consequentially, because others could look at what I had studied and make of it what they could, if, for example, they wanted to be able to disagree with me.[4]

The contemporary methodology of conversation analysis has maintained Sacks's pioneering focus on the details of actual interactions and his effort to forestall the process of idealization. Its insistence on the use of data collected from naturally occurring occasions of everyday interaction is paralleled by a corresponding *avoidance of a range of other research methodologies as unsatisfactory* sources of data. These include: (1) the use of interviewing techniques in which the verbal formulations of subjects are treated as an appropriate substitute for the observation of actual behaviour; (2) the use of observational methods in which data are recorded through field notes or with pre-coded schedules; (3) the use of native intuitions as a means of inventing examples of interactional behaviour; and (4) the use of experimental methodologies involving the direction or manipulation of behaviour. These techniques have been avoided because each of them involves processes in which the specific details of naturally situated interactional conduct are irretrievably lost and are replaced by idealizations about how interaction works.

A range of considerations inform this preference for the use of recorded data over subjects' reports, observers' notes or unaided intuition or recollection. Anyone who has examined conversational materials will be highly conscious of the deficiencies of such resources by comparison with the richness and diversity of empirically occurring interaction. For example, although the following sequence is by no means extraordinary, it is difficult to imagine its invention by a social scientist.

```
(1) (NB:VII:2)⁵
    E:    = Oh honey that was a lovely luncheon I shoulda ca:lled you
          s:soo⌈:ner but I:  ⌈l:⌈lo:ved it. It w's just deli:ghtfu⌈:l.     ⌉
    M:          ⌊((f)) Oh:::  ⌋⌊  (    )                            ⌊Well ⌋=
    M:    = I w's gla⌈d      you⌉(came).⌉
    E:              ⌊'nd yer f:⌊friends ⌋'re so da:rli:ng,=
    M:    = Oh:::⌈: it w'z:       ⌉
    E:          ⌊e-that P-⌊a:t isn'she a do:⌈:ll?⌉
    M:                                      ⌊iYe⌋ h isn't she pretty,
          (.)
    E:    Oh: she's a beautiful girl.=
    M:    = Yeh I think she's a pretty gir⌈l.
    E:                                    ⌊En' that Reinam'n::
          (.)
    E:    She SCA:RES me.=
```

Not only is it impossible to imagine the above being invented, it is similarly inconceivable that it could be recollected in such detail either by an ethnographer or by an actual participant. And, even if it could be recollected, it could not be heard again and again. Moreover, as Sacks notes, it can be difficult to treat invented or recollected sequences as fully persuasive evidence for analytic claims.[6] And even if they are accepted, such inventions or recollections can tell us nothing about the frequency, range, variety or typicality of the conversational procedures within the fragment.

The intuitive invention of data is subject to an additional problem which has nothing to do with complexity, but everything to do with the way unaided intuition tends to typify the ways interaction happens. Consider (2) below:

(2)　　A:　　I have a fourteen-year-old son.
　　　　B:　　Well that's alright.
　　　　A:　　I also have a dog.
　　　　B:　　Oh I'm sorry.

Although (2) is simple enough, it is not the way we imagine interaction happens. If it had been invented, it might have been used to show what is meant by incoherent interaction. But in fact (2) is taken from a conversation in which the would-be tenant of an apartment (A) is describing circumstances to the landlord (B) which might disqualify the rental and, viewed in this context, the datum is perfectly coherent and sensible. The myriad ways in which specific contexts (e.g. particular social identities, purposes and circumstances) are talked into being and orientated to in interaction vastly exceed the comparatively limited, and overwhelmingly typified, powers of imaginative intuition.

A similar range of issues arises in relation to experimentally produced data. The success of social-psychological experiments is strongly dependent on the experimenter's ability to identify, control and manipulate the relevant dependent and independent variables. Not only is this extremely difficult to accomplish without some form of experimenter contamination, but also it is unlikely that an experimenter will be able to identify the range of relevant variables without previous exposure to naturally occurring interaction. Moreover, without such exposure the experimenter will find it difficult to extrapolate from experimental findings to real situations of conduct, nor will it prove easy to determine which (if any) of the experimental findings are artefacts of the experimental situation, since such a determination can only be achieved by systematic comparison with naturally occurring data. In sum, the most straightforward procedure has been to work with naturally occurring materials from the outset. Naturally occurring interaction presents an immense range of interactional variations in terms of which systematic comparisons may be used both to check and to extend particular analyses.

Thus the use of recorded data is an essential corrective to the limitations of intuition and recollection. In enabling repeated and detailed examination of the events of interaction, the use of recordings extends the range and precision of the observations which can be made. It permits other researchers to have direct access to the data about which claims are being made, thus making analysis subject to detailed public scrutiny and helping to minimize the influence of personal preconceptions or analytical biases. Finally, it may be noted that because the data are available in 'raw' form they can be reused in a variety of investigations and can be re-examined in the context of new findings. All of these major advantages derive from the fact that the original data are neither idealized nor constrained by a specific research design or by reference to some particular theory or hypothesis.

Part XVI

Theoretical Perspectives in Sociology

Many different theoretical outlooks exist in sociology, although they tend to converge on a similar range of basic problems and issues. Reading 74 provides a succinct description of the tenets of one of the most influential bodies of thought from the nineteenth century, that of Karl Marx and Friedrich Engels. Human social life, Marx argues, is organized above all in terms of the practical requirements whereby material production is carried on. Changes in the social frameworks of production have profound consequences for all the other major institutions of society.

Marx and Engels did not recognize a separate discipline of 'sociology'. Their writings span whole areas of what would now be recognized as distinct disciplines of sociology, economics, history and philosophy. They were specifically hostile to the work of Auguste Comte, who first coined the term 'sociology' and regarded himself as its prime founder. Emile Durkheim, by contrast, drew heavily upon Comte's work and sought to consolidate the establishment of sociology as a distinctive and specific social science. According to Durkheim (Reading 75), sociology is the study of social facts: objectively given conditions of social life. Social facts, he declared in a famous statement, should be treated as 'things'. Established patterns of social life, in other words, have a solidity and a resistance to the individual will on a par with material objects in the natural world. We might think of ourselves as the creators of social institutions, but in fact the more enduring of such institutions predate our individual lives and are 'external' characteristics of the environments in which we move.

Max Weber, the third great classical influence upon modern sociology, took a different position again (Reading 76). Weber rejected the type of viewpoint expressed by Durkheim, arguing instead that social activity has to be understood in terms of the meanings which social behaviour has for those involved. Unlike objects in nature, human beings are purposive, reasoning agents, whose activities are not governed by mechanical considerations. To know why a person acts as he or she does involves interpreting the meaning of the action for that individual. Although sociology in this sense is 'subjective', Weber stated, it none the less strives for clear and verifiable accounts of human social life.

The acknowledged founders of sociology were all male and none of them gave any particular attention to the position of women in society, or to questions of gender more generally. Such issues, however, were discussed in nineteenth-century social thought, as the selection from Harriet Taylor Mill demonstrates (Reading 77). Together with her husband, John Stuart Mill, Harriet Mill took up the challenge of women's emancipation. Women, she argued – and this was certainly true at the time at which she wrote – are educated to accept one dominant aim: making a satisfactory marriage. Once they start to embrace a wider range of social objectives, however, and move out from the confines of the domestic setting, they have the capability radically to change modern civilization. If marriage were abolished, she suggested, women could be placed on an equal par with men and many other desirable social changes would follow.

The following three pieces all concern traditions of social theory which have become particularly influential in the twentieth century. George H. Mead (Reading 78) is the originator of what has come to be called 'symbolic interactionism' (he himself did not use that term). Symbolic interactionism shares elements with Weber's standpoint, accentuating as it does the meaningful qualities of social activity. According to this perspective, social interaction is symbolic in nature. In contrast to Weber, however, Mead wrote extensively upon the self, arguing that social interaction is vital to the emergence of self-consciousness in the human individual. The individual first of all experiences her- or himself not in an immediate way, but by means of the attitudes and reactions others assume.

Functionalism and structuralism rank as two of the most influential theoretical approaches in modern sociology. Durkheim's writings provided the prime inspiration for the emergence of functional analysis, although some aspects of his writings also became incorporated within structuralism. Dorothy Emmet (Reading 79) offers a lucid description of the concept of function. Functional analysis, she declares, consists essentially in relating one element of a larger system to the overall workings of that system. Studying the function of an organ in the body, therefore, would mean showing what contribution that organ makes to the life of the organism as a whole. Analysing the function of a social item, such as a religious practice, means showing how such a practice contributes to the overall continuity of the social order.

Like functionalist analysis, structuralism (Reading 80) distances itself from interpretation of human action in terms of intentions or reasons. As a theoretical tradition, structuralism has its origins in the study of language, particularly as pioneered by the linguist Ferdinand de Saussure. Saussure argued that the structural components of language are not actually contained in specific instances of speech. Language (*langue*) consists of sets of rules and strategies which language users have to employ if they are to generate grammatical speech and to understand others.

Structuralists have suggested that the structural qualities of social systems can be understood in a parallel fashion. According to this view, the structural characteristics of human societies are not best represented, as in functionalism, as parts of a 'visible' social unity. Rather, 'structure' should be understood as the rules and conventions which 'stand behind' observed regularities in social activity.

This theme is further developed in the final selection in the volume (Reading 81). Most of the above standpoints either stress that social phenomena are independent of the intentions and reasons individuals have for what they do, or emphasize such reasons and intentions to the exclusion of structural influences. We need to develop an outlook in sociological theory which acknowledges the structural features of social systems, yet gives full recognition to the significance of 'meaningful' action. Such a perspective implies a reassessment of the relation between sociology and common-sense beliefs, since such beliefs are core elements of the meaningful activities of social actors.

Karl Marx and Friedrich Engels

The Materialist Conception of History

In the social production of their life, men enter into definite relations that are indispensable and independent of their will, relations of production which correspond to a definite stage of development of their material productive forces. The sum total of these relations of production constitutes the economic structure of society, the real foundation, on which rises a legal and political superstructure and to which correspond definite forms of social consciousness. The mode of production of material life conditions the social, political and intellectual life process in general. It is not the consciousness of men that determines their being, but, on the contrary, their social being that determines their consciousness. At a certain stage of their development, the material productive forces of society come in conflict with the existing relations of production, or – what is but a legal expression for the same thing – with the property relations within which they have been at work hitherto. From forms of development of the productive forces these relations turn into their fetters. Then begins an epoch of social revolution. With the change of the economic foundation the entire immense superstructure is more or less rapidly transformed. In considering such transformations a distinction should always be made between the material transformation of the economic conditions of production, which can be determined with the precision of natural science, and the legal, political, religious, aesthetic or philosophic – in short, ideological forms in which men become conscious of this conflict and fight it out. Just as our opinion of an individual is not based on what he thinks of himself, so can we not judge of such a period of transformation by its own consciousness; on the contrary, this consciousness must be explained rather from the contradictions of material life, from the existing conflict between the social productive forces and the relations of production. No social order ever perishes before all the productive forces for which there is room in it have developed; and new, higher relations of production never appear before the material conditions of their existence have matured in the womb of the old society itself. Therefore mankind always sets itself only such tasks as it can solve; since, looking at the matter more closely, it will always be found that the task itself arises only when the material conditions for its solution already exist or are at least in the process of formation. In broad outlines Asiatic, ancient, feudal and modern bourgeois modes of production can be designated as progressive epochs in the economic formation of society. The bourgeois relations of production are the last antagonistic form of the social process of production – antagonistic not in the sense of individual antagonism, but of one arising from the social conditions of life of the individuals; at the same time the productive forces developing in the womb of bourgeois society create the material conditions for the solution of that antagonism. This social formation brings, therefore, the prehistory of human society to a close.

READING 75

Emile Durkheim
The Field of Sociology

The proposition according to which social facts are to be treated as things – which is the very foundation of our method – is one which has stimulated great opposition. It has been considered paradoxical and scandalous for us to assimilate the realities of the social world to those of the external world. Such criticism involves a singular misunderstanding of the meaning and application of this assimilation: the object of this was not to reduce the higher to the lower forms of being, but on the contrary to claim for the higher forms a degree of reality at least equal to that which is readily granted to the lower. We do not say that social facts are material things, but that they are things by the same right as material things, although they differ from them in type.

Just what is a 'thing'? A thing differs from an idea in the same way as that which we know from without differs from that which we know from within. A thing is any object of knowledge which is not naturally controlled by the intellect, which cannot be adequately grasped by a simple process of mental activity. It can only be understood by the mind on condition that the mind goes outside itself by means of observations and experiments, which move progressively from the more external and immediately accessible characteristics to the less visible and more deep-lying. To treat the facts of a certain order as things thus is not to place them in a particular category of reality, but to assume a certain mental attitude toward them; it is to approach the study of them on the principle that we are absolutely ignorant of their nature, and that their characteristic properties, like the unknown causes on which they depend, cannot be discovered by even the most careful introspection.

With the terms thus defined, our proposition, far from being a paradox, could almost pass for a truism if it were not too often misunderstood in the human sciences and especially in sociology. Indeed, one might say in this sense that, with the possible exception of the case of mathematics, every object of science is a thing. In mathematics, since we proceed from simple to more complex concepts it is sufficient to depend upon mental processes which are purely internal in character. But in the case of 'facts' properly so called, these are, at the moment when we undertake to study them scientifically, necessarily unknown *things* of which we are ignorant; for the representations which we have been able to make of them in the course of our life, having been made uncritically and unmethodically, are devoid of scientific value, and must be discarded. The facts of individual psychology themselves have this character and must be seen in this way. For although they are by definition purely mental, our consciousness of them reveals to us neither their real nature nor their genesis. It allows us to know them up to a certain point, just as our sensory knowledge gives us a certain familiarity with heat or light, sound or electricity; it gives us confused, fleeting, subjective impressions of them, but no clear and scientific notions or explanatory concepts. It is precisely for this reason that there has been founded in the course of this century an objective psychology whose fundamental purpose is to study mental facts from the outside, that is to say as things.

This is all the more necessary in the case of social facts, for consciousness is even more helpless in knowing them than in knowing its own life. It might be objected that since social facts are our own creations, we have only to look into our own mind in order to know what we put into them and how we formed them. But, in the first place, the greater part of our social institutions was bequeathed to us already formed by previous generations. We ourselves took no part in their formation, and consequently we cannot by introspection discover the causes which brought them into being. Furthermore, when we have in fact collaborated in their genesis, we can only with difficulty obtain even a very confused and a very distorted perception of the true nature of our action and the causes which determined it. When it is merely a matter of our private acts we know very imperfectly the relatively simple motives that guide us. We believe ourselves disinterested when we act egoistically; we think we are motivated by hate when we are yielding to love, that we obey reason when we are the slaves of irrational prejudices, etc. How, then, should we be able to discern with greater clarity the much more complex causes from which collective acts proceed? For, at the very least, each one of us participates in them only as an infinitesimal unit; a huge number of others collaborate with us, and what takes place in these other minds escapes us.

Thus our principle implies no metaphysical conception, no speculation about the fundamental nature of being. What it demands is that the sociologist put himself in the same state of mind as physicists, chemists or physiologists, when they enquire into a hitherto unexplored region of the scientific domain. When he penetrates the social world, he must be aware that he is penetrating the unknown. He must feel himself in the presence of facts whose laws are as unsuspected as were those of life before the development of biology; he must be prepared for discoveries which will surprise and disconcert him.

READING 76

Max Weber

Meaning and Interpretation in Sociology

The term 'sociology' is open to many different interpretations. In the context used here it will mean that science which aims at the interpretative understanding of social behaviour in order to gain an explanation of its causes, its course and its effects. It will be called human 'behaviour' only in so far as the person or persons involved engage in some subjectively meaningful action. Such behaviour may be mental or external; it may consist in action or omission to act. The term 'social behaviour' will be reserved for activities whose intent is related by the individuals involved to the conduct of others and is orientated accordingly.

(1) 'Meaning' is used here in two different senses. First, there is actual conduct by a specific actor in a given historical situation or the rough approximation based on a given quantity of cases involving many actors; and, second, there is the conceptually 'ideal type' of subjective meaning attributed to a hypothetical actor in a given type of conduct. In neither sense can it be used as an objectively 'valid' or as a metaphysically fathomable 'true' meaning. Herein lies the distinction between the behavioural sciences, such as sociology and history, and the orthodox disciplines, such as jurisprudence, logic, ethics or aesthetics, whose purpose it is to determine the 'true' and 'valid' meaning of the objects of their analysis.

(2) The line between meaningful and merely responsive (i.e. subjectively not meaningful) behaviour is extremely fluid. A significant part of all sociologically relevant behaviour, principally purely traditional behaviour . . ., fluctuates between the two. Meaningful, i.e. subjectively understandable, conduct does not figure at all in many cases of psychophysical processes, or, if it does, is recognizable only by the expert; mystical experiences which cannot be adequately communicated in words are never fully understandable for anyone who is not susceptible to such experiences. On the other hand, the ability to perform a similar action is not a precondition to understanding; it is not necessary 'to be Caesar in order to understand Caesar'. To be able to put one's self in the place of the actor is important for clearness of understanding but not an absolute precondition for meaningful interpretation. Understandable and non-understandable parts of a process are often inextricably intertwined.

(3) All interpretation strives, as does science generally, for clarity and verifiable proof. Such proof of understanding will be either of a rational, i.e. logical or mathematical, or of an emotionally emphatic, artistically appreciative, character. Rational proof can be supplied in the sphere of behaviour by a clear intellectual grasp of everything within its intended context of meaning. Emphatic proof in the sphere of behaviour will be supplied by complete sympathetic emotional participation. Direct and unambiguous intelligibility is rational understanding of the highest order, especially in mathematically and logically related propositions. We understand plainly what it means when anyone uses the proposition $2 + 2 = 4$ or the Pythagorean theorem in reasoning or argument, or when a chain of reasoning is logically executed in accordance with accepted ways of thought. In the same way we understand the actions of a person who tries to achieve a certain goal by choosing appropriate means, if the facts of the situation on the basis of which he makes his choice are familiar to us. Any interpretation of such rationally purposeful action possesses – for an understanding of the means employed – the highest degree of proof. Not with the same accuracy, but still accurate enough for most purposes of explanation, it is possible to understand errors (including problem entanglements) to which we ourselves are susceptible or whose origin can be detected by sympathetic self-analysis. On the other hand, many ultimate *goals* or *values* towards which experience shows that human behaviour may be orientated often cannot be understood as such, though it is possible to grasp them intellectually. The more radically they vary from our own ultimate values, the more difficult it is for us to understand them through sympathetic participation. Depending

upon the circumstances of a particular case, it must then suffice to achieve only a purely intellectual understanding of such values or, failing that, a simple acceptance of them as given data. As far as is possible, the conduct motivated by these values can then be understood on the basis of whatever opportunities appear to be available for a sympathetic emotional and/or intellectual interpretation at different stages of its development. Here belong many zealous acts of religion or piety which are quite incomprehensible to those not susceptible to such values; as well as the extreme rationalistic fanaticism typical of the exponents of the 'rights of man' theories which are abhorrent to those who, for their part, emphatically repudiate them.

As our susceptibility grows, the more readily are we able to experience such true passions as fear, anger, ambition, envy, jealousy, love, enthusiasm, pride, vengeance, pity, devotion and other desires of every kind, as well as the irrational behaviour issuing from them. Even when the degree of intensity in which these emotions are found far surpasses our own potentialities for experiential understanding, we can still interpret intellectually their impact on the direction taken by our behaviour as well as the choice of means used to implement it. For purposes of systematic scientific analysis it will be convenient to represent all irrational, emotionally conditioned elements of conduct as deviations from a conceptually pure type of goal-orientated behaviour. For example, an analysis of a crisis on the stock exchange would be most conveniently attempted in the following manner: first, a determination of how it would have run its course in the absence of irrational factors; second, using the foregoing as a hypothetical premise, the irrational components are then singled out as 'deviation' from the norm. In the same way, the determination of the rational course of a political or military campaign needs first to be made in the light of all known circumstances and known goals of the participants. Only then will it be possible to account for the causal significance of irrational factors as deviations from the ideal type.

The construction of a purely rational 'goal-orientated' course of conduct, because of its clear understandability and rational unambiguity, serves sociology as an 'ideal type'. Thus we are aided in our understanding of the way in which actual goal-orientated conduct is influenced by irrational factors of every kind (such as emotion, errors) and which then can be classified as deviations from the original hypothesized behaviour.

Only in this respect and because of methodological efficiency can the method of sociology be considered 'rationalistic'. Naturally, this procedure may not be interpreted as a rationalistic bias on the part of sociology, but simply as a methodological device. Neither can it be considered as evidence of the predominance of rationalism in human existence. To what extent the reality of rationalism does determine conduct is not to be considered here. That there is a danger of rationalistic interpretations in the wrong place will not be denied. Unfortunately, all experience confirms the existence of such a danger.

(4) On the other hand, certain 'meaningless' (i.e. devoid of subjective meaning) processes and phenomena exist in all sciences of human behaviour. They act as stimuli, or effects, and they either encourage or inhibit human conduct. Such 'meaningless' behaviour should not be confused with inan-

imate or non-human behaviour. Every artefact (e.g. a machine) acquires meaning only to the extent that its production and use will serve to influence human behaviour; such meaning may be quite varied in its purposes. But without reference to such meaning the object remains completely unintelligible.

What makes this object intelligible, then, is its relation to human behaviour in its role of either means or end. It is this relationship of which the individual can claim to have awareness and to which his conduct has been orientated. Only in terms of such categories does an understanding of objects of this kind arise.

READING 77

Harriet Taylor Mill
The Social Character of Gender

If I could be Providence for the world for a time, for the express purpose of raising the condition of women, I should come to you to know the *means* – the *purpose* would be to remove all interference with affection, or with anything which is, or which even might be supposed to be, demonstrative of affection. In the present state of women's mind, perfectly uneducated, and with whatever of timidity and dependence is natural to them increased a thousandfold by their habit of utter dependence, it would probably be mischievous to remove at once all restraints, they would buy themselves protectors at a dearer cost than even at present – but without raising their natures at all. It seems to me that once give women the desire to raise their social condition, and they have a power which in the present state of civilization and of men's characters, might be made of tremendous effect. Whether nature made a difference in the nature of men and women or not, it seems now that all men, with the exception of a few lofty minded, are sensualists more or less – women on the contrary are quite exempt from this trait, however it may appear otherwise in the cases of some. It seems strange that it should be so, unless it was meant to be a source of power in semi-civilized states such as the present – or it may not be so – it may be only that the habits of freedom and low indulgence on which boys grow up and the contrary notion of what is called purity in girls may have produced the appearance of different natures in the two sexes. As certain it is that there is equality in nothing now – all the pleasures such as they are being men's, and all the disagreeables and pains being women's, as that every pleasure would be infinitely heightened both in kind and degree by the perfect equality of the sexes. Women are educated for one single object, to gain their living by marrying – (some poor souls get it without the churchgoing. It's the same way – they do not seem to be a bit worse than their honoured sisters). To be married is the object of their existence and that object being gained they do really cease to exist as to anything worth calling life or any useful purpose. One observes very few marriages where there is any real sympathy or enjoyment or companionship between the parties. The woman knows what her power is and gains by it what she has been taught to consider 'proper' to her state. The woman who would gain power by such means is unfit for power, still they do lose this power for paltry advantages and I am astonished it has never occurred to them to gain some large purpose; but their minds are degenerated by habits of dependence. I should think that 500 years hence none of the follies of their ancestors will so excite wonder and contempt as the fact of legislative restraints as to matters of feeling – or rather in the expression of feeling. When once the law undertakes to say which demonstration of feeling shall be given to which, it seems quite consistent not to legislate for *all*, and to say how many shall be seen and how many heard, and what kind and degree of feeling allows of shaking hands. The Turks' is the only consistent mode. I have no doubt that when the whole community is really educated, though the present laws of marriage were to continue they would be perfectly disregarded, because no one would marry. The wisest and perhaps the quickest means to do away with its evils is to be found in promoting education – as it is the means of all good – but meanwhile it is hard that those who suffer most from its evils and who are always the best people, should be left without remedy. Would not the best plan be divorce which could be attained by any *without any reason assigned*, and at small expense, but which could only be finally pronounced after a long period? Not *less* time than two years should elapse between suing for divorce and permission to contract again – but what the decision will be must be certain at the moment of asking for it – unless during that time the suit should be withdrawn.

(I feel like a lawyer in talking of it only! O how absurd and little it all is!)

In the present system of habits and opinions, girls enter into what is called a contract perfectly ignorant of the conditions of it, and that they should be so is considered absolutely essential to their fitness for it!

But after all the one argument of the matter which I think might be said so as to strike both high and low natures is – who would wish to have the person without inclination? Whoever would take the benefit of a law of divorce must be those whose inclination is to separate and who on earth would wish another to remain with them against their inclination – I should think no one – people sophisticate about the matter now and will not believe that one *'really would wish to go'*! Suppose instead of calling it a 'law of divorce' it were to be called 'proof of affection' – they would like it better then.

At this present time, in this state of civilization, what evil could be caused by, first placing women on the most entire equality with men, as to all rights and privileges, civil and political, and then doing away with all laws whatever relating to marriage? Then if a woman had children she must take charge of them, women could not then have children without considering how to maintain them. Women would have no more reason to barter person for bread, or for anything else, than have men. Public offices being open to them alike, all occupations would be divided between the sexes in their natural arrangements. Fathers would provide for their daughters in the same manner as for their sons.

All the difficulties about divorce seem to be in the consideration for the children – but on this plan it would be the women's *interest* not to have children – now it is thought to be the woman's interest to have children as so many ties to the man who feeds her.

Love in its true and finest meaning, seems to be the way in which is manifested all that is highest best and beautiful in the nature of human beings – none but poets have approached to the perception of the beauty of the material world – still less of the spiritual – and hence never yet existed a poet, except by inspiration of that feeling which is the perception of beauty in all forms and by all means which are given us, as well as by *sight*. Are we not born with the *five* senses, merely as a foundation for others which we may make by them – and who extends and refines those material senses to the highest – into infinity – best fulfils the end of creation – that is only saying, *who enjoys most is most* virtuous. It is for *you* – the most worthy to be the apostle of all the highest virtues to teach such as may be taught, that the higher the *kind* of enjoyment, the *greater* the *degree*, perhaps there is but one class to whom this *can* be *taught* – the poetic nature struggling with superstition: you are fitted to be the saviour of such.

READING 78

George H. Mead
Self and Society

The self has a character which is different from that of the physio-logical organism proper. The self is something which has a develop-ment; it is not initially there, at birth, but arises in the process of social experience and activity, that is, develops in the given individual as a result of his relations to that process as a whole and to other individuals within that process. The intelligence of the lower forms of animal life, like a great deal of human intelligence, does not involve a self. In our habitual actions, for example, in our moving about in a world that is simply there and to which we are so adjusted that no thinking is involved, there is a certain amount of sensuous experience such as persons have when they are just waking up, a bare thereness of the world. Such characters about us may exist in experience without taking their place in relationship to the self. One must, of course, under those conditions, distinguish between the experience that immediately takes place and our own organization of it into the experi-ence of the self. One says upon analysis that a certain item had its place in his experience, in the experience of his self. We do inevitably tend at a cer-tain level of sophistication to organize all experience into that of a self. We do so intimately identify our experiences, especially our affective experi-ences, with the self that it takes a moment's abstraction to realize that pain and pleasure can be there without being the experience of the self. Similarly, we normally organize our memories upon the string of our self. If we date things we always date them from the point of view of our past experiences. We frequently have memories that we cannot date, that we cannot place. A picture comes before us suddenly and we are at a loss to explain when that experience originally took place. We remember perfectly distinctly the picture, but we do not have it definitely placed, and until we can place it in terms of our past experience we are not satisfied. Nevertheless, I think it is obvious when one comes to consider it that the self is not necessarily involved in the life of the organism, nor involved in what we term our sensuous experience, that is, experience in a world about us for which we have habitual reactions.

We can distinguish very definitely between the self and the body. The body can be there and can operate in a very intelligent fashion without there being a self involved in the experience. The self has the characteristic that it is an object to itself, and that characteristic distinguishes it from other objects and from the body. It is perfectly true that the eye can see the foot, but it does not see the body as a whole. We cannot see our backs; we can feel certain portions of them, if we are agile, but we cannot get an experience of our whole body. There are, of course, experiences which are somewhat vague and difficult of location, but the bodily experiences are for us organized about a self. The foot and hand belong to the self. We can see our feet, especially if we look at them from the wrong end of an opera glass, as strange things which we have difficulty in recognizing as our own. The parts of the body are quite distinguishable from the self. We can lose parts of the body without any serious invasion of the self. The mere ability to experience different parts of the body is not different from the experience of a table. The table presents a different feel from what the hand does when one hand feels another, but it is an experience of something with which we come definitely into contact. The body does not experience itself as a whole, in the sense in which the self in some way enters into the experience of the self.

It is the characteristic of the self as an object to itself that I want to bring out. This characteristic is represented in the word 'self', which is a reflexive, and indicates that which can be both subject and object. This type of object is essentially different from other objects, and in the past it has been distinguished as conscious, a term which indicates an experience with, an experience of, one's self. It was assumed that consciousness in some way carried this capacity of being an object to itself. In giving a behaviouristic statement of consciousness we have to look for some sort of experience in which the physical organism can become an object to itself.

When one is running to get away from someone who is chasing him, he is entirely occupied in this action, and his experience may be swallowed up in the objects about him, so that he has, at the time being, no consciousness of self at all. We must be, of course, very completely occupied to have that take place, but we can, I think, recognize that sort of a possible experience in which the self does not enter. We can, perhaps, get some light on that situation through those experiences in which in very intense action there appear in the experience of the individual, back of this intense action, memories and anticipations. Tolstoy as an officer in the war gives an account of having pictures of his past experience in the midst of his most intense action. There are also the pictures that flash into a person's mind when he is drowning. In such instances there is a contrast between an experience that is absolutely wound up in outside activity in which the self as an object does not enter, and an activity of memory and imagination in which the self is the principal object. The self is then entirely distinguishable from an organism that is surrounded by things and acts with reference to things, including parts of its own body. These latter may be objects like other objects, but they are just objects out there in the field, and they do not involve a self that is an object to the organism. This is, I think, frequently overlooked. It is that fact which makes our anthropomorphic reconstructions of animal life so fallacious. How can an individual get outside himself (experientially) in such a way as to become an object to himself? This is the essential psychological problem of selfhood or of self-consciousness; and its solution is to be found by referring to the process of social conduct or activity in which the given person or individual is implicated. The apparatus of reason would not be complete unless it swept itself into its own analysis of the field of experience; or unless the individual brought himself into the same experiential field as that of the other individual selves in relation to whom he acts in any given social situation. Reason cannot become impersonal unless it takes an objective, non-affective attitude towards itself; otherwise we have just consciousness, not *self*-consciousness. And it is necessary to rational conduct that the individual should thus take an objective, impersonal attitude towards himself, that he should become an object to himself. For the individual organism is obviously an essential and important fact or constituent element of the empirical situation in which it acts; and without taking objective account of itself as such, it cannot act intelligently, or rationally.

The individual experiences himself as such, not directly, but only indirectly, from the particular standpoints of other individual members of the same social group, or from the generalized standpoint of the social group as a whole to which he belongs. For he enters his own experience as a self or individual, not directly or immediately, not by becoming a subject to himself, but only in so far as he first becomes an object to himself just as other individuals are objects to him or in his experience; and he becomes an object to himself only by taking the attitudes of other individuals towards himself within a social environment or context of experience and behaviour in which both he and they are involved.

READING 79

Dorothy Emmet

The Notion of Function

Social theorists, as well as those concerned with describing social behaviour, are often guided, deliberately or implicitly, by some model of society. By 'model' is here meant a way of representing a complex of relationships the adoption of which affects how the subject is approached. The form of representation may contain an implicit analogy, and it is necessary to watch this to see that it is not carried to a point where it may mislead. One model of society, developed by Hobbes, compares it with an artefact. Those who have used this model have been thinking primarily of a deliberately and purposively contrived 'device of government' doing what it is intended to do. Another model has been that of society as an organism, but this, taken in the common-sense meaning of an organism, i.e. a body like a human or animal body with a unitary life process and probably a single centre of consciousness, is now generally regarded as misleading. There is, however, another kind of model of society which seems to be very much alive at present. This looks on a society as a single system of interrelated elements with mutual adjustments and corrections, and it examines the 'functions' of social institutions by trying to see how they contribute to maintaining this unity.

This kind of model uses a type of description which is not couched in terms of conscious purpose or intention. In some cases, whether we consider this as a type of teleological or as a type of mechanistic description may be largely a matter of words. Yet even when such an explanation is being presented as a form of mechanistic description, there is no doubt that the terminology of 'function' has certain teleological associations, if not implications, and it is well to be aware of what these are, and to be able to see in any particular instance how much is being built on them.

The notion of 'function' is applicable where

(a) the object of study can be considered as forming a system taken as a unitary whole;

(b) the unitary whole must be ordered as a differentiated complex, in which it is possible to talk about 'part–whole' relationships;

(c) the parts will be elements which can be shown to contribute to fulfilling the purpose for which the ordered whole has been set up, or, if it has not been purposefully set up, to maintaining it in a persisting or enduring state.

(The word 'contribute' here need carry no connotation of intention, or even of effort. I have used it, because it suggests a part–whole relationship, and to avoid the clumsiness of saying the parts 'play a part'.) I have included (c) as a general requirement in addition to (b), because the notion of function does not seem able, so to speak, to stand on its own feet. This is clearly so in the cases where we can speak of some part performing a function in a given whole when the whole itself is thought of as having a purpose; for instance, the function of a bit of the mechanism of a piece of apparatus can be described in relation to the purpose for which the apparatus has been constructed. In this way, the notion of function might be said to be indirectly teleological, and is commonly so used, both where the complex whole has been designed for a purpose, and where the way in which the parts of the whole work together makes it look as if it were designed. But where the purpose is not specified, or where we are reluctant to ascribe deliberate purpose at all, as in the case of biological organisms, the unexpressed presumption is likely to be that the function of an element is to be considered as the way in which it helps the system to persist and maintain itself in some form of recognizable continuity.

Here it looks as if a value judgement was being made, and perhaps not clearly recognized. Is the maintenance and stability of the system being taken as *desirable*, so that functions of elements in contributing to it are taken as thereby commendable? If so, this would introduce a teleology of values as implicit in a functional description. Or are we simply saying that, *taking some system for granted* as a complex whole, some element does in fact help maintain it? If the latter is all that is being said, then the statement that some element has a certain function might be looked on as no more than a statement of fact; it might even be said that it could be translated into a plain statement of results, as if we were to say that the statement that the function of the heart is to circulate the blood need mean no more than that the result of the heart beating is that the blood circulates: a statement in terms of efficient causality with no teleological implications. But I do not think this will quite do, since to talk about a 'function', and not only about a 'result', will be to consider the process with reference to a unitary system with a persistent structure. This assumption of an ordered context means that if we say that *x* has a function, we are in fact saying more than that *x* has the consequence *y*. It has the consequence *y* within a system the efficiency or maintenance of which depends (*inter alia*) on *y*.

READING 80

John Sturrock

Saussure and the Origins of Structuralism

We can say . . . that any word in a language is a sign, and that language functions as a system of signs.

Saussure analysed the sign into its two components: a sound or acoustic component which he called the *signifier* (*signifiant* in French), and a mental or conceptual component which he called the *signified* (*signifié*). In this analysis, be it noted, things themselves, for which linguistic signs can be asked to stand when we want to refer to the world around us, are ignored. The signified is not a thing but the notion of a thing, what comes into the mind of the speaker or hearer when the appropriate signifier is uttered. The signifier thus constitutes the material aspect of language: in the case of the spoken language a signifier is any meaningful sound which is uttered or heard, in the case of the written language it is a meaningful mark inscribed on the page. The signified is the mental aspect of language which we often deem to be immaterial, even though it is certain that within the brain a signified is also a neural event. Signifiers and signifieds can be separated in this way only by the theorist of language; in practice they are inseparable. A truly meaningless sound is not a signifier because it does not signify – there can be no signifier without a signified; correspondingly, no concept can be said to exist unless it has found expression, that is to say been materialized, either inwardly as a thought or outwardly in speech – there can be no signified without a signifier. . . .

The distinction between signifier and signified . . . can also be applied in situations other than the analysis of the constituent signs of natural language. We have experience in our daily lives of a great many signs that are not verbal ones: of pictures and diagrams, for instance. And it is a fact that any object whatsoever, be it natural or artificial, can become a sign provided that it is employed to communicate a message, i.e. to *signify*. The flower that grows only to blush unseen can never be a sign since there is no one present to turn it into one. But within a culture flowers can be and are used as signs: when they are made into a wreath and sent to a funeral, for example. In this instance, the wreath is the signifier whose signified is, let us say, 'condolence'. (There can be no precise signified for a wreath because the language of flowers is too loose, at any rate in our culture; but equally there can be no wreath without a significance of some kind.)

The nature of the message conveyed by signs such as wreaths of flowers is one determined by the culture in which the sender and recipient live. Flowers have no *natural* significance, only a cultural or conventional one. . . . When they are employed as signs they enter into what is often referred to as a *code*, a channel of communication linking the two parties to any such cultural transaction. . . . The study of signs in general, and of the operation of the vast number of codes in any culture which enable us to interpret these signs satisfactorily, is now practised under the name of semiology in France and other European countries, and of semiotics in the United States. It was Saussure, again, who first called for the institution of such a general science of signs.

He also introduced two other pairs of contrasted terms which are important to any understanding of the style of thought we are faced with. In the study of language he distinguished first of all between what he called *langue* and *parole*, or 'language' and 'speech'. *Language* is the theoretical system or structure of a language, the corpus of linguistic rules which speakers of that language must obey if they are to communicate; *speech* is the actual day-to-day use made of that system by individual speakers. This distinction can usefully be compared to the rather better-known one popularized more recently by the American grammarian Noam Chomsky, who distinguishes between our linguistic *competence* and our linguistic *performance*, meaning respectively the theory of language we appear to be able to carry constantly in our heads and the practical applications we make of it. For Saussure the linguist's proper job was to study not speech but language, because it was only by doing so that he could grasp the principles on which which language functions in practice. This same important distinction emerges, in the work examined in this [discussion], as one between *structure* and *event*, that is to say between abstract systems of rules and the concrete, individual happenings produced within that system. The relation between one and the other, and the question of which should take precedence – do structures precede events, or events structures? – has been much debated.

A second and, for my purposes here, final Saussurian distinction is that between the *synchronic* and *diachronic* axes of investigation. It is permissible to study language – to take Saussure's own subject – along two radically different axes: as a system functioning at a given moment in time, or as an institution which has evolved through time. Saussure himself advocated the synchronic study of language, by contrast with the diachronic studies of the linguists who were his predecessors in the nineteenth century. They had been preoccupied by the history of particular languages, by etymologies, phonetic change and the like, and had never stopped to try and work out the total structure of a language, freezing it at a set moment of its evolution the easier to comprehend the principles on which it functioned.

Synchronic, or structural, linguistics thus introduced a revolutionary shift in perspective. It would have recognized that a total study of language must combine both perspectives, but it was prepared to ignore the diachronic perspective in order to set linguistics on a sounder, more productive footing. Structuralism as a whole is necessarily synchronic; it is concerned to study particular systems or structures under artificial and ahistorical conditions, neglecting the systems or structures out of which they have emerged in the hope of explaining their present functioning. . . .

Another influence on structuralism to be traced to Saussure's linguistics is not a matter of vocabulary, but is the most profound – and also the most elusive – of all. A crucial premise of Saussure's theory of language is that the linguistic sign is 'arbitrary'. It is so in two ways: the signifier is arbitrary inasmuch as there is no natural, only a conventional, link between it and the thing it signifies (not the signified in this case). There is no property common to all trees, for instance, which makes it logical or necessary that we should refer to them as 'trees'. That is what we, as anglophone persons, call them by agreement among ourselves; the French choose differently, they refer to them as *'arbres'*. But language is arbitrary at the level of the signified also, for each native language divides up in different ways the total field of what may be expressed in words, as one soon finds out in the act of translating from one language to another. One language has concepts that are absent from another. The example which linguists like to give of such arbitrariness is that of colour terms, which vary greatly from one language to another, even though the colours themselves form a continuum and, being determined naturally by their wave frequency, are universal.

The extremely important consequence which Saussure draws from this two-fold arbitrariness is that language is a system not of fixed, unalterable essences but of labile forms. It is a system of relations between its constituent units, and those units are themselves constituted by the differences that mark them off from other, related units. They cannot be said to have any existence within themselves, they are dependent for their identity on their fellows. It is the place which a particular unit, be it phonetic or semantic, occupies in the linguistic system which alone determines its value.

Those values shift because there is nothing to hold them steady; the system is fundamentally arbitrary in respect of nature and what is arbitrary may be changed.

'Language is a form and not a substance' was Saussure's famous summation of this quite fundamental insight, an insight without which none of the work done by [Claude] Lévi-Strauss, [Roland] Barthes and the others would have been feasible. Structuralism holds to this vital assumption, that it studies relations between mutually conditioned elements of a system and not between self-contained essences. It is easiest once more to instantiate this from linguistics. There is nothing essential or self-contained about a given word; the word 'rock', let us take. That occupies a certain space, both phonetically and semantically. Phonetically it can only be defined by establishing what the limits of that space are: where the boundaries lie if it crosses which it changes from being the word 'rock' to being a different sign of the language – 'ruck', for instance, or 'wreck', which abut on it acoustically. Semantically, we can only delimit the meaning of the signifier 'rock' by differentiating it from other signs which abut on it semantically, such as 'stone', 'boulder', 'cliff'.

In short, without difference there can be no meaning. A one-term language is an impossibility because its single term could be applied to everything and differentiate nothing; it requires at least one other term to give it definition. It would be possible, if rudimentary, to differentiate the entire contents of the universe by means of a two-term code or language, as being either *bing* or *bong* perhaps. But without the introduction of that small phonetic difference, between the two vowel sounds, we can have no viable language at all.

READING 81

Anthony Giddens

Sociology and the Explanation of Human Behaviour

The 'sociological' direction of modern philosophy involves a recovery of the everyday or the mundane. Our day-to-day activities are not merely inconsequential habits, of no interest to the student of more profound matters, but on the contrary are relevant the explication of quite basic issues in philosophy and in social science. Common sense is thus not to be dismissed as merely the inertia of habit or as a set of semi-formulated ideas of no importance to social analysis. To develop this observation further, however, we have to enquire a little more deeply into what common sense is. We cannot necessarily understand the term 'common sense' in a common-sense way.

Although no doubt more finely honed distinctions could be made, I shall distinguish two basic meanings of 'common sense'. One of these I call 'mutual knowledge' and separate from what can simply be called 'common sense' understood generically. By mutual knowledge I refer to knowledge of convention which actors must possess in common in order to make sense of what both they and other actors do in the course of their day-to-day social lives. Meanings are produced and reproduced via the practical application and continued reformulation in practice of 'what everyone knows'. As I would understand it, the programme of ethnomethodology consists in the detailed study of the nature and variations of mutual knowledge. Mutual knowledge refers to the methods used by lay actors to generate the practices which are constitutive of the tissue of social life. It is in substantial part non-discursive. That is to say, to use [Ludwig] Wittgenstein's phrase, it consists of the capability to 'go on' in the routines of social life.

Not having any place for a concept of mutual knowledge, naturalistic social science presumes that the descriptive terminology of social analysis can be developed solely within professionally articulated theories. But in order to generate valid descriptions of social life, the sociological observer must employ the same elements of mutual knowledge used by participants to 'bring off' what they do. To be able to generate veridical descriptions of social activity means in principle being able to 'go on' in that activity, knowing what its constituent actors know in order to accomplish what they do. . . . The implications of the point are rich. All social analysis has a 'hermeneutic' or 'ethnographic' moment, which was simply dissolved in traditional mainstream social science.

There is one way in which a grasp of the inescapably hermeneutic character of social science provides an answer to the question of its enlightening possibilities. That is to say, we might suppose . . . that what is 'new' in social science concerns only descriptions of forms of life (either in unfamiliar settings in our own culture, or in other cultures). In the view of the naturalistic social scientist, of course, the claim that social analysis can be no more than ethnography is absurd . . . But it is a proposition that deserves to be taken seriously. For there is a sense in which lay agents must always 'know what they are doing' in the course of their daily activities. Their knowledge of what they do is not just incidental but is constitutively involved in that doing. If they already not only do know, but in at least one sense *must* know what they are doing, it might seem that social science cannot deliver 'findings' with which the actors involved are not already familiar. At a minimum we must accept that the conditions under which the social sciences can deliver enlightenment to lay actors are more complex than was presumed in naturalistic social science.

What forms, then, might such enlightenment assume? The following considerations provide the basis of an answer.

1 It has to be accepted that the ethnographic tasks of social science are indeed fundamentally important. That is to say, all of us live within specific cultures which differ from other cultures distributed across the world, and from others 'recoverable' by historical analysis. In modern societies we also all live in specific contexts of larger cultural totalities. The 'news value' of the ethnographic description of culturally alien settings is certainly a significant element in social science.

2 Second, social science can 'display' – that is, give discursive form to – aspects of mutual knowledge which lay actors employ non-discursively in their conduct. The term 'mutual knowledge' covers a diversity of practical techniques of making sense of social activities, the study of which is a task of social science in its own right. As I have already mentioned, it can be construed as the task of ethnomethodology to provide such a 'display' of the taken-for-granted practicalities of our conduct. We might also instance, however, the writings of Erving Goffman as of singular importance in this respect. Perhaps more than any other single writer, Goffman has made clear how complicated, how subtle – but how routinely managed – are the components of mutual knowledge. We might also remark that the whole of linguistics is concerned with the 'display' of mutual knowledge. Linguistics is about what the language user knows, and must know, to be able to speak whatever language is in question. However, most of what we 'know' in order to speak a language, we know non-discursively. Linguistics tells us what we already know, but in a discursive form quite distinct from the typical modes of expression of such knowledge.

3 A matter of very considerable significance – social science can investigate the unintended consequences of purposive action. Actors always know what they are doing (under some description or potential description), but the consequences of what they do characteristically escape what they intend. A nest of interesting problems and puzzles is to be found here, and I

shall only discuss them briefly. Naturalistic versions of social science depend for their cogency upon the observation that many of the events and processes in social life are not intended by any of the participants involved. It is in the 'escape' of social institutions from the purposes of individual actors that the tasks of social science are discovered. In this respect we must in some part continue to defend the version of social science advanced by the 'mainstream' against more 'interpretative' conceptions. A characteristic failing of those traditions of thought which have done most to bring into focus the significance of mundane social practices is that they have ignored altogether the unintended consequences of social activity. But it would be futile to imagine that the issue was adequately handled in naturalistic social science. For the naturalistic sociologist, the unintended character of much social activity is wedded to the view that social life can be analysed in terms of the operation of factors of which social actors are ignorant. But it is one thing to argue that some of the main parameters of social activity are unintended by those who participate in that activity; it is quite another to presume that, consequently, individual agents are acted upon by 'social causes' which somehow determine the course of what they do. Far from reinforcing such a conclusion, a proper appreciation of the significance of the unintended consequences of action should lead us to emphasize the importance of a sophisticated treatment of the purposive nature of human conduct. What is unintentional cannot be even characterized unless we are clear about the nature of what is intentional; and this, I would argue, also presumes an account of agents' reasons.

There are several different types of enquiry that relate to the role of unintended consequences in human action. For example, we might be interested in asking why a singular event occurred in spite of no one's intending it to occur. Thus a historian might pose the question: why did World War I break out, when none of the main parties involved intended [its] actions to produce such an outcome? However, the type of question with which naturalistic social scientists have traditionally been preoccupied concerns the conditions of social reproduction. That is to say, they have sought to demonstrate that social institutions have properties which extend beyond the specific contexts of interaction in which individuals are involved. The connection between functionalism and naturalism has specific application here. For the point of functional explanation has normally been to show that there are 'reasons' for the existence and continuance of social institutions that are quite distinct from the reasons actors might have for whatever they do.

In recent years, partly as a result of a renewed critical examination of functionalism, it has become apparent that an account of institutional reproduction need not, and should not, have recourse to functional interpretations at all. Human social systems do not have needs, except as counterfactually posited 'as if' properties. It is perfectly appropriate, and often necessary, to enquire what conditions are needed for the persistence of a given set of social institutions over a specified period of time. But such an enquiry invites analysis of the mechanics of social reproduction, it does not supply an explanation for them. All large-scale social reproduction occurs under conditions of 'mixed intentionality'. In other words, the perpetuation of social institutions involves some kind of mix of intended and unintended outcomes of action. What this mix is, however, has to be carefully analysed and is historically variable. There is a range of circumstances which separate 'highly monitored' conditions of system reproduction from those involving a feedback of unintended consequences. The monitoring of conditions of system reproduction is undoubtedly a phenomenon associated with the emergence of modern society and with the formation of modern organizations generally. However, the intersection between intended and unintended consequences in respect of institutional reproduction is variable and in all instances needs to be concretely studied. A double objection can be made to explaining social reproduction in terms of statements of the form 'the function of x is . . .'. The first is, as already stated, that such a statement has no explanatory value, and can only be rendered intelligible when applied to social activity in the form of a counterfactual proposition. The second is that the statement is ambiguous in respect of intentionality. In conditions in which reproduction is 'highly monitored', the tie between purposes (of some agents) and the continuity of social institutions will be direct and pervasive. Where an unintended feedback operates, the mechanics of the reproduction process will be quite different. It is normally essential to distinguish the difference.

Notes

Reading 1

1 Anthony Giddens, *Sociology*, 3rd edn (Cambridge: Polity Press, 1997).

Reading 2: The Sociological Imagination and the Promise of Sociology

1 Mills uses language that would now be regarded as sexist. Virtually all authors in the field of sociology today recognize that words like 'he' and 'his', when used to mean human beings as a whole, are an expression of gender power – and that such usage should be avoided.

Reading 5: Civil Inattention and Face Engagements in Social Interaction

1 R.K. White, B.A. Wright and T. Dembo, 'Studies in adjustment to visible injuries: evaluation of curiosity by the injured', *Journal of Abnormal and Social Psychology*, 43 (1948), p. 22.
2 Ibid., pp. 16–17.
3 H. Viscardi Jr, *A Man's Stature* (New York: John Day, 1952), p. 70.
4 From Simmel's *Soziologie*, cited in R.E. Park and E.W. Burgess, *Introduction to the Science of Sociology*, 2nd edn (Chicago: University of Chicago Press, 1924), p. 358.
5 H. Melville, *White-Jacket* (New York: Grove Press, n.d.), p. 276.

Reading 6: Embarrassment and Interactional Organization

1 C. Darwin, *The Expression of Emotions in Men and Animals* (London: Julian Freidman, 1979), p. 330 (first published 1872).

Reading 7: Time, Habit and Repetition in Day-to-Day Life

1 W. James, *The Principles of Psychology* (New York: Dover, 1950), vol. 1, pp. 112, 121.

2 T.H. Huxley, *Lessons in Elementary Physiology* (London: Macmillan, 1866), quoted in James, *Principles of Psychology*, vol. 1.
3 A. Marwick, *Britain in the Century of Total War* (London: Bodley Head, 1968).
4 James, *Principles of Psychology*, vol. 1, p. 122.
5 J.S. Bruner, *On Knowing: Essays for the Left Hand* (Cambridge, MA: Harvard University Press, 1979), pp. 6–7.

Reading 11: Sickness and Health in Pre-Modern England

1 J.H. Turner (ed.), *The Rev. Oliver Heywood, 1630–1702* (Brighouse, Yorks: 1881–5), vol. 3, p. 207.
2 E.J. Chimenson (ed.), *Elizabeth Montagu, Her Correspondence from 1720 to 1761* (London: 1906), vol. 1, p. 33.
3 A. Macfarlane (ed.), *The Diary of Ralph Josselin* (Oxford: 1976), p. 21.
4 R. Latham and W. Matthews (eds), *The Diary of Samuel Pepys* (London: 1971–), vol. 5, p. 10.
5 L.A. Marchand (ed.), *Letters and Journals of Lord Byron* (London: 1982), vol. 2, p. 58.

Reading 13: History of Old Age: From Antiquity to the Renaissance

1 Simone de Beauvoir, *Old Age*, trans. Patrick O'Brian (Harmondsworth: 1977), p. 100.
2 Konrad Lorenz, 'La place des anciens ches les animaux sociaux', *Communications*, 37 (1983), p. 7.
3 Georges Condominas, 'Aînés anciens et ancêtres en Asie du Sud-Est', *Communications*, 37 (1983), p. 63.
4 Louis-Vincent Thomas, 'La viellesse en Afrique Noire', *Communications*, 37 (1983), p. 85.
5 Ibid.

Reading 17: It's Normal to be Queer

1 For more information on the Internet, see Reading 28.

Reading 18: What Do We Mean When We Talk About the Body and Sexuality?

1 H. Ellis, *The Psychology of Sex* (London: William Heinemann, 1946), p. 3.

Reading 19: Irregular Work, Irregular Pleasures: Heroin in the 1980s

1 J. Helmer, *Drugs and Minority Oppression* (New York: Seabury, 1975), p. 12.
2 R. Hartnoll, R. Lewis and S. Bryer, 'Recent trends in drug use in Britain', *Druglink*, 19 (Spring 1984), pp. 22–4.

Reading 26: Visualizing the News

1 P. Schlesinger, *Putting 'Reality' Together: BBC News* (London: Constable, 1978), pp. 160–1.

Reading 30: Why Do Marriages Break Down?

1 M. Rheinstein, *Marriage, Stability, Divorce and the Law* (Chicago: University of Chicago Press, 1972), p. 274.
2 B. Berger and P. Berger, *The War over the Family* (London: Hutchinson, 1983), p. 166.
3 J. Bernard, *The Future of Marriage* (New York: Bantam, 1973), p. 52.

4 A study carried out by the authors between 1982 and 1984 upon which their discussion is based.
5 Berger and Berger, *War over the Family*, p. 166.

Reading 31: Household Spending, Personal Spending and the Control of Money in Marriage

1 J.E. Todd and L.M. Jones, *Matrimonial Property* (London: HMSO, 1972).

Reading 34: The Development of Ethnic Awareness and Identification

1 G.M. Vaughan, 'Concept formation and the development of ethnic awareness', *Journal of Genetic Psychology*, 103 (1963), pp. 93–103.
2 P.A. Katz, M. Sohn and S.R. Zalk, 'Perpetual concomitants of racial attitudes in urban grade schoolchildren', *Developmental Psychology*, 11 (1975), pp. 135–44.
3 F.E. Aboud and F.G. Mitchell, 'Ethnic role-taking: The effects of preference and self-identification', *International Journal of Psychology*, 12 (1977), pp. 1–17.
4 Vaughan, 'Concept formation'.

Reading 36: 'There Ain't No Black in the Union Jack'

1 R. Ellison, *Shadow and Act* (New York: Random House, 1964), p. 263.

Reading 37: The Legacy of Empire: The British Case

1 Salman Rushdie, 'The new empire within Britain', *New Society*, 9 (December 1982), pp. 417–21.
2 Tom Nairn, *The Break-Up of Britain* (London: Verso, 1981), p. 269.
3 Gary P. Freeman, *Immigrant Labor and Racial Conflict in Industrial Societies* (Princeton: Princeton University Press, 1979), p. 277.
4 As a representative of the British Joint Council for Welfare of Immigrants, an immigrant rights organization, put it (John Plummer, 'Racism – built into immigration control', *Searchlight*, 45 (1979), p. 8).
5 Sarah Spencer, 'The implications of immigration policy for race relations', in S. Spencer, ed., *Strangers and Citizens* (London: IPPR/Rivers Oram Press, 1994), p. 27.

Reading 38: Marx and Weber on Class

1 K. Marx and F. Engels, 'Manifesto of the Communist Party', in *Selected Works* (London: 1968), p. 35.
2 K. Marx, *Capital*, vol. 3 (Moscow: 1959), pp. 582 ff.
3 K. Marx and F. Engels, *The German Ideology* (London: 1965), p. 61.
4 M. Weber, *Economy and Society* (New York: 1968), vol. 2, pp. 926–40, and vol. 1, pp. 302–7.
5 Ibid., vol. 2, p. 928.
6 Ibid., p. 927.

Reading 39: The Old Boy Network

1 C. Erickson, *British Industrialists: Steel and Hosiery, 1850–1950* (Cambridge: Cambridge University Press, 1959).

Reading 40: The Middle Classes in Modern Britain

1 M. Savage, J. Barlow, P. Dickens and A.J. Fielding, *Property, Bureaucracy and Culture: Middle Class Formation in Contemporary Britain* (London: Routledge, 1992).

2 J. Goldthorpe, 'On the service class: Its formation and future', in A. Giddens and G. MacKenzie (eds), *Social Class and the Division of Labour: Essays in Honour of Ilya Neustadt* (Cambridge: Cambridge University Press, 1982); also J. Goldthorpe, *Social Mobility and the Class Structure in Modern Britain* (Oxford: Oxford University Press, 1987).

Reading 41: Is There a British Underclass?

1 A. Giddens, *The Class Structure of Advanced Societies* (Hutchinson: 1973).
2 J. Rex and S. Tomlinson, *Colonial Immigrants in a British City* (Routledge: 1979).
3 K. Auletta, *The Underclass* (Random House: 1982).
4 C. Murray, *The Emerging British Underclass* (IEA: 1990).
5 W. Wilson, *The Truly Disadvantaged* (Chicago: University of Chicago Press, 1987).
6 F. Field, *Losing Out* (Blackwell: 1989).
7 R. Lister, 'Concepts of poverty', *Social Studies Review*, 6(5) (May 1990).
8 R. Miles, *Racism and Migrant Labour* (Routledge and Kegan Paul: 1982).
9 N. Abercrombie and A. Warde, *Contemporary British Society* (Polity Press: 1988).
10 D. Smith, *Racial Disadvantage in Britain* (Penguin: 1977).
11 P. Sarre, 'Race and the class structure', in C. Hammet et al. (eds), *The Changing Social Structure* (Sage: 1989).
12 S. Field, 'Trends in racial inequality', *Social Studies Review*, 2(4) (March 1986).

Reading 42: The Labour Process

1 D. Gallie, *In Search of the New Working Class: Automation and Social Integration Within the Capitalist Enterprise* (Cambridge: Cambridge University Press, 1978), p. 51; D. Gallie, *Social Inequality and Class Radicalism in France and Britain* (Cambridge: Cambridge University Press, 1983), p. 58.
2 H. Braverman, *Labor and Monopoly Capital: The Degradation of Work in the Twentieth Century* (New York: Monthly Review Press, 1974), p. 58.
3 B. Jones, 'Work and flexible automation in Britain: review of developments and possibilities', *Work Employment and Society* 2(4) (1988), p. 453.

Reading 47: Information Technology and the 'Information Society'

1 Information Technology Advisory Panel, *Learning to Live with IT* (London: HMSO, 1986).
2 B. Goudzwaard, *Aid for the Overdeveloped West* (Toronto: Wedge, 1975), p. 4.

Reading 53: Military Conscription and Citizenship

1 Victor Kiernan, 'Conscription and society in Europe before the war of 1914–18', in M.R.D. Foot (ed.), *War and Society* (London: Elek, 1973), p. 142.
2 Isaac Deutscher (discussing Jean Jaurès), *The Prophet Armed: Trotsky 1879–1921* (New York: Vintage, n.d.), p. 477.
3 Ibid., p. 406.

Reading 54: Women and War

1 S. Saywell, *Women in War* (New York: Viking, 1985), p. 38, italics added.
2 Ibid.
3 K.J. Cottam, 'Soviet women in combat in World War II: The ground forces and the navy', *International Journal of Women's Studies*, 3/14 (1980), pp. 345–57.

Reading 55: Inequality and Selection in Education

1 A.H. Halsey, A.F. Heath and J.M. Ridge, *Origins and Destinations: Family, Class and Education in Modern Britain* (Oxford: Clarendon Press, 1980).

2 J. Goldthorpe (with C. Llewellyn and C. Payne), *Social Mobility and Class Structure in Modern Britain*, 2nd edn (Oxford: Clarendon Press, 1987). See Figure 3.1 (Goldthorpe).

Reading 59: Challenging Secularization Theory

1 R.N. Bellah, *Beyond Belief* (New York: Harper and Row, 1970), p. 237.
2 D. Martin, *A General Theory of Secularization* (New York: Harper and Row, 1978).
3 K. Dobbelaere, *Secularization: A Multi-Dimensional Concept*, Current Sociology Series, 29 (Berkeley, CA: Sage, 1981).
4 C.Y. Glock, 'The religious revival in America?', in J. Zahn (ed.), *Religion and the Face of America* (Berkeley, CA: University of California Extension, 1965), p. 82.
5 N.J. Demerath III, 'Trends and anti-trends in religious change', in E. Sheldon and W.E. Moore (eds), *Indicators of Social Change* (Berkeley, CA: Russell Sage, 1968), pp. 368–9.
6 Ibid., p. 368.
7 H. Wheeler, 'The phenomenon of God', *Center Magazine*, 4 (1971), p. 8.
8 Ibid., p. 454.
9 E. Durkheim, *The Elementary Forms of Religious Life* (New York: Collier Books, 1961 [1912]), p. 474.

Reading 60: Radical Islam

1 A. Jarisha, *Shari'at Allah Hakima* (Cairo: 1977), ch. 2.
2 *al-Da'wa*, April 1977, pp. 4, 42.

Reading 62: Durkheim on the Origins of Religion

1 E. Durkheim, *The Elementary Forms of Religious Life*, pp. 1–2.
2 Ibid., p. 3.
3 Ibid., p. 119.
4 Ibid., p. 134.
5 C. Lévi-Strauss, *Structural Anthropology*, vol. 2 (London: Allen Lane, 1973), p. 48.
6 Durkheim, *Elementary Forms*, p. 206.
7 Ibid.
8 Ibid., p. 207.
9 Durkheim, *Textes* (Paris: Minuit, 1975), vol. 2, p. 27.
10 R. Aron, *Les étapes de la pensée sociologique* (Paris: Gallimard, 1967), p. 361.
11 Durkheim, *Elementary Forms*, p. 347.

Reading 63: What is a Revolution?

1 R.E. Park, *Society* (Glencoe, IL: Free Press, 1955), p. 36.
2 J. Baecheler, *Revolution* (New York: Harper and Row, 1975), p. 91.
3 S. Neumann, 'The international civil war', *World Politics*, 1/3 (1949), p. 333n.
4 E.K. Trimberger, *Revolution from Above: Military Bureaucrats and Development in Japan, Turkey, Egypt and Peru* (New Brunswick, NJ: Transaction, 1978), p. 12.
5 C.J. Friedrich (ed.), *Revolution* (New York: Atherton, 1966), p. 5.
6 S. Huntington, *Political Order in Changing Societies* (New Haven, CT: Yale University Press, 1968), p. 264.
7 T. Skocpol, *States and Social Revolutions: A Comparative Analysis of France, Russia and China* (Cambridge: Cambridge University Press, 1979), p. 4.
8 P. Calvert, *Revolution* (London: Macmillan, 1970), p. 15.

451

Reading 64: Reinventing the Global Village

1 T. Skocpol, *States and Social Revolutions: A Comparative Analysis of France, Russia and China* (Cambridge: Cambridge University Press, 1979), p. 4.
2 M. Kundera, 'The tragedy of Central Europe', *New York Review of Books*, 26 April 1984, p. 33.
3 M. Gorbachev, speech at Stanford University, 4 June 1990.
4 M. Foucault, *Language, Counter-Memory, Practice* (Ithaca, NY: Cornell University Press, 1977), pp. 154–7.

Reading 66: Urban Disasters and Megacities in a Risk Society

1 D. Harvey, *The Urban Experience* (Oxford: Blackwell, 1989).
2 M. Douglas and A. Wildarsky, *Risk and Culture* (Berkeley, CA: University of California Press, 1982).
3 U. Beck, *Risk Society* (London: Sage, 1992), p. 55.
4 R. Sylves and T. Pavlak, 'The World Trade Center disaster: A normal accident?', in T. Horlick-Jones (ed.), *New York City and Urban Emergency Management*, special issue of *Disaster Management*, 6/3 (1994).
5 S. Sassen, *The Global City: New York, London, Tokyo* (Princeton, NJ: Princeton University Press, 1991).
6 A characteristic of 'late' (or 'high') modernity in which, in sociological terms, agency is progressively freed from structure. A number of authors have pointed to the negative aspects of this fragmentation of traditional social structures; however, recent work has suggested that reflexivity may have a number of positive effects. In particular, it may bring a 'deepening of the self', in which new possibilities emerge for individuals to reflect critically upon their social conditions of existence.
7 A. Giddens, *The Consequences of Modernity* (Cambridge: Polity Press, 1990).
8 Beck, *Risk Society*.
9 D. Harvey, 'Introduction', in S. Zukin, *Loft Living* (London: Radius, 1988).
10 I. Burton, R. Kates and G. White, *The Environment as Hazard* (New York: Oxford University Press, 1978).
11 A. Kirby, 'Towards a new risk analysis', in A. Kirby (ed.), *Nothing to Fear: Risk and Hazards in American Society* (Tuscon: University of Arizona Press, 1990).
12 T. Horlick-Jones and D.K.C. Jones, 'Communicating risks to reduce vulnerability', in P. Merriman and C. Browitt (eds), *Natural Disasters: Protecting Vulnerable Communities* (London: Thomas Telford, 1993).
13 Beck, *Risk Society*.

Reading 73: Conversation Analysis

1 E. Durkheim, *The Rules of Sociological Method* (London: Routledge and Kegan Paul, 1982 [1897]).
2. H. Sacks, 'Sociological description', *Berkeley Journal of Sociology*, 8 (1963), pp. 1–16.
3 H. Sacks, unpublished lectures, transcribed and indexed by G. Jefferson (University of California at Irvine, 1964–72).
4 Ibid.
5 Transcription conventions: a single left bracket [indicates the point of overlap onset; a single right bracket] indicates the point at which an utterance or utterance part terminates *vis-à-vis* another; (.) indicates a tiny 'gap' within or between utterances . . . probably no more than one-tenth of a second; :: colons indicate prolongation of the immediately prior sound – the length of the colon row indicates length of the prolongation; WORD upper case indicates especially loud sound.
6 H. Sacks, 'Methodological remarks', in J.M. Atkinson and J.C. Heritage (eds), *Structures of Social Action: Studies in Conversation Analysis* (Cambridge: Cambridge University Press, 1984).

Sources and Acknowledgements

The editor and publishers wish to thank the following for permission to use copyright material:

Philip Allan Publishers Ltd. for Joan Chandler, 'Women Outside Marriage', *Sociology Review*, 2:4, April (1993); Mike Savage, 'The Middle Classes in Modern Britain', *Sociology Review*, 5:2, November (1995); Andy Pilkington, 'Is There a British Underclass?', *Sociology Review*, 1:3, February (1992); and Geoffrey Walford, 'Education and Private Schools', *Sociology Review*, 3:2, November (1993); Allyn & Bacon for material from Erving Goffman, *Encounters: Two Studies in the Sociology of Interaction* (1961) Bobbs-Merrill. Copyright © Allyn & Bacon; Blackwell Publishers for material from Georges Minois, 'Introduction' to *History of Old Age: From Antiquity to the Renaissance*, Sarah Hanbury Tenison (1989) Polity Press, pp. 1–7; Serge Moscovici, *The Invention of Society: Psychological Explanations for Social Phenomena*, W. D. Halls (1993) Polity Press, pp. 37–43; Nicholas Abercrombie and Alan Warde, 'The Labour Process', pp. 45–61, and 'Inequality and Selection in Education', pp. 360–8, in *Contemporary British Society: A New Introduction to Sociology* (1995) Polity Press; Christine Geraghty, *Women and Soap Opera: A Study of Prime Time Soaps* (1990) Polity Press, pp. 9–17; Christian Heath, 'Embarrassment and Interactional Organisation' in *Erving Goffman, Exploring the Interaction Order*, eds. Paul Drew and Anthony Wootton (1988) Polity Press, pp. 136–60; John Kingdom, *Government and Politics in Britain* (1991) Polity Press, pp. 253–60; and Martin Shaw, *Post-Military Society: Militarism, Demilitarism and War at the End of the Twentieth Century* (1991) Polity Press, pp. 175–7; Deirdre Boden for material from 'Reinventing the Global Village' (1990) Unpublished ms. (Department of Sociology, Washington University); BSA Publications Ltd. for material from

Jan Pahl, 'Household Spending, Personal Spending and the Control of Money in Marriage', *Sociology*, 24:1 (1990); Cambridge University Press for material from Emile Durkheim, 'The Field of Sociology' in *Emile Durkheim: Selected Writings*, ed. Anthony Giddens (1972); The Economist for 'Are men necessary?', *The Economist*, 23.12.95–5.1.96, pp. 121–3; 'It's normal to be queer', *The Economist*, 6.1.96, pp. 78–80; 'Time to adjust your set', *The Economist*, 23.12.95–5.1.96, pp. 29–31; 'Home sweet home', *The Economist*, 9.9.95, pp. 25–7; Dorothy Emmet for material from *Function, Purpose and Powers: Some Concepts in the Study of Individuals and Societies* (1972) 2nd edn, Macmillan, London; The European for Birna Helgadottir, 'Eastern Europe tires of capitalist promises', *The European*, 7–13 Dec. (1995) p. 11; Fourth Estate Ltd. for material from Roy Porter and Dorothy Porter, *In Sickness and in Health: The British Experience 1650–1850* (1988) pp. 2–6; The Free Press, a division of Simon & Schuster, for material from Erving Goffman, *Behavior in Public Places: Notes on the Social Organization of Gathering*. Copyright © 1963 by The Free Press; Johan Galtung for material from his article, 'The Green Movement: A Socio-Historical Exploration', *International Sociology*, 1:1 (1986); Anthony Giddens for material from *The Class Structure of the Advanced Societies*, 2nd edn (1980) Unwin Hyman; Gower Publishing Company Ltd. for material from P. E. Willis, *Learning to Labour: How Working Class Kids get Working Class Jobs* (1977) Saxon House, pp. 22–9; The Guardian for George Monbiot and Tim Radford, 'Last warning on Earth', *The Guardian*, 14.12.95; and Chris Brewster, 'You've got to go with the flow', *The Guardian*, 22.4.95; HarperCollins Publishers for material from Jane Dowdeswell, *Women on Rape* (1986) Thorsons; Harvester Wheatsheaf for material from Jean Bethke Elshtain, *Women and War* (1987) pp. 173, 177–8; the Independent for Andrew Brown, 'And the word was all male', *The Independent*, 31.5.95; and David Cohen, 'Could you be a fitness junkie?', *The Independent*, 4.12.95; Kluwer Academic Publishers for Tom Horlick-Jones, 'Urban Disasters and Megacities in a Risk Society', *GeoJournal*, 37:4, Nov. (1995) pp. 329–34; and Christian Jopke, 'The Legacy of Empire: The British Case', *Theory and Society*, 25 (1996) pp. 476–86; Lawrence & Wishart Ltd. for material from Karl Marx and Frederick Engels, 'The Materialist Conception of History' in *Selected Works in One Volume* (1968) pp. 181–2; Andrew Lownie, Literary Agent, on behalf of the authors, for material from Paul Hewitt with Jane Warren, *A Self-Made Man* (1995); Macmillan Press Ltd. for material from John Scott, *The Upper Classes: Property and Privilege in Britain* (1982); New Statesman & Society for Stuart Weir and Claire Sanders, 'Dangerous Liaisons', *New Statesman & Society*, 6.7.90; Saeeda Cahanum, 'Finishing School', *New Statesman & Society*, 25.5.90; and Anna Pollert, 'Girls, Wives, Factory Lives', *New Society*, 22.10.81; Newsweek, Inc. for Steven Levy with Katie Hafner and Adam Rogers, 'Internet 95', *Newsweek*, 25.12.95–1.1.96, pp. 22–6. Copyright © 1995 Newsweek, Inc.; The Observer for Ruaridh Nicoll, 'Gang babes love to kill', *The Observer*, 12.11.95; and material from Lisa O'Kelly, 'Body talk', *The Observer*, 23.10.94; Office for National Statistics for Crown copyright material; The Open University for material from Jeffrey Weeks, 'The Body and Sexuality' in *Social and Cultural Forms of Modernity*, eds. Robert Bocock and Kenneth Thompson (1992), Polity Press/Open University, pp. 220–4; Open University Press for Richard Ericson, Patricia Baranek and Janet Chan, 'Visualising the news' in *Visualising Deviance: A Study of News Organisation*, eds. R. Ericson, P. Baranek and J. Chan (1987) pp. 270–81; Oxford University Press for material from Gwynn Davis and Mervyn Murch, *Grounds for Divorce* (1988) Clarendon Press. Copyright © 1988 Gwynn Davis and Mervyn Murch; and John Sturrock, 'Introduction' to *Structuralism and Since: From Lévi-Strauss*, ed. John Sturrock (1979). Copyright © 1979 Oxford University Press; Oxford University Press, Inc. for material from C. Wright Mills, *The Sociological Imagination* (1959). Copyright © 1959 Oxford University Press, Inc.; renewed 1987 by Yaraslava Mills; Peter Owen Ltd. for material from Max Weber, *Basic Concepts in Sociology* (1962). Copyright © 1962 The Philosophical Library, New York; Policy Studies Institute for Tariq Modood, Sharon Beishon and Satnam Virdee, 'Conclusion' to *Changing Ethnic Identities* (1994) pp. 111–20; Routledge for material from Paul Gilroy, *There Ain't No Black in the Union Jack: The Cultural Politics of Race and Nation* (1987) Unwin Hyman; Elizabeth A. Stanko, *Intimate Intrusions: Women's Experience of Male Violence* (1985) Routledge and Kegan Paul; and Catherine Marsh, *The Survey Method: The Contribution of Surveys to Sociological Explanation* (1982) Unwin Hyman; Sage Publications Ltd. for material from John Auld, Nicholas Dorn and Nigel South, 'Irregular Work, Irregular Pleasures: Heroin in the 1980s' in *Confronting Crime*, eds. Roger Matthews and Jock Young (1986); Thames and Hudson Ltd. for material from Michael Young, *The Metronomic Society: Natural Rhythms and Human Timetables* (1988); Time, Inc. for material from John Skow, 'The Land: less milk and honey?', *Time*, October 30 (1995); UNESCO for material from David Beetham and Kevin Boyle, *Introducing Democracy: 80 Questions and Answers* (1995) pp. 1–9. Copyright © UNESCO 1995; University of California Press for material from Robert Georges and Michael Owen Jones, *People Studying People: The Human Element in Fieldwork* (1980). Copyright © 1980 The Regents of the University of California; The University of California Press for Jeffrey K. Hadden, 'Towards Desacralizing Secularization Theory', *Social Forces*, 65:3 (1987). Copyright © The University of North Carolina Press; The University of Chicago Press for material from John Stuart Mill and Harriet Taylor Mill, *Essays on Sex Equality*, ed. Alice S. Rossi (1970). Copyright © 1970 University of Chicago Press; and George H. Mead, *Mind, Self and Society: From the Standpoint of a Social Behaviorist*, ed. Charles W. Morris (1934). Copyright © 1934 University of Chicago Press; Virago Press and the author for material from Deborah Tannen, *You Just Don't Understand*, pp. 26–31; Yale University Press for material from Emmanuel Sivan, *Radical Islam: Medieval Theology and Modern Politics* (1985).

Every effort has been made to trace the copyright holders but if any have been inadvertently overlooked the publishers will be pleased to make the necessary arrangement at the first opportunity.

Picture Credits

Index

Note: Page numbers in *italics* refer to comments by the editor.